LAND OF
TEARS

Also by Robert Harms:

*The Diligent: A Voyage Through the Worlds of
the Slave Trade*

*Games Against Nature: An Eco-Cultural History of the
Nunu of Equatorial Africa*

*River of Wealth, River of Sorrow:
The Central Zaire Basin in the Era of the
Slave and Ivory Trade, 1500–1891*

LAND OF TEARS

THE EXPLORATION AND EXPLOITATION OF EQUATORIAL AFRICA

ROBERT HARMS

BASIC BOOKS
New York

Basic Books
Hachette Book Group
1290 Avenue of the Americas, New York, NY 10104
www.basicbooks.com

Printed in the United States of America

First Edition: December 2019

Published by Basic Books, an imprint of Perseus Books, LLC, a subsidiary of Hachette Book Group, Inc. The Basic Books name and logo is a trademark of the Hachette Book Group.

The publisher is not responsible for websites (or their content) that are not owned by the publisher.

Print book interior design by Amnet Systems.

Library of Congress Cataloging-in-Publication Data

Names: Harms, Robert W., 1946- author.
Title: Land of tears : the exploration and exploitation of equatorial
   Africa / Robert Harms.
Description: New York : Basic Books, 2019. | Includes bibliographical
   references and index.
Identifiers: LCCN 2019021576 (print) | LCCN 2019980869 (ebook) | ISBN
   9780465028634 (hardcover) | ISBN 9781541699663 (ebook)
Subjects: LCSH: Africa, Central—History—To 1884. | Africa,
   Central—Colonization—Environmental aspects. | Africa,
   Central—Colonization—Social aspects.
Classification: LCC DT352.7 .H373 2019 (print) | LCC DT352.7 (ebook) |
   DDC 967.031—dc23
LC record available at https://lccn.loc.gov/2019021576
LC ebook record available at https://lccn.loc.gov/2019980869

ISBNs: 978-0-465-02863-4 (hardcover), 978-1-5416-9966-3 (ebook)

LSC-C

10 9 8 7 6 5 4 3 2 1

CONTENTS

INTRODUCTION

FROM A SMALL AIRPLANE, THE Congo basin rainforest appears impenetrable, like a plush green carpet. A closer inspection reveals, however, that it is composed of three distinct layers of vegetation. The middle layer—known as the canopy—is made up of trees between 100 and 150 feet tall. Protruding above it are trees of the emergent layer that have broken through to reach sunlight, attaining heights of up to 200 feet. Below the canopy is the understory, which consists of smaller trees with large leaves to absorb whatever sunlight reaches them. So dense is the vegetation that a raindrop falling on the canopy can take up to ten minutes to reach the ground.

The view from the ground is very different. "The trees are so high that a good shotgun does no harm to parrots or guinea fowls on their tops, and they are often so closely planted that I have heard gorillas growling about fifty yards off without getting a glimpse of them," wrote the missionary/explorer David Livingstone in 1870. The most noticeable feature of the rainforest, however, is the lack of sunlight. Upon entering the forest in 1876, the journalist/explorer Henry Morton Stanley wrote, "We drew nearer to the dreaded black and chill forest called Mitamba, and at last, bidding farewell to sunshine and brightness, entered it. . . . Overhead, the

The French explorer Pierre Savorgnan de Brazza in the Congo Basin rainforest, 1888. *Le Tour du Monde*, 1888, second semester, p. 45.

wide-spreading branches, in many interlaced strata, each branch heavy with broad thick leaves, absolutely shut out the daylight. We knew not whether it was a sunshiny day or a dull, foggy, gloomy day; for we marched in a feeble solemn twilight."[1]

The Congo basin rainforest forms a six-hundred-mile-wide belt that runs east and west along the equator between 4° north latitude and 5° south. Beginning at the shore of the Atlantic Ocean, it stretches eastward for nearly fifteen hundred miles to the mountains and lakes of the Albertine Rift, where it ends abruptly because the rain clouds coming from the Atlantic Ocean drop their remaining moisture as they rise over the mountains. Covering parts of the Democratic Republic of the Congo, the Republic of the Congo, Gabon, Cameroon, Equatorial Guinea, and the Central African Republic, the Congo basin rainforest occupies nearly eight hundred thousand square miles, making it almost as large as the United States east of the Mississippi River. It is the second-largest tropical rainforest in the world, after the Amazon basin rainforest.[2]

The earliest inhabitants of the Congo basin rainforest were people of short stature and reddish-brown skin known generically as Pygmies (although they refer to themselves by specific ethnic labels such as Mbuti or Baka), who developed a hunting and gathering lifestyle in the forest twilight. About five thousand years ago, they were joined by taller black-skinned farmers coming from the northwest who originally settled in natural clearings but later spread out to construct their own clearings, especially after they acquired knowledge of iron smelting around 500 BCE. The earliest farmers who settled in the rainforest shared a common language and a common cultural tradition, but as they dispersed, their ancestral language splintered into roughly 150 distinct, though closely related, languages, and their sociocultural identity subdivided into about 450 separate ethnic groups. The diversity of languages and ethnic identities that the European explorers encountered when they first traversed the rainforest in the late nineteenth century can best be understood as historical variations on a common linguistic and cultural tradition.[3]

That common tradition was especially recognizable in the political organization of the forest peoples. In contrast to the great empires, kingdoms, and chiefdoms of Africa's southern grasslands or the mountain kingdoms of its Great Lakes region, the forest societies were characterized by small-scale political units with flexible forms of leadership and authority. In many cases, the largest political unit was a single village, or even a segment of a village, and the leader was often a self-made "big man" rather than a hereditary chief. The historian/anthropologist Jan Vansina has argued that this distinctive style of political organization was the defining feature that set the forest peoples apart from their neighbors in the mountains and the grasslands.[4]

For centuries, geography conspired to keep strangers out of the Congo basin rainforest. Although European ships first visited the mouth of the Congo River on Africa's west coast in the 1480s, some two hundred miles of rapids prevented them from following

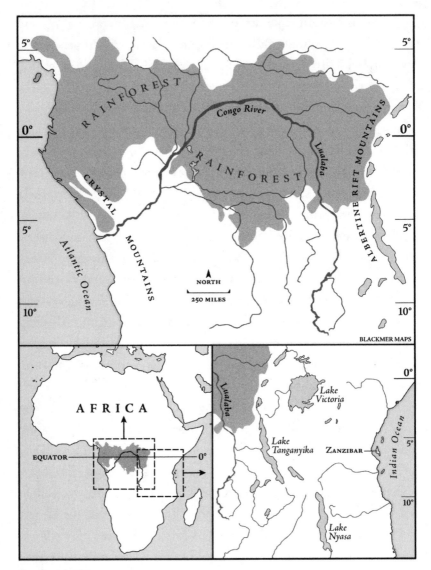

Equatorial Africa

it upstream, and the rugged Crystal Mountains, which run parallel
to the Atlantic coast, discouraged attempts to penetrate the interior
by land. At the eastern edge of the rainforest, the mountains and
lakes along the Albertine Rift sealed it off from the savanna that
stretched eastward to the Indian Ocean. Yet the isolation was never
complete. During the era of the Atlantic slave trade (1500–1870),

an unknown number of forest dwellers who had been captured in local wars or enslaved because of crimes or debts arrived at the Atlantic coast after passing through several sets of African intermediaries along the trade routes. Guns, brass, and cloth entered the Congo rainforest by following the same routes in reverse. Throughout this period, the European slave traders never strayed far from their coastal enclaves.[5]

In the late nineteenth century, however, the relative isolation of the Congo basin rainforest was shattered by intruders from both east and west. From the East African coast came Arab and Swahili traders—subjects of the sultan of Zanzibar—in search of ivory and slaves. They were followed closely by British explorers looking for the source of the Nile, a quest that led Henry Morton Stanley to follow the Congo River downstream to the Atlantic Ocean in 1877 after initially mistaking it for the Nile. The penetration from the west began when the Italian explorer Pierre Savorgnan de Brazza, with support from the government of France, crossed the Crystal Mountains in 1877 to enter the watershed of the Congo River, and when Stanley, who was by then working for the king of Belgium, returned to the mouth of the Congo River in 1879 to build a wagon road around the rapids.

Those explorations from east and west opened the floodgates to the pillage of the human and natural resources of the Congo rainforest. Merchants in search of ivory, captives, and rubber, who operated under the authority of the sultan of Zanzibar, the king of Belgium, or the government of France, entered the rainforest to strip it of its bounty. Ordinary people were flogged, enslaved, imprisoned, and shot; villages were abandoned; fields were left uncultivated; and common intestinal and respiratory diseases became lethal for lack of treatment. Social and political institutions disintegrated as individuals fled from the armed marauders and lived hidden in the forest. In 1905, separate commissions of inquiry sent out by Belgium and France discovered that the inhabitants of the Congo basin rainforest were among the most brutally exploited people on earth. In the short span of thirty years, the intruders had transformed the Congo basin rainforest from a region that they considered terra incognita to a place that reminded one observer of the "land of tears" in Dante's *Inferno*.[6]

The colonial occupation of the Congo basin rainforest was part of a larger process that historians have called the Scramble for Africa, which took place roughly between 1880 and 1900. It was the final phase in a four-hundred-year process of European imperial expansion. During the sixteenth and seventeenth centuries, the Spanish, Portuguese, English, Dutch, and French had seized territories all around the globe to monopolize markets or gain land for European settlements. Africa had largely been exempt from this process, in part because the tropical parts of Africa had disease environments that were deadly to Europeans and in part because the Europeans viewed tropical Africa as a reservoir for captives to fill their slave ships.[7]

In the early nineteenth century, the British and French seized territory at the northern and southern extremities of Africa, both of which had familiar Mediterranean climates, but they avoided the tropical regions, where they were content to conduct trade from small coastal enclaves. In 1870, Europeans controlled only 10 percent of the continent. The European Scramble for Africa in the 1880s was made possible by three developments during the nineteenth century. One was the end of the Atlantic slave trade, a development that prompted Europeans to focus on more legitimate forms of commerce; the second was the European Industrial Revolution, which inspired a search for new sources of raw materials and new markets; and the third was medical advances that made it easier for Europeans to survive in the tropical African environment. In their subsequent partition of the African continent, the Europeans were competing with Arab subjects of the sultan of Zanzibar and Turkish subjects of the Ottoman Empire.[8]

Although boundary adjustments and military expeditions to remote regions of Africa continued until the eve of World War I, most of the European claims on African territory were made during the six-year period between 1885 and 1890. The spark that set off the scramble was the Berlin Conference of 1884–1885, which met to partition the Congo River basin among the French, the Portuguese, and the Congo Free State (a private entity headed by King Leopold II of Belgium). The conference did not accomplish the "paper partition" of the African continent, as some have claimed, but it succeeded in its more limited objectives of dividing the Congo River basin among the European claimants and defining the conditions for making future colonial claims.

From the vantage point of the twenty-first century, it seems inevitable that the industrializing states of Europe would eventually conquer and colonize the equatorial regions of Africa, but it did not necessarily appear that way to the people who were there at the time. In January 1885, when the great powers of Europe (plus the United States and the Ottoman Empire) were meeting in Berlin, two expansionist movements based in Africa seemed to be winning on the ground. In Sudan, an Islamic revolution led by a prophet who called himself the Mahdi was driving out the Egyptians and the Ottoman Turks. In the Congo basin, the Afro-Arab trader and state builder known as Tippu Tip (because of the sound of his guns) threatened to conquer the Congo River Valley down to the Atlantic, and the Europeans understood that there was nobody who could stop him. He backed off, but his threat nevertheless revealed a potential tipping point that could have substantially altered the trajectory of events. To the protagonists of this book, the late nineteenth century was a time when anything seemed possible and no particular outcome was assured.

By the early 1890s, the Congo basin rainforest was being exploited by three different regimes of colonial resource extraction. The eastern third—known as Manyema—was controlled by a coalition of Arab and Swahili traders from the East African coast whose armed caravans scoured the countryside for ivory and captives. It was governed by a loose and ever-changing coalition of the major traders, each claiming his own exclusive trading and raiding territory. The western third—known as the French Congo—was controlled by the government of France, which gave it low priority in the larger scheme of French imperial interests. As a result, the French were loath to make investments in the colony and were largely content with protecting the trade routes and conducting military campaigns to extend the borders.

In between Manyema in the east and the French Congo in the west was an odd entity called the Congo Free State, which was founded in 1885 by King Leopold II of Belgium. After initially experimenting with free trade, Leopold developed a system of granting vast territories (usually much larger than Belgium itself) to Belgian and Anglo-Belgian companies with private armies that forced the inhabitants to strip the forest of its most valuable resources. When the people revolted against the impositions, the Congo Free State's army would step in to support the companies.

The three distinct styles of colonization and exploitation were embodied in their major protagonists, three men whose actions and interactions shaped the earliest structures of colonial rule in equatorial Africa. Henry Morton Stanley laid the groundwork for the Congo Free State, Hamid bin Muhammad (known as Tippu Tip) created the Manyema Empire, and Pierre Savorgnan de Brazza almost single-handedly created the French Congo. All three men had ambiguous identities and shifting loyalties. Stanley was a Welsh-born journalist and explorer who claimed to be an American and later worked for the king of the Belgians. Tippu Tip was a Zanzibari caravan trader of mixed African and Arab descent who proclaimed his allegiance to the sultan of Zanzibar and later to the king of the Belgians. Brazza was an Italian from the Papal States who carved out an empire for France and later converted to Islam and lived in Algeria.[9]

Those three men had divergent agendas and very different ways of relating to the Africans in whose lands they traveled. Tippu Tip moved slowly across the landscape, integrating himself into the local political structures by guile and force. Stanley was always in a hurry, driven to produce results for his European and American patrons, no matter what the cost. Brazza, in contrast, traveled slowly and tried to get to know the people whose lands he crossed. After those three founders departed from equatorial Africa in the 1890s, the fate of its inhabitants was left in the hands of the colonial bureaucrats, rapacious concession companies, and armed trading parties who followed in their footsteps.

By 1900, all three zones of the Congo basin rainforest had adopted variants of King Leopold's system of resource exploitation. In Manyema, the Congo Free State had driven out the principal Arab traders, but instead of bringing in European concession companies, it employed Arab and Swahili agents who collected ivory and rubber for the state while preserving certain aspects of the former Arab system of exploitation. In the French Congo, French concession companies tried to emulate those in the Congo Free State, but they were less successful because of lower levels of investment and military support. The French government claimed that its system of rubber collection was completely different from that in the Congo Free State, but the similarities were too obvious to ignore.

In contrast to the extensive historical literature that treats the Arab zone, the French Congo, and the Congo Free State as isolated entities with separate histories, this book sees all three colonial conquests as aspects of a single process that was spurred by new demands in the global economy and new iterations of Great Power rivalries. The intertwined careers of Stanley, Brazza, and Tippu Tip illustrate this phenomenon. Stanley could not have succeeded without considerable help from Tippu Tip, and the fierce public rivalry between Stanley and Brazza heavily influenced the nature and timing of French colonial claims in equatorial Africa as well as the format of the Berlin Conference. Tippu Tip never met Brazza, but his reluctance to antagonize the French lay behind his decision to refrain from leading his Manyema army down the Congo River to the Atlantic. By taking the entire Congo basin rainforest as the basic unit of analysis rather than a particular colony or imperial power, one can see how the different imperial interests and styles interacted with and influenced one another.[10]

The narrative of imperial exploitation in this book is set in two very different contexts, both of which defy the boundaries of national histories. One is the global context of the world economy and Great Power rivalries. In contrast to recent accounts that focus on forced rubber collection, this one places equal emphasis on the search for ivory. It was ivory, not rubber, that lured Arab and European traders into the Congo basin rainforest, and it was only after the ivory stock was becoming depleted that the search for rubber began in earnest. In the diplomatic arena, the machinations of the British, French, Portuguese, Germans, and Americans were aimed more at positioning themselves in relation to world markets and each other than at building relations with Africa.

The second context is defined by the rainforest ecosystem and the cultures of its inhabitants. The people of the Congo basin rainforest had to make difficult choices of whether to welcome or oppose the intruders and whether to acquiesce to or resist their demands. Their unique form of small-scale political organization had endured for centuries because conflicts had usually involved political units of roughly equal size, and the goal was usually resolution and restitution rather than conquest and pillage. The whole system was threatened when the forest people confronted strangers who made unlimited demands backed by enough firepower to wipe them out. David Livingstone, who traveled in the Congo basin rainforest with an Arab/Swahili ivory caravan in 1870, compared them to "little dogs in the presence of lions."[11]

Embedded in the narrative are three themes that have often been overlooked in the histories of early colonialism in the Congo River basin. The first is the impact of the internal slave trades in Africa and the anti-slavery movements in Europe. Although the trans-Atlantic slave trade was over by 1870, slave trades within Africa that were oriented toward the Nile Valley and the Indian

Ocean continued to supply enslaved laborers to clove plantations in Zanzibar, wealthy households of Cairo, date plantations in the Arabian Peninsula, and various places in the Ottoman Empire. The fight against those slave trades mobilized British and European humanitarians, who lobbied for naval blockades on the East African coast, sponsored a relief expedition to southern Sudan, and created a private crusader army to fight the Arab slavers in the African interior. At the same time, the anti-slavery forces in Britain and Belgium became unwitting allies of King Leopold's imperialistic schemes, which were often justified as anti-slavery projects. Slavery and anti-slavery were thus woven into the discourses of imperialism.[12]

The second theme is resource depletion. The outsiders came primarily to strip the rainforest of its most valuable and accessible resources. The slaughter of the elephants in East Africa created a constantly moving ivory frontier that lured the Arab and Swahili merchants from Zanzibar into the Congo basin rainforest and later attracted European ivory traders who moved in from the west. In a similar way, the depletion of the rubber vines in the rainforest lay behind many of the atrocities of the European rubber concession companies. Because the ivory and rubber frontiers were always moving during this period, the region was constantly in turmoil.

The third theme is local African resistance to the Arab ivory-hunting caravans and the European rubber concession companies. The Arab ivory and slave traders were driven out of Manyema only after one of Tippu Tip's top lieutenants mobilized local forces against them. In the Congo Free State and the French Congo, the humanitarian reformers in Europe were ultimately successful in their fight for administrative reform, but their efforts had little immediate effect on conditions on the ground. The African villagers were left to liberate themselves through flight, rebellion, or destruction of the rubber vines, all of which cut into the profits of the rubber companies. One can only speculate as to whether the reform efforts based in Europe would have succeeded without the fierce and sustained resistance of the African villagers.

To tell the story of the pillage of the rainforest and the devastation of its people in its many facets, the narrative relies on a variety of eyewitnesses who left descriptions of one aspect or another of the larger process. They were a diverse group that included David Livingstone, a Scottish missionary/explorer who entered the Congo rainforest along with the first wave of Arab and Swahili caravans; Alphonse Vangele, a Belgian ivory buyer working for the Congo Free State; John and Alice Harris, British missionaries who exposed the crimes of the Abir rubber company; and André Gide, the French novelist who witnessed the continuing abuses in the French Congo. Figures such as Cardinal Lavigerie, who founded the Anti-Slavery Movement in Europe, and Roger Casement, who cofounded the Congo Reform Movement in Britain, provide perspectives on the humanitarian movements in Europe that sought to influence developments in equatorial Africa.

Insights into the global economic forces that influenced events in equatorial Africa are provided by participant observers such as George Cheney, an ivory trader from Rhode Island who invested his profits in a piano key factory in Connecticut, and Henry Shelton Sanford, an American entrepreneur who lived mostly in Belgium. Hovering behind them all was King Leopold II of Belgium. He never set foot in the Congo River basin, but he engineered the creation of the Congo Free State, a privately held entity more than seventy-five times larger than Belgium itself. Some historians have portrayed King Leopold as a singularly evil genius, but his Congo project could not have succeeded without help from adventurers, commercial interests, national governments, and anti-slavery humanitarians from a variety of nations.[13]

The testimony of the witnesses comes in a variety of forms, including diaries, letters, official reports, public lectures, travel books, and autobiographies. Aside from a few oral accounts by African villagers and a few documents written by Arab traders, the

sources are mainly from Europeans who participated in the colonization of the Congo basin rainforest. The overwhelming majority
of the European travelers shared an implicit sense of racial superiority and a belief in social Darwinism, but they applied these
assumptions in different ways and to different degrees. Father Prosper Philippe Augouard, for example, exhibited a crude racism when
he characterized the Bateke people as "cannibals" who looked like
"veritable savages," but other travelers had views that were more
complex. Henry Morton Stanley, who claimed to be "free of prejudices of caste, color, race, or nationality," nevertheless described
the inhabitants of a village on the border of Manyema as "debased
specimens of humanity." By the time he left the village, however,
he had changed his mind and expressed regret for his "former
haughty feelings." In a similar way, David Livingstone acknowledged his struggle with racial prejudice when he wrote, "Anyone
who lives long among them forgets they are black and feels that
they are just fellow men." Given the wide variation in authorship
and context, each text must be evaluated on its own merits.[14]

Because the travelers' accounts are simultaneously repositories
of historical data and self-consciously constructed representations
of peoples, places, and events, historians of Africa have developed two different approaches to using them. The first is reading
"against the grain," a reference to the practice of mining European sources for data on what Africans were doing and seeking to
uncover the African voices embedded in information recorded by
Europeans. Whereas biographers read the explorers' accounts to
discover what they did and what those actions reveal about their
character and accomplishments, historians of Africa might read the
same accounts to learn what the travelers saw and what they were
told by their African hosts and companions. What the travelers
observed while moving across the African landscape is often more
significant than what they were doing.[15]

The other approach is literary—to interpret the writings of travelers as acts of representation in a specific historical context. The

Danish literary critic Frits Andersen has argued that the common
theme in the diverse body of travelers' writings on the Congo basin
rainforest is the image of "darkness," which stigmatizes the region
as an exceptional place where norms, laws, and rules do not apply.
That image was highlighted in the titles of books such as Henry
Morton Stanley's travelogue *In Darkest Africa* and Joseph Conrad's
autobiographical novel *Heart of Darkness*, and it was reinforced by
unverified tales of African cannibalism and authenticated accounts
of gruesome atrocities carried out by Europeans. In 1906, a popular Magic Lantern slideshow entitled *Congo Atrocities* shocked and
titillated British audiences with a narrative that included claims of
African cannibalism along with examples of European terrorism.
To people in Europe, they were all manifestations of the existential
"darkness" that permeated the Congo basin rainforest.[16]

The analysis presented here seeks to glean information from the
rich trove of travelers' accounts without getting drawn into their
dominant motifs. The terrors described in these pages were instigated by Arab and European enterprises for the purpose of aug-
menting their profits in an increasingly globalized world economy.
If there were unseen forces operating in the rainforest, they were
the universal vices of greed and lust for power. The special charac-
teristics of the forest societies were the result of their relative historical isolation from global markets and their decentralized forms of
political organization, which left them vulnerable to exploitation
by outsiders with guns.

In his innovative and often underappreciated book *Paths in
the Rainforests: Toward a History of Political Tradition in Equatorial
Africa*, the late ethnographer/historian Jan Vansina argued that the
shared cultural tradition of the rainforest dwellers, with its myriad variations, flourished for millennia in equatorial Africa, only
to disintegrate in an astonishingly brief period under the pressures
of colonial occupation. Vansina provided only a brief summary of
that destruction, but the process, as he saw it, unfolded in two
phases. First came the shattering of the forest societies under the

pressure of colonial conquest and commercial exploitation, and then came the forced reconstruction of those societies according to European ideas about how African societies should be organized and governed.[17]

This book explores the first phase of that process. The breakdown of the forest societies proceeded step-by-step through the actions and interactions of a variety of individuals, enterprises, organizations, and governments, all pursuing their own interests. It examines the global forces at work, the major figures involved, and the interlinked processes that led to this outcome. Above all, it explores the complex interplay of humanitarianism and rapaciousness, of development and destruction, and of global demands and local interests, all of which resulted in unspeakable tragedy for the people of the Congo basin rainforest.

CHAPTER 1

MANYEMA

Lake Tanganyika lies in the far interior of the African con-tinent, roughly 1,500 miles from the Atlantic Ocean and 750 miles from the Indian Ocean. As the longest freshwater lake in the world, it stretches 410 miles from north to south. Never more than 45 miles wide and sometimes as narrow as 10, it is nestled at the southern end of an alpine valley that geologists call the Albertine Rift. So deep is the valley that the lake has an average depth of 1,870 feet and a maximum depth of nearly a mile. The moun-tains that rim the west side of the valley, with snow-capped peaks reaching nearly 17,000 feet, create a barrier that makes the weather patterns and ecosystems to the west very different from those to the east. When rain clouds move in from the west, they give up much of their water as they struggle to rise above the mountains. As a result, tropical rainforests predominate west of the Albertine Rift, whereas one finds mostly dry and humid savannas to the east.[1]

During the nineteenth century, the trading town of Ujiji grew up on the east shore of Lake Tanganyika to mark the western ter-minus of the winding caravan road that meandered for nearly a thousand miles across the East African savanna to Bagamoyo, on the Indian Ocean coast. When the British explorer Richard Burton visited Ujiji in 1858, he was disappointed to see little more than "a few scattered hovels of miserable construction surrounded by fields of sorghum and sugar cane." Misled by a German map that listed it as "die Stadt Ujiji" (the city of Ujiji), he had expected a large town with a quay and a marketplace. The quay, he found, was simply a level landing place identifiable by a break in the reedy grasses. A hundred yards up from the lakeshore was the marketplace—a large plot of bare ground where various items were bought and sold in the open air. The town had remained undeveloped because the caravans would purchase trade commodities, dried fish, and foodstuffs and then turn around and leave as quickly as possible.[2]

At the eastern end of the trade route was the small island of Zanzibar. Only sixty-five miles long and nineteen miles wide, it was located in the Indian Ocean just twenty-two miles off the port of Bagamoyo. Since the twelfth century or earlier, it had been inhabited by Swahili-speaking people who practiced Islam, lived in coastal towns, and maintained a mercantile orientation toward the wider Indian Ocean world. During the eighteenth century, Zanzibar and the adjacent Mrima Coast came under the control of the sultanate of Oman (on the Arabian Peninsula at the mouth of the Persian Gulf), and Omani Arab merchants began to migrate to Zanzibar and the Mrima Coast, joining the indigenous Swahili-speaking merchants. Over time, the identities of the two Muslim merchant communities began to merge at the edges as people intermarried, and many Omani Arabs grew up speaking Swahili better than Arabic.

European travelers generally referred to any caravan trader who wore Arab robes and practiced Islam as an Arab, but the missionary/explorer David Livingstone used a variety of terms to describe the caravan traders he encountered in his travels: Arabs, black Arabs, black half-caste Arabs, dark coast Arabs, low coast Arabs, half-caste coast Arabs, and black Swahili Arabs. His terminology hints at the wide range of distinct identities lumped together under the term *Arab*. Livingstone once referred to the Zanzibari caravan trader Khamis wad Mtaa as a "black Swahili Arab," but Tippu Tip, who was a well-known Arab caravan trader, insisted that Khamis was not an Arab. To Livingstone, being an "Arab" was a matter of religion, dress, and lifestyle, but for Tippu Tip, it came down to genealogy and social status.[3]

The monsoon winds in the Indian Ocean made the island of Zanzibar a convenient destination for sailing ships. In the nineteenth century, it attracted vessels from such far-flung destinations as Gujarat, Oman, Hamburg, Liverpool, Massachusetts, and Rhode Island. Zanzibar's central role in the trade of the Western Indian Ocean was confirmed when the British, Germans, French, and Americans established consulates there during the 1830s and 1840s. When Henry Morton Stanley arrived in Zanzibar in 1871 as a journalist working for the *New York Herald,* he described it as the Baghdad of East Africa. "It is the great mart which invites ivory traders from the African interior," he wrote. He was told that five thousand Maria Theresa dollars' worth of trade goods purchased in Zanzibar could be sold for MT\$15,000 in Ujiji (Maria Theresa dollars were silver coins minted by the Hapsburg monarchy that served as the trade currency of the Western Indian Ocean). For the return trip, ivory purchased in Ujiji for MT\$20 per *frasila* (35 lbs.) was worth MT\$60 in Zanzibar.[4]

Prior to 1825, Zanzibar had simply exported whatever ivory African chiefs and traders in the interior sent to it, but in the second quarter of the nineteenth century, caravans organized by Arab and Swahili traders from Zanzibar and financed by Indian merchants living in Zanzibar began traveling into the African interior in search of ivory. Because the tsetse flies that infested the East African savanna spread bovine trypanosomiasis, which was deadly to cattle, horses, and pack animals, the caravans relied on human porters to carry their supplies and merchandise. The growing demand for ivory in Europe and the United States drove up the price by 400 percent between 1825 and 1875, making it profitable to outfit large caravans that traveled long distances. The sharpest increase came between 1867 and 1873, when the price of large Zanzibar tusks at public sales in England jumped 70 percent. In

An ivory caravan crosses the East African savanna, ca. 1880. R. P. Le Roy, *A Travers le Zanguebar*, p. 83.

the 1850s, Zanzibar was exporting about twenty thousand tusks a year, which required the annual slaughter of ten thousand elephants, but by 1875, some forty-four thousand elephants were killed annually to supply the ivory that came to England alone.[5]

The rapidity with which the ivory frontier moved inland is illustrated by the region southwest of Lake Tanganyika, where David Livingstone was traveling in 1867. "Elephants come all about us," he wrote in his diary on April 1. A month later, he wrote, "This is called Mwami country, full of elephants, but few are killed. They do much damage, eating the sorghum in the gardens unmolested." Writing to British foreign secretary Lord Clarendon in December, he noted, "Elephants sometimes eat the crops of the natives and flap their big ears just outside the village stockades." Yet by the time Joseph Thomson of the Royal Geographical Society came through the same area ten years later, the elephants had disappeared. In fourteen months of exploring the lake region of Central Africa, he did not see a single elephant.[6]

As the ivory frontier retreated from the coast during the nineteenth century, the caravans pushed farther and farther into the

East African interior. Arab traders first visited the region of Tabora (some 520 miles from the Indian Ocean coast by a winding footpath) around 1830, and they began to settle there in increasing numbers after 1850. The British explorer Richard Burton described Tabora in 1857 as "the meeting place of merchants and the point of departure for caravans which thence radiate into the interior of Central Inter-tropical Africa." Located in the heart of the territory known as Unyamwezi (i.e., the country of the Nyamwezi people), Tabora was also the central place for hiring caravan porters. Young Nyamwezi men sought employment as porters because it was important to them to earn money to get married and also to become well-traveled and sophisticated in the ways of the wider world. Participation in a caravan became a kind of initiation ritual that turned a boy into a man. Some Nyamwezi porters specialized in traveling the caravan route between Tabora and the coast, while others worked between Tabora and destinations farther inland. A caravan would often travel from the coast to Tabora with one set of porters and then release them and hire a new gang for the next stage of the journey. Caravans traveling west from Tabora first reached Ujiji around 1840, but they initially limited themselves to visits during the dry season because they considered it an unhealthy place to settle.[7]

Contemporaneous with the growth of the ivory trade in the nineteenth century came the expansion of the East African slave trade. The development of clove plantations in Zanzibar in the early nineteenth century broke the worldwide monopoly of the Dutch East India Company, which controlled the clove plantations on the Maluku Islands (a.k.a. the Spice Islands) of Indonesia. Valued for its culinary, medicinal, and aromatic properties, the precious spice was sometimes said to be worth its weight in gold. In 1840, the sultan of Oman moved his capital to Zanzibar, thus initiating a period of "clove mania" as Omani Arabs moved to Zanzibar to seize land from the island's Swahili-speaking inhabitants and start clove plantations worked by enslaved laborers. In 1840, there were roughly seventeen thousand slaves in Zanzibar, and by the 1850s, there were between sixty thousand and one hundred thousand.[8]

The enslaved people in Zanzibar could be divided into four categories. The largest group, rural plantation slaves, generally worked from sunrise to 4:00 p.m. on Saturday through Wednesday, leaving Thursday and Friday free to grow food for themselves and take the surplus to town for sale. The second category, urban slaves, included domestic servants as well as day laborers, porters, and artisans. They were often hired out to various mercantile houses, where they would clean gum copal, break coconuts, load and unload cargoes, or work as carpenters and masons. Upon completing a job, they split their pay with their master. The third category contained the enslaved Circassian, Abyssinian, and Mesopotamian concubines of the sultan. Although slaves, they lived in luxury and bore children who could inherit plantations or even ascend to the sultanate. When Sultan Seyyid bin Sultan died in 1856, all eighteen of his male heirs were sons of enslaved concubines. The final category included trusted slaves who worked as armed guards and trading assistants on caravans. They had a great deal of freedom on the road and could sometimes advance to positions of wealth and power. One prominent example was Khamis wad Mtaa, who grew up in Zanzibar as a slave of the wealthy Abd al-Rahman Sodiq family. He became a successful caravan leader by pioneering the ivory trade in the Maasai country but remained subordinate to his master in Zanzibar.[9]

As with the ivory trade, Zanzibar was the focal point of the Western Indian Ocean slave trade. In 1870, the Customs House records showed an average of twenty thousand captives coming into Zanzibar each year, ten thousand of whom were required annually to replenish the enslaved population. The rest were shipped in Arab-owned sailing ships known as dhows to the Red Sea, the Arabian Peninsula, the Persian Gulf, and other destinations along the rim of the Western Indian Ocean. The British, who had led the fight against the Atlantic slave trade in the early nineteenth

A slave caravan going to Kilwa, ca. 1865. The men are secured by forked "slave sticks," while the women are bound together by ropes around their necks. David Livingstone, *The Last Journals of David Livingstone*, p. 59.

century, imposed treaties on the Omani sultans in 1822 and 1845 that limited the movement of slave dhows. They also sent the Royal Navy's anti–slave trade squadron to the Western Indian Ocean to enforce them, but the effort was ineffectual because the squadron had so few ships. During the period from 1845 to 1860, the effective anti–slave trade patrol along the coast of East Africa often consisted of a single ship, and never more than three. As Admiral Heath told a Select Committee of the House of Commons in 1871, "We have gone on for 25 years and have done no good whatever."[10]

The captives who fueled the East African slave trade did not, as a rule, come from the regions along the central caravan route to Tabora and Ujiji. The powerful chiefdoms in the East African savanna had successfully defended themselves against slavers from the coast, and the ivory caravans needed peaceful passage along the trade route. Instead, the captives came largely from the region around Lake Nyasa, much farther to the south, where Yao slaving parties raided the agricultural populations for captives and sold them to slave caravans run by coastal Arab and Swahili merchants based in the port of Kilwa. From there, the captives were shipped to Zanzibar in dhows. Because the selling price of a captive at the Zanzibar slave market was relatively low and the cost of feeding and moving captives over long distances cut into their meager profits, the Kilwa-based slave caravans seldom traveled more than 350 miles from the coast. When David Livingstone traveled from the Indian Ocean coast to Lake Nyasa in 1866, he encountered several slave caravans and saw abundant evidence of the human destruction caused by slave traders, but west of the lake he passed through territory where no coastal slave traders had ever been seen.

In contrast to slave trade caravans, which stayed within striking distance of the coast, ivory caravans traveled deep into the interior where ivory was cheap. Along the way, they often accumulated captives if they got into wars with the local people or if they purchased people who had been enslaved in local wars. Although many Europeans believed that the captives were being used to carry the ivory to the coast, this was usually not the case. The larger tusks were almost always carried by professional porters, who carried trade goods going in and ivory coming out. Ivory caravans typically contained between five hundred and one thousand people, although some were as large as three thousand. In the normal order of march, the ivory carriers came first, followed by the bearers of cloth and beads. Behind them marched the porters carrying daily supplies, followed by the captives. Enslaved men often marched with their necks secured in heavy forked poles known as "slave sticks," which prevented them from carrying loads. In contrast, enslaved women were often linked together by ropes encircling their necks, an arrangement that gave them enough freedom of movement to carry supplies or small tusks.[11]

The ivory trade subsidized the slave trade in two ways. First, the relatively high prices paid for ivory in Zanzibar made it profitable for large caravans to travel into the far interior, where they could acquire both ivory and captives. Livingstone reported that slave caravans that went beyond Lake Nyasa were profitable only if they also brought back ivory; otherwise, the captives would "eat up all the profits of a trip." The second reason had to do with the credit arrangements that financed the caravans. The Gujarati, British, German, and American trading houses in Zanzibar that advanced trade goods to the caravans expected to be repaid in ivory and did not want captives. When a caravan returned to Zanzibar after several years on the trail, most of the ivory went to the trading houses to repay the loans, but the captives were sold at the slave market for the profit of the caravan traders themselves. The long-distance slave trade was profitable only if the ivory trade covered the basic costs of the caravan.[12]

By 1869, the initial phase of the East African ivory caravan trade was coming to an end. With elephants becoming increasingly scarce in the East African savanna, the Arab and Swahili ivory traders turned to the vast tropical rainforest west of Lake Tanganyika. Their destination was the region that Arab and Swahili traders called Manyema, which stretched from the western shore of the lake to the Lualaba River, a distance of some 240 miles as the crow flies, but perhaps twice as far by the serpentine paths through the mountains and the rainforest. As a name imposed by outsiders, Manyema had no analogue in the local Bantu languages. Many travelers believed it meant "land of forests," but some Europeans, noting the rough similarity to the Bantu term *nyama* (which meant "meat"), claimed without evidence that it was a veiled reference to cannibalism.[13]

The ivory trade in Manyema grew rapidly because it was so lucrative. Ivory purchased for twenty-five cents' worth of copper in Manyema could be sold for MT$120 in Zanzibar. As Livingstone noted in a letter to the British Foreign Office, "The news of cheap ivory caused a sort of California gold fever at Ujiji, and we were soon overtaken by a horde numbering 600 muskets, all eager for the precious tusks." Trading caravans would soon come out of Manyema with as much as thirty-five thousand pounds of ivory per caravan. So much ivory was flowing to Zanzibar that the Indian Ocean port town of Bagamoyo tripled in size from 1867 to 1871.[14]

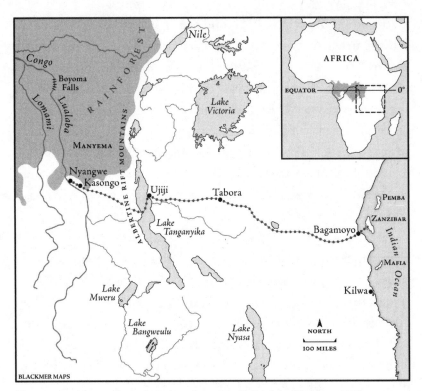

The main trade route from the Indian Ocean to the Lualaba River, ca. 1875

During the 1870s, some of the Arab and Swahili caravan traders who had gone into Manyema settled in towns near the Lualaba River, turning them into commercial centers and thus establishing new bases for future expansion. They would soon be joined by Henry Morton Stanley and Tippu Tip—two travelers who would alter the trajectory of economic and political change in the Congo basin rainforest. At the same time, the ivory-cutting factories along the lower Connecticut River in the United States were expanding their production of ivory-topped piano keys, and an international geographical conference in Brussels, Belgium, was encouraging more European exploration of Africa and increased opposition to the East African slave trade. The impact of those economic and political developments would soon be felt deep in the rainforest of Manyema.

1

Ujiji, Lake Tanganyika, May 1876

When Henry Morton Stanley arrived in Ujiji in May 1876, he rented a flat-roofed, Arab-style house known as a *tembe*, which overlooked the market and Lake Tanganyika. To the south were the tembes of the major Arab traders. He described them as "solid, spacious, flat-roofed structures built of clay, with broad, cool verandas fronting the public roads." The largest was one hundred feet long by twenty-five feet wide and fourteen feet high, with a broad veranda covered with luxurious carpets. To the north were the huts of the *waungwana* (Swahili caravan traders), the *Wanyamwezi* (hired porters from the region of Tabora), the personal slaves of the Arab traders, and the *Wajiji* (the original inhabitants of Ujiji). The town had seen rapid growth since 1869, when it ceased to be the terminus of the caravan route and became a staging area for ivory caravans headed west across Lake Tanganyika into the rainforest of Manyema.[15]

Stanley was going to Manyema to complete the quest of the missionary/explorer David Livingstone, who had spent seven years searching for the source of the Nile River until his death in 1873. Interest in geographical knowledge was exploding in Europe in the late nineteenth century; there were twelve geographical societies in 1870 and twenty-nine by 1890. The International Geographical Congress held in Paris in 1875 attracted fifteen hundred participants from thirty-four countries and featured sessions on how to fill in the gaps in the knowledge about the interior of Africa. In Britain, the search for the ultimate source of the Nile River dominated geographical discussions. The explorer John Hanning Speke had found that the Nile flowed north out of Lake Victoria, but his traveling companion Richard Burton proposed that it originated in Lake Tanganyika, some two hundred miles farther to the southwest. David Livingstone, who had earlier explored the Zambezi River and Lake Nyasa, suggested that the ultimate source of the

The trading town of Ujiji on the east shore of Lake Tanganyika. Note the flat-roofed Arab houses. Edward Hore, *Tanganyika: Eleven Years in Central Africa*, frontispiece.

Nile was a lake called Bemba (later identified as Lake Bangweulu), located southwest of Lake Tanganyika. Eager to solve the world's last great geographical puzzle, the Royal Geographical Society sent Livingstone on an expedition to find the lake and trace its link to the Nile. After a brief visit to Bombay, he landed in Africa on January 28, 1866.[16]

When he reached the area south of Lake Tanganyika in 1867, Livingstone's expedition was on the verge of collapse. Deserted by his hired porters, his party had been reduced to himself and nine African boys known as the "Nassick boys" because they had been rescued from East African slave traders several years earlier and sent to the Nassick missionary school in Bombay. Running low on supplies to barter for food, he sought the aid and protection of Arab and Swahili caravan traders who had come seeking ivory. In August, he began traveling with the powerful Zanzibari ivory trader known as Tippu Tip. After Tippu Tip returned to Zanzibar at the end of 1867, Livingstone traveled with Tippu Tip's cousin Muhammad bin Salih and then with Muhammad's friend and colleague Muhammad bin Gharib, going with him to Ujiji and on to the trading town of Nyangwe in Manyema.[17]

During his two years of travel with Arab and Swahili ivory caravans in the region of Lake Bangweulu, Livingstone gained a reasonably accurate picture of the rivers and lakes in that part of Central Africa. The discharge from Lake Bangweulu took the name Luapula and flowed north to Lake Mweru. Upon emerging from Lake Mweru, it took the name Luvua and ran northwest to join the Lualaba River, which flowed north into the rainforest of Manyema. Livingstone was sure that the Lualaba flowed into the Nile, but he did not know where or how. Accordingly, he had traveled to Ujiji with Muhammad bin Gharib's ivory caravan and then continued on with him into Manyema. He reached the Lualaba River at the trading town of Nyangwe in March 1871, but despite four months of trying, he was unable to procure a canoe to follow the river downstream.[18]

Discouraged by his lack of progress and sickened by the relentless violence of the ivory and slaving frontier, he fixated on a rumor he heard from two Swahili copper traders who told him about four water sources southwest of Lake Bangweulu that were situated less than ten miles apart—two of them flowed north, and the other two flowed south. He associated this description with his schoolboy memories of the Greek historian Herodotus, who had visited Egypt in the fifth century BCE. Herodotus was told by the registrar of Minerva's treasury about the Fountains of the Nile, from which half the water flowed northward into Egypt, and half flowed south into Ethiopia. Herodotus himself had been skeptical of that story and had wondered if the scribe "spoke the real truth," but Livingstone believed that he had stumbled upon Herodotus's Fountains of the Nile. He accordingly abandoned his attempt to follow the Lualaba River north and instead went back to Ujiji to get supplies and organize a new expedition to Lake Bangweulu. When he left Nyangwe on July 20, 1871, he had been living and traveling with ivory and slaving caravans for over four years.

The Arab and Swahili traders who were Livingstone's benefactors and the African chiefs who were his local hosts were never quite sure why he was there. The Victorian fascination with the source of the Nile made no sense to them. When a local chief asked him why he had come so far with no goods to trade, Livingstone replied that he wished to make this country and its people better known to the rest of the world. "We are all children of one father," he told the chief. "People should get to know one another better." Even Tippu Tip, who had come to know Livingstone quite well, found his travels inexplicable. "What did he seek, year after year, until he became so old that he could not travel?" Tippu Tip once asked. "He had no money, for he never gave any of us anything; he bought no ivory or slaves; yet he travelled farther than any of us. And for what?"[19]

Shortly after Livingstone arrived back in Ujiji in October 1871, he encountered Henry Morton Stanley, whom the *New York Herald* had sent to look for him. Livingstone described the encounter as follows: "Susi came running at the top of his speed and gasped out, 'An Englishman! I see him!' And off he darted to meet him. The American flag at the head of the caravan told of the nationality of the stranger. Bales of goods, baths of tin, huge kettles, cooking pots, tents, etc., made me think, 'This must be a luxurious traveler, and not one at his wits end like me.' It was Henry Moreland [*sic*] Stanley, the traveling correspondent of the *New York Herald*."[20]

During the four years that Livingstone had spent traveling with Arab and Swahili slave and ivory traders, he had made no progress at all toward solving the Nile puzzle because, unbeknownst to him, he was not in the Nile watershed at all. Yet by traveling with the Arab trading caravans, he had gained unparalleled insight into the operations, practices, and horrors of the East African slave trade. Along the route from the Indian Ocean coast to Lake Nyasa, he had periodically come upon the bodies of captives who had been killed because they were too weak to walk or had been abandoned to die along the trail because they were ill. In the region west of Lake Nyasa, the ivory caravans of his patrons Tippu Tip and Muhammad bin Gharib included large numbers of captives from hostile encounters with the local inhabitants, but Livingstone nevertheless considered those men to be "gentlemen slavers" who treated their captives humanely. He placed the Ujiji-based traders who went into Manyema in a different category entirely. "This is a den of the worst kind of slave traders," he wrote in his journal.

"The Ujiji slavers, like the Kilwa and Portuguese, are the vilest of the vile. It is not trade, but a system of consecutive murders. They go to plunder and kidnap, and every trading trip is nothing but a foray."[21]

Encouraged by Stanley, Livingstone wrote a long letter to Gordon Bennett, the publisher of the *New York Herald*, describing the operation and impact of the East African slave trade. Stanley would eventually carry it to Marseilles on a French mail steamer, where he transmitted it to the *Herald* by telegraph at a cost of $2,000. The *Herald* published the letter, which took up a page and a half of newsprint, on July 26, 1872, and shared it widely with other newspapers in hopes that they would help defray the telegraph charges. In England, the London *Daily Telegraph*, which billed itself as the "largest, best, and cheapest newspaper in the world," published it on July 29, and other British newspapers picked it up as well. The article appeared just when the British Anti-Slavery Society was mounting a campaign to urge the government to take further actions to stop the Arab-run slave trade in the Western Indian Ocean. Livingstone's letter apparently had an impact because the annual Queen's Speech to the Parliament on August 10 called for the government to take "steps intended to prepare the way for dealing more effectually with the slave trade on the east coast of Africa."[22]

Ten months later, the sultan of Zanzibar, facing the prospect of a total blockade of the island by the British navy, signed a treaty with Britain that called for the immediate cessation of Zanzibar's maritime trade in enslaved Africans, the closing of the Zanzibar slave market, and protection for captives liberated from the dhows. Although the treaty forced the slave dhows to alter their routes to avoid the stepped-up British navy patrols, it did not bring about an appreciable reduction in the total volume of the Indian Ocean slave trade. Between 1860 and 1890, the British navy boarded about a thousand dhows and liberated some twelve thousand captives, but the smuggling of enslaved Africans continued until the end of the nineteenth century. The British abolitionists, however, counted the Zanzibar anti-slavery treaty as a rare moment of triumph for their cause, and they credited Livingstone for his contribution.[23]

During the four months that Stanley and Livingstone spent together, Stanley developed a deep affection for the older man. Stanley's writings depicted Livingstone as a kind of Victorian-era saint, and Stanley himself came to see Livingstone as his long-sought father figure. Born in Wales in 1841 to an unwed mother, Stanley is listed in the parish records of St. Hilary's Church in Denbigh simply as "John Rowlands, Bastard." After his mother abandoned him at an early age, he grew up in a workhouse, where he received a rudimentary education. At the age of seventeen, he signed on as a deckhand on a Yankee cotton ship sailing from Liverpool to New Orleans, where he took the name Henry Stanley, after the local cotton-shipping magnate Henry Hope Stanley, and concocted a story by which the elder Mr. Stanley had adopted him in a private ceremony. After serving in both the Confederate and Union armies during the Civil War, he found work as a journalist covering the frontier wars and the Colorado gold rush before landing a job as a traveling correspondent for the *New York Herald*. In Ujiji, he at last found the father he had been looking for all his life. "When I fell sick with the remittent fever, hovering between life and death, he attended me like a father," wrote Stanley. Years later he wrote, "I seem to see through the dim, misty, warm, hazy, atmosphere of Africa, always the aged face of Livingstone, urging me on in his kind, fatherly way."[24]

After Stanley and Livingstone parted in March 1872, Livingstone went southwest to Lake Bangweulu to look for the Fountains of the Nile, assisted by a caravan supplied by Stanley. He died from fever and anal bleeding at Lake Bangweulu on May 1, 1873, without finding the mythical fountains. His African assistants removed his organs, preserved the body with salt and a smokehouse process, sewed it into a canvas bag covered with tar, and carried it all the way to Bagamoyo, on the Indian Ocean coast, where it was loaded onto a British warship and taken to England. On April 16, 1874, Livingstone's body reached the docks in Southampton, England. Among the dignitaries there to meet it was Henry Morton Stanley.

Disregarding the four years that Livingstone had spent traveling with Arab ivory and slave traders, the British public acclaimed him as a champion crusader against the East African slave trade. At his funeral at Westminster Abbey on April 18, 1874, the dean of Westminster spoke of Livingstone's "burning indignation and fierce determination" to expose and strike a fatal blow to the slave trade. "He grappled with it as with the coils of a deadly serpent," intoned the minister, "and it recognized in him in turn its most formidable foe. Each strove to strangle the other, and by that struggle he perished." Livingstone's tomb in Westminster Abbey was inscribed with a quotation from an unsent letter that he had written to *New York Herald* publisher Gordon Bennett in April 1872, which ended with the words "All I can add in my loneliness is, may Heaven's richest blessing come down on everyone—American, English, or Turk—who will help heal the open sore of the world."[25]

Stanley returned to Africa in 1875 to complete Livingstone's quest for the source of the Nile, after persuading the London *Daily Telegraph* and the *New York Herald* to cosponsor the expedition. Despite his filial reverence for Livingstone, his route showed that he had never taken Livingstone's theories about the Fountains of the Nile seriously. Instead of heading southwest to Lake Bangweulu, Stanley traveled northwest to Lake Victoria to double-check Speke's observation that the Nile emerged from the northern end of that lake. He then went to Lake Tanganyika, where he was able to verify the 1874 finding of Verney Lovett Cameron (a British explorer sponsored by the Royal Geographical Society) that the lake's outlet flowed west toward the Lualaba instead of northeast toward Lake Victoria. It remained for Stanley to tackle the biggest puzzle of all— the course of the Lualaba River. For that, he would have to go into Manyema and visit Nyangwe, the frontier trading town that was fast becoming the major commercial center on the Lualaba.

Based on his previous experiences as a young reporter in the gold-mining towns of Colorado, Stanley instinctively understood the similarities between the ivory trade in Manyema and the American Wild West. "The fever for going to Manyema to exchange tawdry beads for its precious tusks," he wrote, "is the same kind as that which impelled men to the gulches and placers of California, Colorado, Montana, and Idaho; after nuggets to Australia and diamonds to Cape Colony. Manyema is at present the El Dorado of the Arabs and the *Wamrima* [i.e., coastal] tribes." Stanley also grasped the economic geography of the ivory trade. Ivory purchased in Manyema for a penny's worth of copper per pound was sold for MT$1.42–1.71 a pound in Zanzibar. Stanley had noted in 1871 that it was "only four years since the first Arab returned from Manyema with such wealth of ivory, and reports of the fabulous quantities found there, that ever since the old beaten tracks of Karagwah, Uganda, Ufipa, and Marungu have been comparatively deserted."[26]

Stanley's caravan left Ujiji on August 25, 1876, and headed west for Nyangwe. Containing 132 people, it had diminished considerably due to deaths and desertions since departing from Bagamoyo fifteen months earlier with 356 people, and two of his three white companions had died. Several Arab traders offered to accompany him with their armed trading parties, but Stanley had refused because Ujiji traders had a bad reputation in Manyema. That decision proved fortunate because Stanley's caravan was neither threatened nor molested on the two-month journey from Ujiji to Nyangwe.

2

Brussels, Royal Palace, September 12, 1876

Nearly three weeks after Stanley left Ujiji for Manyema, an international conference convened at the Royal Palace in Brussels,

Belgium. It carried the bland title of "The Brussels Geographical Conference," but its agenda was far more ambitious than the name suggested. Delegations came from the six greatest European powers—England, France, Italy, Germany, Austria-Hungary, and Russia—as well as from Belgium, a country slightly smaller than the state of Maryland. The British delegates included Thomas Fowell Buxton, the grandson of the great abolitionist; Bartle Frere, who had negotiated the 1873 anti–slave trade treaty with the sultan of Zanzibar; and Admiral Leopold Heath, who had commanded the Royal Navy's anti–slave trade squadron in the Indian Ocean. There was also William Mackinnon, a shipping magnate from Liverpool, and the explorer Verney Lovett Cameron, who had crossed Africa from east to west in 1874–1875. From Germany came its two greatest living explorers, Gustav Nachtigal and Georg Schweinfurth, as well as the president of the Berlin Geographical Society. The French delegation included the president of the Paris Geographical Society and the Marquis de Compeigne, who had done some preliminary exploration along the Ogowe River near the Atlantic coast. As a group, the delegates were a mixture of explorers, armchair geographers, and anti–slave trade activists.[27]

At the opening session, King Leopold II explained that the conference was being held in Brussels because Belgium was a neutral country that was centrally located. "Needless to say, in bringing you to Brussels, I have not been motivated by selfish designs," he told the delegates. "No, gentlemen, if Belgium is small, she is happy and satisfied with her lot. I have no other ambition than to serve her well." He then outlined the purpose of the conference in terms that were both grandiose and vague: "The subject which brings us together today is one of those that merit the attention of the friends of humanity. To open up the only parts of the globe where civilization has not yet penetrated, to pierce the darkness in which entire populations are enveloped, is a crusade worthy of this age of progress." As he continued on, it became clear that he was speaking about the equatorial regions of Africa.

At the time King Leopold II spoke, Belgium had been an independent country for only forty-six years, born of a Catholic revolt for independence from Protestant Holland. But independence had come at a heavy price: when the major European powers agreed to recognize Belgium's borders in 1839, they took away half of Luxemburg and half of Limburg, and the break with Holland cut off Belgium's access to the Asian markets served by the Dutch East India Company. Even before Leopold II succeeded his father to the throne, he was scheming to "aggrandize Belgium" by attacking Holland or invading the Rhineland, but he abandoned those ideas as unrealistic. Instead, he focused on the extension of the fatherland by means of colonial expansion. "It is on distant shores," he wrote, "that we need to recover our lost half-provinces."[28]

When Leopold II was enthroned as the second king of Belgium in December 1865, he was already concocting schemes for overseas adventures. His first objective was China. "My dream is to create a world-wide Belgium company with headquarters in Brussels," he wrote, "which would, in time, become for China what the [British] East India Company has become for the Indian subcontinent." Unable to find investors, he abandoned the plan and tried to buy part of the South Pacific island of Borneo, but the Dutch rejected his offer. He then tried to create a private company that would lease the Philippines from Spain for ninety years, thus providing access to markets in China and Japan, but Spain declined. In July 1875, Leopold was talking with the British about establishing a colony in New Guinea. By this time, he had long given up on trying to interest the Belgian government in his colonial adventures. These were his personal projects, which he pursued using his powers of persuasion, his personal fortune, his status as king, and a handful of Belgian government officials who were personally loyal to him. He conducted all the negotiations in strictest secrecy, which is why the delegates at the Brussels Geographical Conference did not question him when he presented himself as a humanitarian with no ulterior motives.[29]

Historians have long debated what motivated the king of a small European country to engage so energetically in colonial adventures. To the Belgian historian Jean Stengers, Leopold's imperialism was "economic imperialism in its purest form." Stengers argued that Leopold was motivated less by personal greed than by the belief that overseas territories offered economic opportunities for European nations. Leopold was a great admirer of the Dutch colonial empire in the East Indies, which produced huge profits for the Dutch treasury. With Belgium cut off from those markets after 1830, the king wanted to create a similar entity that would enrich Belgium. But another Belgian historian, Vincent Viaene, has pointed out that King Leopold's schemes had political, social, and nationalistic dimensions as well. A colony that provided a market for Belgian manufactured goods would also provide jobs for Belgian factory workers, and the need for colonial administrators and military officers would provide employment opportunities for the Belgian middle class. Moreover, the possession of a colony would turn "little Belgium" into an imperial metropole, and Brussels would become the capital of an empire, complete with broad boulevards and imposing monuments. That is why Leopold talked about transforming the Belgians from a nation of grocers and lawyers into "an imperial people."[30]

With his colonial schemes in the Far East going nowhere, Leopold turned his attention toward Africa. On August 22, 1875, he wrote to Baron Lambermont, his confidant in the Ministry of Foreign Affairs: "For the moment, neither the Spanish, nor the Portuguese, nor the Dutch are inclined to sell. I will discretely inquire about whether there is something to be done in Africa." It was the equatorial regions of Africa that interested Leopold the most, in part because they remained largely unexplored. As the conference approached, the king was aware that Stanley was in the process of exploring the Lualaba. He was also aware of Cameron's theory that the Lualaba ran into the Congo River because he had made an incognito visit to Cameron in London in May 1876. Having sent a delegate to the International Congress of Geographical Sciences in Paris at the beginning of August, Leopold was well informed about the French expedition led by Pierre Savorgnan de Brazza that was exploring the Ogowe River in hopes of finding a more accessible route between the Atlantic Ocean and the heart of Africa.[31]

A month before the opening of the Brussels Geographical Conference, King Leopold wrote a confidential letter to the Belgian delegation. Instead of writing about geography, he focused on the slave trade within Africa, which, he estimated, was enslaving more than one hundred thousand people a year. It was the duty of the European countries to lance that infected sore by forming an international organization with headquarters in Belgium and branches in the different member countries. The organization would raise money in the different countries for building a series of interlinked stations for scientific research and hospitality to European explorers. Even though most of the money would come from the various member countries, the executive committee in Belgium would be responsible for the overall direction of the project.[32]

Emile Banning, the secretary of the conference, elaborated on the anti-slavery theme in his report on the conference. The efforts by England to end the maritime slave trade were laudable, he said, "but there exists in the present day a universal conviction that the trade can only be destroyed on the actual scene of its ravages." He was proposing to attack the slave trade on African soil. "Opening up Africa to science, Christianity, commerce, and civilization," he wrote, was the "only system which can result in the *complete and definitive abolition* of the slave trade" [emphasis in original].[33]

We can only speculate as to why King Leopold would put so much emphasis on the anti-slavery cause, given that Belgium had never participated in the Atlantic slave trade and had no tradition of anti-slavery activism. One possible reason was that it gave the Geographical Conference a higher humanitarian purpose that could arouse the passions of the participants. A second reason was to attract the support of the British, who had taken the lead in suppressing the Atlantic slave trade in the first half of the nineteenth century and who were the only maritime power attacking the slave trade along the east coast of Africa. It was no accident that the British delegation included the leading activists against the East African slave trade. Leopold would later admit that the anti-slavery emphasis was mainly a ploy to attract British support.[34]

When the delegates gathered at the Royal Palace in Brussels on September 12, Leopold outlined the three goals of the conference. The first was to designate two bases of operation—one on the East African coast opposite Zanzibar and one at the mouth of the Congo River. A line drawn at 6° south latitude would pass near both places, and so Leopold was, in effect, defining the area of operation as the broad band of equatorial Africa that stretched from the Atlantic to the Indian Ocean. The second goal was to identify routes into the interior along which to build a series of scientific and hospitality stations that would be the front line in the fight to suppress the African slave trade. The third goal was to establish an international organization with an executive committee that would oversee the stations and direct the work of the various national committees. Telling the delegates that they were engaged in a "crusade worthy of this age of progress," he noted that he would be happy if "Brussels became the general headquarters of this civilizing movement."

When the conference concluded on September 14, the delegates had ratified all of the major ideas that Leopold had outlined earlier in his confidential memo. The area of operation was the band of territory from the Atlantic to the Indian Ocean that stretched from roughly ten degrees north to ten degrees south of the equator. The locations of the proposed interior stations were left vague, but the group specifically mentioned Ujiji and Nyangwe as potential sites. They also agreed to form an "International Commission of Exploration and Civilization of Central Africa" consisting of two delegates from each of the member countries and to organize a series of national committees whose major tasks would be generating interest and raising money. The organization would be administered by an executive committee composed of a president and four members chosen by the conference. When Bartle Frere proposed that King Leopold should be elected president, the delegates burst into applause.

Belgium was the first member country to set up a functioning national committee of the "International Association for Abolition of the Slave Trade and Opening Up Central Africa." When King Leopold addressed the national committee members in the Royal Palace on November 6, he began by talking about slavery. "The slavery that still continues over a considerable portion of the African continent is a festering sore which all friends of civilization must desire to see eliminated," he proclaimed. He told the delegates that they were building "an international association to put a stop to this odious traffic, which is a disgrace to the age in which we live, and to tear away the veil of darkness that still hangs over Central Africa." He also explained his strategy for fighting the internal African slave trade: "We are convinced that if we succeed in opening roads and establishing stations on the tracks followed by the slave merchants, this odious traffic will be ended." He did not explain how the mere existence of hospitality stations staffed by a handful of Europeans would accomplish that goal.[35]

National committees soon began to spring up in a variety of European countries, even ones that had not been invited to the Brussels conference. The Paris Geographical Society approved the establishment of a French national committee at a special meeting on October 16. The French committee maintained a degree of independence, preferring to support French projects that were not linked to the association in Brussels. The Germans formed a national committee, known as the German African Society, in December. The Netherlands, Russia, Austria, Italy, Switzerland, Spain, and Portugal all formed national committees in early 1877. At a meeting of the American Geographical Society in New York on May 22, 1877, the members approved the formation of a national committee. The resolution read, "The American Geographical Society approves the plan conceived by His Majesty the King of the Belgians for the exploration and civilization of the interior of Africa and the suppression of the slave trade." The society nominated Henry Shelton Sanford, the former US ambassador to Belgium, as its representative to the International Commission in Brussels.[36]

In Britain, the Royal Geographical Society ran into opposition from both the Foreign Office and the Home Office when it tried to form a national committee of King Leopold's International Association. The Home Office pointed out that suppression of the internal African slave trade was a matter for national governments that was far beyond the capacity of any private organization. After intense debate, the Royal Geographical Society decided to withdraw from Leopold's association, a development that motivated King Leopold to reevaluate his emphasis on suppressing the slave trade. Right after the Brussels conference, the organization was called "The International Association for Abolition of the Slave Trade and Opening Up Central Africa." Once the British withdrew, however, Leopold dropped the emphasis on the slave trade and adopted the neutral title of the "International African Association." He was using a vaguely defined international organization with scientific and humanitarian pretensions as a vehicle for advancing his own agenda in Africa, even though the agenda itself had not yet been worked out.[37]

3

Manyema Territory, October 1876

In October 1876, when Henry Morton Stanley was trekking through Manyema toward Nyangwe, he noticed that the "Wild West" atmosphere that David Livingstone had described in 1871 was beginning to be organized into a regular system of trade and tribute that was undergirded by a new form of political authority. "We met two waungwana from Kasongo," Stanley wrote in his diary on October 17, "who gave us news of the late massacre of an entire caravan on the road to Kasesa by Manyema treachery, and the departure of Tippu-Tib—Hamed Hamudi—to avenge the massacre." Stanley's entry makes it clear that the person most responsible for imposing the new political order in Manyema was the Zanzibari ivory trader Tippu Tip.

Hamid bin Muhammed of the clan El Murjebi, who came to be known as Tippu Tip, was usually referred to as an Arab, but he had the appearance of a person of mixed ancestry whose facial features and dark skin struck many Europeans as more African than Arab. "Contrary to widespread opinion," wrote the Belgian lieutenant Alphonse Vangele, "Tippu Tip is not an Arab; he is a person of mixed-blood from Zanzibar with pure Negroid traits." Similarly, the Austrian explorer Dr. Oscar Lenz wrote, "He is not of the pure Arab race; his complexion is very dark, without being a true Negroid type." By Tippu Tip's own account, his paternal great-grandfather had come to East Africa from Oman and settled on the Mrima coast opposite Zanzibar, and his paternal great-grandmother had been born to an African mother and an Omani Arab father. That is perhaps why Salim bin Muhammad, who was one of Tippu Tip's top lieutenants (and, by one account, his brother-in-law), claimed that Tippu Tip's father was a "half-caste Arab."[38]

Tippu Tip's maternal ancestry is more difficult to trace. According to his friend and biographer Heinrich Brode, Tippu Tip's mother belonged to a prominent Omani Arab family from Muscat that had immigrated to Zanzibar. But Tippu Tip himself told a more complex story about his maternal grandfather, a trader from the Mrima coast who had traveled far into the East African interior and purchased an enslaved girl from the Tetela country named Darimumba, who became his concubine. She bore him a daughter named Bint Habib, who later married Tippu Tip's father and became Tippu Tip's mother. He recounted that his grandmother, Darimumba, had told him stories about the Tetela country when he was a boy. A third version of Tippu Tip's maternal ancestry was given by Salim bin Muhammad, who claimed that Tippu Tip's birth mother was an enslaved African woman from the Mrima coast.[39]

Tippu Tip's ambiguous appearance sometimes put him at a disadvantage when dealing with Europeans who apprehended the world according to the racial prejudices of their time. Charles Eliot, the British consul in Zanzibar, wrote that Tippu Tip's features "were of the African type and produced at first an impression that he was a low-caste hybrid; but this impression was dispelled by his polite and dignified manner and his flow of speech." During his years in the interior of East and Central Africa, however, Tippu Tip's appearance proved to be an asset on more than one occasion when he acquired authority by claiming to be a distant kinsman of an African chief. He could be an African or an Arab, depending on the needs of the moment.[40]

It is possible to know quite a bit about Tippu Tip because near the end of his life he wrote his autobiography in the Swahili language using Arabic characters, and his friend in Zanzibar, the German doctor Heinrich Brode, wrote a biography based on the Swahili manuscript with additional details from his interviews. In his autobiography, Tippu Tip proudly portrayed himself as an ivory trader but never mentioned trading in slaves, an omission that clearly bothered the Europeans who collaborated in the publication of his autobiography and his biography. W. H. Whitely, who translated the autobiography from Swahili into English, tried to play down Tippu Tip's slave-trading activities. "There may be those who feel embarrassed at Tippu's part in slave trading," wrote Whitely, "but this was for him—as one may read—a minor consideration." But Charles Eliot, the British consul general of Zanzibar, was less diplomatic. "It must be admitted that Tippu Tip was a slave trader," he wrote. Then he added mysteriously, "Much remains untold."[41]

The history of Tippu Tip's family mirrored the growth of the inland caravan trade in nineteenth-century East Africa. His paternal grandfather had been one of the pioneers of the caravan route running from Zanzibar to Tabora and on to Lake Tanganyika. Tippu Tip's father, Muhammad bin Juma, had been raised in Tabora, which was the most important trading center between the coast and Lake Tanganyika. Tabora was also the inland headquarters of the Omani Arab caravan traders, who, according to the British explorer Richard Burton, "in many cases, settle here for years, remaining in charge of their depots while their factors and slaves travel around the country and collect items of traffic." The Arabs lived comfortably, and even splendidly, in Tabora. Their large single-story houses had shady outside verandas and spacious inner courtyards, and they received regular supplies of merchandise, comforts, and luxuries from the coast. A wealthy Arab merchant typically lived surrounded by his wives, concubines, and slaves, who were sometimes trained in various crafts and skills.[42]

It was common among mobile caravan traders to have households in more than one location, each presided over by a wife. In Tabora, Tippu Tip's father had married the daughter of the principal wife of Fundi Kira, the powerful Nyamwezi chief who governed the region in which Tabora was located. The marriage produced a financial payoff when Fundi Kira made his new son-in-law his agent for selling his considerable stores of ivory. In Zanzibar, Muhammad bin Juma had married Bint Habib al-Wardi, who reportedly gave birth to Tippu Tip sometime between 1837 and 1840. Tippu Tip grew up in Bint Habib's household in Zanzibar speaking Swahili, which he learned to write using Arabic letters. Throughout his life, he was more comfortable speaking Swahili than Arabic, and he sometimes used an Arabic-speaking interpreter in his meetings with Arabs.[43]

At the age of eighteen, Tippu Tip went on a caravan trip with his father that took him to Tabora and on to Ujiji. After that, he began trading on his own. In 1860, he borrowed merchandise worth a thousand Maria Theresa dollars from an Indian merchant in Zanzibar and traveled inland to purchase ivory. When he saw that the trade was going poorly, he continued farther and farther inland until he came to a place where ivory was abundant and cheap. The trip resulted in enormous profits.

For his next trip, which began in 1863, he went to twenty different Indian merchants in Zanzibar and borrowed trade goods worth thirty thousand Maria Theresa dollars. Arriving in the region southwest of Lake Tanganyika in 1867, he entered the territory of a chief named Nsama, who had a lot of ivory but was reputed to be a treacherous person who had previously killed and robbed a number of Arab and Swahili merchants. When Tippu Tip and his entourage entered Chief Nsama's fortified town, they were ambushed by Nsama's soldiers, who shot arrows at them. They responded by firing their muskets, which were loaded with buckshot for fighting at close quarters. As Nsama's soldiers rushed them in a tightly packed formation, they were quickly gunned down. "They died like birds," Tippu Tip wrote. In Nsama's warehouses they confiscated over thirty tons of ivory and an equal weight in copper from the Katanga copper mines. In subsequent encounters with chief Nsama's forces, they acquired about a thousand captives.[44]

During the war with Nsama, Hamid bin Muhammed picked up the nickname that he would proudly carry for the rest of his life. As he described it, "The name Tip Tip had been given to me by the locals who had fled to Urungu. They said they had seen many waungwana [Swahili caravan traders] and had seized their goods, but this man's guns went 'tiptip' in a manner too terrible to listen to. That is how I got my name Tip Tip." So important was the moniker to him that he later entitled his autobiography *The Story of Hamid bin Muhammed el Murjebi, Known as Tippu Tip.*[45]

On July 29, 1867, Tippu Tip met David Livingstone, who had come to the region south of Lake Tanganyika in search of Lake Bemba, but whose progress had been impeded by the war between Nsama and Tippu Tip. Writing about the encounter three decades later, Tippu Tip described it as follows: "Some of my men went out searching for the enemy, but before they reached their objective, they made contact with an Englishman, a big fellow, by the name of Livingstone, his first name David. . . Some of my men brought him to my camp, while others carried on the war against Nsama. As for Livingstone, he had neither goods nor rations. Said bin Ali and I took him in." Tippu Tip later described the way he aided Livingstone's explorations: "He wanted guides to take him to Lake Mweru. He went and came back, now anxious to visit Kazembe's. We gave him guides to take him there, and picked out one of our kinsmen, Said bin Khalfan, to go as far as Kazembe's." Tippu Tip departed in December 1867 to return to Zanzibar, leaving Livingstone under the care and protection of his colleagues and relatives. He never saw Livingstone again.[46]

Tippu Tip left Zanzibar on his third ivory-buying trip early in 1870. It would last twelve years. After considering competing offers from two mercantile establishments in Zanzibar, he accepted MT$50,000 worth of trade goods on credit from Taria Topan, an Indian Muslim who was one of the wealthiest merchants in Zanzibar. He expressed a clear preference for getting his financing from Muslims, perhaps because any financial disputes could then be settled in Islamic courts according to Sharia law, whereas the Indian Hindus were more likely to seek relief from the British Consular Court in Zanzibar. Under Topan's patronage, the chain of finance behind Tippu Tip's trading trip stretched around the Western Indian Ocean rim from Zanzibar to Gujarat.

While many Zanzibar-based traders were aiming their caravans toward Manyema, Tippu Tip followed a different route. His first objective was the area southwest of Lake Tanganyika that he had visited on his previous trip. He stayed about a month with Chief

Nsama, whom he had vanquished in 1867. David Livingstone, who was by then in the Lake Bangweulu region in search of the Fountains of the Nile, heard rumors that "Tippu Tip is reported to be carrying it with a high hand in Nsama's country, insisting that all the ivory must be brought as his tribute." Moving southwest from Chief Nsama's territory, Tippu Tip came to the border of Chief Kazembe's country, where he found the path blocked by Kazembe's soldiers. He decided to vanquish Kazembe just as he had earlier defeated Nsama. After a month of fighting, his soldiers reached Kazembe's town and killed him, capturing a large quantity of guns and ivory and countless captives. Nsama and Kazembe had been the two most feared and powerful chiefs in the region, and Tippu Tip had defeated them both.[47]

Tippu Tip next headed north to the Tetela territory southwest of Manyema. He noted that ivory could be purchased very cheaply, a sure sign that no ivory traders had previously been in the area. He gained favor with the Tetela chief Kasongo Rushie by claiming that his maternal grandmother had been a woman of the Tetela royal family who had been enslaved by the Luba and sold to Tippu Tip's grandfather. Tippu Tip's biographer Heinrich Brode considered the story a "well-prepared tissue of lies," but it apparently worked because Kasongo Rushie appointed him as the new chief and announced that all tusks should be brought directly to him. In the next two weeks, two hundred tusks arrived, and two or three more came in every day. As he had done with Chief Nsama, Tippu Tip was collecting ivory as tribute instead of purchasing it.[48]

In early 1874, Tippu Tip took his caravan northeast to the Lualaba River and the trading town of Nyangwe, the commercial heart of Manyema. Because there was continuing friction in Nyangwe between the traders from Zanzibar and those from the Mrima Coast, he was asked to stay and be the town's chief, but he was more interested in continuing on to the town of Kasongo, thirty-five miles to the southeast, where his close relative Muhammad bin Said (known as Bwana Nzige) lived. Arriving at Kasongo,

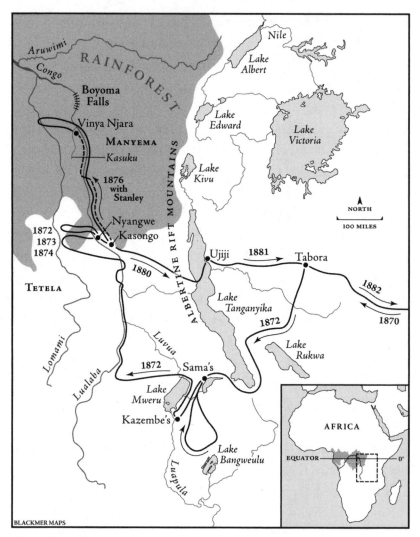

Tippu Tip's third trading journey, 1870–1882, including his travels with Stanley in 1876

he found the Arab and Swahili traders beset with problems. The local people were engaged in organized resistance against them by refusing to bring them sufficient quantities of food for sale and by helping their captives escape. Tippu Tip himself lost two hundred captives and was unable to recover even one because the local villages were operating a kind of "underground railroad" to move escaped captives far away.

Portrait of Tippu Tip by Herbert Ward, ca. 1890. Herbert Ward, *Five Years with the Congo Cannibals*, p. 169.

When Tippu Tip met with the major Arab and Swahili traders in Kasongo, they gave him full authority to solve their problems. He decided on war and fought the locals for three months until they submitted and gave the traders complete authority. The local people were expected to supply work parties for whatever tasks the

Arabs needed, and all ivory—even the smallest tusks—had to be brought in as tribute. Soon food was plentiful again, as the region produced abundant rice. People would come from as far away as Nyangwe to buy rice, sometimes paying for it with ivory. Tippu Tip was now the undisputed ruler of Kasongo, and his merchant empire was becoming a political empire.[49]

4

Ivoryton, Connecticut, United States, 1874–1876

The 220-acre tract of land in Essex, Connecticut, owned by Comstock, Cheney & Co., manufacturers of ivory combs, billiard balls, and piano keys, was fast becoming a company town with a store, a boardinghouse, and a row of Gothic houses for the company officers. Between 1874 and 1876, the company built a three-story factory building and two two-story factory buildings (known collectively as the "lower factory") along the Falls River for working ivory. A quarter of a mile upstream, it added a three-story building (known as the "upper factory") for fashioning wooden piano keys that would be topped with ivory veneers. It was clear that the company was moving into the production of piano ivories in a major way.[50]

The very name of the company encapsulated the complexity of producing ivory products on an industrial scale. Samuel Comstock had been working with ivory since 1832, when he started a factory for making ivory combs and toothpicks in partnership with his brother. For waterpower to drive the circular saws and other machinery, the factory was built along the Falls River, a modest stream that ran into the Connecticut River, four miles away. When the brothers' partnership broke up in 1847, Samuel moved upstream and began acquiring dam and water rights, including the right to dig a large ditch to divert water from the river for manufacturing purposes. In 1851, he purchased 220 acres of farmland adjoining his shop that would be the site of future company buildings. During this period of acquisition, Samuel was often strapped for money, and in 1853, he had to borrow a thousand dollars from his father-in-law. He received a much-needed infusion of funds in 1860, when George Cheney, an ivory trader from Providence, Rhode Island, invested $3,500 to purchase one-quarter of his company. In return, he made Cheney a full partner and changed the name of his enterprise to Comstock, Cheney & Co.

George Cheney had begun his career as an ivory trader. In 1850, at the age of twenty, he made his first trip to Zanzibar as the supercargo (head trader) on the *Sacramento*, one of several ships owned by Rufus Greene of Providence, Rhode Island. The voyage was less than successful, and the ship returned with $6,000 worth of unsold merchandise. The captain, John Congdon, blamed it all on George Cheney. "He often talks of the next voyage," the captain wrote in his journal. "If they ever send him again as supercargo, I shall be mistaken. He hardly sells a thing, and never buys without coming to me for my judgment on all." But George Cheney could not easily be fired because he was courting Rufus Greene's daughter Sarah. He returned to Zanzibar on one of Rufus Greene's ships in 1851, but this time he was no longer the supercargo. It is difficult to discern if he had any real duties at all.[51]

In March 1853, Cheney set out for his third voyage to East Africa accompanied by Sarah, his wife of one week. The couple spent nearly two years in Zanzibar, where Cheney bought ivory, cloves, and gum copal (a tree resin used for making varnish); supervised the hired day laborers who packed the merchandise for shipping; and cleared the merchandise through the Zanzibar Customs House. He also sold bales of *merikani*, a white cotton cloth produced in Salem, Massachusetts, and barrels of gunpowder to Swahili and Arab caravan traders who carried them far inland in their quest for ivory. By the time he left Zanzibar on June 19, 1855, he had become a skilled trader.

The exchange of Massachusetts cloth for East African ivory seemed like a perfectly respectable transaction, but underneath the

surface, the trade was deeply entangled with slavery. The Massachusetts mills produced cloth from cotton harvested by enslaved
Africans in the American South, and the East African caravans
transported both ivory and captives, with the profits from ivory
subsidizing the slave trade. The New England ivory traders who
traveled to Zanzibar understood those connections very well, and
even ordinary Americans were not unaware of the ivory trade's
unsavory implications. In 1844, Rev. Alexander Sessions of Salem
had been forced to deny rumors that Richard P. Waters, the American consul in Zanzibar, was a slave trader. In a letter to the consul,
Reverend Sessions tried to play down the importance of the rumors. "Let not this allusion to remarks assume an undue importance
to your mind," he wrote.[52]

George Cheney left for his fourth and final trading voyage in
1857, when he accompanied his father-in-law, Rufus Greene, to
Zanzibar. For two years, the two men purchased ivory, gum copal,
and cloves that were carried to Providence on Rufus Greene's ships,
and they sold cotton cloth, gunpowder, and other New England
products to the Arab and Swahili caravan traders. Greene was
delighted by the favorable trading conditions in Zanzibar. "Every
facility is allowed to all agents of the foreign [mercantile] houses
resident there," he wrote to US assistant secretary of state Frederick
Seward. "I have never been in any country or city where the person or property of foreigners was so secure or safe as in Zanzibar.
I resided there two years, and during that time my transactions in
trade exceeded two hundred thousand dollars." There is no record
of how much money George Cheney made on that trip, but a few
months after his return to Providence in February or March of
1860, he purchased one-quarter of Samuel Comstock's ivory comb
manufacturing business.[53]

Soon, Samuel Comstock's farm was being transformed into
a company town. Between 1867 and 1874, he sold land near his
large house to the company's officers in order to create a long line
of Gothic houses along the main street. In 1872, Comstock built

the company store, which sold groceries and general merchandise, and had an assembly hall on the second floor for company functions and public activities. When the men's boardinghouse became inadequate to house the workers, the company moved a former seminary building to a site near the lower factory to use as a boardinghouse, and it later added a boardinghouse for women. During the 1870s, the company had about forty-five employees working at the lower factory, which consumed nine thousand pounds of ivory per month, and 150 workers making wooden piano keys at the upper factory.[54]

The infusion of George Cheney's money had allowed the company to make the transition from ivory combs and toothpicks to piano keys and billiard balls. Piano production in Europe and the United States increased tenfold between 1850 and 1900 as the increasing mechanization of piano manufacturing greatly reduced the selling price. The growing desire of respectable American households to have pianos can be seen in the official statistics of manufactures for 1860, which listed twenty-one thousand pianos produced annually in a country of thirty-one million people. An article in the *Atlantic Monthly* in July 1867 noted that "almost every couple that sets up housekeeping on a respectable scale considers a piano only less indispensable than a kitchen range."[55]

The American piano industry, which had been producing about 2,500 mediocre-quality pianos annually in the 1830s, had received a major boost in the 1840s when Jonas Chickering's factory in Boston started manufacturing an improved piano with a one-piece cast-iron frame concealed inside the wooden exterior. When the factory burned down in 1852, the company replaced it with a five-story structure that was, at the time, the largest industrial building in the United States. The following year, a German immigrant named Henry Steinway and his sons opened a small piano-making shop in New York City. Like Jonas Chickering, Steinway used a cast-iron frame, but he improved the sound by stringing the strings in a different way and increasing the tension so that they resonated better on the sounding board. Within a few years, Steinway pianos began showing up in concert halls, and a Steinway debuted with the New York Philharmonic in 1861.[56] Although Steinway and Chickering differed on many aspects of piano design, they agreed that the white piano keys should be topped with ivory veneers, even though some American manufacturers were still using mother-of-pearl or tortoiseshell. Ivory-topped piano keys had the smooth but slightly tacky feel that concert pianists preferred.

The other rapidly growing use for ivory was for billiard balls. In 1850 Michael Phelan of New York City, one of America's best billiard players, noted the extraordinary rapidity with which the number of billiard rooms and players had increased during his career. Whereas billiard tables had once been the exclusive amusement of the very rich, urban billiard rooms where people of modest means could play were becoming popular. Phelan remembered a time when there were not more than sixteen accessible billiard tables in all of New York City, but by 1850, there were over four hundred, and new billiard rooms had also opened in New Orleans, Philadelphia, and Boston. The growing popularity of billiards was in evidence as far away as Chicago, where almost every saloon in the city put in one or more billiard tables between 1858 and 1859.[57]

The growth of Comstock, Cheney & Company was mirrored by Pratt, Read & Company in Deep River, Connecticut, some four miles away. When the Pratt Brothers Company, the Julius Pratt Company, and the George Read Company amalgamated in 1863 to form Pratt, Read & Co., all three were already producing piano keys. The consolidated company owned three dams along Deep River plus the town reservoir, which gave it plenty of waterpower for its machinery. With the piano key business booming, Pratt, Read erected a new and larger factory in 1866. Some of the money for the expansion came from Rufus Greene, who had invested a considerable sum in the Pratt Brothers Company in 1860 and had become a trustee. The two competing ivory companies were thus intertwined at the highest level.

Taken together, Comstock, Cheney & Company and Pratt, Read & Company had a near monopoly on the production of piano ivories in the United States, and they were major producers of ivory billiard balls and combs. The investments from the ivory traders George Cheney and Rufus Greene indicated the increasing vertical integration of ivory trading in Zanzibar with the manufacture of ivory products in Connecticut. Cheney and Greene knew very little about sawing ivory or managing a factory, but they knew a great deal about the globalized web that connected the Connecticut River valley to East Africa. At the other end of that web were the Arab and Swahili caravans that traveled deep into the heart of Africa in search of ivory and captives.

5

Riba Riba, Manyema Territory, October 5, 1876

After crossing the watershed that divides the streams flowing east toward Lake Tanganyika from those flowing west toward the Lualaba River on October 5, 1876, Henry Morton Stanley observed a gradual increase in the extravagance of the vegetation. Trees were one hundred feet tall, vines were as thick as cables, and thorns were like hooks of steel. "At Manyema," he wrote, "the beauty of nature becomes terrible, and in the expression of her powers she is awful." Traveling through villages on the southern fringes of the Manyema rainforest, he also noticed that square and rectangular huts with wattle-and-daub walls topped by gradually sloping roofs had replaced the round huts with tall conical roofs that were typically found east of Lake Tanganyika. That small ethnographic detail, readily visible to a passing traveler, was emblematic of the distinctive cultural traditions of the forest dwellers.[58]

From Lake Tanganyika all the way to the Atlantic Ocean lived people who spoke closely related languages and organized themselves in localized political units. They were led by individuals who displayed their leadership skills by developing social networks and amassing wealth rather than by hereditary chiefs. Stanley recognized that the Manyema form of political organization, which differed dramatically from the large chiefdoms in the East African savanna or the mountain kingdoms of the Great Lakes region, had left the people of Manyema at a disadvantage against outsiders with guns. "The Arabs have refrained from kidnapping between the [Lake] Tanganyika and the sea," he wrote, "but in Manyema, where the natives are timid, irresolute, and divided into small, weak tribes, they recover their audacity, and exercise their kidnapping propensities unchecked."[59]

The major exception to that generalization was the Lega people, who lived in the forest north of the trade route. Although they had a decentralized political system, a voluntary association known as Bwami linked their independent villages together and thus facilitated the mobilization of warriors in times of danger. When a trading party led by one of Muhammad bin Gharib's lieutenants arrived in Lega country in 1870, thousands of warriors gathered to oppose it. The head trader announced, "We come to buy ivory, and if there is none we go away." But the Lega replied, "Nay, you come to die here," and unleashed a volley of arrows. When the traders responded with gunfire, the Lega fled, but the ivory traders generally avoided Lega villages after that.[60]

The Bwami association served primarily to teach and uphold the central principles of Lega social and political life. Young men or women who wished to be initiated into Bwami had to obtain tutors and learn the relevant proverbs (out of a repertory of well over a thousand) that outlined the Bwami philosophy and moral code. They also learned how to interpret the abstract sculptures and masks that served as mnemonic devices for Bwami teachings. In order to advance through the ranks of the Bwami association, young initiates had to seek mentors in the higher ranks and mobilize financial and moral support from their kin to sponsor initiation ceremonies. Reaching the highest rank—Kindi—was a lifelong quest, normally achieved by only one or two people in each village. As the only Bwami members allowed to own ivory sculptures, holders of the Kindi rank referred to themselves as *nenemulamba* (the owners of the ivory) and wore hats topped with hairs from an elephant's tail. Consequently, the Lega found it unthinkable to sell ivory to Arab traders.[61]

While passing through Lega villages in 1876, Stanley admired the skill of the blacksmiths and the artisanship of the cane furniture in the houses. Although he was unaware of the Lega tradition of producing abstract sculptures, he took note of the "curiously carved bits of wood" and the "handsome carved spoons" that he saw in the houses. He did not see any ivory sculptures because they were normally kept hidden and were displayed only during Bwami ceremonies. Stanley also observed that the Lega had "much traditional lore" that was communicated from one generation to another, a clear allusion to Bwami proverbs and moral philosophy. He was frustrated, however, by their lack of curiosity about the outside world. "They have been imprisoned for generations in their woods," he wrote in his diary, "and the difficulty of making way through these forests which surround them is the sole cause why they know naught of the outside world or the world outside knows aught of them. It appears to be synonymous with the Forest Country." Stanley failed to understand that with their rich cultural and intellectual life, the outside world had little to offer them.[62]

With the notable exception of the Lega, people in Manyema had placed little or no value on elephant tusks prior to the arrival of the Arab ivory caravans in the 1860s. Elephants had previously been hunted for their meat. Unlike the elephant hunters in the grasslands of East Africa, who would attack an elephant with spears, the people in the rainforest of Manyema generally relied on a kind of deadfall trap consisting of a heavy log suspended above a trail, with a spear attached to one end. Forest elephants often traveled along the same forest paths that the people used, and when an elephant's foot touched the trip-cord, the spear was driven into the elephant's neck by the weight of the log. Although straight tusks were sometimes used as doorposts or pestles, most tusks were simply stashed in the villages or hidden in the forest. Tusks that were rotted and gnawed by rodents could sometimes be found at places where an elephant had once been killed, indicating that the hunters had not found it worthwhile to carry them back to the village.

Because ivory had such little value in Manyema, the first Arab traders could buy a tusk for a few strings of beads and take it to Ujiji, where they received weight-for-weight in beads, thick brass wire, and calico. As more traders from Ujiji invaded Manyema, however, the price rose, creating a demand for larger quantities of trade goods. Caravans coming directly from Zanzibar carried large quantities of imported beads, which were in high demand. A caravan led by the Zanzibari trader known as Juma Merikani arrived in Manyema in October 1870 with an immense store of beads and copper; and the trader Abed bin Salim brought in seven thousand pounds of beads three months later.[63]

In contrast, Arab traders based in Ujiji had only limited access to trade goods from Zanzibar, so they resorted to other means to obtain ivory. Muhammad bin Gharib's caravan brought Lunda captives that it had earlier obtained south of Lake Tanganyika. Muhammad had planned to trade them for ivory, but the Manyema people rejected them, claiming that they were thieves and criminals. Running short on trade goods, some of Muhammad's trading parties would hold the village headman hostage until the villagers brought ivory to pay the ransom. Other traders engaged in direct plunder. In June 1870, Livingstone passed through nine villages that had been looted and burned by ivory traders from Ujiji. In October, he encountered four different trading parties that were getting all their ivory by fighting. "Plunder and murder is Ujijian trading," he noted in his diary. Two years later, he summed up the ivory trade in Manyema as follows: "When parties leave Ujiji to go westward into Manyema, the question asked is not what goods they take, but how many guns and kegs of gunpowder. If they have two or three hundred muskets and ammunition in proportion, they think success is certain."[64]

On October 17, 1876, Stanley's caravan reached the Lualaba River and began to follow it north to Nyangwe. Coming to the village of Mkwanga, Stanley met two black Zanzibaris from Kasongo, Tippu Tip's town, who told him that Tippu Tip was away on a military mission after local villagers had massacred one of his trading parties. The next day, October 18, Stanley came to Mwana Mamba's town, where several Arab and Swahili traders lived. He was conducted to the veranda of Said el-Mazrui's compound. It was there he met Tippu Tip.

Here is how Stanley described the meeting in his diary: "Heartily welcomed by Arabs and natives. Saw the redoubted Hamed bin Mohammed, alias Tibu Tib, a fine handsome ~~black~~/dark man of Arab extraction in the prime of life who, next to Said bin Habib, is the first of Arab explorers." Two things are noteworthy about this entry. The first is that Stanley was not sure how to describe the skin color of Tippu Tip; he first wrote "black" and then changed it to "dark." The second thing is that he recognized Tippu Tip as a fellow explorer. In his book *Through the Dark Continent*, Stanley elaborated on the meeting: "He was a tall, black-bearded man of Negroid complexion, in the prime of life, straight, and quick in his movements, a picture of energy and strength. He had a fine intelligent face, with a nervous twitching of the eyes, and gleaming white and perfectly formed teeth. He was attended by a large retinue of young Arabs, who looked up to him as chief, and a score of waungwana and *Wanyamwezi* [hired porters] followers whom he had led over a thousand miles through Africa. With the air of a well-bred Arab, and almost courtier-like in his manner, he welcomed me to Mwana Mamba's village."[65]

Tippu Tip's account of the encounter, written many years later, focused on a story that Stanley did not mention. "One afternoon Stanley appeared," wrote Tippu Tip. "We greeted him and welcomed him and gave him a house. The following morning we went to see him, and he showed us a gun, telling us, 'From this gun fifteen bullets come out.' Now, we knew of no such gun firing fifteen rounds, neither knew of one nor had seen such. I asked him: 'From a single barrel?' He said they came from a single barrel, so I asked him to fire it so I could see. At that, he went outside and fired twelve rounds. Then he took a pistol and fired six rounds. He came back and sat down on the verandah. We were amazed! I asked him how he loaded the bullets, and he showed me."

Tippu Tip had been impressed by Stanley's Winchester model 1866 lever-action rifle, which could fire fifteen rounds without reloading. It was one of the many advances in American firearms technology that had come out of the Civil War. The muskets of the Arab and Swahili ivory traders could intimidate the people of Manyema, but the repeating rifles being developed in the West had the capacity to put the ivory traders out of business.[66]

Sitting on Said el-Mazrui's veranda, Stanley asked the Arab and Swahili traders why the two British explorers who had previously come to Nyangwe—Livingstone and Cameron—had failed in their efforts to purchase canoes to explore the Lualaba River. The traders said that it was the fault of Mwinyi Dugumbi, the acknowledged headman of Nyangwe, who refused to allow them to purchase canoes because he feared that the British consul in Zanzibar would hold him responsible if anything bad happened to them. Stanley was not convinced. The real reason, he surmised, was that Livingstone and Cameron's porters had been terrified to leave the established caravan routes and head into uncharted territory, and so they had plotted at night with Dugumbi and the other Arab traders to block the purchase of canoes.

The key to a successful mission, Stanley believed, was Tippu Tip. If Tippu Tip and his armed followers accompanied them long enough to place a good stretch of unknown country between themselves and the Arab trading towns, then the porters would have to stay with the expedition out of fear that they would not be able to safely make their way back if they deserted. He thus approached

Tippu Tip with a request that the trader should accompany him with an armed entourage for sixty days of marching in return for a fee of five thousand Maria Theresa dollars. According to Stanley's account of the meeting, Tippu Tip protested that he did not have enough men at his disposal at the moment, and he was worried that he would not return home alive. "If you white men are desirous of throwing away your lives," said Tippu Tip, "it is no reason we Arabs should. We travel little by little to get ivory and slaves, and are years about it—it is now nine years since I left Zanzibar—but you white men only look for rivers and lakes and mountains, and you spend your lives for no reason, and to no purpose."[67]

Tippu Tip gave us a different version of the discussion, noting that Stanley had offered him seven thousand Maria Theresa dollars to accompany him on the trip. In reply, Tippu Tip showed Stanley his enormous stores of ivory and said that a mere MT$7,000 would not tempt him to make the trip. "I shall go from good will," he told Stanley, "and it won't be MT$7,000 that seduces me from here." Tippu Tip's version made an important point about status and dignity. If Tippu Tip had accepted Stanley's original offer, he would have become Stanley's employee; if he went out of friendship, then they were equals, and Stanley was in his debt. Tippu Tip agreed to accept reimbursement for his expenses but wanted nothing that could be construed as payment for his services. According to Stanley's diary, they reached an agreement that Stanley would pay MT$5,000 to cover Tippu Tip's expenses.[68]

The deal was struck, and Tippu Tip agreed to accompany Stanley for sixty days of marching with 140 riflemen and seventy spearmen, along with about five hundred porters and camp followers. The armed guard was partly for protection against attack but also to intimidate any of Stanley's porters who harbored thoughts of running away. Stanley was overjoyed. He wrote in his diary, "Tippu Tip is the most dashing and adventurous Arab that has ever entered Africa, and to ensure success in this exploration, I could not have done better than to have secured his aid in exploring a dangerous country. Few tribes will care to dispute our passage now." Stanley clearly understood that Tippu Tip would make the difference between success or failure of his mission.[69]

Before parting, Stanley and Tippu Tip agreed to meet up in Nyangwe a few days later. During four days of marching to Nyangwe, Stanley passed destroyed villages that were the result of the Arab traders' battles to establish dominance over the local population. He estimated that the population was perhaps half of what it had been a few years earlier, the rest of the people having been killed or enslaved or having migrated out of the area. Wade Safini, one of the Zanzibari captains of Stanley's expedition, told him that eight years earlier the region had been thickly populated with fields, villages, goats, and pigs. "You can see what the country is now for yourself," Safini told Stanley.[70]

While waiting for Tippu Tip to arrive in Nyangwe, Stanley wrote a long dispatch to the *New York Herald* and the London *Daily Telegraph* on the subject of the slave trade in the East African interior. After recounting the details of several local slaving forays that he had recorded in his diary, he quoted Abed bin Salim, one of the original Arab inhabitants of Nyangwe, as saying that such raids took place between six and ten times a month. Tippu Tip later confirmed that general picture when he told Stanley, "Slaves cost nothing. They require only to be gathered. And that is the work of Mwinyi Dugumbi and Mtagamoyo."[71]

There were differences of opinion as to what happened to the people who were captured in the raids. Stanley painted a picture of an integrated slave-trading network stretching from Nyangwe to Zanzibar, but Tippu Tip saw the slaving activities in Manyema in more localized terms. He pointed out that Mwinyi Dugumbi and Mtagamoyo had no cloth, beads, or merchandise. "They obtain their ivory by robbing," he told Stanley. "They attack the simple peoples of Nyangwe right and left. Twelve or fifteen slaves then caught are sold for 35 pounds of ivory. Mwinyi Dugumbi has 100 to 120 women, Mtagamoyo has 60." Although many of the people captured in the raids would be exchanged for ivory, others would be retained in trading centers such as Kasongo, Nyangwe, and Ujiji to serve as servants, concubines, porters, and food producers for Arab and Swahili traders. That analysis is supported by John Kirk, the British consul in Zanzibar, who reported that captives from Manyema and Lake Tanganyika were not known in Zanzibar.[72]

In concluding his article, stanley noted that the treaty Britain had signed with the sultan of Zanzibar in 1873 prohibited only the transportation of captives by sea. He observed that the inland slave trade was just as bad, and he strongly condemned the subjects of the sultan who engaged in it. "I charge them with being engaged in a traffic especially obnoxious to humanity—a traffic founded on violence, murder, robbery, and fraud. I charge them with being engaged in a business which can be called by no other name than land piracy, and which should justly be as punishable as piracy on the high seas." A week after writing that dispatch, Stanley's caravan left Nyangwe, traveling under the protection of Tippu Tip, who was perhaps the biggest slave trader of all.

6

Nyangwe, Manyema Territory, November 5, 1876

For both Stanley and Tippu Tip, traveling north from Nyangwe would take them into unknown territory. The previous trips to the north by Arab and Swahili traders had all been failures. Mtag-amoyo, the head trader for Mwinyi Dugumbi (the headman of Nyangwe), had organized a land expedition into the Lega country. A member of that party described the Lega country to Stanley and Tippu Tip as "a forest land where there is nothing but woods, woods, and woods for days and weeks and months. There was no end to the woods." The forests, he said, were populated by fearsome creatures such as boa constrictors, enormous ant colonies, leopards, and gorillas, and the people were hostile to strangers. The Arab

traders had given up on traveling north, he said, because they had
lost nearly five hundred men in three attempts.[73]

Leaving Nyangwe on November 5, 1876, Stanley's party numbered 154 after recruiting some additional porters in Nyangwe,
whereas Tippu Tip's party totaled about 400 people, including a
hundred armed Nyamwezi guards, some Ruga-Ruga mercenaries
armed with spears, and a hundred armed slaves from Manyema
and surrounding territories who carried flintlock muskets. The
composition of Tippu Tip's caravan showed that the era when
hired Nyamwezi porters and guards dominated the caravan trade
was coming to an end, as locally obtained captives were gradually
replacing the Nyamwezi. The two parties planned to travel overland parallel to the Lualaba to get around the two known sets of
rapids. For the first few miles, the going was easy because Nyangwe
itself was in open country, but only ten miles to the north they
entered the endless rainforest.

"Another difficult day's work in the forest and jungle," wrote
Stanley in his diary on November 9. "Our caravan is no longer the
tight compact force which was my pride, but utterly disorganized;
each one scrambling to the best of his ability through the woods."
He also noted that the forest was so dark that sometimes he could
not read the words he had written in his field notebook. Tippu
Tip, who had never before traveled through the rainforest, gave
a remarkably similar description. "We left Nyangwe," he wrote,
"and went north through the forest where one cannot see the sun
for the size of the trees, except in the clearings for cultivation or
villages. We were in difficulties because of the mud." Perhaps the
best description of the rainforest was written by Livingstone six
years earlier: "The sun, though vertical, cannot penetrate, except
by sending down at mid-day thin pencils of rays into the gloom.
The rain-water stands for months in stagnant pools made by the
feet of elephants; and dead leaves decay in the damp soil and make
the water of numerous rivulets the color of strong tea. The climbing
plants, from the size of a whipcord to that of a man-of-war's hawsers,

are so numerous the ancient path is the only passage. When one of the giant trees falls across the road, it forms a wall breast-high to be climbed over, and the mass of tangled ropes brought down makes cutting a path round it a work of time which travelers never undertake."[74]

On November 19, the expedition rejoined the Lualaba River on the far side of the rapids and put the sections of Stanley's forty-foot rowboat together. From then on, Stanley and Tippu Tip would travel in the boat with the crew while the others traveled overland on the west side of the river, where the forest was less dense. Stanley told his followers that he hoped to meet people who would sell him dugout canoes. However, the people in the river villages not only refused to sell them canoes but also tried to block their passage. "The natives could not be induced to assist," he wrote in his diary the following day, "and we had to take canoes by force."

In Stanley's book *Through the Dark Continent*, he described finding abandoned, damaged canoes and repairing them and then, after being attacked on the water by a flotilla of canoes, capturing thirty-eight canoes in a single night. Stanley's diary, however, gives the impression that canoes were seized a little at a time as they descended the river. "The young fellows whom I sent to search the expedition out were attacked by a large party who threw four spears at them," he wrote on November 24. "By running to the river and seizing a canoe, they saved themselves." On December 20, he noted, "Made a night expedition and captured four large canoes. Sent a land expedition to search for the enemy; wounded one man. I killed one yesterday who was probably a chief or an influential person, for weeping and sorrow was great, and since then they have become utterly unnerved."[75]

Tippu Tip's version of the events is in substantial agreement with Stanley's diary: "I harried the locals and captured several dugout canoes and goats," wrote Tippu Tip. "One day I took six or seven canoes and countless goats. We went on until we reached the river Kasuku, at the point of its confluence with the Congo from the south. By this time we had obtained sufficient boats for Stanley and his loads. We stayed on the Kasuku for twelve days, when Stanley said to me, 'Now you return, you have already done me a great service these last four months. Let us, however, make one effort to get two large dugouts sufficient to take my donkeys.' We stayed up all night on the island to lie in wait for the locals until we got two dug-outs large enough."[76]

By the testimony of both men, they were plundering and shooting their way down the Lualaba. The European explorer and the Arab ivory trader had very different objectives, but they seemed to be in agreement on the question of tactics.

The final stop for the combined parties was the town of Vinya Njara. After smallpox had broken out among the canoe travelers, they hoped to convalesce in the town, but when they approached it, they were met with arrows that killed one of Stanley's men and wounded several others. The expedition made a camp outside the town and launched an attack the next morning. As the townspeople fled, Stanley's party occupied the town and fortified it against a counterattack. Two days later, the land party arrived to reinforce the defenses and help drive the townspeople from the surrounding forest. For the next week, they occupied the town unmolested while their sick and wounded either recovered or died.

Stanley and Tippu Tip said their goodbyes on December 28, 1876, following a banquet given by Tippu Tip and a farewell dance performed by Tippu Tip's Nyamwezi porters. As with many pivotal moments in Stanley's travels, we do not know exactly what happened because the two men have left divergent accounts. Stanley's diary records that he gave Tippu Tip a promissory note for MT$2,600, even though he had earlier promised to pay MT$5,000 plus food for 140 men, with any further rewards being strictly voluntary. Tippu Tip, for his part, claimed that Stanley had originally promised him MT$7,000. The voluntary gifts are also a matter of dispute. Stanley recorded giving parting gifts of a silver goblet, a wooden box, a gold chain, 30 *doti* (120 yards) of cloth, 2 *frasila*

(70 pounds) of beads, 6,300 cowrie shells, 1 pistol, 200 rounds of ammunition, and 2 coils of brass wire. In his autobiography, Tippu Tip did not mention those gifts, but he recounted that Stanley had promised to send him a large sum of money, a watch, and other presents. A dozen years after the parting, Tippu Tip told the British adventurer James Jameson that Stanley had promised to send him his watch, his gun, and other presents but had not followed through. When Tippu Tip complained to Stanley, the explorer replied that he had sent him a gun via the sultan of Zanzibar and a fine suit of clothes via Taria Topan, Tippu Tip's creditor, but they had sent them on to Tippu Tip under their own names and had failed to credit Stanley for the gifts.[77]

Whereas Stanley's account of their parting focused on payments and gifts, Tippu Tip emphasized that Stanley's Zanzibari porters had refused to continue and were on the verge of mutiny until Tippu Tip, after consultation with Stanley, told them that he would shoot anybody who tried to desert Stanley's fleet and join his caravan. Tippu Tip gave an almost identical account to the Belgian traveler Jérôme Becker in 1881 and to James Jameson in 1888. Stanley indirectly confirmed it in a dispatch to the *New York Herald* on September 5, 1877, in which he stated, "It was an anxious period, this of our parting, for I feared that there would be a mutiny, but my young men were staunch and too well trained to desert me at this critical period." It was apparently their fear of Tippu Tip, not their staunchness or their training, that kept Stanley's crew from deserting.[78]

On December 28, 1876, Stanley's party headed down the Lualaba River: the forty-foot cedar rowboat was followed by twenty-two dugout canoes, which the Zanzibari porters named after British navy warships that called in Zanzibar, while Stanley gave them names like *Telegraph*, *Herald*, and *Livingstone*. Two days later, Stanley wrote in his diary, "I hope to God there are no tremendous cataracts ahead; with steep hills on both sides of the river, such a place would indeed be a chasm." Five days later, the fleet encountered the first of seven waterfalls in a sixty-two-mile stretch during which the river dropped two hundred feet. That series of waterfalls is known today as Boyoma Falls, but it was known throughout the colonial period as Stanley Falls because Stanley had named it after himself.[79]

When the flotilla reached the first waterfall, it had to stop while fifty men took axes and cut a road through the forest that was one mile long by twenty feet wide in order to drag the canoes around the first two falls. The dugout canoes were incredibly heavy because of their thick bottoms, and they were even heavier if the wood had absorbed a lot of water. Stanley's largest canoe (which he had captured on January 2) was eighty-five feet, three inches long and must have weighed over four tons. Over the next three weeks, the process would be repeated five more times. At the last cataract, they constructed two hundred yards of wooden rails topped with log rollers to drag the canoes over jagged rocks. It had taken them twenty-two days to travel sixty-two miles.[80]

While they were traversing the seven waterfalls, Stanley noticed that the course of the river was changing. Between January 3 and January 19, 1877, the river had flowed north-northeast, which indicated that it could possibly flow into the Nile. By taking boiling points to calculate the altitude, he reckoned that they were about a hundred feet higher than the Nile. The next day, however, the river ran due north, and beyond the sixth cataract the course shifted to north-northwest. Then, on January 24, it took a sharp turn to the west-northwest, heading away from the Nile. Stanley calculated the altitude as 1,511 feet, which was below the level of the Nile. If his calculations were correct, then there was no way that the Lualaba could flow into the Nile. He was beginning to think that he was in the watershed of the Congo River, not the Nile.

CHAPTER 2

COMPETITION FOR THE ATLANTIC COAST

To a ship sailing along the Atlantic coast of Africa, the powerful stream of brown water surging into the blue-green ocean is visible as far as ninety miles out to sea. The water comes from the Congo River, which pours nearly two million cubic feet of water into the ocean per second, making it the second most powerful river in the world (after the Amazon). Located just six degrees south of the equator, the river's mouth is seven miles wide, providing an easy entrance to a broad estuary, which has been known to Europeans ever since the Portuguese maritime explorer Diogo Cão arrived there in 1482. When he returned in 1485, he sailed his fleet of three caravels up the estuary for about a hundred miles until his route was blocked by Yellala Falls. There, he made an inscription on a stone that read, "Here arrived the ships of illustrious John II, King of Portugal—Diogo Cão, Pero Anes, Pero da Costa." Diogo Cão had no way of knowing that the falls that stymied him were just the first of a series of waterfalls and rapids that continued for two hundred miles.

Nearly four centuries later, no European expedition had successfully penetrated beyond the rapids. That is why the European maps of Africa in the 1870s still had a huge blank spot in the middle. The Tuckey Expedition, sent out by the British Admiralty in 1816, had sailed up the Congo River estuary to Yellala Falls and then set out on foot to carry sections of two disassembled thirty-five-foot rowboats around the rapids and use them to explore the Upper Congo. During a month of travel through the Crystal Mountains, it suffered from difficulties in hiring porters, exhaustion, and violent fevers. After passing Isangila Falls and seeing a stretch of open water ahead, they declared "mission accomplished" and headed back to their ship. They had advanced up the river for about fifty miles beyond the stone marker that Diogo Cão had left in 1485. When the explorer Richard Burton visited the Congo River estuary in 1863, he got as far as Yellala Falls but no farther.[1]

The contrast between the fiercely competitive and highly publicized search for the source of the Nile and the apparent lack of European interest in the course of the Congo is striking. It probably had more to do with mythology than geography, for no ancient mysteries or fountains of Herodotus were ever associated with the Congo River. The Congo, for all the power of its waters, was still viewed in Britain as a poor cousin of the Nile. As David Livingstone had noted in 1872 when he looked at the Lualaba (Upper Congo) River in Nyangwe, "I am oppressed by the apprehension that, after all, it may turn out that I have been following the Congo; and who would risk being put into a cannibal pot and converted into a black man for it?"[2]

Even though the cataracts near the Atlantic coast kept the Europeans from reaching the Upper Congo for nearly four centuries, they did not prevent Africans on the Upper Congo from trading with the coast. Enslaved Africans from beyond the cataract region were arriving at the coast by land routes as early as 1529. Over the next three centuries, the Congo River estuary was a regular calling place for Portuguese, Dutch, English, French, and American slave ships that carried some 276,000 captive Africans across the Atlantic to lives of slavery in the New World (while much larger numbers of captives were taken out of nearby coastal ports both north and south of the Congo River). Even though the British outlawed the Atlantic slave trade in 1807, the treaty they signed with Portugal in 1817 allowed for the slave trade to continue unabated in the regions south of the equator, which included the Congo River estuary.[3]

When the Hungarian naval lieutenant Ladislas Magyar visited the Congo estuary in 1848, he reported that "the quantity of the merchandise imported from Brazil and the Caribbean in the warehouses of Porto de Lenha is unbelievable. It is destined for the slave markets on the upper river and its numerous tributaries." By then, British anti–slave trade ships were patrolling south of the equator, but with severe restrictions. The Anglo-Portuguese Treaty of 1842 had given British ships the right to intercept Portuguese slave ships on the high seas south of the equator, but they could not interfere with ships at anchor or within cannon shot of the coast. Magyar remarked that "despite their efforts, the British cruisers hinder only a very small part of that infamous traffic."[4]

The closing of the Brazilian slave ports in 1850 and the Cuban slave ports in 1862 finally brought the Atlantic slave trade to an end, but even then it wound down slowly. When Richard Burton visited the Congo River estuary in 1863, he saw five slave trading depots run by independent Portuguese traders at a place called French Point. He had arrived during a "dull time" when there were no captives in the barracoons, and so the traders busied themselves buying peanuts and palm oil while waiting for the arrival of the next slave caravan. Burton learned that the profit on agricultural commodities was only 50 percent, whereas the profit on captives was 500 percent. A few days later, he arrived at Porto de Lenha, which he described as the "chief slaving settlement on the Congo." Because he did not see any captives, Burton concluded that "slave exportation is practically dead."[5]

A blockade of the Congo River estuary by the British navy's anti–slave trade squadron from 1863 to 1865 finally ended the trans-Atlantic slave trade in the Congo estuary. When British missionaries visited Porto de Lenha in 1879, they reported that "the last traces of the barracoons there have only recently disappeared." South of the Congo River, however, captives were still being marched to the Atlantic port of Ambriz to be shipped to the nearby Portuguese island of São Tomé as so-called contract laborers who worked on the sugar and cocoa plantations on seven- to ten-year contracts. Very few of them, if any, ever returned home.[6]

With the slave trade winding down after 1850, there was anticipation among European traders that the mouth of the Congo River would become an important site for what the British called "legitimate trade." By the 1870s, a brisk trade in ivory, rubber, palm oil, palm kernels, and animal hides had grown up in the Congo River estuary. At the mouth of the river, the port of Banana was home to Dutch, French, Portuguese, and British trading houses, the largest being the Dutch Trading Company, which employed fifty to sixty Europeans. The company steamship *Afrikaan* visited every two months, bringing a variety of European trade goods, and a steamship from Hamburg came every month to deliver gin, rum, and barrels of low-quality gunpowder. The trade goods were carried up the estuary in the Dutch Trading Company's thirty-five-ton steamboat *Zaire*, which supplied ten company trading establishments as well as a number of independent Portuguese and Afro-Portuguese traders.[7]

Portugal, whose sovereignty over the coast of Angola was recognized by the Anglo-Portuguese Treaty of 1817, began pressing the British to recognize its claims over the mouth of the Congo River after midcentury. The British steadfastly refused, even though they were not advancing any claims of their own. In 1876, however, the British opened negotiations on that question with the Portuguese. By then, the status of the Congo River basin was about to become a highly contentious international issue. The negotiations were still ongoing when Henry Morton Stanley descended the Congo River in 1877.[8]

1

Upper Congo River, February 7, 1877

On February 7, 1877, Stanley observed that the river was flowing southwest, a complete reversal of its earlier course. It had made an enormous U-turn. The mystery was now solved. He was traveling on the Congo River toward the Atlantic Ocean. Stanley's conclusions were confirmed the next day when he visited the village of Rubunga and asked the old chief the name of the river. At first, the chief replied, *"Ibari,"* which simply meant "river" (as opposed to the terms for tributaries, streams, and creeks). When pushed to be more specific, the chief replied, *"Ikutu ya Congo,"* a phrase that Stanley translated as "the River Congo."[9]

In his eagerness for confirmation that he really was on the river that the British called "Congo," Stanley had heard what he wanted to hear. For the rest of his trip, he never met another African who referred to the river as *"Ikutu ya Congo."* The peoples along the upper river called it by names such as *Ibari* or *Ebale*, which meant "river," while the people living nearer to the river's mouth called it *Nzali, Njari,* or *Nzadi*, all of which also meant "river." Stanley later acknowledged that whereas every small stream or tributary in equatorial Africa had its own name, the great water was everywhere known simply as "the river." The Portuguese had called it the Zaire, using a corruption of the African term for river, and the British had called it the Congo, after the old Kongo Kingdom that had formerly controlled the river's estuary. A French map from 1764 split the difference by naming it "Congo or Zaire."[10]

Geographers would later learn that much of Africa between the Atlantic coast and Lake Tanganyika was covered by a high plateau that tilted slightly toward the southwest. There was a depression in the center of the plateau—the remnant of an ancient lake— that was shaped like an enormous washbasin set in a bathroom

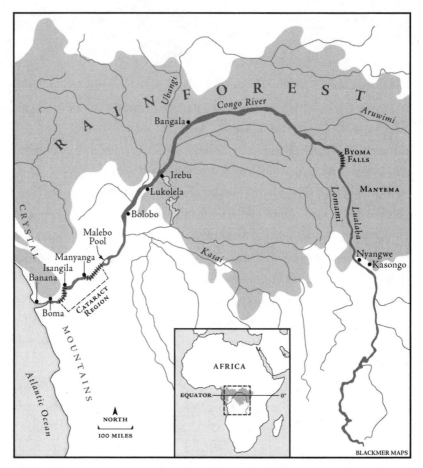

The Lualaba and Congo Rivers from Nyangwe to the Atlantic, 1876–1877

countertop. The *cuvette centrale*, as the Belgians later called it, was about nine hundred miles across, and it determined the shape of the Lualaba/Congo River system. Confined within the basin, the river initially flowed north, made a long, lazy curve to the west, and then flowed south-southwest. Overall, it described a U-shaped arc through the equatorial rainforest. After arriving at the savanna region south of the forest, it made a sharp right turn to cut through the surrounding plateau and escape toward the Atlantic coast.

While the members of Stanley's expedition noted changes in the physical geography as they went along, they were aware that the economic geography was changing as well. On February 1, at the mouth of the Aruwimi River, Stanley's expedition had been attacked by a fleet of forty-four canoes containing warriors armed with spears. After driving off the attackers with withering gun-fire, Stanley discovered a temple of ivory—a round thatched roof that stood on thirty-three ivory pillars. He ordered his men to seize all the ivory they could lay their hands on, including ivory pestles, war horns, and mallets. It would be the last time they saw any ivory that appeared to have little commercial value. On February 9, some of Stanley's crew spotted four ancient Portuguese muskets in a village. Stanley was told that they had been purchased from black traders from Bangala, located downstream, who came up once a year to buy ivory. When Stanley spread out his assort-ment of trade goods to purchase food, he found that people wanted mainly brass rods, which he cut from the coils of thick brass wire. He had stumbled onto the fact that brass rods were the primary currency of the Upper Congo River trading system.[11]

As the expedition continued downriver, Stanley received more confirmation that they were in the Atlantic Ocean trading zone. Ever since leaving Nyangwe, his battles had been fought against people who attacked with spears and arrows. But on February 13, when Stanley and his men were approached by a dozen large canoes, they found sixty to seventy muskets pointed at them. After a brief battle, the attackers retreated because their muskets could not match the firepower of the expedition's Winchester and Sny-der repeating rifles. The next day, as the expedition approached the trading town of Bangala, Stanley engaged in what he called the "fight of fights" against a fleet of war canoes containing men armed with some three hundred muskets firing homemade mus-ket balls of copper and iron. After driving off the attackers, the expedition faced only one more river battle during the rest of the trip. News traveled fast along the river, and the downriver villages had apparently decided that further canoe battles against Stanley's expedition were futile.

The war fleet that attacked Stanley at Bangala was armed with over three hundred muskets, indicating that they were within the Atlantic coast trading zone. Henry M. Stanley, *Through the Dark Continent*, vol. 2, p. 300.

Seven years later, an inhabitant of Bangala named Muélé recounted the Bangala view of the battle. When the sun was at high noon, he said, the people spotted a flotilla of dugout canoes of an unidentifiable design led by a large boat such as they had never seen. The bodies of the crew members were covered with white cloth, even their heads. The strangest thing, however, was that the two men who appeared to command the fleet had skin that was white like the clay they used to make pottery. They seemed to have the same form as regular people, but their hair and faces seemed strange. The older one had flat gray hair and eyes the color of water. When the fleet stopped at an island in the river instead of approaching the town in the fashion of a regular trading party, the people of Bangala were sure that the mysterious newcomers had hostile intentions. That conclusion was confirmed when a canoe approached Stanley's fleet and heard him barking orders in Swahili, a language that they had never before heard. They therefore assembled their war canoes and launched an attack. During the battle, they were shocked by the power of the expedition's rifles.

Their wooden shields were penetrated as if they were bananas, and their hardwood canoes cracked and filled up with water. Bullets penetrated the mud walls of houses along the riverbank, and goats wandering in the gardens fell as if hit by lightning. "After the expedition escaped," said Muélé, "we heard no more about them."[12]

Stanley's explanations for why his flotilla was being attacked changed as he moved down the river. On the stretches of the river just before and after Stanley Falls, he seemed to believe that the local people wanted to eat him. "We were followed by six or seven canoes who pulled lustily after us and called out to others hidden behind the small island to advance and eat us," wrote Stanley in his diary on January 3. "A few harmless shots allayed their rage for our flesh." Stanley's highly embellished descriptions aside, it seems more likely that he was attacked because his canoes were transgressing ethnic monopolies over certain stretches of the river. Stanley frequently referred to the people who were attacking him as "savages" and "cannibals," but it might have been more useful to see them as part of the diminishing number of Africans who were still living outside of the influence of global trade. His trade goods seemed to have little value to them, which would explain why the people were not eager to sell him food, fish, and goats. The beads, cloth, and brass that he carried had little intrinsic value for people who were not in the habit of using them. The value of trade goods was, in part, culturally determined according to the prestige that came from possessing them, but in the heart of the equatorial rainforest, no system of attributing prestige values to foreign goods had yet developed.

By the time he reached the large river town of Bangala, however, Stanley was once again in a region that was accustomed to international trade. The Congo River basin, he learned, was organized into a series of overlapping trading zones, with different ethnic groups claiming trading monopolies on different stretches of the river. The traders from Bangala went upriver to purchase ivory at a series of towns just below the confluence of the Aruwimi, but they did not go all the way to the Aruwimi itself. To sell their ivory downriver, the Bangala traders were permitted to descend as far as the town of Irebu, but the people of Irebu were not permitted to travel above Bangala. Such complex trading arrangements had developed over time and become customary. Is it any wonder that the sudden appearance of Stanley's imposing flotilla of approximately twenty-three canoes was greeted with hostility?

Stanley later took stock of the battles he had fought since leaving Nyangwe: "We have attacked and destroyed 28 large towns and three or four score villages, fought 32 battles on land and water. We obtained as booty in wars over $50,000 worth of ivory, 133 tusks and pieces of ivory." That record of violence would have astonished the two British travelers who had traveled in Manyema ahead of Stanley. Both David Livingstone and Verney Lovett Cameron had been willing to alter their travel itineraries to avoid conflict. Livingstone had usually traveled with a small party of followers or with the large caravans of Arab and Swahili ivory traders such as Tippu Tip, Khamis wad Mtaa, and Muhammad bin Gharib. By going wherever his hosts were going and traveling at their pace, he spent more than seven years wandering about equatorial Africa without solving his geographical puzzle.[13]

In a similar way, Verney Lovett Cameron, who had crossed Africa by land ahead of Stanley's expedition, had wanted to travel west from Manyema in 1874 to look for a mysterious lake he had heard about, but the local chief refused to let strangers with guns travel through his country. "Although I could have obtained sufficient men from Nyangwe and Tippu Tip to have easily fought my way through," he wrote, "I recognized it as my duty not to risk a single life unnecessarily; for I felt that the merit of any geographical discovery would be irretrievably marred by shedding a drop of native blood except in self-defense." Instead, he traveled to the Atlantic coast with the caravan of an Afro-Portuguese slave and ivory trader, arriving at the Angolan port of Benguela in November 1875. By so doing, he managed to cross Africa from east to west

without fighting any battles but also without making any significant geographical discoveries beyond identifying the drainage outlet from Lake Tanganyika.[14]

For Stanley, in contrast, completing his mission in a timely fashion was paramount. His reputation for brutality notwithstanding,
he normally avoided battles whenever possible. When searching for
Livingstone in 1871, he found the trade route between Tabora and
Ujiji blocked by the Nyamwezi chief Mirambo because of a trade
dispute. While the Arab and Swahili caravans waited months for
the dispute to be resolved, Stanley improvised a new route to Ujiji
that bypassed the troubled area. In a similar way, when his Congo
River flotilla was approaching Irebu, Stanley chose to avoid conflict
when some individuals in a canoe fired shots at his party from a
distance. "The river was wide enough," he wrote. "Channels innumerable afforded us means of escaping from their mad ferocity."[15]

When faced with obstacles or danger that would imperil his
mission, however, Stanley kept going in situations where Livingstone or Cameron would have paused or turned back. As a former
soldier and a war correspondent who had covered the American
frontier wars, the British Abyssinian campaign in Ethiopia, and the
British Ashanti campaign in the Gold Coast, he understood how
to win skirmishes against larger forces by using modern firepower
and tactics. "Perceiving we had sufficient cause to begin war," he
wrote in his diary on December 18, 1876, "we made a stockade."
To Stanley, an exploring expedition was much like a military mission in which success was paramount and casualties or collateral
damage were taken for granted. The war analogy even extended to
his practice of seizing canoes, ivory, and goats as booty.

One African traveler who would have endorsed Stanley's
approach was Tippu Tip. Like Stanley, he preferred peaceful
engagement, but if attacked or blocked, he made sure that he came
out the winner. After parting with Stanley on the Lualaba River
on December 27, 1876, Tippu Tip's party had headed west toward
the Lomami River, where they traded copper bracelets for ivory,

heading back to Nyangwe only after they had run out of copper. The return trip proved hazardous. "From the time we left Lomami until we reached the Congo," wrote Tippu Tip, "we were engaged in fighting every day." Stanley would have understood.[16]

Stanley's assessment that his expedition was now within the Atlantic Ocean trading zone was confirmed on February 18, when he spotted an African canoe with fifteen paddlers wearing loincloths of red blanketing. The canoe was carrying trade goods up the river. The most popular trade items for this part of the river, he learned, were red blanketing, Madras cloth, prints, soft beads, white beads, shells, guns, powder, and flint stones for muskets. On February 21, his expedition camped on a small island opposite a settlement, and people came out to look at their trade goods—the different kinds of cloth they carried were in demand, as were brass tacks, brass bands, brass wire, plates, cups, knives, and mirrors. The men came armed with old American flintlock muskets decorated with brass tacks and brass bands. It was clear that trade in items from overseas had been established long before the arrival of Stanley's expedition.

As Stanley descended the river, he began to map out the trading towns and ethnically exclusive trading zones that organized commerce along the Upper Congo River. The traders at Bangala, for example, were permitted to descend the river as far as Irebu, but no farther. At that point they had to sell their ivory and other products to the Bobangi traders who controlled the river trade between the equator and the cataract region of the Lower Congo. At junctions where major tributaries flowed into the Congo River, there was usually a Bobangi market town that controlled the trade along that tributary. Anybody who was not a member of the appropriate ethnic alliance or who did not have the requisite kinship or "blood brother" connections was subject to attack, as Stanley had learned when he fought the "fight of fights" near Bangala.[17]

Stanley decided to bypass the major Bobangi trading towns such as Irebu, Lukolela, and Bolobo. The river was normally five to eight miles wide and sprinkled with chains of elongated islands that divided the riverbed into a series of parallel channels, making it almost impossible to see from one bank to the other. While passing Irebu on the far side of the river, Stanley noted that "Providence had kindly supplied us with crooked byways and unfrequented paths of water which we might pursue unmolested." At Lukolela, the islands briefly disappeared and the river narrowed to about two miles wide, giving the town a commanding view of the river. Stanley passed by Lukolela without comment, even though it was a major trading center.

By avoiding the Bobangi trading towns, Stanley missed a chance to learn more about the trading system of the Upper Congo. When he returned to Irebu five years later, he was impressed by the sophistication of the ivory traders. "They knew the varied lengths of the *sina* ("long" of cloth) and the number of mitako (brass rods) they were worth, whether savelist, florentine, unbleached domestic, twill, stripe, ticking, blue and white baft; the value of beads per thousand strings, as compared to uncut pieces of sheeting or kegs of gunpowder or flintlock muskets, short or long," he wrote. "They could tell by posing on the arm, what profit on an ivory tusk purchased at Langa Langa would be derived by sale at Stanley Pool."[18]

He also missed a chance to learn more about operations of the Bobangi commercial system. The departure of a fleet of Bobangi trading canoes from Lukolela was described six years later by another traveler: "Five large canoes had been selected, each to be manned by twenty-five stalwart paddlers," he wrote. "All the ivory (some tusks weighing ninety pounds) was carried down and laid along the bottoms of the dugouts; then the bales of fish and *chiqwange* [cassava loaves] were snugly stowed, also bundles of *ngula* (powdered redwood). Everything is packed so that the canoe is kept perfectly trim all the time. The slaves to be sold downstream are led down and crowded together in a sitting posture and securely handcuffed on the bottoms of the dugouts. When all the canoes were properly loaded and in perfect trim, Ndobo gave the order."[19]

The largest Bobangi trading town was Bolobo, whose population Stanley would later estimate at ten thousand. As the expedition passed Bolobo without stopping, Stanley remarked on the "scores of native canoes passing backwards and forwards, either fishing or proceeding to the grassy islets to their fish sheds and salt making." He feared that they would have another conflict, but it did not materialize. "Though they looked at us wonderingly," he wrote, "there was no demonstration of hostility." There was a reason why people looked at him "wonderingly," and it had nothing to do with his white skin, which was now a deep tan from the tropical sun. A century later, elders in Bolobo could still recall the people's astonishment at seeing Stanley's rowboat. People on the Congo River always paddled their dugout canoes standing up and facing forward, but in Stanley's rowboat, the oarsmen were sitting down and facing backward. For the people of Bolobo, it was an unforgettable sight.[20]

As Stanley traveled downstream, the character of the river changed. On March 8, it contracted to twenty-five hundred yards wide, becoming fast and deep as it ran between hilly banks up to six hundred feet high. It changed again on March 13, when it widened to resemble a lake with sand bars and wooded islands. He had arrived at Malebo Pool, which was approximately twenty-two miles long and fourteen miles wide. He promptly named it Stanley Pool. At the west end of the Pool was a roaring waterfall that forced him to pause. Communicating largely by pantomime, a Bateke chief named Gamankono led Stanley's boats in his canoe to within a hundred yards of the first broken water above the falls and then motioned for them to head for shore. As they made camp near the roar of the falls, Stanley was unaware that he was at the beginning of a two-hundred-mile stretch of rapids and waterfalls in which the river fell over nine hundred feet as it cut through the Crystal Mountains to reach the sea, some three hundred miles away.

2

Malebo Pool, Congo River, March 13, 1877

When Stanley arrived at Malebo Pool on March 13, 1877, he failed to grasp that he was at the key juncture of Africa's west coast ivory trade. Malebo Pool was the place where the canoe-loads of ivory from the Upper Congo were sold to brokers, who in turn sold them to caravan traders who took them overland to the Atlantic coast. Stanley did not realize that the genial Chief Gamankono, who guided him to see the falls, was one of the biggest ivory brokers at the Pool. It was not until his next expedition four years later that he fully appreciated its role as a depot of the west coast ivory trade. Arriving at a village of ivory traders on the north shore of the Pool in July 1881, Stanley reported, "A number of them were, engaged in counting brass rods and sorting cloths, while many a fine ivory tusk gleamed white on the ground nearby. Groups of buyers and sellers were seated around, discussing the merits of their respective properties." The traders directed Stanley to the village of his former guide, Chief Gamankono, where he met a Bobangi trading party of four hundred men who had come to the Pool to sell their ivory. In 1877, however, Stanley was too focused on his immediate goal of descending the river to observe the extensive ivory trade going on all around him.[21]

The ivory trade at Malebo Pool was a relatively recent phenomenon. The British missionary William Holman Bentley was told in 1881 by ivory traders at the Pool that during the era of the Atlantic slave trade, large numbers of captives had been carried down to the Pool by the Bobangi traders in their large canoes. The Bobangi did not mount slaving operations themselves but instead used their vast trading network to purchase prisoners of war, debtors, people accused of witchcraft, people accused of crime, women accused of adultery, and victims of kidnapping and to transport them downstream. At the Pool, the captives were sold to "middlemen" traders who turned them over to Kongo and Bateke caravan operators, who marched them to the Congo estuary and nearby coastal ports. As the Atlantic slave trade wound down after the close of the Brazilian slaving ports in 1850, the price of slaves dropped sharply, causing the Bobangi trade with the Pool to almost grind to a halt.[22]

Bentley was told that Kongo traders from the territory of the old Kongo Kingdom began coming to the Pool looking for ivory sometime around 1866. Soon the entire Bobangi trade network was focused on buying up all the ivory available on the Upper Congo and bringing it to the Pool. Bentley's date for the beginning of the ivory trade seems essentially correct, given that Richard Burton had visited a number of Congo estuary trading establishments in 1863 without mentioning any ivory. In 1869, the Dutch Trading Company set up its African headquarters at Banana, at the mouth of the Congo River, and the ivory trade had been growing ever since.[23]

When the French missionary Prosper Philippe Augouard arrived at the Pool in 1881, he reported that "Stanley Pool is incontestably the greatest ivory market on the west coast of Africa. The village of Mfwa, where I stayed, is the central market where 80–100 tusks a day are sold. The inhabitants of Stanley Pool buy ivory from the Bobangi, who bring it down the river, and they sell it on the spot to the Bakongo, who transport it to the markets of Zombo and San Salvador." He was saying, in effect, that Malebo Pool was to western equatorial Africa what Zanzibar was to eastern equatorial Africa. The two centers of the ivory trade mirrored one another. The bulk of the ivory from elephants killed in the equatorial regions of Africa flowed to one trading center or the other.[24]

There were two main ivory trade routes from the Pool to the coast, neither of which closely followed the course of the Congo River. The northern route went west to the Niari Valley, a 125-mile-wide depression that served as a passage through the Crystal Mountains between the inland plateau and the coast. The route then bifurcated, with one branch going to the coastal port of Cabinda and the other to Boma, some seventy miles up the Congo estuary from the mouth of the river. The southern route went through the trading town of Tungwa to San Salvador, the capital of the once-powerful Kongo Kingdom, and then on to the coastal port of Ambriz. Slave caravans from Malebo Pool also traveled the southern route: some went to Ambriz, where the captives were shipped to São Tomé, while others were taken to Lembelwa, about twenty-five miles north of San Salvador, to be sold for domestic purposes.[25]

The rulers of the Kongo Kingdom had once controlled the southern trade routes all the way from the Pool to the Atlantic coast, but half a century of civil wars beginning in the 1660s had caused the kingdom to splinter into its component provinces, each with its own royal court. Even after the kingdom was restored in the early 1700s, the king's power was more symbolic than operational. In the 1850s and 1860s, the provinces themselves split into shifting combinations of their component parts. As a result, petty chieftaincies dominated the political landscape by 1870. The local chiefs enjoyed almost complete autonomy, and the king's control of the trade routes did not extend beyond taxing the caravans that passed through the royal capital of San Salvador. By 1877, when Stanley arrived at the Pool, the trade routes to the coast traversed the territories of a number of local chiefs, who would allow caravans to pass only if there were previously negotiated agreements and generous customs payments.[26]

When an ivory caravan from the Pool arrived at a European trading establishment on the coast or along the Congo estuary, it halted while the caravan captains donned their finest coats, hats, and multicolored umbrellas. Marching to the accompaniment of a double clapper-less bell that produced two tones when struck with a rod, they advanced toward the trading house. Before beginning trade, they had engaged the services of a local broker/interpreter, who had set up a trading session. In the ensuing negotiations, the unit of account was the gun, although guns were not necessarily exchanged. If the agreed-upon price for a certain tusk was five guns, for example, the seller would then pick out five guns' worth of cloth, brass, gunpowder, and other items. Bargaining could go on for days, during which time the porters would receive food and grog from the traders while the caravan captains received a variety of presents.[27]

When Stanley arrived at the falls at the lower end of Malebo Pool on March 13, 1877, he made a decision that almost proved fatal to the expedition. He was 214 miles by straight-line distance from the river port of Boma in the Congo estuary; by the modern road that now winds through the Crystal Mountains, the distance is 285 miles. He calculated his latitude at 4°39′, which is not far off from the 4°19′ on modern global positioning systems, but he seemed to have lost track of his longitude since November 27, 1876, when he lost his chronometer in one of the battles on the Lualaba River. He would later learn that he was seventy miles closer to the coast than he thought he was.[28]

An overland dash to the coast was possible because the expedition was now in open grassland country south of the equatorial rainforest. The Crystal Mountains, which ran parallel to the coastal plain, formed a rugged barrier, but they never exceeded thirty-two hundred feet in elevation. The expedition had crossed much higher mountain ranges in the earlier stages of the trip. Given that Stanley's caravan usually traveled from six to twelve miles a day when on the march, it should have been able to walk to the coast in a little over a month, especially if they lightened their loads. Instead, Stanley decided to drag the heavy dugout canoes around the waterfalls, shoot the rapids, and then paddle to the mouth of the Congo. He not only kept his large canoes but had two new ones built to replace ones that were lost in the rapids. Because of that decision, the expedition would spend the next four and a half months dragging the canoes around waterfalls and shooting treacherous rapids before it finally abandoned the river and struck out overland for the river port of Boma.

Stanley's crew dragging a dugout canoe around the first cataract below Malebo Pool. Henry M. Stanley, *Through the Dark Continent*, vol. 2, p. 339.

There are several possible explanations as to why Stanley made that unfortunate choice. One is that Stanley arrived at the Pool believing that only two waterfalls stood between him and the coast. On February 18, he wrote in his journal, "It may be that there are no more than the cataract of Sundi and the Falls of Yellala, otherwise I cannot account for the ascent of these trading canoes and such extensive possession of cloths and guns so far up the river." Stanley failed to realize that the trading system on the Upper Congo, where goods and traders traveled by water, was very different from the system in the Lower Congo region, where everything traveled by land routes to bypass the cataract region.[29]

Whether because of haste or language problems, Stanley failed to obtain sufficient information from the very people who were in the best position to know how to get from the Pool to the coast—the local ivory traders. Although he had failed to recognize that the genial Chief Gamankono was a major ivory trader, he properly identified Ngaliema, the chief of the village nearest the falls, as an ivory trader. "The King of Ntamo was very urgent that we should return at some future time and make trade with him, but opposed to our proceeding higher up the river and his village," Stanley wrote in his diary. "This arose, of course, from a fear that he would lose his profits." Stanley seemed to be in such a hurry to find a way around the falls that he failed to collect information on the overland trade routes that bypassed the cataract region entirely.[30]

Stanley would later blame his decision on inaccurate information. Just before he'd left the Pool, the chief of Ntamo had told him that there were only three cataracts, which he called the father, the mother, and the child, whereas Stanley would later count the total number of cataracts at thirty-two. "Had I the least suspicion that such a terrible series of falls were before us, I should never have risked so many lives and such amount of money," Stanley wrote in his diary on July 18, "but the natives, whether from ignorance or interest, constantly cheered us with reports that only one or two remained, after which we might lie in the canoes and glide dreamily down river without danger."[31]

But why did Stanley choose to believe the repeated reports of open water just beyond the next rapids? One reason was that he was determined to map the course of the Congo River. Despite all the difficulties of getting around the cataracts, he did not abandon the river until Isangila Falls, which had been reached by the Tuckey Expedition in 1816, thus making it possible for him to claim that the entire river had now been mapped. Perhaps a more important reason, however, lies in his diary entry of July 18, when he noted that he had arrived at the Pool with 133 tusks and pieces of ivory worth approximately $50,000 that he had obtained as booty in his battles. In the end, nearly all of that ivory was lost during his passage through the cataract region due to the loss of twelve canoes in the rapids and thefts by his crew. If Stanley had aligned himself with the existing trading system and bartered his tusks for overland passage to the coast, a lot of misery and death might have been avoided.

The four and a half months of shooting rapids and dragging canoes around waterfalls were by far the most difficult part of the entire trip. In his diary, Stanley summed up the work as follows: "Hauled our canoes and boat up a mountain 1,500 feet high, then over the mountains six miles, then lowered them down the slope to the river, lifted by rough mechanical skill our canoes up gigantic boulders 12, 15, and 20 feet high, then formed a tramway over these boulders to pass the falls of Massassa, Nzabi, and Zinga."[32]

On August 1, the exhausted and hungry crew abandoned their canoes at Isangila Falls and began to march the final eighty-two miles to the river port of Boma. Their problem now was finding enough food. The party had been reduced to 115 people by deaths and desertions, but they still consumed a large amount of food each day. Stanley grew so fearful that they would not have enough strength to make it to Boma that he sent out runners with letters to any English, French, or Portuguese traders that they might find. The letters read, "We are now in a state of imminent starvation. We can buy nothing from the natives, for they laugh at our kinds of cloth, beads, and wire."

Stanley's expedition was starving in a region where food was plentiful. The markets near Isangila Falls were later described by the British traveler Harry Johnston. "They are generally held every four or eight days," he wrote. "The natives will often come a hundred miles to attend one of these big markets, and there are generally over a thousand present. They bring sheep, goats, pigs, Muscovy ducks, and fowls for sale or barter. At the markets between Isangila and Manyanga, five hundred eggs may be bought at a time. The natives also sell fresh vegetables, pumpkins, sweet potatoes, and even a wild cabbage, bananas, plantains, pineapples, groundnuts, sugar cane, maize, kola-nut, tobacco, and *kikwange* [cassava]." From Johnston's description, it appears that the region could have easily provided all the food Stanley's party needed.[33]

The problem was that he lacked the proper trade goods. Stanley was now in a region long accustomed to international trade, and the customers were very particular. "Beads are almost useless," Stanley wrote in his diary on August 2, "brass wire not in demand, nothing but cloth, of which we have so little that it is like the widow's cruse of oil." Two days later he noted, "One peck of potatoes cost four yards of cloth; beads and shells or wine of not much value here; the cloth is so plentiful that it is almost worthless." The next day he passed through a district containing sixteen or seventeen villages. "The people are amiable but terribly extortionate," he wrote, "and so keen on trading that my people get more and more emaciated." The following day, August 6, he approached a market and heard that cowrie shells were in demand, so he gave each crew member forty cowries to buy food. Finally, on August 7, the relief party he had requested arrived from Boma with four sacks of rice, two sacks of potatoes, three large loads of fish, five gallons of rum, and assorted smaller items such as jelly, a tin of fruit, and three bottles of Indian pale ale. "The long war against famine is over," Stanley wrote in his diary.

Two days later, on August 9, his caravan marched into Boma, where he met four Portuguese traders, an agent of the Dutch Trading Company, and the captain of the steamship *Kabinda*. He would later note that Boma's total European population included two Englishman, two Dutchmen, one German, one Frenchman, and twelve Portuguese. The steamship took his entire expedition to the Atlantic port of Cabinda, north of the river's mouth. From there, Stanley accompanied his crew back to Zanzibar by ship around the southern tip of Africa. Then he departed for Europe via Aden and Egypt.[34]

When Stanley left the Congo River, he knew that he had lived out David Livingstone's worst nightmare by proving that the Lualaba was really the Congo and not the Nile. Yet by mapping the course of the Congo River, he had made a discovery with momentous consequences for the subsequent course of European imperialism in equatorial Africa. Ever since Speke had discovered that the Nile flowed from Lake Victoria, the question of its ultimate source was of interest mostly to a handful of members of the Royal Geographical Society. The fierce competition among the explorers for recognition and fame was more about British elite rivalries and Victorian fantasies than about filling in the remaining blank spaces on the map of Africa.

After Stanley's trip, it was clear that the Luapula River flowed out of Lake Bangweulu to Lake Mweru, where it came out as the Luvua, which flowed into the Lualaba. After passing Boyoma Falls, the Lualaba was called the Congo, which flowed without obstruction for a thousand miles to reach Malebo Pool, and then passed through two hundred miles of cataracts before flowing peacefully through the Congo estuary for the final one hundred miles to the Atlantic. David Livingstone had spent the last seven years of his life in the basin of the Congo, not the Nile. What he had unwittingly accomplished was to clear the way for Stanley to map the Congo River basin. By the time Stanley's exhausted and hungry expedition arrived at the river port of Boma, the last big blank spot on the European map of Africa had begun to be filled in.

3

Upper Ogowe River, August 1877

On August 9, 1877, the day that Stanley's caravan staggered into Boma, a French expedition led by twenty-five-year-old Pierre Savorgnan de Brazza was camped some three hundred miles to the north-northeast. It was on the Ogowe River, which runs roughly parallel to the equator in what is now Gabon. As the largest river between the Niger and the Congo, the Ogowe was thought to be a direct route into the heart of Africa. After moving up the river for five hundred miles during twenty months of travel, Brazza's expedition had arrived at the limit of navigation. Having reached his

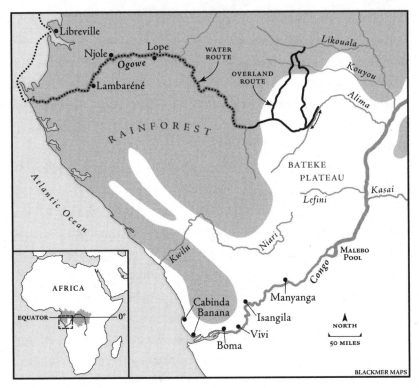

Brazza's first expedition, 1875–1878

destination, he did not like what he had found. "We have demonstrated," wrote Brazza in his official report, "that this waterway,
on which geographers had based high hopes for penetrating the
depths of the African continent, is enclosed in a very secondary
basin that slopes toward the Atlantic." Just when Stanley was savor-
ing his success, Brazza's mission looked like a failure.[35]

The circumstances into which Pietro Savorgnan di Brazza
(a.k.a. Pierre Savorgnan de Brazza) and John Rowlands (a.k.a.
Henry Morton Stanley) were born could not have been more different. Pietro's father could trace his noble lineage as far back as
the Roman emperor Septimus Severus, and his mother was from a
noble Venetian family that was descended from Marco Polo. Pietro grew up in Rome, which was part of the independent Papal
States and not yet a part of the Kingdom of Italy. In order to fulfill

his dream of becoming a naval officer, his parents sent him to a Jesuit high school in Paris that prepared young men for the military academies. After graduating from the French naval academy at Brest in 1870, he was assigned to the ship *Venus*, which was part of the French South Atlantic fleet. The *Venus* followed the routes of the old anti–slave trade patrols, stopping in Senegal, Gabon, Cape Town, and South America. It would occasionally stop at Libreville, Gabon, a settlement that the French had founded for the captives that they liberated from slave ships. On one of those trips, Brazza obtained permission to make a short visit to an African village along the Ogowe River.

In 1874, while still on the *Venus*, he wrote to the minister of the marine in Paris to propose an expedition to explore the Ogowe. In his proposal, Brazza stressed the commercial potential of the river and also the scientific benefits of the exploration. In a supplement to the original proposal, he added a third reason for going. He noted that his journey would bring him to "a completely unknown country, where the British and the Germans push on in their desire to be the first explorers. It is highly desirable that France should not cede to others the honor of this exploration, whose point of departure is in French territory." As a young man who had just become a naturalized French citizen a month earlier, he showed a burst of patriotism for his adopted land. The reason why the ministry took his proposal seriously was that the minister of the marine, Admiral de Montaignac, had known Brazza and his family since Brazza was thirteen and had helped Brazza to gain admission to the French naval academy even though he was a foreigner. With the support of Admiral de Montaignac, the Ministry of the Marine agreed to provide financial backing to the venture, with additional resources to be provided by the ministries of education and commerce. The Paris Geographical Society and the French national committee of King Leopold's International African Association contributed smaller amounts. Even so, the funds would pay for less than half of the expedition's expenses. The rest would come from Brazza himself.[36]

Brazza left Bordeaux in August 1875, accompanied by a quartermaster, a doctor, and a naturalist. In Senegal, he picked up thirteen Senegalese marines; at the French-controlled port of Libreville, Gabon, on the Atlantic coast, he purchased two large dugout canoes and hired four interpreters with knowledge of different West African languages. The core of the expedition was thus composed of four Europeans and seventeen Africans. From Libreville, they took the French steamboat *Marabout* down the coast to the Ogowe and up the river for 150 miles to Lambaréné, where the English trading house of Hatton & Cookson occupied a series of warehouses and the Carl Woermann trading company from Hamburg had a smaller establishment. Both companies purchased ivory, ebony, and rubber.

Brazza brought with him 156 trunks of supplies and trade goods that weighed between 50 and 110 pounds each, making it necessary to obtain a fleet of dugout canoes and paddlers to continue the journey. For two months, Brazza met regularly with Renoke, the chief of Lambaréné, to bargain over the price of canoes, the wages of paddlers, and the gifts for the chiefs and canoe captains. After many bargaining sessions that Brazza described as "interminable," he finally concluded a deal after resorting to ruses such as sending his associate upstream to bargain for canoes with a rival chief and loading some unneeded trunks onto a trading steamer to give the impression that he was planning to return home with his trade goods. On January 13, 1876, the expedition left Lambaréné in ten large canoes that were fifty to fifty-five feet long and three feet wide, manned by a hundred hired paddlers.[37]

From information he collected at Lambaréné, Brazza understood that he was in a region where ethnic identities were highly localized and political authority was decentralized. The Enenga people at Lambaréné, for example, occupied no more than a few villages scattered along a few miles of the riverbank; the Apingi people, farther up the river, made up only eight or ten villages; and the Okanda people at Lope occupied only thirty villages plus a few hamlets. There were few powerful chiefs who could offer the expedition safe passage over a large region. Chief Renoke at Lambaréné exerted some personal influence over the riverine populations for about two hundred miles upstream, but his influence was on the wane. He had once exerted extensive control over the river traffic, but the end of the Atlantic slave trade and the arrival of the European trading houses had undermined his influence. Farther up the river, most villages, regardless of their ethnic affiliation, were completely independent. The local chiefs competed for power by attempting to control the trade along certain stretches of the Ogowe. For Brazza, the situation mandated that he should travel slowly and try to form relationships with local chiefs as he went along.[38]

Despite their ethnic diversity, the populations that Brazza encountered along the Ogowe could be divided into two broad categories—those who were primarily river people and those who were primarily land people. The river peoples such as the Enenga in Lambaréné were fishers, traders, and skilled canoemen who could shoot rapids going upstream. But they were indifferent farmers who got their agricultural products from villages of enslaved cultivators that they had established inland from the river. When Brazza's associate Dr. Noel Ballay visited the inland villages, he concluded that the slaves did not seem particularly unhappy and that they were considered almost like members of their masters' families. Although he had correctly observed that the idiom of kinship was used to define the place of slaves in the larger society, he missed the more subtle point that the slaves were always considered to be permanent junior members of the group. When a slave referred to his or her master as "father," it was a sign of subordination, not affection.[39]

The Akélé people, who lived a dozen miles upstream from Lambaréné, were primarily land people, even though some of their villages lined the Ogowe River. The distinction became clear when the expedition encountered rapids and found that the Akélé paddlers were afraid to shoot them, whereas the Enenga paddlers were skilled at handling rapids. As land people, the Akélé were great elephant hunters who organized large-scale hunting parties and constructed elephant-pit traps along forest paths. During the dry season, an enterprising man living in a riverside village would form a small caravan made up of his slaves, his wives, and members of his extended family in order to travel inland on winding forest paths to exchange European merchandise for ivory and rubber. Ivory was a high-value product that could profitably be transported by porters over long distances, whereas rubber was gathered only in places within easy travel of the river because its value was relatively low. After leaving the Akélé country, Brazza's party came to an area where people were just beginning to collect wild rubber by making incisions in the rubber-bearing *landolphia* vines that grew wild in the rainforest. As they went farther up the river, no rubber was being collected at all because the Europeans had only recently started buying wild rubber.[40]

By the time the expedition arrived at Lope on February 9, 1876, it was in bad shape. Seven canoes had been lost or damaged while shooting rapids, the trunks of goods had been soaked, and the paddlers from Lambaréné did not want to go any farther, especially now that their contracts had expired. Brazza paid them and sent them home. He could not hire new paddlers because the rainy season was starting and people were reluctant to travel. After building a warehouse for storing the trade goods, he spent a year headquartered in Lope, sending his associates back to Lambaréné and Libreville to pick up extra supplies while he made small excursions in the region by land and water and tried to develop contacts with the peoples farther up the river. Such a strategy got Brazza into trouble with the chiefs of Lope, who wanted a more exclusive relationship.[41]

Lope was the site of a major slave market. Every February slave merchants from the upper Ogowe descended upon Lope to trade with the Enenga traders from Lambaréné who came up in canoes loaded with European merchandise. Chief Renoke himself was a regular attendee. The Atlantic slave trade was finally over, and the slave market at Lope was largely for domestic demand. Some of the captives purchased at Lope ended up in the agricultural villages of river peoples such as the Enenga of Lambaréné, while others were taken down the Ogowe to Cape Lopez, on the Atlantic coast. There, some of them were purchased by Afro-Portuguese slave traders to become so-called contract laborers on the coffee and cocoa plantations on the island of São Tomé, less than two hundred miles away; others were taken to the Gabon estuary to work in agricultural villages or as domestic slaves.[42]

During his time in Lope, Brazza had many opportunities to observe the operations of the slave trade on the Ogowe River. On one of his excursions, he met a canoe fleet carrying 182 captives. He was unable to help them, but he did manage to get them released from their wooden handcuffs in case a boat overturned in the rapids. During the high slave market month of February at Lope, he noted that the Enenga traders from Lambaréné were not bringing enough European trade goods to purchase all the captives that were for sale. When the trade goods ran out, the Enenga traders went back to Lambaréné to resupply, but some slave traders from Lope were beginning to descend toward Lambaréné themselves, something they had not done in the past. Because Brazza had released his hired paddlers, he decided to purchase forty captives, enough to man two large canoes. His plan was to set them free immediately and offer them jobs, but he could afford to purchase only a few with his available trade goods because he was being charged the higher prices that reigned at the coast.[43]

After the annual Lope slave market was over, however, Brazza bought eighteen captives who were about to be taken down the river, paying for them with a letter of credit good for merchandise in the European trading houses of Lambaréné. He organized a public ceremony in which the slaves could gain their freedom by touching the French flag. He told them that they were free to depart if they wished, or they could stay with him as free laborers and work for wages. All of them chose to stay. However, a few months later when Brazza arrived in the Aduma country where the captives came from, almost all of them left the expedition to return to their home villages. Some of them had been sold by the very relatives that they were now returning to, and Brazza worried that they would be sold again. In his chagrin, he missed the larger point that the liberated slaves had gone back to their extended families for the same reason that they had earlier remained loyal to him: they had no other place to go. In societies organized on the basis of kin groups, there was no place for autonomous individuals.[44]

On March 18, 1877, Brazza left Lope with a new fleet composed of seven large canoes with eighteen to twenty paddlers each, twenty midsize canoes, and six small ones. In the sixteen months that had passed since he had arrived at Lambaréné by steamboat, he had advanced only some two hundred miles along the Ogowe River. Before Brazza left Lope, Chief Renoke from Lambaréné, who had come up for the annual slave market, called a meeting of chiefs from up and down the Ogowe and urged them to give Brazza safe passage through their territories. In his speech, the chief noted that the Ogowe was segmented into exclusive trading zones, the limits of which were marked by shrines that visited misfortune on people who went beyond the boundaries of their zone. He asked the chiefs to allow Brazza's expedition to bypass the boundaries marked by the shrines. Chief Renoke had no political authority farther up the river, but he was respected as a prominent ritual specialist.[45]

As the expedition moved up the river, it lost members. Many of the hired paddlers arrived at their home villages and left the expedition. More seriously, a smallpox epidemic broke out that was being spread by Brazza's paddlers, who carried the disease to their home villages. The expedition was delayed for a month in the village of Dumé while Dr. Ballay helped treat the sick and Brazza tried to hire new paddlers. Brazza finally left Dumé on July 22, 1877, and in early August he reached the point at which the Ogowe was no longer navigable, even by a small canoe. It had taken them twenty months to follow the course of the river for 350 miles after debarking from the steamboat in Lambaréné.

During those twenty months, Brazza had developed a style of exploration that was influenced by David Livingstone, whose writings he had read. Brazza would go into the territory of a certain ethnic group and make contact with the most influential chiefs. He would give them a variety of gifts, including cast-off costumes and fake jewelry from the Imperial Theatre of the Tuileries in Paris. He would stay as long as necessary to establish good relations with the chiefs and then ask them to provide guides and porters or paddlers as far as the territory of the next group. Brazza would sometimes stay weeks or months in a single territory.[46]

If negotiations failed to achieve the desired result, Brazza would resort to theater. Realizing that powerful chiefs were considered to be powerful magicians, he would give the local chiefs a very impressive display of fireworks and military rockets and then threaten to call war down upon them if they did not cooperate. At one point, Brazza was trying to hire a new set of paddlers to take his party upstream, but the canoemen refused because it was the season to make trading trips downstream. Brazza paid a local shrine priest a large quantity of merchandise to put a curse on any downstream travel, thus, in effect, closing the river. Brazza told the chiefs that the curse would not be lifted until he had enough paddlers to continue his trip.[47]

After reaching the limit of canoe navigation on the Ogowe in August 1877, Brazza decided to continue eastward on foot. His goal, he wrote, was to reach "the mysterious regions that extend between the upper Nile and Lake Tanganyika," a clear reference to the Great Lakes region of equatorial Africa. The minister of the marine had defined Brazza's objective as the lakes mentioned by David Livingstone and Samuel Baker (a British explorer of the upper Nile). Both Brazza and the minister were apparently looking for a lake; neither of them mentioned the Congo River.[48]

Traveling on foot posed a new set of challenges. The hired canoe paddlers from the Ogowe had all gone home, as had all but two of the freed slaves. The Senegalese marines, who were accustomed to traveling by boat, balked at the prospect of overland travel. After consolidating their supplies and discarding everything that was dispensable, they still had ninety chests and bales of cloth to transport. Porters were hard to find because this was a region where trade caravans were unknown; the few trade goods that made it this far from the coast were traded from village to village. Brazza's only option was to hire a group of porters to go as far as a certain village and then hire another group for the next stretch. The negotiations for hiring a new group of porters would take as long as five days. With insufficient numbers of porters, they often had to go back over the same ground three times to move all their supplies.

Frustrated by the lack of progress, Brazza decided to purchase slaves to use as porters, but this time he would not set them free until the voyage was over. Brazza's reports are vague as to how many slaves he purchased and used in this way, but given the labor requirements of the expedition, it must have been at least thirty. When the rainy season arrived, the expedition built huts and established a base camp to wait it out. The final difficulty for the Europeans in the party came when their shoes wore out. They broke open a metal chest with soldered seams only to discover that water had seeped in and ruined the spare shoes. From then on, Brazza and his French colleagues would march barefoot, just like their African guides and porters. In the eight months since reaching the limit of navigation on the Ogowe, they advanced less than a hundred miles.

4

Brussels, June 20, 1877

Expectations were high when the International Commission of King Leopold's International African Association (IAA) held its first annual meeting in Brussels in June 1877. Nine European countries plus the United States were represented. The Russian and Portuguese delegates were unable to attend, and the British had withdrawn under pressure from the Home Office and the Foreign Office. The British member of the Executive Committee, Bartle Frere, had gone to South Africa to become Britain's high commissioner for Southern Africa, and the vacancy would be filled by the American businessman Henry Shelton Sanford. Sanford had no experience in Africa, but by the end of the meeting, he was enthusiastic about the association. "With no aims of conquest or aggrandizement, with no special interests to promote other than those of civilization and humanity," he wrote, "I hope that the whole united effort on two sides of the Atlantic will be to further the international plan of action with the certainty that its results will redound to the common good of all."[49]

During two days of meetings, the delegates elaborated on plans for building stations in equatorial Africa. The hospitality functions of the stations would include receiving European travelers, providing them with scientific instruments and provisions, and supplying guards and interpreters for their travels. The scientific research to be conducted at the stations would include making astronomical and meteorological observations; collecting geological, botanical, and zoological specimens; making maps; preparing vocabularies and grammars of African languages; and collecting ethnographic information. In contrast to the Brussels Geographical Conference a year earlier, where the suppression of the slave trade had been a major emphasis, that subject was now barely mentioned. The new approach was based on the idea that by opening up territory and creating better conditions for commerce, the slave trade would somehow wither away on its own.

The location of the first station generated much debate. The Dutch favored the Congo River estuary, where the Dutch Trading Company had a large establishment; the Austrian delegates proposed going up the Nile in the footsteps of the German traveler

Georg Schweinfurth; and the Spanish delegates wanted to follow the Zambesi River through Portuguese territory to Lake Nyasa. In the end, the mouth of the Congo River, a clear favorite of King Leopold II, was rejected because of the insalubrity of the climate and the lack of information about paths to the interior. Instead, the group decided that Zanzibar should be the point of departure and that the path into the interior should follow the familiar caravan route to Tabora, Ujiji, and Nyangwe. The delegates noted that there were now Catholic and Protestant missions on the Mrima coast opposite Zanzibar, a Swiss trading establishment near Tabora, and English establishments at Ujiji that would be supportive of the association's project. By 1877, the territory between Zanzibar and Lake Tanganyika was no longer terra incognita where only explorers ventured. Missionaries and merchants had followed in their wake.

The initial IAA station, it was decided, would be established at or beyond Nyangwe, and it would be the first in a line of stations advancing westerly toward the Atlantic Ocean. Their presence would open up "a vast region of unknown country" and perhaps help to trace the course of the Congo River to its mouth. None of the delegates knew that Stanley was closing in on the mouth of the Congo as they spoke. Their ignorance was understandable, given that he had gone to Africa in search of the Nile.

In Britain the Royal Geographical Society sought to capitalize on the wave of enthusiasm generated by Leopold's initiative, even though it had withdrawn from the International African Association. They began to solicit money to set up an African Exploration Fund for the scientific examination of the resources of Africa and the best routes to the interior. The Royal Geographical Society was now less interested in answering arcane questions such as the ultimate source of the Nile than in furthering British commercial interests. At a meeting in the Egyptian Hall of Mansion House (the official residence of the lord mayor of London) on July 19, 1877, which was attended by such luminaries as the lord mayor and the archbishop of York, the president of the Royal Geographical Society told the audience that Central Africa could supply the "whole world with cotton, sugar, and every other tropical product." He added that Central Africa could provide a new market of almost unlimited capacity for British manufactured products. There were, he said, "millions of barbarous or semi-civilized people who are ready to become customers."

The British explorer Verney Lovett Cameron followed, telling the crowd that Africa would soon become the new Spice Islands. He had walked for long distances along the valley of the Lualaba in the shade of nutmeg trees, where the ground was "literally covered with nutmegs." Africans produced much more food than they could possibly consume, he said, as evidenced by the fact that trading caravans of up to five thousand people could always purchase enough food. Following the presentations, the members unanimously adopted a resolution stating that "the commercial interests of this country are to a large extent involved in the development of intercourse and legitimate trade with the out-ports to the fertile but little-known regions of Central Africa."[50]

The major impediment to developing this commerce, according to the speakers, was the continuing violence of the internal African slave trade, which claimed between fifty thousand and one hundred thousand lives a year. Britain's recent treaty with the sultan of Zanzibar was a failure because it recognized slavery as a domestic institution even while forbidding slave trading on the seas. The archbishop of York told the crowd that Africa was a land of great fertility and riches and that "if commerce could be planted there, the slave traffic would wither away of its own accord." He introduced a resolution stating that compiling more information regarding the lesser-known regions of Central Africa was a preliminary step toward suppressing the slave trade. After Thomas Fowell Buxton, who represented the Anti-Slavery Society, seconded it, the resolution was approved. A third resolution was passed that praised the efforts of the British missionary societies "to spread the

humanizing influence of Christianity in Africa by the establishment of permanent mission stations in the distant interior." Exploration would thus pave the way for commerce and Christianity,
which would somehow bring about the end of the slave trade.

Although the Royal Geographical Society's African Exploration Fund operated independently from Leopold's International
African Association, the rhetoric and strategy employed by the
two organizations seemed to echo the words of David Livingstone. In a lecture before the members of Cambridge University
in 1857, Livingstone had told the audience, "Those two pioneers of
civilization—Christianity and Commerce—should ever be
inseparable." Twenty years later, David Livingstone lay buried in
Westminster Abbey, but his rhetorical formula of "Christianity,
commerce, and civilization" was enjoying a resurrection. Emile
Banning, the secretary of the Brussels Geographical Conference,
had repeated that formula but added the word "science." Where
both the International African Association and the Royal Geographical Society went wrong was in failing to acknowledge that
global commerce was already practically everywhere in Africa. As
the ivory caravans in Manyema showed, its effects were not necessarily desirable. Humanitarian discourse in Europe was often
strangely divorced from the realities in Africa.[51]

The International African Association's expedition to found its
first station was financed and organized by the Belgian national
committee. Its personnel consisted of two Belgian army officers, a
Belgian naturalist, and an Austrian explorer. Their mission was to
establish a station in Manyema, either at Nyangwe or somewhere
beyond. They left Southampton, England, on October 18, 1877,
on a vessel of the Union Mail Steamship Company that took them
around the Cape of Good Hope and reached Zanzibar on December 12. The following day they met Henry Morton Stanley, who
was about to board a British India Steam Navigation Company
ship for Aden. Stanley had arrived two weeks earlier to repatriate
the 108 surviving members of his crew. When he met the Belgian

expedition, it was the first time he had ever heard of the International African Association.[52]

5

Bateke Plateau, March 30, 1878

At the end of March 1878, Brazza's caravan reached the Bateke Plateau, less than one hundred miles from where they had abandoned the Ogowe River. "The country presents itself, in effect, in the form of a desert with sand for soil," wrote Brazza. The plateau was broken up by deep gorges with protruding granite rocks, exposing the geological structure of Kalahari sands resting on a base of granite. In this specialized ecosystem, he found tracks of a lion, an animal that was unknown along the Ogowe, and he later spent a night listening to lions roar in the distance. Rainfall was plentiful, but because the rain quickly filtered down through the Kalahari sands, streams were rare, and people got their water from deep wells. The expedition would sometimes walk a whole day without crossing a stream. The banana groves that lined the Ogowe valley had disappeared. The only visible vegetation, other than the ubiquitous prairie grasses, was the palm trees that provided shade for the villages. In that desertlike environment, the expedition sometimes found it necessary to purchase water and firewood.[53]

The Bateke Plateau is a geographical oddity in that the grassy vegetation built on undulating sand dunes is surrounded by tropical rainforest to the east, west, and north. Brazza referred to the people living on the plateau as Bateke, although anthropologists have subsequently made a distinction between the eastern Bateke (also known as Tio), who lived on the plateau, and the western Bateke, who lived in the low country to the west. People on the plateau cultivated cassava and a kind of fine-grained millet similar to the fonio produced in the Fuuta Jaloo highlands of West Africa. Brazza was impressed by the carefully cultivated fields, in which as many as thirty to forty people worked together using implements that he had never seen along the Ogowe.[54]

After traveling through a region where European trade goods had been scarce, he found an abundance of white salt from Europe, cloth, and other trade items on the Bateke Plateau. The one European product that was missing from the repertory was guns. As was the case in East Africa, the traders reserved the guns for themselves. The foreign goods were brought in by Laadi traders from the Niari Valley who were part of the western Bateke group that lived at a lower elevation in lands with more rivers and trees. The people of the plateau purchased cloth and other European goods primarily in exchange for captives, which they obtained from the lands to the north. Laadi caravans of 50–100 men regularly traveled the length of the plateau to distribute their products, although Brazza crossed paths with a caravan that contained at least 150 men.[55]

Brazza was now in a region where it was easier to hire porters to supplement his nucleus of enslaved carriers, but he found it a mixed blessing. The hired Bateke porters seemed to have designs on stealing his merchandise in collaboration with local chiefs and villagers. He had several tense confrontations, but in the end the hired porters and villagers always backed down because the expedition had guns and they did not. Brazza carried a Winchester model 1866 lever-action rifle similar to the one used by Stanley, and when the situation got tense, he would find a pretext to fire fourteen shots in rapid succession just to demonstrate what it could do.

In the Bateke country, Brazza heard about the Alima River that flowed to the east-northeast, and he made a reconnaissance mission to see it. As his party approached the Alima, Brazza noticed three changes. First, the trade goods in the villages no longer came from the southwest but from the northeast via the Alima. Second, it became impossible to hire Bateke porters and guides because they feared the Bobangi traders (whom Brazza called Apfuru, using the Bateke term), who had established trading villages along the Alima. Brazza attributed this fear to the fact that the Bobangi were tall, strong, and well fed, but it was more likely because the Bobangi had muskets and the Bateke did not. Without the labor provided by hired porters, Brazza's enslaved porters had to go back and forth over each stretch several times to transport all the baggage. The third change was that food, especially cassava, was increasingly scarce as they approached the Alima, forcing Brazza to limit the cassava rations to half a pound a day. Arriving at the Alima, he learned that cassava was scarce because so much of it was sold to the Bobangi traders who came up the Alima each year at the end of the rainy season. Living in seasonal trading villages that they had built along the river, the Bobangi exchanged smoked fish, European cloth, pottery, palm oil, and salt for cassava and ivory before returning to their homes down the Alima.[56]

Arriving at a Bobangi trading village, Brazza was told by Chief Obemba that the Alima had no rapids and that after six days of travel, it reached a body of "water without end" from whence came the guns and gunpowder. Being unaware of the U-shaped trajectory of the Congo River, and not knowing that the Congo was eight to ten miles wide, Brazza did not associate the mysterious body of "water without end" with the Congo River. Instead, he imagined that the Alima flowed into Lake Chad. As evidence, he pointed to the black mineral salt that was carried up the Alima by the Bobangi traders. In contrast to the local vegetable salt extracted from the flowers of palm trees on the Bateke Plateau, the black salt brought by the traders was clearly of mineral origin. Brazza associated it with the salt works in Wadai, west of Lake Chad, mentioned by the German explorer Gustav Nachtigal, not realizing that the black mineral salt actually came from Mboko, just two hundred miles to the north. Lake Chad, in contrast, was seventeen hundred miles away.[57]

Having decided to descend the Alima in canoes, Brazza returned to his base camp to pick up the rest of his porters and supplies. When the full caravan arrived at Chief Obemba's trading village on the Alima two weeks later, Brazza discovered that the

Bobangi traders he had seen earlier had hastily left in twelve large canoes loaded high with baskets of cassava. With the traders gone, Brazza was able to buy eight dugout canoes with the help of Chief Obemba. Even though some of the canoes were old and needed repair, he paid a high price: a total of eight muskets, eighty boxes of gunpowder, 550 yards of cloth, two hundred bells, one hundred mirrors, one hundred necklaces, and assorted other items. As he prepared to depart, he was repeatedly warned that the Bobangi claimed a monopoly on trade along the Alima. They would not allow foreigners to travel on their waterway, especially ones with merchandise.

As Brazza's fleet began to descend the river, they observed that the Bobangi had abandoned some of their trading camps in order to concentrate their forces at the most strategic points along the river. Throughout the first day they were fired on from almost every village they passed and were pursued by armed Bobangi in dugout canoes. Brazza's enslaved porters, who had been forced by necessity to become paddlers, flattened themselves on the bottom of the canoe once the shooting started, forcing the Senegalese marines to put down their guns and paddle.

Brazza's party spent the night on a sandbank, where they set up defensive positions at first light. As the sun rose, they saw thirty dugout canoes filled with men armed with muskets that separated into two groups to attack from both flanks. Brazza's expedition had only fifteen rifles, but they were French-made 1874 Chassepot bolt-action rifles that fired metallic cartridges and had fast-twisting rifling for increased accuracy. They were far superior to the smooth-bore flintlock muskets used by the Bobangi. When the Bobangi canoes reached a spot about forty yards away, both sides opened fire. The rapid fire and accurate shooting of the Senegalese marines caught the Bobangi by surprise and forced them to retreat. The battle had lasted only a few minutes.

Bobangi oral traditions about that battle reveal some important context that was missing in Brazza's account. A Bobangi chief named Bolunza had acquired a monopoly over the commerce along that stretch of the Alima, giving him authority over the seasonal trading villages and the marketplaces in the larger villages downstream. Chief Obemba, who facilitated the sale of canoes to Brazza, was a subordinate chief who was jealous of the wealth and power of Bolunza and wanted to challenge him. Obemba's position would be strengthened if Brazza succeeded in descending the river. The oral traditions depict Obemba's action in aiding Brazza as treason, and they depict Bolunza as a local hero who was committed to blocking Brazza's passage.[58]

The oral traditions state that during the battle, Chief Bolunza stood at the front of the lead canoe holding a war charm called *Makuba* over his head to render him invulnerable to bullets. Bobangi fighters were cut down all around him by the gunfire of the Senegalese marines, but Bolunza was untouched. That latter point was confirmed by Brazza. "I will always remember the man who was in the lead canoe, upon which we concentrated our fire," wrote Brazza. "He never ceased to stand tall and wave a charm above his head. He was preserved from the bullets that rained around him."[59]

When the firing stopped, Brazza had to make a decision. His party could try to slip past the Bobangi attackers while they were regrouping, or they could abandon the Alima altogether. Brazza reasoned that if they continued on, the attacks would increase as they approached the heart of Bobangi territory, and he had only fifteen guns and a dwindling supply of ammunition. After three days on the sandbank during which they heard rumors that the Bobangi were preparing for another attack, they decided to abandon their canoes and escape on foot. They reduced their baggage to what the porters could carry in one trip, sinking seven chests in the river. Fearing that the Bobangi were planning a new attack the next morning, they left during the night, leaving bonfires burning to mask their retreat. They slogged through the swampy forest of the river valley in the dark. By morning they had reached the beginning of the hills that lined the Alima valley, and by evening they were out of the reach of the Bobangi.

Brazza would later have second thoughts about his decision to abandon the Alima. Speaking to the Paris Geographical Society in 1879, he said, "I have regretted not following my first inspiration [i.e., to move ahead] ever since I learned from the travel writings of Stanley, that, in less than five days, we would have reached the waters of the Congo rather than a lacustrine impasse, which would have left us at the mercy of the Bobangi." But three years later he blamed the hostility of the Bobangi on Stanley. "You will recall," he wrote to the minister of the marine, "that Stanley had gone down the Congo, leaving no other memory of his passage than the thirty-two battles in which he took part. Myself, suffering from the backlash of the *hostility he had sown*, had to fight against the Bobangi, who are the masters of the Congo." While Stanley made a convenient scapegoat, it would be more accurate to conclude that Stanley and Brazza both encountered hostility because they were foreigners trying to trespass upon a commercial monopoly. The only difference was that Brazza turned back, whereas Stanley fought his way through.[60]

Not wanting to give up his mission, Brazza planned to continue traveling eastward on foot, but local hostilities kept pushing him to the north. He was thus traveling roughly parallel to the Congo River, which was less than 150 miles away. He did not realize that every river he crossed ran into the Congo. When some of the porters were too exhausted to continue, he divided his expedition, sending his two French companions back to the Ogowe with the ailing porters and continuing on with ten enslaved porters and six Senegalese marines. By the end of July, he reached the Licona (a.k.a. Kouyou) River and encountered Bobangi traders who wore imported cloth and carried guns. Brazza was told that they periodically came up the Licona in fleets of fifty to one hundred canoes and then split up to go up the different tributaries. They would attack villages with their guns and take away captives to sell as slaves. Brazza was told that the captives were taken away to faraway countries and never seen again. In his confusion about equatorial African geography, he did not realize that they were being taken to the Congo River and then downstream to Malebo Pool.[61]

In early August 1878, Brazza and his men heard bird songs that presaged the coming of the rainy season, which would turn the plains into swamps. They could have built huts and waited out the rainy season, as they had done the year before, but their trade goods were running low and their health was deteriorating. Noting that it was three years since he had left France, Brazza decided to turn back. The farthest point the expedition had reached was near a river he called Leboi Ocoua, which meant "river of salt." The local people made salt by a process of evaporation from the salty water that flowed down from hills with salt-rich soil. This was the black salt that he had seen along the Alima when he had wrongly concluded that it came from the region of Lake Chad. He later told the Paris Geographical Society that he had been confused about the course of the Congo River, and it was only after he had left Africa and read Stanley's book *A travers le continent mystérieux*, published in 1879, that it suddenly became clear to him that all of the rivers he had crossed since reaching the Bateke Plateau flowed into the Congo. He had been within 150 miles of the Congo River for several months without realizing it.

For the return journey, he selected a westward route that he believed would get him to the upper Ogowe in the shortest time, but the enslaved porters preferred to retrace their steps and travel in familiar territory. When Brazza insisted, seven of the porters deserted, leaving him with only three porters and the Senegalese marines. They abandoned most of their remaining supplies, including the instruments for fixing their location, and continued on with their reduced crew. On September 9, 1878, they rejoined Brazza's two remaining French colleagues (the naturalist had gone home earlier) and the remaining enslaved porters who were waiting for them on the upper Ogowe. The dugout canoes were still at the

same spot where they had left them. The trip down the Ogowe
went rapidly, especially after some local chiefs provided them with
skilled paddlers to help them shoot the rapids. At Lope, Brazza was
pleasantly surprised to find several chests of supplies waiting for
him. They had been sent by Leopold II, the king of the Belgians.[62]

CHAPTER 3

THE GRAND HIGHWAY OF COMMERCE

IF YOU TOOK A MAP of Africa in the 1870s and colored in all the parts controlled by the European powers, you would find that the areas under European control were mostly located at the northern and southern extremities of the continent—places with a Mediterranean climate that was hospitable to European settlers. In the north, France controlled the parts of Algeria between the Mediterranean Sea and the Atlas Mountains; at the southern tip of Africa, Britain controlled the Cape Colony and the fertile strip of land between the Indian Ocean coast and the Drakensberg Mountains. In tropical Africa, the Portuguese, French, and English controlled a number of trading enclaves along the coasts and major rivers, while small settler colonies for freed slaves had been established by the British in Sierra Leone and by the Americans in Liberia. Even counting the extensive colonial spaces in northern and southern Africa, European nations controlled less than 10 percent of the continent.

All of that was about to change. In many parts of Africa, European expansion would follow a relatively straightforward path by moving inland from long-established coastal enclaves. The major exception was the Congo River watershed. Although it covered an area the size of Western Europe, the Congo River watershed had been completely unexplored prior to Livingstone and Stanley, two accidental travelers who were looking for the Nile, not the Congo. The map used at the Brussels Geographical Conference in 1876 still showed a huge blank spot that encompassed the entire Congo watershed.

The region entered the European consciousness only after Stanley, coming from the east, emerged from the mouth of the Congo River in 1877 and made the course of the Congo River known to the Western world, while Brazza, moving in from the west, was trying to determine whether the Ogowe River offered a pathway into the heart of the rainforest. Although the paths of the two explorers passed within 150 miles of each other, the results of their expeditions were very different. After returning to Britain to write a book about his adventures, Stanley was recruited by King Leopold II of Belgium to build a road around the rapids of the Lower Congo River and establish permanent stations at key points on behalf of a syndicate called the Upper Congo Study Committee, which was headed by King Leopold. Brazza, after failing to obtain new funding from the French Ministry of the Marine, was sent by the semiautonomous French national committee of King Leopold's International African Association to build a station on the Ogowe, ostensibly for scientific and humanitarian purposes. Although they were fierce rivals working for separate organizations, both men were operating under the umbrella of King Leopold II.

Whereas Stanley tried to fulfill his contract with King Leopold to the letter, Brazza was pursuing his own agenda. The two men followed different routes to Malebo Pool, the beginning of a thousand-mile stretch of navigable water on the Congo River. Brazza's route took him to the Bateke Plateau, the nearly treeless plain that provided a break in the rainforest. After dealing with numerous petty chiefs in the rainforest, he discovered that the Bateke Plateau was a single polity under the authority of a king who bore the title Makoko. Going far beyond his instructions, Brazza concluded a treaty by which the Makoko ceded his kingdom to France and agreed to fly the French flag. Although Stanley and others would later claim that the Makoko's authority was exaggerated and that he did not intend to sign away his country, the treaty changed the nature of European consciousness of the Congo River basin. What had once been a competition between Stanley and Brazza for imperial bragging rights would quickly become a race to claim territory and gain recognition from the major European powers.

1

Brussels, September 17, 1877

From his palace in Brussels, King Leopold II had eagerly followed the progress of Henry Morton Stanley's expedition. After hearing no news for over a year, he took great interest in the report in the London *Daily Telegraph* on September 17, 1877, that Stanley had emerged from the mouth of the Congo River. The king immediately sent telegrams to the *Daily Telegraph* and the *New York Herald*—the cosponsors of Stanley's expedition—congratulating them for their "great service to science and civilization." From subsequent articles published in October and November, the king learned that Stanley was shifting his focus from geographical puzzles to commercial schemes. "Setting aside the contributions of our expedition to Geography," wrote Stanley, "the greatest discovery it has made is in the great field for trade it has opened to the world." Stanley described towns two miles long with broad streets between rows of neat, well-built houses that lined the banks of the Congo River. "I know of no part of Africa so thickly inhabited," he wrote. "Every thought seems engrossed with trade, and fairs and markets are established everywhere." Stanley concluded that "the Congo is, and will be, the grand highway of commerce to West Central Africa."[1]

After reading the *Daily Telegraph* articles, King Leopold resurrected his earlier plan for the International African Association to build a station along the Lower Congo, and he believed that Stanley would be the best person to oversee the project. In a letter to the Belgian ambassador to London, Leopold emphasized that his strategy needed to be indirect and subtle because the English would oppose him if he tried to claim territory. He accordingly proposed "a purely exploratory mission which will offend no one and provide us with some posts down in that region . . . which we can develop when Europe and Africa have got used to our presence on the Congo." Just to make sure that his intention was clear, Leopold added, "I do not want to expose myself or alarm the English, nor do I want to miss this opportunity to obtain a piece of this magnificent African cake."[2]

Wanting to get in touch with Stanley as soon as he arrived in Europe, Leopold asked his friend Alfred Rabuad, president of the Marseille Geographical Society, to invite Stanley to Marseilles to give a lecture. When the explorer arrived in Marseilles on his way home from Zanzibar on January 13, 1878, he was greeted by Rabaud along with two emissaries of King Leopold's International African Association—Baron Greindl and Henry Shelton Sanford. The two emissaries met with Stanley for six hours the next day and invited him to meet with King Leopold in Brussels for further talks. As Stanley summarized that meeting seven years later, "I was made aware that King Leopold intended to undertake something substantial for Africa and that I was expected to assist him." Stanley declined, saying that he was eager to get to England and write a book about his expedition.[3]

One reason why Stanley was reluctant to get involved with King Leopold was that he hoped to persuade the British government to claim sovereign rights over the Congo River basin. In a dispatch to the London *Daily Telegraph* written from Luanda, Angola, shortly after he emerged from the mouth of the Congo River, Stanley had observed, "I feel convinced that the Congo question will become a political question in time. As yet, however, no European Power seems to have the right of control. Portugal claims it because she discovered its mouth; but the great powers—England, America, and France—refuse to recognize her right." He then urged England to proclaim sovereignty over the Congo River basin "at once."[4]

His advice was not heeded. As Stanley wrote in his diary, "I delivered addresses, after-dinner speeches, and in private have spoken earnestly to try to rouse them and adopt early means to secure the Congo basin for England. Even as late as October, November, and December [1878], as I went lecturing through the United Kingdom, I continued trying to impress upon them that someday they would regret not taking action, but it was no use." Many years later, Stanley's widow, Dorothy, echoed his frustration: "He spoke in all the commercial centers, especially in Manchester and Liverpool, setting forth the immense advantages to trade of such an enterprise. He had audiences with such public men as would listen, or seem to listen. But the government and the people of England turned a deaf ear."[5]

Stanley's efforts to drum up British interest in the Congo River basin were hindered by two factors. The first was that Stanley's reputation for violent encounters had made him toxic in England, where he was viewed as a product of the American Wild West who stood in stark contrast to the saintly Livingstone and the gentlemanly British explorers such as Burton and Cameron. The most important factor, however, was the belief in the Foreign Office that the tropical areas of Africa were best left as free trade zones as long as access for British merchants could be guaranteed. A confidential Foreign Office memorandum proposed to "confine ourselves to securing the utmost possible freedom of trade on that [west] coast, yielding to others the territorial responsibilities." That attitude was on display in 1876, when the Foreign Office rejected Verney Lovett Cameron's declaration of a British protectorate over the Congo River basin because it felt that opening the interior of equatorial Africa to British companies was unlikely to be profitable in the present generation.[6]

It was not until August 10, 1878, after his book *Through the Dark Continent* had gone to press, that Stanley finally traveled to

Brussels to meet with King Leopold II. Stanley was received with full honors, dining at the palace on Monday, attending a banquet in his honor given by the Belgian Geographical Society on Tuesday, and dining with the king again on Wednesday. Instead of simply building stations for the International African Association, Stanley proposed building a railway from the Congo River estuary to Malebo Pool and placing steamboats on the Upper Congo to conduct trade. The king seemed pleased with Stanley's plan and sought subscribers to form a company that would invest 27 million Belgian francs in a railway and steamboats. The major problem was that the company would be building a railroad through territory that it did not control. Stanley tried to assure the potential investors that he could sign treaties with the local chiefs guaranteeing their property rights along the rail line, but two major industrialists backed out at the last minute, scuttling the deal.[7]

The king then developed a more modest plan that would proceed in three stages: stage one would be a philanthropic and scientific organization that would build stations, survey territory, and sign treaties to lay the groundwork for building a railroad; stage two would be a transportation company that would build the railway to Malebo Pool; and stage three would be a trading company that would put steamboats on the Upper Congo and establish a commercial operation. The investors met in Brussels on November 25, 1878, and formed a syndicate known as the Upper Congo Study Committee, which would operate for three years to implement stage one. In its organizational structure, it was entirely separate from the International African Association. King Leopold was elected honorary president of the Study Committee, and Col. Maximilien Strauch, one of Leopold's most loyal advisors, was chosen as president. Stanley agreed to head up the Study Committee's operations in Africa, and he accordingly signed a three-year contract with the committee that was renewable for two additional years. This was in addition to the five-year personal service contract he had earlier signed with King Leopold. Stanley's tasks were to build three stations between the Congo River Estuary and Malebo Pool, conduct a survey for building a railroad, and explore the commercial possibilities of the Upper Congo. Exploration in equatorial Africa was rapidly giving way to commercialization.[8]

The Study Committee was initially financed by Belgian and Dutch capital. The largest investor was King Leopold himself, who invested 265,000 Belgian francs from his personal fortune; the second was the Dutch Trading Company with 130,000 francs; then came two members of the Belgian nobility with 50,000 and 25,000 francs, followed by smaller investors. When the total value of the subscriptions fell well short of the million francs the king had hoped for, he sent Stanley to Britain, where he solicited over 100,000 francs' worth of investments. Soon thereafter, the Dutch Trading Company went bankrupt, leaving King Leopold as the only large investor in the syndicate and giving him new freedom to redefine the Study Committee's mission.[9]

With its strong financial base, the Study Committee prepared to send out the best-equipped expedition ever to set foot in tropical Africa. The committee purchased five steam-powered riverboats ranging from twenty-four to sixty-five feet in length, two steel barges, prefabricated buildings, portable toilets, and a long list of supplies such as tents, cloth, beads, wire, tools, masts, oars, sails, ropes, oils, paint, zinc sheets, boards, nails, drills, forges, gunpowder, and medicines. To transport the men and equipment to the Congo River, the committee chartered two steamships: the *Albion* would go to Zanzibar via the Suez Canal (which opened in 1869) to pick up porters and armed guards, while the *Barga* would sail directly to the Congo River with the supplies. Arriving in Zanzibar, Stanley hired a crew of sixty-eight Zanzibari porters, fifty of whom had earlier accompanied him on his journey across Africa. He also met with the sultan and left gifts and money to be forwarded to Tippu Tip. Then the *Albion* returned to the Mediterranean with Stanley and the Zanzibari porters in order to sail down the coast of West Africa to the mouth of the Congo River.[10]

When the *Albion* arrived at Gibraltar on June 26, 1879, Colonel Strauch was waiting to present Stanley with a radically new vision of the Study Committee's objectives. Although he encouraged Stanley to sign treaties with local chiefs and build stations, as previously agreed, he now wanted Stanley to secure as much land as possible for each station and try to attract Africans to settle there. It was unlikely that Africans would want to leave their homes to settle near the stations, but what Colonel Strauch apparently had in mind was to purchase slaves, declare them free, and settle them near the stations to produce food and work as wage laborers.

Once the Congo River stations were established, Colonel Strauch wanted Stanley to extend their authority over the neighboring chiefdoms and to organize the stations and their dependencies into a "Confederation of Negro freedmen." Despite the high-sounding rhetoric, Colonel Strauch emphasized that "there is no question of granting the slightest political power to Negroes. That would be absurd. The white men, heads of stations, retain all the powers." The stations would be responsible to the president of the confederation, who would be a European appointed by King Leopold, and who would reside in Europe. "It is not a question of Belgian colonies," Strauch told Stanley. "It is a question of creating a new state, as big as possible, and running it." Stanley dismissed the idea as wildly unrealistic. "It would be madness for one in my position to attempt it," he wrote to Colonel Strauch. "All we can hope at present is to win suffrage to live and move about without fear of violence." As harebrained as Leopold's scheme sounded at the time, a variant of it would come to fruition six years later with the establishment of the Congo Free State.[11]

2

Paris, January 24, 1879

Two weeks after Stanley left Brussels to begin his mission to the Congo River, Pierre Savorgnan de Brazza addressed the Paris

Geographical Society in a lecture hall at the Sorbonne. He had just returned from his three-year expedition up the Ogowe River to the Bateke Plateau. After giving a detailed narrative of the expedition, he came to the big question that was on the minds of the armchair geographers in the audience—how could he have spent months within striking distance of the Congo River without knowing it? The answer, in short, was that even though he knew where he was in relation to the Atlantic coast, he had no information about the course of the Congo River. "I could not imagine that the Congo rolled its majestic waves in front of me in the direction of the rising sun," he told the crowd. It was not until he returned to France and saw the large fold-out map in Stanley's book that the picture became clear. "As soon as I learned about the path followed by that explorer," he said, "all was suddenly illuminated. The series of rivers that I had crossed all ran into Stanley's Livingstone [Congo] River." Having owned up to his mistake, he issued a challenge for the future: "The geographical conquest of that immense continent will require great effort. French explorers will not fail in this essential task." Then he added, "For my part, I am ready to get back on the trail."[12]

Despite the meager geographical results of his three-year expedition, Brazza was honored upon his return to France. In addition to receiving a gold medal from the Paris Geographical Society, he was made an officer of the French Academy and a knight of the Legion of Honor, and the French navy promoted him to sublieutenant. More than honors, however, he wanted financial backing for a new expedition. In his report to the minister of the marine, he tried to generate support by advocating the suppression of the slave trade and the development of new forms of commerce. "The future of the country near the upper Ogowe is linked to the question of the slave trade," he wrote. "The day when it no longer absorbs the activity of the tribes that participate in it, they could use their natural aptitudes for transporting indigenous products in their dugout canoes. Only then can the tribes of the back country exploit the natural riches of their forests." But his patron at the Ministry of the Marine, Admiral de Montaignac, had retired, and the ministry was not interested in sponsoring a new expedition.[13]

Brazza's best option was to seek financial support from the French National Committee of the International African Association. Although the French national committee operated under the umbrella of the IAA, it maintained a high degree of independence. The French committee had raised private money for its own projects and obtained a grant of 100,000 francs from the French government for exploration in Africa. At a meeting of the French national committee in Paris on July 25, 1879, there was strong sentiment in favor of Brazza's plan to reach the Congo River by way of the Ogowe and the Alima and to plant the French flag at Malebo Pool ahead of Stanley's arrival. The French had learned that Stanley had left Gibraltar in June on a secretive mission to the mouth of the Congo River. Unaware that he was working for King Leopold, they assumed he was planning to establish stations for the British.[14]

King Leopold learned about the French national committee's plan to send Brazza to Malebo Pool only because Henry Shelton Sanford, the American businessman who was a member of the IAA executive committee, was present at the Paris meeting. In an effort to secure Brazza's services for the Upper Congo Study Committee, the king invited him to Brussels to receive the Order of Leopold award for his exploration of the Ogowe. During three days of meetings at the king's residence in Laeken (a suburb of Brussels), Leopold tried to persuade Brazza that it was better to work for an international syndicate such as the Study Committee than to work for the French national committee of the IAA. Leopold understood that he could control the activities of the Study Committee, whereas he had only minimal influence over the French national committee. According to popular accounts, Brazza responded haughtily, "Sir! I am a French officer!" thus proclaiming his loyalty to his adopted country. But two decades later, Brazza would recall that he refused the king's offer because he had been put off by the secretive nature of the Study Committee's mission and was reluctant to work under Stanley's authority.[15]

The discussions in Brussels gave Brazza second thoughts about becoming an agent of the French national committee of the IAA, since he now understood that the IAA and the Upper Congo Study Committee, although two separate organizations, were connected through King Leopold and Colonel Strauch. At a meeting of the French national committee of the IAA on November 27, Brazza outlined a scheme for laying claim to vast portions of the Congo River basin in the name of France. The committee balked at the plan because its IAA charter required it to be nonpolitical, but Brazza persisted. "Give me 10,000 francs," he told the committee, "and in three months I will plant the French flag on the banks of the Congo."[16]

The problem of jurisdiction was resolved when Brazza obtained some modest support from the Ministry of Foreign Affairs, the Ministry of Education, and the French navy. He was now working under the auspices of both the IAA and the French government. The IAA station to be established on the Ogowe, which was intended for scientific and humanitarian purposes, would give him cover to plant the French flag in the Congo River basin, even though the French government had not asked him to do so. Although he was working primarily for the French national committee of the IAA, he could use his status as a naval officer to claim that he was a representative of the French government. Despite his dual affiliation, he was basically operating on his own.

Brazza left Libreville, Gabon, on March 8, 1880, to take the steamboat *Marabout* up the Ogowe River to Lambaréné, as he had done on his earlier trip. His crew consisted of three French navy personnel, ten Senegalese marines, and four interpreters. At Lambaréné he hired canoes and paddlers, choosing only people who agreed to make the entire trip. Although it had taken him two years to reach the Ogowe's limit of navigation on his earlier trip, this time he made it in about three months. On June 13, he raised the French flag to signify the founding of a French station on the upper Ogowe that would become known as Franceville. Leaving behind a small crew to receive the people who would come out to build the station, Brazza departed on June 22 with a crew of five Senegalese marines and seven porters that he had picked up in Libreville. He had learned on his previous trip that locally hired porters tended to desert after a few days, whereas complete strangers were more likely to stay with the expedition because it was their best guarantee of returning home.

Brazza had originally talked about heading east to the Alima River and following it until it joined the Congo, but memories of his battle with the Bobangi traders discouraged that strategy. Armed with the detailed map of the Congo River that was included in the pocket of Stanley's book, he would instead cross the Bateke Plateau and march directly south toward Malebo Pool. On July 20, the party reached the Lefini River and followed it eastward until they arrived at Chief Ngampéré's village on July 30. Even though the village was small, its chief was clearly an important figure. He wore a massive copper collar signifying that he was a "chief of the crown" who was ritually responsible for the fertility and well-being of the surrounding territory. Ngampéré had been installed in that office by the Makoko, the great chief of the Bateke, who had authority over the Bateke Plateau. Brazza was told that the Makoko lived at Mbe, about twenty miles southeast of Ngampéré's village. He was held in such high respect that his subordinate chiefs approached him on their knees. This was the first time Brazza had ever heard of the Makoko.

Up until this point, Brazza had been dealing with small, independent chiefs typical of the decentralized political culture of the rainforest societies, but now he encountered a kingdom with a sovereign ruler and subordinate chiefs that was more characteristic of the savanna region to the south. Surrounded on three sides by forests, the dry grasslands of the Bateke Plateau were a geographical and political anomaly. It was as if the southern savanna had protruded northward into the Congo basin rainforest. Even though modern linguists consider the Bateke language to be a "forest language," the inhabitants of the plateau had a savanna-style political system.[17]

Brazza wanted to head directly south toward Malebo Pool, but the Bateke chiefs who served as his guides kept urging him to follow the Lefini River east toward its junction with the Olumo. A map that a local chief drew on the ground with a stick, which Brazza duly copied into his diary, showed the Lefini River running into the Olumo, which ran into the Ncouna, none of which he could locate on Stanley's map. Brazza had not realized that *Olumo* was just a local name for the Congo River, and *Ncouna* was the local name for Malebo Pool. Leaving part of his men and supplies behind for faster traveling, he headed overland for Chief Ngampei's town, on the west bank of the Olumo (i.e., Congo) River.

At nine o'clock in the evening on August 15, 1880, Brazza saw the Congo River for the first time, even though he did not realize that was what he was looking at. "In the faint light of the moon," he wrote in his diary, "we saw the immense sheet of water of the Olumo unroll in front of us. It was a grandiose spectacle." As his party entered the riverside village of Ngampei by moonlight, Brazza realized that it was not like the Bateke villages that dotted the Bateke Plateau. He had noted in his diary that the people of Ngampei were known as *"Bateke maballe,"* but he did not know that the latter term was derived from *ebale,* the Bobangi word for the Congo River. The villagers were the "Bateke of the Congo River," whose culture was heavily influenced by the Bobangi. Their canoes, paddles, water flasks, mats, and baskets, and the copper decorations on their muskets, all reflected the Bobangi style. Remembering his previous violent encounter with Bobangi traders on the Alima, Brazza was on high alert and took an inventory of his weapons, but the night passed peacefully.[18]

The next afternoon Brazza met with Chief Ngampei. After the usual ceremonial greetings, Brazza said that he had been sent by the great chief of the white people to find a place to build a commercial station in order to open up the country for white traders

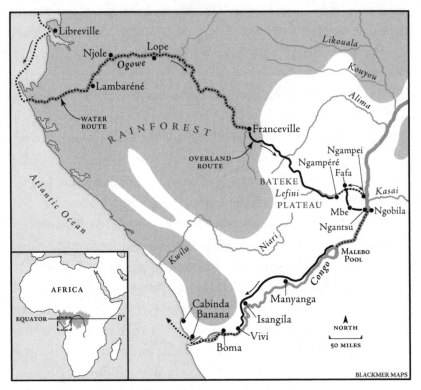

Brazza's second expedition, 1880

and their products. The whites would bring in an abundance of cloth and other European goods to trade for local ivory and rubber. Ngampei responded that the whites were welcome to come and build a station wherever they liked.

Then Chief Ngampei told Brazza an extraordinary story. He said that in the past, the Bateke people had been united under a strong ruler, but after that ruler died, each chief had gone his own way, creating a chaotic political landscape. He was reciting a variant of a widely known Bateke myth about a time when all the Bateke chiefs lived together in a great capital city under the watchful eye of their king, but after the king's death, they had all dispersed. Various versions of the myth had been used to explain Bateke disunity over the past centuries, and therefore the myth spoke to a general condition of decentralized power rather than a specific event. Chief Ngampei, however, added a new wrinkle by suggesting that perhaps the great chief of the whites would come and restore the mythical lost unity of the Bateke.[19]

Why would Chief Ngampei seem willing to turn over sovereignty to a white stranger? Brazza probably interpreted the statement in the light of European nineteenth-century racial thought, which would have seen it as an acknowledgment of white racial superiority. But Chief Ngampei saw his statement in very different terms. The Bobangi along the Congo River believed that dead ancestors occasionally returned and walked the earth as ghosts, who appeared as white. Black and white were not seen as immutable racial categories but rather as transient states of being. This belief was common throughout the region and was also held by the Kongo people along the Lower Congo River. So when Chief Ngampei suggested that a white chief would restore the mythical lost unity of the Bateke, he was most likely referring to the return of a former Bateke chief from the spirit world. In any case, he was certainly not advocating subordination to the government of France.[20]

Getting permission from the Bateke chief for a station was the easy part. Brazza knew that the Europeans would never break into the Congo River trade unless they reached an agreement with the Bobangi—the masters of the Congo River. He therefore asked Chief Ngampei to take a message to the Bobangi. Using a theatrical stunt that he had probably used before, and would use many times afterward, he approached the chief with a bullet in one hand and a piece of cloth in the other. The Bobangi had a choice, he said. If they chose the cloth, it meant that they wanted peaceful trade. If they chose the bullet, it meant war. The chief replied that he needed to consult with some Bobangi chiefs and would have their reply in two days.

While Brazza waited for the reply, he remained on alert because he feared that the Bobangi were mobilizing to attack him, as they had done on the Alima during his first expedition. The arrival of a new group of Bobangi traders the next day seemed to confirm his suspicions. They had purchased cassava along the Alima River and had now come to Ngampei's village in their canoes to trade it for dried fish and tobacco. Brazza stayed out of sight as the trading session proceeded peacefully. Had he tried to talk to the Bobangi traders instead of hiding from them, he might have learned that the Olumo River was actually the Congo and that he was only five days' travel by canoe from Malebo Pool. Still worried that the Bobangi might be planning to attack him, Brazza's party left the next day and retraced their steps to Fafa, a village on the Lefini River that they had passed through earlier. Away from the Congo River, he was back to his original plan: he would travel south across the Bateke Plateau to reach Malebo Pool. His first destination would be Mbe, the capital of the Bateke Kingdom.

3

Mbe, Bateke Plateau, August 28, 1880

On August 28, 1880, Brazza's expedition left Fafa and trekked southward for thirty miles along the flat and nearly treeless Bateke Plateau. Brazza was going to Mbe, where he would meet the great Bateke chief who bore the title Makoko. In an account Brazza wrote two years later, he credited Ngampéré, the chief who wore the massive copper collar, with delivering an invitation from the Makoko. According to Brazza's story, Chief Ngampéré told him, "The Makoko has known for some time about the great white chief of the Ogowe; he knows that his terrible guns have never been used to attack, and that peace and abundance follow in his footsteps. He has charged me to carry the words of peace and guide his friend." That story became enshrined as the official account of the origins of Brazza's visit to the Makoko. But that invitation is not mentioned in Brazza's diary, and Brazza's story fails to explain why Ngampéré had initially sent Brazza east toward the Congo River rather than south to Mbe, the Makoko's capital.[21]

In contrast to the surrounding rainforest, the Bateke Plateau was a barren grass-land because its sandy soil does not retain water. *La Tour du Monde*, 1888, second semester, p. 55.

The historian Jan Vansina has suggested a very different scenario. He argues that the Makoko did not want to meet with Brazza and had accordingly ordered the chiefs along the Lefini to guide Brazza toward Chief Ngampei, on the Congo River, in order to deflect him from Mbe. It was most likely Ngampei who decided that if Brazza wanted permission to build a trading station on the Congo River, then he needed to get approval from the Makoko in Mbe. Evidence for this scenario can be found in the words of the treaty that Brazza signed with the Makoko. It begins, "King Makoko, who is sovereign over the lands between the mouth of the Lefini and Ncouna [Malebo Pool], having ratified the cession of territory made by Ngampei for the establishment of a French station . . ." Those words suggest that Chief Ngampei had sent Brazza to the Makoko to ratify the trade agreement.[22]

As the expedition approached the Makoko's village, Brazza summarized his goals in his diary. His first goal was to locate the most practical route between the Atlantic coast and the Upper Congo River and secure it for France. His second goal was to acquire rights for France over the Bateke Plateau, which he saw as the transition zone between the Atlantic coast and the Upper

Congo River. His third goal was to plant the French flag at Malebo Pool, which was the meeting point between the open waters of the Upper Congo River and the rapids of the Lower Congo. Given that Brazza's only official task was to select sites for one or two stations to be built by the French national committee of the IAA, the agenda that he outlined was entirely his own.

Brazza referred to the Makoko's domains as the "Kingdom of Makoko" and noted that it encompassed the Bateke Plateau from Malebo Pool in the south to the Lefini River in the north, which gave it a dimension of roughly 150 miles north to south and 100 miles east to west. The political structure of the Makoko's kingdom has been described by historian Henri Brunschwig as "feudal" because the real power was in the hands of the dozen or so "chiefs of the crown," who wore massive copper collars. Brazza referred to them as feudal lords, but this kingdom was very different from the kingdoms of medieval Europe because the Makoko's powers were above all spiritual and magical. He was the master of *Nkwe Mbali*, the national spirit that was honored every fourth day by a day of rest (called *Nkwe Mbali*) and by a special ritual at the Makoko's court. It was said that the king could unleash lions upon the objects of his wrath or send torrents of rain to wash away the crops and houses of his enemies. One early French explorer described the Makoko as the "Pope of the Bateke," an analogy that Brazza, who had grown up in Rome under the authority of the Papal States, could appreciate.[23]

The major power exercised by the king was to appoint a new lord when an old one died and provide the copper collar for the installation ceremony, but the king had little power to give orders to the lords once they were installed. Instead, he served as a clearinghouse for information and frequently sent out runners to carry news (but not orders) to the various lords. When called upon, he mediated disputes between the lords, but his power to do so was limited. While Brazza was on the Lefini River, two of the most important Bateke lords were at war with one another, and the king was helpless to do anything about it.[24]

The king's only direct authority was over the inhabitants of the village of Mbe, where he served as the village headman as well as the king of the larger realm. Mbe was described in the 1880s as "a small village, not very prosperous looking, with houses falling in ruins." The royal compound contained two houses for the king and huts for his twelve wives and eight slaves—paltry numbers for an African monarch. Although the king collected tribute from his subjects, much of it came in the form of food or locally woven raffia cloth, and the capital displayed few signs of conspicuous wealth. Because most of the inhabitants of Mbe were members of the royal family who did not do agricultural labor, the village was dependent on irregular supplies of food sent in as tribute from the surrounding regions. The relative poverty of Mbe was in stark contrast with the prosperity of the Bobangi trading towns along the Congo River and the Bateke trading towns at Malebo Pool.[25]

As Brazza's party approached Mbe, they halted at a waiting area, where they were told to dress in their finest clothes while messengers went ahead to alert the king to their arrival. Nobody entered Mbe unannounced. When all was ready, Brazza's group made its entrance, preceded by a clarion and a French flag. After they arrived inside the stockade of the royal compound, the reigning Makoko, whose personal name was Iloo, came out, preceded by his wives. Wrapped in a large piece of cloth and adorned with a large copper collar and copper bracelets on his arms and legs, the Makoko sat on a cushion that was placed on a lion skin. As the king who could reputedly command the lions, the Makoko alone had the right to sit on a lion skin, and he held a monopoly on the skins of any lions killed in his realm.

After the appropriate ceremonies and greetings, the guides recounted the story of Brazza's travels to Ngampei on the Olumo

River, where he had discussed the possibility of building a French station. Brazza then explained that when he learned that the Makoko was the ruler of all the land between Ngampei and Malebo Pool, he traveled to Mbe to discuss the possibilities for future relations between France and the Bateke Kingdom. As the meeting came to a close, the king retired to his house, and the guests were served a meal of cassava, pistachios, and sorghum. The hosts apologized for the meager amount of cassava and explained that elephants had recently devastated the cassava fields.

Over the next two weeks, Brazza had numerous discussions with the king and the major officials at Mbe. After outlining the possibilities for increased trade offered by the French, he recounted how he had offered the Bobangi on the Olumo River the choice of peace or war but had not received a response. To resolve that problem, the king sent for Opoontaaba, who was his prime minister, and for Ngobila and Ngantsu, whose towns faced each other on opposite banks of the Congo River and who thus controlled the flow of trade. In the structure of the Bateke Kingdom, Ngobila was a lord who wore a copper collar while Ngantsu was a mere land chief. Ngobila had great influence over the Bobangi because they paid tolls to him when they went to trade at the Pool. During discussions of the trading networks, the prime minister drew a map in the sand that made Brazza realize, for the first time, that the Olumo River was the Congo. "I can finally locate myself on Stanley's map," he wrote in his diary.[26]

After two weeks of ceremonies and discussions during which the Makoko called in some of his most important chiefs and officials for consultation, the agreement was ready to be concluded. Although Brazza's previous agreements with chiefs had been oral pronouncements accompanied by a public ceremony, he decided that this one called for a written and signed treaty because the Makoko was the first chief he had encountered who commanded a large territory. The authority of the numerous petty chiefs in the rainforest rarely extended beyond their own village, but the

Makoko, in contrast, was the recognized ruler of the entire Bateke Plateau. In a ceremony on September 10, 1880, Brazza wrote out two copies of the treaty in French and signed his name at the bottom while the Makoko made an X.

The Makoko Treaty contained two clauses. The first was the ratification of Chief Ngampei's cession of a plot of land along the Congo River for a trading station. Since most of the discussion that preceded the signing of the treaty concerned the advantages of trade with the French, it is not surprising that the Makoko would agree to let Brazza build a station. The king had shared with Brazza his understanding that the French were like the Bobangi insofar as they appeared to be dedicated exclusively to commerce. What the Makoko clearly had in mind was that the whites should be a commercial counterweight to the Bobangi and would thus create a competitive situation from which the Bateke could profit. The Bobangi traders never challenged the authority of the Bateke chiefs along the Congo River, such as Ngantsu and Ngobila, and therefore the king saw no political risk in letting French traders come. If the French were like the Bobangi, they would not be a problem.[27]

The second clause is the most significant. It reads, "The King Makoko . . . having made the cession of his territory to France, to whom he cedes his hereditary rights of supremacy; desiring, as a sign of that cession, to fly the colors of France, I give him a French flag." If the words are taken at face value, then it appears that the Makoko ceded both his territory and his sovereign powers to France, which is something that no sovereign king would voluntarily do. It is difficult to understand why the king signed the treaty. Oral traditions collected by Jan Vansina recount that the king and his prime minister were initially wary of Brazza and that the prime minister had energetically opposed the treaty, but the Makoko overruled him.[28]

How are we to explain the Makoko's actions? One possible explanation is that Brazza failed to properly translate or explain that part of the treaty, and therefore the king was unaware that he was doing anything more than making an X on a simple trade agreement. But that explanation fails to address why the king agreed to fly the French flag. Although flags, as symbols of national sovereignty, were previously unknown in that part of Africa, the Makoko was a specialist in ritual and symbolism and was certainly aware that flying the French flag had some kind of larger meaning. Moreover, the king gave Brazza a piece of sod, representing the land of the Bateke. The symbolism of the sod would seem to represent more than just selling a small plot of land for a trading post. To Brazza, it represented the entire kingdom.

Given that the Makoko's power was largely spiritual and magical, it is not difficult to imagine that three factors beyond the temporal realm may have influenced the king's thinking. The first was the myth of lost Bateke unity, which Brazza heard again when he was in Mbe. Brazza was told that after the formerly unified kingdom broke up, the reigning Makoko had created the feudal lords to keep the Bateke from descending into anarchy. Embedded in the myth was a longing to recover the lost unity that may or may not have ever existed. The second factor was that during the negotiations the Makoko consulted in a dream with his ancestor four generations back. Given that the Bateke conceived of their history as a recurring cycle of two generations—the first and the last—in which everything in between them was erased, then going back four generations would have taken the Makoko into a deep mythical time when the kingdom was remembered as unified. The third factor was the association made by Chief Ngampei between Brazza's "great white chief" and the spirits of deceased Bateke kings, a notion that was also suggested by the Makoko's prime minister. That association may have been on the mind of the Makoko as well. Putting the three factors together, we can surmise that the Makoko was hoping to restore the mythical lost unity of his kingdom by seeking the spiritual support of a great white (i.e., ancestral) chief. Flying the French flag would give him an extra level of spiritual protection. As the "Pope of the Bateke," the Makoko would have viewed the agreement largely in spiritual terms. He would not have

knowingly placed himself under the secular administrative authority of the French government.[29]

The 110-word treaty that Pierre Savorgnan de Brazza signed with
the Makoko of the Bateke on September 10, 1880, was one of those
tipping points in the history of equatorial Africa whose significance
would become apparent only later on. Unlike the British protectorate treaties signed by Verney Lovett Cameron from 1874 to 1875,
which languished in the file cabinets of the British Colonial Office,
this one was instrumental in setting off the European scramble for
equatorial Africa. Historians may claim that by 1880 the colonial
partition of the African continent was all but inevitable, given the
increasing importance of African commodities for the industrializing economies of Europe and the growing imbalance of military
power between Europe and Africa. But the partition of equatorial
Africa took place in a particular way at a particular time, with very
particular and tragic results. If one follows that twisting and tangled
path, then Brazza's Makoko Treaty becomes a key focal point.

4

Ngantsu's Town, Upper Congo River, September 14, 1880

Brazza left Mbe immediately after signing the Makoko Treaty and,
two nights later, slept at Chief Ngantsu's town on the west bank
of the Congo River. The river was less than a mile wide at that
point, and the towns of chiefs Ngantsu and Ngobila nearly faced
one another across the water. Ngobila was a territorial lord whose
authority over the Congo River stretched along the west bank from
the Alima River to Malebo Pool. In practice Ngobila exercised his
authority mainly by collecting tolls from the Bobangi and Likuba
traders who passed by his town. It was most likely Ngobila who
had initiated Stanley's thirty-second and final battle on the Congo
River on March 9, 1877, because he saw that Stanley was trying to
pass by his town without stopping to pay the toll.[30]

Brazza spent a week trying to make contact with Bobangi traders but without success because they were as wary of him as he was of them. Finally, on September 19, four large Bobangi canoes appeared that held about thirty men each and carried a total of sixty guns. They were returning upriver to the Alima after a trip to Malebo Pool. After they beached their canoes, they entered the town in a ceremonial parade to greet Chief Ngantsu. Brazza approached them and began to speak through his interpreter. He told them a story about two white men who had come to equatorial Africa. The first one came down the Congo River in canoes and fought a series of battles in which he killed many people with his powerful guns. The second white man went to the upper Alima River, where he paid an exorbitant amount of merchandise to buy some canoes, but, despite his generosity, he was viciously attacked. Realizing that he would have to kill many people if he continued down the Alima, he retreated and traveled by land in order to maintain the peace. When the two white men returned to Europe and reported to the great chief of the white people, the first was condemned for his violence and demoted while the second was praised for his peaceful conduct. In a thinly disguised form, Brazza was talking about Stanley and himself.

Brazza was taking liberties with the facts. In his official report on his first expedition, he had explained that he had abandoned his descent of the Alima because he'd had only fifteen guns and had been running low on ammunition. After returning to France, he had written, "If we had known that the Alima would have led us to the Congo in five days, we would not have hesitated to force our way through in order to return to the coast via the Congo." The story about the great chief of the whites condemning Stanley while praising Brazza was another convenient piece of fiction. Writing in his diary, Brazza justified it by noting that Stanley had been pilloried in the European press for his violent encounters, whereas he himself had received praise for his peaceful diplomacy.[31]

Without revealing that he was the second white person in the story, Brazza told the Bobangi traders that he had been sent to prepare the way for white traders who wanted to buy ivory and rubber. Holding up his two hands, he said that in one hand was war and in the other was commerce. If they chose war, the Congo River would run red with Bobangi blood; but if they chose peace, they could profit from trading directly with the whites. The Bobangi canoe captains replied that they preferred trade over war. Their trips to Malebo Pool, they said, were long and hard. It would take sixteen days of hard paddling to get home to the Alima. If the whites would set up a commercial station in the region to buy their ivory and rubber, they would welcome it. They also mentioned that rubber was abundant in their country, but the Bateke traders at the Pool did not buy it.

At this point Brazza sent for French flags to give to the four canoe captains, but Chief Ngantsu stepped in to forbid it. In order to preserve his position of authority over the Bobangi, the chief wanted to retain exclusive possession of the French flag. When Brazza tried to give the captains a gift of beads, Ngantsu insisted on being the one to hand them out, thus preserving his position as the middleman between Brazza and the Bobangi. Brazza was furious but could do nothing. The incident suggests that Chief Ngantsu, who had been present at Mbe when the Makoko Treaty was signed, did not feel that any of his sovereignty had been transferred to France. He was not ceding his authority to Brazza.

Brazza's encounter with the four Bobangi canoe captains made him realize that the best way to make an agreement with the Bobangi was to go through Ngobila, who was superior in rank to Ngantsu. When six Bobangi canoes arrived from Malebo Pool on September 21, Brazza retreated to his hut and sent word to Ngobila, who arrived the next morning along with sixteen canoes carrying two hundred Bobangi, each armed with a musket. When the meeting started, Brazza again told the story of the violent white man and the peaceful white man and said that he had been sent by the chief of the whites to promote peaceful trade. He held up bullets in his right hand and cloth in his left hand and asked them to choose war or peace. When they chose peace, he had his men dig a hole. He threw the bullets into the hole, saying that he was "burying war." Then he filled in the hole and planted a flagpole with a French flag. "Let war be banished until this tree that I have planted grows up and bears bullets for fruit," he intoned. After a five-volley salute by his Senegalese marines, he handed out French flags to the Bobangi chiefs. This time Ngantsu did not try to stop him. Half an hour later, a Bobangi canoe flying the French flag was on its way to Malebo Pool.

A week later, Brazza left Ngantsu's town for Malebo Pool in two large canoes provided by Ngobila, who also supplied four Bateke canoemen. On the fourth day, they arrived at Malebo Pool and soon received a visit from Ngaalio, whom Brazza described as the Makoko's representative at Malebo Pool. Ngaalio, who was the brother of the Makoko's prime minister, had arrived at the Pool the previous year with two hundred armed men to collect tribute from the Bateke chiefs who had set themselves up as ivory brokers at the Pool. The Pool was only five days' travel from the Bateke capital at Mbe over a path that crossed the Bateke Plateau. The Makoko had established villages along the route that were settled by his former slaves so that travelers passing between the Pool and Mbe could find food and lodging along the way. When Brazza had been negotiating with the Makoko at Mbe a month earlier, he'd seemed unaware that he was only five days by land from Malebo Pool.

Even though the senior Bateke chief at the Pool was Ntsuulu, who wore a large copper collar that signified his status as a feudal lord, it was the Makoko's tax collector who mobilized the Bateke chiefs at the Pool to meet with Brazza and give him permission to build a station. The agreement was reached in a single meeting on October 3, 1880. Although Brazza had come to obtain a small plot of land for a station, he claimed that he needed more time to pick the right spot, and so he was claiming the entire north bank of the Pool in the name of France. After he wrote out the treaty and signed it, four Bateke chiefs came forward to make an X. One was Ngaalio, the tax collector, who made his mark as a representative of the Makoko; then came Ngia Sa, whose copper collar signified that he was a Bateke lord. Two lesser chiefs followed. As a sign of France's possession of the territory, Brazza planted the French flag and gave out French flags to all the Bateke chiefs who controlled parts of the north bank. As payment for the territory that he was claiming, he gave gifts to the assembled chiefs, and a separate gift was to be sent to the Makoko at Mbe. Then Brazza wrote out another piece of paper promoting Malamine, one of his Senegalese marines, to the rank of sergeant and naming him chief of the French station at the Pool. He would be assisted by two Gabonese sailors.

Brazza stayed at the Pool for two more weeks, holding conversations with the Bateke chiefs and urging them to refuse to cooperate with Stanley when he came. Brazza was surprised to learn that no word of Stanley's progress had reached the Pool, but he wanted to make sure that Stanley would not be welcome when he arrived. Still hoping to find an easy overland route to the Atlantic, he headed straight toward the coast instead of following the rapid-strewn Congo River. Finding that the terrain was interrupted by mountains, he turned south toward the valley of the Congo River, which he followed toward the Atlantic coast. When two British missionaries arrived at Malebo Pool after Brazza had departed, they were met with such hostility from the local population that they retreated down the river. They had apparently met the reception that Brazza had planned for Stanley.[32]

5

Vivi, Lower Congo River, September 27, 1879

Five chiefs were waiting at the Vivi landing when Henry Morton Stanley arrived at four o'clock in the afternoon of September

27, 1879. They wore items of secondhand European clothing that included a red English military tunic, a black frock coat, a brown coat that once belonged to a London club, and hats of felt and silk. "See what a ready market lies here for old clothes," he wrote in response to the sight. Stanley's expedition had arrived at Boma, the chief port along the Congo River estuary, on August 22, 1879. After unloading their equipment and supplies and storing them in warehouses owned by Dutch, English, and French trading firms, Stanley continued up the river to Vivi in a steam launch with a party of three Europeans and ten of the hired Zanzibaris.[33]

The Vivi district lay along the estuary of the Congo River just below Yellala Falls, and it was on the high riverbank that Stanley wanted to build the first station for King Leopold's Upper Congo Study Committee. Although oceangoing ships could not advance beyond Boma, situated thirty miles down the estuary, small river steamers could make it all the way to Vivi, which marked the limit of navigation. Much of the Vivi district consisted of rock-strewn slopes and jagged hilltops that were, in Stanley's words, "barren, mean, and worthless." Stanley, however, was not looking for agricultural land but for a point of departure for the interior. He was more interested in what a road from Vivi might promote than in what Vivi itself could provide.

After greeting Stanley, the chiefs asked him what he wanted. He told them that he needed enough land to build houses and gardens and wanted the right to build a road on which his people and others could pass unobstructed by the local chiefs. After each chief received a gift of a bottle of gin, they left to consult on the matter. When the meeting reconvened the next morning, the five chiefs agreed to Stanley's conditions provided that they were adequately compensated. The bargaining went on for four hours before Stanley agreed to make a down payment of thirty-two pounds' worth of cloth plus two pounds a month in rent. Afterward, Stanley praised the bargaining acumen of the chiefs. "In the management of a bargain," he wrote in his book, "I should back the Congolese native

against Jew or Christian, Parsee or Banyan, in all the round world."
Noting that some unthinking people might consider the Africans
unsophisticated, he added, "Unsophisticated is the very last term
I should ever apply to an African child or man in connection with
the knowledge of how to trade." His diary entry, however, was
more subdued: "I am not altogether pleased with my purchase," he
wrote. "It has been most expensive in the first place, and the rent is
high. However, necessity has compelled me to it."[34]

Vivi Station was completed by January 24, 1880, but then
the most difficult work began. The expedition needed to build a
wagon road that ran roughly parallel to the Congo River rapids
for fifty-two miles from Vivi to a point beyond Isangila Falls that
marked the beginning of an eighty-mile stretch of open water. The
road would roughly follow the route that Stanley's expedition had
traveled on foot in 1877 during its descent of the Congo River.
On this road, they would transport two river steamboats and a
steel barge, using a heavy steel wagon pulled by mules and whatever manpower was available. The boilers, engines, and other heavy
parts would be removed and transported separately. Stanley estimated that the heavy steel wagon would be able to advance about
one mile per day once the road was finished.

To construct the wagon road through the rugged terrain of
the Crystal Mountains, Stanley employed gangs of men to pul-
verize rocks with crowbars and sledgehammers in order to build
the roadbed, and he ordered large boulders blasted with dynamite.
Vivi chiefs who watched Stanley instruct the workers on how to use
a sledgehammer gave him the nickname Bula Matari, a Kikongo
term meaning "breaker of rocks." The name quickly spread up the
river to Isangila and Malebo Pool. On the Upper Congo River,
however, where Kikongo was no longer spoken, Stanley was known
as "Tandley," a direct transliteration of "Stanley" into the local
Bantu languages where the letter combination *st* was unknown.[35]

To scout out the wagon road and make contact with the local
chiefs, Stanley undertook a reconnaissance mission. Arriving at the

large town of Nsanda, he had a meeting with thirty chiefs from the surrounding area. Like the chiefs of Vivi, they were dressed in bright-colored imported cloth covered by cast-off coats from London and Paris clubs and English and French military uniforms. Their heads were adorned with low-crowned felt hats and old military caps. Stanley explained to them that he wanted their permission to build a road through their territory and wished to hire local men to help with the construction. The chiefs replied that the road would be a good thing because it would bring trade. They would give him permission in return for a satisfactory payment. Stanley later grumbled that he had paid £150, which he considered a "prodigal expenditure of money," for a "right of way through a territory generally unoccupied, and of no present use to any person."[36]

When Stanley arrived at Isangila, which would be the terminus of the first section of his road, he found that news about his arrangements with the chiefs of Vivi and Nsanda had preceded him. After a meeting with the Isangila chiefs, he was offered land for a station in return for comparable payments. Beyond Isangila was eighty miles of open water, interrupted only by some minor rapids, followed by a new series of rapids and waterfalls. Stanley planned to build stations at Isangila and Manyanga—the two ends of the open stretch—and leave a steamboat to ferry supplies and people back and forth. Beyond Manyanga, he would have to build another road to Malebo Pool.

While the negotiations for treaties went quickly, the construction of the first section of the wagon road progressed much more slowly. On September 20, 1880, Stanley reported, "We have made three bridges, filled up a score of ravines and gullies at the crossings, graded six hills, cut through two thick forests of hardwood, and made a clear road thirty-eight miles long." Along this road, he was transporting tools, prefabricated buildings, supplies for the stations, a steel barge, and two steamboats. The *Royal* was a thirty-foot steam launch with a mahogany cabin and silk curtains that had belonged to King Leopold II, and the *En Avant* was a

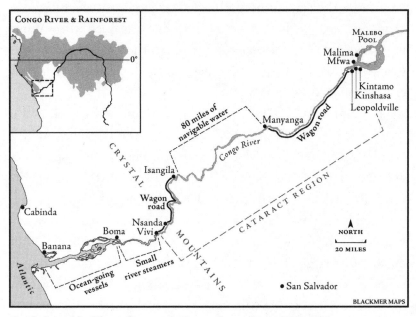

Stanley's road-building efforts on the Lower Congo River, 1879–1882

forty-three-foot paddle-wheel steam launch that was effective in shallow water. The *Royal* alone weighed nearly four tons. Stanley's regular crew consisted of 14 Europeans, most of whom were occupied with operating the steamboats and were "utterly useless to me in the road-making," and 106 African workmen—mostly Zanzibaris, Krumen from Sierra Leone, and workers from the Atlantic port city of Kabinda—all of whom were far from home and thus unlikely to desert. The contract workforce was assisted by as many as 200 locally hired laborers, with the number varying according to the location and the tasks.[37]

On November 2, they began to haul the boats up the steepest hill that they had yet encountered. Four block-and-tackle pulley sets were tied to sturdy trees along the road, and the *En Avant* was fastened to the steel wagon with sturdy straps. A five-inch-thick hawser rope normally used to secure ships at a dock was attached to the wagon, along with several smaller three-inch ropes. Working in the fashion of sailors, the crew pulled to the refrain of "ho heave yo." The wagon moved slowly and jerkily up the hill while crew members put blocks behind the wheels to keep it from rolling backward. An hour later the *En Avant* reached the top, and then the process was repeated to haul up the *Royal*. The boilers and engines were brought up the next day.

By Saturday, November 6, the expedition had established a camp at the foot of Ngoma Mountain. In the distance, Stanley could see Isangila Falls, which marked the end of the first section of roadbuilding. He wrote that every mile was "marked by rapids, careening swiftly towards the cataracts of Inga." This was the section that is known today as Inga Falls—a series of rapids and waterfalls where the Congo River drops 315 feet in nine miles. With a median discharge of 1.5 million cubic feet of water per second, it is, in terms of volume, the largest waterfall in the world. A wagon road that bypassed Inga Falls would be a major accomplishment.

Sunday, November 7, 1880, was a day of rest. Stanley bathed, shaved, and dressed in his finest Sunday clothes. Then he sat down to read. His reverie was interrupted when a messenger arrived with a note that read, "Count Savorgnan de Brazza, Ship's Sub-Lieutenant." An hour later, a tall white man with dark complexion appeared. As Stanley later described him in his book, Brazza was "dressed in a helmet, naval blue coat, and feet encased in a brown leather bandage." He had a following of fifteen men armed with Winchester repeating rifles. However, Stanley gave a less charitable description of his meeting with Brazza in a speech to the Stanley Club (an organization of Americans in Paris who had followed his exploits) in 1882, when he described Brazza as "a man without shoes who was unremarkable except for a worn-out military coat and a head covering, followed by a small troop of men each carrying 125 lbs. He was not, as you can well imagine, an imposing figure." Later in that speech, he described Brazza as "shoeless, lost, and poor."[38]

Despite Stanley's mocking tone, he must have been stunned to discover that the repeated warnings about Brazza that he had

Stanley's crew hauling the hull and boiler of a steamboat up a steep hill. Henry M. Stanley, *The Congo and the Founding of Its Free State*, vol. 1, p. 228.

received from King Leopold and Colonel Strauch had been prescient. On December 30, 1879, Colonel Strauch had written to Stanley that Brazza was about to return to the Ogowe to build a station at the limit of canoe navigation. From there, it was only fifty miles overland to the upper Alima, which Brazza could follow to the Congo and then travel down to Malebo Pool. Colonel Strauch believed that Brazza planned to beat Stanley to the Pool, and he urged Stanley to advance as rapidly as possible in order to get to the Pool ahead of Brazza.[39]

Replying on February 6, 1880, Stanley rejected the idea. "I beg leave to say that I am not a party in a race to Stanley Pool," he wrote, using the name that he had given to Malebo Pool, "and I do not intend to visit it again until I can arrive with my 50 tons of goods, boats, and other property, and after finishing the second station." Stanley estimated that he could march to the Pool in fifteen days, but he saw no benefit in doing so, since it was already well established that he had been the first European to set eyes on it. Stanley failed to understand that this was no longer a competition for bragging rights; it was now about territorial claims and future colonies.[40]

Stanley revisited the issue on June 14, 1880, when he wrote to Colonel Strauch that even though it would take him a long time to reach Stanley Pool at his present pace, he believed that he would get there before Brazza. King Leopold responded in July that as soon as the Manyanga Station was established, Stanley should take a light caravan and get to the Pool ahead of any competitors. He should choose a station site, sign treaties for the land, and construct some rudimentary buildings to show possession. He could then leave some men in charge of the Pool Station and return to Manyanga to continue work on his wagon road. On October 25, Stanley replied to Colonel Strauch that he remained focused on the original plan to build the stations and the road and that he did not expect the road to reach Isangila before mid-December. That news made King Leopold uncomfortable. "The king wants

Mr. Stanley to advance rapidly to Stanley Pool," wrote Colonel Strauch to Stanley. He added, "The day the expedition arrives at Stanley Pool will be a great day. All of Africa will lie before him." When Brazza walked into the camp at Ngoma Mountain, Stanley must have realized that by stubbornly sticking to his step-by-step approach, he had been outflanked.[41]

During the three days that Brazza spent at Stanley's camp, the two explorers conversed as best they could. Stanley's French, by his own description, was "abominable," and Brazza's English was "not the best." Brazza told Stanley that he had marched overland from the upper Ogowe to the upper Alima and descended the Alima for a short distance before leaving it to head south to the Lefini River. The mention of the Alima was more about laying a claim than accurately recounting his travels, given that Brazza's diary shows that he had stayed well south of the Alima. Brazza told Stanley that he had visited Malebo Pool and left a small contingent there, but he said nothing about his treaty with the Makoko or his treaty with the Bateke chiefs at the Pool. Brazza's account of his travels was a carefully crafted narrative designed to lay claims without alerting Stanley to his larger goals. Stanley observed that Brazza spoke with the air of a man who had nothing to conceal but who revealed nothing of his future intentions.[42]

After resting for three days at Stanley's camp, Brazza set out to follow Stanley's wagon road to the Vivi Station, where he took one of the Upper Congo Study Committee's river steamers to Banana, at the mouth of the river. From there, he caught a mail steamer to Gabon in order to return to the Ogowe River, where his IAA station was being constructed. Brazza's diary for that period has not been preserved, so we cannot know his immediate thoughts about Stanley. In a letter he wrote to the French committee of the IAA when he arrived at Banana on December 8, he barely mentioned meeting Stanley. "On November 9, I arrived at Ndambi Mbongo, Stanley's advance station," he wrote. "Three days later, I was at Vivi, his original station."[43]

By February 1881, Stanley's wagon road had been completed to Isangila, where he built a camp and later a station. The two steamboats ferried supplies to the upper end of the eighty-mile stretch of open water, where they planned to build the Manyanga Station. Stanley signed a treaty with the local chiefs for a site about five miles from the great Manyanga market, which attracted eight to ten thousand people when it met every nine days. Slaves, ivory, rubber, copper, oil, pigs, sheep, and goats were for sale as well as European imported goods such as salt, cloth, pottery, glassworks, and ironworks. African caravans from the coast bound for Malebo Pool stopped at the Manyanga market, which seemed to be at an economic transition point between the zone where cloth and beads were the main currency and the zone where copper and brass rods were in demand. They would exchange their cloth for brass rods and continue on to the Pool, whereas caravans traveling from the Pool to the coast did the opposite. Stanley's crew constructed a corrugated iron warehouse to store supplies and was beginning work on the wagon road to Malebo Pool. By mid-July, Stanley was finally ready to set out with a small caravan to march to Malebo Pool.[44]

6

Malebo Pool, Congo River, July 27, 1881

As Stanley's caravan approached Malebo Pool on July 27, 1881, they saw a small group of men coming toward them holding a French tricolored flag on a staff. Stanley described the leader as "a dashing-looking Negro" wearing a sailor uniform with noncommissioned officer stripes on his arm. He was Sergeant Malamine, the Senegalese marine whom Brazza had installed as chief of the French station at Malebo Pool. Malamine handed Stanley a copy of Brazza's treaty with the Makoko and a copy of the document by which Brazza had taken possession of the north bank of Malebo Pool in the name of France. Stanley was not surprised to see the

NGALYEMA, CHIEF OF KINTAMO.

Ngaliema was the most powerful chief on the south bank of Malebo Pool and the
wealthiest ivory trader along the lower Congo River. Henry M. Stanley, *The Congo and
the Founding of Its Free State*, vol. 1, p. 306.

treaty, since the two British missionaries who had earlier been
driven away from Malebo Pool had described it to him, but he was
not sure what to make of it.[45]

When Stanley asked his old friend Chief Gamankono if the
Makoko was the great king of all the country, the chief replied,
"There is no great king anywhere. We are all kings—each a king
over his own village and land. But no one has authority over

another chief. Makoko is an old chief; he is richer than any of us; he has more men and guns; but his country is Mbe." In a similar way, Chief Ngaliema on the south shore of the Pool told the British missionaries, "I have not sold my country to the Makoko. I am chief here, and I shall do as I like in my own country." The limitations of the Makoko's authority were experienced firsthand by Sergeant Malamine, who had settled in the north-shore village of Mfwa and invoked the name of the Makoko in asking for food. When none was forthcoming, he was eventually forced by hunger to relocate to Kinshasa, on the south shore of the Pool, even though it was outside the jurisdiction of his treaty.[46]

Despite Malamine's document stating that the Makoko had ceded the north shore of the Pool to the French, Stanley went to the north-shore village of Malima to see his old friend Chief Gamankono, who said that he and his sons had no objection to Stanley's building a station in Malima. By the next morning, however, everything had changed. Sergeant Malamine had come into the village at dusk and talked with the chiefs. Soon thereafter, the town crier walked through the street telling people not to speak with Stanley's people or sell them any food. Chief Gamankono apologized to Stanley for the sudden change of heart but explained that another chief had insisted that Stanley should leave.

Stanley's party began its retreat from Malebo Pool when he got word that Chief Ngaliema, who had made blood brotherhood with Stanley in 1877, had invited him to visit. Ngaliema lived at Kintamo, on the south bank of the Pool, and was thus outside the jurisdiction of Brazza's treaty. He had been born in a Bateke village a hundred miles north of Malebo Pool, but after being driven from his home as a young man because of accusations of witchcraft, he had obtained permission from the indigenous Mbundu chiefs to settle on the south bank of the Pool. Ngaliema had prospered in the ivory trade, and by investing his profits in slaves, guns, and gunpowder, he had become the most powerful chief on the south bank of the pool. In his warehouses he had 150 tusks weighing between fifty and ninety pounds each and stacks of European trade goods, including velvets, silks, blankets, glassware, crockery, and brass rods. Stanley estimated that Ngaliema was richer than all the chiefs between Boma and Malebo Pool combined. As an ivory broker, Ngaliema had strong reservations about allowing Stanley to build a station at Malebo Pool. As the discussions dragged on, Stanley returned to Manyanga to supervise the building of the second segment of the wagon road to the Pool, leaving ten of his Zanzibari crew with Ngaliema as a sign of good faith.[47]

Ngaliema was getting considerable pressure from other traders and chiefs to reject Stanley's overtures. When the Kongo caravan traders learned that Ngaliema was considering inviting Stanley to build a station at the Pool, they warned the chief, "If that is the case, we come no more; the country is dead. It will be no place for trade for us if the white man comes." Ngaliema also faced opposition from the Mbundu chiefs living on the south bank of the Pool, who were the traditional owners of the land. They told him, "Is this the way you behave after we gave you ground to live on and trade; that you take upon yourself to say who shall come into the country? Very well, we shall kill your trade, your markets shall be closed, and you will die of hunger." Under pressure from the real owners of the territory, Ngaliema expelled his Zanzibari guests and told them to carry word to Stanley that he should not try to build a station on the south bank.[48]

Stanley's mission was rescued by the intervention of another chief who bore the title Makoko, even though his ethnicity was Mbundu and not Bateke (apparently, the title was not ethnically exclusive). In a rare stroke of luck, Stanley had stumbled onto the Makoko who was the lord of the land along the south bank of the Congo River up to the Pool. Like the Makoko at Mbe, he had no power to give orders to lesser chiefs, but his spiritual authority commanded great respect. When he received Stanley, he sat on a mat covered with a leopard skin. Pointing to the skin, he said that it was proof of the authenticity of his title because only a Makoko could possess a leopard skin. Stanley did not know that a leopard skin indicated a lower rank than a lion skin. The Makoko at Mbe, for example, sat on a lion skin, whereas his lords sat on leopard skins.[49]

After the greetings and formalities, the Makoko explained that he had objected to Stanley's negotiations with Ngaliema for building a station because Ngaliema was a mere stranger living on Mbundu land and was not a proper land chief. Stanley apologized for the mistake, pleading ignorance of the subtleties of chiefly authority, and asked for permission to build a station at the Pool. After an exchange of gifts, the Makoko introduced Stanley to a man who was the brother of an Mbundu chief who had authority over some territory on the south shore of the Pool. He then gave Stanley a sword as a symbol of his support.

Relations between Stanley and Ngaliema remained tense because the Mbundu chiefs on the south bank of the Pool suspected that Ngaliema had attempted to sell the country to Stanley. On December 24, 1881, Ngaliema and a dozen chiefs met with Stanley to discuss the rumors. Both Ngaliema and Stanley denied that there was ever a deal to sell the country. Having been informed about a local custom for settling such disputes, Stanley had one of his assistants paint a white chalk stripe along each of Ngaliema's arms to signify that he was innocent. Surprised by Stanley's knowledge of the local custom, the arbitrator of the meeting announced that Stanley could "build everywhere as much as you like; the country is free and open, and all of us are now your friends."[50]

Stanley's diplomatic maneuvers at the Pool belied his reputation in Europe for crass brutality. Reports from two missionaries in 1881 depicted a very different person from the one who had fought thirty-two battles while descending the Congo River in 1877. Father Augouard reported an incident at the Pool in which a group of armed men trapped him in a marshy area for several days. Augouard wrote that "Mr. Stanley, with his three white men and seventy Zanzibaris armed with 14-shot rifles could have easily swept the place clean in less than ten minutes, but he did not want to rely on violence." Similarly, a British Baptist missionary reported that his friendly reception by the western Bateke "was doubtless due in a good measure to Stanley's friendly and gentle treatment of them." Stanley explained his new attitude toward violence in a letter to Colonel Strauch in January 1882: "A trial of force by the natives would be our ruin so far as future prospects are concerned. Blood once shed is a bar to future peace and commerce."[51]

Stanley's agreements with the Bateke and Mbundu chiefs at Malebo Pool nevertheless fell short of King Leopold's expectations. In August 1881, Colonel Strauch urged Stanley to begin organizing the riverine peoples politically and to found stations that would become the capitals of the tribal states. To that end, Stanley should sign treaties of alliance with the African chiefs that specified that the Upper Congo Study Committee would act on their behalf in foreign dealings. The goal, Strauch emphasized, was to create a federation of such states under the patronage of the Study Committee. By September, however, King Leopold was not sure that Stanley had gotten the message. "In your next letter to Stanley," Leopold wrote to Strauch, "insist on the necessity of getting the native chiefs to recognize the supremacy of our stations, so that in Europe we may have these stations recognized by the [European] Powers as free towns." He added, "If our stations were recognized as free communities extending as far as possible on the banks of the Congo, we should have made a first big step towards the establishment of a commercial and transport enterprise." But Stanley, who had done everything in his power to convince the chiefs that he was *not* trying to buy their country, ignored the king's request.[52]

On New Year's Day 1882, large crowds collected at Kintamo (Ngaliema's town) and Kinshasa (where Sergeant Malamine was staying) to see the first steamboat on the Upper Congo River. It had been brought to Malebo Pool in pieces along the wagon road and reassembled. From the Pool, the paddle wheeler *En Avant* could go up the river for a thousand miles to Stanley Falls without encountering obstructions. By the end of February, the main house for the station was completed. It was a two-story wattle-and-daub structure built on a terrace cut out from the side of a sandy hill about ninety feet above the river. Warehouses and housing for the other Europeans were being built on the terrace, while huts for the Zanzibaris were built at the bottom of the hill. The *En Avant* and a steel whaleboat were kept at the beach. Stanley named the new station Leopoldville.[53]

While Stanley was celebrating the accomplishment of his original assignment to build three stations linking the Congo River estuary to Malebo Pool, King Leopold was writing a letter to Stanley expanding the definition of his mission. After assuring Stanley that "Belgium desires no territory in Africa," he ordered Stanley to obtain as much land as possible for the Study Committee. Without wasting a minute, Stanley should sign treaties placing all of the African chiefs between the mouth of the Congo and Stanley Falls under the authority of the Study Committee. The king noted that Brazza had brought all the chiefs at Malebo Pool under his authority in a short time, and he worried that if the Study Committee did not quickly establish its authority over the region, other countries would move in, and the Study Committee's entire investment would be wasted.[54]

King Leopold's second concern was the lack of commercial activities. He had been upset when the chartered steamship *Barga*, which had carried the original supplies for the expedition to Africa, returned empty. He had apparently expected a shipload of ivory. Once Stanley was established at the Pool, the king ordered him to purchase "all the ivory that is found in the Congo." Stanley had identified four main centers of the ivory trade at the Pool— two on the north shore and two on the south—that together had about two hundred tusks total at any given time, but the ivory was being sold to African overland caravan traders as fast as it came in, thus limiting opportunities for the Belgians. The best way to get control of the ivory trade, Stanley believed, was to go directly to the Bobangi trading towns on the Upper Congo and purchase the ivory before it arrived at the Pool. He told Strauch a story about a Bobangi princess named Eela who came to the Pool with thirteen large tusks. She had planned to sell some of them to Ngaliema and the rest to Stanley, but Ngaliema seized all the tusks. "Never mind, Eela," Stanley told her. "I am going up to your own country, and then you can sell to me as much as you like."[55]

On April 20, 1882, Stanley left on the steamboat *En Avant* to establish contacts with the populations of the Upper Congo. After twenty-eight hours of steaming, he arrived at the place where Ngobila's town and Ngantsu's town faced each other across the Congo River. Both chiefs had accepted French flags from Brazza the previous year. In contrast to Brazza, who had spent considerable time with Ngantsu on the west bank, Stanley stopped at Ngobila's town, which was on the east bank. Whatever he thought of Brazza's treaty with the Makoko at Mbe, Stanley was clearly trying to avoid antagonizing the French until the issue was sorted out in Europe. After his missteps in his negotiations with Ngaliema at the Pool, Stanley had learned that the populations in the riverside towns were not necessarily the customary owners of the land but were sometimes interlopers who had received permission to settle on land claimed by somebody else. In the case of Ngobila, it turned out that the Bateke lord was living on land claimed by the Mfunu people, whose chief, Gandelay, lived inland from the river. After several days of discussions, a formal gathering at Ngobila's town was arranged for May 1.

The chiefs came in their most impressive finery. Chief Gandelay was carried in a hammock surrounded by drummers and musicians with ivory horns. Also arriving was Ngantsu, who came from the other side of the river in three canoes accompanied by drums, bells, and horns. When the meeting began, Ngobila explained that Stanley wanted a plot of land at Ngobila's town to build a station. The Bateke lord noted that he had no objection to the station, but he was a mere ivory trader, whereas Chief Gandelay was the real owner of the land, and his consent was required to seal the deal.

Then Chief Ngantsu spoke. Because he lived on the west bank of the river in the territory of the Makoko, he possessed full rights to the land on which his village stood. Ngantsu said that if Gandelay refused to allow Stanley to build a station, then Stanley was welcome to cross the Congo River and build in his town. "We will make plenty of trade," he added. Finally, it was Chief Gandelay's turn to speak. He said that if Ngobila accepted Stanley into his town, then he would accept Stanley as well. Stanley then introduced Lt. Eugene Janssens, who would be the chief of the new station. Janssens selected a plot about eight hundred yards below the town that commanded an excellent view of the river in both directions.

Leaving Janssens to build the station, Stanley returned to the Pool, arriving at the Leopoldville Station on May 9. Because he was returning from his first voyage on his steamboat, he received a warm welcome from the local chiefs. But underneath the polite greetings, there was a battle of wills and wits between the Bateke ivory brokers at Malebo Pool and the Europeans who wanted to break into the ivory trade. The Bobangi traders from the Upper Congo initially sided with the Europeans because they were bringing ivory to the Pool faster than the Bateke ivory brokers could bring in enough cloth, brass, and beads to barter for it. As a result, they were forced to buy cassava at exorbitant prices in order to feed themselves while they waited weeks or months for more trade goods to arrive from the coast. The arrival of European traders, they believed, would bring more trade goods and more competition to the Pool. Moreover, if European ivory buyers settled on the Upper Congo, then the Bobangi traders would no longer have to make the arduous journey to Malebo Pool. They were willing to abandon the Pool entirely if a more convenient market could be found.[56]

Léon Guiral, a Frenchman who arrived at the Pool in April 1882 to replace Sergeant Malamine as the head of the French station, quickly understood that the Bateke ivory brokers were fearful of being displaced by white traders. "Even though the inhabitants of the Pool have displayed warm feelings toward the commander of the French," he wrote, "it would be an error to believe that they are ready to renounce their commercial advantages in our favor." Guiral's insights help to clarify some of the unanswered questions about Brazza's Makoko Treaty. The Makoko at Mbe, who was largely a spiritual leader, had little to lose by forming what he viewed as a predominantly spiritual alliance with a foreign power. The Bateke chiefs at Malebo Pool, in contrast, were wealthy traders who jealously guarded their monopoly control over the major choke point in the entire Congo River trading system. As a result, the treaty they signed with Brazza allowed only for a spot to build a station at some point along a nine-mile stretch of the riverbank.[57]

The chiefs at Malebo Pool were worried that the days when the ivory trade was dominated by Bobangi canoemen, Bateke ivory brokers, and Kongo ivory caravans were numbered. "If we let the white men into the country, they will soon make an end of us," a Kongo chief told the missionary Bentley. "It is bad enough to have them on the coast." That sober prediction was echoed in a letter from King Leopold to Colonel Strauch on June 13, 1881, that noted ominously, "Africa is more than ever the object of competition from all the industrial and commercial countries who are struggling to find new outlets for their products. We can expect fierce competition on their part. That is a sufficient incentive for Mr. Stanley to proceed with all haste."[58]

CHAPTER 4

HOMEWARD BOUND

B ETWEEN JUNE AND NOVEMBER 1882, three well-known travelers with ambitious plans and ambiguous national identities
returned to the countries where they owed allegiance or had contractual obligations. Pierre Savorgnan de Brazza, the Italian who
had become a French citizen, returned to France; Henry Morton
Stanley, a Welshman who was widely presumed to be an American, returned to Belgium; and Tippu Tip, who had family ties to
Omani Arabs and Nyamwezi East Africans, returned to the island
of Zanzibar, where he had been born. All three travelers went to
consult with their overlords and plan their next steps. By then, the
three men were no longer explorers but were state builders.

For all three men, the consultations foreshadowed bigger
changes to come. Arriving in Belgium, Stanley discovered that the
blandly named Upper Congo Study Committee had been replaced
by a new entity called the International Association of the Congo.
Like its predecessor, it was run by King Leopold II and his administrator, Colonel Strauch, but it had shed any pretensions of international cooperation. Despite its name, its only known member
was King Leopold. Brazza returned to France determined to get
the French government to ratify his Makoko Treaty, thus making
France a recognized colonial power in equatorial Africa. In this
effort, he was inadvertently aided by Henry Morton Stanley. As

the rivalry between the two men was displayed in the French press, Brazza became a national hero and a symbol of a myth of "gentle French colonialism" that contrasted with Stanley's brutality. Brazza's newfound celebrity was the key to persuading the French parliament to ratify the treaty with virtually no debate. When Tippu Tip returned to Zanzibar, he found himself caught between the sultan of Zanzibar, who wanted him to continue exporting his ivory through East Africa, and the Europeans, who wanted to purchase his ivory and ship it out to the Atlantic coast in their steamboats. The sultan tried to secure Tippu Tip's loyalty by offering to make him the governor of Tabora, but Tippu Tip preferred to govern his own empire.

The issues under discussion had implications that went far beyond exploration and trade; they were becoming more and more about laying claims to large parts of equatorial Africa. Yet it would have been difficult to imagine in the waning months of 1882 that within two years the nations of Europe would gather to carve up equatorial Africa, a region as large as Europe itself that had been terra incognita to the outside world only five years earlier.

1

Paris, June 23, 1882

The largest amphitheater at the Sorbonne held eighteen hundred people, and it was already full by 7:30 p.m., half an hour before the lecture was scheduled to begin. Soon several hundred people were jostling for positions around the doors, in the hallways, and up the staircase. The Paris Geographical Society had distributed four thousand tickets in hopes of attracting a large audience, and well over half of them were redeemed. When Ferdinand de Lesseps, the president of the Paris Geographical Society, opened the session at eight o'clock, the main speaker was not on the stage because he was trapped among the throngs of people who had come to hear his talk. Pierre Savorgnan de Brazza's previous lecture to the Paris Geographical Society nearly three years earlier had been a more staid affair, attracting a small audience of scientists and armchair explorers. What brought the crowd out on this warm June evening was not so much the desire to hear about new geographical discoveries—the major geographical puzzles relating to the Congo River basin had already been solved by Stanley—but rather to hear about the treaty that Brazza had signed with King Makoko in equatorial Africa. The news that Brazza had persuaded an African king to sign over his country to France had gripped the popular imagination. They also wanted to hear how Brazza, with his meager funding and tiny contingent of African marines and porters, had outmaneuvered the lavishly funded expedition led by Henry Morton Stanley.[1]

Brazza had been extremely busy following his encounter with Stanley at Ngoma Mountain in November 1880. Continuing on to the Atlantic coast, he had caught a steamship back to Gabon. Then he followed the well-traveled route up the Ogowe River by steamship to Lamberéné and then by dugout canoe to Franceville, where the French national committee of the IAA was building a station. The IAA had an elaborate plan to transport a dismantled steamboat to Franceville and then carry it overland fifty miles to a station on the upper Alima. From there, the steamboat could travel down the Alima to the Congo River and on to Malebo Pool. Brazza learned that the project had stalled in Gabon because the boilers had been lost and new ones had to be ordered from Europe. Moreover, the Bobangi were still preventing the French from descending the Alima. The French National Committee of the IAA had established a small station on the upper Alima, but the French station chief, Antoine Mizon, had fought gun battles with villages along the Alima, thus arousing the hostility of the population and rendering the Alima route temporarily inhospitable. The French flags that Brazza had passed out to Bobangi traders at Ngantsu's town in 1880 apparently had not reached the upper Alima.[2]

Those problems encouraged Brazza to look for alternatives to
the Ogowe-Alima route and to focus more on Malebo Pool itself.
He organized and sent out a relief expedition to carry loads of beads
overland to the Senegalese sergeant Malamine and the two Gabonese sailors who were maintaining the French presence at the Pool.
They would use the beads to buy needed supplies. In the absence of
regular supplies, they had been supporting themselves by hunting
game and selling the meat, and they wore locally obtained cloth to
preserve their well-worn uniforms for official occasions. The French
station, which had come to be known as Brazzaville, consisted of a
small hut in the village of Ntchoulou that Sergeant Malamine had
purchased with his own money.[3]

Brazza was determined to find an overland route between the
Pool and the coast that bypassed Stanley's wagon road. Traveling
with a small party of Senegalese marines and porters, he found that
the valley of the Niari River provided a pathway between the Pool
and the coast that was less challenging than the rugged valley of
the Lower Congo River. The Niari Valley had long been used by
Bateke slave and ivory caravans, and Brazza's good relations with
the Bateke proved useful in locating this route. Having decided
that the Niari Valley provided better access to the Malebo Pool
than the Ogowe-Alima route that had been his previous focus,
Brazza was ready to return to France.[4]

Two weeks after he arrived in Paris, Brazza was standing in
front of an overflow crowd at the Sorbonne. Because his command
of French grammar was shaky and his French vocabulary was not
extensive, the general secretary of the Paris Geographical Society
had penned the final version of Brazza's speech. Sticking close to
his text, Brazza spoke in French with a heavy Italian accent. His
lecture drew stark contrasts between Stanley and himself: "speed
and slowness, boldness and caution, strength and weakness." He
told the crowd that Stanley had descended the Congo River "at
the speed of an arrow" in 1877 while remaining ignorant of the
immense region and its numerous peoples. Brazza's own travels, in

contrast, had proceeded slowly, giving him time to learn the local languages and get to know the people. In the process, he had abolished trade monopolies, united diverse peoples into a single trading system, and fought against slavery. Above all, he had built trust and gained a reputation for peaceful penetration of the interior. When he planted the French flag at Franceville, he told the audience, the people understood that it was a symbol of liberty and peace.[5]

Then Brazza told the story of his visit to the Makoko, along with embellishments for dramatic effect. In Brazza's telling, the invitation from the Makoko said, "Makoko has for a long time known about the great white chief of the Ogowe. He knows that his terrible guns have never been used in attacks, and that peace and abundance follow in his footsteps." Brazza did not explain why that fulsome invitation was not mentioned in his diary or why he had waited a full month before going to the Makoko's capital at Mbe, even though it was only two days' travel away. He continued the embellishments when he characterized the Makoko's palace as the "Tuileries of the Makoko," even though other French explorers would later describe it as poor and unimpressive.[6]

In explaining why the Makoko had ceded his territory to France, Brazza credited Stanley. He told the crowd that the Makoko knew nothing of white men except for slave traders on the coast and the echo of Stanley's guns along the Congo River. Because he did not wish to go to war against two different parties of white men, he decided to befriend whoever inspired the most confidence. Given a choice between Stanley and Brazza, the king had chosen the latter. Brazza was claiming that Stanley's warlike behavior had driven the Makoko into his arms.

Brazza's explanation is suspect. Of the thirty-two battles that Stanley reported during his descent of the Lualaba and the Congo Rivers in 1877, only one of them was fought along the stretch of the Congo River controlled by the Bobangi and the Bateke. That battle took place on March 9, 1877, when Stanley's fleet was attacked by Bobangi canoes, probably on orders from Chief Ngobila. Stanley's diary records that three of his people were wounded in the row-boat and another was wounded in a canoe before the attackers were driven off, but it gives no indication as to how many Bobangi might have been killed or wounded. Brazza's diary entry for July 30, 1880, confirms that he had heard about the battle but gives no details. Instead, he records a story about Stanley's unsuccessful attempt to sell his donkey during his passage down the river over two years earlier. Brazza added, almost as an afterthought, "He fought a battle against the Bobangi." It is noteworthy that the donkey—and not the battle—was the focal point of the story in his diary.[7]

Local stories about Stanley's passage seemed to focus on the wondrous and the bizarre, as evidenced by the story told at Bolobo about Stanley's men paddling backward. Brazza's diary records only one other story about Stanley's descent, and it is about Stanley trying to maneuver his canoes around the waterfalls at Malebo Pool. Stanley's attempt to navigate the falls seemed memorable to the Bateke because it struck them as supremely foolhardy, if not totally insane. But there is no evidence in Brazza's diaries that the Bateke were terrified of Stanley's guns. The Makoko at Mbe, who was in regular communication with the Bateke chiefs at Malebo Pool, must have known that Stanley's passage across the Pool in March 1877 had been a peaceful one. Stanley wrote in his diary that "we encountered very peaceable people in canoes who spoke kindly and came near," and the next day he made blood brotherhood with Chief Ngaliema of Ntamo. Blood was being comingled but not shed. It seems that most of Brazza's information about Stanley's guns and his thirty-two battles came from Stanley's book and not from the Bateke. Brazza's statement at the Sorbonne about the "echo of Stanley's guns along the Congo River" was another of his dramatic exaggerations.[8]

Although Brazza most likely enjoyed his newfound celebrity, he never lost sight of his main goal, which was to persuade the French government to ratify the Makoko Treaty. In August, he laid out the case in his report to the minister of the marine. Two flags were flying on the shores of Malebo Pool, he noted. On the one side was the French flag, which represented France's rights of access to the Congo interior. Across the Pool flew the previously unknown flag of an international humanitarian organization that wanted to become a monopolistic commercial company with sovereign rights. Stanley, he wrote, was signing treaties with the chiefs at the Pool with the goal of squeezing the French out. In the light of those developments, ratifying the Makoko Treaty was the only way to preserve French access to the Congo interior and its commercial possibilities.[9]

Brazza was not optimistic that the government would be interested. Prime Minister Jules Ferry, an advocate of French overseas expansion, had incurred heavy criticism for his invasion of Tunisia in April and May 1881, and his government had fallen in November of that year. Leon Gambetta, another advocate of French expansion, had replaced Ferry, but his government fell on January 26, 1882, having lasted only sixty-six days. By the time Brazza arrived in France in June, he no longer had any allies in high places.

The minister of the marine and colonies, Admiral Jauréguiberry, was not enthusiastic about the Makoko Treaty. When asked by the prime minister of France if it was valid, the admiral made it clear that Brazza had no official standing to negotiate a treaty and had never received any instructions to do so. The admiral sat on the Makoko Treaty for nearly four months before forwarding it to the prime minister on September 26. His cover letter stressed that although the Ministry of the Marine and Colonies had generously provided Brazza with modest material support, it had never given him an official mission. Instead, Brazza worked mainly for the French national committee of the International African Association, whose stations were scientific and humanitarian in nature. When Brazza took possession of the Makoko's territory in the name of France, he was acting entirely on his own. The admiral warned the prime minister that if the treaty were ratified,

France would be obligated to take formal possession of the territory, entailing future expenses that would be hard to estimate. Although the prime minister had the constitutional right to ratify or reject treaties by simple decree, he realized that this one was unique. In the light of Brazza's growing popularity and the continuing discussions of the Makoko Treaty in the French press, the prime minister decided that it would be politically astute to submit it to the Chamber of Deputies.[10]

In his effort to build up public support for the ratification of the Makoko Treaty, Brazza situated his arguments in the context of his rivalry with Stanley. He told his audiences that Stanley traveled like a warrior, accompanied by a legion of armed men, whereas Brazza traveled like a friend who was received with hospitality; Stanley commanded respect with his guns, whereas Brazza was welcomed as a friend. The differences between the two explorers, while real, were vastly overdrawn in Brazza's recounting. Brazza's offers of friendship were always accompanied by the threat of war, and Brazza was not slow to pull out his gun. Just a few days before his encounter with Stanley at Ngoma Mountain, Brazza suspected some locally hired porters of stealing his supplies and fired several shots into a tree at long distance to intimidate them. The fact that Brazza rarely felt it necessary to shoot people spoke to the effectiveness of his intimidation as much as to his diplomatic skills.[11]

Brazza also stoked patriotic fervor by his frequent references to the French flag. He told his audiences that when he had planted the French flag in front of the Makoko's house, he proclaimed it a symbol of friendship and protection. "France is everywhere that this symbol of peace flies," he said he had told the Makoko, "and she will respect the rights of all who are gathered under its protection." When he was handing out French flags to African chiefs along the Congo River and at Malebo Pool, Brazza said he had raised the frightful specter of Stanley. "You know the white person who came here and fought with you?" he asked them. "Well, others are coming who are stronger than him. If you fly the symbol that

I am going to give you, he will not set foot on your territory without your permission, and he will not fire a shot at your people. The French flag will protect you." Whether or not the Bateke chiefs put much faith in the French flag is hard to determine, but it is clear that Stanley himself honored the flag by altering his routes to avoid the regions where it flew, thus giving credence to Brazza's claim.[12]

Although Brazza acknowledged that he and Stanley shared similar goals of opening up equatorial Africa to European trade, he argued that they worked for very different interests. He told the crowds that Stanley was in the service of Belgium's King Leopold, who had political motives underneath his humanitarian pretensions. Brazza then revealed that he himself had political motives as well. "If there is an advantage to be gained by occupying the Congo," he said, "I would prefer that it should be the French flag rather than the 'International' Belgian flag that flies over that magnificent African country." He was already envisioning the colonial partition of equatorial Africa.[13]

Brazza's biggest ally was the French press, which turned him into a national hero and took up his cause. A front-page article in *Le Temps* on September 30 opened by predicting that by the end of the century, the entire world would be under European domination and stated that France needed to be vigilant in claiming her share. Instead of searching out new territories to conquer, however, France should develop the ones it already possessed, beginning with the Congo River basin, a region with great natural wealth in ivory, rubber, palm oil, ebony, and rosewood. After outlining how Brazza had outmaneuvered the lavishly funded and heavily armed Stanley, the article depicted him as a combination of saint and superman: "Without money, without military force, with only the prestige of his moral and intellectual superiority, Mr. Brazza worked wonders. He smashed the barriers to free trade, nearly abolished the slave trade, recruited up to 2,000 canoe paddlers, traced a 120 kilometer road, and was welcomed everywhere as a messenger of peace and prosperity." The article concluded that under such exceptionable conditions, "it would be unpardonable to refuse to ratify the treaty."[14]

The next day, *Le Petit Parisien* filled most of the front page of its Sunday edition with a signed opinion piece entitled "Peaceful Conquest." In contrast to Stanley, who marched through blood like a great conqueror, said the article, Brazza traveled with a handful of African companions and presented himself as a man of peace. By signing treaties and giving out the French flag as a sign of friendship, he had conquered a vast territory without firing a shot. Brazza's treaty, which had been submitted to the Chamber of Deputies, should be ratified as soon as the deputies returned from their recess. There was no time to lose because Stanley, who was financed by millions of francs, had returned to Europe. The article concluded with a plea for the Chamber of Deputies to ratify the Makoko Treaty immediately because it would ensure French access to the largest remaining untapped market in the world.[15]

Other newspapers framed the issue in terms of Anglo-French rivalry. Only two months earlier, Britain had invaded Egypt and abrogated the joint Anglo-French oversight over Egypt's finances. With that incident in mind, *The National* urged the Chamber of Deputies to ratify the Makoko Treaty quickly because, it claimed, the British coveted the territory where Brazza had planted the French flag. Brazza himself echoed this theme when he received the gold medal from the Society for Topography in a ceremony at the Sorbonne. "The previous speaker," he remarked, "has said that the English are everywhere ahead of us. However, there is one place where we have set foot ahead of them; that is the Congo [prolonged applause]. The French flag flies over that country, and the Parliament need only say the word to make it ours forever."[16]

A flurry of articles urging ratification of the treaty appeared in Paris newspapers in late September and early October. Many of them used identical language, which suggests that they came from a common source. *Le Temps* reported on October 4 that "the entire French press, with a warmth that we have never seen in regards to colonial questions, invites the government to ratify the treaty signed by Mr. de Brazza with the people of the Congo River." Two days later the first secretary of the British embassy in Paris observed that "the question has been much discussed in the Paris press during the last ten days, and in each case, the government has been strongly recommended to follow up a plan which promises so much advantage to French colonial trade." By making Brazza—an Italian by birth who spoke thickly accented French—into a national hero, the French press was creating an atmosphere in which opposition to the Makoko Treaty was considered unpatriotic.[17]

2

Brussels, September 29, 1882

When Henry Morton Stanley arrived in Brussels on September 29, 1882, he discovered that he had been kept in the dark for the past three years about whom he was actually working for. The Upper Congo Study Committee, his ostensible employer, had been quietly disbanded in November 1879, just three months after he arrived at the mouth of the Congo River. The Study Committee's biggest outside investor, the Dutch Trading Company, had gone bankrupt, and King Leopold II had used the occasion to reimburse the smaller investors and disband the entire Study Committee, leaving only himself and his administrator, Col. Maximilien Strauch, in charge of the Congo expedition. Long after the Study Committee was disbanded, Colonel Strauch had continued to write to Stanley as if he were still the president of the committee, even though he was actually operating as a proxy for the king. Because Stanley had signed two contracts—one with the Study Committee and another with King Leopold—he was bound to the king for five years regardless of what happened to the Study Committee. But now, he finally understood that he was working exclusively for King Leopold.

Shortly after Stanley's arrival in Brussels, a new organization called the International Association of the Congo (IAC) began to be mentioned in the king's correspondence. "The International Association of the Congo," claimed King Leopold, "is an association of rich philanthropists and men of science who, with no motives other than civilization and a love of progress, seek to open up the Congo basin." Yet none of those men were ever named or identified, and the Belgian historian Jean Stengers has concluded that "the International Association of the Congo was a purely fictive entity: it was nothing but a name, behind which was nobody but Leopold II."[18]

In his meetings with King Leopold and Colonel Strauch, Stanley laid out the accomplishments of his three-year expedition. Despite the success in building five stations and two wagon roads, and putting a steamboat on the Upper Congo River, Stanley told his employer that "the Congo basin was not worth a two-shilling piece in its present state." To put it into profitable order, he told them, "a railroad must be made between the Lower Congo and the Upper Congo, when with its accessibility will appear its value." For such a project to succeed, the builders of the railroad would need to have a charter from Europe giving them the right to govern the land through which the railroad passed and guaranteeing that the guardianship of that land would never be transferred to a rival European power. The railroad would not be profitable, however, unless European businessmen and settlers came to exploit the resources of the Congo River basin, and they would not come unless they could be guaranteed large profit margins. The only way to attract sufficient commercial exploitation of the Congo River basin was to make it a free trade zone with no oppressive tariffs and fees. Maps were brought out, and strategic points for stations and routes for rail lines were identified. Left unmentioned in Stanley's closely censored summary of those discussions was the question of which European power was in a position to make the necessary guarantees.[19]

Brazza's Makoko Treaty had made the project more complicated and perhaps put it in jeopardy. When King Leopold and
Colonel Strauch had first learned about the treaty in May 1881,
the king argued that Brazza had no authority to negotiate treaties.
Brazza had been sent out by the French Committee of the International African Association to found a station at Franceville for
scientific and humanitarian purposes and to scout out a location
for a second IAA station for scientific and humanitarian purposes.
The king now understood that Brazza also had a second mission,
assigned by the French minister of public instruction, to conduct
some purely geographic explorations in equatorial Africa. Neither
of those tasks, he argued, was diplomatic in nature, thus rendering
the treaties outside the parameters of Brazza's missions. By July,
however, the king had adjusted his argument to assert that Brazza's station at Malebo Pool, which was claiming exclusive French
rights of occupation, was officially a station of the French National
Committee of the IAA, an organization of which King Leopold
himself was the president. Accordingly, he wrote letters to both the
head of the French National Committee of the IAA and the French
minister of public instruction demanding that the Malebo Pool
Station should offer all the hospitality and aid to King Leopold's
expeditions that it would offer to the French.

When Brazza arrived in Europe in 1882, King Leopold had
invited him to Brussels in September to discuss the ramifications of
the Makoko Treaty. Brazza, somewhat disingenuously, assured the
Belgian Ministry of Foreign Affairs that the French government
would never ratify it. Leopold, however, did not trust Brazza, and
he wrote a letter to Ferdinand de Lesseps, the president of the Paris
Geographical Society (and also the head of the French National
Committee of the IAA), outlining his objections to the treaty. "I
am afraid," wrote the king, "that it would set [France] on the path
of annexations and conquests, which would lead other nations to
take over the other parts of the Congo in order to monopolize
the trade that is currently open to all." He warned that French

ratification of the treaty would transplant European rivalries into Africa. Instead, he favored lifting the barriers to trade with Africa in a way that brought humanity and European civilization. In other words, he was advocating that the European penetration of Africa should follow the "internationalist" approach of the IAA and the International Association of the Congo, even though that latter organization had only one member—King Leopold himself.[20]

The king and his associates were furious with Stanley for allowing himself to be outmaneuvered by an underfinanced Frenchman despite having received repeated warnings from King Leopold and Colonel Strauch. Baron Solvyns, the Belgian ambassador to London, expressed their feelings: "We find that Stanley was deeply stupid," he wrote. "He should have made sure of the most important place in the Congo—Stanley Pool; and we are surprised that, as a Californian, he was not able to think of fighting his rival by gunshot. He was apparently as kind and easily influenced as these poor wretched savages that are meant to be civilized." Stanley had previously received extensive criticism in Europe for being a product of the American Wild West, but now he was being criticized for not being Wild West enough.[21]

When Stanley arrived in Europe, he could barely contain the hostility he felt toward Brazza. All of his work in building stations, carving out wagon roads through inhospitable terrain, and transporting steamboats to Malebo Pool had been undermined—and nearly negated—by Brazza's treaty. When he had first met Brazza at Ngoma Mountain in 1880, he'd congratulated him on a "brilliant strategy." After the encounter, he wrote in his diary, "He deserves every credit for a brave feat of exploration. It is not a long journey, but the amount of mileage must not be considered. It is the quality and interest of the feat we must bear in mind, and when those are regarded, it will be found that he deserves every honor from those able to decide upon the merits of the feat." It was clear that Stanley had been thinking in terms of gentlemanly competition over the issue of who was the greatest explorer. He had not yet been thinking in terms of dividing up the African continent among the European powers.[22]

Those charitable feelings hardened into bitterness after he learned about the Makoko Treaty and Brazza's treaty with the Bateke chiefs at Malebo Pool. He began to portray Brazza as a chameleon and a fraud: "To all whom de Brazza meets, he is as they wish him to be. With me he is a devoted internationalist; with the Dutch he is intensely amused at the frantic but futile efforts of the Belgians; with the missionaries he has freed slaves by the thousands in a country where there is no slave trade at all; with the French he is the annexator *par excellence*." Stanley elaborated on the competition between the two explorers when he arrived in Brussels at the beginning of October. He told a reporter for the French newspaper *Le Voltaire* that Brazza's explorations were in no way comparable to those of Livingstone, Cameron, or himself. Stanley boasted that he could have accomplished in forty days what had taken Brazza seven years.[23]

In a front-page reply to Stanley's remarks, the Paris newspaper *Le Temps* characterized Stanley as an old-fashioned explorer typical of the bygone age of discovery while depicting Brazza as a new type of explorer better suited to the new imperialism of the late nineteenth century. Brazza, the paper argued, had admittedly gone into territories already explored by others, but he had located the best route between Malebo Pool and the Atlantic coast, had reached Malebo Pool ahead of Stanley, had established friendly relations with the local Africans, and had signed a treaty guaranteeing French priority rights in the Makoko's territory. Stanley, wrote *Le Temps*, was showing bad grace by refusing to recognize Brazza's accomplishments.[24]

On October 19, Stanley was in Paris to speak at a banquet in his honor sponsored by the Stanley Club. Held at the Continental Hotel, the event was presided over by the Paris correspondent for the *New York Herald*. The guests included the American ambassador to France, the American consul general, and the American ambassador to Rome. Given the growing public sentiment in Paris in favor of Brazza's Makoko Treaty, Stanley's speech gave him an opportunity to attack the treaty and the man who had negotiated it. According to *Le Temps*, Stanley had spread the word ahead of time that his speech would deal a "mortal blow" to Brazza's reputation. Because Stanley's contract with King Leopold specified that all public speeches needed the king's advance approval, it can be assumed that Stanley was speaking with Leopold's blessing.[25]

After his opening remarks, Stanley launched into a personal attack on Brazza as an unimpressive figure who did not deserve to be lionized in Europe. "The Sorbonne receives him, France applauds him, and the world—including England—admires him. Gold medals are even now being molded in his honor, painters may now proceed to immortalize him on canvas for admiring posterity." Then Stanley belittled Brazza's geographical discoveries. Brazza's big idea was that one could reach Malebo Pool by going up the Ogowe and then down the Alima to the Congo River. But Stanley noted that by Brazza's own map the straight-line distance between the mouth of the Ogowe and Malebo Pool was 540 miles, whereas the distance between Stanley's Vivi Station on the Congo River estuary and Malebo Pool was only 130 miles. Brazza's discoveries, in short, did not pose a serious alternative to Stanley's.[26]

The key issue of the speech, however, was Stanley's discussion of the treaties Brazza had signed. Stanley said little about the treaty signed with an X by the Makoko at Mbe and instead focused on the treaty Brazza had signed with the Bateke chiefs at Malebo Pool, which ceded nine miles along the northern shore to the French. Stanley noted that the Makoko had received a copy of that treaty, but he was illiterate and could not read it. "What will happen when he realizes the real meaning of the piece of paper that Mr. de Brazza sent him?" Stanley asked. In signing that treaty, the Bateke chiefs believed that they were defining the limits of the territory in which the station would be located, not ceding the entire nine-mile stretch of land to France. "I have spent fifteen years in Africa,"

Stanley said, "and I have never met nor heard about a chief who would give up an inch of his territory." Stanley pointed out that he himself was paying rent on the land for his station at Malebo Pool, just as one would rent land for erecting a building in Paris. It was absurd to think that Brazza could get full ownership of a nine-mile stretch of land for the price of one French flag, two pieces of cloth, and a few strings of beads.

To clinch the point, Stanley told about traveling up the Congo River from Malebo Pool to negotiate a site for building a station at the riverside town of the Bateke chief Ngobila. While he was there, he received a visit from Chief Ngantsu, whose town was across the river, on land ruled by the Makoko at Mbe. When Ngantsu invited Stanley to consider building a station at his town instead, Stanley said that he could not go there because the land had been ceded to Brazza. In Stanley's telling, Ngantsu got visibly angry and denied having ceded any piece of land to a foreigner. He said it was against Bateke customs to do so and added that he would certainly not sell his country for a piece of paper or for gifts from Brazza. Ngantsu insisted that he had offered Brazza the right to rent a plot of land, nothing more.

No sooner had Stanley completed his speech than Brazza entered the banquet hall and sent his visiting card to Mr. Ryan, who was presiding. Wanting to exhibit even-handedness, Ryan invited Brazza to say a few words. Brazza had come prepared with a short statement in English—written for him by a colleague— that he had practiced several times. "This reception of Mr. Stanley having been held in Paris," he began, "I wish to be among those who offer him this welcome. Because it is well to establish that I see in Mr. Stanley, not an antagonist, but a laborer in the same field. Although representing different ideas, our common efforts are converging to the same end—the progress and civilization of Africa." After a few more words, he closed with "I raise my glass to the civilization of Africa by the simultaneous efforts of all nations under all flags." When the applause died down, Brazza approached

Stanley and said, "I have learned, my dear colleague, that you have rudely attacked me in your speech. Before I learn about what you have said, let me shake your hand." As Brazza departed, the president of the banquet said, "Sir, you have exhibited great tact."[27]

Brazza's intervention had been carefully planned and masterfully executed. The article in *Le Temps* the next morning reported nothing of the content of Stanley's speech but reproduced every word that Brazza spoke. Although it characterized Brazza's intervention as a "piece of theatre," it nevertheless rendered the judgment that "the Latin won out over the Anglo-Saxon for his composure." Brazza had spent months cultivating the contrasting images of the crude and bombastic Stanley versus the diplomatic and peaceful Brazza. In an encounter that lasted for less than two minutes, that contrast had been put on display for all to see. Even Stanley's closest allies cringed at his performance. Baron Lambermont, the secretary to the Belgian Ministry of Foreign Affairs, wrote in a telegram that "the exceptionally violent speech of Stanley has produced outrage," and Stanley himself admitted the next day that his attack on Brazza had backfired. "Yesterday's fame has been blotted out by calumny and dispraise," he wrote. Despite his clumsy insults and bitter sarcasm, Stanley had raised some serious questions about the validity of the Makoko Treaty, but in the French euphoria over Brazza's tactful performance, those points were ignored.[28]

Even the cultural and literary magazine *Revue des Deux Mondes*, which had been founded to bridge the cultural gap between Europe and America, heaped approbation on Stanley. In a long article on November 1, G. Valbert noted that Stanley had come to Paris to strike a mortal blow against his adversary, but he had only demonstrated his audacity and his penchant for making extreme and astonishing statements. As for Brazza, the article concluded that "he brought to his service a calm courage and a rare adroitness. This son of a Roman . . . is acclaimed in France as personifying the very qualities that lead to great things: a warm soul, perseverance, and a strong will." Making a link between Brazza's performance and the Makoko Treaty, the article concluded that "the newspapers of all political persuasions are in agreement in demanding that the treaty be ratified." *The Times* of London, however, reported the speech very differently. The article discussed Stanley's critique of the Makoko Treaty and agreed that "a treaty is no treaty if they who have signed it were not aware what they were signing." The article concluded, "No Western State has a moral right to annex vast portions of independent African territory."[29]

In France, however, Brazza-mania was reaching its height. Portraits of him by the celebrity photographer Felix Nadar were popular, and Brazza paraphernalia—including pens, stationery, vases, and commemorative medals—circulated widely. Brazza commemorative dueling swords were manufactured, and restaurants created special menus in his honor. In the ultimate bow to his newfound celebrity, a wax figure of Brazza was being prepared for the Musée Grévin, the French answer to London's Madame Tussaud's.[30]

On November 8, the French business community added its voice to the growing clamor in favor of the treaty when the Paris Chamber of Commerce appealed to the government to ratify it. The next day two Paris banks joined together to form a "Study Society" to make plans for building a railroad from the Atlantic coast to Malebo Pool and creating a large trading company to exploit the resources of equatorial Africa. On November 20, the Marseille Chamber of Commerce issued a statement in favor of ratification.[31]

It was under such conditions that Brazza's Makoko Treaty came before the Chamber of Deputies. The ratification process proceeded at lightning speed. On Saturday, November 18, Prime Minister Duclerc submitted the treaty to the chamber. Acknowledging that he was doing this in response to public opinion, he argued that this was a rare occasion when public opinion and French national interest came together because the treaty was consistent with French interests in advancing commerce and fighting the slave trade. On Monday morning, November 20, a committee was named to study the matter, and it met with Brazza later that same day. "Do not fail to seize the opportunity to take over at minimal cost an immense outlet which will feed our commerce and our industry," Brazza told them. "There exists in Africa a vast inland sea with coastlines that extend for at least 20,000 kilometers and a population estimated at eighty million people. In addition to the wealth that one could extract in the future from the labor of the indigenous population, the passage of time has produced accumulated treasures on the banks of that inland sea that could be exploited the day after tomorrow." After listening to Brazza's arguments in favor of the treaty, the committee approved it unanimously.[32]

The following day, the Chamber of Deputies was in the midst of a debate over the agricultural budget when the presiding officer interrupted it so that the committee's report on the Makoko Treaty could be presented. It was a matter of urgency, he explained. The report was presented by Maurice Rouvier, a Marseilles businessman who had recently served as the Minister for Commerce and Colonies. Rouvier began by stating that Brazza had been sent to Africa by the Ministry of Foreign Affairs, thus depicting his mission as a diplomatic one. Rouvier's definition of Brazza's mission was the exact opposite of the one correctly outlined by the minister of the marine and colonies less than two months earlier, but it gave Brazza the aura of diplomatic standing required for negotiating a treaty. It was a convenient fiction designed to smooth the way for the ratification of the Makoko Treaty.[33]

After redefining the official status of Brazza's mission, Deputy Rouvier sought to define the position of the Makoko. The Makoko, he said, was the sovereign ruler of the Bateke, who had requested the protection of the French flag on September 10, 1880. Rouvier went on to embellish that statement by saying that the Bateke chiefs had requested the protection of the French flag "freely, of their own free will." When Rouvier explained that he was not calling for a military conquest of the Congo but for scientific and commercial stations with only a minimal military presence necessary

for protection, he was interrupted with cries of *"très bien! très bien!"*
The French, he said, would not come as conquerors but as merchants who would buy rubber, gum, wax, ivory, precious metals,
and exotic woods. He was again interrupted with cries of *"très bien!*
très bien!" France, he concluded, would be betraying its own interests if it fell behind other nations in the global movement that was
pulling the Western world toward "regions that only yesterday were
still mysterious." When Deputy Rouvier sat down, nobody stood
up to speak in opposition to the treaty. Without debate, a resolution
to ratify the treaty was adopted on a voice vote with no dissenters.
Then the chamber went back to discussing the agricultural budget.

The French press was ecstatic. The rancorous Chamber of Deputies, which had toppled three successive French governments in
1881 and 1882, had now come together with a unanimous vote.
"The Congo is a remarkable example of the little bit of harmony
that still exists between public opinion and the government's legis-
lation," wrote Gabriel Charmes in the *Revue des Deux Mondes*. "For
the first time in our recent history, we have seen all the political
parties from the extreme right to the extreme left burn with the
same zeal for the same cause." *Le Temps* echoed that theme when
it said that "the Chamber, full of enthusiasm and warm hearts,
abandoned all dissent and became truly French."[34]

The British press, however, scoffed at the treaty. Noting that
the French government had ratified it without first sending out a
commission to ascertain the facts, the Paris correspondent for the
Times of London wrote that "never has a government submitted
to parliamentary ratification a treaty the reality and results of
which it knew so little. The Cabinet knows nothing but what it
has heard from Mr. de Brazza." The French government, the article continued, had undertaken "without any precise preliminary
information, under the mere unreasoning pressure of the public, a
foreign adventure of which it has ascertained neither the utility nor
the consequences."[35]

The day after the ratification vote, Admiral Jauréguiberry ordered the French gunship *Sagittaire* to the mouth of the Congo River to establish a French naval presence at two key ports on the Atlantic coast—Pointe Noire and Cabinda. Both of those ports were possible entryways for a rail line running along the Niari Valley to Malebo Pool. Armed with cannons and lavish gifts for the local chiefs, the captain of the *Sagittaire* signed treaties with the chiefs of the two port towns, thus ensuring that the French would have a direct pathway to Malebo Pool. The presence of the *Sagittaire* made it clear that the French intended to use the Makoko Treaty as a springboard to the possession of a much larger region.

3

Zanzibar, November 22, 1882

Tippu Tip arrived in Zanzibar on November 22, 1882, the day after the French parliament ratified the Makoko Treaty. He had been away for twelve years. From his Manyema headquarters in Kasongo (near the Lualaba River and Nyangwe), he had followed the main trade route to Ujiji (on Lake Tanganyika) and continued on to Tabora and the port city of Bagamoyo, where he took a dhow to Zanzibar. Without pausing to rest, he went straight to see Taria Topan, the Indian Muslim who ran Zanzibar's largest trading house. Having taken out a loan for MT$50,000 in 1870 that was supposed to be repaid after two years, Tippu Tip was now ten years beyond the deadline. Although Islamic law prohibited the charging of interest on loans, Topan could afford to be patient because the loan consisted of trade goods and was to be repaid in ivory, thus leaving ample room for the lender to make a profit by manipulating the barter equivalents. During Tippu Tip's absence, Taria Topan had become the customs master of Zanzibar. All goods and commodities that entered or left Zanzibar passed through the customs house.

Tippu Tip's caravan camp. The screened-off area is the harem. Wilhelm Junker, *Travels in Africa During the Years 1882–1886*, vol. 3, p. 567.

Setting aside the debt issue, Topan directed Tippu Tip to meet with Sultan Seyyid Barghash the next day. Tippu Tip had never met Seyyid Barghash, who by then had been the sultan of Zanzibar for nearly twelve years. The previous sultan, Seyyid Majid, had died in October 1870, shortly after Tippu Tip's caravan left for the interior, and Majid's half brother, Seyyid Barghash, who had been living in exile in India, returned to Zanzibar to take the throne. Topan informed Tippu Tip that Barghash was planning to appoint him the governor of Tabora, which was the major Arab settlement between the Indian Ocean coast and Ujiji, on Lake Tanganyika. Tippu Tip explained that he wanted to go back to Manyema, but Topan warned him that it was not wise to refuse a direct request from the sultan. Tippu Tip realized that when he met with the sultan the next day, he would need to make a strong case for returning to Manyema.

Tippu Tip had been busy since he and Stanley had parted on the Lualaba River in December 1876. While Stanley traveled north toward Boyoma Falls, Tippu Tip went west to the Lomami River, which paralleled the Lualaba. This was new territory for ivory trading: he found stockades made of elephant tusks and saw people pounding plantains with ivory pestles to make a stew, while other tusks were thrown away to rot in the forest. Tippu Tip's trading strategy illustrates the windfall profits that could be obtained on the ivory frontier. He had taken one *frasila* (35 pounds) of beads that cost three Maria Theresa dollars in Zanzibar and exchanged them in Kasongo for five frasila (175 pounds) of copper from Katanga. After giving half a frasila of copper to Stanley, he arrived at the Lomami with 4.5 frasila (158 pounds), which he made into bracelets, each weighing a little over half a pound. Trading at roughly two copper bracelets for a tusk (depending on the size), he purchased two hundred tusks. Tippu Tip's friend Heinrich Brode later calculated that he had turned MT\$3 worth of beads into MT\$10,000 worth of ivory.[36]

The secret of the high profits was that the value of beads increased rapidly as one went farther inland from the coast, just as the value of copper increased with the distance from the mines of Katanga, whereas the value of ivory increased in the opposite direction as one approached the Indian Ocean coast. Tippu Tip's willingness to travel over long distances and go into new areas generated his high profits. Evidence of his success was reported by a missionary from the London Missionary Society who encountered Tippu Tip's caravans near the coast in June 1878. "Both yesterday and today we met large caravans of Nyamwezi carrying ivory to the coast," he wrote in his diary. "They are said to be Tipo-Tipo's men—2,400 in number. Some of the tusks are very large."[37]

As Tippu Tip continued to make trading trips away from his headquarters at Kasongo, he was also building an empire. In the areas he had earlier conquered in his wars with Chiefs Nsama, Kazembe, and others, he was no longer buying ivory but collecting it as tribute. Tippu Tip had left the former chiefs in charge of daily affairs while his appointed tax collectors occupied themselves with collecting ivory and ensuring safe travel along the trade routes. His trading empire operated as a kind of shadow government that kept up the flow of ivory toward Kasongo. Tippu Tip now saw himself as the ruler of a territory and not a mere merchant. When a Baluchi caravan trader named Assani Bundari raided for ivory and slaves in the region southwest of Lake Tanganyika, Tippu Tip fined him 350 pounds of ivory for poaching on his territory. Jérôme Becker, an agent of the International African Association who had several long conversations with Tippu Tip in 1881, described him as "a merchant who doubled as a conqueror and an administrator; and who had carved out a veritable empire in which he reigned as the absolute master with a monopoly on all the sources of ivory. In addition, he had immense plantations worked by thousands of slaves." Despite his state-building activities, Tippu Tip remained nominally a vassal of the sultan of Zanzibar.[38]

Tippu Tip's return to Zanzibar had its origins in a packet of letters he had received in 1879. It contained a letter from Seyyid Barghash, the sultan of Zanzibar, informing him that Henry Morton Stanley had passed through Zanzibar on his way to Egypt in November and December 1877 after completing his descent of the Congo River. It was Tippu Tip's first news of Stanley since the two had parted on the Lualaba River more than two years earlier. The sultan sent Tippu Tip a Winchester repeating rifle like the one that Stanley used. Apparently, Stanley had asked the sultan to convey his rifle to Tippu Tip, but the sultan instead sent it as his own personal gift. Another letter was from Taria Topan, who reminded Tippu Tip that his original loan agreement had called for repayment after two years, a deadline that had long ago passed. The packet also contained MT$3,000 from Stanley and a photograph of the explorer but no letter. Tippu Tip felt slighted—"not even greetings did he send"—and complained that the payment was grossly inadequate because Stanley had promised him MT$7,000 for escorting him down the Lualaba in 1876.

After receiving the packet of letters, Tippu Tip decided to return to Zanzibar in order to maintain good relations with the new sultan's regime. It took another year before his caravan was ready to depart from his headquarters in Kasongo. His original Nyamwezi porters had long ago left after their contracts expired, and he now relied on locally recruited Manyema porters. He later told Jérôme Becker that he departed Manyema with two thousand porters and a thousand armed guards. Even so, he lacked enough porters to carry his enormous stock of ivory, and so he adopted a system whereby the porters carried their loads for four hours, made a camp, and then went back in order to bring the remaining loads the next day.[39]

In February 1881, his caravan arrived at Ujiji, on the eastern shore of Lake Tanganyika, which he had not seen since going there with his father in the late 1850s. It had been a frontier boom town in the 1860s and 1870s and then had begun to decline as a trading town because Manyema ivory was increasingly obtained from tribute instead of trade. When the German explorer Hermann von Wissman passed through Ujiji in 1882, he saw houses standing empty in a state of disrepair, indicating that they had been abandoned for some time. Nevertheless, Ujiji showed signs of its increasing integration into Zanzibar's empire when the sultan appointed Mwinyi Kheri, an Arab merchant and longtime Ujiji resident, as the governor of Ujiji. The sultan had made Kheri responsible for the Arab and Swahili population of Ujiji, whose quarrels and disputes could have repercussions in Zanzibar, but he had no interest in controlling the African chieftaincies that surrounded Ujiji.[40]

The other major change in the Lake Tanganyika region was the arrival of European missions and humanitarian agencies that were establishing permanent stations. Protestant missionaries from the London Missionary Society (LMS) had arrived in 1878, joined in 1879 by the French Catholic White Fathers. South of Ujiji along the eastern shore of Lake Tanganyika, the Belgian branch of King Leopold's International African Association had established its first station. The IAA's original objective in 1877 had been to establish a station at Nyangwe, but its plans were scaled back because of deaths and troubles along the trade route. It settled for building a station at Karema, on the eastern shore of Lake Tanganyika roughly 150 miles south of Ujiji. In 1879, a second IAA expedition built a small fort at Karema called Fort Leopold. A third IAA expedition arrived in Zanzibar in June 1880 to continue building the station. To facilitate the flow of supplies and personnel to the station, the Belgians established a consulate in Zanzibar in 1880 and kept an IAA agent in Tabora.[41]

At Ujiji, Tippu Tip's caravan was slowed down by two factors. The first was that most of his porters were forced recruits from Manyema and, fearful of traveling outside of their home territory, many deserted as soon as they arrived at Ujiji. Tippu Tip took advantage of the situation to replace them with professional Nyamwezi porters. The second problem was difficult relations with the local residents along the route between Ujiji and Tabora. The caravans carried vast amounts of wealth past villages of poor subsistence farmers, and the largest caravans consumed prodigious quantities of food. Moreover, the caravan porters and guards would sometimes steal food or seize local people as slaves. During the early 1880s, there was a rise in resistance against the caravan traders, as chiefs demanded higher tolls and villagers would sometimes kill porters and steal their goods and captives.

Things came to a head when Tippu Tip reached the large town of Rwanda (not to be confused with the modern country of Rwanda), about six hours' march from Ujiji. According to LMS missionaries, hundreds of Tippu Tip's porters and guards fanned out into the cultivated fields, where they stole or burned crops, causing the people of Rwanda to mobilize to drive them back. Tippu Tip's version of the events is somewhat different: "We were attacked for no reason whatsoever," he wrote. "We came at them and fought. After half an hour we drove them off with 26 or 27 of their number dead." But that was not the end of the affair. "We built a stockade immediately and dispatched men to attack their villages," wrote Tippu Tip. "In one day, some fifteen villages that were moated and stockaded were burned. Those that were open, we

left." Several years later, Tippu Tip's associate, Selim bin Muhammad, repeated essentially the same story to the Englishman Herbert Ward but added that Tippu Tip had gained "a considerable
quantity of ivory, the local people being wealthy owing to their
various robberies and the taxes they had for many years imposed
upon passing caravans."[42]

Tippu Tip parked his caravan in the town of Rwanda for six
months while his ivory was being ferried across Lake Tanganyika
little by little. When his caravan was again on the march, Tippu
Tip felt that he was being charged excessive tolls and harassed by
the local villagers. At one place, 150 of Tippu Tip's captives were
stolen, and four of his Nyamwezi porters were killed. Tippu Tip
wanted to launch an attack, but his colleagues advised patience
because they had an enormous amount of ivory to transport and
feared that fighting would only make the journey more difficult.
So Tippu Tip changed his tactics: he paid the tolls and endured
the constant thefts and occasional killings until he reached Tabora
in August 1881 without further warfare. Like Stanley, he could
adjust the level of violence to fit the situation. It had taken him
nine months to travel some three hundred miles from Ujiji to
Tabora with his ivory; Stanley and Livingstone, traveling with a
much smaller and lighter caravan in 1872, had made the trip in
fifty-three days.[43]

Tippu Tip stayed in Tabora for over a year, slowed down by the
death of his father, who owned a compound just outside of Tabora.
His conversations with Jérôme Becker of the International African Association (which advocated the abolition of slavery) revealed
some of the complexities of slavery and abolition in East Africa.
The discussion began when Tippu Tip accused the Europeans of
hypocrisy with regard to slavery. Until recent times, he noted, the
European nations had countenanced slavery, and Russia had only
recently abolished serfdom. Yet as soon as the European nations
outlawed slavery in their own countries, they sought to abolish it
everywhere else. He scoffed at the anti–slave trade treaty that the

British had forced upon the sultan of Zanzibar, noting that slave trading was carried on openly just twenty leagues inland from the port town of Bagamoyo.[44]

After observing that Europeans in Africa employed domestic servants, Tippu Tip asked Becker to explain the difference between a servant and a slave. When Becker answered that a servant was free to leave while a slave was not, Tippu Tip countered that his own domestic slaves had many chances to run away, but they chose to stay with him because he treated them well. He was clearly referring to his armed guards and his household servants, who stayed loyal to him in part because their life was preferable to the alternatives, such as running away and risking reenslavement.

Despite Tippu Tip's attempts to portray slavery as a benign institution, the harsher face of his slaving activities was observed by the LMS missionary Alfred Swann, who met up with Tippu Tip's caravan in late November 1882, when it was about two hundred miles from the coast. Swann's account focused on the captives who were destined for sale at the coast or in Zanzibar. "Here we met the notorious Tippu Tip's annual caravan, which had been resting after the long march through Ugogo and the hot passes of Chunyo," he wrote. "As they filed past, we noticed many chained together at the neck. Others had their necks fastened into the forks of poles about six feet long, the ends of which were supported by the men who preceded them. The women, who were as numerous as the men, carried babies on their backs in addition to a tusk of ivory or other burden on their heads." Swann described the physical condition of the slaves: "Feet and shoulders were a mass of open sores, made more painful by swarms of flies which followed the march and lived on the flowing blood. They presented a moving picture of utter misery, and one could not help wondering how any of them had survived the long tramp from the upper Congo, at least 1,000 miles distant." That was the aspect of the East African slave trade that Tippu Tip preferred not to talk about.[45]

The most intense discussions between Becker and Tippu Tip concerned the IAA's plan to build a station at Nyangwe, which would make it possible for the Belgians to buy Tippu Tip's ivory and ship it to Europe via the Congo River. The straight-line distances from Nyangwe to the east and west coasts were roughly similar, but the Congo route allowed for steamboat transportation over long stretches. Given the difficulties Tippu Tip was having in getting his ivory to Zanzibar with caravans of porters, he was very interested in the idea. When the Belgian captain Emile Storms arrived in Tabora on August 17 on his way to the IAA station at Karema, the discussion of ivory routes resumed. Storms was carrying secret instructions from King Leopold to build a line of stations between Karema and Nyangwe that were to link up with a line of stations to be built by Stanley along the Upper Congo River, thus realizing King Leopold's dream of a line of stations crossing equatorial Africa from east to west. Despite the IAA's pretext of scientific and humanitarian aims, Captain Storms's main goal was to get his hands on Tippu Tip's ivory.

Like Becker, Storms proposed that once the Belgians had a station in Nyangwe, they could purchase Tippu Tip's ivory and ship it down the Congo River by boat. He proposed an arrangement whereby the Belgians would purchase the ivory at Nyangwe for the going price in Zanzibar, minus Zanzibar customs charges. From that base price they would deduct the cost of transportation to the Atlantic Coast. Storms was proposing to reverse the economic geography of equatorial Africa so that the ivory of Manyema would flow to the Atlantic instead of the Indian Ocean. There was something in the proposal for both parties. Tippu Tip would gain from reduced transportation costs, whereas the Belgians would gain by pocketing the money that would have otherwise gone to the customs master in Zanzibar. The big losers would be the sultan of Zanzibar and the customs master, who would be deprived of the substantial customs revenues generated by Tippu Tip's Manyema ivory.[46]

Tippu Tip responded that he would need to seek permission from the sultan before making an agreement. "The country of Manyema over which I rule—both it and I are under the authority of Seyyid," he told Storms. "I can do nothing without his approval." The Belgian replied, "I have no dealings with the sultan. You are the chief of Manyema who has all the authority." In the end, no deal was reached because Tippu Tip refused to undermine the sultan and his customs master.[47]

The Belgian plan to purchase Tippu Tip's ivory at Nyangwe and carry it to the Atlantic coast on river steamers was a fantasy of King Leopold and Colonel Strauch. Already in 1880, when Stanley's wagon road had not yet reached Malebo Pool, Colonel Strauch was pushing him to proceed up the Congo River with all haste in order to reach Nyangwe. Strauch estimated that it took a caravan six months to travel from Nyangwe to Zanzibar if there were no impediments from local chiefs, but it would take only twenty-three days to travel to the mouth of the Congo River by a combination of river steamers and wagon roads. The estimate was wildly unrealistic, but it fueled the king's resolve to establish regular communication with Nyangwe from the Atlantic coast as quickly as possible. The Nyangwe scheme provides an example of how the two international organizations headed by King Leopold—the International African Association and the Study Committee—complemented one another. The IAA would come to Nyangwe from the east coast to build a station that was ostensibly for humanitarian and scientific purposes while the Study Committee, which was really a glorified trade mission, would come in from the West coast and buy ivory.[48]

In June 1881, when Stanley was still in Africa, Colonel Strauch pointedly asked him for a date when he would organize an expedition to Nyangwe. Stanley replied, "Never, during my current contract," and he reminded him that Nyangwe was eighteen hundred miles from Malebo Pool by the river route. Stanley was not opposed to be trading with Nyangwe, but as the only European who had ever traveled from Nyangwe to Malebo Pool, he had a more realistic view of what was possible within a reasonable period of time. The king nevertheless persisted, claiming that once the transportation network between the Atlantic coast and Nyangwe was established, not a single yard of cloth would ever again come to Nyangwe from the Indian Ocean coast, and the large East African ivory caravans would become a thing of the past. When Colonel Strauch ordered fifty more Zanzibari porters to the Congo, he told Stanley that they should be used to transport Belgian officers and their merchandise up the Congo River to Nyangwe. Stanley instead used the Zanzibaris to help transport the paddle-wheeled steamboat *En Avant* to Malebo Pool. The king's dream of diverting the ivory of Manyema to Malebo Pool would have to wait.[49]

On November 23, 1882, the morning after Taria Topan had alerted Tippu Tip to Sultan Seyyid Barghash's plans to appoint him governor of Tabora, Tippu Tip paid a visit to the palace. After hearing the sultan's offer, he revealed that Captain Storms was planning to establish an IAA station in Nyangwe in order to export ivory down the Congo River. He mentioned it in order to show the sultan that his presence in Manyema was indispensable in the current circumstances. The sultan responded, "I had wanted to make you governor of Tabora, but now I think it better that you set off for Manyema without tarrying here." In order to facilitate Tippu Tip's rapid departure, Taria Topan opened his trading firm's warehouse to Tippu Tip and offered him unlimited credit, while the sultan ordered that no caravan could hire porters until Tippu Tip had a full contingent, an order that was designed mainly to block the imminent departure of an IAA supply caravan going to Karema. Despite the efforts of the sultan and Taria Topan to send him on his way, it took Tippu Tip some time to sell all his ivory for a total of £70,000, which made him a very wealthy man. It was not until August 1883—nine months after he had arrived—that Tippu Tip left Zanzibar.[50]

Even though the sultan wanted Tippu Tip to return quickly to Manyema to block the Belgians and ensure that the ivory continued to flow to Zanzibar, he did not offer to make Tippu Tip the governor of Manyema, an act that would have nominally extended the sultan's authority all the way to the Lualaba River. The sultan was content to have governors at Tabora and Ujiji, where there were substantial Arab populations, and to rely on an informal arrangement with Tippu Tip for Manyema. When Tippu Tip was asked by a friend if he wanted to be the governor of Ujiji, he replied, "Did you not know that my chiefdom is Manyema? My domain is larger than Unyamwezi, all Tabora, and the whole of Sukuma. Why should I want a governorship?" The informal recognition of Tippu Tip as the ruler of Manyema satisfied both the sultan and Tippu Tip. It gave Tippu Tip the autonomy and flexibility he needed to run things as he saw fit while still allowing the sultan to claim some influence over the Manyema ivory trade.[51]

The sultan's attitude toward the territories and peoples in the East African interior could be seen in an incident that took place just before Tippu Tip left Zanzibar to return to Manyema. The British consul, John Kirk, approached the sultan to discuss the warfare in the region between the coast and Tabora, which was impeding the ivory caravans, and he proposed that Tippu Tip could mount a military campaign to establish the sultan's control over that country. But the sultan was not interested in the venture because it was far cheaper to secure the key trading towns, where concentrations of wealthy Arab traders had settled, and leave the African chiefs in control of the surrounding territories and peoples. The sultan was maintaining what the historian Philip Curtin has called a "trading post empire" at a time when the Europeans were becoming increasingly interested in claiming territory. As the ruler of a nascent state in the heart of equatorial Africa, Tippu Tip had the option of dealing with the sultan of Zanzibar or with the Europeans who were establishing posts along the Congo River. Or, he could do a little of both.[52]

CHAPTER 5

A TORRENT OF TREATIES

FOR THE FRENCH GOVERNMENT, THE political status of equatorial Africa changed dramatically after the Chamber of Deputies ratified the Makoko Treaty on November 21, 1882, and the Senate followed suit a week later. On December 26, the Chamber of Deputies approved the expenditure of 1,275,000 francs for a new mission to equatorial Africa—more than a dozen times the appropriation for Brazza's previous mission. In the words of French historian Henri Brunschwig, equatorial Africa passed "from the domain of international philanthropy, geography, and religious missions to the domain of nationalistic rivalries."[1]

Although the French government had ratified the Makoko Treaty and provided funds for a new mission to equatorial Africa, it stopped short of establishing an official colony in the Congo River basin. The West African Mission, as its new initiative was called, would be administered by the Department of Public Instruction and not by the Ministry of the Marine and Colonies. Its overall purpose was vaguely defined as "to assure the execution of the arrangements concluded with the Bateke chiefs" by remitting a countersigned copy of the treaty to the Makoko and to sign treaties with other chiefs in order to expand French influence. Brazza was put in charge of the mission and given the vague title of government commissioner. His instructions noted that this title gave him authority "analogous to the governor of a colony," even though he was not officially a governor and the French Congo was not officially a colony.[2]

Two days after the French Chamber of Deputies ratified Brazza's Makoko Treaty, Henry Morton Stanley was on a ship bound for the mouth of the Congo River. The steamer *Harkawway*, which he boarded in Cadiz, Spain, carried fourteen military officers and six hundred tons of supplies and trade goods for his Congo expedition. While in Brussels, Stanley had signed a contract to stay on as head of King Leopold's Congo operations for two more years, but the name of the organization had been changed to the International Association of the Congo (IAC) to give it the aura of a permanent entity. The change in terminology caused great confusion among the king's agents in the Congo River basin, who employed the terms "Study Committee" and "International Association of the Congo" interchangeably.

Stanley's top priority on this expedition was to sign treaties with local chiefs in order to build a firewall against further expansion by the French. Treaties had been a part of Stanley's mission from the very beginning, but the French parliament's ratification of the Makoko Treaty had given the issue a new urgency. The problem for Stanley was that the treaties signed by Brazza were upheld by the government of France, a recognized international power, whereas those signed by Stanley were recognized only by the International Association of the Congo, an entity that was the personal project of King Leopold II. The IAC did not represent the government of Belgium, and the Belgian parliament had no interest in ratifying Stanley's treaties.

The process of treaty making in the Congo River basin varied from place to place because there were four different indigenous political systems. First, there were the large kingdoms in the savanna region south of the rainforest. Near the mouth of the Congo River, the land on the south bank of the Congo River estuary was technically part of the old Kongo Kingdom, even though the kings had lost any direct authority over the chiefs during civil wars in the seventeenth century. Nevertheless, the Kongo king, who had close relations with the Portuguese in neighboring Angola, claimed that any treaties that chiefs signed without his permission were meaningless. In a similar way, the Makoko of the Bateke Kingdom claimed the power to sign treaties on behalf of his subordinate chiefs. The second type of political system was found in the trading towns at Malebo Pool and along the Upper Congo River, where the wealthiest and most powerful traders exercised authority, which was frequently contested by rival traders. The third system was found in the rainforest villages, where authority was held by a local "big man" who wielded power because of his personal wealth, large family, and social networks. Finally, there was the political authority established by the Arab traders in Manyema, who claimed to be under the authority of the sultan of Zanzibar. Treaties that the Europeans signed with the Arabs were not about the cession of sovereignty or territory but about the division of territory and trading zones between two sets of outside intruders.

1

Malebo Pool, March 1883

The form and content of the treaties signed by the International Association of the Congo and its predecessor, the Upper Congo Study Committee, were continuously evolving. The original agreement that Stanley had signed with the chiefs of Vivi, on the Congo River estuary, in September 1879 had simply arranged for leasing a plot of land for a monthly payment and for guarantees of freedom of travel along the trade routes. The return of Brazza to France with the Makoko Treaty in June 1882, however, forced King Leopold to refine his strategy. If France was claiming sovereignty over a vast swath of equatorial Africa, then Leopold needed to claim sovereignty as well. "The terms of the treaties Stanley has made with the native chiefs do not satisfy me," King Leopold wrote to Colonel Strauch on October 16, 1882. "There must be added an article to the effect that they delegate their sovereign rights over the territories." He added, "The treaties must be as brief as possible, and in a couple of articles must grant us everything." The demand for sovereignty made the task of the Association's agents more difficult. As Stanley had stated in Paris, "I have never met nor heard about a chief who would give up an inch of his territory."[3]

Regardless of their specific terms, the treaties were a sham. It is highly unlikely that the full implications of the treaties were understood by the chiefs, who could neither read nor write and who spoke no French or English. It is equally unclear if the chiefs actually controlled all the territory that they ceded in the treaties. To them, signing a treaty often meant little more than receiving a payment in return for making an X on a piece of paper. The charade of treaty making was inadvertently exposed by Capt. Edmond Hanssens (an employee of the IAC) when he wrote to Stanley in 1882, "I bought up the whole confluence of the Ibari-Nkulu, a day's journey upstream and ditto downstream, and four inland along both banks. If Brazza or anyone else came along, he would find the place taken." Hanssens may have claimed that he was buying territory, but he was in fact buying nothing more than marks on sheets of paper.[4]

When Stanley arrived at Malebo Pool in March 1883, his first major task was to consolidate the Association's control over the chiefs on the south bank. Between March 29 and April 9, he signed a series of treaties with the Mbundu chiefs who lived southwest of the Pool and the Bateke chiefs of Kintamo and Kimpoko to form a confederation that was ostensibly for maintaining the peace. According to the treaties, the International Association of the Congo alone had the power to declare war and to arbitrate all disputes that might endanger the peace. It also had the right to approve or reject all European merchants or agents who entered the South Bank Confederation's territory. Henceforth, the flag of

the Association—a solid blue flag with a yellow star in the center—
would fly over the villages of the signatory chiefs every Sunday
morning and on all holidays.[5]

The most contested spot on the south bank was the trading
town of Kinshasa, about eight miles upstream from the Leopoldville Station. It was the home of Chief Ntsuulu, a Bateke lord who
was the highest-ranking vassal of the Makoko at Malebo Pool. He
wore a copper collar and was the only Bateke chief at the Pool who
had the right to sit on a leopard skin, but his authority as the keeper
of the sacred charms was more spiritual than political. The charms
were thought to embody living spirits. When a European visitor
to Chief Ntsuulu's house lit up his pipe, the chief ordered him to
extinguish it immediately before the smoke made the charms ill.[6]

In 1881, when Sergeant Malamine and the two Senegalese
marines that Brazza had left on the north bank to represent French
interests were suffering from shortages of food, Chief Ntsuulu had
invited them to cross over to the south bank and settle in Kinshasa,
even though it was outside the territory defined by the Makoko
Treaty. Isolated and without supplies, Malamine had made his living as a hunter by killing buffalos, elephants, hippopotami, and
antelopes using the fourteen-shot Winchester repeating rifle that
Stanley had given him. When the French natural scientist Leon
Guiral visited Malebo Pool in April 1882, he noted that the famous
"Brazzaville Station" that was being talked about at geographical conferences in Paris consisted of nothing more than Sergeant
Malamine's hut in Kinshasa. Because the Brazzaville Station was
officially under the authority of the French national committee
of King Leopold's International African Association (and not the
government of France), King Leopold put pressure on the French
IAA officials to recall Sergeant Malamine and the two Senegalese
marines to the Franceville Station on the upper Ogowe. After Sergeant Malamine's departure from Kinshasa in May 1882, there
was no longer a French presence at Malebo Pool. A year later, Chief
Ntsuulu joined Stanley's South Bank Confederation and allowed

the International Association of the Congo to build a station in his town.[7]

No sooner had Stanley concluded the treaties for the South Bank Confederation than he received instructions from King Leopold to organize a meeting of all the chiefs along the Lower Congo River from Vivi to Malebo Pool in order to form a political entity to be called the "New Confederacy." The model treaty that accompanied the instructions said that members of the New Confederacy were to fly the Association's flag and that their defense force would consist of locally recruited African soldiers under the command of the IAC. The purpose of the New Confederacy was not stated except for a vague reference to the "civilizing sentiments that motivated the International Association of the Congo."[8]

Stanley found the idea ludicrous. As he wrote to Colonel Strauch, the districts involved were "separate, distinct, and independent one from another. They have no natural communication one with the other except for that which we furnish." Each district, he explained, had from one to ten chiefs, each of which was the sole owner and possessor of the soil. "As Europeans understand the term confederacy," he concluded, "I declare such a confederacy impossible at the present time." Stanley believed that a small-scale confederation such as the one he had established on the south shore of Malebo Pool could be a model for this new kind of state, but it included only 150 square miles and eighteen chiefs, and it could not be replicated on a grand scale. Stanley failed to grasp that King Leopold was less interested in creating a functioning confederacy than a paper confederacy that he could point to in negotiations with private companies and other European nations. A confederation of chiefs stretching from the Congo River estuary to Malebo Pool would be a bulwark against French or Portuguese attempts to lay claims to the Lower Congo.[9]

In August 1883, Stanley left Malebo Pool with a fleet of three steamboats to visit or establish IAC stations along the Upper Congo River. Treaties with the chiefs of large trading towns such as Bolobo and Bangala were problematic because each town was composed of a series of independent villages, each with its own chief. Bolobo consisted of fifteen villages strung out along the riverbank, and Bangala contained twenty independent villages along a twenty-eight-mile stretch of the river. In each case, the chief of one of the villages had signed a treaty in which he claimed to be the chief of the whole town and the surrounding region. In return, he had received substantial gifts of trade goods and leveraged his alliance with the white foreigners to elevate his status above that of his peers.

Arriving at Bolobo, where the IAC had established a station the previous year, Stanley came upon the charred ruins of the station and its warehouse. He learned that all of the villages of Bolobo were at war with the IAC, except for the two that were under the direct control of Ibaka, the chief who had signed a treaty with the Association in 1882. Ibaka was not a hereditary chief but a former slave who had become wealthy in the ivory trade and had taken over the business upon his master's death. That was not an unusual development in Bobangi trading towns, where ambitious and talented slaves were given great latitude by their masters, but Ibaka's rise to the chiefship of the village of Litimba had been strongly opposed by his late master's family, who feared a decline in their own status and fortune.[10]

The treaty that Chief Ibaka had signed with the IAC identified him as the "Superior Chief of the Bolobo District," even though he was at most the first among equals, and even that claim was contested by other chiefs such as Manga and Gatula. In return for the recognition and a "fat present," he had authorized the Association to build a station on a plot of land that turned out to be an ancient burial ground—a place where no Bolobo resident would ever live. Leveraging his relationship with the IAC, he had levied a tax on all the chiefs and traders who came to the station to sell ivory, cutting into their profits and effectively making them his tributaries. Local opposition to Chief Ibaka thus became synonymous

A street scene at Ipoto, one of the component villages of Bangala. The layout of Ipoto was typical of the trading towns along the Upper Congo River. Henry M. Stanley, *The Congo and the Founding of Its Free State*, vol. 2, p. 172.

with opposition to the IAC. When Stanley arrived on August 22, he negotiated with the rebellious chiefs for twelve days with only limited success. He finally managed to bully them into submission by giving them a demonstration of his Krupp gun, a cannon-like weapon that he fired into the river, sending up a large column of water two thousand yards away.[11]

On October 21, Stanley's fleet arrived at Bangala, where he had fought the "fight of fights" when he had first descended the river in 1877. Because the local population still harbored suspicion of him, he was required to go through a blood brotherhood ceremony with the son of Chief Mwata Bwiké before the chief himself appeared and welcomed him. After reaching an agreement on establishing an IAC station at Bangala, Stanley continued on his journey, leaving Camille Coquilhat behind to make the final arrangements and build the station. Coquilhat was disappointed to discover that Mwata Bwiké had no standing army or police force and that his only authority over the other chiefs came from his powers of persuasion. Rather than being a powerful chief, Mwata Bwiké was merely the senior chief in a loose confederation that encompassed no more than thirty thousand people.[12]

Stanley's ultimate objective on his trip up the Congo River was to establish a station on Wana Rusari Island. Located just below the seventh cataract of Boyoma Falls (which he called Stanley Falls), it was nearly a thousand miles by river from the Leopoldville Station at Malebo Pool. Meeting with a group of Genya chiefs on December 1–3, he negotiated limited sovereignty over the island and proprietary rights to all its unoccupied land in return for goods worth £160. Andrew Bennie, a Scottish steamboat engineer, was appointed chief of the Stanley Falls Station, and the workmen soon cleared four acres of ground and built him a rough house. The station would be protected by a garrison of ten Zanzibari soldiers and twenty Hausa soldiers from northern Nigeria. The establishment of the Stanley Falls Station completed the Association's claims to possession of the Upper Congo River, having secured treaty rights at strategic points along the thousand-mile stretch from Malebo Pool to Boyoma Falls. Stanley calculated that it would take fifty-eight days for a steamboat to go up the river from Malebo Pool to Boyoma Falls and thirty days for the return trip.[13]

On December 10, 1883, Stanley left the Stanley Falls Station to return downstream. Despite the temptation to travel beyond the seven cataracts of Boyoma Falls and follow the Lualaba River upstream to Nyangwe, he decided that his primary job was to consolidate the progress made so far. "What was required," he wrote, "was to turn our attention to obtaining the protectorship of the districts between station and station so that we might become masters of one uninterrupted and consecutive territory from the Vivi Station to the Stanley Falls Station." The task of filling in the spaces between the stations was consistent with the evolving strategy of King Leopold, whose terminology was evolving from the "Free States of the Congo" to a singular "Free State." In January 1884, he directed all agents "to ensure the joining of our possessions" in order to form a single state.[14]

With the end of his two-year contract in sight, Stanley left Malebo Pool on March 20 and slowly made his way down the Congo River toward Banana Point, where he would catch a steamship to Europe. When he visited the stations of the Lower Congo, he learned that King Leopold's project to persuade the chiefs to unite in a so-called New Confederacy that controlled the Lower Congo River from Vivi to Malebo Pool had made substantial progress. When Stanley had originally dismissed the project as unrealistic, the king had enlisted Gen. Frederick Goldsmid, a former high-ranking colonial official in British India, to persuade the chiefs along the Lower Congo River to join the New Confederacy. Working with a team of IAC agents, General Goldsmid managed to obtain treaties bearing the marks of more than three hundred chiefs.[15]

The treaties, written in English by Goldsmid, stated that the villages and towns governed by the respective chiefs would be combined into "one united territory to be henceforth and hereafter known as the New Confederacy." The chiefs promised to place their armed forces and their means "under such organization as we shall deem to be best for the common good of the people and welfare of the confederacy." All the chiefs were required to fly the flag of the International Association of the Congo and to respect all treaties made with the Association. In a separate treaty made in October 1883, the chiefs delegated the International Association of the Congo to represent them before the states of Europe. The New Confederacy was nothing more than a ploy by King Leopold to get treaties that he could use to claim diplomatic recognition for the International Association of the Congo. When Colonel Strauch had sent out the model for the New Confederation treaty, he included an excerpt from the book *Le Droit International Codifié* (*International Law Codified*), published in Paris in 1874, so that the IAC agents could make treaties that would be considered valid in international law.[16]

As Stanley continued down the Congo River estuary, he passed through one of the IAC's most intense treaty-making operations. Until 1882, the estuary had been open to a variety of European trading companies and religious missions, but after the ratification of the Makoko Treaty in Paris, the Portuguese had begun making diplomatic moves toward securing control over the river's mouth. To counter Portuguese influence, the IAC had sent Alexander Delcommune to meet with the chiefs near Boma and sign secret treaties that granted sovereignty to the Association. Delcommune later admitted that he had neglected to inform the chiefs "of all the privileges that made up the rights of sovereignty."[17]

The reason for the secrecy was that the ruler of the Kongo Kingdom, who was an ally of the Portuguese, claimed nominal authority over the chiefs. He had sent a letter to the king of Portugal stating that he did not recognize the rights of the International Association of the Congo, only the rights of the king of Portugal. To maintain the secrecy, the IAC refused to allow the chiefs of Boma to have copies of their own treaties for fear that they would fall into Portuguese hands. "If Mr. Delcommune has left copies of these conventions in the hands of the chiefs," said a letter from the Association, "he has committed a most impudent act. No copies should be left with them. One should simply give them signed orders by means of which they may obtain the promised goods."[18]

The Association was buying treaties that would be useful to King Leopold for blocking the efforts of Portugal and France to gain a foothold along the Congo River estuary and for enticing European commercial and transportation companies to invest in the Lower Congo. They were never intended to be serious legal contracts between Association agents and African chiefs. Gen. Frederick Goldsmid told the London *Times* in January 1884 that the treaties had been acquired "for the express purpose of never being enforced, and with the view of preventing anyone else from enforcing them." By then, the scramble for treaties had gone from sham to farce.[19]

2

Franceville Station, Ogowe River, 1883

Because Brazza's third mission was a much larger and more complex undertaking than the first two, he did not leave France until March 20, 1883, three months after the Chamber of Deputies approved the Makoko Treaty. The instructions for the West African Mission, as it was called, were written by Brazza himself. In addition to the primary objectives of returning a countersigned copy of the Makoko Treaty to the Makoko at Mbe and signing treaties with other chiefs, the mission's goals included surveying the territory to look for mines, trees that yielded tropical oils, land suitable for European settlement, or anything else that might be useful to French commerce and industry. It was supposed to take over the existing stations from the French National Committee of the IAA and create new stations along the major communication routes. Finally, it should work to abolish slavery and slave trading. All of those objectives were to be accomplished through conciliation and negotiation, with a minimum of military force.[20]

The treaties that Brazza and his associates planned to sign with local chiefs followed a uniform model. At the top of the treaty were the words "Treaty of Protectorate," and underneath them was the phrase "in the name of France." The preamble that followed said, "In virtue of the powers which have been delegated by Pierre Savorgnan de Brazza, Government Commissioner of the Republic of France in West Africa." Article 1 said "Chief X places his country under the suzerainty and protection of France." Article 2 recognized the authority of the chief over his own territory and promised the aid and protection of France. Despite the language of Brazza's Makoko Treaty ceding "sovereignty" to France, the treaties of the

West African Mission sought only to establish French protectorates over the chiefdoms.[21]

Upon reaching the mouth of the Ogowe River by ship, Brazza followed his customary route, taking a river steamboat to Lambaréné and continuing upstream by dugout canoe. His first goal was to streamline the transportation of goods and supplies from Lambaréné to Franceville, a three-hundred-mile stretch of river interrupted by occasional rapids that caused frequent accidents and loss of cargo. West African Mission agents built a warehouse at Lambaréné, transit stations at the rapids of Njolé and the waterfall at Booué, and another station farther upriver at Boundji. Reaching Franceville, the station he had founded on his second mission, Brazza took it over from the French national committee of King Leopold's International African Association. From that point onward, the IAA no longer had a presence west of the Congo River.

Ever since Brazza's first mission to the Ogowe, he had dreamed of a trade route that went up the Ogowe and overland to the upper Alima and then down the Alima to the Congo River and on to Malebo Pool. That project had been blocked during his first mission by the hostility of the Bobangi traders on the Alima. During his second mission, the IAA had built a small station at Diele, on the upper Alima, but continued Bobangi hostility prevented them from descending the Alima in canoes. Shortly before his return to France, Brazza had marked out a rough overland trail between Franceville and Diele. In order to make the route commercially feasible, however, it was necessary to launch a river steamboat on the Alima. Brazza's colleague Dr. Ballay had obtained the small steamboat belonging to the Geographical Society and had dismantled it for transportation up the Ogowe River to Franceville and then overland to Diele, but the boilers and the ashpan were lost while navigating the rapids and new ones had to be ordered from Europe. In the meantime, Ballay managed to transport the remaining parts to Diele and reconstruct the steamboat, which he named the *Ballay*, with the aid of two mechanics sent out from France.

While he was waiting for the boilers, Ballay received an invitation to meet with some Bobangi chiefs. Arriving at the meeting, he was greeted by Chief Ndombi, who bore scars of a bullet that had passed through his jaw. Ballay suspected that the wound came from the battle with Brazza on July 3, 1878, but was afraid to ask. Chief Ndombi told Ballay that Chief Bolunza, who had led the battle against Brazza, had died recently and that he was now ready to make peace. As a symbol of cooperation, Ndombi offered to sell Ballay an enormous dugout canoe that could hold a hundred paddlers. A price was agreed on, but the negotiations dragged on because some Bobangi chiefs opposed the transaction. That is where things stood when Brazza arrived at Diele in early October 1883 and convoked a meeting with the Bobangi chiefs in which he agreed to pay blood money for the Bobangi deaths in the 1878 battle, thus ending the hostilities. It had taken nearly five years to negotiate safe passage down the Alima River, but in the end, Brazza's method of patient negotiations had paid off.

On October 15, 1883, the Bobangi signaled a new era of cooperation by delivering a large dugout canoe with a capacity of ten tons. The following day, Ballay set off down the Alima with a crew of fourteen men. Despite the agreement he had made with the Bobangi chiefs, he was greeted with fear and suspicion along the Alima, but the reception grew friendlier once he reached the Congo River, where Stanley had recently passed by on his way upstream to help found the station at Bangala. From the mouth of the Alima, Ballay sent a letter to Brazza warning him that when he descended the Alima, he should deny being "Tchougui," a nickname that the Bateke had given to Brazza. The name, which meant "the moon," had been bestowed on Brazza because he took nightly astrological observations. As Ballay wrote to Brazza, "You must absolutely deny that you are 'Tchougui' because the people want nothing to do with him."[22]

On November 20, the replacement boilers and the ashpan arrived at Diele, and the steamship *Ballay* could finally be put into working order. The *Ballay* was a tiny vessel, barely fifteen feet long, with the boilers and smokestack located toward the front, but it was still too big to travel easily on the Alima downstream from Diele because of rocks and other obstacles. Brazza therefore ordered Charles de Chavannes to travel downstream in canoes and build a station, a warehouse, and a wharf near the junction of the Alima and the Leketi, where the water was deeper and more tranquil. The Leketi station would be the embarkation point for steamboats traveling down the Alima to the Congo River and on to Malebo Pool.[23]

On February 18, 1884—nearly a year after Brazza had left France—he set off from the Leketi station to travel down the Alima in the *Ballay*, which was followed by canoes carrying men, merchandise, and supplies. The fleet then traveled down the Congo River to Chief Ngantsu's town, where Ballay had established the first French station on the Upper Congo River. From there, Brazza and his men began marching overland to Mbe. Upon reaching the village where Opoontaaba, the Makoko's prime minister, lived, Brazza sent word to the nearby Bateke capital that he sought an audience with the Makoko. He had come to return a countersigned copy of the treaty that Brazza and the Makoko had concluded four years earlier. The French delegation included Brazza, his brother Jacques (from Rome), Jacques's lifetime friend Attilio Pecile (also from Rome), and Charles de Chavannes, a lawyer from Lyon who served as Brazza's personal secretary. It was an odd French diplomatic delegation because three of the four delegates were more comfortable speaking in Italian than in French.

The next two days were spent in preparation for the ceremony. The Makoko covered his inner courtyard with an immense canopy of red cloth, red being the royal color. On the ground were lion skins for the Makoko to sit upon and leopard skins for the visiting French delegation. There were also cushions for the Makoko and his nine wives that contained charms to keep the person safe. When all was ready, Brazza and his party entered the courtyard preceded by a long line of porters carrying gifts for the Makoko—eight hundred yards of cloth, jewelry, mirrors, a harmonium, a music box, guns, powder, and salt—which were arrayed in the courtyard for all to admire.[24]

The details of the ceremony were recorded by Charles de Chavannes. When everybody was in place, the Makoko came out of his house with his entourage and walked slowly into the courtyard followed by his wives. He had a way of walking on tiptoes that seemed regal and slightly ethereal. After sitting down on his cushion, he rose up and shook Brazza's hand. Then he addressed the crowd in a call-and-response rhythm: "What I told you was true! Yes, it was true. Look at the man who was said to be lost! Look at the man who was said to be dead! Look at the man who was said to be poor! Look at the merchandise and gifts he brought! The people who said those things are liars!" The Makoko did not identify who those liars were, but his words clearly implied that his original treaty agreement with Brazza had created dissention among the Bateke lords and land chiefs. Now the Makoko was trying to use Brazza's visit to crush any further dissent.[25]

The gathering continued the next day, when Brazza returned to remit the countersigned treaty, which was in a crystal case along with letters bearing the seal of France and the signature of the French president. Looking over the assembled lords, dignitaries, and land chiefs, the Makoko sought to establish the fact that he was the supreme ruler of the Bateke Kingdom. He asked, "Who is the owner of the land?" and the crowd responded, "You are!" Libations were passed around for a period of ceremonial drinking and chanting that reminded Chavannes of a Catholic mass. When the chanting subsided, Brazza addressed the Makoko: "You said previously that you would give the French a tract of land [for a station], and that you would place yourself under their protection." The Makoko replied that he remembered making that promise in front of the assembled lords. Then Brazza said, "I carried your words to the great chief of the French, along with the paper on which you made your mark. He has accepted it and signed it in return. And here it is!" With that, Brazza held up the treaty for all to see.

It is worth pausing to reflect on Brazza's exact words as they were recounted by Chavannes in an amphitheater at the Sorbonne nearly fifty years later, with the president of France looking on. The words appear in quotation marks in the text of Chavannes's lecture, as if they were being quoted exactly as they were spoken. According to Chavannes, Brazza reminded the Makoko, "You said previously that you would give the French a piece of land [for a station], and that you would place yourself under their protection." If that is an accurate representation of what Brazza actually said, then he had left out the two most important features. The treaty that Brazza held in his hand called for the cession of a piece of land for a station, as he stated, but it also contained these words: "and makes, in addition, the cession of his territory to France, to whom he cedes his hereditary rights of supremacy." Those words were left out of Brazza's verbal summary. As a lawyer, Chavannes certainly understood the significance of phrases like "cession of his territory" and "cedes his hereditary sovereignty," and he would likely have remembered those phrases if Brazza had spoken them. The absence of those phrases in Chavannes's account raises doubts as to whether Brazza had ever made it clear that the Makoko was ceding all his territory and sovereignty to France.

Brazza's speech was followed by a strange ceremony to certify that the Makoko was really the sovereign over all the lands that he claimed. The king called up the territorial lords one by one and asked, "Who is the owner of the land?" Kneeling on one knee with head bowed, each lord made a promise of fidelity and homage and then answered, "You are!" Then the Makoko called the prime minister to come forward. He knelt before the Makoko with one knee to the ground and one hand touching the soil and listened to the question: "Who is the owner of the land?" He replied, "The land belongs to you. I am your 'wife' [i.e., subordinate partner], and if you die, it is I who will take your brass collar; not for myself, but in order to place it on the neck of the person I select as your successor." When Brazza asked for clarification about the territorial limits of the Makoko's authority, the lords confirmed that the king ruled the west bank of the Congo River from the Alima River in the north to the rapids of the Malebo Pool in the south. Beyond those boundaries, the lords explained, there were no real chiefs, and the people wandered around like sheep. It was a clear reference to the decentralized political systems found in the rainforest.

Then the Makoko began a rant against the Bateke chiefs in attendance who had secretly accepted gifts from Stanley or his agents. Chief Ngantsu was the primary target. Even though he had recently allowed the French to establish a station in his town along the Congo River, he was not completely trusted by the Makoko because he had earlier made the same offer to Stanley. During the ceremony, the Makoko harangued Ngantsu for his disloyalty. In response to an avalanche of criticism, the chief bowed his head and remained silent. In contrast, Ngaalio, who was the Makoko's tax collector at Malebo Pool, tried to defend himself against the Makoko's diatribe, but his shrill voice only brought him ridicule. In the end, he, too, fell silent. To finish the ceremony, Brazza solemnly presented the Makoko with the crystal case containing the treaty.[26]

Noting that Brazza had not yet built a station on the north bank of Malebo Pool, the Makoko promised him the right to build at Mfwa, the ivory-trading town that Stanley had been driven out of in 1880. The Makoko said that if the people of Mfwa would not give Brazza a piece of land, then he would take his magical charms and ritual objects and go with his followers to burn down all the Bateke villages on the north and south banks of Malebo Pool. To facilitate the negotiations at the Pool, the king ordered his prime minister to take Sergeant Malamine and four Senegalese marines overland to the Pool to prepare the way for Brazza, who would arrive by boat with his larger party.

Local events soon intervened to demonstrate that the power of the Makoko and the unity of the Bateke Kingdom that were on display during the ceremonies were largely illusory. A local land chief would not let the prime minister's delegation pass through his territory because, he claimed, the Makoko was in possession of one of his slaves. When the prime minister tried to negotiate a resolution, the chief demanded that the Makoko should come to his village and settle the matter personally. In order to secure safe passage for his delegation, the Makoko traveled to the village in his sedan chair, carried on the shoulders of four porters, to return the slave. The contrast between the ceremonies at Mbe that celebrated the Makoko's power over his appointed lords on the one hand and the refusal of a local Bateke land chief to let the Makoko's delegation pass through his territory on the other vividly illustrated the limits of the Makoko's authority. It also illustrated the vast gulf between spiritual authority, as exercised by the Makoko, and the political power of the land chiefs.

3

Mfwa, North Bank of Malebo Pool, April 29, 1884

Enthusiasm for the French at Malebo Pool had diminished considerably since Brazza had departed in October 1880 and the Senegalese sergeant Malamine had left in May 1882. When Father Augouard, the French Catholic missionary who had made an unsuccessful attempt to establish himself at Malebo Pool in July 1881, returned to the Pool in September 1883, he reported that French flags were nowhere to be seen and that nobody seemed to remember Brazza. Father Augouard tried to distribute the gifts that he had been asked to give out in Brazza's name, but the people refused them, saying that they would not accept gifts from someone they did not know. When he met with the chiefs at the ivory-trading town of Mfwa and tried to invoke the authority of the Makoko and Brazza, they laughed at him. Father Augouard concluded that the Makoko at Mbe "is a petty king such as you find every few steps in Africa, and I have not been able to learn exactly what has become of him."[27]

The town of Mfwa, which the Makoko had selected for Brazza's station, was the largest urban agglomeration on either bank of Malebo Pool. Like many trading towns along the Congo River, it was made up of a number of distinct villages, each with its own chief. Because it was a favored destination for ivory traders from the Upper Congo, visitors from a variety of ethnic groups wandered its streets. Ivory, beer, grain, gum copal, and pottery were for sale in open-air markets, and rifle volleys punctuated the daily calm whenever a new group of traders announced its arrival at the beach. Father Augouard found that the chiefs of Mfwa believed that he was an ivory trader. Although they authorized him to trade, they would not allow him to settle or build a Catholic mission. "The Blacks declare that they do not want any Whites to settle among them, and that we should quickly complete our ivory purchases and then leave immediately," he wrote to French navy commandant Cordier, whose gunship patrolled the mouth of the Congo River. "As for this precious French territory over which so much fuss has been made in the newspapers," he added, "it is simply a joke, and before the vote was taken all the Deputies and Senators should have been sent out to live for a month on roots and water."[28]

It was only because of King Leopold's hesitancy to antagonize the French that the International Association of the Congo had not already built a station at Mfwa. On December 21, 1882, Opoontaaba (the Makoko's prime minister) and his brother Ngaalio (the Makoko's tax collector at Malebo Pool) had signed a treaty with IAC agent Louis Valke, which stated that Opoontaaba was the sovereign chief of all the land between the Pool and the Nkeni River (which ran roughly parallel to the Alima River but was some sixty miles to the south of it). The territory indicated was smaller than the one specified in the Makoko Treaty that Brazza had signed at Mbe, which went all the way to the Alima. Article 1 of Valke's treaty stated that

Leopoldville Station at Malebo Pool, 1884 (from a photograph). Henry M. Stanley, *The Congo and the Founding of Its Free State*, vol. 2, p. 186.

Opoontaaba "recognizes the sovereignty" of the International Association of the Congo; article 2 gave the Association full rights to build stations, make roads, develop plantations, and exploit any products that they might discover in the territory; and article 4 excluded all commercial enterprises that were not authorized by the Association.[29]

Being ignorant of the Bateke custom that a prime minister could never succeed a Makoko, the IAC agents had been under the impression that Opoontaaba had ousted the Makoko and taken over the throne. "One thing Brazza does not know is that the Makoko has been dethroned," wrote Captain Hanssens on January 15, 1883, "and his successor won't hear of the French at any price. A new treaty has been concluded with Valke, and it is we who will have the right of occupation." King Leopold, however, wanted to move cautiously for fear of antagonizing the French government, and Stanley had earlier rejected the idea of establishing a station at Mfwa for the same reason.[30]

When Brazza arrived at Malebo Pool with Chavannes on April 29, 1884, the leadership of the IAC expedition was in flux. Stanley had departed for the Lower Congo and was on his way to Europe, leaving Capt. Seymour Saulez in charge of the Leopoldville Station and A. B. Swinburne in charge of the Kinshasa garrison. Stanley's contract with the IAC was ending, and he was being replaced by Francis de Winton, a retired British major general, who had not yet arrived at the Pool. All three IAC agents at the Pool were British.

Brazza and Chavannes not only planned to reestablish a French presence on the north bank of Malebo Pool, but they also hoped to gain a foothold on the south bank and possibly drive the IAC from Malebo Pool. The idea behind their plan first surfaced at Mbe during the ceremony of remitting the treaty to the Makoko. When Brazza was quizzing the Makoko about the boundaries of his territory, the Makoko reaffirmed his sovereignty over the north bank of the Pool but added that the Bateke chiefs on the south bank, including the chief of Kinshasa, were his vassals as well. Because the Makoko Treaty had already been ratified by the French government, Brazza believed that it would be relatively easy to expand its reach with some new agreements. In the competition between Brazza and King Leopold's International Association of the Congo, Brazza had a huge advantage because his actions were backed up by a major European nation, whereas the IAC was officially recognized by nobody, not even the Belgian government.

After receiving permission from the senior chief to build a French station at Mfwa, Brazza's party selected the site that would become Brazzaville and began clearing the forest. On May 14, several Zanzibari soldiers who worked for the IAC arrived by canoe with some gifts and a letter for Prime Minister Opoontaaba. Chavannes intercepted the letter and discovered that it was a copy of the treaty that Opoontaaba had signed with Lieutenant Valke in December 1882 giving the IAC sovereignty over the Makoko's territory. Now Opoontaaba's double dealings were out in the open. Brazza still wanted to execute his plan to reclaim French rights over the north bank and make claims to Kinshasa and other south bank chiefdoms, but to do that, he needed to confront the Makoko's prime minister.

On May 20, Chavannes crossed the Pool to deliver a letter to Captain Saulez, the IAC's chief of the Leopoldville Station, and caught up with him in Kinshasa. In a meeting that lasted for over three hours, Chavannes made two arguments. The first was that Opoontaaba was a mere representative of the Makoko who had no standing to sign away the Makoko's territory. Therefore, the treaty that Valke had signed with Opoontaaba had no validity whatsoever. Pushing further, he argued that the French could claim rights not only to the north bank, which had been ceded to them by the Makoko Treaty, but to the south bank as well because Chief Ntsuulu of Kinshasa (which was on the south bank) wore a copper collar, signifying that he was a vassal of the Makoko at Mbe. Copper collars, he claimed, were manufactured only by the blacksmiths at Mbe and bestowed by the Makoko upon his lords. Then Chavannes presented a written invitation to the two IAC agents, Saulez and Swinburne, to attend a meeting of Bateke chiefs to be held at Mfwa the next day and to observe the proceedings.

Brazza had arranged the meeting at Mfwa in order to demonstrate to all that Opoontaaba had no authority to sign away the territory and that the Makoko alone had authority over the north bank of Malebo Pool. IAC agents Saulez and Swinburn did not show up, but they sent two Zanzibari soldiers who spoke the Bateke language to observe and report. The meeting was attended mostly by chiefs from the north bank, but it also included Chief Ntsuulu from the south bank, who crossed over from Kinshasa against the objections of the IAC. At the meeting, Prime Minister Opoontaaba stood up and said, "All the land belongs to the Makoko. He has given it to the Commandant [i.e., Brazza] who represents the chief of the Fallha [i.e., French]. The whites on the other bank do not know this, and they have not come." Then Chief Ntsuulu from Kinshasa rose and said, "This land belongs to the Makoko; the land on the other bank belongs to the Makoko as well." Finally,

Opoontaaba stood up again and declared, "The Makoko is my chief. Chief Ntsuulu is my 'wife' [i.e., subordinate partner]. What I know for certain is that I delivered the chiefs of the right bank to the Commandant [i.e., Brazza], and today I deliver those of the left bank."[31]

The instrument for giving official recognition to those verbal declarations was a type of French legal document known as a procès-verbal, which was a certified account of what was said at a meeting. Chavannes, who was a lawyer, prepared the document, which paraphrased the statements of Prime Minister Opoontaaba and Chief Ntsuulu. The next step would be to take a copy of the procès-verbal to Captain Saulez and make a formal claim to Kinshasa and other south bank territories. Brazza assumed that Saulez would reject the claims, but by then the legal foundation to have the French claims recognized in the diplomatic chancelleries of Europe would have been laid. The point of the gathering at Mfwa was not so much to impress the local chiefs, who most likely understood that they were participating in a carefully choreographed performance, but to generate a procès-verbal that would impress the diplomats in Europe.

The day after the meeting, Brazza, Chavannes, and Sergeant Malamine crossed the river to Kinshasa in two canoes flying French flags. Their pretext was to make a courtesy visit to Chief Ntsuulu, who had come to their meeting at Mfwa the previous day, but the real purpose was to deliver a copy of the procès-verbal to Swinburne, the head of the IAC garrison at Kinshasa. After they landed at Kinshasa, Brazza, who was somewhat ill, was carried in a hammock to visit Chief Ntsuulu while Chavannes and Sergeant Malamine went to find Swinburne. What happened after that is difficult to determine because both Chavannes and Swinburne left contradictory accounts.[32]

When the two parties encountered each other near the riverbank, Chavannes said, Swinburne refused to agree to a formal discussion, whereas Swinburne wrote that he welcomed the visitors by passing around a bottle of brandy but that he could not discuss the meeting with the Bateke chiefs because political discussions should be held with Captain Saulez at Leopoldville. Chavannes wrote that the crowd became agitated because Chief Ntsuulu arrived with Brazza and started to shout, "The land belongs to the Makoko," whereas Swinburne's account mentions the two sons of Chief Subila (the chief of one of the component villages of Kinshasa) cursing Brazza and urging Swinburne to have nothing to do with the French. At some point the shouting degenerated into a melee during which somebody apparently punched Chavannes in the nose.

Writing forty-two years later, Chavannes claimed that he could still envisage the "outrageous threat" of that "brutal gesture." Swinburne's account, however, played down the incident and focused on what happened later, when Brazza demanded reparations. "I demand," said Brazza, "that you come to the village and sign a declaration to the effect that one of your men has struck the Secretary of the French Government." Swinburne said he replied, "I have enquired into it, but can find no one to corroborate your statement but yourself and Malamine. I beg to tell you once and for all that we do not recognize any flag but our own, nor do the native chiefs, and that the French flag has never yet fluttered here in Kinshasa and never will." Seeing that they would get no satisfaction, the French party returned to Mfwa after leaving a copy of the procès-verbal for Captain Saulez. The following day Brazza wrote a letter to Saulez saying that "I will consider any attack or insult directed against any chiefs relating to the Makoko as an insult or an attack on the French flag." Although Brazza's party was vastly outgunned by the Association's two garrisons of Zanzibari soldiers, he could nevertheless intimidate the Association agents because his flag represented the power and might of France, whereas the Association's flag represented nobody. Saulez did not want to give the French government a reason to send troops to Malebo Pool.

The row between the French and the Association was not sorted out until Francis de Winton arrived at Malebo Pool. On July 16,

1884, he wrote to Brazza, "I cannot and do not recognize your rights to claim any territory belonging to the Association. Whatever rights you may claim to your country on the north bank, they have always been recognized by the officers at the Association." Although that latter statement was not exactly true, it seemed to calm the situation, and the French thereafter confined themselves to the north bank while the Association stayed on the south bank.[33]

Brazza's ploy had nevertheless achieved its purpose. Brazza and Chavannes had never expected the Association to turn over its stations to the French. What they had gained instead was a procès-verbal of a meeting in which the Makoko's prime minister repeatedly asserted that the land on both banks of Malebo Pool belonged to the Makoko, thus placing it under the purview of the Makoko Treaty. When Chavannes, as Brazza's personal secretary, wrote the final report of the West African Mission two years later, he could point to their claims to the south bank of Malebo Pool as a bargaining chip that had been useful in negotiating a more advantageous delimitation of boundaries between the French government and King Leopold's International Association of the Congo. Like the treaties, the procès-verbal of the meeting at Mfwa had almost nothing to do with the Bateke chiefs; it was all for gaining leverage in the diplomatic meeting rooms of Europe.[34]

The rivalry between the French and the International Association of the Congo had exacerbated deep divisions among the high-ranking officials of the Bateke Kingdom. A few months after the meeting at Mfwa, Prime Minister Opoontaaba openly threatened a revolt against the Makoko, saying that he would cut off his head as well as the heads of Brazza and all the whites who came to his defense. In Kinshasa, Chief Ntsuulu, who supported the Makoko and Brazza, was openly opposed by Subila, a lesser chief who supported the Association. The reason that such a division could persist within a single Bateke town was that Chief Ntsuulu was a Bateke lord whose primary responsibility was the spiritual health of his territory. Chief Subila, on the other hand, was a land chief who had political authority over the day-to-day issues of governance and did not always follow the lead of the lords or the Makoko.[35]

The one person who could see clearly beyond the quarrels between the French and the Association was Prime Minister Opoontaaba. When Chavannes reproached him for accepting gifts from the Association, he replied, "I know well that one day or another the whites on the two banks of the Congo River who quarrel with each other today will end up by making an agreement on our backs. In the meantime, I will take from both sides." He later mused that if he killed the Makoko and was then killed in turn, it would make no difference, because the whites would soon have all the land. Although the Makoko was considered the pope of the Bateke, it was his prime minister, Opoontaaba, who would prove to be the true prophet.[36]

4

Stanley Falls, November 25, 1883

Meanwhile. a second flash point was developing a thousand miles up the Congo River at Boyoma Falls, a series of seven waterfalls along a sixty-two-mile curve of the Lualaba River that Henry Morton Stanley had named Stanley Falls during his descent of the river in 1876–1877. He had picked the seventh cataract as the dividing line where the river changed its name from the Lualaba to the Congo. Stanley did not give the seventh cataract a distinct name, but Tippu Tip referred to it by the English term "Stanley Falls" in his Swahili writings. To minimize confusion, this book will henceforth refer to the seventh cataract as Stanley Falls, while the entire group of seven cataracts will be called Boyoma Falls. Located half a degree north of the equator and roughly a thousand miles from either coast, Stanley Falls is literally in the center of the African continent. The IAC's main rival for control of Stanley Falls was not another European power but a group of Arab and Swahili merchants who were affiliated with Tippu Tip.[37]

Back in November 1883, when Stanley was traveling toward the falls with his fleet of three steamboats to establish the Stanley Falls Station, he had seen an immense flotilla of perhaps a thousand dugout canoes coming toward him. It looked like a moving city. Knowing that he was in the region where he had fought the bulk of his "thirty-two battles" during his original descent of the Congo River, he braced for an attack, but the canoes passed by peacefully and continued downstream. The next day he passed a series of villages that had been reduced to charred heaps and saw canoes planted upright along the riverbank like hollow columns that stood as monuments to the victors. When the villagers told him that they had been attacked at night by strangers who had killed the men and carried off the women and children, Stanley realized that the people in the canoes were refugees.

As he continued up the river, he periodically encountered large fleets of two hundred to three hundred canoes fleeing downstream. Having never before encountered this mode of warfare in equatorial Africa, he began to suspect that the marauders were Arab slave and ivory traders. Stanley's suspicions were confirmed on November 27 when he spotted a large Arab camp with white tents and a fleet of dugout canoes. As his steamboats approached the camp, they were greeted in Swahili, the language of the East African coast, and invited to land near the camp. Soon Stanley's Zanzibari soldiers were shaking hands with the raiding party and speaking with them in Swahili while Stanley, who was fluent in Swahili himself, exchanged gifts with their commanders.

The raiding party that Stanley encountered consisted of three hundred men armed with flintlocks, double-barreled percussion guns, and a few breech-loading rifles, who were accompanied by a roughly equal number of women, followers, and domestic slaves. They were commanded by Kibonge and Karema, two traders in the employ of Abed bin Salim (a.k.a. Tanganyika), who was one of the two biggest Arab traders established in Nyangwe. His employee Kibonge, whose full name was Hamadi bin Ali, was originally from the Comoro Islands off the coast of East Africa. He had been in the employ of Tippu Tip back in 1876, when Stanley and Tippu Tip had traveled up the Lualaba River together. In his book *Through the Dark Continent*, Stanley had described him as "a half-caste man of sturdy form and resolute appearance." Now in the employ of Abed bin Salim, his base of operations was the town of Kirundu, approximately one hundred miles up the Lualaba from the first cataract of Boyoma Falls. The other commander, Karema, had established a camp on the Isle of Katukama, a short distance downstream from the seventh cataract.[38]

Stanley referred to the raiders as "Arabs" because the party had been sent out by Abed bin Salim, but its soldiers were more accurately referred to as *waungwana*, a Swahili term with a complex history. In Zanzibar in the early nineteenth century, the term had referred to locally born freemen (as opposed to slaves or Arabs), but with the influx of slaves into Zanzibar during the nineteenth century, the term began to be applied to the armed slaves and trusted personal assistants of the Arab and Swahili slaveholders. As the ivory trade routes expanded into Manyema in the 1870s, the waungwana who had originally come out from Zanzibar with the trade caravans began to be outnumbered by locally born waungwana who were selected from among the young boys captured in raids. One example of this phenomenon was Hamisi, a young boy who carried Tippu Tip's spare rifle and extra cartridges during battles. Before reaching the age of fifteen, he had traveled with Tippu Tip to Zanzibar, where he had seen the Indian Ocean, the big steamships, and even the sultan.[39]

By the 1880s, a distinct group of Manyema waungwana had emerged. They were usually circumcised, wore whatever Arab-style clothes their meager resources allowed, and knew some of the rudiments of Islam, including which animals were considered unclean. They also learned to speak a distinct Manyema dialect of Swahili that became known as *kingwana*—the language of the waungwana. Such traits set the waungwana apart from ordinary African villagers and townsmen but did not afford them full entry into the select circles of Arab and Swahili traders. In the larger social structure of Manyema, the waungwana formed the intermediate class between the Arab and Swahili merchants on the one hand and the local villagers on the other.

In a letter that Abed bin Salim wrote to the sultan of Zanzibar in May 1884 (six months after Stanley's encounter with Kibonge), he explained that waungwana raiding parties such as the one Stanley had encountered were the avant-garde of Arab expansion beyond Stanley Falls. "Your servant Hamadi [a.k.a. Kibonge] with 400 men went on a journey following the *waungwana*," he wrote, "and they met Stanley, the English American. There was likely to be a clash, but Stanley knew them and they joined together and remained about two days." The letter clearly indicates that the waungwana had led the way and the Arab and Swahili traders had followed in their footsteps. It is also noteworthy that he referred to Kibonge as a servant of the sultan of Zanzibar, thus placing his slaving activities under the sultan's authority.[40]

After spending several hours listening to the stories told by the raiding party, Stanley learned that they had set out sixteen months earlier and had been raiding in the territory downstream from Stanley Falls for about eleven months. Their strategy was to approach a riverside village at night by canoe, surround it, and torch the houses while aiming volleys of musket fire at the fleeing inhabitants. Many of the women and children captured in the raids were then ransomed for ivory that was kept hidden in the forest. After one raid, eighty-five people were ransomed in a single day. Stanley learned that this was the third year in a row that raiding parties organized by Abed bin Salim had ventured below the falls. The raids had netted eight hundred captives and one thousand tusks of ivory in 1881; two thousand captives and fifteen hundred tusks of ivory in 1882; and thirteen hundred captives and twenty-five hundred tusks of ivory in 1883. Over a period of three years, they had destroyed 118 villages on both banks of the Congo River.[41]

In the afternoon, Stanley went to visit the stockade where the captives were held. Inside the enclosure was a series of low sheds extending many rows deep that were crowded with women and children. Those over ten years old were tethered by iron rings around their necks that were linked together by chains, whereas the children were secured by copper rings around their legs. There was not a single adult man to be seen. The ivory was destined for the markets of Zanzibar, but most of the captives would be sent to Manyema to work as agricultural laborers or domestic servants in the growing Arab towns such as Kasongo, Nyangwe, and Kirundu. Many of the boys would be selected to become waungwana and trained as soldiers and porters. The distinctive Manyema pattern of raiding and enslavement observed by Stanley would be noticed by others as well. Capt. W. G. Stairs later noted that "the Arabs attack and capture a village, kill the grown-up men, and make prisoners of all the boys, girls, and women they can; these they carry on with them on their marches, selling the women where they can for ivory and bringing up the boys for raiders and the girls for their harems."[42]

Kibonge and Karema seemed amenable to Stanley's proposal to establish an IAC station at Stanley Falls that would purchase their ivory. They complained about the high prices of the goods that came from the East African coast by way of Ujiji and promised Stanley that they would become the best customers of any European merchants who set up shop at the Stanley Falls Station. Predicting that trading towns such as Nyangwe, Kasongo, Kabambare, and perhaps even Ujiji would get their supplies and trade goods from Stanley Falls in the future, they entertained the fantasy that Stanley Falls could become a second Zanzibar: a great emporium in the heart of Africa where goods from all over the world could be purchased. To aid Stanley in building his station, Kibonge and

Karema provided him with an Arab guide and interpreter who spoke the language of the Genya fishermen at Stanley Falls.

After continuing on to Stanley Falls, gaining permission to build a station, and leaving a small garrison on Wana Rusari Island, Stanley began his return trip to Malebo Pool. He found that the Arab camp had moved downstream since his previous visit, a sure indication that they were not yet establishing permanent settlements downstream from Stanley Falls. During further discussions of the ivory trade with Kinbonge and Karema, he made an agreement to take ten waungwana agents with twenty-nine tusks of ivory to Malebo Pool on his steamboats in order to show them the comparative ease of travel to the Atlantic coast and the range of trade goods that they could obtain for their ivory. After arriving at the Pool and selling their ivory, the ten waungwana traveled along the wagon road to Vivi and then by steamboat to Banana Point, where the river emptied into the Atlantic Ocean. Knowing that the European trading companies carried only the types of goods that were in demand along the Lower Congo, Stanley sent King Leopold an order for a list of articles preferred by the Arabs.[43]

Because the International Association of the Congo and the Arabs were talking about becoming trading partners, Andrew Bennie, the chief of the Stanley Falls Station, would enjoy excellent relations with Karema and Kibonge. In late December 1883, Karema visited the station three days in a row while on his way back to Nyangwe, and he left a sick soldier in the care of Bennie. In April 1884, Bennie traveled 160 miles up the Lualaba River to visit Kibonge at his base of operations in Kirundu. On June 27, some Arabs from Nyangwe arrived at the Stanley Falls Station bringing letters from Abed bin Salim (a.k.a. Tanganyika). "If Stanley comes to the station, salute him on the part of Tanganyika, who cannot come in person to greet him," he wrote, referring to himself in the third person. "Perhaps Kibonge will go to greet him because he wishes to see him. All is well at Nyangwe. Keep an eye on the waungwana; if they steal, send them away and they will never be allowed to return to the Falls." There was also a letter from Karema, who said that he was staying at Kirundu for a while but was sending Bennie a domesticated gorilla as a gift.[44]

Even though his advanced age made it difficult for Abed bin Salim to travel to Stanley Falls, he was reorienting his trade toward the Atlantic coast. In 1884, he started to move his entire store of ivory—about a thousand tusks—toward the Stanley Falls Station because he had been offered a very high price and told that the payment could be remitted directly to Muscat, the capital of Oman, thereby keeping it safe from his Zanzibari creditors. In keeping with his new west coast orientation, Abed's men began flying the International Association of the Congo's flag at various locations between Boyoma Falls and Nyangwe. Other Arab traders, however, saw Abed's move as treason and forced him to take down the Association flag, hoisting the flag of the sultan of Zanzibar in its place. Feeling the pressure, Abed wrote a letter to the sultan in which he reiterated his loyalty and claimed that he had made it clear to Stanley that Boyoma Falls belonged to the sultan. But he also tried to justify his ivory sales to Stanley by claiming that Europe was only forty-five days away from Stanley Falls by water, whereas Zanzibar was six months away by land.[45]

When the sultan of Zanzibar learned that Abed bin Salim's men had sent twenty-nine tusks down the Congo River to the Atlantic Ocean with Stanley, he felt betrayed. He reckoned that the loss of Abed bin Salim's ivory alone would deprive him of £7,000 of customs revenues. He told the French consul that he had aided King Leopold's various International African Association projects for seven years, and now Leopold was trying to encroach upon his richest territory. Having no army of his own in the interior, the sultan depended on Tippu Tip to make sure that all the ivory from Manyema and Stanley Falls would be sold in Zanzibar. "I have learned that the Sultan of Zanzibar provided rapid-firing arms to Tippu Tip with a mission to oppose the establishment of Europeans on the Upper Congo," wrote Ernest Cambier, the IAA's agent in Zanzibar. A similar view was expounded by John Kirk, the British consul in Zanzibar. "Tippu Tip has reached Manyema," he wrote to the British foreign secretary in October 1884. "There is reason to think that besides being a private trader, he is commissioned by the Sultan to watch over Zanzibar's interests and has with him a force of over a thousand guns, sufficient to make his order obeyed." Both Cambier and Kirk understood that the biggest threat to the International Association of the Congo's plans came not from the west but from the east.[46]

5

Wana Sirunga Island, Stanley Falls, December 13, 1884

When Tippu Tip returned to Nyangwe from Zanzibar on May 31, 1884, one of his first tasks was to sternly rebuke Abed bin Salim for selling ivory to the International Association of the Congo and for flying the IAC flag along the Lualaba River. "When he knew he had disobeyed," wrote Tippu Tip to the sultan, "he was sorry." Tippu Tip did not hurry to Stanley Falls but instead sent his son Mwinyi Amani to establish his presence there and prevent any Arabs from selling ivory to the IAC. In the meantime, Tippu Tip was busy restoring his control over his Manyema empire. After spending three months fighting in the region between the Lualaba and the Lomami, where he had traded after separating from Stanley in 1876, he appointed a young armed slave named Ngongo Luteta to oversee the region. Tippu Tip had nothing but the highest praise for Ngongo. "I have never encountered a slave as faithful as Ngongo was toward me," he wrote in his autobiography. "He turned over everything that he acquired to me. I could put him in charge of all my affairs and leave him to exercise his authority over this country." Tippu Tip would later have to reconsider those words.[47]

Tippu Tip then moved south toward the copper mines of Katanga, where he purchased copper at the rate of five pounds of copper for one pound of beads. As he had done before, he would then trade the copper for ivory. "Everywhere I passed, the inhabitants were my loyal subjects," wrote Tippu Tip. In writing that passage, he provided a rare glimpse into the structure of his empire. In the areas that had submitted to his rule, he collected ivory as tribute, and so no trading caravans were required. As more and more territory fell under his control, independent traders such as Abed bin Salim in Nyangwe were forced to seek ivory in new regions that lay beyond Tippu Tip's grasp. That is why the ivory frontier continued to advance toward the Atlantic coast.

On July 3, 1884, a steamboat carrying the ten waungwana agents who had earlier gone downstream with Stanley arrived back at the Stanley Falls Station with the trade goods they had obtained for their ivory. It also brought Arvid-Mauritz Wester, a Swedish lieutenant in the employ of the IAC, to take command of the station. Wester continued Bennie's policy of cultivating good relations with the Arab traders, and on October 18, 1884, he signed a treaty with Tippu Tip's son Mwinyi Amani, who was considered the chief of the Arabs at Stanley Falls. The treaty defined a north-south line at the seventh cataract that divided the Arab territory from the Association's territory. The treaty, which was written in English, stated, "Moni Amani has promised that never an Arab will come in the river below the seventh cataract of Stanley or in any other territory belonging to the Upper Congo Study Committee for fighting, making trade, catching slaves, goats, or chickens." One can question why Mwinyi Amani agreed to sign the treaty, given that his forces could have wiped out the Stanley Falls Station at any time, but the line at the seventh cataract established by the treaty not only kept the Arabs from moving downstream but also kept the IAC from moving upstream toward Nyangwe. The treaty thus created a temporary truce while both sides consolidated their positions.[48]

Tippu Tip arrived at Stanley Falls on December 13, 1884, and set up his camp on Wana Sirunga Island, where his son had settled in October. The island was five hundred meters above the seventh cataract and within sight of Wana Rusari Island, which housed the IAC station. Although the seventh cataract stretched most of the way across the river, it was interrupted by the tip of Wana Rusari Island. Therefore canoes could pass between the Stanley Falls Station and Tippu Tip's island without traversing the waterfall.[49]

When agent Wester heard a rumor that Tippu Tip was planning to breach the seventh cataract and travel down the Congo River, he paid a visit to Tippu Tip's island in an attempt to dissuade him. Tippu Tip told Wester that he had been sent by the sultan of Zanzibar to prevent the Arab and Swahili traders from selling ivory to the Europeans. When Wester tried to convince him of the advantages of selling his ivory by the Atlantic route, Tippu Tip replied that he was aware of the information brought back by the ten waungwana agents, but his orders from the sultan required that all ivory should go to Zanzibar. When Wester mentioned the treaty he had signed with Tippu Tip's son, Tippu Tip dismissed it, saying that Amani did not have the authority to sign treaties on his behalf.

Tippu Tip then proposed that Wester should abandon the station and return down the river with his Hausa and Zanzibari soldiers. He even offered to provide canoes and paddlers to transport the supplies and soldiers down the river. Wester refused, saying that he would rather die than abandon his post. Tippu Tip replied that he would fight if he were prevented from going down the Congo River. The next day Tippu Tip sent seventy-six dugout canoes manned by over seven hundred men to parade past the IAC station. The purpose was clearly to intimidate Wester by showing him what he was up against. Wester had only twenty-eight Hausa and Zanzibari soldiers, and he feared that the Zanzibaris would refuse to fight against a fellow Zanzibari like Tippu Tip. He calculated that there were about three hundred troops in all the Association stations on the Upper Congo that could be called in, but they would be hopelessly outnumbered and outgunned. Three days after the parade of canoes, Tippu Tip paid a visit to the Stanley Falls Station, arriving with a large entourage. He promised Wester that he would not attack the station or any of the villages that flew the Association flag, provided that the Association did not interfere with the activities of the Arab traders. Being in a weak position, Wester had no choice but to agree.[50]

When the British missionary George Grenfell arrived at Stanley Falls just before Christmas 1884, it was clear that the former treaty between Wester and Mwinyi Amani was dead. "We saw the famous Tippu Tip at Stanley Falls," wrote Grenfell. "He had 300 men with him and had sent another 700 down river trading (rather 'raiding,' for we counted twenty burnt villages and thousands of fugitive canoes). He says he has 2,000 more men coming, and talks of making his way down to the Atlantic—says the Sultan of Zanzibar claims all the Congo right down to the sea. Tippu Tip is without doubt the master, at the present moment, of the Upper Congo River."

A detailed description of one of Tippu Tip's raiding parties was given by Lt. Alphonse Vangele, who arrived a month later with a fleet of three steamboats bringing supplies. Arriving at the mouth of the Aruwimi River, some 140 miles below Stanley Falls, he spotted an Arab camp containing two hundred men and forty dugout canoes. After landing at the camp, he was welcomed by Salim bin Muhammad, one of Tippu Tip's top lieutenants. Some people have claimed that Salim was Tippu Tip's cousin, while others claimed that he was Tippu Tip's brother-in-law, but in either case, he was close to Tippu Tip. Salim spoke English very well. He had been to London and was familiar with its sights, such as Hyde Park and Marble Arch. One European who met him described him as "one of the nicest of all Arabs; a gentleman down to the soles of his feet," while another reported that "he invited me to partake of his dinner or midday breakfast more than once, and these little *dejeuners sans fourchette* were among the most agreeable of my experiences during my stay in Africa."[51]

In addition to his charm and his kindness to Europeans, Salim bin Muhammad was the organizer of deadly raids on Basoko

villages along the Aruwimi River. The Aruwimi region was devastated: banana plants had been cut down and houses destroyed,
and there was not a villager in sight. Vangele learned that there was
another Arab camp with two hundred fighters at the mouth of the
Lomami (eighty miles below the falls) and a force of three hundred men fighting between the Lomami and the Lualaba Rivers.
As Vangele continued to steam toward Stanley Falls, he wrote, "All
the countries have been devastated. The natives who resisted were
massacred; the people who are still free fled into the forest or live
precariously on the water in their canoes. The Arab camps overflow
with chained-up captives, mainly women and children, most of
whom are dying of starvation. They serve as ransom for obtaining
ivory and men to transport it to the coast."[52]

Shortly after Vangele's steamboats arrived at the Stanley Falls
Station, Tippu Tip appeared in person to invite him to visit. Arriving at Tippu Tip's island the next day, Vangele, Captain Wester,
and a Swedish traveler named Edvard Gleerup observed that Tippu
Tip had three hundred slaves armed with rapid-fire rifles and that
fifty of the strongest made up his personal bodyguard. He had
about twenty wives with him who originated from all parts of East
Africa. Tippu Tip questioned Vangele about the state of relations
in Europe between the Belgians, the English, the French, the Germans, and the Italians, and he told them of his desire to make a
trip to Europe and visit King Leopold II. Soon the talk turned
to Africa. Vangele mentioned that the Association had concluded
treaties with all the important chiefs between Banana Point (on
the Atlantic coast) and Stanley Falls and that it now claimed sovereignty over all those territories. Tippu Tip responded that all
of equatorial Africa from Zanzibar to Banana Point belonged to
the sultan of Zanzibar and that he, Tippu Tip, had been sent out
as the sultan's envoy to report on the state of affairs in this sector of
the sultan's domains.[53]

Then the conversation turned to more immediate matters.
Tippu Tip said he had been astonished and angered when told that

he could not travel below the seventh cataract, especially after he had helped so many European explorers on their journeys and had taken heavy criticism from his fellow Muslims for helping Christian travelers. Now he was being told that he could not go down the Congo River to trade. Vangele replied that Tippu Tip was free to trade anywhere he liked but that the region between Stanley Falls and the Aruwimi had been devastated by Arab trading parties. Not a single village was still standing, the populations had fled, and there was no food to be purchased. Tippu Tip replied that he ordered his trading parties to avoid fighting, but the orders were not always obeyed. The main problem, he said, was that the local villagers often refused to sell them food, forcing them to follow the example of Stanley and simply seize the food they needed.

Having staked out their respective positions, the two parties were ready for negotiations. Tippu Tip promised to recall the seven hundred men he had operating downstream from Stanley Falls. Tacitly admitting that his trading parties had been supplied with guns but not trade goods, he promised to send a caravan to his headquarters at Kasongo to bring up sufficient supplies of merchandise. In return, he asked the Association to convince the villagers to engage in regular trade with Tippu Tip's trading parties. Vangele replied that because the region had been massively disturbed by Tippu Tip's raiding parties, it was best to wait until life returned to normal before beginning regular trade.

Sensing an opportunity to make a larger point, Vangele added that he was eager to normalize trade in the region because soon there would be a railroad running between the Atlantic coast and Malebo Pool, which would allow goods to travel from Europe to Stanley Falls in about two months. Tippu Tip was not interested. He had earlier rebuked Abed bin Salim for selling ivory to Stanley, and he remained loyal to the sultan of Zanzibar. "I must tell you," he said to Vangele, "that the Sultan of Zanzibar does not want any more Arabs sending their ivory down the Congo River." Before they parted, Vangele tried one more time to promote an alliance with Tippu Tip. "Unite with us and you can become completely independent from Zanzibar," he said. Tippu Tip did not reply.

Vangele left Stanley Falls three days later with his three steamboats to return to the Equator Station. Arriving at the mouth of the Aruwimi River, he again visited the camp of Salim bin Muhammad. Salim confirmed that he had received orders from Tippu Tip to vacate the region and promised that he would be gone in two days. Vangele wanted to stay to make sure that Salim left on time, but the scarcity of food in the devastated region forced him to continue on. As he steamed away, Vangele learned from his Zanzibari soldiers that the Arabs had originally planned to continue raiding downstream as far as Mobeka, some four hundred miles below Stanley Falls and just upstream from the Association's Bangala Station. However, the recall order from Tippu Tip had forced them to change their plans.[54]

During his time at Stanley Falls, Tippu Tip had sent out twenty caravans to trade and raid for ivory. One of them was massacred and returned empty-handed, but the others brought in a total of two thousand frasila (thirty-five tons) of ivory. Because Tippu Tip remained loyal to the sultan of Zanzibar, he needed to carry all that ivory to Zanzibar, a distance of 1,081 miles as the crow flies and much farther by the winding caravan trails. The Swede Edvard Gleerup, who was assisting the IAC at the Stanley Falls Station, traveled to Nyangwe with one of Tippu Tip's ivory caravans in January 1885 and was able to observe the Arab transportation network. The group followed a land route around the seven cataracts of Boyoma Falls to Kibonge's town, where the Arabs had built a transit station with warehouses for goods and supplies. Continuing down the river by canoe, they stopped at a series of way stations that had been set up for feeding and provisioning the trading parties. He reported that armed bands sometimes moved out from those stations to carry out "plunder, massacres, and slave raids" in the interior. From Gleerup's description, it seems that the transportation infrastructure the Arabs were building between Nyangwe and

Stanley Falls was similar in concept to what Brazza had built along the Ogowe and what Stanley had built along the Lower Congo. The only thing missing was the steamboats.[55]

Gleerup described Nyangwe as having ten thousand inhabitants, which was an astonishing number when compared to a few hundred when Livingstone was there in 1871. The rapid growth was due to the influx of captives. Nyangwe was surrounded by plantations worked by slaves and fruit trees brought in from the East African coast. The Arabs had introduced cattle and had donkeys that could be ridden with saddles. From Nyangwe, Gleerup went to Kasongo, Tippu Tip's headquarters, where he was welcomed by one of Tippu Tip's sons. Kasongo had innumerable banana plants and all the fruits and vegetables that one could find in the markets of Zanzibar. Cattle, sheep, and goats were numerous. It is clear from Gleerup's descriptions that Kasongo and Nyangwe were no longer the frontier towns that had been visited earlier by Livingstone and Stanley but had grown into large and prosperous urban centers surrounded by plantations worked by thousands of slaves.[56]

Even with the improved transportation infrastructure, Tippu Tip still had to solve the problem of porters. Although the common myth that the ivory traders enslaved people and forced them to carry ivory to the coast was not accurate in respect to the region between the coast and Ujiji where Nyamwezi and other professional porters were available for hire, it was apparently valid for the region between Stanley Falls and Ujiji. Professional porters were rare at Stanley Falls and throughout Manyema, causing Tippu Tip to rely on enslaved porters who would be sold at the end of the journey. That practice brought heavy criticism from IAC agents, who accused him of launching raids to obtain porters. In response, Tippu Tip devised a new system of caravan transportation. Instead of a single caravan that carried the ivory all the way from Stanley Falls to Zanzibar, he created a system that relied on a series of caravans that operated in relay fashion. One caravan went back and forth between Stanley Falls and Nyangwe, and another traveled back and forth between Nyangwe and Ujiji. What made the new system different from the previous one was that even though the porters were slaves, they would not be sold at the end of the voyage. Once the caravan reached Ujiji and Tabora, it was possible to hire professional porters, although some enslaved porters were apparently used there as well.[57]

It was not until December 1885 that Wester succeeded in signing a treaty with Tippu Tip at Stanley Falls. The document stated that Tippu Tip would not interfere with the white men at the Stanley Falls Station and that both Arabs and whites could trade with the people of the Stanley Falls district, as long as the people were treated humanely. To seal the deal, Wester gave Tippu Tip two tusks from an elephant he had killed with his own gun, and Tippu Tip gave Wester a cow, along with several sheep and goats. An addendum written in Arabic characters stated that Tippu Tip, the Arabs, and their followers had no intention of attacking the local people and that Wester and his men should not attack them either. However, they demanded one exception: they vowed to take vengeance on the Basoko people who had massacred one of their trading parties. Wester accepted the conditions because he knew that he was in a weak bargaining position—Tippu Tip's soldiers could easily wipe out all of the IAC and French stations between Stanley Falls and the mouth of the Congo River if they chose to do so. Under the circumstances, the treaty was better than nothing.[58]

Back in Brussels, King Leopold was pursuing a carrot-and-stick strategy for dealing with Tippu Tip. Following the recommendation of Vangele, who returned to Brussels in 1885, shortly after his encounter with Tippu Tip, the king authorized a hundred Hausa soldiers and two Krupp guns to be sent to the Stanley Falls Station because it was rumored that Tippu Tip was afraid of the Krupps. The carrot included a potential trading partnership and an invitation to visit King Leopold in Belgium. The king would arrange transportation for Tippu Tip and his entourage down the Congo River and on to Belgium by the Atlantic route.

Tippu Tip confessed to being flattered by the invitation, but it put him in a quandary because he had just received letters from the sultan of Zanzibar asking when he would drive the Europeans from Stanley Falls and move down the Congo River. Even though Tippu Tip had enough guns and fighters to accomplish the task, he replied that he could not do anything until the sultan sent him more soldiers and arms from the east coast. Not eager to go to war against the Europeans, he was playing for time because he doubted that the sultan had the capacity to raise an army and send it all the way to Stanley Falls. In fact, the sultan had already sent out a caravan with an enormous quantity of gunpowder and ammunition to supply Tippu Tip, but it had become bogged down between Tabora and Ujiji because of the general state of unrest in the region following the death of the Nyamwezi chief Mirambo. The very existence of the munitions caravan showed that the sultan was deadly serious.[59]

In Zanzibar, the British consul John Kirk was convinced that Tippu Tip would ultimately ally himself with the Europeans against the sultan. "I know of Tippu Tip," wrote Kirk to the Foreign Office in July 1885. "I do not think it probable he would take a part in any attack upon Europeans. On the contrary, I think he personally would be very pleased to trade in ivory with the merchants from the West Coast. The only one to suffer loss would be the Sultan, but as he has done nothing to keep the road to the east coast open, he has no right to complain that traders find a cheaper route." But Tippu Tip, for all his wanderings in equatorial Africa, had always dreamed of retiring someday to the life of a gentleman on the island of Zanzibar, where most of his considerable wealth was stored or invested. Betraying the sultan of Zanzibar might bring him immediate profits, but it would destroy his long-run plans. So when Tippu Tip received a letter from Sultan Said Barghash calling him back to Zanzibar for consultation, he heeded the call. In April 1886, he left Stanley Falls for Nyangwe, where he picked up sixteen tons of ivory to transport to Ujiji, Tabora, and on to Zanzibar.[60]

When Tippu Tip arrived in Zanzibar, he would discover that the equatorial regions of Africa were no longer his for the taking. Instead, they were being divided up among the European powers from the Atlantic to the Indian Ocean. As a result, the political and economic environments that had given rise to his Manyema Empire had irrevocably changed. Those cataclysmic changes were not the result of activities or conflicts in equatorial Africa itself. Instead, they emerged from intense diplomatic maneuvering in Europe and the United States that was grounded in the treaties collected by Brazza's West African Mission and the International Association of the Congo.

CHAPTER 6

CREATING THE CONGOS

U P UNTIL APRIL 1883, KING Leopold II had remained focused on his idea of using treaties with African chiefs to form a "free state" that would be capable of supporting a large European trading company. "Opinion in Europe and America is sympathetic to the project of the [Upper Congo Study] Committee," he wrote in a memo to his administrative aide Colonel Strauch, using the original name of the International Association of the Congo. "We must take advantage of that to act energetically in Africa and obtain the most concessions possible from the chiefs." The goal, Leopold explained, was "to unite them into a vast Indigenous Independent State. Such an Independent State is necessary to provide confidence and security for commerce, and it must be very vast to allow the formation of a great company to exploit its natural products." Realizing that such a state would be highly irregular in the existing international order, the king noted that "there are numerous examples of states founded by individuals without an official mission. A state does not need an official delegation, but for it to exist, it must possess the soil and exercise power over it."[1]

Leopold knew that the success of his Congo Free State would require recognition of its status by other European powers. Stanley brought up that point repeatedly. "I frankly tell you that despite the comparatively strong position of the Association on the Congo, any energetic officer of Portugal or France is stronger with fifty men than we with a thousand," he wrote to King Leopold. "Why? Because we do not understand whether we have the right to resist any aggressive act by Portugal or France by force of arms. Should we do so, what power will uphold us or sympathize with us?" He added, "So long as our status and character are not recognized by European governments, De Brazza with his walking stick, a French flag, and a few words in the presence of the whites of Leopoldville is really stronger than Stanley with his Krupp guns and all material of war, faithful adherents, aid of natives, etc., etc." Stanley even attributed his lack of action against the Arab slave traders at Stanley Falls to the fact that he represented a philanthropic organization that was not backed by a powerful European state.[2]

King Leopold was well aware that his International Association of the Congo, as it was then called, was not recognized by any European state—not even Belgium. He knew that France had made substantial claims on the resources and trade of equatorial Africa (although no other European nation had yet recognized them) and that Portugal was preparing to make similar claims with the backing of Britain. He accordingly devised a two-pronged strategy: first, to prevent other powers from recognizing French or Portuguese claims to the Congo River basin; and second, to persuade one or more of the great powers to recognize his proposed free state. While the scramble to sign treaties with chiefs was accelerating in the Congo River basin, a parallel battle for international legitimacy and recognition was developing in Europe and America.

1

House of Commons, London, April 3, 1883

Jacob Bright, the MP from Manchester, stood up in the House of Commons on April 3, 1883, to introduce a resolution proclaiming that "no treaty should be made by Her Majesty's government that would sanction the annexation by any Power of territories on or adjacent to the Congo." The resolution was aimed squarely at blocking the British Foreign Office's plans to recognize Portugal's jurisdiction over the mouth of the Congo River. Although the Portuguese had been trading along the Congo River estuary below Yellala Falls for nearly four hundred years, they had not made a serious effort to claim jurisdiction over the river until 1876, when they opened negotiations on the issue with Britain. Those negotiations had dragged on inconclusively for five years until the British foreign secretary, Earl Granville, ended them in April 1881. "It would not be desirable to take any steps at the present time in regard to the Congo Question," wrote Granville.[3]

The situation changed in November 1882, when it appeared that Brazza's Makoko Treaty would soon be ratified by the French parliament. In response to the French threat, the Portuguese foreign minister sought to reopen the negotiations with Britain, sending a long letter to the British Foreign Office that arrived on the very day the French parliament ratified the Makoko Treaty. Although the British had no interest in claiming the mouth of the Congo River for themselves (as demonstrated by their previous rejection of Verney Lovett Cameron's treaties with local chiefs), they believed that they could block the French by putting the river under the jurisdiction of Portugal, a reliable ally at the time.[4]

On December 15, Earl Granville proposed a short treaty of six articles. Article 1 gave Portugal jurisdiction over the Atlantic coast between 5°12′ and 8° south latitude, with no mention of how far inland the jurisdiction penetrated. That stretch of coast included the mouth of the Congo River, which was located at 6°1′ south latitude. Article 2 guaranteed freedom of navigation on the Congo River for all nations and prohibited monopolies or exclusive concessions. Articles 3, 4, and 5 dealt with tariffs, the rights of British subjects residing in the territory, and suppressing the slave trade. On December 26, the Portuguese foreign minister responded with counterproposals, and the negotiations were underway. By the beginning of April 1883, when Jacob Bright introduced his resolution of opposition in the House of Commons, it appeared that agreement on a draft treaty was imminent.[5]

King Leopold's International Association of the Congo (IAC) was not a party to the negotiations, even though it possessed stations along the Lower Congo River and had signed numerous treaties with local chiefs. Writing to the British Foreign Office in February 1883, Colonel Strauch outlined the IAC's position. "We are very much alarmed at the negotiations going on between England and Portugal," he wrote. "If the English government installs the Portuguese at the mouth of the Congo, we sincerely hope that they will stipulate with the Portuguese the recognition of the absolute freedom of our roads and stations." He added plaintively, "We have no doubt that the English government will not declare by the stroke of a pen that our works and properties belong not to us, but to Portugal." Two weeks later, Leopold made a direct appeal to his cousin, Queen Victoria: "I beg Lord Granville to prevent the Portuguese from using a treaty with England to destroy our free routes and our free stations."[6]

The cause of protecting the Association's stations along the Lower Congo was taken up by John Kirk, the British consul in Zanzibar, who happened to be in England on leave. Following extensive discussions with King Leopold II in Brussels, he informed the Foreign Office that Leopold would oppose Portuguese occupation by force if necessary. He noted that the Association would soon have fourteen hundred men at its stations, including seven hundred Zanzibaris and four hundred Hausas. Kirk requested that special provisions to protect the Association's stations and roads should be written into the treaty with Portugal. On February 25, 1883, he wrote a memo suggesting that the treaty should limit Portuguese jurisdiction at sixty miles from the coast, leaving the river port of Boma, the Association's stations, and the wagon road to Malebo Pool outside of Portuguese territory.[7]

Despite those pleadings, the British Foreign Office refused to make any special accommodation for the International Association of the Congo beyond the general language about freedom of navigation and the prohibition of monopoly concessions that were already in the draft. To Earl Granville, the Association was little more than an impractical exercise in philanthropy that had no existence in international law. The Foreign Office habitually dealt with states and governments, not with private entities masquerading as states. Earl Granville well understood that the Association was little more than a front organization for the personal ambitions of King Leopold II. "The King of the Belgians is the proprietor of the Association and funds all its money," wrote Granville.[8]

It was not surprising that the opposition to the Anglo-Portuguese Treaty in the House of Commons was led by the MP from Manchester. Popularly known as "Cottonopolis," Manchester was the hub of the Lancashire County cotton cloth industry, which had produced 85 percent of the world's manufactured cloth in the 1830s and had remained the world's most important center of cotton cloth production throughout the nineteenth century. By 1860, some 70 percent of Britain's cotton workers toiled in the mills of Lancashire. With production often outpacing sales, the Manchester cloth merchants were constantly on the lookout for new markets anywhere in the world, including the Congo River. During the three decades from 1850 to 1880, Britain's trade with the Congo River basin had grown from almost nothing to £2 million per year, and much of that trade was in cloth that was manufactured in Manchester.[9]

The Manchester Chamber of Commerce was alarmed by Portugal's aggressive moves toward the Congo River estuary. In November 1882, the chamber had sent a letter to the Foreign Office expressing concerns about the "claims put forward by Portugal on assuming exclusive rights on the River Congo and the bordering states" and adding its apprehensions about Brazza's Makoko treaties. Noting that the mouth of the Congo River was being progressively sandwiched between the French to the north and the Portuguese to the south, the chamber called on the British government to appoint a resident British consul to watch over the "interests and trade of Great Britain on the Congo" and to station a gunboat on the southwest coast of Africa that was at the disposal of the consular agent. Over the next four months, other chambers of commerce weighed in as well: Liverpool, Glasgow, London, Bristol, Birmingham, and more. The groundwork had thus been laid for Jacob Bright to present his resolution in the House of Commons opposing the Anglo-Portuguese Treaty.[10]

Jacob Bright's resolution was an unprecedented parliamentary maneuver, given that treaties were not normally debated until after they had been signed by the diplomats and submitted to Parliament for ratification, but the MP from Manchester wanted to kill the treaty with Portugal before it could gain momentum. In introducing his resolution, Bright claimed that "the territory on the Lower Congo is under the rule of native chiefs and kings. Trade is more absolutely free than in any other part of the globe. As to the general security of the country, merchants make no complaint. They pay an annual tribute and there the matter ends." Along the Congo, he said, "there are no duties and no customs houses, and trade is absolutely free."[11]

The proposed Anglo-Portuguese Treaty, intoned Bright, raised fears that the Portuguese would levy duties as high as 30 percent (as they had done along the Zambezi River) and that they would make trade impossible by requiring passports, papers, tolls, fines, fees, and other petty exactions. Claiming that the poorly paid Portuguese officials were corrupt, Bright warned that "you could hardly look at a bale of goods after it has passed the customs house without paying a fee to somebody." If the potential trade restrictions were not frightening enough, he said, there was always a danger that Portugal would reopen the slave trade to the nearby island of São Tomé and that Catholic Portugal would erect barriers against the British Protestant missionaries who were working in the Lower Congo region.

Bright contrasted the Portuguese record of colonial misrule in Africa with that of King Leopold's International Association of the Congo. The Association, he said, had done great work and had built stations all the way up the Lower Congo and beyond. "There is neither force nor violence," he claimed. "Everything is done by friendly negotiation." Bright's praise for the Association showed the influence of James F. Hutton, a Manchester businessman who had been one of the original investors in King Leopold's Upper Congo Study Committee and who currently served as the Belgian consul in Manchester. Bright was clearly speaking for Hutton and the Manchester Chamber of Commerce when he praised the Association. He did not advocate British recognition of the Association but merely sought to uphold the status quo. "It does not seem that we should be wise in upsetting native rule on the Congo," he concluded.

After the speeches had gone on for some time, Prime Minister William Gladstone took the floor. Noting that Jacob Bright's resolution against the treaty was unprecedented, given that the treaty was still being negotiated, he complained that the resolution would tie the hands of the government. If the government were given enough time to negotiate a more satisfactory treaty, he promised, it would then bring the treaty to the Parliament for full debate and ratification. The promise seemed to satisfy the MPs, and the resolution was withdrawn. Although Jacob Bright's resolution had not passed, he had demonstrated that there was substantial opposition to the Anglo-Portuguese Treaty. The Foreign Office took notice and began to negotiate a new treaty that it hoped would be more acceptable to the British Parliament.

2

Brussels, April 29, 1883

With an Anglo-Portuguese Treaty temporarily blocked, King Leopold began a diplomatic offensive to persuade Britain and France to refrain from making or recognizing rival claims over territory claimed by the International Association of the Congo. He had closely followed the debate in the British Parliament and had observed that the opposition to the treaty was based largely on the fear that the Portuguese would impose duties, fees, and trade restrictions. Reasoning that a guarantee of free and unrestricted trade might get a favorable reception in Britain, he wrote to John Kirk on April 29 proposing that "if England were willing to proclaim neutrality over the mouth of the Congo and acknowledge the neutrality of the Association's stations, we would pledge not to establish customs houses or any tax on our roads." He knew that Britain would never recognize the International Association of the Congo as a sovereign entity, but a proclamation of a neutral zone at the mouth of the Congo River would block Portugal and France and thus create a diplomatic space in which the Association could function.[12]

Three weeks later, King Leopold made the same promise to the British shipping magnate William MacKinnon. "His Majesty requests that you kindly explain to some influential members of Parliament the importance and urgency of recognizing the neutrality of our stations," wrote Colonel Strauch on the king's behalf. "Our stations would make a commitment not to establish any customs in the whole area of their possession or any taxes for the use of the international road connecting them." Despite all the exclusive rights that the Association had claimed in the treaties signed by the African chiefs, Leopold was now using the concepts of neutrality and free trade as bargaining chips to enhance its international standing.[13]

While trying to gain a promise of neutrality from the British, King Leopold was also trying to negotiate an agreement with the French, a difficult task given the well-publicized acrimony between Stanley and Brazza. To conduct secret negotiations, King Leopold relied on Arthur Stevens, a Belgian art critic and dealer who was well known in the cultural salons of Paris. As a young man, Arthur

Stevens had followed his older brother Alfred to Paris and had immersed himself in the art scene while his brother became a successful painter known for his portraits of elegant women. Arthur later moved back to Brussels and established a successful art gallery that introduced the works of new and rising French painters to the Belgian public. As a Belgian who was highly respected by the Parisian cultural elites, Arthur Stevens was an ideal intermediary between King Leopold and French prime minister Jules Ferry. In addition to being the prime minister, Ferry also served as the minister of fine arts.[14]

At the request of King Leopold, Stevens held a series of meetings with Ferry in November and December 1883 in which the two sought to reach an understanding that would help to avoid further clashes between the International Association of the Congo and the French on the Congo River. Early on, Ferry insisted that France would not give official recognition to the Association nor acknowledge its sovereignty. In a letter to Brazza, Ferry explained that the Association "is neither Belgium nor the King of the Belgians; it can have neither a recognized flag, nor regular forces, nor sovereign rights of any kind." Under the circumstances, the best Leopold could hope for was a kind of "good neighbor" agreement in which each side promised to respect the other's territorial claims.[15]

As a crafty negotiator who played on his adversaries' fears, King Leopold quickly discovered that the French were worried about a British takeover of the Congo River. The French prime minister saw Leopold as a naïve dreamer who was running out of money, and he feared that Leopold might try to recoup his losses by selling his stations to a British company or the British government. As evidence of a special relationship between the International Association of the Congo and the British, the French could point to the increasing numbers of Association agents who were British. Brazza warned of the "increase of a British element around Stanley," and Father Augouard warned that the Association "will become British

in the near future, because the Belgian element is today being suc-
cessively eliminated to make way for the British." Those impres-
sions are backed up by numbers: in September 1882, there were 3
British agents out of a total of 43 Association representatives in the
Congo basin, but a year later there were 41 British agents out of
117, creating what agent Louis Valke referred to as a "great British
wave."[16]

What the French prime minister wanted, then, was a guarantee
that Leopold would not sell the Association's stations and treaty
rights to the British. But how could such a pledge be guaranteed?
Leopold's solution was to offer France the right of first refusal. He
inserted the following words into a draft of the agreement: "The
Association, wishing to give further proof of its friendly feeling
toward France, engages to give her the right of preference if, through
unforeseen circumstances, the Association were compelled to sell
its possessions." Because the French were convinced that Leopold
would soon go bankrupt, the agreement would effectively guarantee their eventual possession of the entire Congo River basin.
Leopold, on the other hand, believed that his offer of preemptive
rights would cost him nothing because he had no intention of
going bankrupt.[17]

Prime Minister Ferry had one more demand. Because the
French saw Stanley as an agent for British interests, they wanted
him relieved of any position with the International Association
of the Congo. Stanley's dismissal would not only rid them of a
formidable competitor in Africa but would also exact revenge for
Stanley's speech in Paris heaping ridicule on Brazza. That part
of the agreement was not put in writing, but there was a general
understanding that soon after the agreement was concluded, Stanley would be gone. "The King of the Belgians has sent me assurances that Stanley's recall is already a settled matter," wrote Ferry
to Brazza.[18]

The agreement was finalized by an exchange of letters
between Ferry and Colonel Strauch representing the International

Association of the Congo on April 23 and 24, 1884. France agreed to respect the rights and stations of the Association and to place no obstacles in its way, while the Association declared that if it were ever forced to dispose of its possessions, the option to purchase them would be reserved in the first instance for France. Delimiting the boundaries of the respective territories would be worked out later. It was not an official treaty because France did not officially recognize the International Association of the Congo. The letters nevertheless neutralized the French threat to the Association's stations. Reporting on the completion of the supposedly secret negotiations, *The Times* of London emphasized that "the Association is in no sense a government and has no rights to a flag in the proper sense of the word. It is merely an anomalous agency enjoying certain rights of commercial administration by the sufferance of recognized governments."[19]

3

House of Representatives, Washington, DC, December 4, 1883

On December 4, 1883, both houses of Congress gathered to hear the clerk read the Annual Message from Chester A. Arthur, the twenty-first president of the United States. The message opened with a tour d'horizon of foreign policy issues: fisheries disputes in the Atlantic; the efforts to get France and Germany to import American swine products; and a variety of concerns related to Russia, the Philippines, the Ottoman Empire, Japan, Cuba, Brazil, and Mexico. Just when it appeared that the world survey was complete, the president's message turned to the Congo. "The rich and populous valley of the Congo," intoned the clerk, "is being opened to commerce by a society called the International African Association, of which the King of the Belgians is the president and a citizen of the United States the chief executive officer."

President Arthur's statement was inaccurate in two respects. First, he used the term "International African Association," which was an international philanthropic organization, instead of "Upper Congo Study Committee," which had been a quasi-commercial venture, or "International Association of the Congo," the current name, which was a shadowy organization of murky membership and uncertain purpose. Second, he referred to Henry Morton Stanley as "a citizen of the United States," even though the explorer lacked legal citizenship. He was widely believed to be an American, and that was good enough.

The president's message continued, "Large tracts of territory have been ceded to the association by native chiefs, roads have been opened, steamboats placed on the river, and the nuclei of states established at twenty-two stations under one flag which offers freedom to commerce and prohibits the slave trade. The objects of the society are philanthropic. It does not aim at permanent political control, but seeks the neutrality of the valley." The president concluded that "it may become advisable for us to cooperate with other commercial powers in promoting the rights of trade and residence in the Congo Valley free from the interference or control of any one nation." That single paragraph, buried in a speech that filled eighteen printed pages, was the result of a major diplomatic campaign waged by King Leopold II and his American collaborator Henry Shelton Sanford.[20]

The campaign had begun on June 13, when the king drafted a letter to President Arthur seeking American recognition for his Association. Sanford edited it and translated it into English. President Arthur's sympathetic response encouraged the king to write a second letter, which Sanford carried to Washington and delivered personally. In the letter, Leopold promised the Americans freedom from all customs duties for their future trade along the Congo River. Although the treaties that the Association had signed with the African chiefs were larded with language granting exclusive rights to the Association, Sanford carried with him falsified versions of sample treaties with the exclusivity clauses removed. The king also promised that US citizens would have liberty to acquire or occupy lands in the Congo River basin. That point was aimed squarely at a white American audience. In the aftermath of the Civil War, there was a strain of thought among white Americans that the freed slaves should be repatriated to Africa. Although a modest number of liberated American slaves had been settled in Liberia prior to the Civil War, the vast regions of the Congo basin could absorb many more people. King Leopold was offering the Congo as a resettlement site for former American slaves.[21]

The king's letter was well received in Washington. When President Arthur was preparing his Annual Message to Congress, he invited Sanford to compose the paragraph on the Congo River basin. The draft paragraph was then rewritten to conform to the formal style of the presidential address, but its content was preserved with one exception: Sanford's original paragraph had committed the United States to recognize the "Union of Free States of the Congo" (a nonexistent entity), but President Arthur thought that such a move was premature, given that Americans, including himself, knew almost nothing about the Congo.[22]

Building on the momentum generated by the president's address, Sanford wrote a long article for the *New York Herald* (Stanley's former newspaper), which published it anonymously in the Sunday edition of December 30. The article occupied a full page and displayed a map showing the Association's stations in the Congo River basin. It opened by quoting from the president's annual message and went on to stress the economic benefits of making an agreement with the Association. "It is especially in our cotton goods—the overproduction of which is causing so much trouble and threatening so many disasters, and in which we take the lead—that Africa offers a vast field. Our coarse, unbleached sheetings are the special need of Central Africa, and bear the name of *merikani*." The article then broadened the economic argument to include American hardware, dry goods, and woolen products and put forth the dream of large fleets of free American ships laden with the produce of our factories and returning full of the valuable raw materials of that country.[23]

Three days later, the *New York Times* published another long article that reflected substantial input from Sanford. Expressing pride that the Congo basin was being opened up and developed by Henry Morton Stanley, who was believed to be an American, the article claimed that in time the region "may and probably will be as populous, wealthy, and powerful as the United States." Predicting that US trade with the Congo would someday surpass that with India, it concluded that the "valley of the Congo and the region opened by the labors of the International Association should be made free to the commerce of the whole world," and it urged the Chamber of Commerce to take up the cause. A week later, the Chamber of Commerce of New York City listened to a long presentation on the commercial importance of the Congo River basin from Judge Charles Daly, the president of the American Geographical Society, and approved a resolution that the government of the United States should recognize "the flag of the International Association."[24]

To turn the favorable publicity into political action, Sanford contacted Senator John Tyler Morgan of Alabama. In the wake of the Civil War, Morgan had emerged as a leading southern nationalist, a virulent white supremacist, and an advocate for the mass emigration of former slaves to Africa. He took an interest in the Congo question for two reasons. First, if the Congo River basin became a major market for cloth from the textile mills of Massachusetts, then it would boost the demand for raw cotton from the former Confederate states. Second, he believed that there was not enough room in Liberia to absorb a mass emigration of former American slaves, and he saw the Congo basin as a safety valve for his emigration scheme. As a member of the Senate Foreign Relations Committee, Morgan introduced a resolution on January 21, 1884, calling for the committee to conduct an inquiry into the commerce of the Congo River Valley and submit a report "as to any action that may be properly taken by congress or the executive in the furtherance of our commerce in that quarter." The resolution passed the Senate unanimously.[25]

The committee's inquiry was completed rather quickly because Sanford had brought along a series of documents—including the falsified treaties—for just that purpose. The final report was only ten pages long, but it was backed up by forty-six pages of documents, most supplied by Sanford. The report cited the case of Liberia, where the American Colonization Society had created a colony for the resettlement of freed American slaves, as a precedent for the private "free state" that King Leopold was establishing on the Congo. In order to deflect criticism of the treaties that the International Association of the Congo had signed with Congo chiefs, the report cited the treaties that had been signed with Native Americans by the original English settlers in Massachusetts, Connecticut, New Hampshire, Rhode Island, and North Carolina. It was a clever argument because it forced anybody who questioned the legality of King Leopold's Congo treaties to also question the legality of English settlements in America. The report concluded that "the people of the Congo Country and their benefactors alike deserve the friendly recognition of the United States in their new national character."[26]

On April 10, 1884, the Senate met in executive session—a parliamentary maneuver that rendered the proceedings secret—and approved a resolution that "the Flag of the International African Association should be recognized as the flag of a friendly government." The secrecy took the heat off individual senators who were hesitant to alienate the British by voting for a resolution that undermined Britain's negotiations on the Anglo-Portuguese Treaty. The Senate resolution was followed by an exchange of official declarations on April 18 and 22 between Henry Shelton Sanford for the Association and the American secretary of state. Sanford's declaration stated that the International Association of the Congo agreed to waive import duties on American goods and to guarantee Americans the right to purchase, sell, or lease real estate in the Congo basin. The United States, for its part, recognized "the flag of the International African Association as the flag of a friendly government." After the exchange of declarations, the secrecy was lifted and the American recognition of the International Association of the Congo was announced to the press. The United States had given the Association the formal recognition that the European powers had scorned.[27]

What was the entity that the United States officially recognized? Despite their inconsistent terminology, both declarations stated that "free states" were being established in the Congo River basin under the care and supervision of the Association. The only way to recognize the "free states" was to recognize the International Association of the Congo, an organization that was, in the words of the Belgian historian Jean Stengers, "a fictional entity" that represented no one other than King Leopold II. Willard P. Tisdel, America's first trade representative to the "Free States of the Congo," discovered that fiction when he arrived in Europe in November 1884 and learned, as he put it, that he was "accredited to a country which did not in reality exist."[28]

4

Foreign Office, London, February 26, 1884

Despite King Leopold's successful negotiation with the United States and France, the main threat to his Congo project was still the Anglo-Portuguese Treaty, which was coming up for ratification in the House of Commons on June 26, 1884. The British government had signed the treaty in February, and ratification by Parliament was the final step. The treaty had been substantially reworked following the earlier debate in the House of Commons, and it now contained fifteen articles instead of the original six. It recognized Portuguese jurisdiction over the west coast of Africa between 8° and 5°12′ south latitude, a stretch of coastline that included the mouth of the Congo River, and it gave Portugal jurisdiction over the river's estuary up to Nokki, which was just ten miles downstream from the Association's Vivi Station. By that delimitation of territory, all of the Association's stations were outside the zone of Portuguese jurisdiction. The treaty also called for the suppression of the slave trade and promised freedom for missionaries of any Christian denomination. Despite some minor adjustments in favor of the Association, King Leopold objected to the treaty: he wanted the river port of Boma, which marked the limit of navigability for oceangoing ships, to be outside of Portuguese territory; and he wanted complete freedom from customs and tariffs, not just a clause that offered foreigners the same rights and privileges as Portuguese traders.[29]

As soon as the details of the revised treaty became known, opposition erupted in Britain. As before, it was led by Jacob Bright, the MP from Manchester, and the Manchester Chamber of Commerce, with King Leopold's ally James F. Hutton as its new president. While Bright repeatedly raised questions about the treaty in Parliament, Hutton sent out a circular letter to all the Chambers of Commerce in Britain and all the members of Parliament outlining the case against the treaty. "The king [of the Belgians] is undoubtedly getting up an opposition to the treaty in the House," wrote a Foreign Office official.[30]

To undermine King Leopold's influence, the head of the Africa Division at the Foreign Office, H. P. Anderson, claimed that he had proof that the International Association of the Congo was really a commercial enterprise and not a philanthropic one. Pointing to intercepted treaties between the Association and the chiefs along the Lower Congo that had recently been published by the Portuguese government, he noted that "they not only included sovereign rights to the Company, but gave it an absolute monopoly on trade." Citing the British explorer Harry Johnston, who had recently traveled along the Congo River, Anderson argued that "no one who has seen the agents at work would doubt that the aim of the company has been a gigantic commercial monopoly; far from the roads and stations being open to all, they have been jealously closed against all." Anderson's argument was shelved by the foreign minister, who did not want to complicate the debate on the Anglo-Portuguese Treaty by bringing the International Association of the Congo into it. Instead, he sent Leopold a diplomatically worded note warning him to back off.[31]

As opposition to the treaty grew, Lord Edmond Fitzmaurice, who was both a member of Parliament and the undersecretary of state for foreign affairs, became convinced that it would fail. "It is, I think, beyond doubt that Her Majesty's Government may be beaten on the Congo question in the House of Commons," he wrote on April 23. In order to buy time, he suggested seeking clarification from other European powers as to whether they would sign on to its provisions. The results were not encouraging: France, Holland, and Germany all demanded substantial revisions to better protect their territorial and commercial interests before they would consider signing on.

By May 1884, the Portuguese foreign minister had grown pessimistic about the chances of the treaty being ratified in Britain and devised a backup plan: instead of signing a treaty with Britain and then getting the other European powers to sign on, he would first negotiate a treaty with the other powers and then bring in Britain on the back end. While continuing to negotiate with the British Foreign Office about revisions to make the treaty more acceptable to France, Holland, and Germany, he sent out a circular on May 13 to the other interested powers in which he proposed a conference to hammer out a treaty on the basis of equality of all the powers. Britain did not get an invitation because Portugal was conducting negotiations along two entirely separate tracks.

Lord Granville did not learn about the proposed conference until June 14, when it was mentioned in a letter he received from German chancellor Otto von Bismarck.[32]

On June 26, 1884, the day when the Anglo-Portuguese Treaty was scheduled to come up for ratification in the House of Commons, Lord Fitzmaurice announced that "her majesty's Government has now arrived at the conclusion that the objections taken by some of the Powers to certain portions of the Treaty are of too serious a character to leave any hope of the Treaty being accepted as a whole, and they have therefore informed the Portuguese Government that a ratification of the Treaty would be useless." The Anglo-Portuguese Treaty was now in limbo, leaving the issues of jurisdiction and freedom of trade along the Lower Congo River to be resolved by an international conference.[33]

5

Berlin, May 4, 1883

While negotiating with France and fighting against the Anglo-Portuguese Treaty, King Leopold had also engaged in negotiations with Germany. Following his normal method, Leopold worked through a private intermediary. He had used Henry Shelton Sanford in the United States and Arthur Stevens in Paris, and now he depended on the services of a German banker named Gerson Bleichröder, who lived in Berlin. In his sixties and almost blind, Bleichröder had served for many years as the chief banker for Bismarck and the Prussian State. He had known King Leopold since the two first met in 1877 at the seaside resort of Ostend, Belgium, where Leopold spent his summers. The two men had subsequently maintained an intermittent correspondence on a variety of subjects. "Industry suffers everywhere; it is necessary to create new outlets," wrote the king to Bleichröder in 1878, noting that "the African continent deserves our special attention."[34]

Their correspondence intensified in May 1883, when Leopold asked Bleichröder to help him obtain German recognition of the neutrality of the Association's stations. Although the request went nowhere, Leopold contacted Bleichröder again a year later, following the completion of his agreements with the United States and France. Leopold's plans had changed considerably over the course of the year. No longer content with American recognition of the Association's flag or a "good neighbor" agreement with the French, he now wanted to gain recognition for an "Independent State of Central Africa" that would make its entry into the family of states. "We are right now actively engaged in devising a political constitution and drafting fundamental laws for the new state," he assured Bleichröder. From that point on, Bleichröder served as the intermediary between the Belgian king and the German chancellor.[35]

The timing of Leopold's approach to Germany was fortuitous. Bismarck had become interested in the Congo question in the spring of 1884, when he worked with the German Chamber of Commerce to oppose the Anglo-Portuguese Treaty. The export of German guns, ammunition, and hard liquor to the Congo River had increased rapidly in 1883 and 1884, and the German trading houses operating along the Lower Congo feared that the treaty would limit their trade. Bismarck had first taken notice of King Leopold's International Association of the Congo in late April 1884 when he read that the United States had recognized the flag of the Association. "I see that the Americans have recognized the flag of the International Congo Company," he told the French ambassador. "I do not yet understand the implications of that action because I do not really know what that company is." At that time, Bismarck hoped that King Leopold's International Association of the Congo, with its proclamation of free trade to all nations, might be a useful alternative to Portuguese or French control of the Congo River basin.[36]

At the beginning of June, after Bismarck had formally announced his rejection of the Anglo-Portuguese Treaty, he communicated directly with Leopold II for the first time, giving his conditions for an agreement. Leopold responded by proposing an exchange of declarations such as the ones he had concluded with the United States and France. The model declarations that he sent to Bismarck spoke vaguely of creating "an independent state, stretching from the Atlantic to the possessions of the Sultan of Zanzibar," with the exact boundaries to be determined later. Bismarck was wary of the proposal because he recognized that the Association was essentially demanding carte blanche to do whatever it wanted. To get the negotiations back on track, Bleichröder asked King Leopold to send him a new set of draft declarations along with a map showing the exact borders of the future Congo State. To draw that map, Leopold needed the help of Henry Morton Stanley.

Leopold was spending the summer of 1884 at his royal villa on the beach in Ostend, the transit point between the train to Brussels and the ferry to Dover, England. It was the perfect spot for a meeting with Stanley, who was just then returning from the Congo. On July 29, Stanley disembarked at Plymouth, England, and made his way to London. Four days later, he took the ferry from Dover to Ostend, where he spent several days giving King Leopold a full report on the state of the Congo project. Stanley did not know—and would not find out for some time—that he had already been dismissed from the Association. Believing that all was well, he went to the king's villa on August 7 to help him with a special project.[37]

King Leopold laid out a large map of Africa and asked Stanley to help him plot the borders of a future state in the Congo River basin. Drawing with a red pencil, Stanley outlined the borders of a state that went from 4° north latitude to 6° south latitude and eastward from the cataracts of the Lower Congo to Lake Tanganyika. The boundary lines were strategically drawn to avoid conflicts

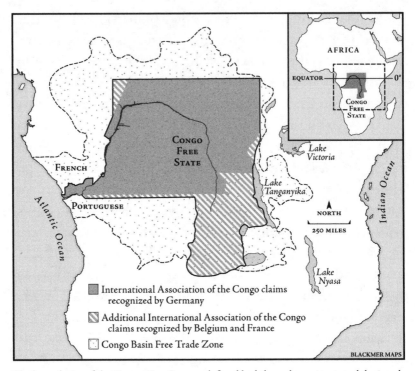

The boundaries of the Congo Free State as defined by bilateral treaties signed during the Berlin Conference in 1884–1885

with the French, the Portuguese, the sultan of Zanzibar, and Tippu Tip. The Manyema trading towns of Kasongo and Nyangwe, as well as the trade route to Ujiji, were outside the borders of the Association's territory, whereas Stanley Falls was claimed by the Association.[38]

The territory thus defined contained roughly seven hundred thousand square miles. It was hundreds of times larger than the combined area conceded in the treaties with the chiefs and roughly sixty times larger than Belgium itself. When the French ambassador to Germany, Baron de Courcel, was shown the map by Bismarck three weeks later, he described the rough outline of Leopold's future state as "an immense parallelogram encompassing the complete course of the river from the cataracts in the west to the region of the great lakes in the east; in other words, all of Central Africa, the nucleus of the continent." The German chancellor did not seem concerned by the enormity of Leopold's proposed state. "It is indeed vast," he told the ambassador, "but it is not up to us to rein in these ambitions, given that the Company guarantees our freedom of trade and that the benefit to us increases with the size of the Company's operations." The French ambassador seemed to agree, in large part because the French anticipated inheriting Leopold's territories. "My conversations with the Baron de Courcel permit me to think that France would not be opposed to the area indicated on the map which your Majesty kindly sent me," the German chancellor informed King Leopold.[39]

One sticking point was the question of what would happen to Germany's freedom of trade in the Congo basin if the Association went bankrupt and sold its territory to France. That problem was solved when Leopold added a sentence to the proposed agreement guaranteeing that Germany's rights of free trade would remain in force even if the territory was sold to another country. The French ambassador ratified that arrangement by a dispatch on September 29 in which the French government pledged to maintain the freedom of commerce promised by the Association if it gained possession of the territory. "I do not know exactly what this Belgian Association is or what will become of it," Bismarck told the French ambassador. "But even if it does not successfully establish itself, it is nevertheless useful for fending off troublesome rivalries and claims that we would find difficult to deal with. We can give it our backing to clear the way."[40]

On November 8, 1884, a convention between the German Empire and the International Association of the Congo was signed by Count Brandenburg, Germany's ambassador to Belgium, and Colonel Strauch for the Association. Article 6 of the convention recognized "the frontiers of the territory of the Association and of the new State, which is to be created, as they are shown in the annexed map." The rough pencil lines that King Leopold and Stanley had drawn in Leopold's seaside villa at Ostend on August 7 were now recognized by Germany as the borders of a future African state.[41]

6

Town Hall, Manchester, England, September 18, 1884

When Henry Morton Stanley rose to speak in the assembly room of the Manchester Town Hall to a rising crescendo of warm applause, he could almost feel a sense of homecoming. When he was a young man of seventeen named John Rowlands, he had passed through Manchester on his way to the seaport of Liverpool, some thirty-five miles away, where he got a job as a deckhand on a ship that had brought raw cotton from New Orleans and returned with cotton cloth from the Manchester mills. After finding employment in New Orleans, he had borrowed his new name from Henry Hope Stanley, the man who owned the largest cotton baling and shipping business in the city. Long before Henry Morton Stanley knew anything about Africa, he had gained an instinctive understanding of the global nature of the cotton industry.

Manchester was the most industrialized city in the world, and its main product was cotton cloth. A visitor in 1808 had described the city as "abominably filthy: the steam engine is pestiferous, the dye houses noisesome, and the water of the river as black as ink." When Alexis de Tocqueville visited Manchester in 1835, he observed that "a sort of black smoke covers the city. Under this half daylight 300,000 human beings are ceaselessly at work." But de Tocqueville also noticed something else: "From this foul drain," he wrote, "the greatest stream of human industry flows out to fertilize the whole world. From this filthy sewer, pure gold flows." Manchester was not only an industrial city; it was also a global city. Using its local resources of water and coal to power its machines, Manchester received raw cotton from such far-flung places as the

United States, India, and Egypt; spun the cotton into yarn using millions of mechanical spindles; and wove it on mechanical looms into cloth to be sold all over the world.[42]

The six weeks since Stanley had returned to England on July 29, 1884, from signing treaties and building stations along the Congo River had been busy ones. He had been a guest of King Leopold in Ostend during August 2–7 and had helped him sketch out a rough map for the future Congo state. In England, he had become popular with the business and merchant community because of his opposition to the Anglo-Portuguese Treaty. Although the Foreign Office had withdrawn the draft treaty in June, it could be brought back at any time. When Stanley met with Foreign Secretary Granville on August 29 to seek British recognition of the Association, he received no encouragement, and so he continued to speak out against the moribund treaty.

On September 18, Stanley spoke in London to a large crowd in the Great Hall of the Cannon-Street Terminus, in an event sponsored by the London Chamber of Commerce. Major figures from the merchant class in London were present, along with T. Fowell Buxton of the Anti-Slavery Society, the Belgian consul, and other dignitaries. Noting that the Anglo-Portuguese Treaty was still under consideration in Britain, Stanley warned that England, which had been a leading advocate of free trade, was on the verge of yielding important commerce "into the hands of the most uncompromising protectionist of the most backward nation in Europe." He was interrupted by cries of "Hear! Hear!" Then he presented the International Association of the Congo as an alternative to Portugal and defended the Association's exclusive treaties as a preemptive move to keep the territory out of the hands of the French and the Portuguese. "Come with your cottons and woolen stuffs, with your trinkets, your beads, and brass wire," he told the crowd, "and trade freely without fear of annoyance from customs and exactions. We wish to secure equal rights to all, and the utmost freedom of commerce." The speech was received with loud cheers.

Following the speech, Stanley was the guest of honor at a dinner sponsored by the London Chamber of Commerce. Among the
forty guests was James F. Hutton, the president of the Manchester
Chamber of Commerce.[43]

A month later, on October 21, Stanley was warmly welcomed
in Manchester, the epicenter of the Industrial Revolution. A lunch-
eon at the Queen's Hotel hosted by Hutton was attended by leading
merchants and manufacturers along with a number of dignitaries,
including Gen. Frederick Goldsmid, who had negotiated the "New
Confederation" treaties with the chiefs on the Lower Congo; the
head of the African Committee of the London Chamber of Commerce; and the German, French, Danish, American, Dutch, and
Brazilian consuls. After the usual opening toasts, Hutton surprised
the crowd by proposing a toast to "His Majesty the King of the
Belgians." He described King Leopold as "a sovereign whose desire
and ambition is to promote the progress and prosperity of the
industry of every country in the world," and the guests responded
with cries of "Hear! Hear!" The International Association, he said,
would guarantee that "there would be absolutely free trade to all
countries in the world." Then Hutton raised a glass for Stanley,
whom he described as "a friend and a benefactor to Manchester
and the industry of Lancashire." He thanked Stanley for his efforts
to "promote the welfare and freedom of the Africans and the prosperity of every country in the world." The guests responded with
hearty applause.[44]

Later that afternoon, Stanley spoke to a crowd of three hundred
at a special meeting of the Chamber of Commerce in the Manchester Town Hall. "If things remain as they are," he told the crowd,
"the future of cotton manufacture is not very brilliant. New inven-
tions are continually cropping up so that your power of producing
is almost incalculable, but new markets for the sale of your products are not of rapid growth." Then he proposed that the Congo
basin offered precisely the new markets that Manchester needed. If
each inhabitant of the Congo basin bought just one Sunday dress,

he said, it would require 320 million yards of cloth. If each inhabitant bought two Sunday dresses and four everyday dresses, it would
come to 3.8 billion yards, with a value of sixteen million pounds
sterling. Then he added in the funeral cloths required for respectable burials and the stores of cloth that prosperous families kept as
a kind of savings account, and he concluded that the Congo basin
offered a market of twenty-six million pounds sterling annually.[45]

To secure that market, he proposed two steps: first, to send a
British navy cruiser to the mouth of the Congo River to prevent
a rival European power from seizing it, and second, to allow the
International Association "to act as guardians of international right
to free trade and free entrance and exit into and out of the river."
To illustrate how this could be done, he read the text of the declaration the Association made to the US government, which said
that the "Free States of the Congo have resolved to levy no customs duties whatsoever" and that the Association is "prepared to
enter into agreements with other nations who desire to secure the
free admission of their products on the same terms as those agreed
upon with the United States." Noting that some European governments believed it was time to establish some form of control over
the Lower Congo, he suggested that the International Association
was "the best and most tolerant form of government for the traders,
which is best for their trading interests, and solves the riddle without clashing with any foregone or preconceived ideas of various
European powers. Here is an Association with a government under
whose flag every nation may compete for the trade of the Congo
basin."

When the cheers died down at the conclusion of his speech,
Stanley held up a document containing the "Manifesto of the International Association" and asked that James Hutton read it aloud.
Hutton replied that, in the interest of time, he would hand a copy
to members of the press, who could publish it for the benefit of all
the citizens of Manchester. The *Manchester Courier* would print a
long summary of the Manifesto the next day, and the Chamber

of Commerce later reprinted the full text, along with the text of Stanley's speech, in a pamphlet. Touting the agreement made with the United States as a model, the Manifesto made two promises. First, that the "Free States" of the Congo would offer free commerce to citizens of all nations; and second, that "the forces at the disposal of the Association would ensure order and tranquility in the territory and do all in their power to prevent slave trading." The "International Association," as it was now being called, promised that "absolute freedom of trade is ensured, with the advantage of a civilized Power to assist them in case of necessity." "By granting entire freedom to trade, and by abolishing customs-house vexations," read the Manifesto, "the Association wishes to attract to their territories commerce and capital."[46]

By the fourth paragraph, the terminology had shifted subtly from the plural term "Free States" that had been used in the agreement with the Americans to the singular term "Free State." King Leopold was now envisioning a singular large state administered by the Association. The Manifesto offered some hints as to how the Free State would be governed. At first, it would be governed from the Association's headquarters in Brussels, which would hire agents from different European countries to man its posts. Once the Free State was established, however, it would be governed by a governor-general, assisted by a legislative council and an executive committee. As for the African population, the Manifesto called for "some consideration for the habits and ideas of the natives in matters of administration and justice. Before laying down new laws and regulations applicable to them, a period of transition must be allowed to pass during which they may continue to follow their own customs."

Meanwhile, after Stanley sat down to loud cheers, Jacob Bright, the MP from Manchester who had led the fight against the Anglo-Portuguese Treaty in the House of Commons, introduced a resolution that "the Chamber of Commerce of Manchester hereby expresses its warm sympathy with the earnest efforts of His

Majesty the King of the Belgians to establish civilization and free trade on the Upper Congo. It also trusts that the Independent State or States proposed to be founded there may be recognized by all nations." The resolution had a particular urgency because an international conference would soon be convening in Berlin to decide the fate of the Lower Congo River. "We do not know what may emanate from that conference," said Bright. "We shall look with great anxiety on what is proposed." He expressed hope that cities all over Britain would pass resolutions in support of Stanley and the International Association of the Congo "in order that those who are assembled around the table of that conference may know that the foremost commercial country in the world is watching their proceedings." The resolution was adopted unanimously.[47]

Although the International Association of the Congo had so far been ignored by the British government, it had just gained official recognition from the merchants and manufacturers of Manchester, the city at the heart of Britain's Industrial Revolution. With the opening of the Berlin Conference approaching, King Leopold's fuzzy idea of creating a Congo Free State was now bolstered by a map, a manifesto, and various levels of recognition from the United States, France, Germany, and the British business community.

Two days later, on October 23, Stanley gave a very different kind of speech in Manchester. The British and Foreign Anti-Slavery Society was meeting to celebrate the fiftieth anniversary of the abolition of slavery in the British colonies. Since that great victory fifty years earlier, membership and interest in the Anti-Slavery Society had dwindled, but now they had a new cause, which they hoped would rekindle the fortunes of their organization. The Society had joined with the Manchester Chamber of Commerce to oppose the Anglo-Portuguese Treaty because they feared that the slave trade might be rekindled if the Portuguese gained control of the Congo River estuary. Stanley was eager to give the speech because associating himself with the anti-slavery cause would enhance the moral authority of the International Association. King

Leopold had always claimed that fighting slavery was one of the goals of his African ventures, and this speech would lend credibility to that claim.[48]

Long before the event began, the Manchester Free Trade Hall, which held five thousand people, was filled to overflowing. The chair of the meeting was James Hutton, who told the crowd that he felt it was his duty as a merchant and as a representative of British commercial interests to express deep contrition for the sins of the past. The dean of Manchester then took the floor and enumerated the successes of the anti-slavery campaigns in the nineteenth century: the abolition of slavery in the British colonies, ending the legal status of slavery in British India, the cessation of the slave trade between Africa and America, the abolition of slavery by France, the emancipation of slaves in the southern states of America, and the abolition of slavery in several provinces of Brazil. The last great battle of the anti-slavery cause, he told the crowd, would be in Africa. The chief object of this meeting, he said, was to "rekindle the enthusiasm in England, and to assist her in carrying the civilizing torch of freedom until its beneficent light should be shed over all the world."

After the opening formalities, it was time for Stanley to speak. For the bulk of his talk, he read from a long dispatch that he had written to the *Daily Telegraph* and the *New York Herald* eight years earlier. It was dated Nyangwe, October 28, 1876. He told the crowd that if a person left the East African island of Zanzibar and headed westward into the equatorial African interior, the activities of slave traders became more and more intense. "Between Bagamoyo and Unanyembe, one sees but retail sales of slaves, in Ujiji I saw large slave droves, and in Uguha, I saw about 800 slaves almost too weak to stand from hunger. In Manyema, I have seen one of the fields whence slaves are obtained, where it may be said that they are grown, reaped, and harvested; or, more correctly, where they are parked, shot, or captured as the case may be."

Stanley went on to link the slave trade to the ivory trade: "The business of purchasing ivory necessitates a demand for human carriers. As voluntary porters are not always to be obtained, they are naturally compelled to purchase slaves to convey the precious material to the coast. Until ivory ceases to be an article of demand, the Arabs are doing the best they can to collect it and bring it to the seaport." Omitted from the talk was any acknowledgment that the biggest slave trader in Manyema was Tippu Tip, who had been a friend and traveling companion to both Livingstone and Stanley.

Stanley then addressed the British campaign to end the seaborne slave trade along the East African coast. "The champions of the Anti-Slavery cause in England, seconded by the government, deserve great credit for having done their utmost to suppress the traffic in slaves on the high seas; but to complete their work, it should be suggested that as long as the trade is permitted in the interior, so certain is it that attempts will be made to continue it at sea." How, then, could the slave trade be ended? Stanley had no easy answer, but he dismissed the suggestion made by some members of the Anti-Slavery Society that England should annex Zanzibar in order to stop the slave trade. "Annexation of Zanzibar to the British dominions, being only a sentimental necessity, cannot be entertained," he told the crowd. When Stanley finished his talk, he moved on to the overflow auditorium at the YMCA, where fifteen hundred people had gathered, and he gave the talk again.

During his two days in Manchester, Stanley had addressed the two issues that most aroused the passions of the business and humanitarian communities—the commercial exploitation of the Congo River basin and the internal African slave trade. Although Stanley argued for keeping the two issues separate, they quickly became fused in the minds of the audiences. The logic was compelling: commercial expansion under European control would boost the prosperity of Manchester and at the same time would end the internal slave trade in Africa. Although Stanley explicitly rejected colonial rule as a solution to slavery, everything he said in his speeches pointed toward that end.

7

Berlin, November 15, 1884

The Berlin Conference of 1884–1885 has been characterized as a major turning point in the history of European colonization in Africa, but analysts disagree as to the exact impact of the gathering. To Kwame Nkrumah, the first president of Ghana, it was the event where the European powers divided up Africa among themselves, but historian William Roger Louis has argued that its actual consequences for Africa were minimal because, apart from the Congo River basin, its ground rules for the partition of Africa were largely ignored. But even if it did not determine the future political structure of Africa as a whole, it certainly decided the fate of the Congo River basin and set off a chaotic scramble in other parts of Africa.[49]

The failure of the draft Anglo-Portuguese Treaty to gain support from the other colonial powers had made an international conference almost a necessity. On October 8, 1884, Germany and France jointly issued invitations to Britain, Belgium, the Netherlands, Portugal, Spain, and the United States to meet in Berlin in November. Invitations to Austria, Russia, Italy, Denmark, Sweden, and Norway went out ten days later, and Turkey obtained a late invitation by claiming that some of the areas under discussion touched upon the dominions of the Ottoman Empire. Many of the thirteen invited countries had no colonial possessions in Africa and no direct interest in the issues at hand, but they could provide useful voices in favor of free trade. The International Association of the Congo did not have formal representation at the conference, but it

The Berlin Conference. Bismarck is seated in the foreground wearing a military uniform. The face to his immediate left is the American delegate Henry Shelton Sanford. Baron Lambermont, the Belgian delegate, is standing by the map, on the left. Universal History Archive/UIG/Bridgeman Images

was represented by an unofficial delegation of Colonel Strauch and Emile Vandervelde.

As the conference approached, Stanley waited in vain for his instructions from King Leopold to go to Berlin, not realizing that he had already been relieved of any official position with the Association. Finally, in late October he received a letter from the American ambassador to Germany, John Kasson, who invited him to join the American delegation along with Henry Shelton Sanford. Since Stanley was still under personal contract to King Leopold, he asked the Association for permission but did not get a reply. "For a reason that eludes me," he wrote to the ambassador, "they forbid me to go to Berlin." The reason was that the Association was afraid he would attack one of the great powers and upset the delicate diplomatic balance. Only after Sanford promised to keep a close eye on Stanley did the Association give Stanley permission to join the American delegation as a technical advisor.[50]

The conference opened on November 15, 1884, at Bismarck's official residence, the former Schulenburg Palace at 77 Wilhelm-strasse, next door to the German Foreign Office. The delegates sat at a U-shaped table in a room dominated by a huge map of Africa. Bismarck welcomed the delegates and read drafts of two propositions to be discussed by the conference at its next meeting. The first proposition was that any European power exercising sovereign rights in the Congo River basin must allow all commercial nations free access that was unfettered by monopolies, discrimination, or taxes. In essence, the Congo River basin was to be a free trade zone for European and American trading companies. Bismarck's second proposition was that all powers exercising rights or influence in the Congo River basin should "cooperate in the abolition of slavery in those localities." That proposition was immediately set aside for later discussion as the delegates focused on the issue of free trade.[51]

Although the idea of a free trade zone in the heart of Africa was appealing to the delegations—especially since most of them had made no claims on the Congo River basin—there remained two problems to be settled. The first was the problem of enforcement. Sir Edward Mallet, the British delegate, pointed out that no Africans were present at the conference, even though the decisions would be of "gravest importance to them." Nevertheless, the British proposed an international commission drawn from the nations at the conference to regulate and enforce freedom of trade.

The issue of enforcement was brought up again in the second session, held on November 19. The American delegate, John Kasson, proposed that the best way to guarantee commercial access to all nations was to put the region under the control of King Leopold's International Association of the Congo. Referencing Stanley's treaties, he argued that the Association had "obtained concessions and jurisdiction throughout the basin of the Congo from the native sovereignties, which were the sole authorities existing there and exercising dominion over the soil or the people." He was arguing, in effect, that the International Association had greater legitimacy and governing capacity than the international commission proposed by the British. Although Kasson, America's ambassador to Germany, was the head of the American delegation, few doubted that the words had been written by the delegation's technical advisor, Henry Morton Stanley. Kasson's suggestion never gained steam, however, because Bismarck declared that the status of the International Association of the Congo was not an issue to be discussed at the conference. It was not mentioned again in the formal sessions until February 23, at the second-to-last meeting of the conference.[52]

The other thorny issue concerned the delimitation of the boundaries of the Congo River free trade zone. It was referred to a special commission composed of delegates from Germany, Belgium, Spain, the United States, France, Great Britain, the Netherlands, and Portugal (i.e., the countries with the most direct interests in Africa). At the second meeting of the commission, Stanley made a presentation. Using a large chart suspended in the room, Stanley described the features of the Congo basin and the territory necessary to secure trade routes to the Atlantic and Indian Oceans. At the next meeting of the commission, Kasson presented a proposed map of the Congo free trade zone. He was careful to state that he was defining an economic and commercial zone, not a political one. The northern and southern boundaries of his proposed zone included slices of territory claimed by the French and the Portuguese, but the biggest change was his proposal to extend the zone eastward to within one degree of longitude of the Indian Ocean coast, leaving only a small coastal strip under the control of the sultan of Zanzibar (who was not represented at the conference). As with Kasson's speech on November 19, there is little doubt that the map had been drawn by Stanley.

Once that map had been officially submitted to the boundary commission, the boundary negotiations shifted to bilateral discussions between governments. The key issue concerned the estuary of the Congo River, which the Association feared would be divided between the French and the Portuguese, thus cutting off the Association's stations from the Atlantic. After extensive negotiations with the French, the Association agreed to abandon its stations in the Kwilu-Niari Valley (which provided an alternative route from the Atlantic to Malebo Pool) if the French would recognize its stations on the south bank of Malebo Pool and pay an indemnity of 5 million francs. Negotiations between the Association and Portugal were more difficult. After Britain, France, and Germany joined forces to issue an ultimatum, Portugal agreed to give up any claims to the north bank and to set the limit of its possessions on the south bank at Nokki, ten miles downstream from the Association's station at Vivi. The upshot of the boundary negotiations was that France lost access to the mouth of the Congo River, Portuguese control of the river's estuary was limited to the south bank as far as Nokki, and the Association gained the north bank as far as Manyanga and the south bank from Nokki onward. Those boundaries would be written into the General Act of the Conference.

The remaining proposition to be discussed, which Bismarck had introduced at the opening session, called for cooperation toward the abolition of the slave trade in the Congo River basin. The slavery issue had not been raised in the preparations for the conference, and it seems to have been added at the last minute as a moral counterweight to the blatant imperialism of the free trade zone discussion. At the end of the conference, the General Act contained a single brief paragraph on the slave trade, declaring that "these territories shall not serve either for a market or a way of transit for the trade in slaves of any race whatsoever. Each of these powers engages itself to employ all the means in its power to put an end to this commerce and to punish those who are occupied in it." This was not a coordinated plan of action against the internal slave trade; its sole purpose was to cloak the imperialist aims of the conference in a fog of moral rectitude.[53]

The conference dealt with several other issues as well. It accepted the British proposal that an international commission should be established to oversee and enforce freedom of trade in the Congo River basin. It also dealt with trade along the Niger River, in West Africa, where the British fought off an attempt to make the lower Niger an international free trade zone similar to the one established for the Congo River basin. The conference also sought to define the legal basis for a European nation to claim sovereignty over an African territory. After much discussion in a special commission, it was agreed that any European power wishing to take possession of territory in Africa should notify the other powers to give them a chance to object or make counterclaims and that colonizing powers should demonstrate effective occupation of the regions they claimed. No European country could simply reserve an African territory for future colonization.

The most significant work of the conference, however, was going on offstage. The conference held only ten formal sessions between November 15, 1884, and February 26, 1885, and they did not usually begin until two or three o'clock in the afternoon, leaving plenty of time for meetings of the special commissions and direct negotiations among the delegations. Although the delegates representing the International Association of the Congo were not allowed to attend the formal sessions, they were extremely active in working behind the scenes to secure recognition from the attending countries. The Association's main task was to obtain formal recognition from all the attending countries. In this effort, it was aided by Bismarck, who had signed a convention with the Association on November 8, exactly one week before the start of the conference. On November 19, the day of the conference's second session, Bismarck privately asked the British ambassador to help the Association become a recognized state, arguing that such a move would protect the Congo basin from a destructive territorial rivalry between France and Portugal.

The British Foreign Office was reluctant to agree because it was not favorably disposed toward King Leopold or the Association and because such a move would be a significant departure from the norms of international law. Nevertheless, as Stanley's speeches to the Chambers of Commerce in London and Manchester showed, there was a considerable body of public opinion in Britain that favored both the Association and the idea of a free trade zone in the heart of Africa. Given that the British government had no inclination to colonize the Congo River basin, British companies hoping to do business along the Congo River believed that a free trade zone administered by the Association offered them the best opportunity. A delegation organized by several major British firms that were trading in the Congo basin even went to Berlin to lobby for the free trade zone, and British protestant missionaries who had built missions in the vicinity of Association stations wrote letters to the Foreign Office in favor of the Association.

In London, the Foreign Office dithered over such questions as whether the Association could be recognized as a state or whether it was an inchoate state in the course of formation, but the dithering came to an end on December 1, when Bismarck told the head of the British delegation that unless Britain recognized the Association, Germany would be unfriendly on other matters, possibly referring to the Niger River or the Nile. When the British foreign secretary presented a proposal for recognition to the cabinet the next day, it was unanimously approved, even though the lord chancellor showed a remarkable lack of enthusiasm, saying that Bismarck was a spoiled child who was unlikely to grant any favors to Britain in return. A formal treaty was signed on December 16, with Britain declaring that "the Government of Her Britannic Majesty . . . hereby recognize the flag of the Association and the Free States under its administration, as the flag of a friendly government."[54]

Other treaties of recognition followed. Italy, Austria-Hungary, and the Netherlands signed in December and Spain in January. France, which had earlier signed an agreement of neutrality but had withheld formal recognition, gave its recognition on February 5, the same day that it reached an agreement with the Association regarding boundaries in the Congo River basin. That was followed by recognition from Russia also on February 5 and Sweden-Norway on February 10. Then Portugal recognized the Association on February 14, the day before it signed the boundary agreement with the Association. Denmark followed on February 23. Ironically, the last country at the conference to recognize the Association was Belgium, which also signed on February 23. By then, only Turkey had not yet completed the negotiations because its delegate was still awaiting instructions from Istanbul.

On February 23, at the penultimate meeting of the Berlin Conference, the subject of the International Association of the Congo again came to the attention of the delegates. To open the session, the chairman read a brief letter from Colonel Strauch to Bismarck announcing that the International Association of the Congo had concluded treaties with all the powers represented at the Conference of Berlin (with one exception) in which they recognized its flag as that of a friendly state or government. It asked the powers at the conference to "consider the accession of a Power whose exclusive mission is to introduce civilization and trade into the center of Africa." One by one, the delegates rose to congratulate the newly recognized colonial state in the heart of Africa. The French delegate expressed hope that "the State of the Congo, now territorially constituted within distinct limits, may soon be able to provide a regularly organized government for the immense territory which it is called upon to develop." Even Said Pasha, the Turkish delegate who was still awaiting instructions from his government, said he had no objection to the new state.

When the welcoming speeches were finished, the delegates moved on to making minor amendments to two articles of the

General Act of the conference. Then the chairman proceeded to a vote, summarizing the content of the chapters already accepted separately and reading the full text of the amendments just adopted. The delegates voted unanimously to accept each chapter and then voted to accept the General Act as a whole.

The final session of the Berlin Conference took place three days later. As each delegate entered the room, he found two copies of the General Act laid out at his place at the U-shaped table. Each delegate would sign both copies, taking one home and leaving the other in Berlin. Bismarck himself presided over the meeting, his first appearance at the conference since the opening session in November. After Bismarck's opening speech, the delegates agreed to dispense with a final reading of the General Act and proceed to the formal signing of the treaties.

Then Bismarck interrupted the proceedings to read a letter from Colonel Strauch declaring that the International Association of the Congo adhered to all the provisions of the General Act. Then Bismarck said, "I believe I express the views of the Conference when I acknowledge with satisfaction the step taken by the International Association of the Congo and acknowledge their adherence to our decisions. The new Congo State is called upon to become one of the chief protectors of the work which we have in view, and trust it may have a prosperous development, and that the noble aspirations of its illustrious founder may be fulfilled." With that, the delegates proceeded to sign their copies of the General Act. The meeting was adjourned at four thirty.[55]

Reading the transcript of that session more than a century later, it is still hard to know exactly what had happened. Had Bismarck and the delegates just accorded the "Congo State," as he referred to the International Association of the Congo, authority over the free trade zone defined by the General Act? Was he speaking for himself or expressing the views of the conference, as he claimed? Article 17 of the General Act called for the formation of an international commission consisting of one delegate from each of the signatory powers to oversee the enforcement of the Act, but no such commission was ever formed. Instead, there seemed to be an unspoken consensus that the territory defined in the Act would be administered by the Congo State, which was the same as the International Association of the Congo, which was the same as King Leopold II.

Historians have searched in vain for a piece of paper that says that the delegates of the Berlin Conference had formally turned the entire Congo River basin over to King Leopold. The British barrister Arthur Keith later acknowledged that the sovereignty accorded to the Congo State did not rest on the Berlin Act itself but rather on the individual treaties that had been signed with the International Association of the Congo. Whatever the legal basis, King Leopold's Congo Free State had achieved a legal existence that was recognized by the United States and the major European powers. As the British ambassador had pointed out on the opening day of the Berlin Conference, the Africans did not get a vote on the matter.[56]

CHAPTER 7

RESCUING EMIN

AT THE CLOSE OF THE Berlin Conference in February 1885, it seemed as if imperialism in Africa was everywhere ascendant. In addition to partitioning the Congo River basin, the conference had created an orderly process by which European nations could lay claim to vast chunks of African territory. On the ground in equatorial Africa, however, the situation was more complex. Along the thousand-mile stretch of the Congo River between Malebo Pool and Stanley Falls, the Congo Free State and the Manyema Arabs were at a stalemate. Although the State and private trading companies were successfully buying ivory between Malebo Pool and the Bangala Station (which was roughly halfway to Stanley Falls), the ivory trade above Bangala was dominated by the Manyema Arabs, who were expanding down the Congo and its tributaries.

At the same time, a roughly parallel situation had developed along the upper Nile, where an Islamic revolutionary movement led by a man who called himself the Mahdi was driving the Ottoman Turks, the Egyptians, and their hired European administrators out of Sudan. One of those administrators was a young German doctor known as Emin Bey, who had been appointed by the khedive of Egypt as the governor of Equatoria, the southernmost province in Sudan. Retreating south along the Nile to Wadelai, he was cut off from all communication with Khartoum and Egypt.

A British-sponsored expedition to rescue him from the south opened up a link between Wadelai (on the Upper Nile) and Stanley Falls (on the Upper Congo), two political and military flash points separated by 458 miles of the densest rainforest in the world. The costly effort to bridge that gap would reconfigure and destabilize the geopolitics of the ivory trade while complicating relations between the Arabs and the Congo Free State. In the aftermath of the European consensus in Berlin, there was growing chaos in the Congo River basin.

1

Kinshasa, Malebo Pool, Congo Free State,
November 17, 1886

"Ivory here is simply asking to be bought," wrote Antoine Swinburne to his employer, Henry Shelton Sanford. "I have to turn it away for want of [trade] goods. Yesterday, I turned away 15 points [of ivory], and this with two opposition trading houses: French and Dutch." He added, "Affairs here at the Pool, so far as we are concerned, are very encouraging. I have now 31 points of ivory, or about 1,300 lbs., ready to send down, all bought in less than a week; and by now, if the goods had been sent up by the State as promised, together with our own efforts, I could have bought ten points a day, and at good prices."[1]

The trading company with the grandiose name "Sanford Exploring Expedition" was the brainchild of Henry Shelton Sanford, the American who had been an enthusiastic supporter of King Leopold's projects in the Congo River basin for over a decade. He had orchestrated the American recognition of King Leopold's International African Association, even drafting a paragraph for President Chester A. Arthur's 1883 State of the Union address, and had been an American delegate to the Berlin Conference of 1884–1885. After the Congo Free State had been recognized by

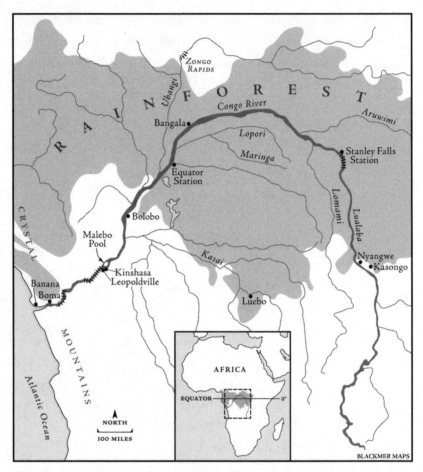

Trading towns in the Congo Free State, 1885–1889

the signatories of the Berlin Act, it was time for Sanford to cash in. He had entertained hopes of an important administrative position in the Congo, but instead Colonel Strauch proposed that the State would facilitate Sanford's efforts to create a commercial company to operate on the Upper Congo River.

Despite the proclamation of the Congo River basin as a free trade zone, King Leopold was interested in corralling as large a share of the Congo basin's commerce as possible. In a letter to his chief administrator in the Congo, written just three months after the end of the Berlin Conference, the king stated, "As for the question of ivory, remember the orders that you have been given to purchase the most possible, and send me your suggestions. Should we give the task to a commercial firm or a company? Or, would it be better to do it all ourselves? In that case, what expenditures are necessary? Wouldn't it be good to buy rubber very cheaply and have it transported to Leopoldville?" But a year later, he was closing State posts on the Upper Congo River and dismissing personnel in order to save money. Under those circumstances, having a friendly private trading firm on the Upper Congo River would be useful.[2]

Sanford had long spoken in rapturous terms about the commercial possibilities of the Congo River basin, but now that his own investments were on the line, he needed a more hardnosed assessment of its potential. He found it in a report written by US Navy lieutenant Emory Taunt, who had been sent by the US government in 1885 to assess the commercial possibilities of the Congo River basin. Taunt noted that Dutch, British, French, and Portuguese companies with stations near the mouth of the Congo River did not travel inland in search of ivory but instead waited for the African ivory caravans to come to them. He had seen caravans of up to six hundred porters carrying ivory to the coast, and the Dutch African Trading Company alone had shipped forty-eight tons of ivory to Europe in the previous six months. Given the number of well-established European companies along the Congo River estuary, Taunt concluded that there were no opportunities there for an American company.[3]

The situation above Malebo Pool, however, was completely different, he reported. There were seven thousand miles of waterways (including tributaries that ran into the Upper Congo River) navigable by steamboat, and no commercial companies were yet operating on the upper river. "In my opinion," concluded Lieutenant Taunt, "the reported wealth of the Upper Congo Valley has *not* been exaggerated. I myself saw rubber, camwood, gum copal, oil palms, ivory, iron, and copper in great quantities on the banks of the main river. . . . Ivory, for a few years, will be abundant; after that, the stock that the natives now have will become exhausted, and, to continue the supply, the elephants must be hunted. The greater part of the ivory now being sold to the traders has, for years past, been used in trade among the different tribes of the interior; it was probably found on dead elephants; some little of it trapped." Taunt concluded that trade on the Upper Congo would increase immeasurably once a railroad had been built around the rapids of the Lower Congo, but he felt that there was an opportunity for American firms to establish themselves on the upper river ahead of the completion of the railroad. He cautioned, however, that "no immediate return can be looked for, as it will take time to establish factories and to learn the ins and outs of the trade."[4]

Taunt's report gave Henry Shelton Sanford the assurance he needed to solicit investors and form a commercial company. When his efforts to attract American investors failed, he found Belgian investors and registered the company in Antwerp under the name Sanford Exploring Expedition (SEE). The original capital was $60,000, of which Sanford personally invested $15,000. The Congo Free State promised to aid the company by providing porters to transport goods to Malebo Pool, offering low-cost transportation on state steamers, and leasing several recently abandoned State stations to the company. Sanford hired Lieutenant Taunt to head the company's Congo Operations.[5]

Despite promises of aid from the Congo Free State, the company experienced a series of disappointments after arriving at the mouth of the Congo River in July 1886. The state charged exorbitant rates for transporting SEE merchandise on state steamers in the Congo River estuary, and porters for carrying goods overland to Malebo Pool were scarce and expensive. Despite the State's promise to furnish four hundred porters a month, only sixty-nine loads of material arrived at Malebo Pool during the first six months of operations. When the SEE recruited independent porters, the State impressed many of them into its own service. The company got so desperate that one of its agents began purchasing slaves and

An ivory caravan carrying tusks from Leopoldville to Matadi, 1892. Collection Royal Museum for Central Africa, Tervuren, unknown photographer, 1892

"liberating" them on condition that they would work as porters for the company. As for stations, the State reneged on its promise to lease the recently vacated State station at Kinshasa but allowed the SEE to lease the abandoned State stations at Equator and Luebo for a period of five years.[6]

Even before Lieutenant Taunt arrived in the Congo to set up the company's operation, he had discovered that the SEE would face commercial competition from the Congo Free State. On the ship SS *Cabo Verde* sailing to the Congo, he met the Congo Free State agent Alphonse Vangele, who told him that he had orders from King Leopold to purchase ivory along the Upper Congo. Taunt felt that King Leopold was playing a "double game" and wrote to Sanford that it "must be stopped." Vangele reached Malebo Pool on August 28 and obtained use of the steamboat *Henry Reed*, which the State had leased from the American Baptist Mission Society, for a trip up the Ubangi River. On the way, he stopped at the abandoned Equator Station (which he had founded in 1883) to build a warehouse that would serve as his base of operations for the next two years. From there, he went up the Ubangi River as far as the rapids of Zongo, returning to the Equator Station on November 4, 1886. The official purpose of the trip was to explore the Ubangi and sign treaties with chiefs, but he also bought thirty-six hundred pounds of ivory.[7]

When the SEE agents Swinburne and Taunt arrived at Malebo Pool in September 1886, they found that they had competition from the New Dutch Trading Company and a French company. In addition, there were long-established African ivory buyers such as Stanley's friend Chief Ngaliema. Ivory came to the Pool from the upper river, carried by Bobangi traders in large canoes to Mfwa and Kimpela on the north bank and to Kintambo and Kinshasa on the south bank. Taunt noted that the price of ivory at Malebo Pool—formerly very cheap—was rising because of the increased competition. When he learned that ivory could be purchased at Bolobo—a week's travel upriver—for ten to fifteen *mitakos* (brass rods) a pound, he concluded that it was best to purchase it as far from the Pool as possible in order to get better prices.[8]

The first SEE agent to establish himself on the Upper Congo River was E. J. Glave, a former agent for the International African Association and the Congo Free State, who took over the State's abandoned Equator Station in January 1887. As an ivory buyer and an avid big-game hunter, Glave took a keen interest in the habits of the elephants in the heart of the equatorial rainforest. In contrast to the beasts of the East African savanna, the forest elephants were usually found in thick tropical foliage. They normally roamed in families of two or three animals but sometimes in herds as large as two or three hundred. They were constantly on the move because an elephant would eat six to eight hundred pounds of food a day.

A herd of fifty elephants would typically be scattered over a patch of two to three acres. Often the foliage was so thick that the hunter would be within thirty or forty yards of an elephant herd for five or six hours without getting a clear shot at one of the elephant's vital spots. On one occasion, Glave learned about a herd of a hundred elephants feeding a few miles from the Equator Station. "We crept close to them," Glave reported, "but they were in the midst of a thick undergrowth, and we could only discern their whereabouts by an occasional glimpse of their great bodies through the foliage, or the raising of a trunk as one of them would snap off a branch in order to pluck from it some delicate sprout which had caught his eye. But, all around us, the rustling among the big leaves and the waving of the slender shrubs denoted their presence."[9]

It was not until August 1887 that Glave gained the use of the company's steamboat *Florida* and began to travel the inland waterways in search of ivory. His first trip was to the basins of the Maringa and Lopori Rivers. Traveling up the Maringa, he purchased ivory in every village, often very cheaply. In one case, he purchased a seventy-five-pound tusk for beads and shells worth about one dollar. Many of the tusks were old, having been hidden underwater in the river for years. Glave reported that many of the tusks came from hunters called "Bambutu" who inhabited the extreme headwaters of the river. They killed elephants with spear traps and pitfall traps and attacked them with heavy spears. He was no doubt referring to the Bambuti Pygmies. On that trip, Glave purchased about two tons of ivory.[10]

In addition to its Equator Station post on the Upper Congo River, the SEE took over the abandoned government post at Luebo, some five hundred miles up the Kasai River (a major tributary of the Congo). The ivory trade at Luebo was not profitable because of competition from Portuguese ivory merchants coming north from Angola, but wild rubber extracted from the *landolphia* vines in the forests promised to be more profitable. People would make an incision in the rubber vines and attach a small calabash to catch the drops of latex, which was then poured into a larger vessel and exposed to heat and smoke so that it could congeal into rubber balls. A flintlock musket could be traded for a hundred pounds of rubber, a small barrel of gunpowder could purchase fifty, and two yards of cotton cloth could purchase five and a half pounds of rubber.[11]

The Sanford Exploring Expedition took an interest in the rubber trade from the very beginning. Shortly after Taunt arrived at Malebo Pool in October 1887, he sent a sample of rubber to Henry Shelton Sanford. "I send you a ball of Luebo rubber," he wrote on November 26. "The natives rub the sap on their bodies, and when dry, they take it off and form a ball. Forty of these balls cost one bead." By March 1888, the company had received sixty-one hundred pounds of rubber in balls weighing 2.25 pounds each. In search of new markets in the United States, Sanford contacted companies such as the Converse Rubber Company and the Boston Rubber Shoe Company, but no contracts were ever signed.[12]

By 1888, the SEE had invested a substantial amount of money in its Congo venture but had seen very little in return. Sanford estimated that the company had purchased twelve to fifteen tons of ivory, but most of it had not yet been sold in Europe, most likely because of difficulties in obtaining porters to carry it to the Atlantic coast. When the impatient Belgian investors began to discuss liquidation of the SEE, Sanford tried to form a new company based on American investors. He told interested American businessmen that in a single year the company could purchase 100–150 tons of ivory and 40–50 tons of rubber, but he had no takers. With the American economy expanding, investments in the Congo seemed unnecessarily risky. In December 1888, the Sanford Exploring Expedition was taken over by the Société Anonyme Belge, which acquired all of its equipment and contracts. Sanford had gambled that King Leopold's assistance would compensate for his lack of capital, and he had lost. The main effect of his aborted project was to put much of the commerce of the Upper Congo firmly in Belgian hands.[13]

2

Stanley Falls Station, Upper Congo River,
September 27, 1886

When the steamboat *A.I.A.* (*Association Internationale Africaine*) approached to within half a mile of the Congo Free State's station at Stanley Falls on September 27, 1886, the crew noticed that no flag was flying. The station looked deserted, and the two large earthen-walled houses for the State agents had been scorched by fire. The small military camp beside the station was still intact, but the people who emerged from the huts were wearing white robes instead of Congo Free State uniforms. One of them waved a long pole holding the flag of Zanzibar. By then, it was clear that the station was in the hands of Tippu Tip's Arab colleagues and their Manyema soldiers. Fearing an attack from land and water, the steamboat made a U-turn and began its retreat. A cry of "hurrah!" went up from the riverbank, and a barrage of rifle fire harassed the boat as it headed downstream. The next day the *A.I.A.* was alerted by fishermen that a white man had taken refuge in the nearby village of Yariembi. Stopping at the village, they found Walter Deane, the Stanley Falls station chief, in a hut where he was being cared for by friendly villagers after spending thirty days hiding in the rainforest to elude capture and certain death.[14]

The State station had been built in December 1883 on Wana Rusari Island near the seventh cataract of Stanley Falls. It was just five hundred yards downstream from the island where Tippu Tip had established his camp. The treaty that the International Association of the Congo had signed with the Arabs in October 1884 had established the seventh cataract as the dividing line between the Arab and Association territories, but that arrangement had not lasted more than a few months. At the time, the Association lacked the goods or personnel to engage in serious trade, and the station served mainly as a placeholder for its territorial claims. The main

Tippu Tip (right) at Stanley Falls with his half brother Bwana Nzige. CPA Media—Pictures from History / Granger—

job of the agents was simply to survive until a commercial infrastructure could be established.[15]

Very little had changed since the Berlin Conference had acknowledged the territorial claims of the Congo Free State. IAC agents became State agents; two 75 mm Krupp guns were sent to enhance the security of the Stanley Falls Station; and a new treaty signed by Tippu Tip in December 1885 stated that both the Arabs and the Congo Free State could trade freely anywhere in the Stanley Falls District as long as they treated people humanely and refrained from slave raiding. In February 1886, State agent A. M. Wester, who had signed the treaty with Tippu Tip, was replaced by Walter Deane, a former lieutenant in the British army, and in April, Tippu Tip departed for Zanzibar, leaving his half brother Muhammad bin Said (a.k.a. Bwana Nzige) in charge. Having too many Manyema soldiers and caravan porters to live on a small island, Bwana Nzige had built a settlement on the south bank of the Congo River, just opposite the island that housed the State station. Deane had received strict orders to avoid conflict if at all possible, given that his small contingent of thirty-two hired Hausa soldiers and forty hired Bangala soldiers was vastly outnumbered by the Manyema soldiers of the Arabs and that the two Krupp guns served more for intimidation than for serious defense against a sustained attack.

Despite the weakness of his position, Deane did not shrink from getting into conflicts with the Arabs by giving sanctuary to the enslaved concubines of Arab traders. In one case, an Arab named Khamis entered the State station and seized his concubine, who had sought sanctuary there. In response, Deane and twenty soldiers went to Khamis's village, burned it down, and made off with the woman and all the ivory. Although it was a small conflict, it had larger symbolic significance in signaling which group of foreign invaders had true authority at Stanley Falls. Deane bragged that his actions in defense of enslaved women had earned him a certain authority in the eyes of the local populations at the expense of the Arabs, while Bwana Nzige, in seeming agreement, complained that the Arabs' authority over their own slaves was being undermined by Deane.[16]

The tension between Walter Deane and Bwana Nzige came to a head in June 1886, when a slave concubine who had been beaten by her master sought sanctuary at the State station. Bwana Nzige came to the station the next day to demand that she be returned to her master. According to the missionary George Grenfell, who witnessed the encounter, Deane said that he would not force her to return against her will. Bwana Nzige then became agitated and asked Deane whether he could "take care of his head," a taunt that Deane understood as a threat. Deane later claimed that he had offered to pay a large ransom for the woman, but Grenfell's account makes no mention of it. As relations between the state and the Arabs soured over the next month, Deane stuck to his position that any slave seeking sanctuary at the station would receive it.[17]

On August 24, 1886, a force of four hundred to five hundred of Bwana Nzige's Manyema soldiers attacked the station, having crossed over to the island during the night. Because of its strong stockade, the fortified station fought off repeated attacks for three days, but with ammunition running low, the hired Bangala soldiers deserted and headed downstream in canoes during the night. The next evening most of the Hausa soldiers followed them down the river, leaving Deane with no alternative but to evacuate the station. After blowing up the station to prevent the Arabs from getting any of the remaining weapons and gunpowder, the two State agents and four remaining Hausa soldiers swam across a narrow branch of the river to spend the night hiding in the surrounding forest. Deane's colleague, a Belgian lieutenant named Dubois, drowned in the crossing.[18]

After that, the State's Stanley Falls Station remained unoccupied, and the Bangala Station—some five hundred miles downstream from Stanley Falls—became the farthest inland extension of the Congo Free State's trading zone. Although there was talk about mounting a military expedition to reestablish the Stanley Falls Station, the State lacked the capacity to challenge Bwana Nzige and his Manyema soldiers. With both the Congo Free State and Tippu Tip gone from Stanley Falls, the Arab traders there were free to resume their former pattern of raiding and trading. Instead of focusing their activities on the Congo River itself, however, the raiding parties went into the forest toward the headwaters of the smaller rivers that drained into the Congo. Herbert Ward, an agent of the SEE, reported that if one went up the tributaries toward their headwaters, one would inevitably find Arab-led trading and raiding parties.[19]

3

Zanzibar, September 25, 1886

The idea of sending a British expedition to bring relief to Emin Bey, the beleaguered governor of Equatoria province in Sudan, was first proposed in a telegram from Frederick Holmwood, the acting consul general in Zanzibar, on September 25, 1886. The War Office in London replied that such an expedition would be the height of folly. Soon, however, public opinion in Britain began to support a relief expedition because Emin was seen as a hero in the fight against the Arab slave trade in Sudan, which funneled black-skinned captives from southern Sudan to slave markets in Khartoum and Cairo.

On October 29, 1886, the *Times* of London published a letter that Emin Bey had written to Charles Allen, the secretary of the Anti-Slavery Society. It said, in part, "Ever since the month of May 1883 we have been cut off from all communication with the world. Forgotten and abandoned by the [Egyptian] government, we have been compelled to make a virtue out of necessity. . . . I suppose that in Egypt or Khartoum, we are believed to be dead, and for this reason they have not sent us any steamer." On November 5, the executive committee of the Anti-Slavery Society passed a resolution that read, "In view of the services rendered by Dr. Emin Bey, both in the suppression of the slave trade, and in administering for a considerable period a settled and peaceful province of Egypt, the Committee considers that the position of Emin Bey presents a very strong claim upon her majesty's government." The resolution urged that the British government should "be sparing of neither exertion nor expense in order to rescue him from the destruction which seems to await him."[20]

The man at the center of the controversy called himself Emin Bey, but he was born as Eduard Schnitzer into a middle-class Jewish family in Prussia. His father died when he was five years old, and his mother subsequently married a Lutheran and was baptized, along with her children. Edward completed his medical studies in Berlin in 1864 but was disqualified from practicing medicine in Germany because he let too much time elapse before applying to take the state medical examination. He then moved to Montenegro and joined the Ottoman Turkish service as a quarantine officer at

the port of Antivari but left in 1870 to join the staff of the Ottoman governor of northern Albania.

When the governor died in 1873, Schnitzer returned to Prussia, but in December 1875, he arrived in Khartoum, Sudan, where
he called himself Emin Effendi and claimed that he was a Turk
who had studied medicine in Germany. Emin was comfortable
in Sudan because it was under the control of Egypt, which was a
self-governing province of the Ottoman Empire. He started a medical practice and collected specimens of plants, animals, and birds
for museums in Europe. It was there that he discovered collecting
was his true passion. Because he was fluent in the Ottoman dialect
of Arabic, the Turco-Egyptian administration of Sudan recruited
him to be a government medical officer in the newly established
Equatoria Province, the southernmost province in Sudan.[21]

In August 1877, the British persuaded Khedive Ismail, the Ottoman viceroy of Egypt and Sudan, to sign a Slave Trade Convention
with Britain in which he pledged to end the sale or purchase of
slaves in Sudan. Shortly thereafter, Emin was appointed governor
of Equatoria Province, with the rank of *bey*. Due to Emin's efforts,
the slave trade in Equatoria was almost eradicated by 1879, and
many of the Khartoum-based slave traders had left the province.
But Emin was not satisfied, because the slave trade from Bahr-el-
Ghazal province, located northwest of Equatoria, continued. "I do
not even know where my frontier lies on the side toward that nest
of slaves, the Bahr-el-Ghazal province," he wrote. "The capture of
slaves and the slave caravans which travel daily from the southern
districts northward to the Bahr-el-Ghazal territory are undeniable
facts."[22]

His more immediate concern, however, was the rebellion
against the Egyptian occupation of Sudan led by a Muslim religious figure who called himself the Mahdi. "A year ago," Emin
wrote in 1882, "a certain Muhammad Ahmad, who had been held
by the Arabs to be a kind of prophet, on account of his contem-
plative life, suddenly gave out himself to be the Mahdi—the last

prophet—and commenced his new career by sending letters to the Governor-General and the governors and chiefs of the tribes, requiring them to recognize his superior (spiritual) authority and be ready to obey his orders." Over the next three years, the Mahdists' power grew steadily as their armies moved from victory to victory.[23]

On April 18, 1885, Emin received a packet of letters sent out by Karam Allah, the commander of the Mahdi's army in the Bahr-el-Ghazal. It contained a copy of a letter written by the Mahdi announcing that Khartoum had been taken on January 25 and a letter from Karam Allah saying that if Emin did not surrender, the Mahdist forces would march on Emin's provincial headquarters at Lado, on the White Nile. With Lado running dangerously short of grain, the military officers there decided to evacuate all the women, children, and civilians to the south, leaving only the soldiers. By July 10, Emin had established a station at Wadelai, located on the White Nile just north of its exit from Lake Albert. He was now less than three degrees north of the equator. Although Emin was cut off from all communication with Khartoum, he had a steamboat that could navigate on both the Nile and Lake Albert, and he could send letters to Zanzibar via the kingdom of Bunyoro, located southeast of Lake Albert.

Abandoned by the Egyptian government, Emin was running his own independent polity, which he had no intention of abandoning. On April 17, 1887, he described his situation: "Things go on with us in the same way as before. We sow, we reap, we spin, and live day after day as usual. I have been obliged to evacuate Lado, as it was impossible for me to supply the garrison there with corn, but as a set-off to the loss of this station, I have been able to reoccupy the district of Makraka." He closed the letter by reiterating his position about leaving. "I should like here again to mention that if a relief expedition comes to us, I will on no account leave my people. We have been through troublous times together, and I consider it would be a shameful act on my part were I to desert them. All we would ask England to do is to bring about a better understanding with Uganda [i.e., the Kingdom of Buganda], and to provide us with a free and safe way to the coast. This is all we want. Evacuate our territory? Certainly not!"[24]

Even though Britain had established an informal protectorate over Egypt following its invasion in 1882, its main interest was to protect the Suez Canal and oversee the Egyptian government's finances. Britain had neither the desire nor the capacity to interfere in the affairs of the Turco-Egyptian Sudan, where the forces of the Mahdi were dominant. When the British government refused to send a military expedition to rescue Emin, the shipping magnate William MacKinnon took it upon himself to organize the Emin Relief Committee as a private venture. The Relief Committee's thirteen members included Henry Morton Stanley, James F. Hutton (the ex-president of the Manchester Chamber of Commerce), John Kirk (the British consul general in Zanzibar), and Horace Waller (a former expedition colleague of David Livingstone). At the initial meeting of the Committee on December 29, 1886, Stanley was appointed leader of the expedition and given carte blanche in terms of selecting the route, the personnel, and the equipment. The exact goal of the expedition remained vague. One option was simply to bring guns, ammunition, and supplies to Emin so that he could hold out in Equatoria for a while longer; the other option was to evacuate him and his men to Zanzibar and repatriate them to Egypt. The final decision would be up to Emin.

Immediately after the meeting, Stanley took the overnight ferry to Belgium to meet with King Leopold the next morning. Even though Stanley had earlier been relieved of his duties to the International Association of the Congo, he still had personal contractual obligations to Leopold II that required him to obtain the king's permission. His discussions with the king focused on two issues. The first was the choice of a route. Instead of marching overland from Zanzibar to southern Sudan, Stanley proposed going to Zanzibar to pick up hired guards and porters, then taking a steamship around the southern tip of Africa to the mouth of the Congo River, and then going up the Congo and Aruwimi Rivers on steamboats as far as the rapids of Yambuya, located 70 miles northwest of Stanley Falls. From there, they would trek for 322 miles through the rainforest to Lake Albert and on to Wadelai to find Emin (the true straight-line distance from Stanley Falls to Wadelai was 458 miles and much farther by winding paths). Stanley preferred this route because he could make use of steamships and steamboats and also because the Zanzibari porters would quickly be so far from home that they would not be tempted to desert.[25]

King Leopold had his own reasons for preferring the Congo River route. First, the expedition would help to reestablish the Congo Free State's influence in the Stanley Falls region, and second, the idea of annexing Equatoria to the Congo Free State was on his mind because it would give the Free State direct access to the commerce along the Nile. Leopold even considered paying Emin £1,500 a year to govern Equatoria on behalf of the Congo State. Leopold's view prevailed because he refused to let Stanley lead the expedition unless he took the Congo route. MacKinnon, who favored an overland trek from Zanzibar, reluctantly agreed to supply a steamship to carry Stanley and his hired guards and porters from Zanzibar around the Cape of Good Hope to the mouth of the Congo River. Once the expedition reached Malebo Pool, King Leopold would provide the entire fleet of Congo Free State steamboats and whaleboats to carry Stanley and his men up the Congo River and then up the Aruwimi to the rapids at Yambuya.[26]

The second issue involved the Congo Free State's relations with Tippu Tip. Stanley was aware that Tippu Tip had recently arrived in Zanzibar and would be there when he came to pick up the porters. The Congo River route was not feasible if the Arabs at Stanley Falls were hostile to the expedition because they could cut off its food supplies or attack it in order to capture the guns and the ammunition it was carrying to Emin. Stanley planned to meet with Tippu Tip and demarcate separate spheres of influence for the State and the Arabs so that the two groups could coexist peacefully.

Accompanied by seven European assistants recruited from Britain, Stanley arrived in Zanzibar on February 22, 1887, after picking up 61 Sudanese soldiers in Cairo and 13 Somali soldiers in Aden. He carried with him a letter from the khedive of Egypt promoting Emin to the rank of pasha, which is why he was known to the expedition as Emin Pasha. In Zanzibar, Stanley picked up 620 soldiers and porters who had been recruited in advance by the acting British consul general, Frederick Holmwood. His most important task, however, was to reach an agreement with Tippu Tip. The two men had not seen each other since they parted near Stanley Falls more than ten years earlier.[27]

Despite the ascendency of the Arab and Swahili traders in the Stanley Falls region, Tippu Tip had gotten a very sober assessment of the broader geopolitical realities in East Africa when he arrived in Zanzibar on November 28, 1886. Ever since the Berlin Conference, German interests had been aggressively claiming territory on the African mainland. In 1885, Germany had annexed the region north of Lake Nyasa, thereby challenging both the sultan's formal claims and Britain's informal claims over the region. The Anglo-German Agreement signed on November 1, 1886, had recognized the sultan's control only over Zanzibar, Pemba, and two other small islands and a strip along the coast that stretched inland for a mere ten miles. "Hamed, you must forgive me," the sultan told Tippu Tip, "but I really do not want the hinterland at all. The Europeans here in Zanzibar want to steal from me. Will it be the hinterland? Those who are dead, who see nothing of this, are at peace. You, too, are a stranger to it. You will see what is involved." "When I heard Seyyid's words," wrote Tippu Tip in his autobiography, "I knew that it was all up." Although the collapse of the sultan's claims on the African interior was disheartening to Tippu Tip, it freed him to rethink the future of his Manyema empire.[28]

In his book *In Darkest Africa*, Stanley portrayed his meeting with Tippu Tip at the British consulate as a dramatic encounter in which he did not know if he was meeting an old friend or a new enemy. He described Tippu Tip as the "uncrowned king of the region between Stanley Falls and Tanganyika Lake [a straight-line distance of 484 miles], commanding many thousands of men." Tippu Tip, for his part, described the meeting in more business-like terms. He noted that Stanley flattered him by saying that he had originally planned to sail directly to the west coast of Africa, but, having heard that Tippu Tip was in Zanzibar, he had come this way instead. The flattery was a lie; Stanley had planned to use armed porters from Zanzibar from the very beginning.[29]

The negotiations over separate spheres of influence quickly reached an impasse because King Leopold had insisted that the authority of the Congo Free State should extend all the way to Stanley Falls while Tippu Tip insisted on keeping the posts that the Arabs had established downstream from the falls. The British consul Holmwood urged Tippu Tip to abandon the downstream posts to avoid the threat of attack by Congo State's armed steamers, but Tippu Tip seemed confident that he could maintain his position against such an attack. Prior to Stanley's arrival, he had sent off a caravan carrying fifteen hundred percussion-cap muskets, two hundred breech-loading rifles, and a full complement of ammunition to Stanley Falls, where three thousand Manyema soldiers armed with guns were mustered to protect the falls from an attack by the Congo Free State.[30]

It is not certain when the idea of appointing Tippu Tip as the Congo Free State's governor of the Stanley Falls District first came up, but it seemed a good compromise. In that way, the State could gain nominal possession of the Arab posts below Stanley Falls, and Tippu Tip could gain European recognition of his author-ity over territory that he already controlled. A second advantage for Stanley was that Tippu Tip would accompany the relief expe-dition to Stanley Falls and recruit additional porters for the trek through the rainforest to Lake Albert. A third advantage was that the appointment would encourage Tippu Tip to sell some of his ivory to the Congo Free State. After a long discussion, Tippu Tip told Holmwood to work out the details with Stanley and draw up the agreement.

The contract said that "the Congo State appoints Hamed-bin-Mohammed al Murjebi, Tippu Tip, to be Wali [i.e., governor] of the independent State of the Congo, at Stanley Falls District." He was to fly the flag of the Congo State at the Stanley Falls Station, maintain the authority of the State downstream to the mouth of the Aruwimi River, and suppress the slave trade. He would receive a resident officer of the Congo State to act as his secretary in all his communications with the governor-general of the Congo. For his services, Tippu Tip would receive a salary of thirty pounds a month. He was free to "carry on his legitimate private trade in any direction and to send his caravans to and from any places he may desire." Before signing the contract, Tippu Tip sought authorization from the sultan of Zanzibar. "Seyyid advised me to go, and to go as far as they wanted," recounted Tippu Tip. "I complained about the wage they were giving me, thirty pounds a month. But he maintained that I should go, even for ten pounds a month, and I would still be able to carry on my business." The proffered salary was indeed a pittance compared to the considerable wealth of Tippu Tip. Before leaving Zanzibar with Stanley on February 25, he instructed his agent to send MT$30,000 worth of trade goods to Manyema.[31]

There was a second contract as well, which would also be consequential. This one dealt with the porters that Tippu Tip was to furnish to the expedition once it reached the Stanley Falls region. They would transport relief supplies overland for Emin Pasha and carry out his reported seventy-five tons of ivory, worth about £60,000. Article 7 of this second contract was very explicit: "All of these men, if loaded with ivory at the Nyanza Albert, shall deposit the said ivory at the Congo and within the District of Stanley Falls as the officer in charge shall direct." Article 8 allowed Stanley to reengage the men for a second trip if all of the ivory could not be evacuated on the first one. The contract called for Tippu Tip to supply "a number of able-bodied men in Hamid bin Muhammad's employ" but did not specify the number. It also stated that Tippu Tip should supply each man with a gun and a hundred bullets but that Stanley would supply the gunpowder.[32]

On February 25, just three days after Stanley had arrived in Zanzibar, the steamship *Madura*, provided by McKinnon's British-India Steam Navigation Company, steamed southward with Stanley and his seven European assistants, Tippu Tip and his entourage, and the hired soldiers and porters. Over the next three weeks, they traveled around the southern tip of Africa, with a brief stop at Cape Town and then on to Banana, at the mouth of the Congo River. From there, they traveled up the Congo River estuary to Matadi on steamboats chartered from the New Dutch Trading Company, the British Congo Company, and the Portuguese Companhia Portugueza do Zaire. Then they followed the caravan road around the rapids to Malebo Pool.[33]

Herbert Ward, an employee of the Sanford Exploring Expedition, encountered the caravan on March 28, 1887. As he described it, Stanley led the caravan, riding on a mule with silver-plated trappings. Behind him came Somali soldiers in white robes and braided waistcoats, Zanzibari soldiers with guns and ammunition belts, Sudanese soldiers with dark hooded coats and rifles on their backs, and Zanzibari porters carrying boxes of ammunition and sandy-colored blankets. Altogether, the caravan contained about seven hundred people and stretched out along the trail for four miles. "An abrupt turn of the narrow footpath," wrote Ward, "brought into view the dignified form of the renowned Tippu Tip, as he strode along majestically in his flowing Arab robes of dazzling whiteness, carrying over his left shoulder a richly decorated sabre, which was an emblem of office conferred on him by His Highness the Sultan of Zanzibar. Behind him, at a respectful distance, followed several Arab sheiks, whose bearing was quiet and dignified. In response to my salutation, they bowed most gracefully."[34]

Stanley (on the donkey) and Tippu Tip (to his right) on the caravan trail from Matadi to Malebo Pool. Note the porters carrying sections of the steel boat. *Illustrated London News*, January 25, 1890.

It took the caravan exactly a month to arrive at Malebo Pool on April 21. Stanley had requested the use of all the Congo Free State's steamboats to carry his entourage upriver, but he found that only the *Stanley* was in working order. The *En Avant*'s steam engine was no longer working, but it could be towed as a barge. Learning that the *Peace*, belonging to the (British) Baptist Missionary Society, and the *Henry Reed*, belonging to the American Baptist Foreign Missionary Society, were at the Pool, Stanley requisitioned both of them from the missions and threatened to seize them if they refused. He also commandeered the *Florida*, belonging to the San-ford Exploring Expedition, even though it lacked an engine and had to be towed. To this fleet, he added several whaleboats to be towed as barges. Because of a shortage of boats, a good portion of the supplies was left behind at the Pool.[35]

By the time the fleet reached Bolobo, some two hundred miles upstream from Malebo Pool, on May 12, it was clear that the three small steamers were not capable of transporting the entire entourage up the Congo River to Yambuya. Stanley therefore decided to divide his expedition into three groups: Tippu Tip's people, numbering roughly one hundred, would go directly to Stanley Falls on the *Henry Reed*. The Emin Pasha Relief Expedition would be divided into an advance guard of 375 men using the *Stanley* and the *Peace*, while the remaining 125 men would remain in Bolobo to be brought up on the second trip when the steamers returned to Malebo Pool to pick up the rest of the supplies. They would form the rear column.

On June 12, 1887, Stanley and his advance guard arrived at the mouth of the Aruwimi, some nine hundred miles from Malebo Pool but one hundred miles short of Stanley Falls. Following his plan to avoid the Arab-controlled territory, they proceeded up the Aruwimi for a hundred miles until the Yambuya rapids blocked their further advance. There, Stanley constructed his base camp. Stanley's advance guard would then proceed east through the equatorial rainforest toward Lake Albert, following the rapid-filled valley of the Aruwimi/Ituri. They would travel mainly on foot and would use locally confiscated dugout canoes where feasible. Meanwhile, the steamers returned to Malebo Pool to pick up the supplies that had been left there and the 125 men who had been left at Bolobo. According to Stanley's plan, when the rear column arrived at the Yambuya camp, it would be joined by six hundred Manyema porters to be supplied by Tippu Tip, and they would then follow Stanley's trail through the rainforest to Lake Albert.

4

Yambuya Camp, Congo Free State, June 28, 1887

Stanley left the Yambuya camp with the advance guard on June 28, 1887. The column consisted of 414 men with 360 rifles. The Sudanese served as soldiers, while the Zanzibaris carried loads, mostly ammunition. In addition, the caravan was carrying a steel rowboat in sections for crossing bodies of water and a Maxim gun, which was the world's first true machine gun. He left Maj. Edmund Barttelot in charge of the Yambuya camp, along with 129 Zanzibaris and Sudanese, who would soon be joined by the 125 men left behind in Bolobo and the 600 porters to be provided by Tippu Tip. That combined group would constitute the rear column. Stanley estimated that he would be back in five months. In the meantime, the rear column had instructions to follow Stanley's trail as soon as the steamboats brought up the rest of the men and supplies and Tippu Tip delivered the porters.[36]

For the next five months, the advance guard struggled to march through the rainforest toward Lake Albert. Stanley described the forest: "Great trees, rising as high as an arrow shot toward the sky, uniting their crowns, interlacing their branches, pressing and crowded one against the other, until neither sunbeam nor shaft of light may penetrate it." The description by Thomas Parke, the expedition's medical officer, was less lyrical. "We were now marching through dense primeval forests," he wrote, "in which we often passed several days without a glimpse of the sun, oppressed with the persistent odor of decomposing vegetation; frequently wading through stinking miasmatic swamps and stagnant elephant pools."[37]

As he had done when traveling down the Lualaba with Tippu Tip in 1875, Stanley divided the expedition between the companies that traveled by land and those that traveled by water. Stanley's account of the expedition gives his usual colorful and self-serving narrative, but the diary of Arthur J. Mounteney Jephson provides a more candid account of the events. As a former cadet in the British Merchant Navy, Jephson was often in charge of the river travel. The frequent rapids prevented the expedition from traveling for long stretches by dugout canoe, but the steel boat, which could be taken apart and carried overland around waterfalls, proved very useful, and they sometimes seized canoes, which could sometimes be hauled around the rapids but often had to be abandoned at the next waterfall.[38]

On July 4, Jephson wrote, "Stanley had seen five canoes loaded with food going downstream and had fired on them. Four got away, but one put into the opposite bank. . . . It contained a goat, native cloth . . . and 13 large jars of palm oil." On July 5, they came upon a camp where the villagers hurriedly ran into the forest. "We took what food we wanted and towed eleven canoes across to the other side of the river. Stanley was camped in a large deserted village—the people from whom we took the canoes were probably the inhabitants of the village who had fled upon hearing of our being in the neighborhood." On July 16, Stanley, traveling in the steel boat, pursued a canoe with four men and shot one of them, causing the other three to jump overboard. By the time he secured the canoe, the wounded man had bled to death. They threw his body into the river, washed the blood out of the canoe, and filled it with their loads.

When the expedition approached a riverside village, the villagers would usually flee. "It is wonderful how the natives clear out from every place before us," wrote Jephson. The major problem throughout the march was finding food to feed the roughly four hundred members of the expedition. Unable to purchase sufficient food, the expedition took to seizing hostages and trading them for food or simply raiding villages and fields. The main staple food in this region was cassava (i.e., manioc), a root crop that can remain in the ground for up to a year without spoiling. The expedition would dig up the cassava fields and take all the ripe cassava. "Today, half the expedition went over to Maguai and brought back quantities of manioc from the fields at the back of the village," wrote Jephson. "Nelson followed on the track of some men with goats, but did not get them; he came, however, upon villages with quantities of Indian corn [i.e., sorghum] done up in baskets and brought it all into camp."[39]

The companies that marched overland sometimes encountered impenetrable rainforest. On July 27, Jephson wrote, "The road had to be cut through solid jungle, but we struck elephant tracks in the afternoon and got along pretty well." The problem with elephant tracks, Jephson learned, was that sooner or later they always led through swampy ground. But there was another problem as well. On July 23, Jephson was following an elephant track when he encountered a fence that had a small opening for the path. As he went through the opening, the ground gave way under his feet, and he fell into a wedge-shaped hole about eight feet deep. He had fallen into an elephant trap. On August 8, he wrote, "This country must be swarming with elephants; one passes their tracks all day long." Because of the density of the rainforest, however, he almost never saw an elephant.[40]

On July 23, Stanley captured another dugout canoe and found in it a broken sword of the type carried by many of the Arabs. It was a sure sign that Arab ivory traders had been there ahead of them. On August 31, a party of twenty Manyemans approached Stanley's camp, bringing them a gift of a fat goat. They were attached to a larger Arab ivory-collecting party headed by Uledi Balyuz, known locally as Ugarrowa, who commanded several hundred armed men. The Manyemans said that Ugarrowa had a semipermanent camp twenty marches farther up the Aruwimi River. On September 16, as Stanley's expedition approached the camp, Ugarrowa arrived with six canoes, drums beating and horns blaring, and bringing them presents of goats, chickens, rice, and plantains. He explained that he was a native of Zanzibar who had gone to seek his fortune in Manyema and had settled at Kirundu, on the Lualaba River. Two years previously, he had left Manyema to search for ivory in the rainforest along the Ituri River (which runs into the Aruwimi). For the past year, he had been living in a settlement built on an abandoned village after driving out the inhabitants. After resting up at Ugarrowa's camp for two days, and leaving fifty-four sick and weakened porters with him to recover, Stanley moved on.[41]

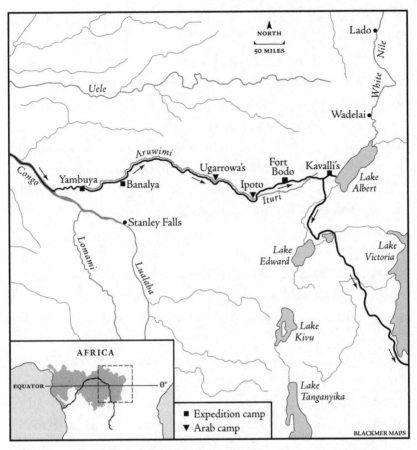

Route of the Emin Pasha Relief Expedition, 1887–1889

On October 18, Stanley's expedition arrived at an Arab camp at Ipoto, which was built in a large clearing of at least seven hundred acres. They were welcomed by a Manyema man named Khamis, a lieutenant of Kilonga-Longa, who was away seeking ivory and was not expected to return for three months. Both Khamis and Kilonga-Longa were under the authority of Abed bin Salim, a major Arab ivory trader who lived in Nyangwe. There were no Arabs in the camp, only Manyemans. The soldiers were young men who were not paid a salary but received a small commission on the ivory they obtained. While the relief expedition was at the camp, an ivory-raiding party returned with sixteen tusks obtained by raiding villages and seizing ivory that was stored in huts or hidden in the forest.[42]

After ten days at Kilonga-Longa's camp at Ipoto, Stanley set out for Lake Albert, leaving behind twenty-nine men who were too sick or weak to travel. Because river travel was no longer feasible, they disassembled the steel boat and stashed it in the woods. Stanley set off with Manyema guides who had agreed to accompany his expedition for fifteen marches. On December 4, the 160th day since leaving Yambuya, they broke out of the rainforest and found themselves in what Jephson described as "one of the loveliest lands we had seen," with waving green grasses on undulating hills with herds of cape buffaloes and elands. On December 8, they entered a long, broad valley that was completely under cultivation, with great fields of sorghum, millet, bananas, sweet potatoes, Indian corn, and beans. Jephson wrote that it was "a very land of Goshen."[43]

On December 13, 1887, nearly six months after leaving Yambuya, they spotted the waters of Lake Albert. The expedition had accomplished its first objective, but at great cost. According to Jephson's figures (which differ slightly from those of Stanley), of the 389 men who had left Yambuya, only 169 were still with the group. Of the original group, 56 had been left behind at the camp of the Arab trader Ugarrowa, 24 had been left at the camp of Kilonga-Longa, 120 were lost by death or desertion, and another 20 were simply missing.[44]

Stanley had earlier sent messages to Emin Pasha, asking him to withdraw to the southern end of the lake and wait for the relief expedition, but neither Emin nor his steamboat, the *Khedive*, had been seen there for several years. After waiting two days on the shore and discovering that food was scarce, they returned to the forest and cleared the ground to build a stockaded camp they called Fort Bodo, sending out parties to reclaim the survivors who had been left behind at Arab camps along the route. Then they began to plant fields. While waiting for their crops to grow, they survived by looting the countryside. When they learned on January 21, 1888, that there was a settlement in the forest with a plentiful supply of Indian corn, they attacked it and shot two people, causing the others to flee. They then made off with eight tons of grain.[45]

By the beginning of April 1888, Stanley returned to the lake with the steel boat to try to make contact with Emin. Stopping at Kavalli's town, on the plateau high above the lake, Stanley was given a letter that Emin had written a month earlier, telling him to wait at Kavalli's for Emin's arrival. Being impatient, Stanley moved down to the lakeshore. On the evening of April 28, Emin arrived on the steamer *Khedive*. Even though it was late in the day, he went ashore to greet Stanley, who uncorked three bottles of champagne that he had carried all the way through the rainforest to celebrate the occasion. Over the next ten days, Stanley presented Emin with a variety of options: to evacuate to Zanzibar and return to Egypt by ship; to stay on as King Leopold's governor of Equatoria, which would then be annexed to the Congo Free State; or to remain as he was, but with an infusion of fresh supplies. Emin said that he needed some time to visit his posts and discuss the issues with his people.

Stanley was finally ready to return to his original camp at Yambuya in hopes of locating the rear column and bringing the rest of the men and supplies to Lake Albert. He left Fort Bodo on June 16, 1888, with 113 Zanzibaris and 95 carriers furnished by Emin Pasha. On August 8, they reached Ugarrowa's old camp and found it deserted. Two days later, they caught up with Ugarrowa's party, which was returning to Manyema with six hundred tusks weighing about thirteen tons, after having run out of gunpowder. Ugarrowa gave Stanley a gift of three large canoes that he could use to transport his party downstream. There was no doubt that the Arab traders and their Manyema followers had been successful in scouring the Ituri rainforest for ivory.[46]

5

Stanley Falls District, Congo Free State, June 17, 1887

Tippu Tip had arrived at Stanley Falls on the steamer *Henry Reed* on June 17, 1887, just two days after Stanley's advance guard had first arrived at Yambuya to prepare for their march through the rainforest. After greeting his Arab kinsmen and colleagues and raising the flag of the Congo Free State over his headquarters, he started gathering porters who would accompany the rear column, which would follow Stanley's trail to Lake Albert. According to Tippu Tip's contract with Stanley, he was to provide an unspecified number of porters from his headquarters at Stanley Falls to join the rear column of the Emin Pasha Relief Expedition. Stanley would later claim that Tippu Tip had agreed to provide six hundred porters, but that figure seems to have been a verbal understanding rather than a contractual obligation.[47]

Tippu Tip's initial attempt to send porters to the rear column's camp at Yambuya ended in failure. In July, he assembled a group of five hundred Manyema porters and took them down the Congo to the mouth of the Aruwimi in fifty canoes. But the Genya canoemen he had hired were reluctant to go up the Aruwimi to Yambuya because it was foreign territory to them. At the first night's camp along the Aruwimi, four members of Tippu Tip's group were killed and others captured in an attack by local villagers. In retaliation, Tippu Tip's soldiers destroyed the hostile village, but the canoemen refused to go any farther, claiming that they were ill with fevers and dysentery. With his gunpowder running low, Tippu Tip ordered the canoe fleet to return to Stanley Falls.[48]

During August and September, Tippu Tip made two attempts to send porters to Yambuya by overland routes, but each resulted in failure and yielded a total of only ten porters. Then, Salim bin Muhammad, one of Tippu Tip's top lieutenants, arrived at Yambuya

Tippu Tip (seated, center) meeting with his Arab chieftains at Stanley Falls. Herbert Ward, *Five Years with the Congo Cannibals* (1891), p. 165.

on September 26 with forty porters and confessed that Tippu Tip had not been able to provide any more. The problem was that the Manyema porters had refused the assignment after hearing rumors about the excessive weight and size of many of the loads carried by Stanley's Zanzibari porters. They had also heard rumors about the harsh treatment that the Zanzibaris received from Major Barttelot in the Yambuya camp. The only way to solve the problem, Tippu Tip believed, was to bring in a new set of porters from Kasongo, promise them lighter loads, and put them under the command of an Arab commander. In order to find more porters, Tippu Tip left Stanley Falls during the first week of November 1887 to travel up the Lualaba River to Kasongo.[49]

During the months when the rear column had been waiting at Yambuya for the porters, the Arab ivory caravans had been busy. Selim bin Muhammad, one of Tippu Tip's lieutenants, established a camp a short distance away from the expedition's camp. Lacking a stock of trade goods, he apparently obtained ivory by raiding. By May 1888, his Manyema troops were raiding up to fifteen days' march from Yambuya to the north and northwest as well as along the Aruwimi down to its junction with the Congo. Many of the tusks he brought in had cracks and blisters from the fires that burned the villages, thus giving evidence of how they were obtained. When the State steamer *A.I.A.* arrived at the Yambuya camp, Selim bin Muhammad arranged to have fifteen hundred pounds of tusks carried by the Belgians to Stanley Falls.[50]

The ivory raids also captured people. Many of them were held until they were ransomed with ivory, but others were taken away as slaves. "Nasaro bin Sef, with a large number of captives roped together, and some five or six hundred pounds worth of ivory, came down from Abdullah's further camp, seventeen days up this river," wrote Herbert Ward in his diary on March 5, 1888. The next day, he wrote, "This morning Selim's men, to the number of eighty or so, are going to attack a big village down the river, to raid it, and to capture slaves, which in due course of time will be sold for ivory." Tippu Tip had pledged to end raiding and slave trading in the region downstream from Stanley Falls, but he knew that he was powerless to stop it, even when his own lieutenant was doing the raiding.[51]

Tippu Tip returned to Stanley Falls on May 22, 1888, after recruiting porters at Kasongo. He told Major Barttelot, who had come to Stanley Falls to consult with him, that he had been able to get four hundred men for the relief expedition but no more. He had secured their agreement by promising them that they would carry half loads and work under the supervision of an Arab commander. Tippu Tip himself wanted no payment for the services of the porters, but Mwinyi Somai, who was to serve as their commander, should receive £1,000 plus any ivory he collected en route. Tippu Tip went to the Yambuya camp on June 4 to supervise the weighing of the loads and the preparations for the rear column to follow Stanley's blaze marks through the rainforest.[52]

On June 11, 1888—almost a year after Stanley's advance guard had left Yambuya—the rear column left the Yambuya camp to follow his trail. They had heard nothing from Stanley since he had left on June 28 of the previous year, and during that time, over eighty of the Zanzibari and Sudanese porters had died in the Yambuya camp. The expedition struck out due east through some of the thickest rainforest in the world, following the line of the Aruwimi River. "Our road was very bad," wrote William Bonny, "and the marching difficult, consisting of forest, swamp, marsh, and river the whole distance." The group was divided into four companies that marched separately. Stanley had promised to leave blaze marks and cut-down trees to indicate the route, but the trail was frequently lost, and the different companies became separated. The 430 Manyema porters, accompanied by about 200 follow-ers (including their wives and personal slaves), lagged behind the Zanzibaris despite carrying lighter loads. At the beginning, it took them four days to cover the same ground the Zanzibaris covered in three, and then they stopped and demanded five days of rest. Instead of an orderly march, they were, in Major Barttelot's words, "all over the place."[53]

The company of Zanzibaris commanded by Major Barttelot was having the greatest difficulty. Fourteen men deserted on June 15 with twelve loads, and three more Zanzibari men and a boy deserted with their loads and rifles on June 22. The following day, Barttelot's personal valet absconded, taking Barttelot's revolver and seventy-five rounds of ammunition. The problem, it seemed, was Major Barttelot himself. His colleague William Bonny, who suf-fered no desertions or lost loads with his own company of Zanzi-baris, later wrote in his official report that "the major was simply hated, not feared, by every Arab and the whole of the people belonging to them, and this feeling of hatred was brought about by himself through his mannerism and want of tact. He did not understand the Arabs, who could buy or sell him at their pleasure, and the wonder is that he was not shot or knifed months ago."

In the end, it was a Manyema headman who shot Barttelot. Early in the morning on July 19, when the expedition was camped at Banalya, a Manyema woman was beating a drum and singing, as she did every morning. Furious that the woman was disturbing his sleep, Barttelot sent his steward to tell her to stop, but she continued to drum and sing. He then took out his revolver and approached the woman as if to strike her. At that moment, a single shot was fired from a nearby house by Sanga, a Manyema headman who was in charge of ten porters. Then the camp erupted in chaos as many of the Manyema porters fled with their loads, leaving only 183 Manyema porters out of the 430 who had left the Yambuya camp five weeks earlier. Sanga and his commander, Mwinyi Somai, ran away and headed for Stanley Falls to plead their case to Tippu Tip.

James Jameson, an officer of the rear column, followed them to Stanley Falls, arriving on August 2 to discuss the situation with Tippu Tip. He had two main goals: to void the labor contract with Mwinyi Somai and to punish the man who had killed Major Barttelot. The killer, who was already in custody at Stanley Falls, was tried before a tribunal of Arabs and Europeans and executed by a firing squad. Jameson also needed a new set of Manyema porters and a person to command them who had sufficient authority. Tippu Tip surprised Jameson by suggesting that he himself could mount an expedition to rescue Emin Pasha in exchange for a fee of £20,000, but he would insist on traveling via the familiar trade route to Ujiji and from there strike out to the north toward Lake Albert. Reluctant to abandon Stanley's orders for the rear column to follow Stanley's route through the rainforest, he asked Tippu Tip to give him a canoe and paddlers to take him to Bangala to consult with State officials. During the trip, he contracted hematuric bilious fever and died, thus ending the negotiations.

The rear column remained stalled at Banalya until August 17, 1888, when Stanley strode into the camp. Nearly fourteen months had passed since he had left the camp at Yambuya with the advance guard, promising to be back in five months. He was shocked by what he found. As he later described it in the *New York Tribune*, "We found, to our grief and horror, that Major Barttelot had been shot, that Mr. Troup had been invalided home, that Mr. Jameson was away at Stanley Falls, and Mr. Ward was detained at Bangala." More seriously, he found that 164 Zanzibaris and Sudanese were either dead, deserted, or missing, and 42 of those remaining were sick or dying in the camp. That left only about 60 men out of the original 270 who were able to carry loads. He also found that only about one-third of the supplies were left. Some had been sent down to the Bangala Station for storage, but much had simply disappeared.[54]

To prepare for the march to Lake Albert, Stanley met with the remaining Manyema headmen and told them that they were free to stay with the expedition or leave. Three headmen, with 20 carriers each, agreed to stay and joined the porters that Stanley had brought with him from Lake Albert and the surviving Zanzibari porters in the rear column. When the group set out on August 21, it contained 283 carriers with 230 loads. Anticipating losses through injury, desertion, or illness, Stanley was sure that the excess porters would be needed. Four months later, the rear column arrived at the expedition's Fort Bodo camp to join the advance guard.[55]

When the combined expedition arrived at Kavalli's town, overlooking Lake Albert, on January 16, 1889, they learned that Emin's situation had worsened considerably during their long absence. Some of his Egyptian officers had mutinied and taken him prisoner, and then the forces of the Mahdi had begun to move south along the Nile toward Lake Albert, motivated in part by the arrival of Stanley's expedition. Fearing that Stanley was coming to claim their country, they were mobilizing to stop him. The Mahdists had taken Lado, Emin's old station, causing the other stations along the Nile to be evacuated for fear of attack. In order to consolidate their support against the Mahdist forces, the rebellious officers freed Emin and sent him to Wadelai, where he was free to do as he pleased, although he no longer had any authority.

Under such circumstances, many of Emin's followers decided to evacuate Equatoria and make their way to Zanzibar and eventually to Egypt, even though Emin himself continued to vacillate. On February 17, Emin Pasha and sixty-five followers arrived at Stanley's camp at Kavalli's to begin the evacuation process. Throughout February and March, the camp grew to over a thousand people. During the hasty evacuations of the stations along the Nile, most of Emin's legendary stores of ivory had been looted or abandoned. All that remained were sixty tusks to be used for paying the Manyema porters.[56]

On April 10, 1889, Stanley's expedition left Kavalli's for the march to the coast. In his diary, Arthur Jephson described the caravan as being three miles long, rendered gay and colorful by the flags and brightly colored clothes of the Zanzibaris and the Egyptian women. Emin and the other refugees from Equatoria were followed by the Zanzibari porters, the locally recruited porters, and the cattle that the expedition had obtained in its cattle raids. Of the people who had originally left Zanzibar with Stanley, only 230 remained. When the local porters deserted, leaving portions of their loads strewn along the route, Stanley sent Jephson to raid the people living higher up the mountains. "We were chiefly to catch people for carriers and to get cattle," wrote Jephson in his diary.[57]

Two days later, the caravan halted for four weeks because Stanley was ill with gastritis. The men passed the days by conducting raids for food and for captives to serve as carriers. On April 20, Jephson reported, "This morning Stanley told us to count over the slaves, chiefly women and children, whom our people had caught, and hand half of them over to the Pasha to give to his people. This Stairs and I did, and handed over 20. We brought them over to the Pasha's house. Upon my word, it was a most shameful scene. . . . Orders are, however, orders, and we must obey them in spite of the heartrending scenes and shameless brutality we see in these raids." On May 6, he wrote, "Shookri Aga, the Zanzibaris, and the Pasha's people returned today bringing with them numbers of slaves. The Pasha's people must now have over 150 natives that they have caught as slaves."[58]

Although Jephson reported such incidents with a degree of Victorian stoicism, he was quickly becoming disillusioned with Emin. "Now that Emin Pasha, who has been represented as one of the champions of Anti-Slavery, who is supposed to have kept slavery far from him and his people, has come into our camp," he wrote in his diary, "scenes of the most disgraceful cruelty, constant beatings, constant shrieks of women, and constant desertions are a daily occurrence. . . . One's heart gets sick and a strong indignation rises in one when one thinks how the sympathies of Europe have been tricked and played with, and how we have been duped into giving our best energies toward helping and rescuing a man and his people utterly unworthy of our help or even our sympathy."

As the caravan moved south and east over the next four months, it experienced a generally friendly reception from the local people because Stanley's Zanzibari soldiers helped drive away raiders coming from the kingdom of Bunyoro who had previously entered the territory, seized cattle, and captured the salt marshes near Lake Edward. "Our expedition was supported with grain, bananas, and cattle by voluntary contributions of the kings and peoples," wrote Stanley in his report to the consul in Zanzibar. "Not a bead or a yard of cloth was demanded from us. Such small gifts of cloth to the chiefs that we gave were given of our own accord." Jephson, who can be regarded as a reliable witness, did not contradict Stanley's account.[59]

The size of the caravan was constantly changing. It had left Kavalli's on April 10 with 570 refugees from Equatoria. By August 5, it was down to 414, and by October 4, down to 311. It arrived at Bagamoyo, on the Indian Ocean coast, with 290 refugees. Of the 280 missing persons, 80 had perished from ulcers, fevers, or fatigue, while 200 were left with local chiefs along the way to recover. On the other hand, local Africans who had been afraid to travel to the coast because of the dangers of the route attached themselves to the caravan until it numbered 1,000 travelers.[60]

6

Bagamoyo, Indian Ocean Coast, December 4, 1889

As the Emin Pasha Relief Expedition approached the Indian Ocean coast, Stanley sent letters ahead to inform the British consul in Zanzibar and the Germans in Bagamoyo of the group's impending arrival. The British sent the HMS *Turquoise* and the HMS *Somali* to Bagamoyo to transport the caravan to Zanzibar, while the Germans sent the warships *Sperber* and *Schwalbe*. Long known as the major port for ships going to Zanzibar, just twenty-two miles away, Bagamoyo had been the headquarters of German East Africa ever since the Anglo-German Treaty of 1886 had shrunk the domains of the sultan of Zanzibar.

When Stanley's caravan reached the ferry at the Kingani River, just outside of Bagamoyo, on December 4, 1889, it was met by Maj. Hermann von Wissman, the German imperial commissioner for East Africa, who accompanied Stanley and Emin into Bagamoyo on horseback. They were taken to the mess house for German officers and given a lunch on the upstairs veranda, which had been decorated with palm fronds. Fine champagne flowed freely, but Stanley diluted it with German mineral water in order to stay sober.[61]

A banquet was held that evening in the central dining room on the second floor. Wine flowed freely, and the band from the *Schwalbe* played during the dinner. Major Wissmann, Stanley, and Emin Pasha gave speeches, accompanied by numerous toasts. Emin, who was among his German countrymen for the first time in many years, thanked the English philanthropists who sponsored the relief expedition, the Germans for the splendid reception, and His Imperial Majesty Kaiser Wilhelm II for sending him a gracious message of welcome and congratulations. Shortly after finishing his speech, Emin slipped out of the room.

Just minutes later, there was a cry that Emin was lying unconscious on the street below. He had apparently walked out of a low window, thinking it was the door to the second-story veranda. Nobody knows exactly why it happened, but three factors may have been at play. First, Emin was not used to buildings with more than one story. Second, the cataracts on both of his eyes made him extremely nearsighted. Captain Hirschberg, who sat next to him at the banquet, reported that Emin had to raise the food to within three or four inches of his eyes in order to see it. Third, he was not accustomed to drinking alcohol, having lived in Muslim countries for many years. The champagne that Stanley had offered him at Kavalli's on Lake Albert may have been the first alcohol he had tasted in years.[62]

Emin was carried unconscious to the German hospital. Several of his ribs were broken, and it appeared as if he had an extensive fracture at the base of his skull. The next day he was conscious enough to complain of soreness all over his body, and his ears oozed a bloody fluid. Two days later, he developed bronchopneumonia. On December 10, he showed signs of improvement, but the bloody discharge from his ears did not cease until the twentieth day. Dr. Thomas Parke, from the Relief Expedition, attended to him until he himself fell ill and was transported to the French hospital in Zanzibar, leaving Emin in the care of German doctors. By January 25, 1890, Emin was well enough to write a letter to his cousin. "I am still at Bagamoyo," he wrote, "because the fracture of the skull, which was the result of my fall, has left some serious aftereffects, although, thanks to the devoted care, I am restored sufficiently to be able to take short walks." Then Emin informed his cousin that he had no intention of returning to Egypt or Europe. "I intend to leave here in a few days to resume scientific work," he wrote, "and for this purpose I propose to apply for an extension of leave from Egypt."[63]

With Emin unable to travel, the Relief Expedition had sailed to Zanzibar on a fleet of British and German ships on December 6, just two days after Emin's fall, leaving behind Dr. Parke and about twenty people from Emin's personal entourage. While in Zanzibar, Stanley paid wages to the surviving Zanzibaris (or their masters, in the case of slaves) and set up a relief fund for the widows and orphans of those who died. A few days later, Stanley, the European officers, and 260 Egyptian and Sudanese refugees sailed for Egypt, arriving in Cairo on January 16, 1890. In an eerie replay of his earlier quest for David Livingstone, Stanley was returning home without his prize.[64]

In his report to the British consul in Zanzibar, Stanley made an inventory of the staggering losses of the expedition. Only one of the thirteen Somalis engaged at Aden had survived the expedition. Of the sixty Sudanese enlisted in Cairo, seven had earlier been sent home from the camp at Yambuya, and twelve returned to the coast with the expedition. Of the 620 Zanzibaris, only 225 returned—55 were killed in skirmishes on the trail between Yambuya and Lake Albert; 202 died of starvation, ulcers, dysentery, and exhaustion; 2 were executed for selling their rifles and ammunition to buy food; and the remaining 106 deserted. Of the Europeans, Barttelot was shot and Jameson died of fever, but the others returned home.[65]

Perhaps the best balance sheet of the mission was given by Jephson in his diary. Just before the expedition left Lake Albert for the coast, he wrote: "Look at the lives we have lost. Major Barttelot and some 450 of our own people, to speak nothing of some hundreds of Manyema and many hundreds of natives we have killed, and whose villages we have destroyed in forcing our way here. Look again at the numbers we shall lose between here and Zanzibar, and the natives we shall probably kill. On the other hand, what have we done in return for all this? We have Emin Pasha—not, alas, the Emin Pasha we all imagined him to be—and some 50 Egyptian employees, with their wives, concubines, families, and slaves, the off-scouring and dregs of Cairo and Alexandria. Is what we have got an equivalent of what we have lost? Ten thousand times, no."[66]

The Emin Pasha Relief Expedition was the greatest disaster in the Victorian-era exploration of Africa, inflicting death and destruction on the members of the expedition and the people along its route. It was nevertheless consequential for three reasons. First, it reconfigured the political and economic relations between the Congo Free State and the Manyema Arabs by making Tippu Tip the governor of the Stanley Falls District. Second, it opened up the route through the rainforest between the Upper Congo and the Upper Nile. Third, the fallout from Tippu Tip's involvement in the Relief Expedition would ultimately force him to leave Manyema.

CHAPTER 8

THINGS FALL APART

WHILE STANLEY AND HIS EMIN Pasha Relief Expedition struggled through the rainforest, the Congo Free State was moving to dominate the ivory trade on the Upper Congo River. The battle was waged on two fronts. Along the Upper Congo River between Malebo Pool and the Bangala Station, the State competed for ivory against private European companies. Although the 1885 Berlin Act had guaranteed free trade throughout the Congo River basin, King Leopold took advantage of the growing anti-slavery sentiment in Europe to sponsor an anti-slavery conference in which he mobilized support for imposing tariffs on private companies. The second front was in the region near Stanley Falls. After the appointment of Tippu Tip as the governor of the Stanley Falls District made it possible for Europeans to purchase ivory from the Manyema Arabs, the State not only sought to dominate that trade by making exclusive deals with Tippu Tip, but it also confiscated ivory collected by other Manyema raiding parties.

Given the rivalries between the Congo Free State and the private trading companies on the Upper Congo, and the parallel rivalries between Tippu Tip and the major Arab traders along the Lualaba, the ivory trading system as a whole was in a delicate balance, held together in part by Tippu Tip. When he was forced to return to Zanzibar in 1890 to defend himself against a lawsuit filed by Henry Morton Stanley, that balance became more difficult to maintain. The struggle over ivory was further exacerbated when the Anti-Slavery Movement in Europe sought to send a modern-day crusader army to the Congo to fight the Arab slave trade. Because the Manyema raiders sought both ivory and slaves, the Congo Free State could justify aggression against the raiders in the name of anti-slavery. Thus did anti-slavery sentiment in Europe translate into an anti-Arab sentiment in the Congo.

1

Stanley Falls, Congo Free State, May 18, 1888

While the rear column of the Emin Pasha Relief Expedition was still waiting at the Yambuya camp for porters, the steamboat *A.I.A.* arrived at Stanley Falls on May 18, 1888, carrying Lt. Guillaume Van Kerckhoven, the Congo Free State's agent at Bangala. It was the first sign in nearly a year that the State was still interested in maintaining a working relationship with Tippu Tip. The State had earlier sent out two agents from Brussels to be Tippu Tip's assistants, but one of them had died at Leopoldville, and the other had become so sick at Leopoldville that he had to be sent home.[1]

Tippu Tip decided to take advantage of Van Kerckhoven's visit to sell some of his ivory. He asked Van Kerckhoven to take two thousand to three thousand pounds of ivory down the river to sell it to the commercial houses at Malebo Pool or send it to Europe for sale. Van Kerckhoven readily agreed, but the deal fell apart the next day when Antoine Greshoff of the New Dutch Trading Company arrived on his steamboat the *Holland* with a large stock of trade goods. Over the next five days, Greshoff bought five tons of ivory, paid for as follows: one-third paid with gunpowder (one-half paid immediately, and the other half in four to five months), one-third paid for with cloth, and one-third to be paid in shillings in Zanzibar. The transaction showed how Tippu Tip mixed barter

Tippu Tip's ivory stock at Stanley Falls, ca. 1890. Bridgeman Images

with credit arrangements and international currency exchanges. When Greshoff left with the ivory, he promised to return quickly and establish a trading station at Stanley Falls.[2]

Outflanked by the Dutch, Van Kerckhoven realized that the nature of the ivory trade along the Upper Congo River was changing. The State's approach had focused on its agent Alphonse Vangele, who traveled the waterways in his steamboat and purchased ivory from villagers and African ivory merchants. Now, however, commercial companies such as the New Dutch Trading Company and the Sanford Exploring Expedition were establishing posts along the Upper Congo to buy ivory from African villagers and local ivory traders. By 1888, the private companies accounted for the majority of the ivory that came down to Malebo Pool, and Van Kerckhoven feared the Congo Free State was being squeezed out.

That analysis was seconded by J. R. Warner, the engineer on the State's steamer *A.I.A.*, who observed that the companies had been buying up the "dead ivory" that the local villagers had hidden in the forest or buried under the floors of their houses to await an opportunity for trade. Now, however, when the local hunters killed an elephant, they would immediately take the tusks to the nearest trader in order to get the higher prices paid for clean, white ivory. "Were Tippu and his Manyemas even now to descend the Congo and raid some of the villages below Upoto," wrote Warner, "I doubt if he would get enough ivory to pay for his powder, as these villages are visited every two or three weeks by the trading steamers of the Sanford Company and the Dutch house, who buy up the ivory as fast as the natives can procure it." Under such circumstances, Van Kerckhoven believed, the State's best option for profiting from the ivory resources of the rainforest was to buy ivory from Tippu Tip and the other Arab ivory hunters.[3]

In an attempt to gain an edge in the ivory trade with Tippu Tip, the State sent the former International African Association agent Jérôme Becker to Stanley Falls in February 1889 to make a deal with Tippu Tip for forty tons of ivory. To pay for it, the State deposited £10,000 in gold with Taria Topan, Tippu Tip's commercial agent in Zanzibar. Two days after Becker arrived at Stanley Falls, Greshoff of the New Dutch Trading Company came up in the *Holland*, only to learn that all of Tippu Tip's ivory had been promised to the State. When the Dutch company protested that the Berlin Act did not permit the State to engage in commerce, the State claimed that it had arranged the purchase of the ivory on behalf of an unnamed European company. As the deposit in Zanzibar revealed, however, that unnamed company was the Congo Free State itself.[4]

In his autobiography, Tippu Tip portrayed the year 1889 as a banner year for his ivory trade. "We stayed on at Stanley Falls," he wrote. "Every month, two or three European steamboats arrived, and they left loaded with ivory; sometimes they were unable to carry the entire stock. Stanley Falls was becoming populated with Europeans, and anything you wanted to buy was available. Stanley Falls became a great port, where you could find anything you wanted. Belgian and French companies arrived and established factories. My God! It was magnificent!" As a symbol of the growing

Tippu Tip's grand canoes going down the Congo, 1889. Engraving, J. Bell after Herbert Ward, *The Illustrated London News*, December 21, 1889, Yale Center for British Art, Paul Mellon collection.

importance of Stanley Falls to the economy of the Congo Free State, Governor-General Camille Janssen arrived on October 25, 1889, to meet with Tippu Tip.[5]

Although Tippu Tip's ivory was contracted to the Congo Free State, the other Arab ivory traders were free to make deals with the European commercial houses. The companies now had plenty of trade goods in stock, and they would advance the goods to Arab traders in return for the promise of ivory to be delivered later. Whatever reservations some Europeans may have had about the Arabs' methods of obtaining ivory were quickly forgotten in the rush to get ivory from Stanley Falls. As the available stocks of "dead ivory" near the waterways were being exhausted by the steamboats of the European companies, the Arab traders and their Manyema followers were moving into previously untapped regions along the Aruwimi and Uele rivers northeast of Stanley Falls, as Stanley had observed during the Emin Pasha Relief Expedition.

If Tippu Tip was satisfied with the state of the ivory trade, he nevertheless found the geopolitical situation troubling. Since he had left Zanzibar with Stanley to aid the Emin Pasha Relief Expedition in February 1887, all the equatorial regions of Africa, from the Atlantic to the Indian Ocean, had been divided up among the European powers. The Congo Free State and the French colonies of Gabon and Congo covered the territory from the Atlantic Ocean to Lake Tanganyika, and now the region east of Lake Tanganyika had been partitioned between the Germans in the south and the

British in the north. "This is what they said to me," wrote Tippu Tip to his brother in Zanzibar. "We were astonished on hearing this extraordinary news."[6]

Even the Congo Free State began contesting the boundaries of Tippu Tip's authority. He had been under the impression that his authority as governor of the Stanley Falls District extended downstream from Stanley Falls to the Free State's Bangala Station five hundred miles away, but the Belgians claimed that it extended only one hundred miles downstream to the mouth of the Aruwimi River. To make sure that there was no ambiguity about the downstream limits of Tippu Tip's authority, Lieutenant Van Kerckhoven founded a military camp at Basoko, the gateway to the Aruwimi, without first informing Tippu Tip. In dealing with the Congo Free State, Tippu Tip found comfort in advice he had received from James Jameson of the Relief Expedition: "The Englishman said that I was not the man belonging to the Belgians, but that I, an independent man, was to look after my own affairs, and added that they, the Belgians, had made me the governor of a place actually belonging to me."[7]

In Manyema itself, Tippu Tip's authority was contested by some of the major Arab traders. Although the ivory traders in Manyema were commonly referred to as "Arabs," only about forty of them were true Arabs who could trace their ancestry back to the states around the Persian Gulf; the rest were waungwana, the Swahili-speaking African Muslims from Zanzibar or the East African coast. Still others were people from Manyema who had adopted Islam and Arab dress. When James Jameson traveled with Tippu Tip along the Lualaba River from Kasongo to Stanley Falls, he gained a sense of the political geography of Manyema. Tippu Tip, he was told, controlled Kasongo (in the south) and Stanley Falls (in the north) but not the riverside towns in between. Nyangwe, the largest of the Lualaba trading towns, was divided into three separate towns, controlled respectively by Mwinyi Mohara, Said bin Abed, and Said bin Habib.[8]

When the Arab ivory traders had first come to Manyema in the 1870s, there was much quarrelling and fighting among them, Jameson was told, but those conflicts had been settled, and each Arab chief now controlled a separate outlying district where his followers raided for ivory and slaves. The three greatest Arab chiefs in Manyema were Tippu Tip at Kasongo, followed by Said bin Abed and Said bin Habib, both at Nyangwe. After them were lesser chiefs such as Kibonge, who recognized the authority of Said bin Abed, and Mwinyi Mohara, who was deferential to Said bin Habib. None of those chiefs owed any particular allegiance to Tippu Tip, and they acted in concert with him only when there was a common cause.[9]

Despite the fractured and contested power structure, Jameson made the claim that "Tippu Tip owns the whole of Manyema." He did not elaborate, nor did he define the boundaries of Manyema, but he apparently meant that Tippu Tip was the dominant Arab authority in the region along the Lualaba River from Kasongo to Stanley Falls. Tippu Tip's claim to authority rested partly on his connections in Zanzibar, which gave him privileged access to credit, arms, and trade goods. Tippu Tip's lieutenant, Salim bin Muhammad, told Herbert Ward that Tippu Tip invested most of his profits in land and houses in Zanzibar and that he had lent large amounts of trade goods and guns to lesser Arab traders in order to keep them in his debt and thus to retain his authority over them.[10]

Tippu Tip was nevertheless in a difficult position if he tried to assert the authority of the Congo Free State over the Arab traders in order to prevent them from raiding for captives or ivory. Upon his arrival as the governor of the Stanley Falls District, he found that followers of Said bin Habib had "spoiled the river" down to the mouth of the Aruwimi by their raids and had caused the riverine villages to be deserted. During his failed attempt to bring porters to Yambuya in 1887, he had spent twelve days coaxing people to return to their villages, but many villages remained deserted because the people were afraid. A year later, he told Lieutenant Van

Kerckhoven that both Said bin Habib and Said bin Abed refused to recognize his authority as governor.[11]

Even though he had great wealth and numerous armed followers, Tippu Tip felt insecure about his position in the contentious politics of Manyema. In March 1889, he wrote to the British consul in Zanzibar: "Tell him [the Belgian king] to send me some arms. Now all the Arabs are my enemies. They say I am [the one] who gave all the places of the mainland to the Belgian king. What I earnestly wish from the Belgian King is that he should not leave me alone." He made a similar statement to Van Kerckhoven, saying, "The new Sultan of Zanzibar has completely abandoned me. I am like a bird without wings perched on a branch of a tree that my enemies want to cut down. . . . My hope rests in our Sovereign [i.e., King Leopold II], and I will do everything to earn his favor."[12]

Two developments in Zanzibar forced Tippu Tip to interrupt his trading activities at Stanley Falls and make a trip to the East African coast. The first was the death of Sultan Seyyid Barghash in Zanzibar on March 27, 1888, and his replacement by his younger brother, Seyyid Khalifa. The other development was more urgent. As Tippu Tip described it in his autobiography, "Then came news from Europe, from the king of the Belgians, informing me of serious news from Stanley, who had informed him that I was responsible for the death of the Major [Barttelot], that I had broken the agreement, and that retribution for the Major would be exacted from me. Further, the funds with Taria Topan had been blocked. A serious lawsuit had been filed against me!"[13]

The lawsuit caught Tippu Tip by surprise. His communications with Stanley had been cordial up to that point, and there had been no indication that Stanley held him responsible for Major Barttelot's death. The idea of the lawsuit seemed to have taken shape in Stanley's mind when he was in Zanzibar settling the accounts from the Emin Pasha Relief Expedition and learned that Taria Topan, who was Tippu Tip's commercial agent in Zanzibar, held £10,000 in gold that had been deposited for Tippu Tip by the Congo Free

State. On December 19, 1889, Stanley's lawyer lodged a claim at the British Consular Court charging Tippu Tip with failing to provide porters for the expedition and demanding £10,000 in indemnities. With Tippu Tip at Stanley Falls, the court postponed the full hearing until he could appear to defend himself. In the meantime, the judge issued an order freezing Tippu Tip's funds.[14]

In Brussels, King Leopold had an interest in the case because the frozen funds had come from the Congo Free State. A Belgian trader in Zanzibar sent copies of the court documents to the king with a commentary that cast doubt on Stanley's case. "The contract between Stanley and Tippu Tip seems very vague to me," he wrote. "The responsibilities of the parties to the contract are not well defined; neither the number of porters nor the dates when they are to be delivered is fixed." Upon receiving the documents, the king urged Tippu Tip to hurry to Zanzibar to defend himself and unblock the money. A short time later, Tippu Tip received the official summons from Judge Cracknall of the British Consular Court in Zanzibar, requiring him to appear within six months or forfeit the money.[15]

Tippu Tip left Stanley Falls in May or June 1890 to make the long trip to Zanzibar. Arriving at Mtowa, on the western shore of Lake Tanganyika, he encountered the British missionary Alfred Swann. "I found him bursting with indignation," wrote Swann, "on account of a letter he had received from officials at Zanzibar requiring his presence at the Courts to defend himself in an action brought against him by Stanley for damages." Tippu Tip pointed to the letter and exclaimed, "Look at that! It is a note ordering me to be at the coast in two months. Stanley accuses me of hindering him on his journey to find Emin Pasha, and alleges that this was the cause of Barttelot's death. If I had wished to stop him, I should not have played with the matter by sending 400 men instead of 600 as per contract; I should have killed him years ago. I do not simply *hinder*; I *destroy*! If I assist, it is at all costs."

Concerned about missing the court's deadline, Tippu Tip asked Swann to write a letter on his behalf to Judge Cracknall asking for more time. The missionary agreed. "Tippu Tip, Mohamed bin Khalfan, and Bwana Nzige, with Nassur bin Seif, are coming to Zanzibar," wrote Swann. "They will leave in two months and come peaceably—at least they have asked me to inform the Consul to that effect." To speed up his rate of travel, Tippu Tip arranged for the ivory his caravan was carrying to be stored in Ujiji while he went on ahead. After being delayed at Tabora by illness, he arrived in Zanzibar on July 20, 1891.[16]

During the months that passed between the filing of Stanley's complaint and Tippu Tip's arrival in Zanzibar, new evidence had appeared that weakened Stanley's case. Stanley's own published account of the Emin Pasha Relief Expedition, *In Darkest Africa; or, the Quest, Rescue, and Retreat of Emin, Governor of Equatoria*, sought to portray Tippu Tip's character and actions in a negative light, but it nevertheless showed that Tippu Tip had indeed supplied porters. Then came the publication of the diaries and letters of Major Barttelot and James Jameson in 1890, which further undercut Stanley's claims. Their information was highly credible because both men had died in the Congo and could not have revised their narratives in the light of later events.[17]

Upon arriving in Zanzibar, Tippu Tip had his lawyer prepare a declaration that rebutted Stanley's accusations and made counterclaims demanding reimbursement for the extra supplies that he had provided to the expedition. The day after Tippu Tip delivered the declaration, the lawyer for the Emin Pasha Relief Expedition appeared before the court and withdrew the lawsuit, thus freeing up the blocked funds. The main effect of the lawsuit was to bring Tippu Tip back to Zanzibar at a delicate time for relations between the Congo Free State and the Arabs in Manyema. Remaining in Zanzibar, he built a large house in Stone Town overlooking the sea at a point not far from the sultan's palace. By 1895, he would be the second-largest landowner in Zanzibar (after the sultan), owning seven clove plantations that were worked by as many as ten thousand slaves. He would never return to Manyema.[18]

2

Paris, Église du Saint Sulpice, July 1, 1888

The Église du St. Sulpice was the second-largest church in Paris, only slightly smaller than the Cathedral of Notre Dame. Cardinal Lavigerie, the founder of the White Fathers missionary society (so called because they wore white Maghreb-style cassocks), was delivering a major address on the position of the Catholic Church regarding the internal slave trades in Africa. As the Archbishop of Algiers, he had fought for years against the trans-Saharan slave trade that carried captives from the West African Sahel to North Africa, but recently he had turned his attention to equatorial Africa, where the White Fathers had taken over two stations on the shores of Lake Tanganyika—Karema and Mpala—from King Leopold's International African Association in 1885.[19]

Lavigerie told the crowd that whereas slavery had gradually disappeared from the Americas, slaving and slavery were increasing in the heart of Africa. When the White Fathers first arrived at the borders of Manyema ten years earlier, he told the audience, that province was the most populous in the region, entirely covered with villages and fields. "Today," he told the audience, "the slavers of Tippu Tip have turned the greatest part of that region—a region one-third as large as France—into a sterile desert, where one finds only the bones of the dead as testimony to the previous inhabitants."[20]

After giving vivid and horrifying descriptions of slave raids and slave caravans in equatorial Africa, based largely on the writings of Livingstone and Cameron, Cardinal Lavigerie called for an army of crusaders. "It is my belief," he said, "that five or six hundred

European soldiers, well organized and well officered, would be sufficient to suppress slave-hunting and slave-selling in the higher table lands of the African continent." Reminding his listeners of the medieval Crusades, he made an urgent call for a new crusade: "I appeal to you, the Christian young men of all the countries of Europe, and I ask: what should hinder you from reviving . . . the noble achievements of your forefathers? Why should we not see, with the sanction of the Church and her pastors, a renewal of the unselfish devotion which was the glory of past ages?" Cardinal Lavigerie was calling for the formation of a military-religious order of a type not seen in Europe since the Late Middle Ages.[21]

At the end of July, Cardinal Lavigerie was in London to address the British and Foreign Anti-Slavery Society at Prince's Hall, Piccadilly, one of the largest venues in the city. The advance publicity had billed the event as a "Crusade Against the Slave Trade." Lord Granville, the former British foreign secretary, presided over the meeting, and the luminaries on the platform included the explorer Verney Lovett Cameron and Horace Waller, who had accompanied Livingstone on the Zambezi expedition. Seated in the audience was King Leopold II, who had crossed the English Channel from his seaside villa in Ostend for the occasion.[22]

Attired in a long black cassock with red buttons, a red skullcap, and a red silk girdle, and with a massive gold cross hanging by a chain around his neck, Cardinal Lavigerie spoke in French, raising his voice slightly when he wanted to invoke pity or indignation and punctuating his speech with long pauses. At one point, he held up a double-forked "slave stick" to illustrate the horrors of the slave caravans. He began his address by talking about the trans-Saharan slave trade, which he had fought for years as the archbishop of Algiers, but he quickly came to his main subject: the slave trade from Manyema to the East African coast.

"The slave trade in the Sahara is nothing in comparison with . . . the heart of Africa," he told his audience. He then went on to link the East African slave trade to the ivory trade. "Ivory (which is the principal object of their commerce) was abundant in the extreme, for no one had ever come to seek it so far. In certain provinces, such as Manyema, they found it in such enormous quantities that they used elephant tusks to fence in their gardens and make supports for their primitive huts. It was through ivory that the ruin of this unfortunate country began. . . . Without pity, without mercy, these brigands fell upon the inoffensive population, massacred all who resisted, put the others in chains, and by threats or by force obliged the men to serve as beasts of burden as far as the coasts, where they were sold with the ivory they carried." Then Cardinal Lavigerie called for an armed force of five hundred resolute Europeans to join his crusade to fight the slave traders and made a stirring appeal to all the women present to bring their influence to bear on their husbands, fathers, and brothers to join his crusade.[23]

The British and Foreign Anti-Slavery Society found itself in an awkward position. Its method had always been to mobilize the *moral* force of public opinion, not actual military force, and to put pressure on established governments instead of taking unilateral action. After the cardinal left abruptly at the end of his speech because he was suffering from an attack of neuralgia, the meeting went on to pass a series of resolutions that condemned the Arab slave trade but did not mention a crusade or a military force. So embarrassed was the Anti-Slavery Society by Cardinal Lavigerie's remarks that when it printed an English translation of his speech, it left out his plan to organize a new crusade. The only reason we know that the cardinal attempted to recruit volunteers is because the speech was reported by the London *Daily News*.[24]

Before heading to Brussels for his next major speech, Cardinal Lavigerie stopped in Ostend to visit King Leopold at his villa. The king appreciated the cardinal's efforts to stir up public opinion against the Arab slave traders, but he had two concerns. The first was that any independent armed forces that entered the territory of the Congo Free State should not be freebooters but should operate under the authority and guidance of the king and the Free State's government. The second concern was that the name of Tippu Tip, which had been invoked in the cardinal's speech in Paris, should not be mentioned in Brussels. Tippu Tip was now the governor of the Stanley Falls District of the Congo Free State, and the king did not want him portrayed in a bad light.

On August 15, the cardinal spoke at the Église Saints Michel et Gudule, the largest Catholic church in Brussels. After firing up the crowd with a speech similar to the ones he had given in Paris and London, he focused his attention on Belgium: "You have been asleep, Catholics of Belgium. . . . You have not poured all your effort into the battle against barbarism, which was, for you, an obligation." He then called for a hundred volunteers to fight the slave traders and a million Belgian francs to purchase a steamboat for Lake Tanganyika. The next day more than fifty young men signed up for the crusade. On August 25, Cardinal Lavigerie founded the Belgian Anti-Slavery Society and appointed Lieutenant General Jacmart, a former commander of the Belgian École Militaire, as its head. In announcing the formation of the new organization, Lavigerie stated that its goal was to eradicate slavery and slaving in the Congo, by force if necessary.[25]

Six months after the organization's founding, seven hundred young men had signed up to be modern crusaders, and there were local chapters in Antwerp, Brussels, Ghent, Liège, Namur, and several other major Belgian cities. There would soon be nineteen chapters, which worked to mobilize public opinion and to raise money and volunteers. The plan was to send a volunteer army to Lake Tanganyika to block the trade in slaves from Manyema toward the east African coast. However, with growing unrest and warfare in the region east of the lake making the caravan routes unsafe, the Society began to explore the idea of sending its volunteer army up the Congo River by steamboat from Malebo Pool to Stanley Falls and then on to Nyangwe by canoe. From there, they would travel to Lake Tanganyika by the overland caravan routes. By June 1889, the Congo River option had hit a snag. In a letter addressed to all the young volunteers who had answered Cardinal Lavigerie's call, the president of the Society explained that despite the Congo Free State's willingness to transport the crusaders on its steamboats, it lacked the capacity to do so. The general asked all the volunteers to be patient while the directors of the Society worked out a route to Lake Tanganyika and a means of transportation.[26]

Although Cardinal Lavigerie's activities had not yet sent any crusaders to Africa, they were very successful in putting pressure on European governments to address the humanitarian issues raised by the slave trade from Manyema to East Africa. The British, especially, were feeling pressure from the British and Foreign Anti-Slavery Society, now newly energized by Cardinal Lavigerie, as was King Leopold. Because the epicenter of slave-hunting activities lay mostly in the Congo Free State, the British government suggested to King Leopold that he should convene a conference of major powers to discuss ways to coordinate their actions against the slave trade. It originally suggested a small conference attended by the five major naval powers, but Leopold, who quickly warmed to the idea, insisted that it should be attended by all the signers of the Berlin Act of 1885. What the British did not understand at the time was that Leopold *needed* all of the signers of the Berlin Act, because he intended to use the slave trade conference to amend the Berlin Act itself.[27]

When the Slave Trade Conference opened in Brussels on November 18, 1889, it aroused a great deal of public interest. A forked-stick slave yoke was on display, and the Belgian Foreign Office distributed information it had gathered on the horrors of the slave trade. Cardinal Lavigerie sent a set of documents about the history of his Anti-Slavery Movement to each delegate, and the publication *Bruxelles Attractions* organized a public lecture on the slave trade at the Palais de la Bourse. The Belgian minister of foreign affairs opened the conference with these words: "The work which you are about to undertake is great and pure. It is generous, it is disinterested. It does not even entail the gratitude of those races . . . whose safety it is your mission to organize." The participants in the conference included Henry Shelton Sanford, who represented the United States, and John Kirk, who represented the sultan of Zanzibar.[28]

Prior to the opening of the conference, the Congo Free State released a report on the political and military measures that the Congo Free State had taken to suppress the slave trade. Focusing on the Arab slave trade in Manyema, the report outlined the construction of military posts between Bangala and Stanley Falls and the formation of army units composed of local troops who had received military training. It emphasized the post at Bangala and the new post established at Basoko, at the mouth of the Aruwimi, to halt the Arab advance. Finally, the report noted the appointment of Tippu Tip as the governor of the Stanley Falls District. Recognizing that the appointment had not had the desired effect of ending slave raiding in the Stanley Falls District, the report claimed that the move "had contributed in a certain measure to limit the horrors of slave hunting." In effect, the report portrayed the military expansion of the Congo Free State as synonymous with the fight against slavery.[29]

Once the conference got underway, the sessions followed the Belgian plan to look first at the regions of Africa where slaves were captured, then the slave routes by land and water, and finally the destination countries where the slaves were sold and dispersed. The main slave-capturing zone discussed at the conference was Manyema, although the delegates also defined a larger "slave trade zone" that included Africa from 20° north latitude to 22° south. King Leopold did not personally attend the conference, but he followed its proceedings extremely closely and intervened through his delegates when it seemed opportune. As the conference continued, there seemed to be a general agreement that the territories that had been parceled out in treaties since 1885 needed to be more effectively occupied by the European colonizers. This would require more government stations, military posts, and better transportation systems. In this way, anti-slavery sentiments were being seamlessly transformed into imperial projects.[30]

At the session on May 10, 1890, a proposal was introduced that argued that the Congo Free State would be especially handicapped in trying to carry out the recommended measures because it was forbidden by the Berlin Act of 1885 from levying customs duties on imports. The proposal stated, "In view of . . . the expenses imposed upon them by the present treaty in consequence of the suppression of the slave trade, the signatory powers allow the imposition of import duties upon merchandise imported into the abovementioned states and possessions [i.e., the basin of the Congo]." The proposal was assigned to one of the subcommissions of the conference for further study.[31]

The General Act of the Brussels Slave Trade Conference was passed on July 2, 1890, after more than seven months of speeches and deliberations. Article 1 listed the measures necessary to combat the slave trade within Africa, including government stations, military posts, roads, railroads, telegraph lines, and restricting the importation of modern firearms. According to the Conference, colonial occupation was now the answer to the continuing problem of the slave trade. After the Act was voted on and passed, a special declaration was introduced. Acknowledging that the General Act imposed new obligations on the powers with possessions in the "conventional basin of the Congo," and that meeting those obligations would require new financial resources, it allowed any powers that had possessions in the Congo River basin to establish duties on imported goods at a rate not to exceed 10 percent. Although small parts of the "conventional basin of the Congo" were claimed by Portugal, France, Britain, and Germany, the vast majority of the territory in question belonged to the Congo Free State.[32]

King Leopold had scored a major victory. Five years earlier in Berlin, he had gained control of the Congo River basin by promising a free trade zone. Now, he had annulled that promise and gained the right to impose import duties, gaining new revenues that he could use any way he wished. The declaration by no means obligated him to spend the money on fighting the slave trade. King Leopold had skillfully used the genuine anti-slavery sentiment that had been stirred up in Europe by Cardinal Lavigerie and others to reverse the Berlin Act and gain new powers for the Congo Free State. In addition, the conference had given him a moral justification for driving the Arabs out of Manyema. He had only to wait for the right time.

3

Stanley Falls District, Congo Free State, June 1890

When Tippu Tip departed from Stanley Falls in May or June 1890, he left his nephew Rashid bin Muhammad (the son of Bwana Nzige) as the acting governor of the Stanley Falls District. To make it official, the Congo Free State had sent Rashid a letter of appointment. Prior to receiving the appointment, Rashid had been collecting ivory along the lower Lomami River (which entered the Congo seventy miles downstream from Stanley Falls), and he was often in residence in the village of Isangi, at the confluence of the Lomami and the Congo Rivers. J. Rose Troup of the Emin Pasha Relief Expedition, who spent several days at Rashid's camp in April 1888, described him as follows: "He carried himself well, with a self-reliant pose and an air of command. I was at once struck with the awe which he inspired among his subordinates, who looked upon him as a veritable chief and commander. . . . He was always robed in spotless white, wearing the usual long, flowing Arab garment with a pure white turban that set off his fine face well." Tippu Tip's business affairs were left to Muhammad bin Ali, whom Jameson had earlier described as "Tippo Tib's chief sheik at the falls."[33]

It was an inopportune time for Tippu Tip to leave Manyema, because the Congo Free State had been getting very aggressive in its quest for ivory. The State's military camp at Basoko, at the mouth of the Aruwimi River, marked the new downstream boundary of Arab authority. Between Basoko and the State station at Bangala, the Arab traders and their Manyema soldiers were permitted by the treaty to trade but not raid. Lieutenant Van Kerckhoven, the State agent at the Bangala Station, believed that the Arab and Swahili traders obtained all their ivory by theft and pillage without giving any merchandise in exchange, and therefore the State had the right to confiscate it. In April 1891, the State agent at Stanley Falls, Isidore Tobback, sent a letter to two Arab ivory traders informing them that "the king does not like it [ivory] to go to foreigners or anywhere out of his country, and this is a great matter which will not please him." To soften the tone, he added, "Anything you want from us, let us know, and we will send it to you, even if it is [worth] 100 *frasilas* of ivory."[34]

In 1891, King Leopold appointed Van Kerckhoven to lead a military expedition that followed the Uele River (which ran parallel to the Aruwimi about 120 miles farther north) in order to extend the boundaries of the Congo Free State up to Emin Pasha's old headquarters at Lado, on the Nile. Van Kerckhoven was given fourteen European officers and a contingent of six hundred African soldiers, a number that swelled to one thousand by 1892. In March 1891, the soldiers assembled at Bumba, on the Congo River about a hundred miles downstream from Basoko, from where they marched north until they reached the Uele. Moving eastward along the Uele and up some of its tributaries, they would attack Arab raiding parties and confiscate their ivory. An attack by Van Kerckhoven on October 24, 1891, netted eight hundred tusks of ivory, while a subsequent attack a few days later killed eighteen hundred people in an Arab camp.[35]

Lt. Louis-Napoleon Chaltin, one of the expedition's officers, described a surprise attack that he launched on an Arab/Manyema camp: "One day, toward dawn, we surprised the camp of traders who were still sleeping," he wrote. "A whole caravan of slaves, ivory, flags, arms, and ammunition were seized. Only a few of the traders managed to flee." Another officer, Lt. Pierre-Joseph Ponthier, launched a surprise attack on an Arab/Manyema camp along the Mokongo River (a tributary of the Uele) and then pursued the fleeing Manyema forces for the next two days in an effort to wipe them out. "In short," he reported, "the [Manyema] bands along the Mokongo have suffered not only a defeat, but a veritable disaster from which they will not soon recover."[36]

Arab and Manyema trading parties were not the only victims of the Van Kerckhoven expedition. While fighting for three weeks against a group of forest dwellers who shot poisoned arrows at them, the Free State forces captured 370 men and women, plus a large number of children. According to a declaration by two British members of the expedition, Van Kerckhoven had all the men and women tied to each other and placed in a line. Then he ordered them to be shot. When a friendly chief named Semis begged Van Kerckhoven to spare them, he replied that they had given him a lot of trouble, and he was tired of them. Then he gave the orders, and they were all shot. The children were given to friendly chiefs as slaves.[37]

The Van Kerckhoven expedition attracted attention because of its brutality and the enormous quantities of ivory it seized. On February 3, 1892, Sayf bin Hamed, the son of Tippu Tip, wrote to his father about a trader named Ismail, who told him that "the Belgians had taken away all his ivory and killed many men, and that only a few had escaped." Ismail attributed the attack to a European named "Barestendi." The transliterated name in that letter undoubtedly referred to "Bula-Matende," the African nickname for Van Kerckhoven. The expedition's records confirm that a detachment led by officers Ponthier and Daenen had launched a surprise attack on Ismail's camp in which they captured him and seized ten tons of ivory.[38]

The Manyema raiding parties that Van Kerckhoven attacked along the Uele had been sent out by the major Arab ivory traders established at Stanley Falls and along the Lualaba. The commercial agent Charles Doré reported that the Van Kerckhoven expedition had seized five hundred tusks belonging to Tippu Tip and seven hundred belonging to Rashid, Tippu Tip's nephew who was the acting governor at Stanley Falls. The commercial agent Arthur Hodister reported that Rashid was ruined financially, having lost 500,000 Belgian francs' worth of ivory when a State agent identified only as "Mr. N." confiscated fourteen hundred tusks from him. The Arab traders not only lost money but were left unable to repay the advances they had received from the New Dutch Trading Company and the Société Anonyme Belge (which had taken over the former Sanford Exploring Expedition). At Nyangwe, the Arab chieftain known as Mwinyi Mohara reported that the Van Kerckhoven expedition had attacked his caravans on the Uele, killing his men and confiscating his ivory. He claimed that he had lost more than 1.5 million francs' worth of ivory. In all, European traders estimated in 1892 that the Free State confiscated nine and a half tons of ivory from followers of Tippu Tip, Rashid, Mwinyi Mohara, and others.[39]

Perhaps the Arab trader most affected by the Van Kerckhoven expedition was Hamadi bin Ali, known as Kibonge. Originally from the Comoro Islands, he was described in 1892 as a rich and powerful Arab trader who could mobilize five thousand guns and was independent of Tippu Tip. In September 1892, the State heard rumors that Kibonge's business partner, Said bin Abed, was returning from the upper Uele after amassing several hundred tons of ivory. Lacking enough porters to carry it, he had stashed most of it in depots along the route. The State agent Fivé alerted Van Kerckhoven to search for this rich cache. When Said was more than three months late in returning from his expedition, Kibonge told a State agent that the Congo Free State, having confiscated Tippu Tip's ivory, was now going after his. The total amount of ivory confiscated by the Van Kerckhoven expedition is not known, but in August 1892, the Belgian publication *Le Mouvement Géographique* carried the following notice: "Important cargoes of ivory coming from the territories explored by Mr. Van Kerckhoven continue to arrive . . . at the State post at Bumba, where they are stored in warehouses and shipped to Leopoldville on State steamers. It is estimated that many tons of ivory valued at several million francs have already passed through Bumba."[40]

In the absence of Tippu Tip, the aggressive actions of the Congo Free State were causing political turmoil in the Arab zone. At Stanley Falls, Rashid was under strict orders from Tippu Tip to avoid violence, and he had meekly acquiesced when the Free State made off with his ivory, but the State actions had left him feeling beaten and sad. "If the State wants us to leave the territory," he told a Belgian commercial agent, "what can we say? We will leave and return to Muscat." But other Arab traders, who were independent of Tippu Tip, advocated resistance to the State's actions. The first casualties of the Arab resistance would be Belgians working for a newly formed company, the Syndicat Commercial, whose operations were directed by Arthur Hodister. During the months of March, April, and May 1892, Hodister and other commercial agents from the Syndicat Commercial fanned out along the Lualaba between Kirundu and Kasongo to discuss setting up stations to buy Manyema ivory. The idea was that the stations would save the Arab ivory traders the trouble of carrying their ivory to Stanley Falls or Zanzibar. At Kirundu, the Syndicat received a warm welcome and purchased nearly a ton of ivory, but at Riba-Riba, the next trading town farther up the Lualaba, they were met with skepticism. The chief of Riba-Riba was Muhammad bin Amici, called Nserera, who was subordinate to Mwinyi Mohara in Nyangwe. Nserera told the expedition that it must first gain the approval of Mwinyi Mohara before he would negotiate with it.[41]

Arriving in Nyangwe, Hodister learned that much had changed since James Jameson of the Emin Pasha Relief Expedition had visited the town four years earlier. Mtagamoto bin Sultani (known as Mwinyi Mohara) was now the undisputed chief of Nyangwe since Said bin Habib had died while on a journey to Zanzibar, and Said bin Abed had been driven out and forced to relocate to Kirundu. In 1891, it was said that Mohara commanded four thousand rifles and that he controlled the ivory trade along the middle Lomami River. Commercial agent Doré believed that Mohara was as powerful as Tippu Tip and more feared. When Hodister met with Mwinyi Mohara in Nyangwe, he learned that the Arab chief was furious about his losses to the Van Kerckhoven expedition. He had not only lost a great deal of ivory but also more than a hundred of his men. "The expedition along the Uele attacked my caravans; my men have been killed; and my ivory was taken," he told Hodister. "All the whites are the same. They are bad for the Arabs. I don't want any of them in my town." He then ordered Hodister to leave Nyangwe immediately and never come back.[42]

Returning toward Stanley Falls, Hodister was riding a horse, accompanied by three Belgian agents of the Syndicat Commercial riding donkeys and followed by a caravan of porters. As they approached Riba-Riba, they were met by an armed force of Manyema followers of the major Arab traders. Hodister dismounted and approached the leader of the group to discuss the matter, but shots rang out, and Hodister fell dead. Then his three companions were also shot and killed. Although the attack was organized by Chief Nserera at Riba-Riba, there was little doubt that the orders for it came from Mwinyi Mohara in Nyangwe. When the State agent Isidore Tobback had passed through Kirundu on May 12, just two or three days before the attack on Hodister, he was shown letters that Mwinyi Mohara had sent to all the Arab chieftains along the Lualaba, urging them to expel the whites from Manyema. The attack on Hodister's party signaled a larger insurrection of the Arab traders along the Lualaba against the Congo Free State. As *Le Mouvement Géographique* reported in October 1892, "Mwinyi Mohara, Nserera, and Kasuku have declared war; Kibonge has defected; and Sayf is being urged to leave the Falls. How much longer will Rashid remain loyal?" Shortly after that article was published, another European was killed in

Manyema. It was a German traveler known to the world as Emin Pasha.[43]

A bizarre chain of circumstances had brought Emin to Manyema. After recovering in Bagamoyo from his fall at the German banquet, Emin wanted to pursue his passion for collecting biological specimens, but he lacked the funding to do so. He accepted an offer from Hermann von Wissman, the German imperial commissioner for East Africa, to lead an expedition into the interior to sign treaties with local chiefs. On April 26, 1890, just five months after Emin had arrived in Bagamoyo with Stanley, his German expedition was ready to depart for the interior. Emin's orders were to secure the territory along the southern shore of Lake Victoria and all the territory between Lake Victoria and Lake Tanganyika, "so as to frustrate England's attempts at gaining an influence in those territories."

Even before Emin's party reached Lake Victoria, however, the British and German governments signed a new treaty settling the boundary dispute. After a copy of the treaty was sent to Emin on September 7, it became clear to him that there was no longer a need to block the British. At the beginning of December 1890, Wissmann ordered Emin to return to the coast at all speed. "There was a letter from Herr von Wissmann, disapproving of all I have hitherto done and directing me to hurry on and return to the coast, as great changes are imminent," Emin wrote to his sister on April 5, 1891. "So this is what it has come to, and I am given my leave. Well, I do not blame them; they have no more need of me, and that is the end of it."[44]

Wissmann's letter liberated Emin to pursue his passion for collecting. Sending most of his party to the Indian Ocean coast, he traveled northwest toward Lake Albert with a small group of soldiers and porters to explore the territory and collect specimens, retracing in roughly reverse order the route he had followed with Stanley. Then he headed west into the Ituri rainforest, following in reverse the route of the Emin Pasha Relief Expedition. "At last I have solved what has long been puzzling me, viz., the existence of the primeval forest west of the Albert Nyanza near Mosongua, etc," he wrote to his sister. "It is an extension of this. The dark stretches of the forest, standing out in marked contrast to the savanna, look curious, and I can readily understand how the natives of the grasslands regard the dark forest and its mysteries with awe." The rainforest proved to be a specimen collector's paradise, filled with exotic birds, butterflies, snakes, and even a rare species of red mice.

On January 29, 1892, Emin received two messengers from a Manyema ivory trader named Ismaili, who invited him to his station in the Ituri rainforest. Ismaili was a headman working for Said bin Abed, one of the most powerful Arab traders in Manyema, who had recently moved down the Lualaba from Nyangwe to settle at Kirundu with Kibonge. On March 6, the porters sent by Ismaili arrived at Emin's camp. With their help, Emin crossed into the Congo Free State and arrived at Ismaili's camp on March 12. On May 28, his party left for Said bin Abed's camp at Ipoto, arriving on June 18 only to find that Said bin Abed was absent, having gone to Kirundu with two hundred guns to join the Arab revolt against the Congo Free State and the followers of Tippu Tip.[45]

On August 1, Emin's expedition left Ipoto, accompanied by Ismaili and occasionally joined by Said bin Abed himself. After two months of marching through the mud and swamps of the rainforest, the caravan arrived at Kinena, about 175 miles west of Kirundu. Said told Emin to stay with Ismaili at Kinena while he went ahead to Kirundu to seek permission for Emin to join him there. The penultimate entry in Emin's diary, written on October 22, 1892, shows that Emin was aware of the unrest along the Lualaba resulting from the Van Kerckhoven expedition. "Mwinyi Mohara wants to fight," he wrote. "A friendly letter from Bwana Kibonge, alias Hamadi bin Ali: I am to come soon." But, unbeknownst to Emin, Kibonge had also sent a letter to Chief Kinena, ordering him to kill Emin.

What happened next is known only from the later testimony of Ismaili. On October 23, 1892, Chief Kinena, Ismaili, and others went to Emin's dwelling and asked him to send his soldiers to collect plantains at groves about an hour's march away. Once Emin's soldiers were gone, two men grabbed Emin's arms. Chief Kinena looked him in the face and said, "Pasha, you must die!" Emin asked, "Who are you that you should condemn a man to death?" Kinena answered, "The order is not mine. Kibonge sent it. He is my master; him, I must obey." When Emin protested that he had received a letter from Kibonge promising him free passage, Chief Kinena showed Emin the other letter from Kibonge that condemned him to death. Four men then pinned Emin to the ground, lying on his back, while a fifth slit his throat. A few hours later, Emin's severed head was placed in a box and sent to Kibonge.[46]

Kibonge's motives for ordering Emin's death are not completely clear, given that Emin was not a threat to his interests. From a broader perspective, however, it is apparent that Emin's death was collateral damage from the Van Kerckhoven expedition. Dr. Oscar Baumann, who had visited Tippu Tip at Stanley Falls in 1886, explained the connection as follows: "Bloody engagements took place. Van Kerckhoven stormed several Arab camps and captured valuable stores of ivory. Naturally, the Arabs were embittered beyond measure. . . . If Said bin Abed himself had wished to shield Emin, he could hardly have done so in the face of his infuriated Manyema or the fugitive bands scattered by Van Kerckhoven."[47]

The killing of the agents of the Syndicat Commercial in May 1892, followed by the killing of Emin Pasha in October, were sure indications that a state of war existed between the Congo Free State (represented by Rashid at Stanley Falls and Sayf at Kasongo) and the other Arab settlements along the Lualaba. The only person who had the stature to mediate that conflict was Tippu Tip, but he was far away in Zanzibar defending himself against the lawsuit filed by

Henry Morton Stanley. In the absence of such a calming influence, events moved inexorably toward all-out war.

4

Ivoryton, Connecticut, July 1894

By the 1890s, the two Connecticut ivory factories that produced combs, piano keys, and billiard balls were no longer getting their tusks exclusively from Zanzibar. With Comstock, Cheney & Co. and Pratt, Read & Co. each consuming roughly ten tons of ivory per month, they needed more tusks than Zanzibar could supply. In July 1894, Pratt, Read began experimenting with ivory coming from the mouth of the Congo River (known as "Congo ivory"), making 1,489 sets of piano key veneers cut from twenty-eight Congo tusks over the next six months. "I wish you would tell me just what you think of the Congo ivory," wrote W. H. Arnold of the Arnold, Cheney ivory importing company to George L. Cheney, the general manager of Pratt, Read, in November 1894. Two months later, he reiterated the point: "If we are to be up to date, it is very important to study this Congo ivory and find out just how good or bad it is, and what properties of it we can use."[48]

By the middle of 1895, the Congo River ivory was beginning to prove its value. "I hope that every effort will be made to continue the use of Congo ivory," wrote Arnold on June 12, 1895. "We are advised of large arrivals of Congo ivory at Antwerp, and think that the price will further decline at the next sales." During 1896, the ivory importing company purchased 7,840 pounds of ivory from their agent in Zanzibar and 7,900 pounds of Zanzibar ivory from London, but they also bought 6,100 pounds of Congo ivory from Antwerp. In 1898, the Pratt, Read ivory factory bought 70,052 pounds of Congo ivory while the Comstock, Cheney

Tusks arriving at the Comstock & Cheney factory in Ivoryton, Connecticut, 1890. Pratt, Read Corporation Records, Archives Center, National Museum of American History, Smithsonian Institution.

factory bought 26,666 pounds. Together, the two companies purchased nearly 50 tons of Congo ivory in 1898 alone.[49]

In some respects, the distinction between Zanzibar ivory and Congo ivory was meaningless because Tippu Tip and the ivory hunters in the forests of Manyema were shipping elephant tusks to both coasts. Ivory arriving in Europe or the United States was identified according to the African port where it was shipped, not the specific place where the elephant had been killed. If Tippu Tip sold a load of ivory to a European firm on the Congo River, it was labeled Congo ivory; if he sent it to Zanzibar, it was labeled Zanzibar ivory. This point is best illustrated by a story that the missionary George Grenfell sketched out in his diary in 1888. According to the story, a hunter killed an elephant in the Stanley Falls region and sold one tusk to European traders on the Congo River and the other tusk to Arab traders from Zanzibar. The story traced the divergent routes followed by the two tusks until they ended up lying side by side on a London dock.[50]

During the 1880s, the land occupied by Comstock, Cheney & Co. had become known as the "Village of Ivoryton" in celebration of the ivory products it produced. As the company grew, it built more houses to rent to its employees, owning eleven houses in 1881 and twenty-nine ten years later. To get workers, the company paid agents at Ellis Island in New York City to direct newly arrived immigrants toward Ivoryton, where they would find housing on the company property. Up until 1885, the workers were mostly Scandinavian and German immigrants, but after that, they were mostly Italians and Poles. By 1899, the company buildings occupied thirty acres of land and boasted about one hundred thousand square feet of factory space. To accommodate its six hundred employees, the company owned forty tenement houses and a boarding house that could accommodate sixty people.[51]

Turning an elephant tusk into ivory veneers for piano keys was a complex process involving many steps. The first was the *selection* of the tusks for the piano trade. The company wanted mature tusks, weighing forty pounds or more, which were free from spots, streaks, cracks, or rings. Then came *junking*, in which the tusk was sawed into four-inch lengths with a fine-toothed band saw. In the *blocking* stage, the cross section of the four-inch cylinder was marked with a series of rectangles, working out from the center and leaving wedges in between. Then came *parting*, in which the rectangular blocks were cut out of the cylinders with a circular saw. The wedges between the blocks were used to make toothpicks, ear cleaners, or tool handles. In the *slitting* phase, the blocks were sliced into one-sixteenth-inch-thick strips with circular saws, using a back-and-forth motion similar to cutting slices of meat in a butcher shop. Then came *chemical bleaching*. To give the keys on a piano keyboard a uniform whiteness, the ivory strips were bleached in a hydrogen peroxide solution for up to seventy-two hours before being washed in warm water and then sent to the drying chambers.

The final step in seasoning the ivory veneers was *sun bleaching*. Since the 1840s, ivory cutters had known that exposure to sustained sunlight and heat would whiten the ivory and accelerate the activity of the chemical bleach. To accomplish this effect, the company used bleaching houses, which were long glass buildings built on metal frames. They were a bit like greenhouses, except that the primary face of the bleach house was a slanted roof that ascended at a forty-five-degree angle from the ground to a height of eleven feet. Wooden trays of ivory veneers were exposed to sunlight for up to a month or more, depending on the season, during which time the veneers were regularly turned to whiten each edge. Only then were they ready to be matched, trimmed, and glued onto the wooden keys with hot glue. In 1899, the bleach houses of Comstock, Cheney were a total of thirty-five hundred feet long.[52]

Although Comstock, Cheney & Co. was best known for its piano keys, it did not neglect the production of ivory billiard and pool balls. The company claimed a patented process of bleaching and seasoning the balls, which, it claimed, made them more durable and less likely to crack than those from other manufacturers. Using this method, the company produced billiard balls in diameters ranging from 2¼ inches to 3 inches and pool balls from 2⅛ to 2⅜ inches in diameter. Nevertheless, the company favored piano keys because an average adult African tusk would produce only four or five billiard balls, whereas it could yield fifty to fifty-five complete keyboards of ivory veneers.[53]

Three miles east of Ivoryton, the Pratt, Read Company in Deep River was prospering as well. When the main factory and surrounding shops were destroyed by fire on July 31, 1881, the company replaced them with a four-story factory equipped with the latest machinery and supported by a machine shop, a blacksmith shop, drying houses, a matching house (for matching the ivory veneers), bleach houses, and an office building, all situated on a fifty-acre tract owned by the company. At the time of the fire, the company employed about 160 workers. The management of the two ivory companies was interconnected: George A. Cheney, who became president of the Comstock, Cheney Company in 1878, was the cousin of Benjamin Arnold, who became president of the Pratt, Read Company in 1877, and was the father of George L. Cheney, who became the general manager of Pratt, Read in 1892.[54]

In 1899, the newspaper *The Deep River New Era*, in a burst of local boosterism, summed up the growth of Ivoryton, Connecticut, as follows: "The village of Ivoryton, which a few years ago was almost wilderness, is now one of the most beautiful villages in the state, and this has been accomplished mainly through [Samuel Comstock's] efforts." The darker side of the ivory trade, however, was revealed by Henry Morton Stanley in his 1889 report to the British consul in Zanzibar. "People in England have not the slightest idea what the present fashion of ivory collecting . . . means," he wrote. "Bands consisting of from 500 to 600 Manyema, armed with Enfield carbines, and officered by Zanzibar Arabs and Swahili, range over that immense forest east of the upper Congo, destroying every district they discover, and driving such natives as escape the sudden fusillades into the deepest recesses of the forest." He then outlined the basic operations of the raiding parties: "In the midst of a vast circle described by several days' march in every direction, the ivory raiders select a locality wherein plantains are abundant, prepare a few acres of rice, and while the crop is growing, sally out by twenties or forties to destroy every village within the circle. . . . Thus, the land becomes denuded of ivory, but, unfortunately, also, it becomes a wild waste."[55]

No sooner had Stanley written that report than the Congo Free State began seizing ivory by force of arms from the Arab raiding parties. Even a jaded imperialist like Stanley knew that the prosperity of a town such as Ivoryton, Connecticut, was built on the suffering and death of people in the Congo River basin.

5

Nyangwe, Manyema Territory, March 4, 1893

When dawn broke over the Lualaba River, a fleet of one hundred large dugout canoes paddled by Genia fishermen arrived at the landing near the Congo Free State's military camp on the swampy ground near the west bank. They had come to ferry the State soldiers across the Lualaba to attack the town of Nyangwe, the major emporium for the trade in ivory and slaves in equatorial Africa. Sidney Langford Hinde, a Canadian-born captain in the Congo Free State's army, described Nyangwe in 1893 as "a finely-built Arab town of 25,000 or 30,000 inhabitants."[56]

The audacious river crossing by the Genia canoe fleet caught the Arabs in Nyangwe and their Manyema followers by surprise. The State forces had been camped on the west bank of the Lualaba for six weeks but had not attempted to cross, being mostly content to fire a few musket shots across the river, which was about a thousand yards wide at the narrowest point. The puff of smoke that signaled that a bullet was coming gave the defenders a chance to duck for cover before they heard the sound of the gun. Mwinyi Mohara, the undisputed chief of Nyangwe, had been killed three months earlier in a clash with State forces west of the Lualaba, leaving the town's leadership in uncertain hands. After landing on the east bank of the Lualaba and climbing the embankment to enter the town, the Free State forces were astonished to find almost no opposition. "We succeeded in landing and in taking the greater part of the town, scarcely firing a shot," wrote Hinde. "By ten o'clock that evening, we had fortified ourselves in the higher part of the town." Nine days later, a revolt broke out that was put down by the State forces. Fearing further uprisings, the Free State forces burned the greater part of the town. By the time the bulk of the State forces left Nyangwe on April 17, Hinde could report that in six short weeks, Nyangwe "had been reduced from a well-built town of about thirty

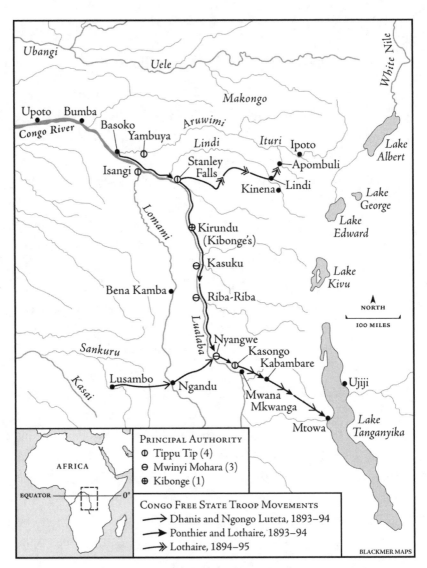

The war between the Manyema Arabs and the Congo Free State, 1892–1895

thousand inhabitants to one large fortified house with a soldiers' camp around it."[57]

The war between the forces of the Manyema Arabs and those of the Congo Free State in 1892–1893 was something that authorities on both sides had sought to avoid. When Tippu Tip left Manyema in May or June 1890 to travel to Zanzibar, he had left his nephew

Rashid in charge of Stanley Falls, while his son Sayf governed his larger empire from his headquarters in Kasongo, some 350 miles to the south. In the trading towns along the Lualaba River between Tippu Tip's two power centers, Arab chiefs such as Mwinyi Mohara and Kibonge were in full revolt against the State and its agents. By Sayf's calculations, however, the chief threat to his trading empire came not from the State agents at Stanley Falls or from the rebellious Arab chiefs along the Lualaba River but from Ngongo Luteta, the Tetela slave whom Tippu Tip had placed in charge of his operations along the upper Lomami, to the southwest of Kasongo.

The dynamics of the ivory trade required that the trading territory should constantly expand, and Ngongo Luteta's expansions to the west had brought him into conflict with the Congo Free State, which had established a post at Lusambo, on the Sankuru River, in 1890. The Lusambo post could be reached by a steamboat traveling east along the Kasai River and then continuing up the Sankuru. Like the State military camp at Basoko, at the confluence of the Congo and Aruwimi Rivers, which served to check the Arabs' westward advance in the Stanley Falls region, the Lusambo post, as the headquarters of the Lualaba District, was there to check the Arab advance in the southern end of the Arab Zone.

While the State was erecting military barriers against Arab expansion, Ngongo Luteta was expanding his operations southwest into the Luba territory, making the great Luba chiefs Lumpungu and Mpania Mutombo his vassals. In 1890, his forces were defeated in a clash with the Free State forces, and two years later, while he was carrying out another expedition to the southwest, he was defeated in a battle with State forces led by the commissioner of the Lualaba District, Francis Dhanis. Following that defeat, his vassals Lumpungu and Mpania Mutombo secretly submitted to the State. With his position weakened by the loss of his two powerful vassals, and not wanting to continue sending his ivory to Sayf in Kasongo, he entered into an alliance with Dhanis and permitted the Congo Free State to build a post at his capital, Ngandu, on the Lomami River.

According to Dhanis, Ngongo told him, "What have the Arabs done for me? . . . They want all my ivory, and they have taken it all and given me nothing. Everything I have, I obtained by my own strength." It would be easy to dismiss Dhanis's report as a self-serving fantasy except that it corresponds with Tippu Tip's own characterization of Ngongo. "I had never seen a slave with obedience like his," wrote Tippu Tip in his autobiography. "Everything he got, he brought in. I kept him informed about all my business and left him in charge in the [Kasongo Rushie's] kingdom." By 1892, however, Ngongo Luteta was seeking to break free of his Arab overlords, even if doing so required making an alliance with the Congo Free State and giving it a large stockpile of ivory.[58]

In Kasongo, which was Tippu Tip's headquarters in Manyema, Sayf saw the defection of Ngongo Luteta as a major betrayal. He was not only losing control of a large territory but also losing the ivory income from that region (in 1886, for example, Ngongo had delivered thirty-two tons of ivory to Tippu Tip in Kasongo). Moreover, if Ngongo could defect without paying a price, others might follow his lead. Following a long-standing Arab custom, Sayf sent a messenger to Ngongo with a hoe and a rifle cartridge and asked him to choose. If he chose the hoe, it was a sign of submission, but if he chose the cartridge, there would be war. Ngongo Luteta replied by sending a velvet cloth for Sayf's burial shroud. Soon, Sayf was marching with an army estimated at ten thousand men into the region between the Lualaba and the Lomami. His goal was to punish the rebellious Ngongo, who was not only his political subordinate but also his father's slave.[59]

In an attempt to head off a war, the Congo Free State's representative at Kasongo, Jean-François Lippens, wrote a letter to Commandant Dhanis on Sayf's behalf that made two demands. First, the State should withdraw its post from Ngongo's capital. Sayf would accept a State post on the Lomami, but he insisted on choosing the site himself. Second, the State should remain neutral in the upcoming war between Sayf and Ngongo. The letter argued that the State was not prepared for a war against an Arab force that had fifteen thousand guns. At the time, the State had four hundred Hausa soldiers, Ngongo Luteta had two thousand guns, and Chief Lumpungu, Ngongo's former vassal, had three thousand guns. Echoing Lippens's letter, the State sent orders to Commandant Dhanis on December 3, 1892, instructing him to maintain a defensive posture and try to avoid any conflict with the Arabs. At the same time, a letter from Tippu Tip arrived at Stanley Falls ordering Rashid and Sayf to maintain amicable relations with the Congo Free State.[60]

Despite the reluctance of both the Congo Free State and Tippu Tip to go to war, the dynamics on the ground were leading toward a showdown. Feeling an obligation to punish Ngongo Luteta for his treachery, Sayf's Manyema forces crossed the Lomami River into Free State territory but were driven back. Then the combined forces of the Congo Free State, Ngongo Luteta, and Lumpungu crossed the Lomami into Tippu Tip's territory in pursuit of Sayf, even though they had no authorization to do so. The State forces now included six European officers, four hundred Hausa soldiers employed by the Congo State, and twenty-five thousand African allies, many of them armed with spears and bows. As they marched toward the Lualaba, they encountered the army of Mwinyi Mohara, the chief of Nyangwe who had come to the aid of Sayf. In a series of battles in December 1892, they killed Mohara and exterminated his forces, capturing five thousand guns. On January 28, 1893, the State forces approached the Lualaba River and saw Nyangwe on the other side. Then, on March 4, they crossed the Lualaba in canoes and took Nyangwe.[61]

The next objective of the State forces was Kasongo, a town of twenty thousand that had been Tippu Tip's headquarters but was now under the authority of his son Sayf. Located thirty-five miles south of Nyangwe and nine miles inland from the Lualaba,

Kasongo, Tippu Tip's capital in Manyema, as sketched by James Jameson in 1888. The town was abandoned in 1892 after being attacked by Congo Free State forces. James Jameson, *The Story of the Rear Column of the Emin Pasha Relief Expedition*, p. 254.

Kasongo's population had recently tripled to around sixty thousand, swelled by the people who had fled from Nyangwe, as well as the forces of Bwana Nzige (who had driven the State from Stanley Falls in 1886), the forces of Said bin Abed (who had accompanied Emin Pasha on his last journey), and those of Muhammad bin Amici, called Nserera (the chief of Riba-Riba who had orchestrated the killing of Hodister). Sayf's people were scrambling to build defenses because it had never occurred to them that Kasongo might come under attack.

Approaching Kasongo on April 22, the main body of the State forces took a wrong path and approached the city from the rear while other columns attacked from the main road. Caught between the two attacking forces, the town's defenders retreated, along with crowds of women, children, and slaves. Within two hours, the State forces had captured the main points in the city. "Kasongo is a much finer town than even the grand old slave capital Nyangwe," wrote Captain Hinde. "Here we found many European luxuries, the use of which we had almost forgotten: candles, sugar, matches, silver and glass goblets and decanters were in profusion. We also took about twenty-five tons of ivory; ten or eleven tons of powder; millions of caps, cartridges for every kind of rifle, gun, and revolver perhaps ever made; some shells; and a German Flag taken by the Arabs in German East Africa." They also found a metal box containing Emin Pasha's papers, including his diary for the period from January to October 1892. But they did not find Sayf or any of the other Arab chiefs, who had all escaped with the retreating soldiers.[62]

In the Stanley Falls region, where Rashid governed on behalf of the Congo Free State, the State forces at the military camp at Basoko (at the mouth of the Aruwimi) became more aggressive after they learned that Dhanis was marching on Kasongo and Nyangwe. In order to secure the lower Lomami as a barrier against Arab/Manyema expansion, they traveled up the Lomami in two State steamers and discovered that the Arab post at Bena Kamba had been abandoned. Marching east to the Lualaba by land, they found that Riba-Riba (where Hodister's expedition had been attacked a year earlier) had been hastily abandoned and partially burned in anticipation of their attack. Returning on May 6, 1893, to the Lomami, where the steamer *Ville de Bruxelles* awaited them, they received a message from Stanley Falls that Rashid had joined the Arab revolt and the State garrison there was under attack. They arrived at Stanley Falls in time to inflict a major defeat on the Arabs, taking fifteen hundred prisoners, but Rashid escaped. Although both the State and the Arabs fought using locally recruited troops, the State soldiers had the advantage of being trained for warfare by experienced military officers, whereas the fighters in the Arab armies were mostly ivory-and-slave raiders who had never faced serious military opposition.[63]

On June 25, a steamer arrived at Stanley Falls with Hubert Lothaire, the commissioner of the Bangala District, and Pierre-Joseph Ponthier (recently promoted to captain), accompanied by two hundred Bangala troops. On June 28, with their force augmented by one hundred troops recruited at Stanley Falls, they went

up the Lualaba in fifty canoes commandeered from the Genia
fishermen to dislodge the remaining Arabs. When they arrived
at Kirundu—Kibonge's town—they found it abandoned. Continuing up the Lualaba in the direction of Nyangwe, they fought
a battle against the combined forces of Rashid and Kibonge on
July 10 in which they captured six thousand to seven thousand
prisoners, but Rashid and Kibonge escaped. State troops caught
up with Rashid and Kibonge again on August 16, but again they
escaped. After that, Rashid and Kibonge split up. Rashid moved
southeast to Kabambare, on the main trade route between Ujiji
and Nyangwe, while Kibonge moved due northeast to establish
himself on the upper Lindi. After three months of fighting on the
Lualaba, Lothaire returned to Bangala with more than thirteen
tons of ivory that he had seized. Ponthier and his Bangala troops
continued up the Lualaba to join Dhanis at Kasongo.[64]

After the fall of Nyangwe and Kasongo, Rumaliza, the Arab
chief of Ujiji, arrived from Lake Tanganyika with a large army.
First settling at Kabambare, halfway between Lake Tanganyika
and the Lualaba, he then advanced toward the Lualaba and built
several forts south of Kasongo as a staging area for retaking the
town. When Rumaliza's forces were driven out of those forts
between mid-October and mid-November 1893, they retreated to
the east, toward Lake Tanganyika. In late November 1893, State
forces attacked a makeshift Arab fort near Mwana Mkwanga. Sayf
was severely wounded in the battle, and he died a few days later.

On January 25, 1894, State forces took Kabambare, where they
received the surrender of Said bin Abed and Rashid, but Rumaliza, the Arab chief of Ujiji, escaped across Lake Tanganyika and
pledged his loyalty to the Germans, who now controlled Ujiji.
Abed was acquitted by a military court for the killing of Emin
Pasha, and Rashid was deported to the Kasai region of the Congo
Free State and put in charge of an agricultural project. He was later
sent back to Zanzibar by ship to prevent him from ever returning
to Manyema.[65]

When Commandant Dhanis left the Congo in 1894, Lothaire took over as the commander of the Arab Zone and was charged with eliminating the remaining pockets of Arab resistance. An important Arab force commanded by Kibonge was still operating in the region east of Stanley Falls, on the upper Lindi, which ran parallel to the Aruwimi. Lothaire's forces captured Kibonge at the town of Lindi and executed him on January 1, 1895, for ordering the killing of Emin Pasha. Five days later, they intercepted a letter from the British ivory trader Charles Stokes informing Kibonge that he was on his way with guns and ammunition. Then they went after Stokes, capturing him in his tent near Apombuli and seizing sixty German Mauser repeating rifles, eight breech-loading Snyder rifles, an assortment of cartridges and caps, and 350 kilos of gunpowder. They also located scattered depots containing more than seven tons of ivory. Stokes was taken to Lindi and tried by a hastily assembled military tribunal, which convicted him of providing arms and ammunition to slavers. He was hanged at dawn on January 15.[66]

News of Stokes's summary military execution caused an outcry in Britain because Stokes, as a British citizen, should have been tried as a civilian and given the right to appeal. Responding to diplomatic pressure from the British, the Congo Free State tried Lothaire for murderous homicide at the Court of Appeals in Boma, Congo, where he was acquitted. When the British protested, Lothaire was retried by the Supreme Council of the Congo Free State in Brussels, where he was again acquitted. Lothaire claimed that the execution of Stokes was a necessary part of the battle to drive the Arab slavers out of the Congo Free State, but many in Britain and Germany saw it as a fight over the stockpiles of ivory.

With the Arab ivory traders in retreat throughout Manyema, the Congo Free State moved in quickly to exploit the resources of the Manyema rainforest. Those efforts were observed by E. J. Glave, who arrived at Kasongo on January 2, 1894, after traveling with a small caravan along the main trade route via Lake Tanganyika and Kabambare. He was there as a journalist to write a series of articles for *The Century Magazine*, published in New York City. Although he died of a fever before completing his journey, the magazine published his journal posthumously.

Arriving at Kasongo, Glave wrote: "Kasongo shows signs of having been a most important town, certainly the largest I have yet seen in Africa. For a square mile, the ground is covered with masses of large clay or sun-dried brick of houses, which contained numerous rooms. Each Arab *mgwana*, or man of any importance whatever, had a large house for himself and wives; their followers and slaves lived elsewhere." Then he described what had become of the town. "The houses are now in utter ruins. A broad road running from west to east, thirty feet wide, was kept clear of grass when Kasongo was occupied. The large houses were built on each side of the way. Now a prolific outburst of foliage threatens to hide every vestige of this famous place. Only a few *waungwana* [plural form of *mgwana*] of minor importance are here now; all others have gone to settle, by order, near the Congo Free State Station at New Kasongo, on the Lualaba."

Two days later, Glave arrived at Nyangwe, which now consisted of little more than a Congo Free State station and a large military camp. "In connection with the station," he wrote, "there are 5,000 auxiliaries [irregular African troops], who are sent all over the country to beat the natives into submission. They go in bands of 1,000 men, women, and children, and all belongings, settle upon a suitable spot in a rich district, and then bring the natives under their control and prepare the way for a white man to establish a post." The head of the Free State post told Glave that the area around Nyangwe could produce fifteen tons of rubber a month when more villages were brought under State control and that ivory was brought in as tribute and also for sale.[67]

After Glave visited the Stanley Falls Station from February 11 to 19, he observed: "The State conducts its pacification of the country after the fashion of the Arabs, so that the natives are not gainers at all. The Arabs in the employ of the State are compelled to bring in ivory and rubber, and are permitted to employ any measures considered necessary to obtain this result. They employ the same means as in days gone by, when Tippu Tip was one of the masters of the situation. They raid villages, take slaves, and give them back for ivory. The State has not suppressed slavery, but established a monopoly by driving out the Arab and *waungwana* competitors." Glave cited the example of a Swahili trader named Kayamba, "who now is devoted to the interests of the State, catching slaves for them and stealing ivory from the natives of the interior." He also mentioned that after two soldiers were killed at the State post on the Lomami River, "Arabs were sent to punish the natives. Many women and children were taken, and twenty-one heads have been brought to the falls and have been used by Captain Rom [the Stanley Falls station chief] as decoration round a flower bed in front of his house."

The State's demands for rubber were seen as particularly oppressive. "When a village does not consent to make rubber," wrote Glave, "the *mgwana* [Arab/Swahili official] of that particular district is empowered to fight the offending village and to kill and take prisoners, which is quite general." Arriving at Basoko (at the mouth of the Aruwimi River), Glave heard war drums threatening the State post and noted that the surrounding area was in full revolt. In one attack, the rebels had killed twenty-two State soldiers in three hours. "It is the natural outcome of the harsh, cruel policy of the State," he wrote, "wringing rubber from these people without paying for it. The revolution will extend." That prediction was confirmed when he arrived at Bumba on February 27 and found that the station chief was away on a war expedition. "The persistent badgering of the natives for rubber and ivory has led to the revolt," observed Glave. "All are agreed on this point."[68]

In the aftermath of the war in Manyema, different participants expressed widely varying views on its impact. In his report to King Leopold II, Commandant Dhanis characterized the war as an effort to end the East African slave trade. "The annihilation of Arab power has brought about the complete suppression of the devastating bands which, in order to procure slaves, have been ravaging the country with fire and sword, from the Uele in the north down to the Sankuru in the south. With them, the slave trade disappears from the regions they exploited, and very soon, we may hope, it will no longer exist in the Congo State." But Captain Hinde emphasized the way the war had changed the political geography of Manyema. Speaking to the Royal Geographical Society in London on March 11, 1895, he told the crowd, "The political geography of the Upper Congo basin has been completely changed as a result of the Belgian campaign among the Arabs. It used to be a common saying in this part of Africa that 'all roads lead to Nyangwe.' This town, visited by Livingstone, Stanley, and Cameron, until lately one of the greatest markets in Africa, has ceased to exist, and its site, when I last saw it, was occupied by a single house."[69]

CHAPTER 9

CONCESSION COMPANIES AND COLONIAL VIOLENCE

D URING THE 1890S, THE CONGO Free State and the French
Congo formed a study in contrasts of colonial governance.
The Congo Free State, which was the private property of King
Leopold II of Belgium, was intended from the beginning to be a
moneymaking venture. As such, it required investments in infrastructure, equipment, administrators, and military personnel, all
of which were intended to produce a profit in a timely fashion.
The quickest way to generate income was to strip the rainforest of
its marketable resources. The Manyema Arabs had shown the way
by raiding villages for ivory and for captives who could be ransomed with ivory or retained as slaves. The Congo Free State had
piggybacked onto this system by buying up Tippu Tip's ivory and
attacking Arab trading parties to seize their stockpiles.

While the Congo Free State was carrying on a war over ivory
against the Arabs in Manyema and along the Uele River, it was
also seeking to exploit the natural resources of the regions between
Malebo Pool and Stanley Falls. Because elephants in the dense
tropical rainforest were hard to locate and approach, even hunters
armed with the latest model rifles found them difficult to kill. As a
consequence, ivory was proving to be a boom-and-bust commodity

in that the first traders to arrive in a region bought up vast stores of "dead ivory" that had been accumulated over many decades. Thereafter, they could purchase only the ivory from freshly killed elephants, which caused the volume to decrease rapidly.

The Congo Free State needed a more sustainable approach to exploiting the natural resources of the Congo basin rainforest. Stanley had recommended botanical resources such as rubber, which were more sustainable than animal resources. But wild rubber was difficult to locate and harvest, and sufficient quantities would not be forthcoming without attractive prices. The State concluded that only a system of forced production could yield mass quantities of wild rubber without paying market prices and that such a system could be put in place only by a large entity such as the Congo Free State or large concession companies with total control over the land and the people.

The frenetic activity of the Congo Free State formed a contrast to the French territory that stretched from the north-south line of the Congo and Ubangi Rivers to the Atlantic Ocean. On August 1, 1886, in the wake of the Berlin Conference, the French proclaimed it the Colony of Gabon and Congo and, on April 30, 1891, renamed it the Colony of the French Congo. To avoid confusion, the colony will be referred to hereafter as the French Congo. Until 1898, it was administered by Pierre Savorgnan de Brazza with minimal personnel whose job was mainly to maintain peace along the trade routes. The African population was not taxed, and government revenues came mostly from duties on imports and exports collected at ports along the Atlantic coast. Although there was talk about developing the transportation infrastructure to facilitate trade between the coast and the Congo River basin, nothing was done for lack of funding. Even though Brazza was the commissioner-general of the French Congo, he was frequently away from his headquarters in Libreville, Gabon, sometimes for as long as two years. The colonial regime administered by Brazza was environmentally sustainable, but it was not politically sustainable in Paris, where the

French parliament demanded higher levels of exploitation and profit.

1

Brussels, Place de la Bourse, February 14, 1888

One hundred thousand shares of Congo Free State bearer bonds went on sale at the Brussels Stock Exchange on February 14, 1888. This was the first of three installments designed to raise 150 million Belgian francs for the Congo Free State. Each bond bore a face value of 100 francs and was redeemable in ninety-nine years. Although its face value grew by 5 francs each year, the increase was not true interest because it did not compound. The special appeal of the bonds, however, lay in the lottery, which would be held six times per year. Each drawing chose twenty-five shares for immediate redemption at premium prices, with the winning bond receiving 200,000 francs. Some observers in the Belgian financial community found the scheme "interesting," but the major financiers at the Brussels Stock Exchange dismissed it as "bizarre."[1]

The bond scheme was a sign of King Leopold's financial desperation. "His Majesty repeats ten times per hour that we are going bankrupt, that he doesn't know how he can pay his expenses, that the bankers won't lend him any more money, etc., etc.," wrote Albert Thys, the king's secretary for colonial affairs, on September 27, 1885. "Our Gracious Sovereign is like this all the time." By 1886, the Congo Free State was so strapped for money that it closed the majority of its stations on the Upper Congo River and recalled most of its agents. Under those circumstances, Leopold saw no alternative but to seek assistance from the government of Belgium, which agreed to issue the bonds but not to guarantee them. Instead, a consortium of banks led by the Société Générale de Belgique guaranteed the bonds.[2]

After the initial release of 100,000 shares of Congo Free State bonds in February 1888 at 83 francs each, their value began to fluctuate wildly, forcing Leopold to buy shares himself to keep the price up. The second installment, consisting of 600,000 shares, went on sale a year later, but by then the bonds from the first issue were selling at well below the 84-franc offering price for the second issue. Only about 260,000 shares of the second installment were ever sold. The third installment, consisting of 800,000 shares, was not released, and trunks filled with the unissued bonds were stored in Leopold's private residence. As his financial situation grew more precarious, the king often appeared distracted. One day, as he paced back and forth, his wife cried out, "But, Leopold, you will ruin us with your Congo!"[3]

The financial relationship between the Belgian government and the Congo Free State had been defined in 1885, when Leopold sought approval from the parliament to be both the king of Belgium and the sovereign of the Congo Free State. During the negotiations, Leopold won support by absolving the Belgian government of any financial responsibility for the Congo. Prime Minister Auguste Beernaert assured parliament that the Congo Free State was the king's personal project, which had nothing whatsoever to do with the Belgian government. By the beginning of May 1885, both chambers had passed the resolution, which read, "His Majesty Leopold II, King of the Belgians, is authorized to be the head of the state founded in Africa by the International Association of the Congo. The union between Belgium and the new State of Congo will be exclusively a personal one."[4]

King Leopold had inherited a personal fortune of 15 million Belgian francs (one Belgian franc was equal to one French franc). When he invested his personal money in the Congo Free State, it entered the Free State's budget in the category of special funds, which remained under Leopold's control, overseen by Baron Auguste Goffinet, who also managed the king's personal fortune. The special funds account was augmented by money left over from the defunct

International African Association and a portion of the money from the sale of Congo Free State bonds. In contrast, the general funds in the Congo Free State's budget came from ivory sales, export duties, taxes, bonds, and direct loans. Leopold's objective was to finance his Congo venture as much as possible with other people's money.[5]

When the Congo Free State bonds failed to provide the anticipated funds, Leopold sought to persuade the Belgian government to give him a direct loan. His major financial asset was the Congo itself. In a dramatic gesture, he wrote a will leaving the Congo Free State to Belgium after his death in return for a loan of 25 million francs. Sixteen years earlier, Leopold had pledged the Congo to France in the event that his venture went bankrupt, and now he was pledging it to Belgium to avoid that very bankruptcy. The loan was issued in 1890 with no interest for ten years, after which time the Belgian government would have the right to take over the Congo if it chose to do so. As a condition of the loan, Leopold could not take out any other loans without the written permission of the Belgian government.

While searching for funds in Belgium, Leopold was developing plans to extract more revenue from the Congo Free State itself. Although State agents were aggressively seizing stockpiles of ivory from the Arabs, Leopold knew that it was a diminishing resource. In 1885, Stanley had outlined the case for exploiting the vegetable products of the rainforest. "Ivory," he wrote, "stands but fifth in rank among the natural products of the basin. The total value of the ivory supposed to be in existence in this region today would but represent . . . 30,000 tons of India-rubber. If every warrior living on the immediate banks of the Congo and its navigable affluents were to pick about a third of a pound in rubber each day throughout the year . . . and convey it to the trader for sale, £5,000,000 worth of vegetable produce could be obtained without exhaustion of the wild forest productions."[6]

From the beginning, the Congo Free State had laid claim to the products of the land. The first decree ever published in the

Bulletin Officiel de l'État Indépendant du Congo was the ordinance of July 1, 1885, which stated that "vacant land must be considered as belonging to the state." Vacant land was later defined as all land that was not under direct habitation or cultivation—in other words, all land outside of villages and cultivated fields. However, the land that the State considered vacant was not necessarily considered vacant by the local populations. As the missionary Charles Padfield explained, "In this district there is no such thing as 'unoccupied land.' The term is a complete misnomer. It is impossible to find a part of the forest which is not claimed under native law and custom." The purpose of the Congo Free State's decree, however, was not to seize individual plots of land from African villagers but to lay a legal foundation for future claims to the rubber, ivory, and other products of the forest that lay beyond the villages and fields.[7]

There remained the question of how to organize the collection of wild rubber and other forest resources. Leopold discussed this issue with Charles de Chavannes, the lieutenant governor of the French Congo, during a conference in Brussels in 1890, which had been convened to set import duties for the Congo River basin. The two men met at the royal palace. After a bit of opening conversation, Leopold began a long monologue in which he talked about all the money he had spent in developing the Congo and how the mineral-rich region of Kwilu-Niari, on which he had pinned great hopes for recovering his investments, had been taken over by France. At length he came down to his main question: "How can we best exploit the labor of the natives?"

Chavannes responded by reverting to stereotyped views of Africans that would become common during the colonial period. He said that the "natives," as he called them, had an "outdated mentality that caused them to prefer hunger to work in daily life." He added that the concept of saving money was completely foreign to them. After receiving their salary for one or two days of work, he said, "they return to their instinctive laziness for as long as they can until the money runs out." The king was probably unaware that Charles Lemaire, the commissioner of the Equator District of the Congo Free State from 1890 to 1893, had a very different view of African workers. "Superficial observers have frequently reported that the black man has no desire to work," wrote Lemaire. "That is an error: we can observe that the black man has no desire to work for nothing; in other words, he desires to enjoy the fruits of his labor, and . . . he does not differ, in this respect, from the white man in any way."[8]

Chavannes had two suggestions for King Leopold. The first was that the competition among small trading houses in both Congos would drive up the prices they paid for African resources and would thus encourage the Africans in their "indolent ways." The solution was to base the economy on large companies with effective monopolies. His second suggestion was to impose a system of forced labor on the Africans. Such forced labor, he argued, could be considered the equivalent of required military service in European countries, and it was simply a normal tax that the Africans must pay in exchange for the "benefits that European civilization had brought them at great expense." Chavannes told the king that his suggestion would never be accepted in France, where, he noted, "humanitarian ideals dominated all else, even basic logic. But perhaps in Belgium my suggestions would be better received." King Leopold listened thoughtfully and then complimented him on his answer.[9]

The legal foundations of the Congo Free State's monopoly on rubber gathering were outlined in a decree of October 30, 1892, which gave the State the exclusive right to collect rubber in a series of river basins both north and south of the bend of the Congo while reserving the Lomami River and the Lualaba above Stanley Falls for future exploitation. In order to mobilize and exploit African labor, the decree stated that Africans in the defined regions who gathered rubber would be required to give a portion of it to the State as a tax. On December 5, the king issued a new decree requesting the administration of the Congo Free State to take all

measures that it deemed useful or necessary to ensure the exploitation of the resources of the rubber regions. "For a long time," stated
the decree, "the administration has believed that it has the right to
demand from the natives taxes in the form of labor, and the power
to delegate that right to private companies without specifying the
nature and level of these expectations, nor the means to employ
to enforce them." That decree, which was never published in the
Bulletin Officiel, became the legal basis for forced rubber gathering
in the Congo Free State.[10]

Leopold's decision to focus on rubber came at a time when
demand for rubber in Europe and the United States was growing
rapidly. In 1871, the United States had imported roughly five thousand tons of rubber, which was 50 percent of the world's rubber
trade. The major uses were for rubber shoes and boots, followed by
industrial uses such as gaskets and belts, followed by ponchos and
raincoats. A major development came in 1888, when John Boyd
Dunlop of Belfast applied for a patent on pneumatic bicycle tires
to replace the inch-thick solid rubber tires then in usage. In 1895,
the French rubber manufacturers Edouard and André Michelin
entered a motor car equipped with pneumatic tires in the Paris-
Bordeaux race. The trip used up twenty-two inner tubes, but the
vehicle made it to Bordeaux. After that, tires and inner tubes would
propel the expanding demand for rubber. The world capital of the
rubber industry in the late nineteenth century was Akron, Ohio,
where the B. F. Goodrich Company was incorporated in 1880, the
Diamond Rubber Company began in the 1890s, Goodyear started
in 1898, and the Firestone Tire and Rubber Company in 1900.[11]

By 1892, King Leopold had found investors to form companies that would exploit the rubber resources of the Congo. The
Anglo-Belgian India Rubber Company, known by its acronym
"Abir," received an oval-shaped concession that covered twenty-five
thousand square miles south of the bend in the Congo River, and
the Société Anversoise received a concession of twenty-two thousand square miles in the Mongala River basin, north of the Congo

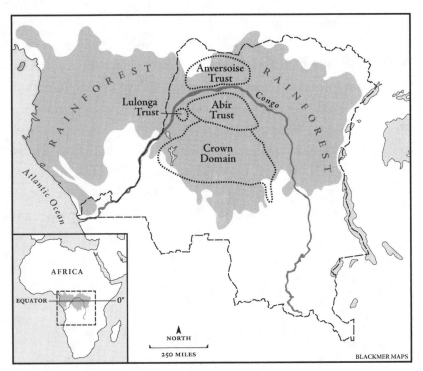

Rubber Concession Territories in the Congo Free State, 1892–1899

River bend. Each of these concessions was roughly twice the size of Belgium. Within their concession areas, the companies held the exclusive right to exploit all the products of the forests for a period of thirty years. They also enjoyed "rights of police," which allowed them to create and use private armies, and "powers of detention," which allowed them to operate private prisons and labor camps.[12]

Abir was founded with British capital that came from a group of investors led by Col. John Thomas North, a British financier who had made a fortune investing in nitrate mines in Chile. Of the company's two thousand capital shares, eighteen hundred were held by British investors. In addition, there were two thousand bonus shares (*actions de jouissance*) that had no face value but nevertheless received dividends. If the company made a profit in a given year, the capital shareholders received 6 percent interest on their investment, and the remaining profits were divided equally

among the bonus shares, half of which were held by the Congo
Free State. In short, the Congo State would receive a generous
share of the profits without investing any money. The Anversoise
Company, in contrast, had twenty-five hundred capital shares but
no bonus shares. The main shareholders were Alexander de Browne
de Tiège, an Antwerp banker with close financial ties to King Leopold, and Constant de Browne de Tiège, Alexander's brother. By
the end of 1892, the legal, financial, and corporate structures were
in place to launch an assault on the rubber resources of the Congo
Free State and on the people who lived in the rubber concession
regions.[13]

2

Equator Station, Congo Free State, December 1890

Charles Lemaire arrived at the Equator Station in December 1890
to begin his assignment as the first commissioner of the newly created Equator District. His major task was to institute forced rubber
gathering. The circular from Governor-General Camille Janssen,
which had gone out to all the district commissioners in the Congo
Free State on March 27, 1890, declared, "The king believes that a
series of small military and fiscal posts need to be established at
judiciously chosen points. These posts . . . would have the task of
introducing the harvesting of rubber to the natives . . . and requiring them to bring in their produce."[14]

In contrast to elephant hunting, which could be accomplished
only by professional hunters with the aid of elaborate deadfall traps
and pit traps, rubber gathering could be done by ordinary villagers.
The wild rubber in the forest came mainly from the *landolphia*
vine, which looked remarkably similar to a number of other vines
that did not bear rubber. A rubber gatherer would go deep into the
forest in search of a suitable vine. Then he would cut an incision in
the vine and hang a small earthen pot under it to catch the latex

as it dripped out. To coagulate the latex without recourse to large pots and smoke, he would rub it onto his arms, chest, and stomach so that the heat from his body solidified the liquid. Then he would peel off the coating of rubber and shape it into a ball. If the vine did not yield sufficient latex, he would move on to find another one. The next time he went to collect rubber, he would have to go deeper into the forest to find an untapped vine. With each rubber gathering trip, the job became more difficult. As the Sanford Exploring Expedition had learned at its post at Luebo, people were willing to collect rubber during the agricultural off-season if the price was right. However, a regime of forced, year-round rubber gathering was a different matter entirely.

Instead of following the governor-general's instructions, Lemaire sent out his own circular in 1892, proclaiming a State monopoly on rubber purchases but avoiding any mention of forced rubber gathering. Lemaire's recalcitrance caught the attention of Edmond Van Eetvelde, who had replaced Colonel Strauch in 1890 as King Leopold's right-hand man in Brussels for administering the Congo. Van Eetvelde told the governor-general that Lemaire should collect detailed information on the rubber resources of the Equator District and "make every effort to collect the greatest possible quantity of rubber throughout his entire district."[15]

The dispute became irrelevant in 1893 when a certain Mr. Engerieth arrived in the Equator District carrying a letter of introduction from Van Eetvelde. "The bearer of this letter is Mr. Engerieth, the head of the Anglo-Belgian India Rubber Company [i.e., Abir] in your district," read the letter. "Mr. Engerieth and his assistants have been given the task of installing stations on the Lopori and the Maringa. . . . As you know, the State is committed to establish a certain number of posts and turn them over to the company, along with the territory around them for a radius of 15 miles. The placement of these posts should be well chosen to facilitate the harvest of the products." Lemaire was further instructed to construct buildings of local materials for the posts, supply the posts

Balls of rubber drying on racks at the Abir post of Baringa. E. D. Morel, *King Leopold's Rule in Africa*, p. 24.

with arms and ammunition, and introduce the company agents to the local chiefs.[16]

By the end of 1894, the Abir headquarters at Basankusu (at the junction of the Maringa and Lopori Rivers) was functioning, and a second post had been established at Bongandanga, some 120 miles up the Lopori. When the Abir agents, accompanied by fourteen armed sentries, arrived at Bongandanga, they made an agreement with the local chiefs: Abir would help them to expel the Ngombe immigrant groups who were intruding into their territory if they would bring rubber in return. The villagers worked willingly at first, but later, when they tired of the rubber work, they learned that their names had been written down and that those who failed to bring in their required quota of rubber every fortnight would be punished. With resistance to Abir growing, the company placed armed sentries in each village in the vicinity to ensure the collection of rubber (the term "sentries" is used here to distinguish armed company employees from the "soldiers" who worked for the State). During 1894, the post at Bongandanga brought in two tons of rubber per month.

Abir established six more posts during 1895 and 1896, each with one or two European agents and a contingent of armed sentries. An old man described the beginning of the rubber work in one of the villages near the Baringa post. "The sentries came to us to make us work rubber," he recounted. "But we refused this rubber work, and they went to tell the European, and he said, 'You go and fight against them.' And they came to fight us with their guns. We sent one of our men, whose name was Ngila, to tell the white man that he should stop fighting against us. We accepted the rubber work, and we went to work." During 1896, the Abir concession exported 190 tons of rubber.[17]

During the years 1898–1900, Knud Jespersen, a commander of the State police, traveled extensively in the Equator District and observed the conditions in both the State-controlled areas and the Abir-controlled areas. His memoir provides a rare glimpse of the way the State and the rubber company established control over the territory and domination over the populations. Jespersen was initially sent to a State post along a tributary of the Ruki River. The lieutenant in charge of the post was backed up by 150 African soldiers, about a third of whom had been recruited from the Equateur District (the rest were Tetela and Luba recruits from the Kasai River region). In response to their arrival, the local population had fled the immediate territory around the post after first burning down their huts. To establish control of the countryside, the State officer sent out contingents of twenty to twenty-five soldiers commanded by African officers to five designated regions. Each soldier was armed with a single-shot Albini rifle (which was the standard infantry rifle of the Belgian army until 1889). In each region, the African officer (either a sergeant or a corporal) settled in the principal village with two or three soldiers and distributed the rest of his soldiers among the neighboring villages, with one or two soldiers in each one. The soldiers were allowed to rule as despots over their villages as long as they produced ivory and rubber.[18]

At the State post, Jespersen observed the delivery of rubber by the soldiers stationed in the surrounding villages. The State officer asked Jespersen to distribute two Albini cartridges to each soldier and to examine the contents of the baskets that the soldiers had placed off to the side. In the baskets, he found about fifty severed hands of all sizes. According to the State military regulations, each soldier was required to justify the firing of a cartridge by producing a human left hand (to prove that the cartridge had been fired in combat). Jespersen noted that many of the hands in the baskets came from people slain in combat, but he also saw hands of children, women, and old people, which had probably been severed from living victims in order to justify the unauthorized expenditure of cartridges. His suspicion was verified when he saw people in the villages with missing hands.

In 1899, Jespersen was ordered to the Abir concession, where a rebellion by the villages around the Lukolenge post (on the Lopori River) had successfully driven out the Abir sentries and captured many guns. Arriving at Abir's headquarters at Basankusu on a State steamer, he observed that the houses were large and rich, with orchards and gardens. The station received all kinds of fine products from Europe: two kinds of flour, Danish butter, Norwegian herring, and alcoholic beverages, including red wine, port wine, whiskey, and champagne. In addition to the headquarters of Abir, there were offices of the Société Anonyme Belge, the Société de l'Ikelemba, and the Anversoise Company (the other major rubber concession company). The arrangement revealed that although the different concession companies and trading companies were competitors, they also worked together for their mutual benefit. Jespersen reported that the companies were under the nominal authority of the Congo Free State, but they considered themselves sovereign in their own territories.[19]

Arriving at the Abir post of Bongandanga after a fourteen-day trip up the Lopori in two enormous canoes with thirty paddlers each, Jespersen learned the bizarre story of the previous Abir agent there. That man had displayed a mental condition that Jespersen referred to as "tropical rage," and he ruled over the neighboring populations like a despot. He set up rifles loaded with blanks around his house and set them off throughout the night to keep people from sleeping. He intercepted all boats going to the five Abir posts farther up the Lopori River and seized their goods at gunpoint, forcing the company to send a contingent of soldiers to arrest him and take him to the company headquarters in Basankusu. "The Lopori River was liberated from a brigand," wrote Jespersen in his memoir, "but there were others who remained."

At the next post, Ekutshi, Jespersen was welcomed warmly, but his Congolese soldiers were restricted to the riverbank, and the Abir agent refused to give them anything to eat. Jespersen learned that although each post was authorized to have twenty-five sentries and twenty-five Albini rifles, the actual numbers were far greater. The European Abir agents would sell some of the rubber and ivory they collected to rival companies for their personal profit. As long as sufficient rubber was collected, Abir closed its eyes to complaints of corruption and mistreatment of the local population, but if the complaints were proven, then the agent was fired and the company washed its hands of the affair. Abir agents received minimal salaries, but they also received a commission on each ton of rubber they produced. Some agents returned home after a three-year contract in Africa with as much as 100,000 francs. Given that Abir was formed with an initial capital of 1 million francs, a bonus of 100,000 francs for a single agent would have been an enormous sum. The agent at Ekutshi told Jespersen that some State military officers worked secretly on behalf of Abir and were paid well for their work. Then he offered Jespersen a bonus of 30,000–60,000 francs if he would ignore the abuses he saw and write a favorable report. Jespersen refused.

The next post Jespersen visited was Iteko. The Abir agent was a man of Anglo-Belgian ancestry who considered himself more refined and cultivated than his fellow agents. He boasted that he did not shoot the villagers for various infractions, as the other agents did. Instead, those who ran afoul of the company were beaten with fists like human punching bags. Around the post, Jespersen noticed Africans with deformed faces, mutilated ears, flattened noses, and gouged-out eyes. The next post was Lokolenge, the place where the revolt against the company had broken out. The agent there conducted himself with the air of a great lord, acting very ceremonious and condescending toward Jespersen. At dinner, the Abir agent got six plates of food, Jespersen got four, and each of his assistants got two.

When Jesperson arrived at Simba, the last Abir post on the Lopori, he met a young agent named Willems, who seemed like a normal person. The son of a doctor, Willems had received a good education but had abandoned it in order to have an African adventure and make some quick money. He condemned the abuses carried out by his superior, who had triggered the rebellion by sending armed sentries into the villages to force people to gather rubber. Because Willems had a good rapport with the local people, Jespersen was able to spend several days visiting nearby villages and talking to the people about the rebellion. He promised them that the abuses would end, but they should first return the guns they had seized. Soon, the guns were returned.

Willems told Jespersen about some of the cruel "games" that the Abir agents played to amuse themselves. One of them was to force African villagers to climb up a tall palm tree and then to climb down headfirst, inevitably falling to their death or serious injury. In a second "game," two villagers would be tied together and thrown into the Lopori River to drift with the current. The Abir agents would then use them for target practice until they either died of the gunshots or drowned. Another agent, who suspected his African concubine of being unfaithful to him, tied her to a tree that contained a colony of fire ants, which swarmed over her and bit her until she died.

Heading back to Basankusu after several months in the Abir concession, Jespersen again encountered the practice of cutting off hands. He stopped at a village where several men told him, "You want us to bring you rubber, but how can we do it? We no longer have hands." They then showed him the stumps of their arms. Arriving back at the Abir headquarters of Basankusu, Jesperson found that the district commissioner of the Equator District was there, another indication of the close working relationship between the company and the State. After submitting his report to the district commissioner, Jespersen returned to Europe for a vacation. There is no evidence that any action was taken on his report.

The general picture that emerges from Jespersen's account is reinforced by the stories told by the people of the Equator District themselves. In 1953, Father Edmond Boelaert, a Catholic missionary with the Sacred Heart Mission in Bamanya, Équateur Province, Belgian Congo, sent out an appeal to teachers, catechists, mission workers, secondary school students, and other literate Africans to write narratives about the arrival of the first whites and forced rubber collecting in their home villages. They were instructed to inform themselves by speaking with their village elders and then write brief narrative accounts. All entries would receive compensation, and the best one would receive a prize of 2,500 francs. In response, Father Boelaert received 280 accounts from various localities in Équateur Province. Eighteen of them concerned the former Abir territory. The following is a small sample. In these narratives, white people are always identified by the nicknames the Africans gave them, not by their European names.[20]

"The war began when a sentry came from the post of Bokongoongolo," wrote Bruno Bafala (from Waka). "He was called Lokwama. He ordered us to harvest rubber. The next day, the white man himself arrived. It was a white agent of the Abir Company. . . . He gave us ten days to start gathering rubber. Then the rubber gathering started, but he killed two persons. We fled across the river and settled at Baringa . . . but a white man from the Abir Company was sent to our place. During the period when rubber was being weighed, there was fighting. They fought with guns, and we fought with arrows. The guns were pistols, and then came Albini rifles."

The account written by Ferdinand Bokamba (from Loma) focused on the recruitment of sentries by the company: "We suddenly saw a dugout canoe downstream of Lomako. In it was a white man named Lokwekwe, his two African assistants, and a lot of food. He settled into one of our straw huts. A week later, he recruited 31 people and dressed them in black clothes with red hats. He told us to call those men 'policemen.' He paid each policeman 4 brass rods. He ordered the people to build him a great house made of adobe." Then came the order to collect rubber. As Bokamba recounted, "After two months, he imposed the harvest of balls of rubber. That order was followed by the arming of the police. Each one received a rifle and instruction on how to use it. . . . Our compatriots collected rubber. Two who did not submit were killed by the white man's police. They killed those who refused to harvest rubber: father, mother, and son."

The account by Hubert-Justin Bompunga (from Bongandanga) emphasized the complicity of the local chief, Lontembe. "At first, we refused to harvest rubber," wrote Bompunga. "But the whites responded with war. Many people were killed. The whites tried to corrupt the chief by offering him goods such as rice, soap, salt, and a variety of other goods. . . . After much misery, [Chief] Lontembe told his people to harvest rubber. Everybody obeyed and began to harvest rubber, but that came after a process that had caused a lot of deaths, because they killed or imprisoned those who did not bring in the required amount."

The account by Leon George Isenge (from Lonola) mentions the rubber company's practice of cutting off hands. "Here at Lonola, the first white man who arrived was Longange. He ordered the chiefs, 'Everybody should bring slabs of rubber.' On market days, he would give people salt or one meter of cloth. If your basket did not contain enough rubber, you were killed in place. Each sentry brought the white man 15–20 mutilated hands taken off dead bodies. Then the white man ordered us to bring the rubber in balls."

The account of Simon Ilonga focused on the region of Simba, on the upper Lopori, where Arabs from Manyema had previously come to collect ivory. He described the beginning of rubber collection as follows: "The whites sent a sentry to impose the collection of rubber. The villagers were furious and started to attack those men. The villagers took refuge in the forest. . . . The whites armed their sentries with rifles, and they mistreated the villagers just as the Arabs had done previously. . . . The Bongando became furious and declared, 'Come, we will act as we did before [against the Arabs]. We give them our wives, we give them food, we do the work they demand of us, and then they decide to kill us! No! We must kill those men and some whites.' When night arrived, they stopped the sentries of the whites, seized their rifles, and killed a number of them. Then they fled into the equatorial forest."

The final account excerpted here comes from Nicolas Afolembe. Like the previous one, it refers to the Bongando people who lived in the vicinity of Simba, on the upper Lopori: "After the departure of the Arabs," he wrote, "they were replaced by the whites who came for rubber. The elders call that time 'the era of the Abir Company.' Each village had a sentry sent by the whites to force the people to collect rubber. Because of that, the people suffered. . . . At each weighing of the rubber, if the rubber of the sentry or the people under his authority was insufficient, the sentry was punished with the *chicotte* [hippopotamus-hide whip] or prison. That is why the sentries killed many people. Before going to the weighing, they verified if the weight of each person's harvest was sufficient. A person who came up short was killed. As a result, many people were killed."

Each village in the Abir concession had its own unique stories of the imposition of rubber gathering. Yet when taken together, they are remarkably similar. Even though many villages and villagers resisted the demands, their resistance was brutally crushed. The late nineteenth century was a particularly devastating time for the people who lived on the upper Lopori River. Having endured the ivory impositions of the Arabs and their Manyema followers, they were then subjected to the rubber impositions of the European colonizers.

3

Ndobo, Anversoise Concession, January 1900

Edgar Canisius, an American adventurer with previous service in the South Pacific and three years with the Congo Free State, returned to the Congo in 1899, this time as an employee of the Société Anversoise. His trip from the port city of Boma, the capital of the Congo Free State, illustrates how much the Congo had changed since the time of the Berlin Conference in 1885. The first change was that he traveled from Boma to Malebo Pool by train. When he had first come to the Congo in 1896, he was able to travel by train only as far as Kimpasse and then did a fifteen-day trek to Malebo Pool. This time, the train went all the way to the Pool. The 242-mile railroad had been built in eight years, using as many as sixty thousand conscripted workers at a time, many of whom were delivered to the work site in chains, like slaves or prison chain gangs. Many of the workers had died from accidents, poor nutrition, lack of shelter, and disease. Although Congo Free State officials would acknowledge only eighteen hundred African deaths resulting from the construction project, local legend held that each railroad tie represented the loss of one African life. Leaving Malebo Pool and going up the Congo River in a State steamboat, Canisius observed that over a hundred steamers were now plying the

Rubber gatherers bring their baskets of rubber to an Anversoise Company post. Note the company agent (front, left) and the three African sentries in company uniforms (front, right). Anti-Slavery International

Upper Congo and its tributaries. They were mostly stern-wheelers, the largest of which could carry 150 tons. The majority of them belonged to the Congo Free State, which enjoyed a near monopoly on the transport business.[21]

Arriving at the Anversoise concession on the north bank of the Congo River in January 1900, Canisius found the region in turmoil. Rubber production had gotten off to a slow start. During 1895–1897, the concession produced only 152 tons of rubber, compared to 516 tons by the Abir concession. In July 1897, the company hired Hubert Lothaire, the Congo Free State's former commandant of the Arab Zone, who had lost his government position in the wake of his summary execution of the British ivory trader Charles Stokes. His military background and reputation for aggressive action were just what the company was looking for.[22]

Lothaire's strategy was to launch a reign of terror on the villages that resisted the rubber quotas. In a declaration published in

1900 in *Le Petit Blue*, a freelance newspaper published in Antwerp, Anversoise agent Joseph Moray described an attack on a peaceful village. "At Ambas, we were a party of thirty under X_____, who sent us into a certain village to ascertain if the natives were collecting rubber, and in the contrary case, to murder all, including men, women, and children. We found the natives sitting peaceably. We asked them what they were doing. They were unable to reply. Thereupon, we fell upon them all, and killed them without mercy." The massacre was just a prelude to the gruesome aftermath. As Moray recounted, "An hour later we were joined by X_____, and told him what had been done. He answered, 'It is well, but you have not done enough!' He thereupon ordered us to cut off the heads of the men and hang them on the village palisades, also their sexual members, and to hang the women and children on the palisades in the form of a cross."[23]

Another Anversoise agent, Louis Lacroix, wrote a letter of confession to the Antwerp newspaper *Nieuwe Gazet*. "I am going to appear before the judge," he wrote, "(1) for having assassinated 150 men and cut off 60 hands; (2) for having crucified women and children; and for having mutilated many men and hung their remains on the village fence; (3) having shot a native with a revolver; (4) for having murdered a native." With multiple witnesses against them, both Moray and Lacroix were convicted on all counts by the Court of Appeals at Boma in September and October 1900. The court also convicted agent Leopold Matthys of imprisoning, starving, and torturing fifty women in the village of Modumbala and thirty more in Mombia, most of whom did not survive the ordeal. Lothaire's reign of terror produced the desired results: rubber production climbed from 93 tons in 1897 to 298 tons in 1898, to 641 tons for the eighteen-month period from January 1899 to July 1900. As director of the company, Lothaire received a commission of 0.10 francs per kilo of rubber produced.[24]

In January 1900, Edgar Canisius met Lothaire at the company headquarters in Mobeka, located at the junction of the Mongala and Congo Rivers, and received instructions to proceed to Ndobo, a post on the Congo River in the eastern part of the company's concession. He spent several weeks at Ndobo, where he had a chance to observe the rubber concession system in action. Canisius estimated that the Anversoise concession was twice the size of Belgium. Governed from the company's headquarters at Mobeka, the concession was divided into five zones, each with a European "zone chief" who supervised the work of the European post agents. Each zone chief received a commission of 0.10 francs for each kilo of rubber produced in his zone. The post agents, he learned, had the right to wipe out villages, kill indiscriminately, and enslave or imprison men, women, and children, as long as they met their rubber quotas. In his discussions with an agent who had been with the company from the beginning, Canisius suggested that perhaps ten thousand Africans had been slaughtered since the company began its Congo operations in 1893. The man replied that twice that number would be more accurate.[25]

There were a dozen villages in the vicinity of Ndobo where the people were required to deliver rubber every fifteen days. An African employee of the company, known as a *capita*, was stationed in each village to ensure that it met its rubber quota. Armed with a musket or a breech-loader, these capitas usually came from other districts of the Congo so that, as outsiders, they had no sympathetic relations with the local populations. They received a salary from the company, but the villagers were expected to supply them with food and shelter. On delivery days, the villagers appeared at the post with their capita, each carrying a basket supplied by the company that was supposed to be filled with balls of rubber.[26]

As each man presented his basket, the white agent inspected it to make sure the quantity of rubber was sufficient and then paid the man in mitakos (brass rods) at the rate of about a penny per pound of rubber. Those people whose rubber fell short were ordered to stand to one side, where they would be flogged with a chicotte. They normally received twenty-five or fifty lashes, depending on the size of the shortfall, but there were instances of up to one hundred lashes. After the whippings were finished, the people were allowed to return to their villages. "The manager of the post," explained Canisius, "had accumulated perhaps no less than a thousand pounds of rubber at the cost of about £4 sterling, including presents to the chiefs and *capitas*. Thus was rubber 'gathered' twice each month at Ndobo."

"The cruel flogging of so many men and boys would probably have had a peculiar effect upon a newcomer," wrote Canisius, "but I was in a measure case-hardened. My experience in the State service during three years had made me familiar with many such, and worse, incidents in Congolese life. For instance, at the government post where I was for a long time stationed, a man had died as a result of an exceptionally severe castigation at the hands of a white official, and elsewhere I had seen blood drawn from the backs of women."

Canisius estimated that about three-quarters of the men in the villages were on the company books (the others presumably being too old or infirm to gather rubber). For those villagers whose names were in the books, rubber gathering occupied nearly all of their time because they had to "search far and wide" in the forest for *landolphia* vines to tap. He described the vines as follows: "In the African jungle, the sap is drawn from a giant creeper (often six inches in diameter at the base), which, shooting upward towards the life-giving light of heaven, twists about the surrounding vegetation—its rivals in the struggle for existence. After reaching the crown of the highest monarch of the forest (often a hundred feet above the ground), the vine rises still further until it is bent back by its own weight to the topmost branches of its original support. Then it climbs along these branches, and those of probably half-a-dozen other great trees, until the machete of the rubber gatherer cuts short its career."

Canisius then described the process of collecting rubber. "The Congo native, when about to gather rubber, generally goes with his fellow villagers far into the jungle. Then, having formed a rough, shelterless camp, he begins his search for the creepers. Having found one of sufficient size, he cuts with his knife a number of incisions in the bark, and, hanging a small earthenware pot below the vine, allows the sap to slowly trickle into it. Should the creeper have been already tapped, the man must climb into the supporting tree at more or less personal risk and make an incision in the vine high above the ground, where the sap has not been exhausted and here he will remain, perhaps the whole of the day, until the flow has ceased." Noting that many rubber gatherers had been killed in falls from the tall trees, Canisius concluded that "few Africans will imperil their lives in rubber-gathering unless under compulsion."[27]

Although the Ngombe people who lived in the vicinity of Ndobo had submitted to the rubber company, the Buja people, who lived farther inland, had resisted the rubber impositions. In late January 1900, a Buja revolt broke out, and in response, two hundred soldiers from the nearest Congo Free State military post arrived and marched inland to the village of Yambata, which they occupied without a fight. Soon thereafter, the company's small steamer arrived at Ndobo with Director Lothaire and fifty sentries to join the State forces at Yambata. Canisius, who accompanied them, noted that Lothaire gave the orders and the State commander merely executed them. Then the soldiers moved out to subdue the region.

On February 11, the expedition arrived at Yalombo, where the company had earlier attempted to establish a post. After building a stockade, the main expedition moved on, and Canisius was left to strengthen the stockade and build a blockhouse. When a column went out on patrol a few days later, it was ambushed, and all but 6 of the 120 men were killed. The Bujas captured more than one hundred rifles and several thousand rounds of ammunition. Canisius and his 30 remaining soldiers abandoned Yalombo a few days later and marched to the company post of Monjoa, which was on a river that ran into the Congo. A few days later, he received orders to return to Ndobo, where the expedition had begun. The operation against the Bujas had lasted six weeks and had killed over nine hundred Buja men, women, and children. It also resulted in the loss of half of the armed forces that had fought for the company and the Congo State. Canisius calculated that if the operation had succeeded in establishing control over the region, it would have netted the company another twenty tons of rubber per month. For the moment, however, the Bujas remained unconquered.

Canisius's final posting in the Anversoise concession was at Akula, just up the Mongala River from the company's headquarters at Mobeka. There, he observed an alternative method of organizing the collection of rubber. Whereas in his previous posting at Ndobo, the company capitas in the villages would accompany the villagers to the post to deliver their rubber, each capita at Akula was given a stock of goods to pay the rubber gatherers directly. Canisius called these men "*capita*-chiefs" because they had their own stocks of trade goods. Instead of paying the rubber gatherers, however, many of the capita-chiefs used the company trade goods to acquire wives and slaves and to attract personal followings. "Some of the *capitas*," wrote Canisius, "had hundreds of armed followers, who went about in bands devastating the villages, ravishing the women, and shooting down the men on the slightest provocation. They held the entire country in a state of terror." He added that "they literally 'ate up' the country by forcing the natives to bring them goats and fowls and other provisions, for which they paid out small quantities of merchandise . . . originally intended as recompense to the rubber gatherers." It goes without saying that the rubber gatherers received nothing at all.[28]

During his months at Akula, Canisius made several journeys into the interior. "Everywhere I went," he wrote, "I found a shocking state of affairs, and the natives dying by famine by the score. Continually harassed and slaughtered at the behest of the white men, they had ceased to plant food products, for they derived no personal benefit from their labors, the *capitas* and soldiers taking everything; consequently, the people were now living like wild beasts in the forest, subsisting on roots, and ants, and other insects."

At Akula, he observed a combined expedition of State and company soldiers under the command of a Lieutenant Braeckman. "The united force then attacked a small tribe known as the Gwakas," he wrote, "and, according to the statement of the lieutenant, killed about 300 of these people. The only charges against the latter were that they had deserted their villages and taken to the jungle and killed one of the *capita*'s men in a scuffle. . . . When the lieutenant returned to Akula, he brought with him many prisoners of war—mostly women—poor, gaunt creatures, ready to drop from hunger and exhaustion."[29]

Canisius left the Congo in April 1901, well before the end of his contract, because of his deteriorating health. After his departure, he was awarded the Star of Service by King Leopold, and he received a 500-franc bonus for his "courage during the four months at Monjoa" by the Anversoise Company's director for the region of the Bujas. His parting words in his memoir noted that "the company for which I had suffered so much is surely tottering to its fall. . . . It is certain that the company's concession has already lost much of its value."[30]

The general picture of massacres, terror, and atrocities painted by Canisius was corroborated at the trials of the three European Anversoise agents in Boma in September and October 1900. In addition to confessing to a variety of crimes, they also described the normal workings of the rubber system. As Agent Moray explained, "When natives bring rubber to a factory, they are received by an agent and surrounded by soldiers. The baskets are weighed. If the baskets do not contain the five kilos required, the natives receive 100 blows with the *chicotte*. Those whose baskets attain the correct weight receive a piece of cloth or some other object. If a certain village contains 100 male inhabitants, and 50 come to the factory with rubber, they are retained as hostages, and a force is sent to bring the 50 unruly natives and burn their village."[31]

In their defense, the agents argued that they were merely carrying out the program of Lothaire and the zone chiefs. Before the trials
began, Lothaire resigned from his position as head of the Anversoise
operations and hastily left the Congo, arriving at the port of Matadi
the day before a steamer sailed and immediately going on board.
When the State judge, F. Waleffe, pronounced the sentences of the
Anversoise agents, he announced his intention to arrest Lothaire
if he ever returned to the Congo because he believed that the convicted agents were merely carrying out Lothaire's orders.[32]

The three European agents were sentenced to prison terms of
fifteen years, twelve years, and ten years, respectively, but one of
them died in prison, and the other two were released after serving only three years. The Court of Appeal in Boma justified the
reduction in the sentences as follows: "The chiefs of the Concession
Company have, if not by formal orders, at least by their example
and their tolerance, induced their agents to take no account whatever of the rights, property, and lives of the natives; to use the arms
and the soldiers which should have served for their defense and the
maintenance of order to force the natives to furnish them with produce and to work for the Company, as also to pursue as rebels and
outlaws those who sought to escape from the requisitions imposed
upon them."[33]

In October 1901, Lothaire returned to the Lower Congo on
a trade mission for Alexander de Browne de Tiège, the Belgian
director of the Anversoise Company. When Judge Waleffe learned
that Lothaire was in the country, he wanted to arrest him, but
the governor-general vetoed the idea because there was no evidence
that Lothaire had personally committed the crimes carried out
by his underlings. After finishing his term, the judge returned to
Belgium and met with King Leopold, who authorized the Congo
Free State judiciary to pursue the case. Judge Waleffe immediately
telegraphed his replacement in Boma to arrest Lothaire, but by
then Lothaire had left for the coast. Commandeering a small state
steamer, the new judge caught up with him at the port of Banana.

Lothaire explained that he was on his way to Luanda, Angola, on some very important business, but he gave his word of honor as a Belgian military officer that he would make himself available upon his return. After the judge accepted his promise, Lothaire caught a Portuguese ship to Lisbon, and from there he made his way back to Antwerp. Once again, he had evaded the rudimentary judicial system of the Congo Free State.[34]

4

Algiers, French Department of Algeria, January 13, 1898

Pierre Savorgnan de Brazza, the commissioner-general of the French Congo, was convalescing in his villa in Algiers when his neighbor, a high Algerian government official named Luciani, stopped by to express his regrets over the announcement that Brazza had been fired. The news caught Brazza by surprise. Just hours before, he and his wife, Thérèse, had enjoyed a lunch at the Winter Palace with the governor of French Algeria, who had apparently been too embarrassed to mention it. Brazza took a carriage to the Café de Bordeaux (which had a subscription to the newspaper *l'Officiel*), where he learned that he was no longer the commissioner-general of the French Congo. He had come to Algeria (which was then an official department of France) in autumn 1897 on a temporary medical leave. A few days after seeing the newspaper announcement, he received a letter from the French minister of colonies that made his medical leave permanent.[35]

By all accounts, Brazza received the news with Roman stoicism, thereby suggesting that he might have suspected it was coming. The French newspapers, which had made Brazza into a national hero in the 1880s, had turned against him by 1897, even trying to emphasize his foreignness by announcing that he had become a Muslim and a Freemason. Bishop Augouard, a missionary in the French Congo, wrote that "his qualities as an administrator are far from equaling his qualities as an explorer. The French settlers blame him for excessive gentleness. It seems that with him, it is always the settlers who are wrong. He would use the resources of the colony to do nothing." A French planter complained that "he keeps on practicing philanthropy, not colonization." Another critic emphasized that the aim of colonization was "the development of the material wealth of the colonized countries and of the colonizers. And this aim will only very occasionally be achieved by talking nicely to the natives." Another newspaper claimed that Brazza "has done nothing in spite of all the means, all the resources, put at his disposal."[36]

Since Brazza's initial appointment in April 1886 as commissioner-general of Gabon and Congo (which were combined into the French Congo in 1891), his low-key approach had contrasted with that of Stanley and the hard-driving administrators in the Congo Free State. Just three months before receiving his commission, Brazza told a crowd of five thousand people at a lecture in Paris that he considered the Congo River basin "a country where the future depends upon the trade and culture of the native peoples. . . . Better than anyone, I know the difficulties in creating a colony without forcing its development, and without wanting to fit a predetermined model." He thus foresaw a long-term process. "To prepare a country for colonization," he said, "is a labor of time and patience."[37]

The French government had tolerated Brazza's leisurely approach because France had many colonies in Africa, and the Congo had never been a priority. In 1893, the minister of foreign affairs reminded Brazza that France's "obligation to concentrate our efforts in other places . . . will indicate the prudent limits that you should not exceed in a country where, until now, our interests are relatively weak." Moreover, the French were confident that Leopold's project would fail and that the Congo Free State would revert to France as outlined in the Anglo-French agreement of 1884. The French government was thus content to let Brazza function as a placeholder while it waited for a chance to enlarge its African empire. Exploiting the territory would come later.[38]

During his twelve years as commissioner, Brazza was frequently absent from his desk in Libreville, Gabon, for long periods of time. After receiving his initial appointment in 1886, he remained in Paris for nine months before departing for Libreville. He then undertook an extended tour of the colony from March 1887 to February 1888 and returned to Paris for eighteen months from November 1889 until April 1891. At the end of 1891, he embarked on a two-year expedition to explore the Sangha River basin (which ran into the Congo River north of the Alima). In January 1895, he began an extended vacation in Algiers and Paris, returning to Libreville in December. In early autumn 1897, he went to Algiers on a medical leave, where he learned of his dismissal.[39]

During Brazza's prolonged absences from Libreville, the day-to-day administration was left to his successive lieutenant governors—Noel Ballay, Charles de Chavannes, and Albert Dolisie—all of whom were his former traveling companions. The French government had originally envisioned that Brazza would be the visionary while the lieutenant governor would see to the daily details of administration. A decree of June 21, 1886, explicitly stated that Brazza should concentrate on "the project of peaceful expansion of which he was the glorious initiator, without being distracted by the obligation to oversee and regulate the thousand details of administration." Yet that division of labor began badly. Ballay, who was the very model of a French civil servant, was continually frustrated by Brazza's administrative style. In 1888, he characterized the colony's administration as "ill-defined, irregular, false, and constantly changing at the whim of the Commissioner General." Ballay resigned in 1889 and later served as governor-general of French West Africa from 1900 to 1902.[40]

As commissioner-general of the French Congo, Brazza's main task was to establish a French presence in the different regions of the colony, which covered an area larger than France, and to do so with a minimal number of colonial administrators. In 1890, there were only twenty-two station chiefs, assisted by thirty-five auxiliary agents, and by 1897 the numbers had increased to fifty-two station chiefs and twenty-six auxiliaries. But even those were not always in place. In 1894, the lieutenant governor complained that only two out of six senior administrators were present in the country; the others were away on administrative furloughs or medical leaves. The job of the station chiefs was loosely defined—fly the French flag, develop good relations with the local people, mediate local conflicts, and encourage the flow of commerce through their territories. Because of the shortage of personnel, the station chiefs rarely ventured far beyond their own posts, leaving the surrounding villages almost undisturbed. As for African personnel, Brazza relied heavily on imported Senegalese soldiers and Dahomean porters. The one area where the administration relied on local African labor was for canoe paddlers to go through the rapids of the upper Ogowe. Rather than tax the African populations, the colonial government relied on duties levied on foreign trade, along with fees for licenses, taxes, and rents paid by European trading companies.[41]

With much of the colony's economic activity concentrated on the coastal plain, the main problem for the French was how to open routes from the Atlantic coast to the Congo River basin. During his early exploration missions, Brazza had traveled up the Ogowe by steamboat to the rapids, then by canoe to its limit, and then had crossed the continental divide by land to reach the Upper Alima, which he descended by boat to the Congo River. Brazza had subsequently developed a workable transportation system by negotiating good working relations with the local chiefs, canoemen, and porters, but he complained that the French colonial officials at the key posts along the route lacked the diplomatic skills and cultural sensitivity to keep the system functioning. In 1893, Brazza began negotiations with a French firm to form a charter company that would have a monopoly on transportation along the upper Ogowe.

The company would receive eleven million hectares of forest (a territory larger than Belgium) and a monopoly over a 435-mile stretch of the river. After long negotiations, the Upper Ogowe Company began to function in 1897, just as Brazza was about to leave the Congo for Algiers.[42]

The only alternative to the Ogowe route was the route from Loango, on the coast, to Brazzaville, at Malebo Pool, via the valley of the Kwilu-Niari River. Brazza believed that canals could be constructed around the major rapids, allowing transportation by river from the coast to within sixty miles of Brazzaville, from where a wagon road could be built. However, the French government had no interest in funding the project, leaving caravans of porters as the only alternative. As with the Ogowe route, Brazza tried to give charters to private companies to create an integrated transportation system. After negotiations with two French companies collapsed, Brazza began negotiations with the New Dutch Trading Company (NAHV) that were still ongoing at the time of his dismissal.[43]

The difficulties of transportation to the interior reached crisis proportions when the French government sought to send a major military expedition commanded by Maj. Jean-Baptiste Marchand up the Congo and Ubangi Rivers to reach the upper Nile in Sudan. The British and the French were both interested in occupying the abandoned Egyptian fort at Fashoda (in southern Sudan) in order to link up their disparate possessions in Africa. Time was of the essence, because the French hoped to occupy the upper Nile while the British were busy fighting the Mahdi rebellion farther north. The supplies for the Marchand Expedition would be sent by ship to the port of Loango and carried by porters along the three-hundred-mile caravan route to Brazzaville, a trip that normally took twenty-five days in the dry season, thirty during the rains. Some three thousand porter-loads of supplies arrived in Loango in May and June 1896, and Brazza was ordered to organize caravans to carry them to Brazzaville. But the caravan route already suffered from a backlog of twenty-five thousand loads sitting in warehouses in Loango. In the end, the expedition was delayed for six months at Brazzaville while waiting for its supplies, and loss of material en route to Brazzaville ranged from 20 to 40 percent.[44]

Because of the difficulties of the routes into the Congo River basin, French trade along the Upper Congo River never developed. In 1893, the only trading companies in Brazzaville were the New Dutch Trading Company and the Belgian Société Anonyme Belge (SAB), after the French firm Daumas-Beraud had sold out to the SAB in 1892. Along the coast and the lower Kwilu River there were three British trading firms, one Dutch, two German, one Belgian, three Portuguese, and two American. The only French firms in the region were Brandon, at Libreville; Ancel Seitz, with posts at Loango and along the Kwilu; and Sajoux, with four posts along the Ogowe. Trade grew slowly from 3.6 million francs in 1890 to 5.3 million francs in 1897. The major products were rubber, ivory, and timber, but the trading companies also installed a few coffee and cocoa plantations along the lower Ogowe. Rubber exports during the 1890s averaged between 500 and 600 tons per year, a paltry amount compared to the 3,746 tons of rubber exported by the Congo Free State in 1899.[45]

Despite its minimal bureaucracy and lack of major infrastructure projects, the colony ran annual deficits, mainly because the French were using it as a staging area for major military expeditions up the Ubangi toward Lake Chad and the upper Nile. In 1896, the colony's revenues were 1.428 million francs, while the French government supplied a subsidy of 1.435 million francs plus a special allocation of a million francs. Even so, the Congo ran a deficit in 1896 of 2.25 million francs, caused largely by the expenses of the Marchand Expedition.[46]

The French minister of colonies gave two reasons for Brazza's dismissal in 1898. First, his government had failed to transport the supplies for the Marchand Expedition to Brazzaville on schedule, and second, his budget deficit was "formidable." But there was another reason, and that was the clamor from French and Belgian companies for the French Congo to adopt a concession system similar to that of the Congo Free State. The same mail that brought Brazza the notice of his dismissal also brought a clue as to the reason for it—a letter from Brazza's longtime secretary saying, "I have just left the Ministry of Colonies . . . A map of the Congo divided into squares like a checkerboard was displayed in all the offices. The entire colony is divided into concessions—forty-two, I was told."[47]

When news got out in the late 1890s that the concession companies in the Congo Free State were making record profits, there was a clamor by French and Belgian investors for similar concessions in the French Congo. The same equatorial rainforest spread across the two Congos, and the inhabitants in both colonies had a similar type of small-scale political organization. During the mid-1890s, Eugène Étienne, a former deputy who was active in the informal pressure group known as the French Colonial Party, wrote a series of articles in *Le Temps* in which he argued for more economic colonization by private companies. During the first months of 1898, some 119 requests for concessions in the French Congo were submitted to the Ministry of Colonies. In response, the minister created an extra parliamentary commission to draw up plans to award concessions in the French Congo. The plan was announced in a circular on May 24, 1899.[48]

Over the next year, forty companies formed, and they obtained concessions that covered 70 percent of the French Congo. The largest concession—the Company of the Sultanates of the Upper Ubangi—was nearly five times the size of Belgium, whereas the smallest—Nkémé-Nkéni—received only twelve hundred square kilometers. Taken as a whole, the value of the shares of the forty companies was 60 million francs, although it is likely that only about 40 million francs were actually subscribed. Nevertheless, given that the French government's total investment in the French Congo between 1890 and 1897 was roughly 13 million francs, an additional 40 million francs of capital was a serious sum.

A significant portion of the capital came from Belgium. Members of the board of directors of Abir and Anversoise made up more than half the directorships in six of the French Congo companies, and there were Belgians on the boards of twenty-nine of the forty French companies. In addition, the Congo Free State itself invested 3 million francs in French companies through front men.[49]

Following Brazza's dismissal in 1898, his designated replacement, Henri de Lamothe, was summoned to Paris to discuss the implementation of a concession system in the French Congo. Returning to Libreville, he brought in a number of French officials who had previously served under him when he was governor of Senegal, while many of the officials already serving in the French Congo, and especially those who had worked closely with Brazza, were ordered back to France to be reassigned. The result was an almost complete turnover of French officials.

In 1899, the new commissioner-general announced a tax of two francs per year on all adult men. Because French money was scarce in the Congo, people were encouraged to pay their taxes in kind. Very little revenue was collected in the first year for lack of a sufficient administrative structure, but the very existence of the tax laid the legal groundwork for coerced rubber gathering by the concession companies in the form of "taxes in kind." There followed a "scramble for the concessions" as the companies sought to occupy their territories as quickly as possible. The territories had been parceled out as spaces on maps, and the concession holders had little idea of the political and geographical realities of their regions. Five of the companies arrived to find that their territories were mostly swamps or contained no significant exploitable resources.[50]

Jules Lefébure, a lawyer at the Court of Appeals in Paris, submitted a doctoral dissertation to the Faculty of Law at the University of Paris in 1904 in which he outlined the legal case for forced rubber gathering. He first argued that "commerce, pure and simple, based on the laws of economics, is insufficient to remunerate the capital expended in a primitive and uncivilized country." As a result, many of the concession companies were considering a forced labor system based on that of the Congo Free State. Acknowledging that the Free State's style of forced labor was little more than slavery, he argued that "taxes in kind" were acceptable if they were limited to a fair payment for the services rendered by the colonial state. However, he warned, "they must not escalate into arbitrary and indeterminate *corvées* paid twelve months of the year." Yet the taxes in kind were merely the opening wedge for a more aggressive system of forced labor. Soon the French Congo would move to emulate the Congo Free State.[51]

5

Antwerp, Belgium, June 27, 1897

When the Belgian ship *Albertville* docked at Antwerp on June 27, 1897, some 267 Africans from the Congo Free State were welcomed to Belgium with music and festivities. Most of the Congolese from the ship were transported directly to the town of Tervuren, but sixty-five soldiers and twenty-four military musicians (mostly buglers) from the group put on a parade in Antwerp. Then they boarded a train for Brussels, where they were greeted at the station by a crowd despite the pouring rain. Finally, they boarded the newly built tramway for the six-mile trip to Tervuren, where they would live for the next two months. They had come to Belgium to be performers in King Leopold's pageant of colonial wealth and power that was known as the Colonial Exhibition of 1897.[52]

The exhibition came just at the time when the Congo Free State was becoming a profitable enterprise, due primarily to increasing revenues from the rubber concession companies. In 1896, the value of the Congo Free State's rubber exports exceeded that of ivory exports for the first time, and by 1900, rubber exports would be worth nearly eight times as much as ivory exports. Because of the growing rubber revenues, the Congo Free State balanced its budget

A model Congolese village at the Colonial Exhibition of 1897 in Tervuren, Belgium.
Collection Royal Museum for Central Africa, Tervuren, photo A. Gautier, 1897.

for the first time in 1896 and often showed a surplus in subsequent years. King Leopold was using the 1897 Colonial Exhibition in Tervuren to showcase the Congo Free State as a great humanitarian project intended to bring commerce and Christian civilization to equatorial Africa.[53]

The exhibition followed upon the success of the 1894 Antwerp International Exhibition, which had featured a Congo pavilion with a diorama of railroads and caravan routes and an exhibit labeled "Congolese rubber: its industrial transformations and manufactured products." The Belgian Anti-Slavery Society's exhibit highlighted the fight against the Arab slave trade in the Congo by displaying a forked-stick slave yoke, chains, and shackles along with captured Arab booty and portraits of Belgian heroes from the military campaign against the Arabs. There was also a Congolese village, constructed beside the Musée des Beaux Arts, where 144 Congolese drawn from a variety of ethnic groups re-created scenes of daily life for the visitors.[54]

The 1897 Colonial Exhibition in Tervuren, in contrast, was an offshoot of the Brussels World's Fair. Originally scheduled for 1895, the fair was postponed for two years to allow King Leopold to complete the buildings and grounds for the Colonial Exhibition at Tervuren. As the Duke of Brabant, King Leopold owned the large park at Tervuren, including the Château de Tervuren, where his sister, Princess Charlotte, had lived until it was destroyed by fire in 1879. In 1895, Leopold ordered the ruins demolished and replaced by the Palace of Colonies for the 1897 exhibition, surrounding it with gardens, pools, and fountains and linking it to Brussels by the new tramway that ran to the main World's Fair site at the Cinquantenaire Park in Brussels.

Complementing the imposing stone edifice of the Palace of Colonies were three "traditional" African villages, with houses built of bamboo and thatch in the Bangala style. Two of them were located along a large pool, with dugout canoes at the waterfront. The third village was away from the water in the trees. Palm trees and other tropical vegetation were planted in and around the villages to give them an air of authenticity. The European visitors were not allowed to enter the villages, but they could watch from behind iron fences, much as they would watch animals in a zoo. A sign proclaimed, "Do not feed the blacks. They are already being fed."[55]

Although the majority of the Congolese at the Tervuren exhibition were men, the group contained at least thirty-five women and a number of children. Ethnically, they were mostly Bangala, with a minority of Ngombe and Basoko. There were also two Mbuti Pygmies from the Aruwimi region and one Manyema Arab with three wives and one son. The Congolese did not actually live in the traditional villages but ate and slept in one of the annexes to the Palace of Colonies. Weather permitting, they spent their days in the villages, doing crafts and daily chores and preparing and eating a noon meal. On a regular schedule, the African soldiers performed military drills or marched in parades, and the musicians played concerts that included bits from popular Belgian songs.

The Congolese performers were normally confined to exhibition grounds, but from time to time they were taken on group excursions to the cinema or the circus in Brussels.

A fourth African village, located away from the other three, was called Gijzegem, named after the town in northern Flanders where Abbe Van Impe ran a school for boys from the Congo. Known as the "civilized village," the houses of Gijzegem displayed a more Western style, and there was a village school. Thirty children dressed in school uniforms occupied the village, where they entertained the visitors by singing Belgian songs accompanied by guitars and mandolins. Because the occupants came from Gijzegem, Belgium—and not directly from the Congo—Abbe Van Impe tried to keep them from mixing with the "raw" Congolese in the other three villages. The purpose of the "civilized village" was to give visitors a vision of what the Congo could become under the benevolent influence of Christianity and Western civilization.[56]

The Palace of the Colonies contained a number of exhibits designed to acquaint visitors with their king's new colony. The long ethnographic hall contained paintings, sculptures, and artifacts that illustrated the material cultures and lifestyles in six different regions of the Congo Free State. Much space was devoted to the colonial economy, with displays of ivory, rubber, tobacco, coffee, exotic woods, and other products. In all, 1.8 million visitors came to Tervuren to see the Colonial Exhibition, as opposed to 6 million who visited the main World's Fair exhibits in Brussels. Visitors to Tervuren could see peaceful and contented "natives" from a distant land that produced wealth for Belgium and King Leopold.[57]

While Leopold was preparing to put a fantasy version of the Congo Free State on display at Tervuren, he was also engaged in a series of secret negotiations to exploit the remaining undeveloped areas of the Congo Free State and to keep a portion of the profits for himself. He kept the plans secret, in part because they belied his depictions of the Congo Free State as a humanitarian venture and in part because the Berlin Act and his loan agreement with the Belgian government had placed limits on what he could do. If successful, his plans would double the amount of intensely exploited territory in the Congo Free State.

On December 4, 1894, Jules de Burlet, the head of the Belgian Council of Ministers, heard a rumor that the king was about to sell 65,637 square miles of land in the Congo Free State to a newly formed company that was controlled by British investors. At a hastily arranged meeting at the palace, the king laid out maps on a table to indicate the location of the three territories he was planning to sell. The largest was Manyema. No sooner had the Arabs been driven out than King Leopold had put the entire territory up for sale. He added a territory around Lake Mai-Ndombe and another around Lake Tumba (both located south of the equator and east of the Congo River). Altogether, the three territories covered an area more than five times the size of Belgium. The king then showed the minister his secret decree of November 30, 1894, which had created a company with the bland name "General Agriculture Company" and a draft of the contract to sell the territories for 6,650,000 francs to a group of investors put together by his old friend Col. John Thomas North. This was not a concession arrangement but an outright sale of land, albeit with certain rights reserved for the Congo Free State. The General Agriculture Company was scheduled to begin its operations on January 1, 1895.[58]

When the full cabinet met the next day, the ministers ordered Leopold to retract the secret decree that had created the company. They gave several reasons. First, the complicated terms of the land sale indicated it was really a disguised loan and was thus forbidden by the king's 1890 loan agreement with the Belgian government. Second, giving such huge territory to British interests might alarm the Germans and the French, who held territory to the east and west of the Congo Free State. Third, if Belgium itself were ever to take over the Congo, "the proposed monopoly might prove a serious difficulty." Bowing to the opposition of the ministers, Leopold withdrew his decree and disbanded the company.[59]

With the land sale off the table, Leopold went back to his maps and defined a territory in the region of Lake Mai-Ndombe that he would exploit for his own purposes. It became known as the Crown Domain. From its beginning, the Crown Domain was shrouded in secrecy. It was created by a secret decree on March 8, 1896, but it was not mentioned in the *Bulletin Officiel* until 1902, when a brief announcement outlined its territorial limits and proclaimed it a legal entity administered by a committee of three people chosen by the king. It did not appear on official maps because parts of it lay in three different administrative districts. State agents from the relevant districts collected rubber with the aid of State soldiers, but the income was credited to the Crown Domain, not the State.[60]

King Leopold's next move was to tighten his grip on the two major rubber concession companies—Abir and Anversoise—that were operating in the Congo Free State. Colonel North died in 1896, and his heirs sold his shares in Abir to an investor from Antwerp, thus eliminating British capital from the company. In 1898, both Abir and Anversoise liquidated and immediately reconstituted themselves under the laws of the Congo Free State in order to avoid Belgian taxes and financial regulations. A look at the new shareholders reveals how intertwined the two companies were. Out of the Abir company's two thousand shares, Alexander de Browne de Tiège, the president of the Anversoise Company, held one thousand shares as a proxy for the Congo Free State and sixty shares in his own name. Similarly, half of the thirty-four hundred Anversoise shares were held by the Congo Free State, with the second-largest shareholder being Alexander de Browne de Tiège, who held eleven hundred shares. Taking the two companies together, the Congo Free State and Browne de Tiège held over 70 percent of the shares.[61]

The money from the concession companies' dividends appeared in the annual budget of the Congo Free State under the heading "Product of the Portfolio," without any designation as to whether it was part of the general funds controlled by the administration of the Congo Free State or the special funds controlled by King

Leopold. Yet it would have been entirely consistent with Leopold's mode of operation for the dividends to be deposited in the special funds account so that he could bring the money back to Belgium if the Congo Free State's budget ran a surplus.[62]

The two rubber concession companies were restructuring their finances at the time when their rubber production and profits were reaching their peak. Abir's production rose from 410 metric tons in 1898 to 539 tons in 1899 and to 701 tons in 1900. At the same time, its profits rose from 2.5 million francs in 1898 to 2.8 million francs in 1899 and to an astonishing 5.9 million francs in 1900. The Anversoise Company, under the aggressive direction of Lothaire, produced 298 tons of rubber in 1898 and 641 tons in the subsequent eighteen months, making a profit of 3.9 million francs in 1898 and 3 million francs in 1899. In addition to the dividends on its shares in the companies, the Congo Free State received a royalty of 300 francs on each ton of rubber exported, an export tax of 25 francs per ton, plus 5 percent of the selling price on the Antwerp market.[63]

As the nineteenth century drew to a close, the budget of the Congo Free State was running an annual surplus, and King Leopold himself was drawing substantial revenues from the Crown Domain. With the budget in surplus, the king began shifting resources from the special funds account to use for projects in Belgium. What remained hidden from the visitors to the 1897 Colonial Exhibition in Tervuren were the sordid details of how those profits were obtained. A major consequence of the secrecy surrounding the true nature of rubber collecting in the Congo Free State was that King Leopold and the officials of the Congo Free State failed to realize that the profits were not sustainable under the reigning system of exploitation.[64]

CHAPTER 10

THE "RED RUBBER" SCANDALS

A T THE BEGINNING OF THE twentieth century, King Leopold's
system of stripping the Congo basin rainforest of its most valuable resources through a combination of Congo Free State actions
and private concession companies seemed to be an economic success story. Two Belgian economists declared that the profits of the
Abir rubber company were "without precedent in the annals of our
industrial companies"; the budget of the Congo Free State was running a surplus; and the Congo Free State's rubber system had been
replicated in the French Congo. Nevertheless, three problems had
arisen that cast doubt on the system's sustainability. The first was
environmental—wild rubber, like ivory, turned out to be a scarce
resource that diminished over time. The second was human—
the system for harvesting rubber had a devastating effect on the
populations subjected to it, resulting in death, flight, and revolt.
The third problem was political, raising the question of how long
metropolitan public opinion and friendly European governments
would tolerate the continuing stories of abuses and atrocities ema-
nating from the two Congos.[1]

Because the Congo Free State had been created by an international conference, interest in its abuses and scandals went beyond
Belgium. In Britain, the Liverpool newspaper editor E. D. Morel
hoped to induce reforms in the Congo by exposing the horrors of

the rubber system. His efforts prompted an investigation by the British consul to the Congo, which was followed by a Commission of Inquiry appointed by King Leopold himself. Morel's book *Red Rubber: The Story of the Rubber Slave Trade Flourishing on the Congo in the Year of Grace 1906* created an indelible public image of the bloodshed and violence that accompanied forced rubber collecting in the Congo Free State.[2]

In France, newspaper reports of colonial atrocities in the French Congo forced the government to send out its own Commission of Inquiry. The members of the Commission were under orders to keep their findings confidential, but a young philosophy teacher named Félicien Challaye published a series of articles about the abuses in the Paris newspaper *Le Temps*. The scandals in the Congo Free State and the French Congo put pressure on the metropolitan governments to initiate reforms, but the greatest threats to the rubber system came from conditions on the ground, where resource depletion and local resistance jeopardized the profits of the rubber companies.

1

Anversoise Concession, Bangala District, 1902

While working for the Anversoise Company, Edgar Canisius noticed a fatal flaw in the Congo Free State's system of forced rubber collection. In contrast to Henry Morton Stanley, who had argued that rubber was a more abundant resource than ivory, Canisius recognized that the *landolphia* vines that supplied most of the rubber in the Congo rainforest were not as numerous or as durable as the State and the concession companies supposed. Unlike temperate-zone forests, which typically are dominated by one or two species of trees, tropical rainforests are characterized by an array of species that intermingle promiscuously. Seven thousand species of flowering plants grow in the African rainforest, and scientists have found as many as one hundred different species of trees in a single test plot the size of three football fields. It follows, then, that specimens of any single species would be found in scattered locations instead of concentrated in certain spots.[3]

"I have seen it stated in official documents and in books written by persons represented to have travelled through the African forests," wrote Canisius in his memoir in 1902, "that there are regions where the jungle is literally a tangled mass of rubber vines. Such stories are ridiculous, for nowhere does the creeper exist in such luxuriance. Like all tropical jungle vegetation, it is scattered over large areas with many other similar plants, which may belong to the same genus, but are not the true rubber vine. On an acre of jungle, one rarely finds two trees of a kind, and the same may be said of the large creepers, or lianas, with which the tropical bush abounds." Canisius understood the practical consequences of this situation. "The stock of rubber vines in those parts of the Congo which have been worked for any length of time," he wrote, "is being rapidly exhausted. Wherever I have been in this vast territory . . . the natives bitterly bemoaned the scarcity of rubber-producing lianas, and piteously begged to be allowed to perform other service than rubber-gathering."[4]

Rubber gatherers developed three methods for meeting their quotas under such conditions. The first was to cut down the rubber vines. Canisius observed that the rubber gatherers, "if pressed for time as they usually are in the Congo in consequence of the threats of the white man and the fear of the Albinis of the soldiers and the muskets of the *capitas*, cut down long lengths of the giant creepers and then subdivide them to make the sap ooze out more quickly." Such practices were so widespread that King Leopold issued a decree in 1904 making it illegal to cut the vines or peel off the bark in order to extract the latex. The second method was to tap vines that produced so-called false rubber, a resinous matter that resembled latex when freshly tapped but which assumed a glossy appearance in the course of drying. This phenomenon was so common

Rubber gatherers tapping a rubber vine. Anti-Slavery International

that Governor-General Théophile Wahis sent out a circular to all district commissioners and zone chiefs in March 1901 complaining that the quality of the rubber was deteriorating because the normal latex from the *landolphia* vine was being mixed with "latex of inferior quality" (i.e., false rubber) or other foreign matter. The third method involved intrusion on the lands claimed by other groups. "Each tribe has only a limited extent of forest, which it can call its exclusive domain," wrote Canisius, "and it consequently very frequently happens, when their own 'bush' is worked out, that the natives from one village penetrate the territory of the other in defiance of tribal usage. . . . In consequence, disputes arise between villages which heretofore, perhaps for quite a long period, have been at peace."[5]

The Anversoise Company tried to keep up its production by making renewed efforts to conquer the Buja country (north of the Congo River), which still had untapped vines. After the 1900 campaign to reoccupy the posts of Yalombo, Yambata, and Monjoa ended in failure, Anversoise evacuated the Buja country until 1903, when Congo Free State soldiers mounted a bloody offensive that lasted six months. Like the previous attempts, this one also failed, in part because the Buja had captured a large number of Albini rifles and cartridges from State and company soldiers during the 1900 war. The State launched another offensive against the Buja in 1904 using a contingent of five hundred to six hundred soldiers.[6]

In March 1904, the Congo Free State suspended the Anversoise Company's concession rights for fifteen years and began to administer the territory directly, using State soldiers to replace company sentries. There were divergent opinions as to why the State did this. The British journalist/traveler Viscount Mountmorres wrote that it was because of "the misconduct and abuse of power of its agents," but Edgar Canisius had a different interpretation. "It is freely stated among the agents of the company," he wrote, "that the magnificent crops of rubber gathered in the Mongala region, which have for a long time equaled sixty to eighty tons monthly, valued in Europe from £20,000 to £25,000, have awakened the avarice and jealousy of that larger monopoly, the Congo Free State, and that the severe 'repression' of atrocities is merely an expedient to compel the company to the beneficent care of *Bula Matari* [i.e., the Congo Free State]." Events soon confirmed Canisius's analysis. Instead of reducing the rubber quotas in recognition of the diminishing supplies, the State officer in charge pushed the production back up to sixty tons per month with a program of murders, imprisonments, and destruction of villages. After he returned to Belgium, the rubber production diminished to around twenty tons per month.[7]

In the Abir concession, the company faced the same diminishing returns as Anversoise, but it adopted a different strategy— adding new posts to fill in the vacant spaces between the old ones. From fourteen posts in 1900, Abir added fifteen new posts in 1902, eleven in 1903, and five more in 1904, but the main result was to hasten the depletion of the rubber vines. Because villagers in areas with insufficient rubber vines often felt they had little choice but to flee, one of the major tasks of the company sentries was to prevent individuals and villages from emigrating. So strong was the company's fear of emigration that Abir required a person to get a permit in order to visit another village, and its agents were instructed to send back any immigrants who came from the territory of another Abir post.[8]

Scattered reports from missionaries provide glimpses into the widespread population movements in the Abir concession in 1902 and 1903. At one post, four chiefs were in prison for trying to emigrate with their villages. At the Dikila post, the Lika people tried to move farther away, but Abir sentries prevented them from doing so. The villages around the Samba post began to emigrate southward, pursued by Abir sentries. The Nsongo Mboyo people, who lived north of the Maringa River, tried to flee the concession, but many of them were caught and deported to the upper Maringa, while six other groups—Likongo, Lianja, Nkole, Yanga-Yanju, Nongo-

Ingoli, and Lofoma—successfully fled south toward the Tshuapa River.[9]

In places where circumstances did not permit people to emi-grate and resettle as a group, they sometimes scattered in small groups and lived in the forest. Missionaries reported in 1901 that the people living inland from the Yala post had abandoned their villages and lived scattered in the forest, a situation that entailed serious health risks. Although the people had lived in the rainforest all their lives, they spent most of their time in the clearings and avoided the dark, damp environment of the forest itself, except for occasional forays for hunting and gathering. Somerville Gilchrist, a missionary with the Congo Balolo Mission who had lived in the Lulonga region for fourteen years, believed that lung and intestinal diseases were the major causes of premature death. Even though sleeping sickness had arrived on the Lopori around 1900, and a smallpox epidemic had ravaged the region from 1899 to 1902, he estimated that deaths from lung and intestinal diseases outpaced deaths from sleeping sickness by twenty to one and deaths from smallpox by forty to one. "The lung and intestinal troubles," he reported, "are without doubt, due, in a very large proportion of the cases, to exposure involved in collecting the [rubber] taxes and in hiding from the soldiers in the forest, as well as the miserable huts the natives now live in because they have neither time nor heart to build better."[10]

It would be easy to dismiss Gilchrist's analysis, since he was not a medical doctor, but a 2004 report by the International Res-cue Committee on the mortality resulting from the warfare that was then raging in the Democratic Republic of Congo confirms his general perspective. Written by a committee that included five medical doctors, the IRC report concluded that the vast majority of the deaths in the war zones were not due to war-related vio-lence but to "easily preventable and treatable illnesses such as fever and malaria, diarrhea, respiratory infections, and malnutrition" that became deadly in the disrupted conditions of the war zones.

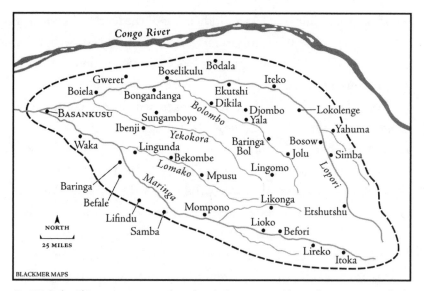

By 1906, the Abir concession was dotted with thirty-two rubber collection posts, which gave the company access to all parts of the territory

Although the exact ratio between violent deaths and those from disease during the colonial rubber wars can never be known, it seems likely that the silent violence of disease was even more deadly than the guns of the Abir sentries.[11]

As the rubber vines grew scarce, rebellions became increasingly frequent in the Abir concession. Along the Maringa River, the country upstream from the Baringa post was so disturbed by fighting in 1897 that the missionaries canceled a planned preaching tour. Farther up the Maringa, an Abir punitive expedition against the Seketulu people resulted in over four hundred killed and numerous prisoners, one hundred of whom died in captivity. Along the Lopori River, large-scale "trading troubles" were reported in 1899 in which five sentries were killed near the Bongandanga post between 1901 and 1902, and Abir sentries put down revolts by the Yamongo, Boonde, and Bofongi. On the Bolombo River (a tributary of the Lopori), the Lilangi, Bokenda, Pukaonga, and Kailanga rebelled but were defeated. It is likely that numerous other rebellions erupted in the Abir concession that were not observed or reported by missionaries. As an indication of the level of violence, a single Abir post in 1903 imported 33 Albini rifles, 126 percussion cap muskets, 17,600 Albini cartridges, 29,255 percussion caps, and 22,755 musket loads.[12]

Forced rubber gathering not only hastened the depletion of the rubber vines but also threatened the very foundations of human subsistence in the rainforest. In the agricultural system known to agronomists as "shifting cultivation," the men needed to clear new fields every three years when the soil in the old ones became exhausted. This was a labor-intensive and time-consuming process that could take up to two months of daily labor. However, with men required to bring in rubber every two weeks, there was no time to clear new fields. Instead, women continued to plant worn-out fields with decreasing yields. That is the most likely explanation for the "terrible famine" that missionaries in the Abir region reported in 1899, and the problem was aggravated by the Abir sentries, who raided gardens and confiscated animals to maintain their lavish lifestyle. Such famines explain why people in the Equator District later referred to the Abir period as *lonkali*, the period of famine.[13]

2

London, House of Commons, May 20, 1903

When the evening sitting of the House of Commons began at 7:30, Herbert Samuel rose to speak about the evildoing in the Congo Free State. Although he was an MP from Yorkshire, a county with no significant ties to the Africa trade, he was nevertheless a member of the Aborigines Protection Society (APS), which had emerged during the 1890s as the leading humanitarian pressure group on British colonial policy. Although the APS lacked a base of broad popular support, it operated as a lobbying group that collected information from the colonies and sent petitions to the Colonial Office seeking remediation on a variety of issues.

In contrast, the British and Foreign Anti-Slavery Society had been strangely silent regarding affairs in the Congo Free State. The relationship between anti-slavery activism and colonialism was a complex one because many of the anti-slavery activists saw colonial rule as the best hope for stamping out slavery and slave trading in Africa. The Anti-Slavery Society's longtime secretary, Charles Allen, had played a key role in initiating the Brussels Anti-Slavery Conference of 1889–1890, which had called on the colonial powers to eradicate slavery from Africa. The conference and the subsequent expulsion of the Arab slave traders from the Congo Free State in 1892–1893 had made King Leopold a hero of the anti-slavery cause. With little work left to do, the Anti-Slavery Society's London office reduced its hours to certain days of the week, and its executive committee began discussions about closing down the organization entirely. It was not until 1902 that the Anti-Slavery Society's new secretary, Travers Buxton, began to support the APS's criticism of the Congo Free State.[14]

On May 20, 1903, Herbert Samuel introduced a resolution in the House of Commons asking the signatory nations of the 1885 Berlin Act to adopt measures to end the colonial abuses prevalent in the Congo Free State. Acknowledging that it was highly unusual for the House of Commons to criticize other countries, he pointed out that the Congo Free State was unique in the history of the world. It had been created at the Berlin Conference by the common consent of all the great powers, and its governance had been entrusted to an individual—the king of the Belgians. "But," he argued, "it was assigned under certain conditions." The first was the "furtherance of the moral and material wellbeing of the natives," and the second was that "the trade of all nations should enjoy complete freedom." By focusing on those two issues, Mr. Samuel was appealing to both the humanitarian and the commercial interests in the chamber.[15]

Neither of these conditions, he charged, had been fulfilled. Following King Leopold's 1892 decree, "the whole of the Congo Free State, with the single exception of a very small portion west of

Stanley Pool, was regarded as a private possession. A large amount of it was worked directly by the State, which had the rubber collected and brought in to its officers, and large tracts had been let to concessionary companies in which the State held half the shares." Turning to the treatment of the African population, he noted that when the Congo Free State was founded, "the world looked on with sympathy, and philanthropists with enthusiasm." After reciting a long list of abuses and atrocities by the State and the concession companies, he noted that the Associated Chambers of Commerce of England had passed a resolution in March asking the government to take action on behalf of British merchants and that the Free Churches had passed resolutions condemning the abuses engendered by the rubber system.

MP Samuel then proposed that an international commission should be established to take steps to abate these evils. To make his own position on human rights clear, he pointed out that he was "not one of those short-sighted philanthropists who thinks that the natives must be treated in all respects on equal terms with white men," but he believed that "there are certain rights which must be common to humanity. The rights of liberty and of just treatment should be common to all humanity."

The resolution was seconded by Sir Charles Dilke, the former undersecretary of state for foreign affairs. Like Herbert Samuel, he was a member of the Aborigines Protection Society. "As to the question of the natives," Dilke told the chamber, "the whole anti-slavery world has been swindled by the Administration of the Congo State." He claimed that the early British supporters of the Congo Free State had been "honest in their original intention; they desired to improve the condition of the natives, but . . . they had been swindled by the Administration of the Congo State." In a single paragraph, he used the phrase "swindled by the Administration of the Congo State" twice. At the conclusion of the debate, a motion was passed that requested "His Majesty's Government to confer with the other Powers, signatories of the Berlin General

Act by virtue of which the Congo Free State exists, in order that measures may be adopted to abate the evils prevalent in that State."

Unsure of how to respond to the resolution, the Foreign Office decided to seek more information on the situation in the Congo. On June 4, just two weeks after the House of Commons debate, it sent a telegram to its consul in Boma, Roger Casement, asking him to investigate the rubber regions of the Upper Congo River. Casement, who had already been planning a trip to that region, left the next day. He had considerable experience in the Congo, having worked for the International African Association and its successor, the Congo Free State, from 1884 to 1886; served as an agent of the Sanford Exploring Expedition in 1886–1887; and organized transportation in the Lower Congo in 1887–1891.[16]

Traveling up the Congo River in the steamboat *Henry Reed*, which he had chartered from the American Baptist Missionary Union, Casement arrived at Bolobo on July 19, 1903. Bolobo was not subject to rubber impositions, but while Casement was there, he heard about refugees from the Crown Domain who had recently settled in the Bolobo area. He spent three days visiting them and listening to stories about killing and mutilation that were so gruesome he initially refused to believe them, even though the very presence of those refugees was evidence that something very bad had happened to them.

"It used to take ten days to get twenty baskets of rubber," a man named Moyo told him. "We were always in the forest, and when we were late, we were killed. We had to go farther and farther into the forest to find the rubber vines, to go without food, and our women had to give up cultivating the fields and gardens. Then we starved. Wild beasts—the leopards—killed some of us when we were working away in the forest, and others got lost or died from exposure and starvation." Moyo then explained what happened when they sought relief from the rubber impositions. "We begged the white man to leave us alone, saying that we could get no more rubber, but the white men and their soldiers said: 'Go!

You are only beasts yourselves. You are *nyama* (meat).' We tried, always going farther into the forest, and when we failed and our rubber was short, the soldiers came to our towns and killed us. Many were shot, some had their ears cut off; others were tied up with ropes around their necks and bodies and taken away." The veracity of those stories was later confirmed by other refugees that Casement interviewed at Lukolela, and by Rev. A. E. Scrivener, a British missionary who had spent three weeks traveling in the Crown Domain.[17]

At Irebu, Casement found that the formerly prosperous trading town, which he had visited in 1887 as an employee of the Sanford Exploring Expedition, had been abandoned and replaced with a military training camp. Much of the population had fled across the Congo River to the French territory to escape the rubber impositions. Going up the Irebu Channel to Lake Tumba, he learned that the State had imposed rubber gathering in 1893 but had abandoned it in 1901 because the rubber impositions had sparked continuous fighting. The rubber period was remembered locally as "the war." A missionary gave him a list of the population of the villages near the lake: Bokaka had declined from five hundred to thirty; Lobwaka from three hundred to thirty; Boboko from three hundred to thirty-five; and on and on. With the villages largely abandoned, people lived "hidden away in the bush like hunted animals, with only a few branches thrown together for shelter, for they have no trust that the present quiet state of things will continue."

Continuing up the Congo to the Lulonga River, Casement noted that it was under the monopoly control of the Lulonga Company, a commercial trading firm that had instituted forced rubber gathering in the same manner as the concession companies. When Casement visited the town of Bolongo, the people complained that there was no rubber left in their district, but the Lulonga Company nevertheless required a fixed quantity each fortnight. Five company sentries were quartered in the town to ensure the rubber supply, and a State force commanded by a white man had briefly occupied the village in May, killing two people. At the next village, Casement found eleven women held prisoner by the sentries until their husbands brought in their quota of rubber. All of this was in a so-called free trade zone.

The main object of Casement's voyage was the Abir concession, outlined by the Maringa and Lopori Rivers, which came together at Basankusu to form the Lulonga. Casement visited the Bongandanga post, some 125 miles up the Lopori from the Abir headquarters at Basankusu. Arriving on August 29, 1903, he saw men from a district about twenty miles away coming to deliver their rubber. As he described it, "They marched in a long file, guarded by sentries of the Abir Company. . . There were everywhere sentries in the Abir grounds, guarding and controlling the natives, many of whom carried knives and spears. The sentries were often armed with Albini rifles, some of them with several cartridges slipped between the fingers of the hands ready for instant use. Others had [percussion] cap guns."

Casement explained what happened when the rubber was weighed. "The rubber brought up by each man under guard was weighed by one of the two agents of the Abir. . . . If the rubber were found to be of the right weight, its vendor would be led off to the cutting store or to one of the drying stores. If the rubber brought by its native vendor was found on the weighing machine to be seriously under the required weight, the defaulting individual was detained to be dealt with in the *'maison des ôtages'* [i.e., house of hostages]." Casement later visited the enclosure in front of the prison. "I counted fifteen men and youths who were being guarded while they worked at mat-making for the use of the station buildings. These men, I was then told, were some of the defaulters from the previous market day, who were being kept as compulsory workmen to make good the deficiency in their rubber."

Casement then went to the home village of some of those men to learn more about their circumstances. "To get the rubber," he wrote, "they had first to go fully a two-days' journey from their homes, leaving their wives, and being absent for from five to six days. They were seen to the forest limits under guard, and if not back by the sixth day, trouble was likely to ensue. To get the rubber in the forests—which, generally speaking, were very swampy— involves much fatigue and often fruitless searching for a well-flowing vine. As the area of supply diminishes, moreover, the demand for rubber constantly increases." On September 3, 1903, Roger Casement left Bongandanga to begin his return journey to Boma. By December 1, he was in London to write his report.[18]

When Casement's report was published by the British government in February 1904, the names of people and places were removed and replaced by letters or symbols to protect the witnesses and avoid leveling unproven charges against State or company employees. Even in this partially redacted form, however, the report painted a devastating picture of the activities of the State and the rubber companies in the Upper Congo. On June 9, the Congo question was again debated in the House of Commons. After listening to a series of speakers demand concrete action, Edward Grey, the liberal spokesman for foreign affairs (and the future foreign minister), spoke in favor of establishing British consulates on the Upper Congo River to monitor the activities of the Congo Free State and called for an international conference to revise the 1885 Berlin Act.[19]

King Leopold was not easily moved by criticism from foreign governments, but he wanted to avoid a reconvening of the Berlin Conference at all costs. To forestall such a development, he reluctantly agreed to send out his own Commission of Inquiry to the Congo. Although he intended it as a mere public relations exercise, the British Foreign Office and a group of Belgian reformers persuaded him to send out an international commission that would conduct a serious and impartial inquiry. The Commission consisted of Edmond Janssens, the assistant attorney general at the Belgian Supreme Court in Brussels; Baron Giacomo de Nisco, an Italian who was chief justice at the Congo Free State's appeals court at Boma; and Edmond von Schumacher, chief of the Department of Justice of the Canton of Lausanne, Switzerland. Their mandate was "to see if, in certain parts of the territory, the natives were subjected to ill treatment either by private individuals or by State agents, to point out practical means of betterment, and to formulate, in case the inquiry reveals such abuses, suggestions as to the best means of putting an end to the same." The Commission had the power to examine documents, call witnesses, and hold open hearings.[20]

The commissioners arrived at Boma on October 5, 1904, and left the Congo on February 21, 1905. For over four months, they traveled up the Congo River and its tributaries by steamer, going as far as Stanley Falls, and making about twenty-five stops to hear testimony and review documents. The commissioners spent nearly five weeks in the Abir concession. On a typical working day, they held a morning session from eight to twelve and an afternoon session from three to seven. The Commission did not include any of the witnesses' testimony in its final report because it "did not consider that the purpose of the inquiry was to fix personal responsibility, but thought it was its duty to examine the condition of the natives rather than individual facts."

The Commission of Inquiry submitted its report to the Congo Free State's administrators in Brussels on October 30, 1905, seven months after it left the Congo. The report presented the Commission's conclusions on a broad range of issues, such as land tenure, taxation, military expeditions, the concession system, and the justice system, and it made suggestions for administrative and legal reforms. On the key issue of taxation, which occupied one-third of the report, the Commission supported the "labor tax" as part of the Congo Free State's civilizing mission. "To civilize a race means to modify its economic and social condition, its intellectual and moral status; it is to extirpate its ideas, customs, and habits and substitute in place of those of which we disapprove the ideas, habits and customs which are akin to ours." As applied to the Africans, the Commission noted, "It is in spite of himself that the native in the beginning must be induced to throw off his natural indolence and improve his condition. A law, therefore, which imposes upon the native light and regular work is the only means of giving him an incentive to work; while it is an economic law, it is at the same time a humanitarian law."

While supporting the general system of forced labor, the Commission proposed modifications to make it less onerous. Among other things, it recommended that forty hours of forced labor per month, as decreed by the State on November 18, 1903, should be interpreted as the *maximum* limit; that only State agents (and not private companies) could exercise rights of police and powers of bodily detention in the concession areas; that Africans should be allowed to pay their "taxes" in other commodities if the wild rubber supplies were exhausted; and that more judges should be appointed to investigate reported abuses.

Although the report gave only brief summaries of the conditions that the commissioners encountered in the Congo, they were sufficient to lend credence to the more detailed reports of Roger Casement and the British missionaries. In terms of the abuses arising from forced rubber gathering, the report singled out the Anversoise, Abir, and Lulonga companies as particularly egregious. "From an examination of documents regarding Mongala [i.e., Anversoise], and a careful enquiry made by the commission in regard to the Abir concession," noted the report, "it appears that acts of the sort of which we are speaking, were very frequent in the territory controlled by these companies. At the different posts in the Abir which we visited, it was never denied that the imprisonment of women as hostages, the imposition of servile work on chiefs, the administration of the lash to delinquents, and the abuse of authority by the black overseers were, as a rule, habitual. Similar conditions have been reported to the Commission from Lulonga."

The commission also acknowledged the depletion of the rubber vines. "Of course, the commission could not form any estimate of the wealth in rubber vines in the forests it saw. . . . Still, it appears undoubtedly true that an exploitation which has continued a certain number of years will lead to a complete exhaustion in those regions contiguous to the native villages." Under those circumstances, the Commission recognized that the task of rubber gathering had become especially onerous for the Africans. "In the majority of cases, he must make a journey every fortnight which takes two or three days, sometimes more, in order to reach that part of the forest where he can find the rubber vines in sufficient quantity. There, for a certain number of days he leads an uncomfortable existence. . . . He must carry what he has gathered to the State post or to the company, and not until then does he return to his village, where he can tarry only two or three days before the time for the next delivery is close at hand. . . . It is hardly necessary to remark that this state of affairs is a flagrant violation of the law of 'forty hours.'"

One thorny problem addressed by the Commission of Inquiry was depopulation. The Commission acknowledged that the system of forced rubber gathering had resulted in considerable loss of life through killing, displacement, malnutrition, and disease, but it believed that the main causes of depopulation were the epidemics of smallpox and sleeping sickness that had swept along the river valleys of the Congo River basin in the 1890s. That observation was accurate for the towns along the Congo River itself. In 1900, the Catholic mission at Kwamouth was abandoned after it lost six hundred children to sleeping sickness, while Tchumbiri was so reduced by sleeping sickness that the Baptist mission considered abandoning it. Neither of those towns was subjected to rubber quotas. Further up the river at French Lukolela, smallpox reduced the population from one thousand to fifty.[21]

What the Commission failed to acknowledge, however, was that the epidemics were a direct consequence of the increased travel and mobility resulting from the activities of the State and the European companies. The river steamers often carried smallpox-infected soldiers and company employees, and they harbored infected tsetse flies that spread sleeping sickness. By focusing on smallpox and sleeping sickness—diseases that afflicted the strong as well as the weak—the Commission failed to give enough weight to the more quotidian deaths from malaria, intestinal diseases, and respiratory diseases, which could become deadly when people were malnourished, ill housed, and exhausted.[22]

The other side of the demographic equation was lower birthrates. The missionaries charged that women used abortion to avoid having children so that it would be easier to flee from military expeditions. The Commission acknowledged that abortion was practiced in the rubber-producing regions but attributed it to "a superstitious idea encouraged by sorcerers." Both explanations could be true because abortions were generally talked about in mystical terms even though they were undertaken for practical reasons. By focusing on abortion, however, the Commission missed the role of gonorrhea (which can cause pelvic inflammatory disease in women and epididymitis in male testicles) and syphilis (which can cause miscarriages and stillbirths in women and epididymitis in men) in reducing the birthrate. The spread of those diseases increased significantly with the movement of State soldiers and company sentries through the rubber areas.[23]

Neither the missionaries nor the Commission of Inquiry attempted to estimate the total number of deaths from the system of forced rubber gathering. Although depopulated or abandoned villages were frequently observed in the rubber areas, it was difficult to determine how many of the former inhabitants had been killed as opposed to being displaced or scattered. The refugees from the Crown Domain who settled in the hinterland of Bolobo showed that people would migrate long distances to find safety, and the governor of the French Congo claimed in 1900 that thirty thousand people from the Abir concession had crossed the Congo River to seek refuge.[24]

Other critics, however, ventured estimates. Edgar Canisius was told by an agent that as many as twenty thousand people had been killed in the Anversoise concession between 1893 and 1900, and one can speculate that perhaps an equal number were killed in the subsequent wars against the Buja, bringing the total to as much as forty thousand. For the Abir concession, the Belgian anthropologist and historian Daniel Vangroenweghe has estimated that "thousands" of Congolese were killed and "tens of thousands" died from punishments and reprisals for failing to bring in enough rubber. The British reformer and newspaper editor E. D. Morel estimated in 1906 that the population of the Congo Free State as a whole had decreased by a *minimum* of 1.5 million since 1890 from violence, forced labor, malnutrition, and disease, although he acknowledged that his computation "can only be hypothetical." Roger Casement, on the other hand, thought that Morel's estimate was too low and that the true number was closer to three million. Given that no census of the Congo Free State was taken before or immediately after the rubber wars, the numbers must remain a matter of speculation.[25]

3

Baringa, the Abir Concession, December 1904

King Leopold's Commission of Inquiry declined to publish the testimony upon which its conclusions were based, but some of the British missionaries in the Abir concession wrote out transcripts of their testimony and sent copies to E. D. Morel in Liverpool, who published them in a pamphlet entitled *Evidence Laid Before the Commission of Inquiry*. John and Alice Harris of the Congo Balolo Mission provided some of the most riveting testimony. They had been married in England in 1898, and their honeymoon trip had been a voyage to the Congo Free State to begin their mission work, initially near the Abir post at Bongandanga, and later at Baringa, which was also in the Abir concession.

Alice had a Kodak camera, which she used to document the curiosities she encountered in Africa. "I use my camera to take photos of the nature, the strange insects, the interesting animals," Alice wrote to her sister in 1900. "The other use I am making of my camera is this; we have seen several small children and young people with a hand missing, sometimes both hands. . . . I will keep taking these photos as a kind of documenting process, and then I will send them back to the Regions Beyond missionary headquarters in London to see what they make of them. In my heart I fear that this points to a far greater evil than we can yet understand." Yet she was reluctant to cast blame on King Leopold. "I cannot imagine that King Leopold would put up with anything out of order," she wrote, "were he to discover that his men were not fulfilling his wishes for good governance. He had promised to free the natives here from the Arab slavers. In that light, we must be careful as we work, careful to preserve the truth and not spread gossip or innuendo."[26]

By the time the Commission of Inquiry came to Baringa in December 1904, the Harrises had gathered ample evidence that their earlier suspicions were true. John presented evidence on a number of specific murders and atrocities that had taken place under the administrations of two recent Abir agents. Then he discussed "irregularities common to all agents" and gave examples from his own experience. He described public floggings in which men received one hundred strokes with the chicotte and noted that the imprisonment of men, women, and children had resulted in many deaths in prison or immediately after release. He also discussed the irregular taxes imposed by the agents and charged that "the whole of the villages were absolutely under their despotic control." There was the dramatic testimony of Chief Lontulu, who brought 110 twigs of different lengths to represent men, women, and children who had been killed by the Abir sentries.

Missionary Alice Seely Harris in the Congo. Anti-Slavery International

After hearing evidence of two hundred murders in four nearby villages, the commission agreed to accept the following as a true general statement: "That hundreds of people have been killed in this district for rubber, and that I could prove it by multitudes of witnesses."[27]

Alice Seeley Harris confirmed the parts of her husband's testimony that she had personally witnessed and then talked about the women prisoners at Bongandanga. "If a certain village or villages were short," she said, "a number of the women from those places would be seized and put in prison until the men made up their deficiencies. This was the recognized method of the Abir agent, who often told me that this was the best way to get the 'taxes' brought in." Alice also described the caravans of rubber gatherers that passed by her mission station. Coming from thirty to forty miles away and guarded by armed sentries, they had the appearance of a prison gang. She also reported seeing rubber workers carried away by their friends after being severely whipped with the chicotte.[28]

The testimony of the British missionaries was later reinforced by Viscount Mountmorres, who was making an extensive tour of the Congo Free State as a special correspondent for *The Globe* newspaper at the same time that the Commission of Inquiry was conducting its investigation. Instead of entering the Abir concession from the west by going up the Lulonga River, as the Commission had done, he entered from the northeast and traversed the Abir territory from east to west. "Partly by land and partly by canoe along the various smaller waterways, I worked from one village to another, visiting the chief trading stations of the company quite unexpectedly," he wrote.[29]

Mountmorres found village life in the Abir concession to be in ruins. "Along the Lopori itself and in all the country south of it along the Maringa, the Yekokora, and the Bolombo, its principal southern tributaries, and in the country lying between them, one scarcely sees a village worthy of the name," he wrote. "Here and there one finds evidence of former considerable settlements with ruins of deserted huts and plantations that have fallen out of cultivation and are being gradually absorbed by the all-devouring tropical bush. . . . But, for the most part, the population, which seems small, occupies nothing more substantial than the rudest leaf shelters, isolated in groups of two or three in the thickest and least accessible parts of the densest forest."

As for the Abir system as a whole, Mountmorres referred to the Abir sentries as "slave-drivers in one of the cruelest and most oppressive forms of slavery that can be imagined, for it is one in which not the smallest regard is paid for the life, the health, or the comfort of the slave." The European agents, he noted, were largely people who, "for reasons very often to their discredit, are forced to accept service out of Europe at any cost." He learned that one of the Abir agents had previously been dismissed from a company in the French Congo, which "thought he must be a criminal lunatic owing to the atrocities of which he was guilty." Mountmorres concluded that "responsibility must rest with the company in the first instance, although the majority of its agents cannot be absolved for their callous brutality by any attempt to make the company bear their personal and individual responsibility." Although Viscount Mountmorres did not provide evidence to the Commission of Inquiry, which was unaware of his presence in the Abir concession, his report independently reinforced that of the missionaries.

After the Commission of Inquiry departed, conditions in the Abir concession quickly worsened. "Abir is attempting to force rubber with scores of sentries armed with muzzle-loaders," wrote missionary John Harris on March 25, 1905. "Chief Bomolo of Bolemboloko, Chief Isekalongi of Lotoko, and other chiefs have sworn they will die sooner than suffer again as they did before the Commission came. They say, 'Show us where to find rubber and we will work it; if not, come and kill us; we can but die once.'" On April 10, John Harris wrote from Baringa, "We regret exceedingly that the Abir are now reverting to their former methods. The Eleko section, if not also the Luiza section, have left their towns and are hiding in the forest, but we are told the ultimate intention is to migrate to the Tshuapa. . . . It is manifestly clear to us that rubber, as at present demanded, can only be procured by the continued sacrifice of lives, and the shedding of blood, the complete ruin of the forests, and the extermination of the native races." The missionary Edgar Stannard confirmed Harris's assessment by reporting on April 7, "The people have been told that very soon the sentries are coming again to kill more, and if they do not bring in rubber, they will soon be 'finished off.' Of course, we shall report this to the State, but what is the use?"[30]

The biggest threat to Abir's profits was not the Commission of Inquiry but the depletion of the wild rubber vines in the rainforest. When John Harris took a one-hundred-mile trip through the rainforest, he did not see a single live rubber vine, although he saw a lot of dead ones. When the missionary Charles Padfield traveled along the Maringa River, he was told that the rubber was finished. One man told him, "We sent seeking rubber until we met the people of the Tshuapa, and then we went towards the Ikelemba, and then the white man told us to cut the vines, and we cut them, and then we dug up the roots, and now what is there left?" By 1905, 90 percent of Abir's rubber was reportedly coming from the headwaters of the Tshuapa River, a previously untapped region lying outside the boundaries of the Abir concession.[31]

In August 1905, the Congo Free State sent soldiers to the Abir concession to force an increase in rubber production, much as it had done the previous year in the Anversoise concession. Two companies of State soldiers from the military camp at Irebu toured the Abir concession, stopping at each village and threatening to come back and make war if they did not produce rubber. Pleas that there was no rubber were ignored. Instead of lowering the quota on each village, they raised it. In October, a third military company began touring the concession in a similar fashion. But it was a wasted effort. Figures from the thirty largest Abir posts show that monthly rubber production fell from nineteen tons in August 1905 to seventeen tons in January 1906 and to seven tons in April 1906. With the Congo Free State investing considerable resources in the rubber production of Abir, there were rumors that the State was planning to take over the concession as it had previously done with Anversoise.[32]

On September 12, 1906, the Congo Free State formally took over the concessions of both Abir and Anversoise, promising to pay the companies 4.50 francs per kilo of rubber delivered to Antwerp until 1952. At the time of the agreement, the price of rubber at Antwerp was 13.5 francs per kilo, leaving a considerable profit for the State, especially considering that the State owned half the shares of the two companies. State military forces had already occupied the Anversoise concession in 1904 and the Abir concession in 1905, and so the formal agreements in November 1906 simply legalized the status quo. The two major concession territories were now fully in the hands of the Congo Free State.[33]

King Leopold's Crown Domain, located south of the Abir concession in the region of Lake Mai-Ndombe, had largely been shielded from negative publicity because of its remote location and State secrecy. Nevertheless, hints of its existence had occasionally leaked out to the wider world. In 1899, some missionaries had ascended the Ruki/Busira/Tshuapa River to make contacts with the people. When they unknowingly entered the Crown Domain, they picked up an unwanted escort of thirty State soldiers, who would not let them speak to the people or even buy food from them. After a month of trying unsuccessfully to build relationships with the people of the area, the missionaries gave up and went back down the Ruki in their canoes.[34]

The next missionary to enter the Crown Domain was Rev. E. A. Scrivener, a British Baptist missionary from Bolobo, who visited it in 1903. While there, he heard stories about the coming of the State to this formerly remote area. The people were living in peace and quietness, Scrivener was told, when white men with rifles came in from Lake Mai-Ndombe and told people to bring in rubber. A small reward was offered, but it was gradually reduced until they were told to bring in the rubber for nothing. When they tried to refuse, "several were shot by the soldiers, and the rest were told with many curses and blows to go at once, or more would be killed."[35]

As Scrivener recounted the story: "Terrified, they began to prepare food for a fortnight's absence from the village, which the collection of rubber entailed. The soldiers discovered them sitting about. 'What, not gone yet?' Bang! Bang! Bang! And down fell one and another dead in the midst of wives and companions. There is a terrible wail, and an attempt is made to prepare the dead for burial, but this is not allowed. All must go at once to the forest. . . Many died in the forests from exposure and hunger, and still more from the rifles of the ferocious soldiers in charge of the post. In spite of all their efforts, the amount fell off, and more and more were killed."

"I was shown around the place," Scrivener reported, "and the sites of the former big chiefs' settlements were pointed out. A careful estimate made of the population of, say, seven years ago [i.e., 1896] to be 2,000 people in and about the post, within the radius of, say, a quarter of a mile. All told, they would not muster 200 now, and there is so much sadness and gloom that they are fast decreasing." When the Commission of Inquiry took testimony from Scrivener at Bolobo on November 7, 1904, he told it that the new State agent in the part of the Crown Domain that he had visited had ended the massacres and atrocities, but the rubber system itself remained oppressive. The villagers still had to go several days' march into the forest to find rubber and then carry it to the nearest government station, which was sometimes a great distance away.[36]

Cassie Murdoch of the British Baptist mission in Bolobo made a seven-week, 450-mile journey through the Crown Domain in July and August 1907, and he reported that things had gotten worse as the wild rubber became depleted. He confirmed Scrivener's view that the massacres and atrocities that accompanied the early stages of forced rubber gathering had largely subsided but maintained that the "cruel and grinding system" of forced rubber gathering remained. "The Crown Domain west of Lake Leopold II [i.e., Lake Mai-Ndombe] has been depopulated to an alarming extent," he wrote. "There are evidences of it everywhere. I passed through at least three districts which had once contained very large towns, but which are now completely empty. . . . There cannot be the least doubt that this depopulation is due directly to the State. The number of people they shot or otherwise tortured to death must have been enormous. Perhaps as many or more of those who escaped the rifle died from starvation and exposure." Murdoch acknowledged that it was difficult to determine the death toll. "I am far from affirming that all that number of people have been butchered," he wrote. "Some are now living in the *Domaine Privé* [i.e., outside of the Crown Domain], and others have built small hamlets in little out-of-the-way corners in an attempt to hide themselves from the rubber tax and from the depredations of the soldiers."[37]

For those people who remained under State control, Murdoch reported, the rubber tax "demands from twenty to twenty-five days of labor every month. . . . It was some time before I made the discovery that in the Crown Domain west of Lake Leopold, there is no rubber. . . . I also found that the rubber is collected from the *Domaine Privé* in forests from ten to forty miles beyond the boundary of the Crown Domain. . . . I have made a careful calculation of the distance the people I have met have to walk, and I find that the average cannot be less than 300 miles, there and back. . . . The rest of the time is used in hunting for vines and in tapping them when found." Even so, their efforts were not always successful. "Two days after I left the Domain on my way back," he wrote, "I saw some men returning empty handed. They had been hunting for over eight days and had found nothing. What the poor wretches would do, I cannot imagine."

4

Paris, February 16, 1905

On February 16, 1905, a front-page story in the Paris scandal-sheet *Le Matin* reported that several drunken colonial officers in the French Congo had blown up an African man with a stick of dynamite. They were celebrating Bastille Day in Brazzaville on July 14, 1904, with a huge feast and generous libations. When all were thoroughly drunk, they decided on an experiment to see the effect of dynamite on a black man. According to the newspaper, "The drunken officers heartily applauded such an ingenious idea, and their joy knew no bounds when the originator of that proposition . . . carried out his invention." They seized a young African man, tied him up, and fastened the stick of dynamite to his back. Then they got the idea to force it into his anus, causing him to vomit. "The blast rang out," went the article, "projecting bloody debris, body parts, and intestines over a great distance." Soon newspapers all over France reproduced all or part of the story, bringing it to millions of readers.[38]

As might be expected from a scandal newspaper, *Le Matin* got many of the details wrong. The incident did not happen in Brazzaville but at Fort Crampel, nearly eight hundred miles to the northeast; it took place in 1903, not 1904; the victim was not an innocent bystander but a man already condemned to be executed; and the dynamite was attached to his neck. Nevertheless, the shocking essence of the story was correct, and it revealed unsavory happenings in the French Congo. The dynamite story was followed by stories in more respectable newspapers that examined the poor quality of administrative personnel in the French Congo, the abuses in recruiting porters, the injustices in collecting taxes, and the many rebellions. Since the public was well aware that a Belgian Commission of Inquiry had recently conducted investigations in the Congo Free State, there began to be calls for a similar commission to investigate the situation in the French Congo.[39]

In order to silence the newspapers, and to avoid being lumped together with the Congo Free State in international opinion, the French minister of colonies set up a Commission of Inquiry. Envisioning a routine investigation that would make some bland, bureaucratic recommendations, he appointed Etienne Dubard, a veteran colonial inspector who was chief of service for the inspector general of colonies, to lead the commission. When Dubard refused the job because of poor health, the government offered the position to Pierre Savorgnan de Brazza, who had been living in retirement in Algiers ever since being dismissed as governor-general of the French Congo seven years earlier.

Brazza was not the preferred choice of the minister of foreign affairs, who feared that he would be difficult to control, but after the president of France mentioned his name and Brazza personally lobbied several cabinet ministers, he was offered the job. Gustave Binger, the Africa director at the Ministry of Foreign Affairs, later complained that the cabinet had favored Brazza without thinking things through because they thought he could rally public support for the government. But if the ministry was wary of Brazza, the newspapers were ecstatic. "I am almost embarrassed to congratulate the Minister for sending M. de Brazza to discover the Congo for a second time," opined the editor of *Le Siècle*. "It is almost inconceivable that such a simple idea could enter the brains of French politicians."[40]

Brazza accepted the job on the condition that he could pick his own team of investigators. Besides Brazza, the principal members of the commission included three people from the office of the inspector general of colonies, three colonial administrators with experience in Africa, one member from the Ministry of Foreign Affairs, and one from the Ministry of Colonies. Perhaps the most unusual pick was Félicien Challaye, a thirty-year-old philosophy teacher in a Paris secondary school, who served as Brazza's personal secretary and accompanied him at all times. Challaye had completed two years of advanced study in philosophy at the University of Berlin and had subsequently received a grant to undertake two trips through the "peripheral" parts of the world. His published letters in the magazine *Cahiers de la Quinzaine* denouncing colonial brutality in Indochina had caught the attention of journalists at the Paris newspaper *Le Temps*. For purposes of the Congo trip, he was credentialed as a reporter for *Le Temps*, and his articles would provide a candid look at the situations observed by the Brazza Commission. As the only member who was not connected to the French government or the military, he was not bound by the normal code of silence.[41]

According to their confidential instructions, the commissioners were to draw a sharp distinction between the concession system in the French Congo and the one in the Congo Free State and to stress that the principles that underlay the French system were completely different from those of the Free State. The instructions also claimed that the colonial army in the French Congo existed solely to keep the peace and not to force people to bring in rubber. The commissioners were ordered to collect information discreetly on the Congo Free State for comparative purposes, but they were warned not to carry any documents or notes with them if they entered Free State territory, for fear that they could fall into the wrong hands.[42]

The administrative structure of the French Congo in 1905 was very different from the one that Brazza had left in 1898. The capital and seat of administration had moved from Libreville to Brazzaville in 1904, after the Congo Free State's completion of the railway from Matadi to Malebo Pool had liberated Brazzaville from its isolation. Because of French military advances up the Ubangi River and north to Lake Chad, the French Congo was now divided into four separate regions: Gabon, Middle Congo, Ubangi-Chari, and Chad. All of them were under the authority of the commissioner-general in Brazzaville.[43]

Before arriving at the mouth of the Congo River, the Commission made an excursion up the Ogowe River to Njole, the limit of navigation for river steamboats. This was the region that Brazza had turned over to the Société du Haut Ogooué, which had received a monopoly on trade in return for developing an integrated transportation system along the upper Ogowe. When the commissioners arrived at Njole, they were greeted by a crowd of chiefs who seemed happy to see Brazza but had complaints about the concession company. Although the SHO operated like a normal trading company in that it imported European goods and traded them for rubber, the chiefs complained that the prices it charged for its merchandise were much higher than before it had been granted its monopoly. They also complained about the head tax, which they referred to as a "fine." To escape the tax, many of the people had abandoned their riverside villages and built new villages hidden in the forest. These complaints, however, were mild compared to what the commission would find in the Congo River basin.[44]

The Commission resumed its trip along the Atlantic coast to the estuary of the Congo River, where it disembarked at the Congo Free State's port of Matadi. From there, they took the Free State's railroad to Malebo Pool and then a steamboat across the Pool to Brazzaville, the new capital of the French Congo. The commissioners received a "correct," if tense, welcome from the commissioner-general, Émile Gentil, but Brazza felt that Gentil was doing everything he could behind the scenes to impede the work of the Commission. On May 20, 1905, the Commission left Brazzaville on the steamboat *Albert Dolisie* to go up the Congo River. "As soon as we left Brazzaville," wrote Brazza to the journalist Paul Bourde, "the obstruction began—an underground plot of which I still do not know the full extent was hatched by the Minister of Colonies in order to hamper the work of the mission."[45]

At a brief stop in French Lukolela, the commissioners found the local people in full revolt against the concession company that had established itself in the region. Continuing on, they left the Congo River to go up the Ubangi and steamed through a region with an estimated population of eight hundred thousand Bonjo people but not a single French administrative post. The French concession company was the only colonial authority in the region. Challaye noted that the company took advantage of the situation to "tyrannize the blacks and exploit them harshly." The company sentries forced the men to collect rubber, seized their wives, and bombarded them with a thousand demands.

In response, the Commission was told, a group of Bonjo rebels had hatched a plot to send a gift of chickens, attractive female slaves, and palm wine to the Senegalese agent in charge of a company post. When the company personnel were drunk, the rebels invaded the post, broke into the warehouse, and seized the guns and ammunition. Some rebels already had arms and ammunition

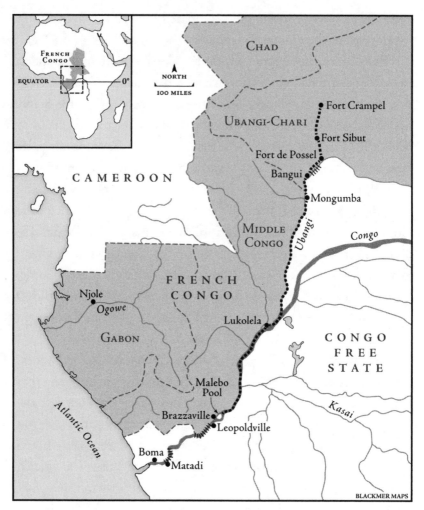

The Brazza Commission's travels from Malebo Pool to Fort Crampel, 1905

that they had received from the company in exchange for ivory and rubber. As the revolt spread, twenty-four of the company's African agents were killed. To put down the revolt, the French colonial government had sent a company of Senegalese soldiers, who were not used to fighting in thick forest with narrow paths that made them susceptible to ambushes. It was "impossible to approach the enemy, or even to see them," wrote Challaye. The tactics of the Bonjo rebels along the Ubangi were similar to those of the Buja rebels in the Anversoise concession in the Congo Free State. In both cases, the rebels were extremely successful.[46]

After a stay in Bangui, which marked the limit of steamboat navigation, the Commission continued up the Ubangi in whaleboats that could pass the rapids. Arriving at Fort de Possel on June 30, it left the river to travel straight north by land toward Lake Chad. The commissioners were now traveling through a savanna region with tall, thin grass punctuated by small trees and tall earthen termite mounds. Riding on horseback, the commissioners were going to Fort Sibut and then to Fort Crampel, their final destination, 150 miles north of the Ubangi River. This was the main caravan route to get supplies to Fort Lamy, the capital of Chad, and the people who lived near the route were conscripted to serve as caravan porters. In the immediate area, there were barely twelve thousand men available to transport 360 tons of supplies per year, and many of them lived three days' walk from the caravan route. When people tried to move farther away to avoid porterage, the government established posts and military camps to prevent them from emigrating.[47]

Challaye noted that when Émile Gentil, the current commissioner-general of the French Congo, had first led an expedition through this territory in 1895, he had described the region as flourishing. "The villages are numerous," Gentil wrote, "surrounded by immense plantations of millet and manioc. Abundance and prosperity is everywhere." Traveling in 1905, Challaye was disturbed by what he was seeing. "What a lamentable contrast between the opulence of yesterday and the misery of today!" he wrote. "No more villages. Barely a few huts around the French posts. No more plantations; the porters are unable to find even minimal food. It is extremely difficult, even for the whites, to buy a few chickens at a good price. Everywhere is desert; everywhere is famine."[48]

Brazza, for his part, was frustrated by his inability to gain accurate information. "Every effort was made, during my passage through this region, to prevent me from gaining information. Had

I not succeeded in developing personal and direct relations with the natives despite this obstruction, it would have produced the unbelievable situation that my passage through this region would have supported, in the name of France, an approval of all the atrocities that have been committed here."[49]

Arriving at Fort Crampel on July 18, Challaye noted that the region around the fort was under the control of a concession company, which had provoked a revolt among the population. In 1904, the company had arrested a local chief because his people had failed to bring in the required amount of rubber. After the chief died in prison a month later, the people revolted and killed twenty-seven African agents of the company. When the French colonial army came with its Senegalese soldiers to put down the rebellion, they found the whitened skulls of the dead agents filled with balls of rubber. Challaye thought it was a fitting symbol to express the cause of the revolt.[50]

Back in Bangui on August 10, the Commission took whaleboats to Mongumba to gain more information about an incident involving women prisoners that Brazza had begun investigating during his earlier passage through Bangui. According to Challaye, the basic facts were as follows: In April 1904, the French administrator at Bangui needed to increase the collection of the head tax. He sent out a state agent, along with a force of "regional guards"—an armed force recruited from the local region that was hostile to the riverside populations. The regional guards were in many ways similar to the "sentries" recruited by Abir and Anversoise in the Congo Free State. The state agent settled in the village of Mongumba and sent out two regional guards to each village to force the chiefs to bring in rubber. The guards brutalized the inhabitants and raped the women, causing many of the villagers to flee across the Ubangi River to the Congo Free State.

To keep people from fleeing, the state agent sent out his regional guards to the surrounding villages to seize women and children as hostages until the men brought in rubber, which the state agent handed over to the concession company (further evidence that tax collecting was a mere pretext to force people to bring in rubber for the company). Because the company deemed the quantity of rubber insufficient, the women were sent to Bangui, where fifty-eight women and ten children were locked in a storage building twenty feet long with no opening except for the door, where they were fed only occasionally. Twenty-five of them died in the first twelve days, and the rest were moved to a larger building. But they still had insufficient food, and the deaths continued. When a French doctor arrived in Bangui and heard cries coming from the building, he demanded that it be opened. Inside, he found thirteen women and eight children clinging to life; the rest were dead. Altogether, forty-five women and two children had died in prison in Bangui, and several of the survivors died soon after their release.[51]

Brazza took a personal interest in this case and compiled a thick dossier with a report and forty-two auxiliary documents that he sent to the minister of colonies via a Belgian ship ahead of the departure of the Commission. He summarized his findings as follows: "I have the honor to inform you that during May 1904 the methods employed by an agent of the administration to collect the tax in kind in the concession territories consisted of having women and children kidnapped and sent to Bangui. There, out of 58 women and 10 children, 45 women and 2 children were dead after five weeks." Brazza added: "I believe it my duty to call your attention to the significance of this affair because the incident in question is not isolated. To the contrary, the kidnapping of women in the native villages is routinely used to obtain porters for the route from Fort Possel to Fort Crampel, to speak only of the region I have visited personally."[52]

Descending the Congo River toward Brazzaville with the awe-inspiring but ultimately monotonous rainforest towering on both sides, Challaye felt a desire to reread Dante's *Inferno*. Even though he did not have the book, Dante's images, words, and phrases flashed through his head: "Abandon all hope; rivulets of blood;

land of tears; abyss of pain; regions of eternal grievance." He recalled one passage in particular: "I see in the valley new suffering, new torments, new executioners." He concluded his meditation by writing, "For as long as I live, I will retain the sadness of having seen a genuine hell with my own eyes."[53]

By August 21, the Commission was back in Brazzaville just in time for the opening of the trials of George Toqué, the former chief administrator at Fort Crampel, and his assistant Ferdinand-Leopold Gaud—the two men implicated in the notorious dynamite incident. Each was accused of various individual crimes in addition to their collaborative one. Asked by the judge to describe the larger context in which the crimes occurred, Toqué described the methods of obtaining porters: raids on villages and the kidnapping of women and children who were not released until the porters completed their journey. In 1901, Toqué said, he had stumbled onto a hostage camp hidden in the bush and found the dead bodies of 20 women and another 150 dying of hunger. The same methods, he said, were used to collect the taxes.[54]

The dynamite incident was taken up on the second day. The victim was a man named Pakpa, who had worked for the French as a guide. He had been accused of intentionally leading regional guard troops into an ambush, where two of them were killed and several others wounded. After Toqué had sent orders to Gaud to arrest Pakpa and execute him with a firing squad, Pakpa was arrested on July 12 and put in the pit at Fort Crampel. Because of the French tradition of liberating prisoners on Bastille Day, July 14, Gaud asked Toqué what should be done with the three prisoners in the pit. Toqué suggested liberating the other two but hesitated about whether to liberate Pakpa. Finally, he said to Gaud, "Do what you want." Gaud then brought Pakpa out of the pit with the aid of a regional guard, attached the stick of dynamite to his neck, and blew him up.

As the trial in Brazzaville wound down, the defense lawyer pleaded for understanding the difficult situation of the two young colonial administrators, who were responsible for transporting three thousand loads per month to Fort Crampel without a workable system for obtaining porters. In the end, both men were found guilty of some of the charges against them, and each was sentenced to just five years in prison because of the extenuating circumstances. Some people in France may have thought that the sentences were too light, but the French officials in Brazzaville were outraged that the two men had been sentenced at all.

By the time the Commission left Brazzaville for the coast on August 29, Brazza had been confined to his room with an illness for ten days. To get to the steamboat that would take the Commission across Malebo Pool to board the train at Leopoldville, the staff prepared a hammock to carry him, but he insisted on walking, leaning heavily on his cane. Challaye, who had been Brazza's constant companion during the trip, summed up Brazza's feelings as the former explorer left the Congo for the last time. "An immense sorrow increased the burden of physical and intellectual fatigue from which he suffered," wrote Challaye. "He saw a despotic and greedy Administration imposing ill-considered or vexatious taxes. . . . He saw concessionary companies, cynical and rapacious, seeking to reconstitute a new slavery, seeking to force poorly remunerated labor upon the natives by threats or violence. . . . From these sinister discoveries, de Brazza suffered from the bottom of his heart. They hastened his end."[55]

5

England, a Church Parish Hall, 1906

As the lamps were dimmed in the parish hall, the Magic Lantern show began. "The Congo Atrocities: A Lecture to Accompany a Series of 60 Photographic Slides for the Optical Lantern," announced the title slide. It noted that the narration had been written by William Riley (of Riley Bros. Ltd.) and revised by

Men holding up severed hands in the Abir concession. The missionary John Harris is on the right. Anti-Slavery International

E. D. Morel and Rev. John H. Harris. The slide failed to mention that most of the photographs had been taken by Alice Seeley Harris, although that information was disclosed later in the narration.

The event was sponsored by the Congo Reform Association, an organization founded in March 1904 by Roger Casement and E. D. Morel. As a former shipping clerk for Elder-Dempster shipping lines in Liverpool, Morel had become alarmed by trade statistics showing large quantities of guns and ammunition going to the Congo and rubber coming back. In 1903, he quit his job to work full time as the editor of the *West African Mail*, a weekly trade journal that mixed shipping schedules and trade statistics with articles critical of the Congo Free State. In a series of meetings with Roger Casement beginning in December 1903, the two men drew up plans for an organization that focused on reforming the Congo Free State. It would be headed by Morel, with support from such diverse figures as H. R. Fox Bourne of the Aborigines Protection Society, Henry Grattan Guinness of the Regions Beyond Missionary Union, and the Liverpool merchant John Holt.

The Congo Reform Association represented a curious amalgamation of business interests, secular humanitarianism, and religious fervor. As an advocate for universal human rights, Morel expressed his belief in "the right of the native to his land and to the fruits of his land; his right to sell those fruits to whomsoever he will, and his right as a free man to his freedom—those are the real principles at stake." The "freedom" of which Morel spoke referred primarily to freedom to trade with British merchants and not to political rights or self-government, thus making it easy for the Belgians to dismiss him as an agent for the Liverpool and Manchester Chambers of Commerce. Reverend Guinness, in contrast to Morel, had emphasized the role of missionaries in fulfilling their "civilizing mission" by ending such heathen practices as slavery, polygamy, and cannibalism through Christian conversion and mission education. Taken together, the different strands of thought coexisted in an uneasy alliance that fit within David Livingstone's famous framework of "Christianity, Commerce, and Civilization."[56]

Following its inaugural meeting in Liverpool on March 23, 1904, the Congo Reform Association saw its main mission as disseminating information about the Congo via the "Special Congo Supplement" in the *West African Mail* and a steady stream of book-length pamphlets written by Morel. Although Morel fantasized that this movement would become as big as the anti–slave trade movement in the nineteenth century, he lacked experience in grassroots mobilization. When Alice and John Harris returned from the Congo on furlough in late 1905, the CRA decided to send them out on a speaking tour to drum up support from evangelical churches. The key to the tour's success would be the Magic Lantern slides based on Alice's photographs. When Morel worried that the missionaries would prioritize their religious goals over humanitarian ideals, John Harris replied, "You appeal to the more educated classes and politicians; what I want to do is appeal to the popular mind."[57]

In 1906, two different versions of the Congo Atrocities Lantern Show were being presented in chapels and meeting halls all over

Britain. The first was presented by Alice and John Harris. Using a text written mostly by Alice, they sometimes presented together and sometimes separately. When they worked together, Alice gave the narration in her clear voice that hinted of her upbringing in Wiltshire County in southwest England, while John helped with special effects. Alice later explained that when she showed the slide of the hippopotamus-hide whip, John would "snap the *chicotte* across the stage as I spoke, slap it down hard across the plank flooring to make my point. Pain. Suffering. Frothing at the mouth. That was our point!" Alice added, "Manipulation is not always a bad thing, I decided. We needed to arouse sympathy. We could not have it said that people in Britain were unaware of the atrocities. We reminded our audience that Britain had abolished the slave trade in 1833, and it was now 1906, and there were thousands of people across the waves who deserved the same benefit."[58]

The Riley Brothers' set of glass slides, in contrast, could be purchased or rented from optical lantern dealers, complete with a text for the narrator. The Riley Brothers Company, which was the largest lantern show outfitter in the world, had amassed a collection of thousands of glass slides, which they organized into sets and supplemented with written narration. Their "Congo Atrocities" slide set invoked both a human rights framework, which focused on violations of the Berlin Act, and a religious framework, which focused on the cruelty and evil of King Leopold's system. Depicting the Africans as savages and cannibals, it emphasized the great "civilizing mission" that had been betrayed by the greed of King Leopold II. A few excerpts illustrate the flavor and tone of the presentation.[59]

As the title slide disappeared, the screen showed a map of Africa that highlighted the Congo Free State. "Ladies and Gentlemen," intoned the narrator. "For some time past, the eyes of a great number of people in Great Britain and America have been turned on that immense tract of country in the heart of Africa known as the Congo Free State. Ever since the formation of that State, there have been some who have suspected the intentions and the good faith of its founder, but during recent years . . . the revelations that have now been made public surpass in horror the wildest dreams of the prophets of evil. It is high time that the conscience of this country was thoroughly aroused, and I therefore beg you to follow me closely as I lay before you, briefly but clearly, the startling indictment against the sovereign of the so-called 'Free State.'"

Slide number six showed King Leopold II. "One man in Europe had set his heart on the prize. It was Leopold II, King of the Belgians. He captivated everybody by his philanthropic schemes for regenerating and saving the African races. His idea was to secure this great district from the grabbers who were seeking to portion out Africa for mercenary ends, and to make it a 'free' state, where the native would enjoy all the blessings of a just and Christian civilization. Stanley fell under the spell of the philanthropic monarch, so did the British Chambers of Commerce, so did the Protestant missionary societies, so did everybody, or almost everybody."

Then came several slides that portrayed the inhabitants of the rainforest as cannibals and savages, thereby reinforcing European notions of "darkest Africa." Although the missionaries had heard unproven rumors of cannibalism, none of them had ever witnessed it. Slide number nine was titled "Entrance to a cannibal village": "[The Congo basin] was a region of isolated tribes and communities, almost the whole of which, except in the south, were confirmed cannibals. . . . Incessant wars and slave raids took place, not with a view to supplying labor, but with the intention of obtaining wives, and above all victims for the cannibal feasts . . . Mrs. Harris's excellent photograph shows the cage-like entrance to a cannibal town, an entrance which could easily be made to act as a trap on occasion." Slide fifteen—"A savage Abir sentry": "The soldiers are themselves savages, and some even cannibals, trained to use rifles, and in many cases they are sent away without any supervision, and they do as they please. When they come to a town, no man's property or wife is safe. . . . The soldier whose portrait is before you has murdered many natives for rubber."

When Alice Seely Harris showed the lantern slide of Nsala looking at the remains of his murdered daughter, grown men would weep. Anti-Slavery International

Slide seventeen—"The chicotte": "We have arrived, therefore, at this point. The king must have rubber, and the native must be forced to produce it. To persuade him to do so, the *chicotte* was introduced, a murderous-looking instrument of hippopotamus hide, five feet long, thickened at one end for convenience of grip. . . . How many men and women have died under its blows, none will ever know . . . Were these the only barbarities? Would to God it had been so! Towns were burnt to the ground, women were outraged, women and children were mutilated; hundreds, thousands, were killed."

The next section of the program—the atrocity photos—featured twelve slides showing hostages, mutilated bodies, and severed hands and feet. The most powerful image showed a father looking at the severed hand and foot of his little daughter, Boali, who had been killed by an Abir sentry. "When we told the story of Boali, the sweet little daughter of Nsala," Alice Harris later recalled, "the place filled with weeping. Grown men worked to restrain their emotion." The show ended with slide number sixty, "The last resort," which showed a British warship that could potentially blockade the mouth of the Congo River to stop the rubber exports. "A great cry for justice and mercy rises from the Congo Forest," proclaimed the narrator. "Can we be deaf to it? Surely not!"[60]

When the lamps were turned up, a designated person in the audience rose to propose a resolution to be forwarded to the secretary of state for foreign affairs and to the local member of Parliament. The model resolution supplied with the slide set read, in part, "This meeting expresses a distinct sense of indignation at the barbarities inflicted upon the natives of the Congo and . . . urges his Majesty's government to utilize, to the uttermost, the resources of British Diplomacy, with a view to the convocation of a renewed Conference of the Powers responsible for the creation of the Congo State." The resolution usually passed by acclamation.

Alice and John Harris gave over three hundred lectures in 1906; the number of Magic Lantern shows using the Riley Brothers' slide set is unknown. The energy generated at the meetings had not been seen since the glory days of the Anti-Slavery Movement in the nineteenth century. Despite the fervor and the petitions generated by the Congo Reform Movement, however, there was little the British government could do. Nevertheless, the evidence published regularly by E. D. Morel and the talk of reconvening the Berlin Conference were beginning to put pressure on members of the Belgian parliament and on King Leopold himself.[61]

CHAPTER 11

THE END OF RED RUBBER

J UST WHEN THE REVELATIONS OF colonial atrocities in the Congo River basin were reaching a crescendo, the trio of explorers and state builders whose actions and interactions had set off the transformation of life in the Congo basin rainforest departed from this world. John Rowlands (a.k.a. Henry Morton Stanley), Hamid bin Muhammed el Murjebi (a.k.a. Tippu Tip), and Pietro Savorgnan di Brazza (a.k.a. Pierre Savorgnan de Brazza) all died during the sixteen-month period between May 10, 1904, and September 14, 1905. Their legacies are still being debated today. All three men were dedicated empire builders who had no qualms about ruling as overlords over the people of the Congo River basin, although they had very different visions of what that entailed. In the end, all three of them lost control of the narratives they had set in motion.[1]

Henry Morton Stanley died in London on May 10, 1904. After returning to Britain from the Emin Pasha Relief Expedition in 1890, he finally received the respect and adulation that he had always craved, even though the expedition itself had been a disaster and had accomplished no discernible purpose. Large crowds awaited him when his ship docked at Dover and again at Victoria Station in London. The Prince of Wales presided over a formal reception for him at St. James Hall, and the Royal Geographical Society booked the Royal Albert Hall—the largest in London—for

Stanley's lecture. Queen Victoria received him at Windsor Castle, and the universities of Oxford, Cambridge, and Edinburgh awarded him honorary doctorates. The historian Edward Berenson has characterized these events as the "Stanley craze" in Britain.[2]

Even though he had spent most of his adult years falsely claiming to be an American, Stanley finally embraced his British roots and became an official British subject in 1892. At the urging of his wife, he served in the House of Commons from 1895 to 1900, although he found the speeches and debates to be tedious. In 1899, he was knighted and became "Sir Henry." His wife petitioned to have him buried in Westminster Abbey near David Livingstone, but the request was denied by the dean of Westminster because of "the violence and even cruelty which marked some of his explorations." Nevertheless, Westminster Abbey agreed to host the funeral service, after which his body would be taken away to be buried elsewhere.[3]

Stanley never again set foot in the Congo after the Emin Pasha Relief Expedition, but he maintained an interest in the affairs of the Free State. In 1896, King Leopold asked him to write a letter to the London *Times* stating that reports of atrocities by Free State officers were merely isolated incidents. Stanley did as he was asked, but he nevertheless acknowledged the veracity of the reports. After hearing more rumors of atrocities, he traveled to Brussels to urge Leopold to send an international commission to investigate, but Leopold angrily rejected the idea. In September 1897, when Stanley went to Belgium to visit the Colonial Exhibition at Tervuren, he requested a meeting with Leopold, but the king refused to see him. The two never met again. When Roger Casement's report on the atrocities associated with forced rubber collecting in the Congo Free State came out in Britain in February 1904, Stanley was too ill to read it, and he died three months later without fully grasping the horrors inherent in the rubber concession system.[4]

Tippu Tip died in Zanzibar on June 13, 1905, following a violent bout of malaria. Since his return to Zanzibar in 1891, he had occupied himself with his plantations, his family, and his friends, but much on the island had changed after the British declared a protectorate over it in 1890. When a pretender to the sultanate with several thousand armed supporters seized the sultan's palace during a succession dispute in 1896, five British warships bombarded it to drive them out. Somehow, one of the green marble treads from the ruins of the palace staircase ended up gracing the doorstep of Tippu Tip's house. The following year, the British abolished the legal status of slavery in Zanzibar. Slaves could petition a British court for a certificate of freedom, but they risked being declared vagrants unless they could prove that they had a place to stay and a means of livelihood. Although few slaves were in a position to take advantage of the decree, it nevertheless initiated a process by which slaves gradually freed themselves by negotiating new work and living arrangements with their former masters.[5]

At the urging of his friend Dr. Heinrich Brode, Tippu Tip wrote his autobiography in Swahili using Arabic characters. Brode transcribed the text into the Latin alphabet and translated it into German. It was published in the 1902 and 1903 annual issues of the *Proceedings of the Institute of Oriental Languages*. Brode's Latinized rendering of Tippu Tip's Swahili text was later translated into English and French. Brode also wrote a German-language biography of Tippu Tip, based on the autobiography and supplemented with information from his interviews with Tippu Tip. It was published in Berlin in 1905, and an English translation was published in London in 1907.[6]

Pierre Savorgnan de Brazza died in a hospital in Dakar, Senegal, on September 14, 1905, while returning home from his inspection mission to the French Congo. The illness that had kept him confined to his room in Brazzaville got worse on the ship back to France. In conversations with his fellow commissioners, he kept repeating the phrase "The French Congo must not become a new Mongala!" referring to the notorious Anversoise concession company in the Congo Free State. French doctors in Conakry, Guinea, recommended that he be taken to the French hospital in Dakar, which had better medicines and equipment. When he was carried off the ship in Dakar with his wife and one aide accompanying him, he waved goodbye to his colleagues as if he were seeing them for the last time. He died the next day, and his body was sent to France for burial. The doctors disagreed as to whether he had died of malaria or dysentery, but his wife, Thérèse, believed that he had been poisoned to prevent him from returning to France to fight for reforms.[7]

Brazza was laid to rest in Paris on October 3, 1905. After a funeral mass at the Basilica of Saint Clotilde, the cortège wended its way through the Place de la Concorde and past the Louvre, followed by a long procession as far as the eye could see. The route was lined with people on both sides, and the windows and balconies of the buildings were crowded with onlookers. When the procession arrived at Père Lachaise Cemetery at 1:15 p.m., the eulogies began.[8]

The minister of colonies, Étienne Clémentel, was the first of four speakers. "Brazza is not completely dead," he told the crowd. "If he is no longer the chief, he has become an example; and, consecrated by his tragic end, his dream of yesterday remains the ideal of tomorrow." Clémentel ended his remarks by invoking French history: "In the course of its long history, France has always looked to something higher. . . . Brazza's great example has been followed by his disciples and his emulators. It prevents us from ever losing hope in the eternal traditions of justice and humanity which are the glory of France." Standing in front of that vast crowd, Clèmentel omitted to mention that he had already disbanded the Brazza Commission and confiscated its documents.[9]

With the original explorers and state builders out of the picture, the fate of the peoples of the Congo basin rainforest was left in the hands of colonial bureaucrats and metropolitan parliaments. On February 20, 1906, the issue of Congo reform was debated in the parliaments of both Belgium and France. Both debates were grounded in the reports of their respective Commissions of Inquiry, yet the outcomes were very different. The overlapping debates revealed a general consensus that colonial rule was here to stay; the only question was what form it should take.

1

Brussels, Chamber of Representatives, February 20, 1906

"Gentlemen," intoned Emile Vandervelde, a socialist politician who was the head of the Belgian Labor Party, "the question which I have the honor of bringing before the House is not a party question. . . . The whole subject resolves itself into this—whether the system adopted in the Congo involves nefarious consequences, as well for the natives, who are its victims, as for Belgium, its alleged gainer." He reminded the representatives that he had brought that same question before the Chamber several times in previous years, but each time he had been accused of being anti-royalist, unpatriotic, and in league with the British while the evidence that he had produced had been dismissed as exaggerated or untrue.[10]

Now, however, the situation was different because he could invoke "the opinion of the three men of conscience, heart, and character who formed part of the Commission of Inquiry which the British government compelled the Congo state to send out." After announcing that copies of the Commission's report would be provided to every member of the Chamber, he lamented that the report was incomplete, because it gave the Commission's conclusions and a brief summary of the evidence but not the testimony itself.

Based on the Commission of Inquiry's report, Vandervelde argued that a "frightful gulf" separated a system of rational colonization from the system that existed in the Congo. "A system of rational colonization," he explained, "would be to recognize native land tenure and to recognize the natives' right of exchanging the products of their free labor on fair terms." The Congo system, in contrast, "is founded upon the confiscation of the land of the natives, upon forced labor, and a system of compulsion which brings about the most frightful abuses." After listing the major forms of coercion as revealed in the report, he asked, "Is there in Belgium a single man who dares to defend the system of hostages, sentries, and punitive expeditions; and who can say that it is right, that it is just, that it is necessary when one burns a village, when one massacres its inhabitants, to kill the innocent as well as the guilty, leaving God to recognize his own?" At that point, applause erupted from the members representing the extreme left.

Then Vandervelde moved on to examine the major beneficiaries of the system—the concession companies and the Crown Domain. As for the concession companies—Anversoise and Abir—he noted that from 1898 to 1903, the Anversoise Company paid an average annual dividend of 425 francs on each 500-franc share. As for Abir, each share paid dividends averaging 1,229 francs from 1898 to 1903. For both companies, the Congo Free State owned half the shares. After quoting a passage from the Commission of Inquiry's report concerning Abir's imprisonment of women hostages and its use of the chicotte, he said, "Add to this, punitive expeditions, burning of villages, the massacre of natives, hands cut off by the sentinels from dead bodies or from people yet alive, and you know the sources of the riches of the shareholders and administrators of Abir."

He then focused his scrutiny on the Crown Domain, which was controlled by King Leopold himself. "Alongside the territories exploited by the concessions," he told the representatives, "we have the astonishing creation that calls itself the Crown Domain. . . . How was this domain constituted? We do not know. How has it been exploited during the last few years? We do not know either, for no European, save the agents of the State, had entered it before 1903." In the absence of hard data, Vandervelde relied on an estimate made by Félicien Cattier, the professor of colonial jurisprudence at the Free University of Brussels, who used the size of the territory to estimate that it had brought 70 million francs of profit to its founder during the ten-year period from 1896 to 1905. Subsequent research has uncovered very few reliable numbers. In 1906, the Belgian minister of justice saw a map of the Crown Domain showing five districts that produced a total of 650 tons of rubber in 1905, which brought in over 6 million francs. In 1957, the Belgian historian Jean Stengers estimated the total revenue from the Crown Domain at 40 million francs for the period of 1901–1907. Because Cattier's figure was based on a longer time span, it may not have been too far off.[11]

To spend the profits from the Crown Domain, King Leopold had created the Crown Foundation, which the Belgian prime minister, Paul de Smet de Naeyer, described in 1903 as an institution to create or subsidize "artistic works, construction projects, and general-purpose institutions in Belgium or the Congo" and to "extend the advantages of the Congo to Belgium." In the absence of any financial records from the Foundation, Cattier's research into real estate transactions revealed that the Foundation had purchased over 18 million francs' worth of real estate in Brussels and Ostend. Added to those were the properties purchased on behalf of the Crown Foundation by Baron Goffinet, the steward of the Civil List, and King Leopold's family estate on the French Riviera, which would bring the total real estate investment to 35 million francs. Other expenditures attributed to the Crown Foundation included 30 million francs for the renovation and expansion of the king's palace at Laeken, 5 million francs for the *Arcade du Cinquantenaire* monument in Brussels, and an unknown amount for the Congo Museum at Tervuren, which was being built on the site of the Palace of Colonies (which had been built for the Colonial Exhibition of 1897).[12]

There were two other sources of funds for the Crown Foundation. The first was outside loans, which had been forbidden by the 1890 loan agreement. After the Belgian parliament voted in 1901 to

The Arcade du Cinquantenaire in Brussels was built in 1905 by King Leopold II and paid for with profits from the sale of Congolese rubber and ivory. Getty Images/Ullstein Bild (from Berliner Illustrirte Zeitung, 1905)

suspend the provisions of that agreement and reserve the question of annexation for another day, Leopold was free to take out new loans on behalf of the Congo Free State. Cattier estimated the total at 130 million francs. Since the accumulated budget deficit of the Congo Free State was 27 million francs, then 103 million francs were left over for the king to spend on real estate and public works in Belgium. The second source of funds was the king's failed 1888 bond scheme. The release of the third and final installment of the bonds, with a total face value of 80 million francs, had been halted in 1890 for lack of public interest, but it was finally released in 1902. As before, the bonds did not sell well, and so the parliament voted in 1903 to convert them to securities, with a face value of 120 francs each, that paid 3 percent compound interest, guaranteed by Congo Free State itself. Even with that modification, sales were slow, and Leopold still had trunks filled with unsold bonds, which he used to pay for projects and services by tearing off the stubs and giving them out like cash. By these methods, he was gaining funds for the Crown Foundation while loading the government of the Congo Free State with debt that would ultimately be repaid by the Belgian government when it took over the Congo.[13]

After outlining the debt situation of the Congo Free State, Vandervelde addressed the claim that the debt was counterbalanced by the rich portfolio of the Congo Free State. "The majority of this stock," he argued, "consists of shares in Congolese companies; there are shares of Abir, of the Anversoise Company, and similar companies. So long as the present system continues, all goes well. As long as the present frantic exploitation of ivory, copal, and rubber continues, all is well. But when the ivory and rubber do not come forward in the same quantities, when the present system of oppression of the natives has disappeared, things will altogether change. Then will the era of deficits commence; then the portfolio will no longer be equivalent to the public debt, and we shall experience all the disadvantages of a state of affairs from which others will have reaped all the profits." At that point, applause erupted from the extreme left.

Vanderveld emphasized that the Congo Free State was not capable of reforming itself. The Commission of Inquiry, he noted, had upheld the system of forced labor and had proposed "insignificant measures" that were "mere palliatives." He had even less faith in the Reform Commission that King Leopold had established in the wake of the Commission of Inquiry's report. The fourteen members of the Reform Commission included seven current officials of the Congo Free State, along with the director of the Kasai Company (in which the Congo State held half the shares) and the director of Abir, who was a close friend of King Leopold. Astonishingly, there was not a single representative of the Belgian Catholic missions.

In the absence of meaningful reform from the Congo Free State itself, Vanderveld argued that it was necessary to consider annexation by Belgium. Harkening back to the 1901 annexation bill that had been suspended (but neither passed nor rejected), he argued that resurrecting it would allow a proper debate on the future of the Congo and clarify the options available to Belgium. "We are, therefore, in precisely the same position as we were in 1901," he told the chamber. He called for a commission to study "the financial consequences which might accrue to Belgium from the ultimate annexation of the Congo and the accomplishment of the necessary reforms to ensure the preservation of the native peoples and the improvement of the moral and material conditions of their existence." In essence, he was asking for a first step toward Belgium taking over the Congo.

The debate resumed a week later and continued for four more days. The prime minister, Paul de Smet de Naeyer, challenged Professor Cattier's figures on both the profits of the Crown Domain and the king's investments in Belgium, and a variety of speakers presented their views about immediate steps and long-range goals. At the end of the debate, there seemed to be a general agreement that Belgium would annex the Congo in the near future; it was just a matter of working out the terms and conditions. On March 2, 1906, the chamber unanimously approved a very short resolution, with the last clause being the substantive one: "The Chamber . . . decides to proceed without delay to the examination of the projected law of 7th August, 1901, on the government of the colonial possessions of Belgium." That was a coded reference to the annexation of the Congo.[14]

During the next four months, diplomatic activity picked up in European capitals to increase the pressure on Belgium to annex the Congo. In London, the foreign secretary, Sir Edward Grey, received a delegation of a dozen people interested in Congo reform at the Foreign Office on November 20. All of them had been invited, but the meeting was staged to make them look like a delegation of independent petitioners. The group included Lord Monkwell, representing the Congo Reform Association; Sir Charles Dilke, representing the liberal MPs in the House of Commons; the bishop of Southwark, representing the Church of England; John Holt, representing the Liverpool Chamber of Commerce; and T. Fowell Buxton, representing the British and Foreign Anti-Slavery Society, which had belatedly become involved in the cause of Congo reform. In his opening remarks, Dilke acknowledged that they were there because "it was the chambers of commerce, the philanthropists, and others who had created the Congo State," and now they were seeking reform of the state that they had helped to create.

The British foreign secretary told the group that action was needed in response to the report of King Leopold's Commission of Inquiry, and the best course of action was annexation by Belgium. However, he cautioned, if the Belgian government failed to annex the Congo, "then I think it will be our duty to sound out the other Powers as to what their view in the matter is." He was, in effect, threatening to reconvene the participants in the 1884–1885 Berlin Conference. Grey's warning to the Belgian government was printed in the *Times* the next morning and reprinted in several Belgian newspapers. King Leopold and the Belgian government could not fail to get the message.[15]

More bad news for King Leopold quickly followed. A dispatch from Belgium's ambassador to Germany on December 3 revealed that if Britain called an international conference on the Congo, Germany would follow its lead. On December 4, a Belgian newspaper reported that US president Theodore Roosevelt had said that he would give serious consideration to a request for an international conference. On December 5, the Belgian ambassador to France delivered a tirade against the British during a meeting with the French foreign minister, only to be told that France would likely side with the British if such a conference were called.

Paul de Favereau, the Belgian foreign minister, was worried that the European great powers were warming to the idea of convening an international conference on the Congo. At the Berlin Conference in 1884–1885, King Leopold had mobilized the great powers in support of his Congo Free State project; now, those same powers were mobilizing to take it away. On December 6, 1906, Favereau told the king that an international conference would probably be held in Britain, and he feared that the outcome would be unfavorable to Belgium. The only way to avoid that fate was the rapid annexation of the Congo by the Belgian government. He then proposed that the government of Belgium should make an announcement to that effect. The king replied, "I have no objection to the announcement. The government has said that they favor annexation, and that they are waiting for the right moment to propose it. If a conference is held, we will not attend."[16]

Nearly a year would pass before a treaty declaring that King Leopold II would cede the Congo Free State to the Belgian government was signed on November 28, 1907; nearly another year would pass before the Belgian parliament approved the Colonial Charter, which outlined a system of Belgian colonial administration for the Congo. Those acts cleared the way for Belgium to annex the Congo on November 15, 1908. The negotiations over annexation were long and tortuous, but after December 1906, the outcome was no longer in doubt. Knowing that his personal rule over the Congo was coming to an end, King Leopold secretly formed the Niederfullbach Foundation—a personal foundation registered in Germany—and began transferring assets from the Crown Foundation in an attempt to place them out of the reach of the Belgian government. During the summer of 1908, he ordered his aides to burn the records of his involvement with the Congo Free State.[17]

2

Paris, the French National Assembly, February 19–21, 1906

"Remember, gentlemen, the emotion that overtook the country when we learned of the acts imputed to three colonial bureaucrats named Prache, Gaud, and Toqué." The speaker was Gustave Rouanet, the socialist deputy from the Department of the Seine. He was opening a debate in the French National Assembly that would continue for three days. Having carefully read the reports and documents brought back from the French Congo by the Brazza Commission, Rouanet wanted to share the highlights and introduce a resolution to make all of the documents public. The appointment of the Brazza Commission, he told the deputies, had reassured the public conscience at a troubled moment. "We believed that light— all the light—would be shone on the horrors of the dark continent, and that those responsible would no longer enjoy their impunity." Shouts of "*Très bien! Très bien!*" rang out in the chamber.[18]

Ever since Brazza's death in Dakar on September 14, 1905, the fate of the Commission had been uncertain. Because it was operating on a tight schedule, each of the commissioners had been instructed to write his report during the final ten days at Brazzaville. Then, Brazza was going to combine the individual reports into one final report, but his illness and death prevented it. Before leaving the ship in Dakar, Brazza had appointed Charles Hoarau-Desruisseaux, the inspector-general of colonies, to be his replacement, but that move had not been approved by the minister of colonies.

When the commissioners arrived at the quay in Pouillac (near Bordeaux) on September 22, they faced an onslaught of press coverage. The commissioner-general of the French Congo, Émile Gentil, had left Brazzaville ahead of the Commission to prepare the government's response to the anticipated report and plant stories to discredit the Commission. As a result, individual commissioners were portrayed in the press as biased, naïve, and untrustworthy, and Brazza was accused of plotting to replace Gentil as commissioner-general of the French Congo. In the fog of charges and countercharges, the minister of colonies assembled the commissioners on September 23 and told them that because of Brazza's death, the Commission would be disbanded immediately, and they should turn over all their documents and reports.[19]

The Ministry of Colonies formed a new commission headed by Jean-Marie de Lanessan, a former governor-general of Indochina.

Of the seven members, two were inspectors-general and five were former governors-general of French colonies. Although some partisans of Brazza saw this as a simple attempt to suppress the Commission's work, the minister of colonies, Étienne Clémentel, had a reason to want a serious report. He had been planning for some time to do a major reorganization of the four colonies that made up the French Congo and get a larger budget, and he needed the report to bolster his case.[20]

The Lanessan Commission completed its work in less than three months. Following its penultimate meeting, it sent out a press release on December 10, 1905, which announced that the report would give a lively critique of the administrative system of the French Congo, but it would not blame Commissioner-General Gentil, who "despite his requests, never received the financial means necessary to develop a colony that had been too long abandoned." The report would severely condemn the acts of certain agents of the concession companies, and it would recommend a complete reorganization of the administrative system and the construction of roads and a railroad.[21]

The Lanessan Commission's report was submitted to the minister of colonies on December 19, and he sent it on to the Ministry of Foreign Affairs, where the censors tried to sanitize it by deleting or modifying forty-seven different passages. Even so, they warned that the report revealed violations of the 1885 Berlin Act. Because much of the French Congo lay within the Congo River basin, they were obligated by the Act to "look out for the welfare of the indigenous populations and the improvement of their moral and material conditions." A note written by the censors stated, "Even the revised and partially amended report establishes that we have done things that were not permitted, and we have not done what was prescribed." The implication was that the Lanessan Report should never be released to the public.[22]

The Lanessan Commission's report was divided into four parts. Part One reviewed the evidence of a few selected crimes uncovered by the commission and either dismissed the evidence as inconclusive or absolved Commissioner-General Gentil of any responsibility for them. Part Two dealt with issues of the budget, revenues, and finances, and particularly with the question of taxes paid in money versus taxes in kind. Part Three examined trade, and especially the concession companies. Part Four dealt with the administrative reorganization of the French Congo, proposing changes in the administrative structure, judicial organization, military organization, and transportation.

As for the concession companies, the report focused on their overall impact rather than specific crimes and atrocities. Of the forty original concession companies, thirty-three were still functioning. Only six of them were profitable in 1904, making a combined profit of 2,529,878 francs, while the total balance for the other concession companies was a loss of 12,508,193 francs. From 1899 to 1902, rubber exports had remained steady at 660 tons but rose to 842 tons in 1903 and 1,249 tons in 1904. Still, the results were paltry in comparison to the Congo Free State, which had exported 2,600 tons of rubber in 1904. In the light of the poor performance of the concession companies, the Lanessan Commission recommended (a) that no more concessions be given out, (b) that the government should exert control over the companies to respect the person and liberty of the natives, and (c) that the government should not force the natives to work for the concession companies.[23]

Quickly responding to the recommendations in the report, the minister of colonies issued two decrees on February 11, 1906, outlining a series of reforms. The first decree reorganized the French Congo into three colonies—Gabon, Middle Congo, and Ubangi-Chari-Chad (which was subdivided into Ubangi-Chari and Chad). Each of the three colonies had its own budget, and each was under the control of a lieutenant governor who answered to the commissioner-general in Brazzaville. The second decree called for courts to be established in three troubled but underserved parts of the territory.[24]

Then came a long set of ministerial instructions, which the minister of colonies addressed directly to Gentil. On the question of porters to Lake Chad, he called for the development of a new water route via the Niger and Benue Rivers. As for the concession companies, the minister clarified that the government agents were solely responsible for maintaining the political order and that they should not subcontract the job to the concession companies. He called for separating the collection of the head tax, which was a government function, from the collection of rubber, which was an economic activity. Second, he wanted to establish a service of inspection and control to oversee the actions and practices of the concession companies. Third, he threatened to revoke the charters of concession companies that did not live up to their obligations to treat the Africans humanely. Clémentel had adroitly used the Commission of Inquiry to get the administrative and budgetary reorganization that he wanted while taking minimal steps to deal with the abuses and atrocities uncovered by the Brazza Commission.[25]

Such was the state of affairs when the debate in the National Assembly opened on February 19, 1906. Deputy Rouanet, the speaker, had seen part of the Lanessan Commission's report but not the conclusions. He had also read the reports of the individual members of the Brazza Commission and the supporting documents that they had collected during their inquiry. After summarizing the case of the women hostages in Bangui, Rouanet honed in on the underlying cause. "The harvest of rubber in the form of tax paid to the companies constitutes . . . the primary and incessant preoccupation of the government officials. They receive promotion from the Commissioner-General in proportion to the speed with which they bring in the tax in nature or money." Addressing the minister of colonies, he said, "What you call individual faults, what you consider as isolated events, M. de Brazza proclaimed that it is a system, a regime that has functioned since at least 1901."

Turning to the concession companies, he said. "I cannot recount all the acts of pillage and brutality committed by certain agents of the concession companies. In the Ogowe Company, Mr. Ourson carried out raids on individuals who were held for ransom. . . . In the Upper Ogowe Company, Mr. Treuil tortured many natives to death, and Mr. Puget burned villages and subjected natives to a sadism that is painful to recount." He noted that the Fernand Vaz Company had exported 30,000 francs' worth of forest products without giving the Africans any merchandise in exchange. Rouanet concluded that the concessionary regime was "unworthy of France, unworthy of this country, and unworthy of democracy."

During the second day of Rouanet's impassioned oration, he introduced a resolution that called for the publication of all the reports, documents, and supplementary material collected by the Brazza Commission. "The honor and interests of France," he said, "require that light be shone on the results of the Brazza mission." He sat down to applause from the deputies on the left side of the Chamber.

On the third day came several speakers who defended the government of the French Congo. The main one was Étienne Clémentel, the minister of colonies, who made two main points. First, he promised that the alleged crimes reported by the Brazza Commission would be investigated by the courts in the French Congo. Second, he claimed that the structural problems cited by Rouanet had been addressed by the decrees and instructions that he had issued on February 11. He stressed that he was prepared to revoke the charters of concession companies that did not live up to their obligations. As the debate continued, Clémentel announced that he would accept the publication of the Lanessan Commission's report but that he would not accept the publication of the documents from the Brazza mission. With these assurances, the Chamber voted 345 to 167 in favor of rejecting Deputy Rouanet's resolution. There thus was no parliamentary mandate to publish the reports of either commission.[26]

Despite Clémentel's promise, the Lanessan Commission's report was never released. It was held by the Ministry of Colonies until May 1907, when the Africa director ordered it to be printed in ten numbered copies, each marked "Very Confidential." One copy apparently went to the minister of colonies, and the other nine were locked in a vault. The reports and documents collected by the members of the Brazza Commission were eventually put in a box and sent to the Overseas Section of the French National Archives, a separate facility located on Rue Oudinot in Paris. The box was not given an archive number; it was simply labeled "Afrique Supplement— Mission de Brazza." It sat there unnoticed until 1983, when a master's degree student at the University of Aix-Marseille discovered it and used some of the material in her MA thesis. When the archives from the Overseas Section in Paris were moved to a new facility in Aix-en-Provence in the 1980s, the Brazza Commission material was given a number and quietly integrated into the archives.[27]

One way to evaluate the impact of the reforms introduced by Clémentel is to look at the Mpoko Company, which briefly became the subject of intense administrative and judicial oversight. Located just north of Bangui, it was one of the smaller French concession companies, with a territory about half the size of Belgium. Its director, Gullbrand Schiötz, had previously been the second-in-command of King Leopold's Crown Domain until 1900, when he transferred to the Mpoko Company, bringing thirty Congo Free State soldiers with him. In 1906, a young French colonial administrator named Gaston Guibet arrived in the region to take charge of the government's newly created Mpoko District and keep an eye on the company. Soon after he arrived, he heard reports of atrocities related to rubber gathering and informed Mr. Butel, the government inspector in Bangui.

During 1907, Administrator Gibet, Inspector Butel, and Judge Michelet (the government's magistrate in Bangui) formed a Commission of Inquiry that conducted a series of inspections in the Mpoko concession. Over a period of eighteen months, the commission found evidence of 750 proven murders and 1,500 probable murders in the company's southern zone and a roughly similar number for the northern zone. Mpoko's rubber collection system was almost identical to the systems in the Congo Free State. Armed sentries were stationed in each village, and women were held hostage until the rubber was brought in. Villagers who tried to flee were imprisoned or shot. Workers who failed to bring in their full quotas were whipped or tied to a tree and shot. According to Inspector Butel, "Crime had become a system, which was performed in cold blood and chosen from a catalog of coercion methods according to what was seen to be the most productive."[28]

The accused African sentries and European agents were sent to Brazzaville for trial, where several sentries were convicted of murder and given prison sentences. By the end of 1908, all twenty-seven of the European agents accused of crimes had left the Congo by means of acquittals, health furloughs, or simply skipping out on their bail. In May 1909, the trials came to a sudden end when all the cases were dismissed, apparently on orders from the president of France, who wanted to avoid another Toqué-Gaud scandal. After that, there were no more trials of concession company sentries and agents and no more reports of scandals in the French press.

The scandal nevertheless put the Mpoko Company in jeopardy. The French Congo's newly created Commission on Concessions considered revoking the company's charter but ruled that the crimes did not meet the legal standard for termination. In 1910, Mpoko went out of existence when it was absorbed into the Compagnie Forestière du Sangha-Oubangui as part of a massive merger of eleven concession companies.[29]

3

Aftermath: 1908–1929

The Belgian takeover of the Congo Free State did not result in immediate reforms. The government of Belgium replaced King Leopold as the sovereign authority, but the laws and decrees of the Free State remained in force, and the administrative apparatus remained in place. The reformers in Belgium and Britain had hoped that the Belgian government would invest money in developing the Congo, but instead, the new administration continued to drain resources from the Congo to invest in Belgium. As a result, the Congo Reform Association in Britain continued to put pressure on the Belgian government for meaningful reforms, and the British Parliament again accused the Belgian government of violating the terms of the Berlin Act.[30]

Reform came slowly and in a piecemeal fashion. In 1908, the rubber quota in the Abir concession was reduced to six kilos per year in recognition of the depleted rubber vines. By 1910, the wild rubber supplies were so exhausted all over the Belgian Congo that the government made it legal to cut down the vines and extract the latex by grinding the bark. That same year, it declared an end to the rubber tax and replaced it with a tax paid in Congolese francs, which could be earned in a variety of ways. In 1911, the state revoked the concessions of Abir and Anversoise, giving them grants of land in compensation. The two companies then merged to form the Compagnie du Congo Belge, which operated as a legitimate commercial firm that bought and sold rubber and other products. Despite the decreased rubber revenues, the Belgian government began to invest in the Congo, spending 2 million francs on various projects in 1912. In recognition of the reforms, the Congo Reform Association held its last meeting on June 16, 1913, and passed a resolution proclaiming that "this Association . . . records the belief that its main purposes have now been secured, and that its labors may be honorably brought to a conclusion." The reformers had never been opposed to European colonial rule in Africa; they just wanted an end to the egregious atrocities of the Leopoldian rubber concession system.[31]

The final blow to the rubber regime in the Congo basin rainforest came in 1913, when the rubber plantations in Malaya and Indonesia began to flood the world with high-quality rubber, causing the price of Congo wild rubber to drop from 12 francs

per kilo in 1913 to 4.7 francs in 1914. No longer highly profitable, the rubber trade became insignificant in the Belgian Congo
as the government turned its attention to the gold mines of Kilo
and Moto, which opened in 1905 and 1910, respectively, and
the copper mines of Katanga, which opened in 1911 and would
become the world's largest producer of copper. To get workers for
the copper mines, the Belgians set up a private company called
the Katanga Labor Exchange, which recruited workers from all
parts of the Belgian Congo. One of the major suppliers of recruits
to the Exchange was the Luba chief Lumpungu, who conducted
raids to procure workers and sent them to the mines on three-
year contracts. Lumpungu had once been a slave-raiding vassal of
Ngongo Luteta, and he had apparently continued in his former
ways. Many of his recruits died on the way to the mines; others
never returned to their homes, and their deferred wages were collected by Chief Lumpungu himself.[32]

The French Congo was reorganized in 1910 to become the federation of French Equatorial Africa, which was divided into four
colonies: Gabon, the French Congo, Ubangi-Chari, and Chad.
The subsequent drop in the world price of wild rubber did not drive
the concession companies out of business, in part because they
mounted a major campaign to increase the production of palm
oil, which rose from 70 tons in 1913 to nearly 400 tons in 1918.
Because France needed rubber during World War I, the Compagnie
Forestière du Sangha-Oubangui, which controlled roughly half the
territory in the French Congo, pushed its production up from 180
tons in 1914 to 1,225 tons in 1917 with assistance from the colonial
administration. To make rubber production profitable, the state
reduced the customs payments on rubber exports and negotiated a
45 percent reduction in the cost of shipping rubber to Brazzaville
by riverboat. At the same time, the company cut its costs by reducing its European personnel from 136 agents in 1913 to 18 in 1924.
During the 1920s, roughly 75 percent of the rubber exported from
the French Congo came from the Compagnie Forestière.[33]

When the French novelist André Gide traveled through the Compagnie Forestière concession in 1926, he encountered a particularly cruel form of punishment known as the "Bambio Ball." On September 8, 1926, a work gang of ten rubber gatherers arrived at the company post in Bambio, having failed to bring in their quota the month before. This time they brought in a double amount, but they were punished nevertheless. The "ball" began at eight o'clock in the morning and continued the whole day, with the government administrator and the company agent looking on. The rubber collectors were forced to walk round and round the company post under a fierce sun carrying heavy wooden beams. If they fell down, the guards whipped them with chicottes until they got up. When one man was unable to get up, the administrator said, "I don't give a damn" and ordered the "ball" to go on. The inhabitants of Bambio and the chiefs from the neighboring villages who had come for the market witnessed the whole gruesome spectacle.

The next day, Gide made more discoveries. "Terror reigns, and the surrounding villages are deserted," he wrote. "We talked to other chiefs. When they were asked, 'How many men in your village?' they count them by putting down a finger for each one. There are rarely more than ten." Unable to sleep at night and haunted by thoughts of the Bambio Ball, Gide wrote, "The immense pity of what I have seen has taken possession of me; I know things to which I cannot reconcile myself." André Gide had stumbled upon the last flailing of the rubber concession system in the French Congo. The concession companies had been chartered in 1899 for a period of thirty years. When their concession agreements expired in 1929, they were not renewed. Twenty-four years after the Brazza Commission's investigation, the rubber concession companies were finally out of business.[34]

With the rubber companies gone from the Belgian and French Congos, life in the Congo Basin rainforest did not return to the status quo ante, in part because the colonial chiefdoms imposed by the Belgians and the French had introduced new and more authoritarian forms of local governance. In 1912, the Belgian colonial administration divided the Congo into districts, which were subdivided into territories, which were in turn subdivided into chiefdoms, each one ruled by a government-appointed chief. In the French Congo, the colonial government began forcibly amalgamating small, scattered settlements to create large villages ruled by government-appointed chiefs. It also attempted to abolish the numerous petty land chiefs in order to form large tribes, but it had trouble finding land chiefs who were influential enough to be appointed as tribal chiefs. In regrouping the shattered and scattered populations of the rainforest under the authority of government-appointed chiefs, the Belgian and French colonial governments were not rebuilding traditional rainforest political institutions but creating something entirely different. As a consequence, the centuries-long tradition of small, independent political units in the rainforest led by self-made "big men" faded into history.[35]

Despite further administrative reorganizations, colonial chiefdoms remained in place through 1960, when both Congos gained their independence. The Belgian Congo became the Democratic Republic of the Congo on June 30, 1960, and French Congo became the Republic of the Congo on August 15. During the late 1970s, when I was conducting oral history research along the Upper Congo River, people would frequently describe the colonial chiefdoms as their "traditional" or "customary" system of local rule, unaware of the earlier rainforest tradition of decentralized governance that had been erased and then forgotten. Although the decentralized political systems of the forest peoples had survived the assaults by the ivory hunters and the rubber companies, they had succumbed to the pressure of colonial reformers.

ACKNOWLEDGMENTS

MANY OF THE THEMES THAT have animated and structured this book were first presented in the Jensen Memorial Lectures at the Frobenius Institute at Johann Wolfgang Goethe University in Frankfurt, Germany, in May and June 2006. My discussions with Director Karl-Heinz Kohl, Deputy Director Mamadou Diawara, and their colleagues at the Institute were particularly valuable in helping me to define and frame the project. During my research in various archives in Europe and Africa, I was aided in particular by Maurits Wynants, the late curator of the Henry M. Stanley Archives at the Royal Museum of Central Africa in Tervuren, Belgium, the archivists in the Archives Africaines, housed in the ministry of Foreign Affairs in Brussels, and the archivists at the Archives Nationales d'Outre-Mer in Aix-en-Province, France.

This project owes a huge debt to the many scholars and historians who patiently edited and published the letters, diaries, and reports of many of the characters in this book. The writings of Pierre Savorgnan de Brazza, Henry Morton Stanley, David Livingstone, Emin Pasha, Henry Shelton Sanford, Prosper-Philippe Augouard, Tippu Tip, Wilhelm Junker, Roger Casement, and others became accessible through their efforts. Of special note is François Bontinck's edited translation of Tippu Tip's autobiography, which includes 117 pages of footnotes giving cross-references on the various people, places, and events mentioned by Tippu Tip.

A second debt is to the biographers of many of the key figures in this book. Livingstone, Stanley, Brazza, Tippu Tip, and King Leopold II have all been the subject of well-researched biographies, which have cast important light on their activities, motivation, and character. A third debt is to the historians who have produced valuable syntheses of regional history in equatorial Africa during the late nineteenth and early twentieth centuries. They include Robert O. Collins on Sudan, Norman Bennett and John C. Wilkerson on East Africa, Daniel Vangroenweghe on the rubber concession companies in the Belgian and French Congos, Jules Marchal on the Congo Free State, and Samuel Nelson on the inner Congo basin.

Above all, the project owes a debt to the late Jan Vansina. During his long career of research and writing on the ethnography and history of equatorial Africa, he developed many of the concepts that have influenced the framing and narrative of this book. It is humbling to think that the results of a years-long research project can turn out to be a mere elaboration on a succinct comment once made by Vansina.

The research was made possible by grants from the Yale Center for the Study of Globalization, Fulbright-Hays, and Yale's Whitney and Betty MacMillan Center for International and Area Studies. The research and writing of this book were transformed into a great adventure by my wife, Sandra, who accompanied me on trips to archives in Europe and Africa and managed to maintain her good humor during my long hours at the computer keyboard.

NOTES

INTRODUCTION

1. David Livingstone to Lord Frederick Stanley, Bambarre, Manyuema Country, November 15, 1870, in "Despatches Addressed by Dr. Livingstone, Her Majesty's Consul, Inner Africa, to Her Majesty's Secretary of State for Foreign Affairs, in 1870, 1871, and 1872," 19th Century House of Commons Sessional Papers, Command Papers, vol. LXX (1872), paper no. C 598 (London: Harrison & Sons, 1872), 2; Henry M. Stanley, *Through the Dark Continent*, 2 vols. (New York: Harper & Brothers, 1878), vol. 2, 130.

2. "The Congo Basin Forest," *Global Forest Atlas*, accessed August 28, 2018, https://globalforestatlas.yale.edu/region/congo.

3. Claire Grégoire, "The Bantu Languages of the Forest," in *The Bantu Languages*, ed. Derek Nurse and Gérard Philippson (New York: Routledge, 2003), 349–370; Jan Vansina, *Paths in the Rainforests: Toward a History of Political Tradition in Equatorial Africa* (Madison, WI: University of Wisconsin Press, 1990), 5–6. The ethnographic unity of this vast region was first noticed by the explorer Henry Morton Stanley in 1890. See Henry M. Stanley, *In Darkest Africa; or, the Quest, Rescue, and Retreat of Emin, Governor of Equatoria*, 2 vols. (New York: Charles Scribner's Sons, 1890), vol. 2, 97.

4. Vansina, *Paths in the Rainforests*, 73–83.

5. The segmented trading system is described in Robert Harms, *River of Wealth, River of Sorrow: The Central Zaire Basin in the Era of the Slave and Ivory Trade, 1500–1891* (New Haven: Yale University Press, 1981).

6. Félicien Challaye, *Le Congo Français: La Question Internationale du Congo* (Paris: Félix Alcan, 1909), 107. The phrase *land of tears* comes from *Inferno*, by Dante Alighieri, Canto III. See Dante Alighieri,

Inferno, trans. Henry Wadsworth Longfellow (New York: Modern Library, 2003), 17.

7. On the European Scramble for Africa, see Thomas Packenham, *The Scramble for Africa, 1876–1912* (New York: Random House, 1991); Ronald Robinson and John Gallagher, *Africa and the Victorians: The Official Mind of Imperialism* (New York: St. Martin's Press, 1967); Muriel Evelyn Chamberlain, *The Scramble for Africa* (London: Longman, 1974).

8. On the role of Arabs and Turks, see John C. Wilkinson, *The Arabs and the Scramble for Africa* (Bristol, CT: Equinox, 2015); Mostafa Minawi, *The Ottoman Scramble for Africa: Empire and Diplomacy in the Sahara and the Hijaz* (Stanford, CA: Stanford University Press, 2016); Norman R. Bennett, *Arab versus European: Diplomacy and War in Nineteenth-Century East Central Africa* (New York: Africana, 1986).

9. There are numerous biographies of these figures. On Stanley, see John Bierman, *Dark Safari: The Life behind the Legend of Henry Morton Stanley* (London: Hodder & Stoughton, 1991); Frank McLynn, *Stanley: The Making of an African Explorer, 1841–1877* (New York: Cooper Square Press, 2001), and *Stanley: Sorcerer's Apprentice* (London: Constable, 1991); James L. Newman, *Imperial Footprints: Henry Morton Stanley's African Journeys* (Washington, DC: Brassey's, 2004); Tim Jeal, *Stanley: The Impossible Life of Africa's Greatest Explorer* (New Haven: Yale University Press, 2007). On Tippu Tip, see Heinrich Brode, *Tippoo Tib: The Story of His Career in Central Africa, Narrated from His Own Accounts* (London: Edward Arnold, 1907); François Renault, *Tippo Tip: Un Potentat Arabe en Afrique Centrale au XIXe Siècle* (Paris: Société Française d'Histoire d'Outre-Mer, 1987); Stuart Laing, *Tippu Tip: Ivory, Slavery, and Discovery in the Scramble for Africa* (Surbiton, UK: Medina, 2017). On Brazza, see Général de Chambrun, *Brazza* (Paris: Plon, 1930); Richard West, *Brazza of the Congo: European Exploration and Exploitation in French Equatorial Africa* (London: Cape, 1972); Jean Martin, *Savorgnan de Brazza, 1852–1905* (Paris: Les Indes Savantes, 2005); Isabelle Dion, *Pierre Savorgnan de Brazza: Au Coeur du Congo* (Aix-en-Provence: Archives Nationales d'Outre-Mer, 2007).

10. On the Congo Free State, see Adam Hochschild, *King Leopold's Ghost: A Story of Greed, Terror, and Heroism in Colonial Africa* (New York: Houghton, Mifflin, 1998); Martin Ewans, *European Atrocity, African Catastrophe: Leopold II, the Congo Free State and Its Aftermath* (New York: Routledge Curzon, 2002); Daniel Vangroenweghe, *Du Sang sur les Lianes: Léopold II et Son Congo* (Brussels: Didier Hattier, 1986); Jules Marchal, *L'Etate Libre du Congo: Paradis Perdu: l'Histoire du Congo 1876–1900*, 2 vols. (Borgloon, Belgium: Editions Paula Bellings, 1996); Jules

Marchal, *E. D. Morel Contre Léopold II: l'Histoire du Congo 1900–1910*, 2 vols. (Paris: L'Harmattan, 1996). On the French Congo, see Catherine Coquery-Vidrovitch, *Le Congo au Temps des Grandes Compagnies Concessionnaires, 1898–1930* (Paris: Mouton, 1972). On the Arab Zone, see P. Ceulemans, *La Question Arabe et le Congo, 1883–1892* (Brussels: Académie Royale des Sciences Coloniales, 1959); Bennett, *Arab versus European*; Wilkinson, *The Arabs and the Scramble for Africa*.

11. David Livingstone, *The Last Journals of David Livingstone in Central Africa from Eighteen Hundred and Sixty-Five to His Death*, ed. Horace Waller (New York: Harper Brothers, 1875), 369.

12. See Richard Huzzey, *Freedom Burning: Anti-Slavery and Empire in Victorian Britain* (Ithaca, NY: Cornell University Press, 2012).

13. Neal Ascherson, *The King, Incorporated: Leopold II in the Age of Trusts* (London: Allen and Unwin, 1963); Barbara Emerson, *Leopold II of the Belgians: King of Colonialism* (London: Weidenfeld and Nicolson, 1979); Hochschild, *King Leopold's Ghost*.

14. Johannes Fabian, *Out of Our Minds: Reason and Madness in the Exploration of Central Africa* (Berkeley: University of California Press, 2000), 214–216; Prosper Philippe Augouard, "Voyage à Stanley Pool," *Les Missions Catholiques* 14 (1882): 140; David Livingstone, *Livingstone Letters, 1843 to 1872: David Livingstone's Correspondence in the Brenthurst Library, Johannesburg*, ed. Maurice Boucher (Houghton, South Africa: Brenthurst Press, 1985), 206; Henry M. Stanley, *Through the Dark Continent*, 2 vols. (New York: Harper & Brothers, 1878), vol. 1, 47–48; David M. Gordon, "Interpreting Documentary Sources on the Early History of the Congo Free State: The Case of Ngongo Luteta's Rise and Fall," *History in Africa* 14 (2014): 5–33.

15. Megan Vaughan and Henrietta Moore, *Cutting Down Trees: Gender, Nutrition, and Agricultural Change in the Northern Province of Zambia, 1890–1990* (Portsmouth, NH: Heinemann, 1994), xviii–xxiv. Ann Laura Stoler has urged scholars to take a humbler stance and read "along the grain" before reading against it. Ann Laura Stoler, *Along the Archival Grain: Epistemic Anxieties and Colonial Common Sense* (Princeton: Princeton University Press, 2009), 50–53.

16. Frits Andersen, *The Dark Continent? Images of Africa in European Narratives about the Congo*, trans. William Frost and Martin Skovhus (Aarhus, Denmark: Aarhus University Press, 2016), 14–18, 181; Fabian, *Out of Our Minds*, 221–226. The only known eyewitness account of cannibalism is ambiguous. James Jameson's diary records that he and Tippu Tip witnessed the murder and dismemberment of an enslaved girl (which they themselves had instigated), but he never actually saw the flesh being

cooked and eaten. Jameson died of fever a few months later, and Tippu Tip later denied the whole affair. See James Jameson, *The Story of the Rear Column of the Emin Pasha Relief Expedition* (New York: United States Book Co., 1891), 291; Andersen, *The Dark Continent?*, 240–247; Brode, *Tippoo Tib*, 234–236. On cannibalism as a discourse that was coproduced by Europeans and Africans, see Jared Staller, *Converging on Cannibals: Terrors of Slaving in Atlantic Africa, 1509–1670* (Athens, OH: Ohio University Press, 2019), 7–11. On atrocity accounts, see Robert M. Burroughs, *Travel Writing and Atrocities: Eyewitness Accounts of Colonialism in the Congo, Angola, and Putumayo* (New York: Routledge, 2011), 49–97; Andersen, *The Dark Continent?*, 371–398.

17. Vansina, *Paths in the Rainforests*, 239–248.

CHAPTER 1: MANYEMA

1. United Nations Environment Program, *Africa: Atlas of Our Changing Environment* (Nairobi: UNEP, 2008), 4–11.

2. Richard Burton, *The Lake Regions of Central Africa* (New York: Harper & Brothers, 1860), 309–310.

3. David Livingstone, *The Last Journals of David Livingstone in Central Africa*, ed. Horace Waller (New York: Harper & Brothers, 1875), 173; Tippu Tip, *Maisha ya Hamed bin Muhammed el Murjebi, yaani Tippu Tip, kwa maneno yake mwenyewe*, trans. W. H. Whitely (Nairobi: East African Literature Bureau, 1966), 23.

4. Henry M. Stanley, *How I Found Livingstone* (New York: Scribner, Armstrong & Co., 1872), 5–8.

5. Abdul Sheriff, *Slaves, Spices, and Ivory in Zanzibar* (Athens, OH: Ohio University Press, 1987), 253–256; Burton, *Lake Regions of Central Africa*, 540; Livingstone, *Last Journals*, 350.

6. Livingstone, *Last Journals*, 170–171, 207; Joseph Thomson, *To the Central African Lakes and Back: The Narrative of the Royal Geographical Society's East Central African Expedition, 1878–80* (Boston: Houghton, Mifflin & Co., 1881), 285–286.

7. Burton, *Lake Regions of Central Africa*, xiv, 226–228, 233–235, 314–316; Alfred J. Swann, *Fighting the Slave-Hunters in Central Africa*, 2nd ed. (London: Seeley & Co., 1910), 58.

8. Sheriff, *Slaves, Spices, and Ivory in Zanzibar*, 48–73.

9. James Christie, "Slavery in Zanzibar as It Is," in H. A. Fraser, Bishop Tozer, and James Christie, *The East African Slave Trade and the Measures Proposed for Its Extinction as Viewed by Residents of Zanzibar* (London: Harrison and Pall Mall, 1871), 31–45; Emily Ruete, *Memoirs of an Arabian Princess from Zanzibar* (Zanzibar: Galley Publications, 1998); Livingstone, *Last Journals*, 173, 422. A summary of sources on

Khamis wad Mtaa is found in Tippu Tip, *L'Autobiographie de Hamed ben Mohammed el-Murjebi Tippu Tip (ca. 1840–1905)*, translated and annotated by Francois Bontinck (Brussels: Académie Royale des Sciences d'Outre-Mer, 1974), 198–199.

10. Sheriff, *Slaves, Spices, and Ivory in Zanzibar*, 48–73; Matthew Hopper, "Slaves of One Master: Globalization and the African Diaspora in Arabia in the Age of Empire," in *Indian Ocean Slavery in the Age of Abolition*, ed. Robert Harms, Bernard K. Freamon, and David W. Blight (New Haven: Yale University Press, 2013), 223–240; Minutes of Evidence, July 20, 1871, 53, in "Report from the Select Committee on Slave Trade (East Coast of Africa)," August 4, 1871, *Parliamentary Papers/House of Commons Papers*, vol. 12, 1871, paper 420.

11. For a comprehensive study of the East African ivory caravans, see Stephen J. Rockel, *Carriers of Culture: Labor on the Road in Nineteenth-Century East Africa* (Portsmouth, NH: Heinemann, 2006).

12. David Livingstone and Charles Livingstone, *Narrative of an Expedition to the Zambesi and Its Tributaries* (New York: Harper & Brothers, 1866), 140; "Despatches Addressed by Dr. Livingstone, Her Majesty's Consul, Inner Africa, to Her Majesty's Secretary of State for Foreign Affairs, in 1870, 1871, and 1872," *Parliamentary Papers/Command Papers*, vol. LXX (1872), paper C-598, 19–24; "Memorandum by Kazi Shahabudin respecting the Banians of Zanzibar and the Slave Trade," in *Correspondence Respecting Sir Bartle Frere's Mission to the East Coast of Africa, 1872–73*, Confidential, Printed for the Use of the Foreign Office, July 1873, UK National Archives, Kew, FO881/2270, 181–4.

13. Edouard Foa, *La Traverseé de l'Afrique du Zambeze au Congo Français* (Paris: Librairie Plon, 1900), 193–194; "Manyema," *Encyclopedia Britannica*, 11th ed. (London: Encyclopaedia Britannica Co., 1911).

14. "Despatches Addressed by Dr. Livingstone," 1–5.

15. Stanley, *Through the Dark Continent*, vol. 2, 1–2. On the many meanings of *waungwana*, see Thomas McDow, *Buying Time: Debt and Mobility in the Western Indian Ocean* (Athens, OH: Ohio University Press, 2018), 93–97.

16. Helen Tilly, *Africa as a Living Laboratory: Empire, Development, and the Problem of Scientific Knowledge, 1870–1950* (Chicago: University of Chicago Press, 2011), 36–38. For a comprehensive study of the search for the source of the Nile, see Tim Jeal, *Explorers of the Nile* (New Haven: Yale University Press, 2011).

17. David Livingstone to Roderick Murchison, February 2, 1867, Royal Geographical Society Archives, London, DL 4/4/6.

18. Livingstone to Bartle Frere, July 1868, Royal Geographical Society Archives, London, DL 4/7/2.

19. Livingstone, *Last Journals*, 250; Stanley, *Through the Dark Continent*, vol. 2, 98.

20. Livingstone, *Last Journals*, 400. Henry Stanley had not yet settled on a middle name. At various times he tried Morely, Morelake, and Moreland before selecting Morton. See John Bierman, *Dark Safari: The Life behind the Legend of Henry Morton Stanley* (London: Hodder & Stoughton, 1991), 64, 68.

21. Livingstone, *Last Journals*, 292.

22. Queen Victoria, *The Queen's Speeches in Parliament*, comp. and ed. F. Sidney Ensor (London: W. H. Allen & Co., 1882), 266–270.

23. Matthew Hopper, *Slaves of One Master: Globalization and Slavery in Arabia in the Age of Empire* (New Haven: Yale University Press, 2015), 39, 196–201; Lindsay Doulton, "The Flag That Sets Us Free: Antislavery, Africans, and the Royal Navy in the Western Indian Ocean," in *Indian Ocean Slavery*, ed. Harms et al., 102–103.

24. Stanley, *Through the Dark Continent*, vol. 2, 428–435, 559–560; quotation in Richard Hall, *Stanley: An Adventurer Explored* (London: Collins, 1974), 225.

25. *Morning Post* (London), April 20, 1874. The letter, dated Unyanyembe, South-Eastern Africa, April 9, 1872, was published in London in *The Morning Post*, the *Daily News*, *The Standard*, and the *Daily Telegraph* on April 10 and 11, 1874, and in the *New York Herald* on April 25, 1874; Livingstone, *Last Journals*, 419.

26. Stanley, *How I Found Livingstone*, 460–461.

27. Emile Banning, *L'Afrique et la Conférence Géographique de Bruxelles* (Brussels: Librairie Européenne C. Muqardt, 1877), 119–122.

28. Jean Stengers, "L'Agrandissement de la Belgique: Rêves et Réalités," in *Nouveau Regards sur Léopold I et Léopold II*, ed. Gustaaf Janssens and Jean Stengers (Brussels: Fondation Roi Baudoin, 1997), 237–240. The quotations are in Vincent Viaene, "King Leopold's Imperialism and the Origins of the Belgian Colonial Party," *The Journal of Modern History* 80 (2008): 753–755.

29. Barbara Emerson, *Leopold II of the Belgians: King of Colonialism* (London: Weidenfeld & Nicolson, 1979), 58.

30. Jean Stengers, "King Leopold's Imperialism," in *Studies in the Theory of Imperialism*, ed. Roger Owen and Bob Sutcliffe (London: Longman, 1972), 248–276; Viaene, "King Leopold's Imperialism," 755–757.

31. Jean Stengers, "Leopold II entre l'Extreme-Orient et l'Afrique (1875–1876)," in *La Conférence de Géographie de 1876: Recueil d'Etudes* (Brussels: Académie Royale des Sciences d'Outre-Mer, 1976), 303.

32. Auguste Roeykens, *Léopold II et la Conférence Géographique de Bruxelles, 1976* (Brussels: Académie royale des Sciences Coloniales, 1956), 71–72.

33. Émile Banning, *Africa and the Brussels Geographical Conference*, trans. Richard Henry Major (London: Sampson, Low, Marston, Searle, & Rivington, 1877), 136.

34. Jean Stengers, "Introduction," in *Conférence de Géographie de 1876*, xx–xxi.

35. Banning, *Brussels Geographical Conference*, 162–164.

36. Rutherford Alcock, "African Exploration Fund, August 1877," *Proceedings of the Royal Geographical Society of London* 21, no. 6 (1876–1877), 601–602; Rosaline Eredapa Nwoye, *The Public Image of Pierre Savorgnan de Brazza and the Establishment of French Imperialism in the Congo* (Aberdeen: Aberdeen University African Studies Group, 1981), 50–53; Jean Stengers, "Introduction," xxiii–xxiv; François Bontinck, "Le Comité National Américain de l'A.I.A." in *Conférence de Géographie de 1876*, 490–492.

37. Roger Anstey, *Britain and the Congo in the Nineteenth Century* (Oxford: Clarendon Press, 1962), 61–63; Alcock, "African Exploration Fund," 603–604.

38. Albert Chapaux, *Le Congo: Historique, Diplomatique, Physique, Politique, Economique, Humanitaire & Colonial* (Brussels: Charles Rozez, 1894), 132; Oscar Lenz, "L'Expédition Autrichienne au Congo," *Bulletin de la Société Royale Belge de Géographie* 11 (1887): 221; Herbert Ward, *Five Years with the Congo Cannibals* (London: Chatto & Windus, 1890), 173–174.

39. Tippu Tip, *Maisha*, 69; Ward, *Congo Cannibals*, 173–174.

40. Heinrich Brode, *Tippoo Tib: The Story of His Career in Zanzibar and Central Africa, Narrated from His Own Accounts* (London: Edward Arnold, 1907), v.

41. Tippu Tip, *Maisha*, 5; Brode, *Tippoo Tib*, viii; Stuart Laing, *Tippu Tip: Ivory, Slavery, and Discovery in the Scramble for Africa* (Surrey: Medina Publishing Ltd., 2017), 280–282.

42. Burton, *Lake Regions of Central Africa*, 228–230.

43. On Tippu Tip's use of interpreters, see Oscar Lenz, "L'Expédition Autrichienne au Congo," *Bulletin de la Société Belge de Géographie* 11 (1887): 221–222; James S. Jameson, *The Story of the Rear Column of the Emin Pasha Relief Expedition* (New York: United States Books Co., 1891), 254.

44. For the war against Nsama, see Tippu Tip, *Maisha*, 17–25. An alternative account is given in Andrew Roberts, "The History of Abdullah bin Suliman," *African Social Research* no. 4 (1967): 249–253.

45. Tippu Tip, *Maisha*, 25.

46. Tippu Tip, *Maisha*, 25.

47. Livingstone, *Last Journals*, 461; Andrew Roberts, "Tippu Tip, Livingstone, and the Chronology of Kazembe," *Azania: Archaeological*

Research in Africa 2 (1967): 115–131. For a broader perspective on these events, see Giacomo Macola, *The Kingdom of Kazembe: History and Politics in North-Eastern Zambia and Katanga to 1950* (Hamburg: Lit Verlag, 2002), 136–146.

48. Tippu Tip, *Maisha*, 61–73; Brode, *Tippoo Tib*, 89.

49. Tippu Tip, *Maisha*, 75–79.

50. Anon., *History of Middlesex County, Connecticut* (New York: J. B. Beers & Co., 1884), 357; Donald Malcarne, "Ivoryton: Introduction and History," unpublished manuscript held in the Comstock-Cheney Archives Room at the Ivoryton Library, Ivoryton, CT, 1–11; Anon., "Comstock, Cheney & Co, Ivoryton," unidentified article held in the Comstock-Cheney Archives Room in the Ivoryton Library, 276.

51. Nancy V. Kougeas, "Manufacturer and Merchant: Samuel M. Constock, George A. Cheney, and the Growth of the Ivory Industry in Essex Connecticut, 1827–1872" (MA thesis, Wesleyan University, 1994), 46–59.

52. Philip Northway, "Salem and the Zanzibar-East African Trade, 1825–1845," *The Essex Institute Historical Collections* 90 (1954): 373.

53. Rufus Greene to Frederick Seward, May 4, 1863, in *New England Merchants in Africa: A History through Documents, 1802 to 1865*, eds. Norman Bennett and George Brooks (Brookline, Mass.: Boston University Press, 1965), 522.

54. Anon., *History of Middlesex County, Connecticut*, 357; Malcarne, "Ivoryton: Introduction and History," 1–11; Anon., "Comstock, Cheney & Co, Ivoryton," 276.

55. Arthur Loesser, *Men, Women, and Pianos: A Social History* (New York: Simon & Schuster, 1954), 511–512; Anon., "The Piano in the United States," *The Atlantic Monthly*, July 1867, 82.

56. Loesser, *Men, Women, and Pianos*, 494–496, 512–513; Cyril Erlich, *The Piano: A History* (London: J. M. Dent & Sons, 1976), 58–62.

57. Michael Phelan, *Billiards without a Master* (New York: D. D. Winant, 1850), 122–127; Phelan and Collender, *The Rise and Progress of the Game of Billiards* (New York: Phelan and Collender, 1860), 5, 7–11, 38–40. On Chicago, see *History of Cook County Illinois*, eds. Weston A. Goodspeed and Daniel D. Haley, 2 vols. (Chicago: Goodspeed Historical Association, 1909), vol. 1, 582.

58. Stanley, *Through the Dark Continent*, vol. 2, 77–78.

59. Stanley, *How I Found Livingstone*, 462–463.

60. Livingstone, *Last Journals*, 337.

61. Daniel Biebuyck, *Lega: Ethics and Beauty in the Heart of Africa* (Gent, Belgium: Snoeck-Ducaju & Zoon, 2002), 15–37; Elisabeth

Cameron, "The Stampeding of Elephants: Elephant Imprints on Lega Thought," in *Elephant: The Animal and Its Ivory in African Culture*, ed. Doran H. Ross (Los Angeles: Fowler Museum of Cultural History, UCLA, 1992), 295–302.

62. Henry M. Stanley, *The Exploration Diaries of H. M. Stanley*, ed. Richard Stanley and Alan Neame (London: William Kimber, 1961), 136; Stanley, *Through the Dark Continent*, vol. 2, 133–143.

63. Livingstone, *Last Journals*, 338, 355.

64. Livingstone, *Last Journals*, 318, 333; David Livingstone, *Livingstone's Letters, 1843 to 1872*, ed. Maurice Boucher (Johannesburg: Brenthurst Press, 1985), 204–219.

65. Stanley's Field Notebook, August 21, 1876–March 3, 1877, entry for October 18, 1876, Stanley Archives, Royal Museum of Central Africa, Tervuren, Belgium, no. 18; Stanley, *Through the Dark Continent*, vol. 2, 95.

66. Tippu Tip, *Maisha*, 81.

67. Stanley, *Through the Dark Continent*, vol. 2, 97–99; Stanley, *Exploration Diaries*, 132–133.

68. Tippu Tip, *Maisha*, 81, 89.

69. Stanley's Field Notebook, August 21, 1876–March 3, 1877, entry for November 5, 1876.

70. Henry M. Stanley, *Stanley's Despatches to the New York Herald, 1871–1872, 1874–1877*, ed. Norman R. Bennet (Boston: Boston University Press, 1970), 323.

71. Stanley, *Stanley's Despatches*, 317–327. The letter was dated Nyangwe, October 28, 1876, and was published in the *New York Herald* on October 10, 1877, and in the London *Daily Telegraph* on October 11, 1877; Stanley, *Exploration Diaries*, 134.

72. Stanley, *Stanley's Despatches*, 477–482; Norman R. Bennett, "Introduction to the Second Edition," in Alfred J. Swann, *Fighting the Slave-Hunters in Central Africa*, 2nd ed. (London: Frank Cass & Co., 1969), viii–ix.

73. Stanley, *Through the Dark Continent*, vol. 2, 99–107.

74. Stanley, *Exploration Diaries*, 135; Tippu Tip, *Maisha*, 83; "Despatches Addressed by Dr. Livingstone," 2.

75. Stanley, *Through the Dark Continent*, vol. 2, 184–188; Stanley, *Exploration Diaries*, 140–144.

76. Tippu Tip, *Maisha*, 83.

77. Stanley's Field Notebook, August 21, 1876–March 3, 1877, entries for August 21, 1876, and December 27, 1876; Tippu Tip, *Maisha*, 81, 87; James Jameson, *The Story of the Rear Column of the Emin Pasha Relief Expedition* (New York: United States Book Company, 1891), 300.

78. Tippu Tip, *Maisha*, 85–87; Jérôme Becker, *La Vie en Afrique, ou Trois Ans dans l'Afrique Centrale*, 2 vols. (Paris: J. Lebegue, 1887), vol. 2, 37; Jameson, *The Story of the Rear Column*, 300; Stanley, *Stanley's Despatches*, 379.

79. Stanley, *Exploration Diaries*, 145–146.

80. The large dugout canoe on display at the Royal Museum for Central Africa in Tervuren, Belgium, is seventy-four feet long and weighs 7,716 lbs. Stanley's eighty-five-foot canoe would have been much heavier.

CHAPTER 2: COMPETITION FOR THE ATLANTIC COAST

1. Richard Burton, *Two Trips to Gorilla Land and the Cataracts of the Congo*, 2 vols. (London: Sampson Low, Marston Low & Searle, 1876), vol. 2, 282–302.

2. David Livingstone, *The Last Journals of David Livingstone in Central Africa*, ed. Horace Waller (New York: Harper & Brothers, 1875), 424.

3. David Eltis and David Richardson, *Atlas of the Transatlantic Slave Trade* (New Haven: Yale University Press, 2010), map 98, 141; Leslie Bethell, *The Abolition of the Brazilian Slave Trade* (Cambridge: Cambridge University Press, 1970), 18–19.

4. Quoted in Egide Devroey, *Le Bassin Hydrographique Congolais* (Brussels: G. Van Campenhout, 1941), 66; Bethell, *Abolition*, 187–188.

5. Burton, *Two Trips to Gorilla Land*, vol. 2, 85–86, 92–97, 311.

6. Roger Anstey, *Britain and the Congo in the Nineteenth Century* (Oxford: Clarendon Press, 1962), 15; W. Holman Bentley, *Pioneering on the Congo*, 2 vols. (London: Religious Tract Society, 1890), vol. 1, 42; Catherine Higgs, *Chocolate Islands: Cocoa, Slavery, and Colonial Africa* (Athens, OH: Ohio University Press, 2012), 12, 53.

7. Bentley, *Pioneering on the Congo*, vol. 1, 72–74.

8. Anstey, *Britain and the Congo*, 41–56.

9. On the translation of this term, see Henry M. Stanley, *Stanley's Despatches to the New York Herald*, 1871–1872, 1874–1877, ed. Norman R. Bennet (Boston: Boston University Press, 1970), 357.

10. Henry M. Stanley, *The Congo and the Founding of Its Free State*, 2 vols. (New York: Harper & Brothers, 1885), vol. 1, 2, 202; Jacques Bellin, "Carte des Royaumes de Congo, Angola, et Benguela," in Antoine François Prévost, *Histoire Générale des Voyages*, 19 vols. (Paris, 1754), vol. 4, no. 15.

11. Henry M. Stanley, *The Exploration Diaries of H. M. Stanley*, ed. Richard Stanley and Alan Neame (London: William Kimber, 1961), February 1, 1877, 158–159; Henry M. Stanley, *Through the Dark Continent*, 2 vols. (New York: Harper & Brothers, 1878), vol. 2, 268–278.

12. Camille Coquilhat, *Sur le Haut-Congo*, (Paris: J. Lebègue, 1888), 183–185.

13. Stanley, *Exploration Diaries*, July 18, 1877, 199–200.

14. Verney Lovett Cameron, *Across Africa* (New York: Harper & Brothers, 1877), 279.

15. The notable exception was the August 1875 incident on Bumbireh Island in Lake Victoria, where Stanley's men sailed close to the shore and opened fire on hostile islanders armed with spears and bows, killing thirty-three and wounding over one hundred. This was done to punish them "with the power of a father punishing a stubborn and disobedient son" for an attack on Stanley's landing party three months earlier. See Stanley, *Exploration Diaries*, 76, 93–95.

16. Tippu Tip, *Maisha ya Hamed bin Muhammed el Murjebi, yaani Tippu Tip, kwa maneno yake mwenyewe*, trans. W. H. Whitely (Nairobi: East African Literature Bureau, 1966), 87.

17. For a history and analysis of the Bobangi trading network, see Robert Harms, *River of Wealth, River of Sorrow: The Central Zaire Basin in the Era of the Slave and Ivory Trade* (New Haven: Yale University Press, 1981).

18. Stanley, *The Congo and the Founding*, vol. 2, 22.

19. E. J. Glave, *Six Years of Adventure in Congo-Land* (London: S. Low, Marston & Co., 1893), 128–131.

20. Robert Harms, *Games Against Nature: An Eco-Cultural History of the Nunu of Equatorial Africa* (New York: Cambridge University Press, 1987), 172–173.

21. Stanley, *The Congo and the Founding*, vol. 1, 294–296.

22. Bentley, *Pioneering on the Congo*, vol. 1, 460–461; Harms, *River of Wealth, River of Sorrow*, 24–47.

23. Bentley, *Pioneering on the Congo*, vol. 1, 460–461; Harry Johnston, *George Grenfell and the Congo*, 2 vols. (New York: Appleton & Co., 1910), vol. 1, 91.

24. Prosper Philippe Augouard, "Voyage à Stanley Pool," *Missions Catholiques*, 1882, 141.

25. Harry Johnston, *The River Congo from Its Mouth to Bolobo*, 3rd ed. (London: Sampson Low, 1884), 116; Bentley, *Pioneering on the Congo*, vol. 1, 43.

26. Susan Herlin Broadhead, "Beyond Decline: The Kingdom of the Kongo in the Eighteenth and Nineteenth Centuries," *The International Journal of African Historical Studies* 12 (1979): 615–650; Susan Herlin Broadhead, "Trade and Politics on the Congo Coast, 1770–1870" (PhD diss., Boston University, 1971), 225–228; Anne Hilton, *The Kingdom of Kongo* (Oxford: Clarendon Press, 1985), 221–225.

27. Bentley, *Pioneering on the Congo*, vol. 1, 73–74.

28. Stanley, *Dark Continent*, vol. 2, 507–508; Bentley, *Pioneering on the Congo*, vol. 1, 365.

29. Stanley, *Exploration Diaries*, February 18, 1877, 165.

30. Stanley, *Exploration Diaries*, March 15, 1877, 171.

31. Stanley, *Exploration Diaries*, July 18, 1877, 200.

32. Stanley, *Exploration Diaries*, July 18, 1877, 199.

33. Johnston, *The River Congo from Its Mouth to Bolobo*, 117.

34. Henry Morton Stanley, "Address to the Manchester Chamber of Commerce," in the microform collection *The Nineteenth Century* (Cambridge: Chadwyck-Healey, 1990), title no. 1.1.4678.

35. This section relies heavily on the following published collections of Brazza's letters, reports, and lectures: Pierre Savorgnan de Brazza, *Brazza Explorateur: L'Ogooué 1875–1879*, ed. Henri Brunschwig, Documents pour Servir à l'Histoire de l'Afrique Equatoriale Française (Paris: Mouton, 1966); Pierre Savorgnan de Brazza, *Conférences et Lettres de P. Savorgnan de Brazza sur ses Trois Explorations dans l'Ouest Africaine de 1875 à 1886*, ed. Napoléon Ney (Paris: M. Dreyfous, 1887), re-edition, Heidelberg: P. Kivouvou, 1984); Pierre Savorgnan de Brazza, *Les Voyages de Savorgnan de Brazza: Ogooué et Congo, 1875–1882*, eds. Didier Neuville and Charles Bréard (Paris: Berger-Levrault, 1884). A first-person account of the trip, possibly ghostwritten by Brazza's collaborator Jules-Léon Dutrueil de Rhins, appeared in the Paris magazine *Le Tour du Monde* in 1887, second semester, 289–336, and 1888, second semester, 1–64. Those two articles were reprinted in 1992 as Pierre Savorgnan de Brazza, *Au Coeur de l'Afrique, 1885–1887* (Paris: Phébus, 1992). Brazza's report is in Brazza, *Brazza Explorateur: L'Ogooué*, 165.

36. Brazza, *Brazza Explorateur: L'Ogooué*, 17, 23–24, 29–33.

37. Brazza, *Brazza Explorateur: L'Ogooué*, 53–56. On the length of the canoes, see Brazza, *Au Coeur de l'Afrique*, 42.

38. Brazza, *Brazza Explorateur: L'Ogooué*, 99–100, 117; Brazza, *Au Coeur de l'Afrique*, 63.

39. Brazza, *Au Coeur d'Afrique*, 40; Brazza, *Brazza Explorateur: L'Ogooué*, 100, 104, 127; Robert Harms, "Slavery in the Politically Decentralized Societies of Equatorial Africa," in *African Systems of Slavery*, eds. Jay Spaulding and Stephanie Beswick (Trenton, NJ: African World Press, 2010), 161–172.

40. Brazza, *Brazza Explorateur: L'Ogooué*, 99 fn. 2, 101–104, 117, 129, 158; Brazza, *Au Coeur de l'Afrique*, 46–47, 51.

41. Brazza, *Au Coeur de l'Afrique*, 94.

42. Brazza, *Brazza Explorateur: L'Ogooué*, 100 n. 1, 130; Brazza, *Conférences et Lettres*, 68.

43. Brazza, *Brazza Explorateur: L'Ogooué*, 60–67.

44. Brazza, *Brazza Explorateur: L'Ogooué*, 156, 161; Brazza, *Au Coeur de l'Afrique*, 113–117.

45. Brazza, *Au Coeur de l'Afrique*, 116.

46. Jacques Aldebert de Chambrun, *Brazza* (Paris: Plon, 1930), 51.

47. Brazza, *Brazza Explorateur: L'Ogooué*, 81; Brazza, *Les Voyages de Savorgnan de Brazza*, 90.

48. Brazza, *Brazza Explorateur: L'Ogooué*, 39, 165.

49. Sanford to Latrobe, July 30, 1877, reprinted in François Bontinck, *Aux Origines de l'Etat Indépendant du Congo: Documents Tirés d'Archives Américaines* (Louvain: Editions Nauwelaerts, 1966), 8–16.

50. Rutherford Alcock, "African Exploration Fund, August 1877," *Proceedings of the Royal Geographical Society* 21, no. 6 (1876–1877): 601–615.

51. David Livingstone, *Dr. Livingstone's Cambridge Lectures*, 2nd ed. (Cambridge: Deighton, Bell & Co., 1860), 165.

52. Bontinck, *Aux Origines*, 8–16, 25–26.

53. Brazza, *Conférences et Lettres*, 31; Brazza, *Voyages de Savorgnan de Brazza*, 94; Brazza, *Brazza Explorateur: L'Ogooué*, 132–133.

54. Jan Vansina, *The Tio Kingdom of the Middle Congo, 1880–1892* (London: Oxford University Press, 1973), 3, 11–12.

55. Brazza, *Au Coeur de l'Afrique*, 188–189; Brazza, *Brazza Explorateur: L'Ogooué*, 191.

56. Vansina, *Tio Kingdom*, 258; Brazza, *Brazza Explorateur: L'Ogooué*, 137, 177–178; Brazza, *Conférences et Lettres*, 35.

57. Gustav Nachtigal, *Sahara and Sudan, vol. 4, Wadai and Darfur*, trans. Allan Fisher and Humphrey J. Fisher (Berkeley: University of California Press, 1971), 249; Harms, *River of Wealth, River of Sorrow*, 57–58; Brazza, *Conférences et Lettres*, 34–35.

58. Georges Mazenot, *La Likouala-Mossaka: Histoire de la Pénétration du Haut-Congo, 1878–1920* (Paris: Mouton, 1970), 26–30.

59. Brazza, *Voyages de Savorgnan de Brazza*, 101.

60. Brazza, *Voyages de Savorgnan de Brazza*, 101, 151.

61. Brazza, *Brazza Explorateur: L'Ogooué*, 189; Brazza, *Voyages de Savorgnan de Brazza*, 103.

62. Brazza, *Brazza Explorateur: L'Ogooué*, 198.

CHAPTER 3: THE GRAND HIGHWAY OF COMMERCE

1. London *Daily Telegraph*, September 17, 1877, October 11, 1877, and November 12, 1877; Auguste Roeykens, *Les Débuts de l'Oeuvre Africaine de Léopold II* (Brussels: Académie Royale des Sciences Coloniales, 1955), 283, n. 1. The letters are reprinted in Henry M. Stanley, *Stanley's*

Despatches to the New York Herald, 1871–1872, 1874–1877, ed. Norman R. Bennet (Boston: Boston University Press, 1970), 341–372.

2. The letter is reprinted in Pierre Van Zuylen, *L'Echiquier Congolais ou le Secret du Roi* (Brussels: C. Dessart, 1959), 43–44.

3. *Bulletin de la Société de Géographie de Marseilles*, vol. 2 (1878), 8–9; François Bontinck, *Aux Origines de l'Etat Indépendant du Congo: Documents Tirés d'Archives Américaines* (Louvain: Editions Nauwelaerts, 1966), 27–31; Henry M. Stanley, *The Congo and the Founding of Its Free State*, 2 vols. (New York: Harper and Brothers, 1885), vol. 1, 21.

4. London *Daily Telegraph*, November 12, 1877.

5. Frank Hird, *H. M. Stanley: The Authorized Life* (London: Stanley Paul, 1935), 171. Hird was granted special access to Stanley's papers. Unfortunately, the book has no footnotes, and the date of the diary entry is not given. Henry Morton Stanley, *The Autobiography of Sir Henry Morton Stanley*, ed. Dorothy Stanley (Boston: Houghton Mifflin, 1909), 334.

6. The descriptions of the two battles at Bumbireh Island were published in the London *Daily Telegraph* on August 7 and 10, 1876, while the first mention of the thirty-two battles on the Congo was published in the *Daily Telegraph* on September 17, 1877. John Gallagher and Ronald Robinson, "The Tyranny of Free Trade," *The Economic History Review*, n.s., 6, no. 1 (1953): 14. Draft, Colonial Office, February 8, 1876, UK National Archives (Kew), FO 84/1459, fo. 8–10; Robert S. Thomson, *Fondation de l'Etat Indépendant du Congo* (Brussels: Office de Publicité, 1933), 63.

7. Roeykens, *Les Débuts*, 349–350.

8. The texts of the two contracts are given in Marcel Luwel, *Stanley* (Brussels: Elsevier, 1959), 64–66.

9. Bontinck, *Aux Origines*, 54–55; the Act of Constitution is reprinted in J. Guebels, "Rapport sur le Dossier J. Greindl, Annex V," *Bulletin des Séances, Institut Royal Colonial Belge* 24, no. 2 (1953): 613–618. The British contributions were listed in pounds sterling, which I converted to Belgian francs using a ratio of twenty-five to one, based on the gold values of the two currencies.

10. Henry M. Stanley, *The Congo and the Founding of Its Free State*, 2 vols. (New York: Harper and Brothers, 1885), vol. 1, 68; Th. Van Schendel, *Au Congo Avec Stanley en 1879* (Brussels: Albert Dewit, 1932), 19, 137–139.

11. Stauch's memo is reprinted in Henry M. Stanley, *H. M. Stanley: Unpublished Letters*, ed. Albert Maurice (London: W. & R. Chambers, 1957), 22–23; letter from Stanley to Colonel Strauch reprinted in Stanley, *The Congo and the Founding*, vol. 1, 52–54.

12. The text of Brazza's lecture is given in Piere Savorgnan de Brazza, *Les Voyages de Savorgnan de Brazza: Ogooué et Congo, 1875–1882*, eds. Didier Neuville and Charles Breard (Paris: Berger-Levrault, 1884), 84–108.

13. Pierre Savorgnan de Brazza, *Brazza Explorateur: L'Ogooué, 1875–1879*, ed. Henri Brunschwig, Documents pour Servir à l'Histoire de l'Afrique Equatoriale Française (Paris: Mouton, 1966), 130.

14. Bontinck, *Aux Origines*, 101–102. In 1865, the value of the French franc and the Belgian franc were both set at 0.29 grams of gold by the Latin Monetary Union, which included France, Belgium, Switzerland, and Italy.

15. Jean Autin, *Pierre Savorgnan de Brazza: Un Prophète du Tiers Monde* (Paris: Perrin, 1985), 56–57; Henri Brunschwig, *L'Avènement de l'Afrique Noire* (Paris: A. Colin, 1963), 143.

16. Pierre Savorgnan de Brazza, *Brazza Explorateur: Les Traités Makoko, 1880–1882*, ed. Henri Brunschwig, Documents pour Servir à l'Histoire de l'Afrique Equatoriale Française (Paris: Mouton, 1972), 14–16; Brunschwig, *L'Avèmement*, 143.

17. Claire Grégoire, "The Bantu Languages of the Forest," in *The Bantu Languages*, eds. Derek Nurse and Gérard Philippson (New York: Routledge, 2003), 349–370.

18. Brazza, *Les Traités Makoko*, 31, n. 4.

19. Brazza, *Les Traités Makoko*, 43 and n. 4.

20. Robert Harms, *River of Wealth, River of Sorrow: The Central Zaire Basin in the Era of the Slave and Ivory Trade, 1500–1891* (New Haven: Yale University Press, 1981), 210. When I was doing research among the Bobangi in 1975–1976, rumors spread that I was a long-lost ancestor who had been carried away in the slave trade and had returned to look for his family.

21. Discours fait par M. de Brazza à la Sorbonne le 23 Juin, 1882, Archives Nationales d'Outre-Mer (Aix-en-Provence), Papiers Brazza, PA 16, II, 4; Pierre Savorgnan de Brazza, *Conférences et Lettres de P. Savorgnan de Brazza sur ses Trois Explorations dans l'Ouest Africaine de 1875 à 1886*, ed. Napoléon Ney (Paris: M. Dreyfous, 1887), 150; Maria Petringa, *Brazza: A Life for Africa* (Bloomington, IN: AuthorHouse, 2006), 99.

22. Jan Vansina, *The Tio Kingdom of the Middle Congo, 1880–1892* (New York: Oxford University Press, 1973), 410; footnote by Vansina in Brazza, *Les Traités Makoko*, 36, n. 3.

23. Henri Brunschwig, "La Négotiation du Traité Makoko," *Cahiers d'Etudes Africaines* 5, no. 17: 11; Léon Guiral, *Le Congo Français du Gabon à Brazzaville* (Paris: E. Plon, 1889), 293.

24. See the footnote by Vansina in Brazza, *Les Traités Makoko*, 30, n. 5.

25. Vansina, *Tio Kingdom*, 317, 389–394.

26. Brazza, *Les Traités Makoko*, 29, n. 1; 58, n. 1; and 63, n. 3.

27. Brazza, *Les Traités Makoko*, 63.

28. Brazza, *Les Traités Makoko*, 60, n. 3, and 63, n. 3.

29. Brazza, *Conférences et Lettres*, 159–160; Brazza, *Les Traités Makoko*, 62, n. 3; Charles de Chavannes, *Avec Brazza: Souvenirs de la Mission de l'Ouest-Africaine, Mars 1883–Janvier 1886* (Paris: Librairie Plon, 1935), 241.

30. Harms, *River of Wealth, River of Sorrow*, 133, 138; Vansina, *Tio Kingdom*, 373; Henry M. Stanley, *The Exploration Diaries of H. M. Stanley*, ed. Richard Stanley and Alan Neame (London: William Kimber, 1961), 169.

31. Brazza, *Voyages de Savorgnan de Brazza*, vii.

32. Brazza, *Les Traités Makoko*, 160, 219; W. Holman Bentley, *Pioneering on the Congo*, 2 vols. (London: Religious Tract Society, 1900), vol. 1, 355.

33. Stanley, *The Congo and the Founding*, vol. 1, 130.

34. The diary entry is reprinted in Stanley, *The Congo and the Founding*, vol. 1, 138.

35. Stanley, *The Congo and the Founding*, vol. 1, 147–148, 236–237; Roland Oliver, "Six Unpublished Letters of H. M. Stanley," *Bulletin des Séances, Académie Royale des Sciences Coloniales*, vol. 3 (1957), 351; Robert Harms, *Games Against Nature* (New York: Cambridge University Press, 1987), 172–173.

36. Stanley, *The Congo and the Founding*, vol. 1, 164–171.

37. Stanley, *The Congo and the Founding*, vol. 1, 154–155, 196.

38. Stanley, *The Congo and the Founding*, vol. 1, 231–232; "Banquet du Stanley Club, 18 Octobre, 1882," Archives Nationales d'Outre-Mer (Aix-en-Provence), Papiers Brazza, PA 16, II, 4.

39. Charles Notte, *Document Notte: Stanley au Congo, 1879–1884*, Archives, Doc. 1 (Brussels: Ministère du Congo Belge et du Ruanda-Urundi, 1960), 15.

40. Letter reprinted in Stanley, *The Congo and the Founding*, vol. 1, 159.

41. Notte, *Document Notte*, 37–38, 43–53.

42. Stanley's journal, vol. 1, Congo, 1878–1882, Henry M. Stanley Archives, Royal Museum of Central Africa, Tervuren, Belgium, no. 34, 196.

43. Henry Brunschwig, "Les Cahiers de Brazza (1880–1882)," *Cahiers d'Etudes Africaines* 6, no. 22 (1966): 157–227; Brazza, *Les Traités Makoko, 1880–1882*, 160.

44. Prosper Philippe Augouard, "Voyage à Stanley Pool," *Les Missions Catholiques* 14 (1882): 141; Stanley, *The Congo and the Founding*, vol. 1, 282.

45. The texts of the Makoko Treaty and the possession document are found in Brazza, *Les Traités Makoko*, 279–280. Bentley, *Pioneering*, vol. 1, 366.

46. Bentley, *Pioneering*, vol. 1, 350; Augouard, quoted in Stanley, *Unpublished Letters*, 71.

47. On Ngaliema, see Bentley, *Pioneering*, vol. 1, 461.

48. Stanley, *The Congo and the Founding*, vol. 1, 320.

49. Chavannes, *Avec Brazza*, 158.

50. Stanley, *The Congo and the Founding*, vol. 1, 373. Stanley is quoting from his diary.

51. Augouard, "Voyage à Stanley Pool," 127; Bentley, *Pioneering*, vol. 1, 365; Stanley to Strauch, January 14, 1882, in Stanley, *Unpublished Letters*, 99.

52. Stanley, *Unpublished Letters*, 73; Notte, *Document Notte*, 122–125.

53. Bentley, *Pioneering*, vol. 1, 462–463.

54. Notte, *Document Notte*, 138.

55. Stanley to Strauch, Stanley Pool Station, March 25, 1882, in Letter Book: My Congo Letters, Henry M. Stanley Archives, Royal Museum of Central Africa, Tervuren, Belgium, no. 48, 373–381; Notte, *Document Notte*, 5, 79, 138.

56. Brazza, *Les Traités Makoko*, 74–75.

57. Guiral, *Le Congo Français*, 216–217.

58. Bentley, *Pioneering*, vol. 1, 81; Notte, *Document Notte*, 93.

CHAPTER 4: HOMEWARD BOUND

1. *Le Temps*, June 25, 1882; *Le Figaro*, June 24, 1882.

2. Pierre Savorgnan de Brazza, *Brazza Explorateur: Les Traités Makoko*, ed. Henri Brunschwig, Documents pour Servir à l'Histoire de l'Afrique Equatoriale Française (Paris: Mouton, 1972), 88–89, 262; Pierre Savorgnan de Brazza, *Les Voyages de Savorgnan de Brazza: Ogôoué et Congo, 1875–1882*, ed. D. Neuville and Ch. Breard (Paris: Gerger-Levrault, 1884), xvi.

3. Henry M. Stanley, *H. M. Stanley: Unpublished Letters*, ed. Albert Maurice (London: W. & R. Chambers, 1957), 70–72; Léon Guiral, *Le Congo Français du Gabon à Brazzaville* (Paris: E. Plon, 1889), 234–235.

4. Brazza, *Les Traités Makoko*, 257–277.

5. Discours fait par M. de Brazza à la Sorbonne le 23 Juin, 1882, Archives Nationales d'Outre-Mer (Aix-en-Provence), PA16-II-4.

6. See the map by P. S. de Brazza, "Tracé Provisoire des Itinéraires de l'Ogooué au Congo, 1880," in *Bulletin de la Société de Géographie*, Décembre 1881, reprinted in Isabelle Dion, *Pierre Savorgnan de Brazza Au Coeur du Congo* (Aix-en-Provence: Archives Nationales d'Outre-Mer, 2007), 53.

7. Henry M. Stanley, *The Exploration Diaries of H. M. Stanley*, ed. Richard Stanley and Alan Neame (London: William Kimber, 1961), 169–170; Brazza, *Les Traités Makoko*, 29, 31.

8. Stanley, *Exploration Diaries*, 170; Henry M. Stanley, *Through the Dark Continent*, 2 vols. (New York: Harper & Brothers, 1878), vol. 2, 332.

9. Brazza, *Les Traités Makoko*, 273.

10. Brazza, *Les Traités Makoko*, 150–152.

11. Pierre Savorgnan de Brazza, *Conférences et Lettres de P. Savorgnan de Brazza*, ed. Napoléon Ney (Paris: Maurice Dreyfus, 1877, reprint Brazzaville: Editions Bantous, 1984), 172–174.

12. Brazza, *Conférences et Lettres*, 162, 173–174.

13. Brazza, *Conférences et Lettres*, 173.

14. Edward Berenson, *Heroes of Empire: Five Charismatic Men and the Conquest of Africa* (Berkeley: University of California Press, 2011), 68–72; *Le Temps* (Paris), September 30, 1882.

15. *Le Petit Parisien*, October 1, 1882, and October 4, 1882.

16. Jean Stengers, "The Partition of Africa: L'Impérialisme Colonial de la Fin du XIX-Siècle: Mythe ou Réalité?" *Journal of African History* 3 (1962): 476; *Le Temps*, October 31, 1882.

17. Stengers, "Partition of Africa," 474, n. 15 and 17.

18. Jean Stengers, "King Leopold and the Anglo-French Rivalry, 1882–1884," in *France and Britain in Africa*, ed. Prosser Gifford and William Roger Louis (New Haven: Yale University Press, 1971), 144; Jean Stengers, "Leopold II et l'Association Internationale du Congo," in *Centenaire de l'Etat Indépendent du Congo* (Brussels: Académie Royale des Sciences d'Outre-Mer, 1988), 52; Henry M. Stanley, *The Congo and the Founding of Its Free State*, 2 vols. (New York: Harper & Brothers, 1885), vol. 1, 462.

19. Stanley, *The Congo and the Founding*, vol. 1, 463–465.

20. Charles Notte, *Document Notte: Stanley au Congo, 1879–1884*, Archives, Doc. 1 (Brussels: Ministère du Congo Belge et du Ruanda-Urundi, 1960), 91–113; Stengers, "Partition of Africa," 473.

21. Auguste Roeykens, *Les Débuts de l'Oeuvre Africaine de Léopold II* (Brussels: Académie Royale des Sciences Coloniales, 1955), 222, n. 1.

22. Henry M. Stanley, Journal, vol. 1, Congo, 1878–1882, Henry M. Stanley Archives, Royal Museum of Central Africa, Tervuren, Belgium, no. 34, 196.

23. Stanley to Strauch, Stanley Pool Station, March 25, 1882, Letter Book: My Congo Letters, Henry M. Stanley Archives, Royal Museum of Central Africa, Tervuren, Belgium, no. 48, 379–380; *Le Voltaire*, October 8, 1882, as reported in *Le Temps*, October 8, 1882.

24. *Le Temps*, October 8, 1882; Harrison Wright, ed., *The New Imperialism: Analysis of Late Nineteenth-Century Expansion* (Lexington, MA: D. C. Heath, 1976), vii.

25. Brazza, *Les Voyages de Savorgnan de Brazza*, x, n. 1; *New York Herald*, October 20, 1882; Banquet du Stanley-Club, October 19, 1882, Archives Nationles d'Outre-Mer (Aix-en-Provence), Papiers Brazza, PA 16 II 4.

26. The text of Stanley's speech is found in Banquet du Stanley Club.

27. Banquet du Stanley-Club; Berenson, *Heroes of Empire*, 69.

28. Henri Brunschwig, *L'Avènement de l'Afrique Noire* (Paris: Librairie A. Colin, 1963), 160; Frank Hird, *H. M. Stanley: The Authorized Life* (London: Stanley Paul, 1935), 189.

29. G. Valbert, "M. Savorgnan de Brazza et M. Stanley," *Revue des Deux Mondes* 54 (November 1, 1882): 205–216; *The Times* (London), October 21, 1882.

30. Berenson, *Heroes of Empire*, 70–81. The engraving from the *Almanach du Figaro* was reproduced as the frontispiece to Brazza, *Les Voyages de Savorgnan de Brazza*.

31. Brunschwig, *L'Avènement de l'Afrique Noire*, 159.

32. Assemblée Nationale, Chambre des Deputés, *Débats Parlementaires*, Année 14, 1882, Séance du Samedi, 18 Novembre, 1646–1647. Parts of Brazza's testimony before the committee were quoted during the Senate debate. See Assemblée Nationale, Sénat, *Débats Parlementaires*, Année 1882, Séance du Mardi, 28 Novembre, 1089–1091.

33. Chambre des Deputés, Séance du Mardi, 21 Novembre, 1696–1697; Brunschwig, *L'Avènement de l'Afrique Noire*, 161–162.

34. G. Charmes, "La Politique Coloniale," *Revue des Deux Mondes* 60 (November 1883): 60; *Le Temps*, November 23, 1882.

35. *The Times*, November 30, 1882.

36. Heinrich Brode, *Tippoo Tib: The Story of His Career in Central Africa Narrated from His Own Accounts* (London: Edward Arnold, 1907), 128–129.

37. Arthur Dodgshun, *From Zanzibar to Ujiji: The Journal of Arthur W. Dodgshun, 1877–1879*, ed. Norman Bennett (Boston University: African Studies Center, 1969), 69–70.

38. Norman R. Bennett, "Captain Storms in Tanganyika, 1882–1885," *Tanganyika Notes and Records* 54 (March 1960): 55; Jérôme Becker, *La Vie en Afrique, ou Trois Ans dans l'Afrique Centrale*, 2 vols. (Paris: J. Lebegue, 1887), vol. 2, 34.

39. Becker, *La Vie en Afrique*, vol. 2, 36.

40. Brode, *Tippoo Tib*, 133; Norman R. Bennett, "Mwinyi Kheri," in *Leadership in Eastern Africa: Six Political Biographies*, ed. Norman R. Bennett (Boston: Boston University Press, 1968), 139–164.

41. Dodgshun, *Zanzibar to Ujiji*, ix–xix; Stanley, *The Congo and the Founding*, vol. 1, 39–44; Becker, *La Vie en Afrique*, vol. 1, 403–454; François Bontinck, *Aux Origines de l'Etat Indépendant du Congo: Documents Tirés d'Archives Américaines* (Louvain: Editions Nauwelaerts, 1966), 98–99, n. 151.

42. Beverly Brown, "Muslim Influence on Trade and Politics in the Lake Tanganyika Region," *African Historical Studies* 4, no. 3 (1971): 628; Tippu Tip, *Maisha ya Hamed bin Muhammed el Murjebi, yaani Tippu Tip, kwa maneno yake mwenyewe*, trans. W. H. Whitely (Nairobi: East African Literature Bureau, 1966), 93; Herbert Ward, *Five Years with the Congo Cannibals* (London: Chatto & Windus, 1890), 186–187.

43. Richard Burton, *The Lake Regions of Central Africa* (New York: Harper & Brothers, 1860), xiv, estimates the distance by the trade route as 276 miles, plus 20 percent to allow for detours; Henry M. Stanley, *How I Found Livingstone* (New York: Scribner, Armstrong & Co., 1872), 607.

44. Becker, *La Vie en Afrique*, vol. 2, 45–46.

45. Alfred J. Swann, *Fighting the Slave-Hunters in Central Africa* (London: Seeley, 1910, reprint London: Frank Cass, 1969), 48–49.

46. Norman R. Bennett, "Captain Storms in Tanganyika, 1882–1885," *Tanganyika Notes and Records* 54 (March 1960): 54–55.

47. Tippu Tip, *Maisha*, 109.

48. Notte, *Document Notte*, 52–53.

49. Stanley to Strauch, Second Station, June 12, 1881, in Letter Book: My Congo Letters, Henry M. Stanley Archives, Royal Museum of Central Africa, Tervuren, Belgium, no. 48, 234–236.

50. A. J. Mounteney Jephson, *The Diary of A. J. Mounteney Jephson, Emin Pasha Relief Expedition, 1887–1889* (London: Hakluyt Society, 1969), 79.

51. Tippu Tip, *Maisha*, 111. Becker was under the impression that Tippu Tip had been named the governor of Nyangwe. *La Vie en Afrique*, vol. 2, 448.

52. Brode, *Tippoo Tib*, 158; Philip Curtin, *Cross-Cultural Trade in World History* (Cambridge: Cambridge University Press, 1984), 137–148.

CHAPTER 5: A TORRENT OF TREATIES

1. Henri Brunschwig, *L'Avènement de l'Afrique Noire* (Paris: A. Colin, 1963), 159.

2. Pierre Savorgnan de Brazza, *Brazza et la Prise de Possession du Congo: La Mission l'Ouest-Africain, 1883–1885*, ed. Catherine Coquery-Vidrovitch, Documents pour Servir à l'Histoire de l'Afrique Equatoriale Française (Paris: Mouton, 1969), 225–226.

3. Henry M. Stanley, *H. M. Stanley: Unpublished Letters*, ed. Albert Maurice (London: W. & R. Chambers, 1957), 161; Banquet du Stanley-Club, October 19, 1882, Archives Nationles d'Outre-Mer (Aix-en-Provence), Papiers Brazza, PA 16 II 4.

4. Stanley, *Unpublished Letters*, 160.

5. Text reprinted in C. Denuit-Somerhausen, "Les Traités de Stanley et de ses Collaborateurs avec les chefs Africaines, 1880–1885," in *Le Centenaire de l'Etat Indépendant du Congo: Receuil d'Etudes* (Brussels: Académie Royale des Sciences d'Outre-Mer, 1988), 139.

6. Léon Guiral, *Le Congo Français du Gabon à Brazzaville* (Paris: E. Plon, 1889), 253.

7. Guiral, *Le Congo Français*, 231–233; Henry M. Stanley, *The Congo and the Founding of Its Free State*, 2 vols. (New York: Harper and Brothers, 1885), vol. 1, 495–496, vol. 2, 257–258.

8. Stanley, *The Congo and the Founding*, vol. 2, 197; Charles Notte, *Document Notte: Stanley au Congo, 1879–1884*, Archives, Doc. 1 (Brussels: Ministère du Congo Belge et du Ruanda-Urundi, 1960), 179–183, 193–195; J. L. Vellut, "Les Traités de l'Association Internationale du Congo dans le Bas-Fleuve Zaire (1882–1885)," in *Un Siècle de Documentation Africaine, 1885–1895*, ed. Charles Bils-Lambert (Brussels: Ministère des Affaires Etrangères, 1985), 25–34.

9. Stanley to Strauch, July 12, 1883, in Letter Book: My Congo Letters, Henry M. Stanley Archives, Royal Museum of Central Africa, Tervuren, Belgium, no. 48, 536–537.

10. Robert Harms, *River of Wealth, River of Sorrow: The Central Zaire Basin in the Era of the Slave and Ivory Trade, 1500–1891* (New Haven: Yale University Press, 1981), 157, 220–221.

11. Camille Coquilhat, *Sur le Haut-Congo* (Paris: J. Lebègue, 1888), 84; Charles Liebrechts, *Souvenirs d'Afrique: Congo, Léopoldville, Bolobo, Equateur, 1883–1889* (Brussels: J. Lebègue, 1909), 48–53; Stanley, *The Congo and the Founding*, vol. 2, 63–64; E. J. Glave, *Six Years of Adventure in Congo-Land* (London: S. Low, Marston & Co., 1893), 40–41; Frédéric Orban to Stanley, Bolobo, February 22, 1883, Royal Museum of Central Africa, Tervuren, Belgium, Archives Frédéric Orban, HA.01.0015, no, 7, Copie-Lettres, 362–363.

12. Coquilhat, *Haut-Congo*, 202, 505.

13. Stanley to Strauch, January 27, 1884, in Letter Book: My Congo Letters, 633; Stanley to Strauch, July 18, 1883, in Letter Book: My Congo Letters, 576.

14. Stanley, *The Congo and the Founding*, vol. 2, 166; Jean Stengers, "King Leopold and the Anglo-French Rivalry, 1882–1884," in *France and Britain in Africa*, ed. Prosser Gifford and William Roger Louis (New Haven: Yale University Press, 1971), 142–143.

15. Notte, *Document Notte*, 189; Stanley, *Unpublished Letters*, 161–162.

16. Both treaties are found in the Archives Africaines (Brussels), AI 1377. A version of the New Confederacy treaty is published in Stanley, *The Congo and the Founding*, vol. 2, 197–204. It is roughly inserted into the text without proper explanation or context and appears to have been added at the last minute at the request of Leopold II. A model of the text is found in Notte, *Document Notte*, 190–195.

17. Vellut, "Les Traités," 31. Alexandre Delcommune, *Vingt Années de Vie Africaine*, 2 vols. (Brussels: Larcier, 1922), vol. 1, 165.

18. Vellut, "Les Traités," 32.

19. *The Times* (London), January 5, 1884, 8.

20. Brazza, *Prise de Possession*, 28, 225–226.

21. Modèle de Traité de Protectorat, Chavannes Papers, Archives Nationales de France (Paris), Nouvelles Acquisitions Françaises, 21.048.

22. Charles de Chavannes, *Avec Brazza: Souvenirs de la Mission de l'Ouest-Africaine, Mars 1883–Janvier 1886* (Paris: Librairie Plon, 1935), 120.

23. This is an estimate based on the drawing by Chavannes reprinted in *Avec Brazza*, 144–145. It first appeared in the Paris weekly newspaper *Illustration* on January 23, 1886.

24. Richard West, *Brazza of the Congo* (London: Cape, 1972), 128.

25. There are two eyewitness accounts of this ceremony, both written by Charles de Chavannes. The first is a letter he wrote from Brazzaville on May 4, 1884, reprinted in Brazza, *Prise de Possession*, 341–343. The second is the text of Chavannes's lecture at the annual public meeting of the Académie des Sciences Coloniales held in the Richelieu Amphitheatre at the Sorbonne on April 27, 1731, and published as Charles de Chavannes, "Cinquantenaire de Brazzaville," in Académie des Sciences Coloniales, *Comptes Rendus des Séances* 15 (1931): 39–59 (Paris: Société des Editions Géographiques, Maritimes, et Coloniales, 1932). Parts of the Sorbonne lecture were reprinted in Chavannes's book *Avec Brazza*, 157–162.

26. Chavannes, *Avec Brazza*, 153; Brazza, *Prise de Possession*, 344.

27. Prosper-Philippe Augouard, *Vingt-huit Années au Congo: Lettres de Mgr. Augouard*, 2 vols. (Poitiers: Société Française d'Imprimerie et de Librairie, 1905); Augouard quoted in Stanley, *Unpublished Letters*, 160–161.

28. Guiral, *Le Congo Français*, 228–229; Brazza, *Prise de Possession*, 114–115; Augouard quoted in Stanley, *Unpublished Letters*, 160–161.

29. The text of Valke's treaty was published in Chavannes, *Avec Brazza*, 376–377.

30. Stanley, *Unpublished Letters*, 159–160; Notte, *Document Notte*, 150–151, 182.

31. Chavannes, *Avec Brazza*, 371–375.

32. Chavannes, *Avec Brazza*, 181–184; Marcel Luwel, *Sir Francis de Winton: Administrateur Générale du Congo* (Tervuren, Belgium: Musée Royal d'Afrique Centrale, 1964), 167–170.

33. Luwel, *Francis de Winton*, 172–173.

34. Brazza, *Prise de Possession*, 438.

35. Chavannes, *Avec Brazza*, 241.

36. Chavannes, *Avec Brazza*, 192, 241.

37. Tippu Tip, *Maisha ya Hamed bin Muhammed el Murjebi, yaani Tippu Tip, kwa maneno yake mwenyewe*, trans. W. H. Whitely (Nairobi: East African Literature Bureau, 1966), 116; P. Möller, Georg Pagels, and Edvard Gleerup, *Tre Ar I Kongo* (Stockholm: P. A. Norstedt, 1887–1888), 384–385.

38. F. Bontinck, "La Station de Stanley Falls," *Bulletin des Séances, Académie Royale des Sciences d'Outre-Mer* (1979): 621–623; Tippu Tip, *L'Autobiographie de Hamed ben Mohammed el-Murjebi Tippu Tip*, trans. and ann. François Bontinck (Brussels: Académie Royale des Sciences d'Outre-Mer, 1974), 295–296; Henry M. Stanley, *Through the Dark Continent*, 2 vols. (New York: Harper & Brothers, 1878), vol. 2, 129. Katukama Island is shown on Edvard Gleerup's map of Stanley Falls in *Tre Ar I Kongo*, 288–289.

39. Stanley, *Dark Continent*, vol. 1, 46–53; George Hawker, *The Life of George Grenfell: Congo Missionary and Explorer* (London: Religious Tract Society, 1909), 228–229.

40. Abed bin Salim to Seyyid Barghash, May 16, 1884, UK National Archives (Kew) FO 84/1727, fo. 128–129.

41. Stanley to Strauch, January 27, 1884, in Letter Book: My Congo Letters, 631.

42. Quoted in Melvin E. Page, "The Manyema Hordes of Tippu Tip," *International Journal of African Historical* Studies 7 (1974): 72–73.

43. Delcommune, *Vingt Années*, vol. 1, 43; Stanley to Leopold, January 30, 1884, in Letter Book: My Congo Letters, 657.

44. Bontinck, "La Station des Stanley Falls," 615–630.

45. Kirk to Earl Granville, October 23, 1884, UK National Archives (Kew), FO 84/1679, fo. 85–90; Abed bin Salim to Seyyid Barghash May 16, 1884, UK National Archives (Kew), FO 84/1727, fo. 128–129.

46. Norman Bennett, *Arab versus European: Diplomacy and War in Nineteenth-Century East Central Africa* (New York: Africana Pub. Co., 1986), 217–219; Kirk to Earl Granville, October 23, 1884, UK National Archives (Kew), FO 84/1679, fo. 85–90; P. Ceulemans, *La Question Arabe et le Congo, 1883–1892* (Brussels: Académie Royale des Sciences Coloniales, 1959), 63.

47. Quoted in Bennett, *Arab versus European*, 218–219; Kirk to Earl Granville, October 23, 1884, UK National Archives (Kew) FO 84/1679, fo. 87; Tippu Tip, *Maisha*, 117.

48. Traité d'amitié et de paix avec Moniamani, fils de Tipo-Tip, 10-18-1884, Archives Africaines (Brussels), AI 1377. A partial copy is reprinted in Coquilhat, *Haut-Congo*, 401–403, and in Tippu Tip, *L'Autobiographie de Hamed ben Mohammed el-Murjebi Tippu Tip (ca. 1840–1905)*, trans. and ann. François Bontinck (Brussels: Académie Royale des Sciences d'Outre-Mer, 1974), 159.

49. Tippu Tip, *Autobiographie*, 269, n. 417 fixes the date at December 13, 1884; Bontinck, "Station de Stanley Falls," 628, fn. 8.

50. Coquilhat, *Haut-Congo*, 404–406.

51. Tippu Tip, *Autobiographie*, 269–270, fn. 420; James S. Jameson, *The Story of the Rear Column of the Emin Pasha Relief Expedition* (New York: United States Books Co., 1891), 126, 204; Thomas Parke, *My Personal Experiences in Equatorial Africa, as a Medical Officer of the Emin Pasha Relief Expedition* (London: S. Low, Marston, 1891), 490–491; Herbert Ward, *Five Years with the Congo Cannibals* (London: Chatto & Windus, 1890), 173.

52. J. P. Cuypers, *Alphonse Vangele (1848–1939) d'après des Documents Inédites* (Brussels: Académie Royale des Sciences d'Outre-Mer, 1960), 27.

53. Cuypers, *Alphonse Vangele*, 26–32; Coquilhat, *Haut-Congo*, 404–411.

54. Coquilhat, *Haut-Congo*, 411.

55. Tippu Tip, *Autobiographie*, 136–137; Albert Chapaux, *Le Congo: Historique, Diplomatique, Physique, Politique, Economique, Humanitaire & Colonial* (Brussels: Charles Rozez, 1894), 137–139.

56. Chapaux, *Le Congo*, 137–139.

57. Coquilhat, *Haut-Congo*, 415–416; Tippu Tip, *Autobiographie*, 137.

58. The treaties are reprinted in Tippu Tip, *Autobiographie*, 159–162.

59. Coquilhat, *Haut-Congo*, 415; Tippu Tip, *Autobiographie*, 271, fn. 424.

60. Kirk to Salisbury, July 31, 1885, UK National Archives (Kew), FO 84/1727, fo. 127.

CHAPTER 6: CREATING THE CONGOS

1. Charles Notte, *Document Notte: Stanley au Congo, 1879–1884*, Archives, Doc. 1 (Brussels: Ministère du Congo Belge et du Ruanda-Urundi, 1960), 178–179.

2. Stanley to Strauch, Vivi, May 11, 1884, in Letter Book: My Congo Letters, Henry M. Stanley Archives, Royal Museum of Central Africa, Tervuren Belgium, no. 48, 690–691; Stanley to Strauch, January 27, 1884, in Letter Book: My Congo Letters, 631.

3. Roger Anstey, *Britain and the Congo in the Nineteenth Century* (Oxford: Clarendon Press, 1962), 98.

4. D'Antas and Serpa to Ministry for Foreign Affairs, November 8, 1882, UK National Archives (Kew), FO 84/1802, fo. 261–271.

5. Granville to d'Antas, December 15, 1882, UK National Archives (Kew), FO 84/1802, fo. 393–399.

6. Strauch to Foreign Office, February 5, 1883, UK National Archives (Kew), FO 84/1803, fo. 239–240; King of the Belgians to the Queen, February 22, 1883, UK National Archives (Kew), FO 84/1803, fo. 222–225.

7. Kirk to Hill, February 18, 1883, UK National Archives (Kew), FO 84/1803, fo. 179–187; Kirk memo, February 25, 1883, UK National Archives (Kew), FO 84/1803, fo. 262–266.

8. Anstey, *Britain and the Congo*, 106; Granville, February 24, 1883, UK National Archives (Kew), FO 84/1803, fo. 267–271.

9. Robert Gibb, *Greater Manchester* (London: Myriad Books, 2005), 12–13; Roger Lloyd-Jones and M. J. Lewis, *Manchester and the Age of the Factory: The Business Structure of Cottonopolis in the Industrial Revolution* (London: Croom Helm, 1988), 1; *House of Commons Hansard*, Sitting of Tuesday, April 3, 1883, 3rd series, vol. 27, cols. 1284–1332.

10. Memorial of the Directors of the Manchester Chamber of Commerce to Earl Granville, November 15, 1882, UK National Archives (Kew), FO 84, 1802, fo, 156–160.

11. *House of Commons Hansard*, Sitting of Tuesday, April 3, 1883, 3rd series, vol. 27, cols. 1284–1332.

12. Jean Stengers, "King Leopold and Anglo-French Rivalry, 1882–1884," in *France and Britain in Africa*, ed. Prosser Gifford and William Roger Louis (New Haven: Yale University Press, 1971), 150.

13. Stengers, "Anglo-French Rivalry," 150; Pierre van Zuylen, *L'Echiquier Congolaia; ou, le Secret du Roi* (Brussels: C. Dessart, 1959), 70.

14. "Stevens (Arthur)," in *Biographie Nationale* (Brussels: E. Bruylant, 1866), vol. 23, col. 850–854.

15. Stengers, "Anglo-French Rivalry," 155.

16. Geoffroy de Courcel, *L'Influence de la Conférence de Berlin de 1885 sur le Droit Colonial International* (Paris: Editions Internationales, 1935), 78–79, 98–99; Stengers, "Anglo-French Rivalry," 156–157; Roland Oliver, "Six Unpublished Letters of H. M. Stanley," *Bulletin des Séances, Académie Royale des Sciences Coloniales* 3 (1957): 354–358.

17. Letter printed in Edward Hertslet, ed., *The Map of Africa by Treaty*, 3 vols., 2nd ed. (London: Her Majesty's Stationery Office, 1896), vol. 1, 207–208.

18. Stengers, "Anglo-French Rivalry," 158, fn. 113, 114.

19. *The Times*, London, May 20, 1884.

20. James D. Richardson, *A Compilation of the Messages and Papers of the Presidents, 1789–1897*, vol. 8 (Washington: Government Printing Office, 1898), 170–188.

21. Leopold's letter is reprinted in Robert Stanley Thompson, "Léopold II et Henry S. Sanford: Papiers Inédits," *Congo*, 1930, vol. 2, 302–304. On the falsification of the Vivi treaty, see Stengers, "Anglo-French Rivalry," 128, n. 13. The falsified treaties were printed in *Compilation of Reports of the Committee on Foreign Relations, United States Senate, 1789–1901*, vol. 6 (Washington: Government Printing Office, 1901), 272–276.

22. François Bontinck, *Aux Origines de l'Etat Indépendant du Congo: Documents Tirés d'Archives Américaines* (Louvain: Editions Nauwelaerts, 1966), 143–145.

23. *New York Herald*, December 30, 1883.

24. *New York Times*, January 2, 1884; Bontinck, *Aux Origines*, 155–157.

25. Thomas Adams Upchurch, "Senator John Tyler Morgan and the Genesis of Jim Crow Ideology, 1889–1891," *The Alabama Review* 57, no. 2 (April 2004): 110–131; Joseph A. Fry, *John Tyler Morgan and the Search for Southern Autonomy* (Knoxville: University of Tennessee Press, 1992), 76–79; Joseph A. Fry, *Henry S. Sanford: Diplomacy and Business in Nineteenth-Century America* (Reno: University of Nevada Press, 1982), 144–145; Bontinck, *Aux Origines*, 171.

26. *Compilation of Reports*, 221–276; Thompson, "Léopold II et Henry S. Sanford," 304–307; Lysle Edward Meyer, "Henry Shelton Sanford and the Congo" (PhD diss., Ohio State University, 1967), 81; Bontinck, *Aux Origines*, 187–189.

27. Bontinck, *Aux Origines*, 196, 199–201; Fry, *Henry S. Sanford*, 146–147.

28. The declarations are printed in Hertslet, *Map of Africa by Treaty*, vol. 1, 244–246, and in Bontinck, *Aux Origines*, 200–201; Jean Stengers,

"Leopold II et l'Association Internationale du Congo," in *Centenaire de l'Etat Indépendent du Congo: Recueil d'Etudes* (Brussels: Académie Royal des Sciences d'Outre-Mer, 1988), 52. Tisdel is quoted in Fry, *Henry S. Sanford*, 147.

29. The text of the treaty is found in Roger Anstey, *Britain and the Congo*, 241–246, and in Hertslet, *Map of Africa by Treaty*, vol. 2, 713–714.

30. Anstey, *Britain and the Congo*, 157; H. Percy Anderson, Nature of the King of the Belgians' Co., March 2, 1884, UK National Archives (Kew), FO 84/1809, fo. 233–235.

31. Anderson, Nature of the King of the Belgians' Co., March 2, 1884, fo. 233–235; Anstey, *Britain and the Congo*, 157–158.

32. Bismarck to Granville, June 7, 1884, UK National Archives (Kew), FO 84/1811, fo. 341–345.

33. *House of Commons Hansard*, sitting of June 26, 1884.

34. Fritz Stern, *Gold and Iron: Bismarck, Bleichröder, and the Building of the German Empire* (New York: Knopf, 1977), 402–403.

35. Stern, *Gold and Iron*, 404–407; Marcel Luwel, "Gerson von Bleichröder, l'Ami Commun de Leopold II et Bismarck," *Africa-Tervuren* 11, no. 3–4: 96–97.

36. Jean Stengers, "Léopold II et la Fixation des Frontières du Congo," *Le Flambeau* 46 (1963): 169–170.

37. Henry M. Stanley, *The Congo and the Founding of Its Free State*, 2 vols. (New York: Harper and Brothers, 1885), vol. 2, 206–207.

38. Hertslet, *Map of Africa by Treaty*, vol. 1, map after 246 and reference to the map on 220; map 5 in Robert S. Thompson, *Fondation de l'Etat Indépendant du Congo* (Brussels: Office de Publicité, 1933), 298.

39. Stengers, "Anglo-French Rivalry," 163; Pierre Daye, *Léopold II* (Paris: A. Fayard et Cie., 1934), 212–214.

40. Henry M. Stanley, *Address of Mr. H. M. Stanley* (Manchester: A. Ireland, 1884), 39. Bismarck is quoted in Stengers, "Anglo-French Rivalry," 163.

41. Hertslet, *Map of Africa by Treaty*, vol. 1, 219–220.

42. Quoted in Sven Beckert, *Empire of Cotton: A Global History* (New York: Alfred A. Knopf, 2014), 81.

43. *The Times* (London), September 19, 1884.

44. *Manchester Courier*, October 22, 1884.

45. Stanley, *Address of Mr. H. M. Stanley*, 12–13.

46. *Manchester Courier*, October 22, 1884; Stanley, *Address of Mr. H. M. Stanley*, 35–39.

47. Stanley, *Address of Mr. H. M. Stanley*, 31; *Manchester Courier*, October 22, 1884.

48. Anti-Slavery Society, *Meeting of the British and Foreign Anti-Slavery Society in the Free Trade Hall, Manchester, on the 23rd October, 1884* (Moorgate: Abraham Kingdon & Co., 1884), 1–31.

49. Kwame Nkrumah, *Challenge of the Congo* (New York: International Publishers, 1970), x; William Roger Louis, "The Berlin Congo Conference," in *France and Britain in Africa: Imperial Rivalry and Colonial Rule*, ed. Prosser Gifford and William Roger Louis (New Haven: Yale University Press, 1971), 167–220.

50. Maurice Wynants, "His Majesty Is Out of Town: Les Relations Tendues entre Léopold II et Stanley après la Conférence de Berlin," in *La Mémoire du Congo: Le Temps Colonial*, ed. Jean-Luc Vellut (Tervuren: Musée Royal de l'Afrique Centrale, 2005), 69–70; Robert S. Thompson, "Léopold II et la Conférence de Berlin," *Congo* (1931): 329–330.

51. "Message from the President of the United States Transmitting a Report of the Secretary of State Relative to the Affairs of the Independent State of Congo" (Senate Executive Document no. 196, Serial Volume 2341, June 30, 1886), 23–27.

52. "Report of the Secretary of State," 34; Louis, "Berlin Congo Conference," 202.

53. General Act of the Conference of Berlin, 6.

54. Louis, "Berlin Congo Conference," 200–203; "Report of the Secretary of State," 262.

55. "Report of the Secretary of State," 295–296.

56. Arthur Berriedale Keith, *The Belgian Congo and the Berlin Act* (London: Oxford University Press, 1919), 65.

CHAPTER 7: RESCUING EMIN

1. Swinburne to Sanford, November 17, 1886, Henry Shelton Sanford Papers, Sanford Museum, Sanford, Florida, Box 27, folder 14.

2. E. Boelaert, "La Sanford Exploring Expedition," *Annales Aequatoria* 22 (1959): 126.

3. E. H. Taunt, "Report of Journey on River Congo, Central Africa," Senate Executive Document no. 77, 49th Congress, 2nd session, February 1, 1877, 31–35.

4. Taunt, "Report," 20, 36, 40.

5. François Bontinck, *Aux Origines de l'Etat Indépendent du Congo: Documents Tirés d'Archives Américaines* (Louvain: Editions Nauwelaerts, 1966), 349–353.

6. Joseph A. Fry, *Henry S. Sanford: Diplomacy and Business in Nineteenth-Century America* (Reno: University of Nevada Press, 1982), 157–159; Lysle Edward Meyer Jr., "Henry Shelton Sanford and the

Congo" (diss, Ohio State University, 1967), 174–182; Boelaert, "Sanford Exploring Expedition," 124–125.

7. Taunt to Sanford, July 11, 1886, Sanford Papers, Box 28, folder 1; J.–P. Cuypers, *Alphonse Vangele (1848–1939) d'après des Documents Inédits* (Brussels: Académie Royale des Sciences d'Outre-Mer, 1960), 37–51; Sanford Exploring Expedition, Confidential Memorandum, n.d. (ca. summer 1888), Sanford Papers, box 32, folder 5, 8.

8. Swinburne to Sanford, November 17, 1886, Sanford Papers, box 27, folder 14; Taunt to Sanford, November 26, 1886, Sanford Papers, box 28, folder 2; Taunt to Sanford, September 24, 1886, Sanford Papers, box 28, folder 2; Taunt, "Report," 31–32.

9. E. J. Glave, *Six Years of Adventure in Congo-Land* (London: S. Low, Marston & Co., 1893), 176–177.

10. Glave, *Six Years*, 200; Sanford, Exploring Expedition, Confidential Memorandum, Sanford Papers, box 32, folder 5, 8.

11. Charles Latrobe Bateman, *The First Ascent of the Kasai* (London: George Philip & Son, 1889), 81–90; Bateman to Sanford, June 1, 1887, and June 5, 1887, Sanford Papers, box 24, folder 2.

12. Taunt to Sanford, November 26, 1886, Sanford Papers, box 28, folder 2; Boston Rubber Shoe Company to Sanford, April 14, 1888, Sanford Papers, box 22, folder 4; Converse to Sanford, June 14, 1888, Sanford Papers, box 22, folder 4; Sanford Exploring Expedition, Confidential Memorandum, Sanford Papers, box 32, folder 5, 8.

13. Sanford Exploring Expedition, Confidential Memorandum, Sanford Papers, box 32, folder 5, 7, 10.

14. Camille Coquilhat, *Sur le Haut-Congo* (Paris: J. Lebègue & Co., 1888), 452; J. R. Werner, *A Visit to Stanley's Rear-Guard* (London: William Blackwood & Sons, 1889), 109–114.

15. The treaties are in Archives Africaines (Brussels), A. I. 1377; reprinted in Tippu Tip, *L'Autobiographie de Hamed ben Mohammed el-Murjebi Tippu Tip*, trans. and ann. François Bontinck (Brussels: Académie Royale des Sciences d'Outre-Mer, 1974), 159–163.

16. P. Ceulemans, *La Question Arabe et le Congo, 1883–1892* (Brussels: Académie Royale des Sciences Coloniales, 1959), 74–78.

17. George Hawker, *The Life of George Grenfell, Congo Missionary and Explorer* (London: Religious Tract Society, 1909), 233; Herbert Ward, *Five Years with the Congo Cannibals* (New York: Robert Bonner's Sons, 1890), 201; J. R. Werner, *A Visit to Stanley's Rear-Guard* (London: William Blackwood & Sons, 1889), 95–96.

18. Ward, *Congo Cannibals*, 205–213; Coquilhat, *Haut-Congo*, 457–462.

19. Ward, *Congo Cannibals*, 221.

20. Iain R. Smith, *The Emin Pasha Relief Expedition, 1886–1890* (Oxford: Clarendon Press, 1972), 42–44; *The Times* (London), October 29, 1886; British and Foreign Anti-Slavery Society, November 5, 1886, UK National Archives (Kew), FO 84/1793, fo. 98–99.

21. Emin Pasha, *Emin Pasha: His Life and Work, Compiled from His Journals, Letters, Scientific Notes and from Official Documents by Georg Schweitzer*, 2 vols. (Westminister: Archibald Constable and Co., 1898; reprinted New York: Negro Universities Press, 1969), vol. 1, 1–29.

22. Emin Pasha, *Emin Pasha in Central Africa, Being a Collection of His Letters and Journals*, ed. and ann. G. Schweinfurth (London: G. Philip & Son, 1888), 421–422.

23. Emin Pasha, *Emin Pasha in Central Africa*, 432.

24. Emin Pasha, *Emin Pasha in Central Africa*, 510–511.

25. Frank Hird, *H. M. Stanley: The Authorized Life* (London: Stanley Paul & Co., 1935), 222–223; Henry M. Stanley, *In Darkest Africa: The Quest, Rescue, and Retreat of Emin, Governor of Equatoria*, 2 vols. (New York: Charles Scribner's sons, 1890), vol. 1, 34–35, 391.

26. Smith, *Emin Pasha Relief Expedition*, 78–79.

27. Stanley, *In Darkest Africa*, vol. 1, 57.

28. Richard Huzzey, *Freedom Burning: Anti-Slavery and Empire in Victorian Britain* (Ithaca, NY: Cornell University Press, 2012), 156; Edward Hertslet, ed., *The Map of Africa by Treaty*, 2nd ed., 3 vols. (London: Her Majesty's Stationery Office, 1896), vol. 2, 615–621; Tippu Tip, *Maisha ya Hamed bin Muhammed el Murjebi, yaani Tippu Tip, kwa maneno yake mwenyewe*, trans. W. H. Whitely (Nairobi: East African Literature Bureau, 1966), 121.

29. Stanley, *In Darkest Africa*, vol. 1, 63–65; Tippu Tip, *Autobiographie*, 121–123.

30. Holmwood to Salisbury, February 25, 1887, and Holmwood to Salisbury, March 3, 1887, reprinted in UK Foreign Office, Confidential Print no. 5617, "Further Correspondence Respecting the Relief of Emin Pasha at Uganda, 1887" (May 1888), 32–34, in UK National Archives (Kew), FO 403/79.

31. The text is reprinted in "Further Correspondence," 34, and in Tippu Tip, *Autobiographie*, 164–165; Tippu Tip, *Maisha*, 121–123.

32. A signed copy of the treaty is in the Henry M. Stanley Archives, Royal Museum for Central Africa, Tervuren, Belgium, no. 4801. The text is reprinted in Tippu Tip, *Autobiographie*, 163–164; Wilhelm Junker, *Travels in Africa during the Years 1875–1886*, 3 vols. (London: Chapman & Hall, 1890–1892), vol. 3, 561–562, 566; Stanley, *In Darkest Africa*, vol. 1, 64.

33. Stanley *In Darkest Africa*, vol. 1, 75–76; Tippu Tip, *Autobiographie*, 276, notes 451–452.

34. Herbert Ward, *My Life with Stanley's Rear Guard* (London: Chatto & Windus, 1891), 12–13; Herbert Ward, *Congo Cannibals*, 33–35.

35. Charles Liebrechts, *Souvenirs d'Afrique: Congo, Léopoldville, Bolobo, Equateur, 1883–1889* (Brussels: J. Lebègue, 1909), 169–177.

36. Stanley, *In Darkest Africa*, vol. 1, 133, 498.

37. Stanley, "Mr. Stanley," *The Times* (London), May 3, 1890, 15; Thomas Heazle Parke, *My Personal Experiences of Equatorial Africa as Medical Officer of the Emin Pasha Relief Expedition* (New York: Charles Scribner's Sons, 1890), 497.

38. Stanley, "Mr. Stanley," 15; A. J. Mounteney Jephson, *The Diary of A. J. Mounteney Jephson*, ed. Dorothy Middleton (Cambridge: Cambridge University Press, 1969), 1–3.

39. Jephson, *Diary*, 128, 131.

40. Jephson, *Diary*, 122, 126, 128, 133, 135.

41. Stanley, *In Darkest Africa*, vol. 1, 199; Jephson, *Diary*, 144.

42. Tippu Tip, *Autobiographie*, 240–241; Jephson, *Diary*, 168, 171; Stanley, *In Darkest Africa*, vol. 1, 236–239; Parke, *Personal Experiences*, 124.

43. Jephson, *Diary*, 200–204.

44. Stanley, "Mr. Stanley," 15; Jephson, *Diary*, 206–207.

45. Jephson, *Diary*, 221.

46. Stanley, *In Darkest Africa*, vol. 1, 484–489; Stanley to Euan-Smith, December 28, 1889, UK National Archives (Kew), FO 84/1982, fo. 293–295.

47. Stanley, *In Darkest Africa*, vol. 1, 498.

48. Tippu Tip to Holmwood, July 21, 1887, UK National Archives (Kew), FO 84/1906, fo. 183–193; James S. Jameson, *The Story of the Rear Column of the Emin Pasha Relief Expedition* (New York: United States Books Co., 1891), 122–123; Jameson to Stanley, March 26, 1888, reprinted in Edmund Musgrave Barttelot, *The Life of Edmund Musgrave Barttelot* (London: Bentley & Son, 1890), 387–393.

49. Jameson, *Story of the Rear Column*, 111–123, 129, 141–142, 251; John Rose Troup, *With Stanley's Rear Column* (London: Chapman and Hall, 1890), 151–152, 174–176, 345; Jameson to Stanley, March 26, 1888, reprinted in Barttelot, *Life of Edmund Musgrave Barttelot*, 387–393; letter from Tippu Tip to Sef ben Hamed, reprinted in Tippu Tip, *Autobiographie*, 167–168; Ward, *Stanley's Rear Guard*, 62.

50. Werner, *A Visit to Stanley's Rear-Guard*, 229–235.

51. Ward, *Stanley's Rear Guard*, 84–85.

52. Jameson, *Story of the Rear Column*, 254; Barttelot, *Life of Edmund Musgrave Barttelot*, 239.

53. Jameson, *Story of the Rear Column*, 304–306; Werner, *A Visit to Stanley's Rear-Guard*, 269–273; *Le Mouvement Géographique*, 1888, 82; "Mr. Bonny's Official Report," *The Times*, November 15, 1890, 11; Barttelot, *Life of Edmund Musgrave Barttelot*, 336.

54. Ward, *Stanley's Rear Guard*, 140.

55. Stanley, *In Darkest Africa*, vol. 2, 14.

56. Stanley, *In Darkest Africa*, vol. 2, 121–124, 148; Jephson, *Diary*, 333.

57. Jephson, *Diary*, 343, 346–347; Parke, *Personal Experiences*, 408–409.

58. Parke, *Personal Experiences*, 409–410; Jephson, *Diary*, 343–351.

59. Stanley to Euan-Smith, December 19, 1889, reprinted as "Correspondence Respecting Mr. Stanley's Expedition for the Relief of Emin Pasha," UK Parliamentary Command Papers, Africa, no. 4, 1890 (London: HMSO, 1890), 14.

60. Stanley to Euan-Smith, December 19, 1889, Command Papers, Africa, no. 4 (1890), 15–16.

61. Stanley, *In Darkest Africa*, vol. 2, 453–457.

62. Emin Pasha, *Emin Pasha: His Life and Work*, vol. 2, 2–4; Parke, *Personal Experiences*, 503–507.

63. Parke, *Personal Experiences*, 504–505; Emin Pasha, *Emin Pasha: His Life and Work*, vol. 2, 6.

64. Stanley, *In Darkest Africa*, vol. 2, 473–474; Emin Pasha, *Emin Pasha: His Life and Work*, vol. 2, 16; Jephson, *Diary*, 411.

65. Stanley to Euan-Smith, December 19, 1889, Command Papers, Africa, no. 4 (1890), 16.

66. Jephson, *Diary*, 346–347.

CHAPTER 8: THINGS FALL APART

1. John Rose Troup, *With Stanley's Rear Column* (London: Chapman and Hall, 1890), 212.

2. Pierre Salmon, *Le Voyage de Van Kerckhoven aux Stanley Falls et au Camp de Yambuya (1888)* (Brussels: Académie Royale des Sciences d'Outre-Mer, 1978), 70–71.

3. J. R. Werner, *A Visit to Stanley's Rear-Guard* (Edinburgh: William Blackwood & Sons, 1889), 322–324.

4. On Becker's mission, see P. Ceulemans, *La Question Arabe et le Congo, 1883–1892* (Brussels: Académie Royale des Sciences Coloniales, 1959), 153–162. On Greshoff, see François Bontinck, "Les Archives de la Nieuwe Afrikaanse Handelsvennootschap conserves à Schaarsbergen (Pays-Bas)," *Bulletin des Séances, Académie Royale des Sciences d'Outre-*

Mer n.s., 16, no. 2 (1970): 178–194; Henry Morton Stanley, *In Darkest Africa: The Quest, Rescue, and Retreat of Emin, Governor of Equatoria*, 2 vols. (New York: Charles Scribner's Sons, 1890), vol. 2, 474.

5. Tippu Tip, *Maisha ya Hamed bin Muhammed el Murjebi, yaani Tippu Tip, kwa maneno yake mwenyewe*, trans. W. H. Whitely (Nairobi: East African Literature Bureau, 1966), 129. The quotation is here translated from the French version given by Bontinck because Whitely's English translation of this passage is inaccurate. See Tippu Tip, *L'Autobiographie de Hamed ben Mohammed el-Murjebi Tippu Tip (ca. 1840–1905)*, trans. and ann. François Bontinck (Brussels: Académie Royale des Sciences d'Outre-Mer, 1974), 146–147. On the companies, see Ceulemans, *La Question Arabe*, 196.

6. Tippu Tip to Muhammad bin Masud, undated, but received in Zanzibar on December 21, 1888, reprinted in Tippu Tip, *Autobiographie*, 165–167.

7. Tippu Tip to Muhammad bin Masud, received in Zanzibar on December 21, 1888.

8. François Renault, "The Structures of the Slave Trade in Central Africa in the Nineteenth Century," *Slavery and Abolition* 9, no. 3 (1988): 148.

9. James S. Jameson, *The Story of the Rear Column of the Emin Pasha Relief Expedition* (New York: United States Books Co., 1891), 234, 242.

10. Jameson, *Story of the Rear Column*, 234, 242, 248; Herbert Ward, *My Life with Stanley's Rear Guard* (New York: Charles L. Webster & Co., 1891), 63.

11. Tippu Tip to Holmwood, July 21, 1887, UK National Archives (Kew), FO 84/1906, fo. 183–193; Salmon, *Voyage de Van Kerckhoven*, 60–64.

12. Letter reprinted in Tippu Tip, *Autobiographie*, 169; Ceulemans, *La Question Arabe*, 170.

13. Ward, *My Life with Stanley's Rear Guard*, 134; Tippu Tip, *Maisha*, 129.

14. J. M. Gray, "Stanley versus Tippoo Tib," *Tanganyika Notes and Records* 18 (December 1944): 18–20; Tippu Tip, *Autobiographie*, 290, fn. 522.

15. Quoted in Tippu Tip, *Autobiographie*, 283, fn. 487.

16. Alfred J. Swann, *Fighting the Slave-Hunters in Central Africa*, 2nd ed. (London: Frank Cass & Co., 1969; 1st ed., 1910), 173–174; Swann's letter is quoted in Gray, "Stanley versus Tippoo Tib," 17.

17. The British editions of Stanley's book, *In Darkest Africa*, of Barttelot's book, *The Life of Edmund Musgrave Barttelot*, and of Jameson's

book, *The Story of the Rear Column of the Emin Pasha Relief Expedition*, were all published in 1890.

18. Tippu Tip, *Autobiographie*, 290, fn. 522; François Renault, *Tippo Tip: Un Potentat Arabe en Afrique Centrale au XIXe Siècle* (Paris: Harmattan, 1987), 300–301.

19. François Renault, *Le Cardinal Lavigerie, 1825–1892: L'Eglise, l'Afrique, et la France* (Paris: Librairie Arthème Fayard, 1992), 554–580; François Renault, *Lavigerie, l'Esclavage Africaine, et l'Europe, 1868–1892*, 2 vols. (Paris: E. de Boccard, 1971), vol. 1, 271–275.

20. Cardinal Lavigerie, "L'Esclavage Africain: Conférence Fait dans l'Eglise de Saint-Sulpice á Paris par le Cardinal Lavigerie," pamphlet issued by La Procure des Missions d'Afrique, Paris, 1888, 16.

21. Lavigerie, "L'Esclavage Africain," 20–22.

22. *Daily News* (London), August 1, 1888.

23. Cardinal Lavigerie, "Oration of Cardinal Lavigerie at a Meeting of the Anti-Slavery Society, held in Prince's Hall, London, Tuesday, July 31st, 1888," pamphlet issued by the Anti-Slavery Society, London, 1888.

24. Lavigerie, "Oration of Cardinal Lavigerie," 18–19; *Daily News* (London), August 1, 1888.

25. Quoted in Annelies Feron, "Colonial Enthusiasm and the Anti-Slavery Movement in Belgium during the Anti-Slavery Conference in Brussels in 1889/1890" (MA thesis, Essen University, 2001), English summary, 1.

26. Feron, "Anti-Slavery Movement in Belgium," English summary, 2; *Le Mouvement Antiesclavagiste*, vol. 1 (1889), 238–239.

27. Suzanne Miers, "The Brussels Conference of 1889–1890: The Place of the Slave Trade in the Policies of Great Britain and Germany," in *Britain and Germany in Africa: Imperial Rivalry and Colonial Rule*, ed. Prosser Gifford and William Roger Louis (New Haven: Yale University Press, 1967), 83–95.

28. Miers, "The Brussels Conference of 1889–1890," 102; "Translations of the Protocols and General Act of the Slave Trade Conference Held at Brussels, 1889–1890," UK Parliamentary Command Papers, Africa no. 8A (1890), 2.

29. *Bulletin Officiel de l'Etat Indépendant du Congo* no. 11 (November 1889): 197–209, 210–217.

30. *Le Mouvement Antiesclavagiste*, 1890, 24–25; Miers, "The Brussels Conference of 1889–1890," 108; "Translations and Protocols," 33.

31. "Translations and Protocols," 55–61.

32. "Translations and Protocols," 57, 190–191.

33. Tippu Tip, *Autobiographie*, 149, 216, fn. 177, 284, fn. 492, and 285, fn. 493; Jameson, *Story of the Rear Column*, 161; Ceulemans, *La Question Arabe*, 179, fn. 2; Troup, *With Stanley's Rear Column*, 236–237.

34. Troup, *With Stanley's Rear Column*, 236–237; Ceulemans, *La Question Arabe*, 179, fn. 2; Ceulemans, *La Question Arabe*, 179, fn. 2, 206, 326; Tobback to Muhammad bin Said and Muhammad bin Khalifan, April 2, 1891, UK National Archives (Kew), FO 84/2149, fo. 117–118.

35. Ceulemans, *La Question Arabe*, 283–288, 326–331; *Le Mouvement Géographique*, vol. 9 (1892), 101–103.

36. Chaltin is quoted in L. Lotar, "Souvenirs de l'Uele: Les Arabes des Falls (Deuxième Partie)," *Congo*, vol. 2 (1935): 681; letter from Ponthier in the *Bulletin du Comité de l'Afrique Française*, April 1892, 18.

37. Declaration of Henry Lewis and Davis Moses, Boma, December 24, 1893, UK National Archives, Kew, FO 629/3.

38. Sef bin Mohamed to Hamid bin Mohamed, February 3, 1892, UK National Archives (Kew), FO 84/2232, fo. 263–264; L. Lotar, "Souvenirs de l'Uele," 670.

39. *Le Mouvement Géographique*, vol. 9 (1892): 82, 96, 101.

40. *Le Mouvement Géographique*, vol. 9 (1892), 95, 97; François Renault, "The Structures of the Slave Trade in Central Africa in the Nineteenth Century," 149; Ceulemans, *La Question Arabe*, 329.

41. *Le Mouvement Géographique* vol. 9 (1892): 82.

42. Jameson, *Story of the Rear Column*, 334, 342; Renault, "Structures of the Slave Trade," 164, fn. 5; Tippu Tip, *Autobiographie*, 215, fn. 172; *Le Mouvement Géographique* vol. 9 (1892): 96, 101.

43. *Le Mouvement Géographique* vol. 9 (1892): 97, 101; Ceulemans, *La Question Arabe*, 311.

44. Emin Pasha, *Emin Pasha: His Life and Work, Compiled from His Journals, Letters, Scientific Notes and from Official Documents by Georg Schweitzer*, 2 vols. (Westminister: Archibald Constable and Co., 1898; reprinted New York: Negro Universities Press, 1969), vol. 2, 41–48, 148–151, 174–175; Edward Hertslet, ed., *Map of Africa by Treaty*, 2nd ed., 3 vols. (London: Her Majesty's Stationery Office, 1896), vol. 2, 615–618, 642–651.

45. Emin Pasha, *Emin Pasha: His Life and Work*, vol. 2, 280; Thomas Heazle Parke, *My Personal Experiences in Equatorial Africa as Medical Officer of the Emin Pasha Relief Expedition* (New York: Charles Scribner's Sons, 1891, reprinted New York: Negro Universities Press, 1969), 124; Renault, "The Structures of the Slave Trade," 149, 165, fn. 33; Tippu Tip, *Autobiographie*, 240–241, fn. 280; Jameson, *Story of the Rear Column*, 251.

46. Emin Pasha, *Emin Pasha: His Life and Work*, vol. 2, 294–295.

47. Baumann's article is reprinted in Emin Pasha, *Emin Pasha: His Life and Work*, vol. 2, 292–293.

48. Pratt, Read & Co. to Arnold, January 24, 1895; Arnold to Cheney, November 28, 1894, January 25, 1895, Cheney/Downing Collection, Connecticut River Museum, Essex, CT, box 1, folders 1–3.

49. Pratt, Read & Co. to Arnold, June 12, 1895, November 2, 1896, November 5, 1896, all in the Cheney/Downing Collection, Connecticut River Museum, box 1, folders 1–3; ivory purchase statistics, 1898–1902, in the Pratt-Read Collection, Connecticut River Museum, section G, shelf 6, box 74.

50. Diary of George Grenfell, 1885–1888, June 12, 1888, Baptist Missionary Society Archives, Regent's Park College, University of Oxford, A/18/1.

51. Donald Malcarne, "The Ivory Industry and Voluntary and Involuntary Migration in the Late Nineteenth Century," *North American Archaeologist* 22 (2001): 286–289.

52. David H. Shayt, "Elephant under Glass: The Piano Key Bleach House of Deep River, Connecticut," *IA: The Journal of the Society of Industrial Archaeology* 19 (1993): 48–55.

53. Price list of billiard balls manufactured by Comstock, Cheney & Co., n.d., Cheney/Downing Collection, Connecticut River Museum, Essex, CT, Section G, Shelf 3, Box 74; Shayt, "Elephant under Glass," 40.

54. Curtiss S. Johnson, "From Ivory Combs to Carnegie Hall and Today: The History of the Pratt-Read Corporation," unpublished manuscript in the Pratt-Read Collection, Connecticut River Museum, section G, shelf 6, box 74, 27–35; Malcarne, "Ivoryton: Introduction and History," 9; Nancy V. Kougeas, "Manufacturer and Merchant: Samuel M. Constock, George A. Cheney, and the Growth of the Ivory Industry in Essex Connecticut, 1827–1872" (MA thesis, Wesleyan University, Middletown, Connecticut, 1994), 38.

55. Quoted in Malcarne, "Ivory Industry and Migration," 284; Stanley to Euan-Smith, December 19, 1889, reprinted in "Correspondence Respecting Mr. Stanley's Expedition for the Relief of Emin Pasha," UK Parliamentary Command Papers, Africa, no. 4 (1890), 9.

56. S. L. Hinde, "Three Years' Travel in the Congo Free State," *The Geographical Journal* 5 (1895): 434.

57. Sidney Langford Hinde, *The Fall of the Congo Arabs* (London: Methuen & Co, 1897), 156–157, 171, 180; Hinde, "Three Years' Travel," 434.

58. Dhanis to Governor-General, September 21, 1892, reprinted in Philippe Marechal, *De "Arabische" Campagne in het Maniema-Gebied, 1824–1894* (Tervuren: Musée Royal de l'Afrique Centrale, 1992),

324–326; Tippu Tip, *Maisha*, 117; David M. Gordon, "Interpreting Documentary Sources on the Early History of the Congo Free State: The Case of Ngongo Luteta's Rise and Fall," *History in Africa* 14 (2014): 20–22.

59. Tippu Tip, *Maisha*, 119; Ceulemans, *La Question Arabe*, 348, fn. 3; Norman Bennett, *Arab vs. European: Diplomacy and War in Nineteenth-Century East and Central Africa* (New York: Africana Publishing Co., 1986), 238.

60. Ceulemans, *La Question Arabe*, 350–355; Hinde, "Three Years' Travel," 433; Hinde, *Fall of the Congo Arabs*, 128.

61. Hinde, *Fall of the Congo Arabs*, 124.

62. Hinde, *Fall of the Congo Arabs*, 184.

63. *Le Mouvement Géographique*, Année 1893, no. 16 (July 23), 70, and Année 1893, no. 18 (August 20), 77.

64. Leo Lejeune, *Lothaire* (Brussels: Editions de l'Expansion Coloniale, 1935), 50–62; "Ponthier," in *Biographie Coloniale Belge*, 8 vols. (Brussels: Librairie Falk, 1948), vol. 1, cols. 766–771.

65. Baron Dhanis, "La Campagne Arabe," in *Le Congo Belge*, 2 vols., ed. Louis Franck (Brussels: La Renaissance du Livre, 1929–1930), vol. 2, 82–89. On Rashid, see Renault, *Tippo Tip*, 297–298.

66. René Cambier, "L'Affaire Stokes," *Revue Belge de Philologie et d'Histoire* 30 (1952): 111–119; Josué Henry, "Souvenirs de la Guerre Contre les Arabes," in *Le Congo Belge*, 2 vols., ed. Louis Franck (Brussels: La Renaissance du Livre, 1929–1930), vol. 2, 98–101.

67. E. J. Glave, "New Conditions in Central Africa," *The Century Magazine* 53 (1895–1897): 915.

68. E. J. Glave, "Cruelty in the Congo Free State," *The Century Magazine* 54 (1897): 701–711.

69. Henry Wellington Wack, *The Story of the Congo Free State* (New York: G. P. Putnam's Sons, 1905), 195–196; Hinde, "Three Years' Travel," 442–446.

CHAPTER 9: CONCESSION COMPANIES AND COLONIAL VIOLENCE

1. J. Plas and Victor Pourbaix, *Les Sociétés Commerciales Belges et le Régime Economique et Fiscal de l'Etat Indépendant du Congo* (Brussels: Van Assche, 1899), 72–75.

2. Quoted in P. Ceulemans, *La Question Arabe et le Congo, 1883–1892* (Brussels: Académie Royale des Sciences Coloniales, 1959), 194, fn. 1.

3. Alain Stenmans, *La Reprise du Congo par la Belgique* (Brussels: Editions Techniques et Scientifiques, 1949), 66–75; Plas and Pourbaix, *Sociétés Commerciales*, 72–75; Neal Ascherson, *The King Incorporated: Leopold II in the Age of Trusts* (London: George Allen & Unwin, 1963), 148.

4. Robert Thompson, *Fondation de l'Etat Indépendant du Congo* (Brussels: Office de Publicité, 1933), 290–295.

5. Jean Stengers, "Note sur l'Histoire des Finances Congolaises: Le 'Trésor' ou 'Fonds Spécial' du Roi-Souverain," *Bulletin des Séances, Instutut Royal Colonial Belge*, 1954, 155–195.

6. Henry Morton Stanley, *The Congo and the Founding of Its Free State*, 2 vols. (New York: Harper & Brothers, 1885), vol. 2, 355–356.

7. *Bulletin Officiel de l'Etat Indépendant du Congo*, 1885, 26; E. D. Morel, *Great Britain and the Congo: The Pillage of the Congo Basin* (London: Smith, Elder & Co., 1909), 97. For a critique of the State's position, see E. Boelaert, *L'Etat Indépendant et les Terres Indigènes* (Brussels: Académie Royale des Sciences Coloniales, 1956), 1–22.

8. Charles Lemaire, *Au Congo: Comment les Noirs Travaillent* (Brussels: Imprimerie Scientifique Ch. Bulens, 1895), 39.

9. Charles de Chavannes, *Le Congo Français* (Paris: Librairie Plon, 1937), 215–232.

10. *Bulletin Officiel de l'Etat Indépendant du Congo*, 1892, 307–312; Félicien Cattier, *Droit et Administration de l'Etat Indépendant du Congo* (Brussels: F. Larcier, 1898), 304–307; Félicien Cattier, *Etude sur la Situation de l'Etate Indépendant du Congo* (Brussels: F. Larcier, 1906), 111.

11. Howard Wolf and Ralph Wolf, *Rubber: A Story of Glory and Greed* (Shawbury, UK: Smithers Rapra Publishing, 2009), 318–331. Originally published by J. J. Little & Ives Co., New York, 1936; Steve Love and David Griffels, *Wheels of Fortune: The Story of Rubber in Akron* (Akron, OH: The University of Akron Press, 1999), xiii; Hugh Allen, *Rubber's Home Town: The Real-Life Story of Akron* (New York: Stratford House, 1949), 116–159.

12. E. D. Morel, *King Leopold's Rule in Africa* (London: Heinemann, 1904), 127; Guy Burrows, *The Curse of Central Africa, with Which Is Incorporated 'A Campaign Amongst Cannibals,' by Edgar Canisius* (London: R. A. Everett & Co., 1903), 72; Viscount Mountmorres, *The Congo Independent State: A Report on a Voyage of Enquiry* (London: Williams and Northgate, 1906), 148.

13. William Edmundson, *The Nitrate King: A Biography of "Colonel" John Thomas North* (New York: Palgrave MacMillan, 2011), 99–101; *Bulletin Officiel*, 1893, 29–37; Plas and Pourbaix, *Sociétés Commerciales Belges*, 134–137; Cattier, *Etude*, 191–194; Heinrich Waltz, *Das Konzessionswesen im Belgischen Kongo*, 2 vols. (Jena: Verlag von Gustav Fischer, 1917), vol. 2, 351–354, 372–373.

14. Daniel Vangroenweghe, "Charles Lemaire à l'Equateur: Son Journal Inédit, 1891–1895," *Annales Aequatoria* 7 (1986): 7–8; Waltz, *Konzessionswesen*, vol. 1, 20–21.

15. Vangroenweghe, "Charles Lemaire à l'Equateur," 12–13, 45–46, 50.

16. Edmond Boelaert, "L'ABIR," typescript in the De Ryck Collection of Documents, Memorial Library, University of Wisconsin-Madison, file 6/1, 2–3.

17. Testimony from the Secteur Bolifa, Groupement Boilinga, De Ryck Collection, doc. 26/3/2, 1–2.

18. Jespersen's account was originally published as Knud Jespersen, *En Dansk Officers Kongofaerd*, ed. Kay Larsen (Copenhagen: C. A. Reitzel, 1930). It was translated into French and rendered in the third person by G. Hulstaert in "Le Voyage au Congo d'un Officier Danois: Notes et Commentaires sur les Séjours à l'Equateur de Knud Jespersen (1898–1908)," *Enquêtes et Documents d'Histoire Africaine* 4 (1980): 1–100. See Jesperson, "Voyage au Congo," 1–10.

19. Jespersen's Abir inspection is described in Jespersen, "Voyage au Congo," 10–24.

20. Edmond Boelaert, Honoré Vinck, and Charles Lonkama, "Arrivée des Blancs sur les Bords des Rivières Equatoriales," part 1, *Annales Aequatoria* 16 (1995): 13–20, part 2, *Annales Aequatoria* 17 (1996): 270–308. The testimonies were translated into French by E. Boelaert and Ch. Lonkama. The French texts are also available online as E. Boelaert, H. Vinck, and C. Lonkama, "African Testimonies of the Arrival of the First Whites on the Rivers in the Congolese Equateur Region," Centre Aequatoria, accessed April 16, 2018, http://www.aequatoria.be/04engels/030themes_en/0331temoignages_en.htm.

21. Edgar Canisius, "A Campaign Amongst Cannibals," a special section incorporated in Guy Burrows, *The Curse of Central Africa*, 63–70. On the construction of the railroad, see Jules Marchal, *L'Etat Libre du Congo: Paradis Perdu*, 2 vols. (Borgloon, Belgium: Editions Paula Bellings, 1996), vol. 1, 311–318.

22. Marchal, *Paradis Perdu*, vol. 1, 381–382.

23. E. D. Morel, *King Leopold's Rule in Africa* (London: Heinemann, 1904), 129–130.

24. Morel, *King Leopold's Rule*, 129; Daniel Vangroenweghe, "Le Red Rubber de l'Anversoise, 1899–1900: Documents Inédits," *Annales Aequatoria* 6 (1985): 39–65; Marchal, *Paradis Perdu*, vol. 1, 382–385.

25. Canisius, "Campaign Amongst Cannibals," 72–80; Marchal, *Paradis Perdu*, vol. 1, 382.

26. Canisius, "Campaign Amongst Cannibals," 73–76.

27. Canisius, "Campaign Amongst Cannibals," 77–79.

28. Canisius, "Campaign Amongst Cannibals," 167–168.

29. Canisius, "Campaign Amongst Cannibals," 170–171.

30. Canisius, "Campaign Amongst Cannibals," xiv, 178

31. Morel, *King Leopold's Rule*, 128–133; Vangroenweghe, "Le Red Rubber de l'Anversoise," 39–65.

32. Morel, *King Leopold's Rule*, 132; Marchal, *Paradis Perdu*, vol. 2, 125, says that Lothaire arrived in Belgium in April 1900.

33. Quoted in "Roger Casement's Congo Report," as reprinted in *The Eyes of Another Race: Roger Casement's Congo Report and 1903 Diary*, ed. Seamas O'Siochain and Michael O'Sullivan (Dublin: University College Dublin Press, 2003), 105–106.

34. F. Waleffe, "La Verité sur les Accusations Portées Contra le Grand Roi Leopold II," *Journal des Tribunaux d'Outre-Mer*, 1929, 133.

35. Général de Chambrun, *Brazza* (Paris: Plon, 1930), 217–219.

36. Richard West, *Brazza of the Congo* (London: Jonathan Cape, 1972), 162–163; Isabelle Dion: *Pierre Savorgnan de Brazza: Au Coeur du Congo* (Aix-en-Provence: Archives Nationales d'Outre-Mer, 2007), 78–80.

37. "Assemblée Extraordinaire de la Société pour la Réception de M. P. Savorgnan de Brazza," *Séances de la Société de Géographie* (1886): 49–85; Chambrun, *Brazza*, 162.

38. Catherine Coquery-Vidrovitch, "Les Idées Economics de Brazza et les Premières Tentatives de Compagnies de Colonisation au Congo Francais, 1885–1898," *Cahiers d'Etudes Africaines* 5 (1965): 57.

39. Elizabeth Rabut, *Brazza, Commissaire Générale: Le Congo Français, 1886–1897*, Documents pour Servir à l'Histoire de l'Afrique Equatoriale Française (Paris: Ecole des Hautes Etudes, 1989), 11–12; Maria Petringa, *Brazza: A Life for Africa* (Bloomington, IN: Author-House, 2006), 169.

40. Marie-Antoinette Menier, "Conceptions Politiques et Administratives de Brazza, 1885–1898," *Cahiers d'Etudes Africaines* 5 (1965): 86; Rabut, *Commissaire Générale*, 20.

41. Rabut, *Commissaire Générale*, 23–24, 27–29, 65–68; Jules Lefébure, "Le Régime des Concessions au Congo" (doctoral thesis, University of Paris, Faculty of Law, 1904), 23–24; Menier, "Conceptions Politiques," 88.

42. Rabut, *Commissaire Générale*, 93; Coquery-Vidrovitch, "Idées Economiques," 77–78.

43. Rabut, *Commissaire Générale*, 371–375; Coquery-Vidrovitch, "Idées Economiques," 64–76.

44. Marc Michel, "Auteur de la Mission Marchand: Le Rappel de Brazza en 1897," *Cahiers d'Etudes Africaines* 7 (1967): 152–162.

45. Rabut, *Commissaire Générale*, 295–296, 363–366; Catherine Coquery-Vidrovitch, "L'Echec d'une Tentative Economique: L'Impôt

de Capitation au Service des Compagnies Concessionnaires du Congo Français (1900–1909)," *Cahiers d'Etudes Africaines* 8 (1968): 97; *Bulletin Officiel de l'Etat Indépendant du Congo*, 1900, 41.

46. Rabut, *Commissaire Générale*, 27–28.

47. André Lebon, *La Politique de la France en Afrique*, 1896–1898 (Paris: Plon-Nourrit, 1901), 19; Chambrun, *Brazza*, 219–220.

48. Abraham Ndinga-Mbo, *Savorgnan de Brazza, Les Frères Tréchot, et les Ngala du Congo-Brazzaville, 1878–1960* (Paris: L'Harmattan, 2006), 99; Capitaine Ulysse Marie Alexandre Renard, *La Colonisation au Congo Français: Etude sir les Concessions Acccordées au Congo* (Paris: Imprimerie Kugelmann, 1901), 99. On the French Colonial Party, see C. M. Andrew and A. S. Kanya-Forstner, "The French Colonial Party: Its Composition, Aims, and Influence, 1885–1914," *The Historical Journal* 14 (1971): 99–128.

49. Catherine Coquery-Vidrovitch, *Le Congo au Temps des Grandes Compagnies Concessionnaires, 1898–1930* (Paris: Mouton, 1972), 52; Rabut, *Commissaire Générale*, 27; Daniel Vangroenweghe, "The Leopold II Concession System Exported to the French Congo, with as Example, the Mpoko Company," *Revue Belge d'Histoire Contemporaine* 36 (1906): 326; Jean Stengers, *Combien le Congo a-t-il Coûté à la Belgique?* (Brussels: Académie Royale des Sciences Coloniales, 1957), 278–280.

50. Albert Veistroffer, *Vingt Ans dans la Brousse Africaine* (Lille: Editions du Mercure de Flandre, 1931), 210–220; Coquery-Vidrovitch, "L'Impôt de Capitation," 101–103; Renard, *Etude sir les Concessions*, 119–120; Lefébure, "Régime des Concessions," 276–278.

51. Lefébure, "Régime des Concessions," 101–111.

52. Maurits Wynants, *Des Ducs de Brabant aux Villages Congolais: Tervuren et l'Exposition Coloniale, 1897* (Tervuren: Musée Royal de l'Afrique Centrale, 1997), 120–123.

53. Jean Stengers, *Combien le Congo a-t-il Coûté à la Belgique?* (Brussels: Académie Royale des Sciences Coloniales, 1957), 32–33; Waltz, *Konzessionswesen*, vol. 1, 8–9.

54. Matthew Stanard, *Selling the Congo: A History of European Pro-Empire Propaganda and the Making of Belgian Imperialism* (Lincoln: University of Nebraska Press, 2011), 36–37; *Le Congo à l'Exposition Universelle d'Anvers, 1994* (Brussels: O. de Rycker, 1894), 86.

55. Stanard, *Selling the Congo*, 38.

56. Pascal Dubois, *L'Educaion des Jeunes Congolais en Belgique* (Dessain, 1893), 54.

57. Th. Masui, *Guide de la Section L'Etat Indépendant du Congo a l'Exposition du Bruxelles-Tervuren en 1897* (Brussels: Veuve Monnom, 1897), 265–324.

58. Jean Stengers, "La Première Tentative de Reprise du Congo par la Belgique, 1894–1895," *Bulletin de la Société Royale Belge de Géographie* 73 (1949): 48–63.

59. Stengers, "Première Tentative," 48–63; The Antwerp *Précurseur* quotation was reported in *The Times* (London), January 10, 1895, 5.

60. Cattier, *Etude*, 213; *Bulletin Officiel de l'Etat Indépendant du Congo*, 1902, 151–152; Marchal, *Paradis Perdu*, vol. 1, 123.

61. *Bulletin Officiel de l'Etat Indépendant du Congo*, 1898, Annex, 1–8, 29–37; Cattier, *Etude*, 191–194; Plas and Pourbaix, *Sociétés Commerciales Belges*, 134–137; Burrows, *Curse of Central Africa*, 58, 60; Waltz, *Konzessionswesen*, vol. 2, 374–375.

62. The financial arrangements among the concession companies, the Congo Free State, and King Leopold are difficult to untangle because all the financial records of the Congo Free State were burned in the furnace of the king's palace in Brussels during the summer of 1908. See Stengers, "Note sur l'Histoire des Finances Congolaises," 155; Daniel Vangroenweghe, *Du Sang sur les Lianes: Léopold II et Son Congo* (Brussels: Didier Hatier, 1986), back cover notes.

63. Cattier, *Etude*, 191–194; *Mouvement Géographique*, 1900, 95; Burrows, *Curse of Central Africa*, 58; Marchal, *Paradis Perdu*, vol. 1, 382.

64. Stengers, "Note sur l'Histoire des Finances Congolaises," 183.

CHAPTER 10: THE "RED RUBBER" SCANDALS

1. J. Plas and Victor Pourbaix, *Les Sociétés Commerciales Belges et le Régime Economique et Fiscal de l'Etat Indépendant du Congo* (Brussels: Van Assche, 1899), 136–137.

2. E. D. Morel, *Red Rubber: The Story of the Rubber Slave Trade Flourishing on the Congo in the Year of Grace 1906* (London: T. Fisher Unwin, 1906).

3. Paul Richards, "Africa: The Odd Man Out," in *Tropical Forest Ecosystems in Africa and South America*, ed. Betty Meggers, Edward Ayensu, and Donald Duckworth (Washington, DC: Smithsonian Institution Press, 1973), 22–23.

4. Edgar Canisius, "A Campaign Amongst Cannibals," a special section incorporated in Guy Burrows, *The Curse of Central Africa* (London: R. A. Everett & Co., 1903), 80.

5. *Bulletin Officiel de l'Etat Indépendant du Congo* (Brussels: Hayez, 1904), vol. 20, 1904, 277–281; letter reprinted in Roger Casement, "Le Rapport Casement," ed. and ann. D. Vangroenweghe and J. L. Vellut, *Enquêtes et Documents d'Histoire Africaine* no. 6 (1985): 147; Canisius, "Campaign Amongst Cannibals," 78–79.

6. Jules Marchal, *L'Etat Libre du Congo: Paradis Perdu*, 2 vols. (Borgloon, Belgium: Editions Paula Bellings, 1996), vol. 1, 391.

7. Heinrich Waltz, *Das Konzessionswesen im Belgischen Kongo*, 2 vols. (Jena: Verlag von Gustav Fischer, 1917), vol. 2, 366–368; *Verbatim Report of the Five Days' Debate in the Belgium House of Representatives*, trans. and ann. E. D. Morel (Liverpool: Congo Reform Association, 1906), 21; Viscount Mountmorres, *The Congo Independent State: A Report on a Voyage of Enquiry* (London: Williams and Northgate, 1906), 161; Canisius, "Campaign Amongst Cannibals," 178; Emile Vandervelde, *Les Derniers Jours de l'Etat du Congo: Journal de Voyage, Juillet-Octobre 1908* (Mons: Belgium: la Société Nouvelle, 1909), 119–121.

8. Robert Harms, "ABIR: The Rise and Fall of a Rubber Empire" (MA thesis, University of Wisconsin-Madison, 1973), 42; "Special Congo Supplement to the *West African Mail*," September 1904, 155; Abir Circular no. 38, Basankusu, September 29, 1903, reprinted in Pierre Mille, *Le Congo Léopoldien* (Paris, 1905), 166.

9. "Special Congo Supplement to the *West African Mail*," February 1905, 255–256; Edmond Boelaert, "L'ABIR," typescript in the De Ryck Collection of Documents, Memorial Library, University of Wisconsin-Madison, file 6/1, 10–14.

10. *Regions Beyond*, June 1901, 166; Morel, *Red Rubber*, 72.

11. International Rescue Committee, "Mortality in the Democratic Republic of Congo: Results from a Nationwide Survey Conducted April–July 2004," iv, 11.

12. *Regions Beyond*, March 1897, 128; E. D. Morel, *King Leopold's Rule in Africa* (London: Heinemann, 1904), 158–160; Boelaert, "L'ABIR," 12–14; "Special Congo Supplement to the *West African Mail*," February 1905, 256.

13. Paul Richards, *Indigenous Agricultural Revolution: Ecology and Food Production in West Africa* (Boulder, CO: Westview Press, 1985), 49–62; *Regions Beyond*, 1899, 116, and 1900, 197; "Special Congo Supplement to the *West African Mail*," February 1905, 257; René Philippe, *Inongo: Les Classes d'Age en Région de la Lwafa* (Tervuren: Musée Royal de l'Afrique Centrale, 1965), 24.

14. Kenneth D. Nworah, "The Aborigines' Protection Society, 1889–1909: A Pressure-Group in Colonial Policy," *Canadian Journal of African Studies* 5 (1971): 88–89; Dean Pavlakis, *British Humanitarianism and the Congo Reform Movement, 1896–1913* (Burlington, VT: Ashgate, 2015), 132–133.

15. House of Commons Hansard Sessional Papers, Commons Sitting of Wednesday, May 20, 1903, 4th series, vol. 122, 1289–1333.

16. William Roger Louis, "Roger Casement and the Congo," *Journal of African History* 1 (1964): 101–102.

17. Roger Anstey, "The Congo Rubber Atrocities: A Case Study," *African Historical Studies* 4 (1971): 62–64.

18. The unredacted version of Casement's report is reprinted in Roger Casement, *The Eyes of Another Race: Roger Casement's Congo Report and 1903 Diary*, ed. Seamas O'Siochain and Michael O'Sullivan (Dublin: University College of Dublin Press, 2003), 49–177.

19. "Correspondence and Report from His Majesty's Consul at Boma Respecting the Administration of the Independent State of the Congo," Parliamentary Command Paper, Africa, no. 1 (1904); Louis, "Roger Casement," 112; House of Commons Hansard Sessional Papers, Commons Sitting of Thursday, June 9, 1904, 4th series, vol. 135, 1289–1290.

20. S. J. S. Cookey, *Britain and the Congo Question, 1885–1913* (London: Longmans, 1968), 119–127; *The Congo: A Report of the Commission of Enquiry* (New York: G. P. Putnam's Sons, 1906), 1.

21. Robert Harms, *River of Wealth, River of Sorrow: The Central Zaire Basin in the Era of the Slave and Ivory Trade* (New Haven: Yale University Press, 1981), 231.

22. Karen Kiang and Michael Krathwohl, "Rates and Risks of Transmission of Smallpox and Mechanisms of Prevention," *Journal of Laboratory and Clinical Medicine* 142 (2003): 229–238.

23. *The Congo: A Report of the Commission of Inquiry*, 115–119; on abortion, see Robert Harms, *River of Wealth*, 182–183.

24. Commons Sitting of Wednesday, May 20, 1903, 1297.

25. Canisius, "Campaign Amongst Cannibals," 72; Daniel Vangroenweghe, *Du Sang sur les Lianes: Léopold II et Son Congo* (Brussels: Didier Hattier, 1986), 97; Morel, *Red Rubber*, 173–174. The debate over the number of deaths was rekindled when Adam Hochschild wrote in *King Leopold's Ghost* (New York: Houghton Mifflin, 1998), 233, that "during the Leopoldian period and its immediate aftermath, the population of the territory dropped by nearly ten million people." He based that figure on the colonial government's 1924 estimate (based on an incomplete census) of the population as ten million, combined with the 1919 report of the Belgian Commission for the Protection of the Natives, which estimated that since the beginning of European occupation, the population of the Congo had been reduced by half. The Commission attributed the population decrease to smallpox, sleeping sickness, and venereal diseases, thus leaving the relationship between depopulation and the rubber regime ambiguous. See Congrès Colonial National, *La Question Sociale au Congo: Rapport au Comité du Congrès Colonial National* (Brussels: Goemaere, 1924), 7, 23, 172.

26. Judy Pollard Smith, *Don't Call Me Lady: The Journey of Lady Alice Seeley Harris* (Bloomington, IN: Abbott Press, 2014), 39.

27. Congo Reform Association, *Evidence Laid before the Congo Commission of Inquiry at Bwembu, Bolobo, Lulanga, Baringa, Bongandanga, Ikau, Bonginda, and Monsembe* (Liverpool: Congo Reform Association, 1905), 19–24, 28–29. On the role of missionaries in finding witnesses for the Commission, see Robert Burroughs, *African Testimony in the Movement for Congo Reform: The Burden of Proof* (New York: Routledge, 2019), 75–98.

28. Congo Reform Association, *Evidence*, 25–30.

29. Viscount Mountmorres, *The Congo Independent State: A Report on a Voyage of Enquiry* (London: Williams and Norgate, 1906), 5–161.

30. Congo Reform Association, *Evidence*, 72–75, 88.

31. "Special Congo Supplement to the *West African Mail*," February 1905, 256–267, January 1906, 2.

32. *Official Organ of the Congo Reform Association*, December 1905, 19, January 1906, 2, 7–9, 11, February 1906, 7; *Regions Beyond*, 1906, 256; "Tableau des Impositions Rentrées," De Ryck Collection, document 6/1/5.

33. *Bulletin Officiel de l'Etat Indépendant du Congo*, 1906, 345; *Mouvement Géographique*, 1907, 8. On the major concession and territorial companies, see *The Congo: A Report of the Commission of Inquiry*, 104.

34. Morel, *King Leopold's Rule*, 180.

35. In E. D. Morel, *Affairs of West Africa* (London: Heinemann, 1902), 184–185; Roger Anstey, "The Congo Rubber Atrocities—A Case Study," *African Historical Studies* 4 (1971): 67–68.

36. Congo Reform Association, *Evidence*, 10–12.

37. *The Spectator*, November 2, 1907, vol. 99, 650; E. D. Morel, *What Is Taking Place Now in King Leopold's 'Crown Domain' on the Congo?* (Liverpool: Congo Reform Association, 1907), 6–9, in Edmund Dene Morel Papers, 1892–1915, microfilm: Free University of Brussels, 1961, reel no. 2.

38. *Le Matin* (Paris), February 16, 1905; Paul Rendu, "L'Opinion Publique et la Mission d'Enquête de Brazza au Congo, 1905" (MA thesis, Paris, Sorbonne, 1950), 1–4.

39. Félicien Challaye, *Le Congo Français: La Question Internationale du Congo* (Paris: Félix Alcan, 1909), 121–123; Sophie Romeuf-Salomone, "La Mission d'Enquête de Brazza au Congo, 1905" (MA thesis, Université d'Aix-Marseille, 1984), 12–13.

40. Jean Martin, *Savorgnan de Brazza, 1852–1905* (Paris: Les Indes Savantes, 2005), 193; Henri Brunschwig, "Brazza et le Scandale du Congo Français," *Bulletin des Séances, Académie Royale des Sciences*

d'Outre-Mer, n.s., 23 (1977): 119–120; Rendu, "Opinion Publique," 30–31.

41. Romeuf-Salomone, "Mission d'Enquête," 34–38; Michel Dreyfus, "Preface: Félicien Challaye: Un Pionnier de l'Anticolonialisme," in Félicien Challaye, *Un Livre Noir du Colonialisme: Souvenirs sur la Colonisation* (Paris: Les Nuits Rouges, 1998), 5–6 (originally published in 1935 under the title *Souvenirs sur la Colonisation,* by "Les Amis de l'Auteur"); Rendu, "Opinion Publique," 30.

42. *Le Rapport Brazza: Mission d'Enquête du Congo: Rapport et Documents, 1905–1907,* ed. and ann. Dominique Bellec (Neuvy-en-Champagne: Le Passager Clandestin, 2014), 253–256.

43. Amédée Britsch, *Pour le Congo Français: La Dernière Mission de Brazza* (Paris: L. de Soye, 1906), 5.

44. Challaye, *Congo Français,* 13–15.

45. Martin, *Savorgnan de Brazza,* 198–201; Jean Autin, *Pierre Savorgnan de Brazza: Un Prophète du Tiers Monde* (Paris: Librairie Perrin, 1985), 245–246; Brazza to Paul Bourde, August 24, 1905, published in *Le Temps,* September 27, 1905.

46. Challaye, *Congo Français,* 56–57, 65–66.

47. The organization of porterage was reported in *Le Matin,* February 16, 1905, quoting a former colleague of Georges Toqué. Similar figures were given in the *Bulletin du Comité de l'Afrique Française,* January 1905, cited in Rendu, "Opinion Publique," 23–24.

48. Challaye, *Congo Français,* 92.

49. Britsch, *Dernière Mission,* 14.

50. Challaye, *Congo Français,* 100–101.

51. Challaye, *Congo Français,* 102–104.

52. Britsch, *Dernière Mission,* 13.

53. Challaye, *Congo Français,* 107.

54. Challaye, *Congo Français,* 108–144; Challaye, *Livre Noir,* 61–62.

55. Challaye, *Congo Français,* 146–147.

56. On the Congo Reform Association, see Pavlakis, *British Humanitarianism,* 67–129; Kevin Grant, *A Civilised Savagery: Britain and the New Slaveries in Africa, 1884–1926* (New York: Routledge, 2005), 39–78; E. D. Morel, *E. D. Morel's History of the Congo Reform Movement,* ed. William Roger Louis and Jean Stengers (Oxford: Clarendon Press, 1968), 111–124, 158–168.

57. Grant, *Civilised Savagery,* 60, 67. On missionary photography, see T. Jack Thompson, *Light on Darkness? Missionary Photography of Africa in the Nineteenth and Early Twentieth Centuries* (Grand Rapids, MI: Eerdmans, 2012), 165–206, 229–235; Robert M. Burroughs, *Travel Writing*

and Atrocities: Eyewitness Accounts of Colonialism in the Congo, Angola, and the Putumayo (New York: Routledge, 2011), 86–94.

58. Alice Seeley Harris's voice was recorded in 1970, when she was one hundred years old. The recording is held by Autograph ABP, London ("Alice Seeley Harris, Brutal Exposure: The Congo," Autograph, accessed May 16, 2018, http://autograph-abp.co.uk/exhibitions/brutal-exposure). Smith, Don't Call Me Lady!, 105–106.

59. The list of the slides was reproduced in Thompson, Light on Darkness?, 232; the narration reproduced here was reenacted by Baroness Lola Young and recorded. The recording is held by Autograph ABP, London ("The Congo Atrocities Lecture, Read by Baroness Lola Young," Sound-Cloud, accessed June 10, 2018, https://soundcloud.com/autographabp/the-congo-atrocities-lecture).

60. Smith, Don't Call Me Lady!, 105.

61. Grant, Civilised Savagery, 71.

CHAPTER 11: THE END OF RED RUBBER

1. See Tim Jeal, Stanley: The Impossible Life of Africa's Greatest Explorer (New Haven: Yale University Press, 2007); Stuart Laing, Tippu Tip: Ivory, Slavery and Discovery in the Scramble for Africa (Surrey: Medina Publishing Ltd., 2017); Idanna Pucci, ed., Brazza in Congo: A Life and Legacy (New York: Umbrage Editions, 2009); Florence Bernault, "Colonial Bones: The 2006 Burial of Savorgnan de Brazza in the Congo," African Affairs 109 (2010): 367–390.

2. Edward Berenson, Heroes of Empire: Five Charismatic Men and the Conquest of Africa (Berkeley: University of California Press, 2011), 122–165.

3. Jeal, Stanley, 464.

4. Jeal, Stanley, 443–452.

5. François Renault, Tippo-Tip: Un Potentat Arabe en Afrique Centrale au XIXème Siècle (Paris: l'Harmattan, 1987), 300–306. On the end of slavery in Zanzibar, see Frederick Cooper, From Slaves to Squatters: Plantation Labor and Agriculture in Zanzibar and Coastal Kenya, 1890–1925 (New Haven: Yale University Press, 1980).

6. Heinrich Brode, Autobiographie des Arabers Schech Hamed bin Muhammed el Murjebi genannt Tippu Tip in the series Mitteilungen des Seminars für Orientalische Sprachen an der Königliche Friedrich-Wilhelms Universität zu Berlin, Dritte Abteilung: Afrikanische Studien, vol. 5 (1902), 175–277, and vol. 6 (1903), 1–35. Brode's Latinized version of the Swahili text was later translated into English by W. H. Whitely and published in Swahili and English as Tippu Tip, Maisha ya Hamed

bin Muhammed el Murjebi, yaani Tippu Tip, kwa maneno yake mwenyewe, trans. W. H. Whitely (Nairobi: East African Literature Bureau, 1966). François Bontinck later produced an extensively annotated critical edition with a French translation based on Brode's Swahili text, as Tippu Tip, *L'Autobiographie de Hamed ben Mohammed el-Murjebi Tippu Tip (ca. 1840–1905)*, trans. and ann. François Bontinck (Brussels: Académie Royale des Sciences d'Outre-Mer, 1974). On the biography, see Heinrich Brode, *Tippu Tip: Lebensbild eines Zentralafrikanischen Despoten; nach Zinen Eigenen Angaben* (Berlin: Baensch, 1905); Heinrich Brode, *Tippoo Tib: The Story of His Career in Central Africa, Narrated from His Own Accounts*, trans. H. Havelock (London: E. Arnold, 1907).

7. Félicien Challaye, *Le Congo Français: La Question Internationale du Congo* (Paris: Félix Alcan, 1909), 148–149; Jean Autin, *Pierre Savorgnan de Brazza: Un Prophète du Tiers Monde* (Paris: Librairie Perrin, 1985), 256.

8. Charles de Chavannes, *Le Congo Français* (Paris: Librairie Plon, 1937), 385–391.

9. "Aux Obèsques de M. de Brazza," *Bulletin du Comité de l'Afrique Français*, 1905, no. 10, 176–177.

10. *Verbatim Report of the Five Days' Debate in the Belgium House of Representatives*, trans. and ann. E. D. Morel (Liverpool: Congo Reform Association, 1906), 9–35.

11. Jean Stengers, *Combien le Congo a-t-il Coûté à la Belgique?* (Brussels: Académie Royale des Sciences Coloniales, 1957), 169–170.

12. Félicien Cattier, *Etude sur la Situation de l'Etat Independent du Congo* (Brussels: F. Larcier, 1906), 217–218, 240–241; Stengers, *Combien le Congo?*, 173–174.

13. Cattier, *Etude*, 301–304, 310–311; Stengers, *Combien le Congo?*, 170–171.

14. *Five Days' Debate*, 200.

15. *Times* (London), November 21, 1906, 8.

16. Jean Stengers, "Vers la Reprise du Congo par la Belgique: La Décision," in Jean Stengers, *Congo Mythes et Réalités* (Louvain-la-Neuve, Belgium: Editions Duculot, 1989), 170–173.

17. *Traité de Cession de l'Etat Indépendant du Congo à la Belgique* (Belgium, Parlement: Chambre des Représentants, 1908), 21–23; Robert Senelle, *Léopold II et la Charte Coloniale* (Wavre, Belgium: Mols, 2009), 58, 66–67; Stenmans, *Reprise*, 380–454; Stengers, *Combien le Congo?*, 248–255; Daniel Vangroenweghe, *Du Sang sur les Lianes: Léopold II et Son Congo* (Brussels: Didier Hattier, 1986), back cover.

18. Rouanet's speech is in Assemblée Nationale, Chambre des Deputés, *Débats Parlementaires: Compte Rendu in Extenso*, Année 38 (Janv.–Juin, 1906), 860–867, 884–896. It was reprinted in Jules Saintoyant, *L'Affaire du Congo, 1905* (Paris: Epi, 1960), 139–157.

19. Paul Rendu, "L'Opinion Publique et la Mission d'Enquête de Brazza au Congo, 1905" (MA thesis, Paris, Sorbonne, 1950), 40–63; Saintoyant, *L'Affair du Congo*, 115–119.

20. Henri Brunschwig, "Brazza et le Scandale du Congo Français," *Bulletin des Séances, Académie Royale des Sciences d'Outre-Mer*, n.s., 23 (1977): 116, 124–125.

21. Saintoyant, *L'Affair du Congo*, 119–121.

22. Amédée Britsch, *Pour le Congo Français: La Dernière Mission de Brazza* (Paris: L. de Soye, 1906), 23; *Le Rapport Brazza: Mission d'Enquête du Congo: Rapport et Documents, 1905–1907*, ed. and ann. Dominique Bellec (Neuvy-en-Champagne: Le Passager Clandestin, 2014), 35–36.

23. *Le Rapport Brazza*, 131–132, 151–156, 165, 173.

24. *Journal Officiel de la République Français*, Année 38 (1906): 981–983.

25. *Journal Officiel*, 983–987.

26. *Débats Parlementaires*, 912–927.

27. Sophie Romeuf-Salomone, "La Mission d'Enquête de Brazza au Congo, 1905" (MA thesis, Université d'Aix-Marseille, 1984), 209; *Le Rapport Brazza*, 14, 34–37, 49.

28. The discussion of the Mpoko Company is based on Daniel Vangroenweghe, "The Leopold II Concession System Exported to the French Congo, with as Example, the Mpoko Company," *Revue Belge d'Histoire Contemporaine* 36 (1906): 323–372; Catherine Coquery-Vidrovitch, *Le Congo au Temps des Grandes Compagnies Concessionnaires* (Paris: Mouton, 1972), 177–184; Catherine Coquery-Vidrovitch, "Violences Coloniales au Congo," in *Colonisations et Répressions*, ed. Chantal Chanson-Jabeur, Alain Forest, and Patrice Morlat (Paris: Les Indes Savantes, 2015), 17–33.

29. *Le Rapport Brazza*, 38–39.

30. E. D. Morel, *Red Rubber: The Story of the Rubber Slave Trade Which Flourished on the Congo for Twenty Years, 1890–1910* (Manchester, UK: National Labour Press, 1919), 208–209.

31. *Regions Beyond*, 1909, 82; Marcel Van Den Abeele and René Vandenput, *Les Principales Cultures du Congo Belge* (Brussels: Ministère des Colonies, 1951), 384; *Mouvement Géographique*, 1910, 180, 1911,

286–287, 350–351, 568; Waltz, *Konzessionswesen*, vol. 1, 279–287, vol. 2, 380–391; Morel, *Red Rubber*, 224.

32. Alexandre Delcommune, *L'Avenir du Congo Belge Menacé* (Brussels: J. Lebègue, 1919), 242–243, 250; *Mouvement Géographique*, 1913, 439; Jules Marchal, *Forced Labor in the Gold and Copper Mines: A History of the Congo Under Belgian Rule, 1910–1945*, trans. Ayi Kwei Armah (Popenguine, Senegal: Per Ankh, 1999), 29, 35, 38.

33. Coquery-Vidrovitch, *Grandes Compagnies Concessionnaires*, 368, 370, 439, 462; Georges Bruel, *L'Afrique Equatoriale Française* (Paris: Emile Larose, 1918), 362–363.

34. André Gide, *Travels in the Congo*, trans. Dorothy Bussy (New York: Modern Age Books, 1929, reprint 1937), 56–61; Coquery-Vidrovitch, *Grandes Compagnies Concessionnaires*, 268–269.

35. Jan Vansina, *Being Colonized: The Kuba Experience in Rural Congo, 1880–1960* (Madison: University of Wisconsin Press, 2010), 117; Jan Vansina, *Paths in the Rainforest: Toward a History of Political Tradition in Equatorial Africa* (Madison: University of Wisconsin Press, 1990), 246–248; Report on the Reorganization of the Circumscription Batekes-Alima, Mission Picanon, September 7, 1918, Archives Nationales d'Outre-Mer (Aix-en-Provence), AEF 3 D 4; Affaires Politiques, Réorganisation du Dept. Likouala Mossaka, December 1937, Archives Nationales d'Outre-Mer (Aix-en-Provence), AEF 5 D 37.

INDEX

Page numbers in italics refer to an illustration.

ROBERT HARMS is Henry J. Heinz Professor of History and African Studies at Yale University. He is the author of several books on African history, including *The Diligent: A Voyage through the Worlds of the Slave Trade*, and winner of the Mark Lynton History Prize, the Frederick Douglass Prize, and the J. Russell Major Prize. He lives in Guilford, Connecticut.